S0-AIY-744

LUTHERAN QUARTERLY BOOKS

Editor

Paul Rorem, Princeton Theological Seminary

Associate Editors

Timothy J. Wengert, The Lutheran Theological Seminary at Philadelphia, and Steven Paulson, Luther Seminary, St. Paul

Lutheran Quarterly Books will advance the same aims as *Lutheran Quarterly* itself, aims repeated by Theodore G. Tappert when he was editor fifty years ago and renewed by Oliver K. Olson when he revived the publication in 1987. The original four aims continue to grace the front matter and to guide the contents of every issue, and can now also indicate the goals of *Lutheran Quarterly Books:* "to provide a forum (1) for the discussion of Christian faith and life on the basis of the Lutheran confession; (2) for the application of the principles of the Lutheran church to the changing problems of religion and society; (3) for the fostering of world Lutheranism; and (4) for the promotion of understanding between Lutherans and other Christians."

For further information, see www.lutheranquarterly.com.

The symbol and motto of *Lutheran Quarterly,* VDMA for *Verbum Domini Manet in Aeternum* (1 Peter 1:25), was adopted as a motto by Luther's sovereign, Frederick the Wise, and his successors. The original "Protestant" princes walking out of the imperial Diet of Speyer 1529, unruly peasants following Thomas Muentzer, and from 1531 to 1547 the coins, medals, flags, and guns of the Smalcaldic League all bore the most famous Reformation slogan, the first Evangelical confession: the Word of the Lord remains forever.

Lutheran Quarterly Books

TITLES

Living by Faith: Justification and Sanctification by Oswald Bayer (2003).

A More Radical Gospel: Essays on Eschatology, Authority, Atonement, and Ecumenism by Gerhard O. Forde, edited by Mark Mattes and Steven Paulson (2004).

The Captivation of the Will: Luther vs. Erasmus on Freedom and Bondage by Gerhard O. Forde (2004).

The Role of Justification in Contemporary Theology by Mark C. Mattes

Harvesting Martin Luther's Reflections on Theology, Ethics, and the Church, essays from *Lutheran Quarterly* edited by Timothy J. Wengert, with foreword by David C. Steinmetz (2004).

Bound Choice, Election, and Wittenberg Theological Method: From Martin Luther to the Formula of Concord by Robert Kolb (2005).

Bound Choice, Election, and Wittenberg Theological Method

From Martin Luther to the Formula of Concord

Robert Kolb

WILLIAM B. EERDMANS PUBLISHING COMPANY
GRAND RAPIDS, MICHIGAN / CAMBRIDGE, U.K.

© 2005 Wm. B. Eerdmans Publishing Co.
All rights reserved

Wm. B. Eerdmans Publishing Co.
255 Jefferson Ave. S.E., Grand Rapids, Michigan 49503 /
P.O. Box 163, Cambridge CB3 9PU U.K.

Printed in the United States of America

10 09 08 07 06 05   7 6 5 4 3 2 1

Library of Congress Cataloging-in-Publication Data

Kolb, Robert, 1941-
    Bound choice, election, and Wittenberg theological method: from Martin Luther
to the Formula of Concord / Robert Kolb.
        p.   cm.   — (Lutheran quarterly books)
    Includes bibliographical references.
    ISBN 0-8028-2922-8 (pbk.: alk. paper)
1. Luther, Martin, 1483-1546. De servo arbitrio.   2. Free will and determinism —
History — 16th century.   3. Erasmus, Desiderius, d. 1536. De libero arbitrio diatribe.
4. Free will and determinism — Religious aspects — Lutheran Church — History of
doctrines — 16th century.   I. Title.   II. Series.

    BJ1460.L85K65   2005
    233'.7'092 — dc22

                                                        2005040111

www.eerdmans.com

Contents

Bibliographical Abbreviations   x

Acknowledgments   xii

**Introduction: "One of the Most Famous Exchanges
in Western Intellectual History"**   1

Content and Method in Wittenberg Theology   1

The Reception of *De servo arbitrio* as a Theological Issue   6

**I. "None of My Works Is Worth Anything, Except
Perhaps *De servo arbitrio* . . .": Luther and the
Bondage of Human Choice**   11

Erasmus and Luther: A Feud Waiting to Happen   11

The Nature of *De servo arbitrio*   15

The Roots of Luther's View of Choice   28

The Theology of *De servo arbitrio*   31

   Let God Be God   32

   God Hidden and Revealed   35

   God Chooses His Own   38

   God Saves through the Means of Grace   43

v

Human Beings Are Dependent Creatures	48
All Things Happen by Necessity	52
Human Beings Are Sinners	55
Human Creatures Are Totally Responsible Agents	59
Believers Live a Life of Repentance	61
God Is Not Responsible for Evil	62

II. **Drawing the Spirits in His Path:** *De servo arbitrio* **Wins a (Critical) Following** — 67

The Lutheran Humanists and the Bound Will	67
Pulverizing Free Choice and Seeking a Balance (or Dynamic Tension): Melanchthon on the Freedom of the Will	70
Humanist and Reformer	70
The Loci communes of 1521	76
The Commentary on Colossians	78
The Development of Melanchthon's Thought, 1530-1559	81
Melanchthon's Views in Official Statements of Faith	81
Melanchthon's Views in the Revisions of His Loci communes	84
Predestination	86
Contingency and Necessity	87
Freedom of the Will	91
Reactions to Melanchthon's Teaching in the 1530s and 1540s (or the Curious Lack Thereof)	95
Melanchthon's Last Word on the Freedom of the Will	97

III. **Luther's and Melanchthon's Students Debate the Doctrine of the Freedom of the Will** — 103

The Outbreak of Controversy: The Struggle to Define Wittenberg Theology	103
The Synergistic Controversy	106
The Origins of the Controversy	106
Melanchthon versus Gallus	113

Flacius versus Strigel   118

The Public Polemic Continues   120

The Altenburg Colloquy   128

IV. **Luther's Students Use** *De servo arbitrio*
in Teaching on the Freedom of the Will   135

The Use of *De servo arbitrio* apart from the
Synergistic Controversy   136

The Synergistic Controversy as Setting for the Use
of *De servo arbitrio*   137

   Let God Be God   139

   God Hidden and Revealed   144

   God Chooses His Own   147

   God Saves through the Means of Grace   147

   Human Beings Are Dependent Creatures   151

   Human Creatures Fallen into Sin   156

   All Things Happen by Necessity   161

   Human Beings Are Totally Responsible Agents   164

   Believers Live a Life of Repentance   165

   God Is Not Responsible for Evil   166

V. **"Pious Explanations of Necessity":**
Predestination as Problem in the Wittenberg Circle   170

Initial Treatments of Predestination   171

   The Topic in Loci communes   171

   Marbach versus Zanchi   173

Predestination as Problem in the Wittenberg Late Reformation   179

   Leonhardt Palhöfer's Rejection of Particular Predestination   179

   Nikolaus Selnecker's Rejection of Predestination to Damnation   182

   David Chytraeus's Rejection of Absolute Necessity   190

VI. "God Has Predestined Those Who Cannot Be Lost":
The Formulation of the Lutheran Doctrine of Predestination   198

Cyriakus Spangenberg   198

Spangenberg's Biblical Commentaries   200

Spangenberg's Sermons on Predestination of 1567   205

The Reasons for Spangenberg's Preaching on Predestination   205

The Hermeneutical Basis of Spangenberg's Preaching on
Predestination   209

Spangenberg's Definition of God's Choosing His Children   211

Opposition to Spangenberg   220

Martin Chemnitz   226

Jakob Andreae   236

VII. The Formula of Concord   **244**

The Roads toward Concord   244

The Formula of Concord on Bound Choice and the
Freedom of the Will   248

On God's Eternal Foreknowledge and Election   258

Continuing the Struggle with the Tension between God's
Responsibility and Human Responsibility   265

Conclusion: The Wittenberg Circle's Practice of Theology   271

Researching Reception   272

The Members of the Wittenberg Circle   275

The Students of Luther and Melanchthon   276

Luther and Melanchthon   278

Receiving and Handing Down the Reformers' Message   281

Notes   291

Bibliography   350

Index of Names   371

Index of Subjects   375

Index of Scripture References   378

Bibliographical Abbreviations

ARG	*Archiv für Reformationsgeschichte*
Book of Concord	*The Book of Concord,* ed. Robert Kolb and Timothy J. Wengert (Minneapolis: Fortress, 2000)
BSLK	*Die Bekenntnisschriften der evangelisch-lutherischen Kirche* (Göttingen: Vandenhoeck & Ruprecht, 1930, 1991)
CA	Augsburg Confession, BSLK, 44-137.
CR	Philip Melanchthon, *Corpus Reformatorum. Opera quae supersunt omnia,* ed. C. G. Bretschneider and H. E. Bindseil (Halle and Brunswick: Schwetschke, 1834-60)
FC	Formula of Concord
FC, SD	Formula of Concord, Solid Declaration; see *BSLK,* 829-1100
Jena A	*Tomvs primvs omnivm opervm Reuerendi Patris D. M. L. . . .* (Jena: Rüdinger, 1556-1558).
LQ	*Lutheran Quarterly*
LuJ	*Lutherjahrbuch*
Luther's Heirs	Robert Kolb, *Luther's Heirs Define His Legacy: Studies on Lutheran Confessionalization* (Aldershot: Variorum, 1996)
LW	Martin Luther, *Luther's Works* (Saint Louis and Philadelphia: Concordia and Fortress, 1958-86)
MBW	*Melanchthons Briefwechsel,* ed. Heinz Scheible (Stuttgart-Bad Cannstatt: Frommann-Holzboog, 1977-95)

PL   *Patrologia cursus completus: Series Latina* (Paris and Turnhout:
            Magne, 1859-1963).

RE   *Real-Encyklopädie für protestantische Theologie und Kirche,* ed.
            Albert Hauck (Leipzig: Hinrichs, 1896-1913)

SC   Luther's *Small Catechism;* see *BSLK,* 499-541.

SCJ   *Sixteenth Century Journal*

Sources and   *Sources and Contexts of the Book of Concord,* ed. Robert Kolb
  Contexts   and James A. Nestingen (Minneapolis: Fortress, 2001)

StA   *Melanchthons Werke in Auswahl* [*Studien-Ausgabe*], ed. Robert
            Stupperich, 6 vols. (Gütersloh: Bertelsmann, 1955)

WA   Martin Luther, *Dr. Martin Luthers Werke* (Weimar: Böhlau,
            1883-1993)
  Br   *Briefe*
  DB   *Die Deutsche Bibel*
  TR   *Tischreden*
  Witt A Dt   *Der Erste (-zwo[e]llfte) Teil der Bucher D. Mart. Luth. . . .*
              (Wittenberg: Hans Lufft, 1539-1559).
  Witt A Lat *Tomvs primvs [-septimus] omnivm opervm Reverendi Do-
              mini Martini Lutheri . . .* (Wittenberg: Hans Lufft, 1545-1557).

ZKG   *Zeitschrift für Kirchengeschichte*

Acknowledgments

Larger or smaller portions of the following essays, already published, have been revised and incorporated into this work, and are republished here with the permission of the editors:

"Divine Determination and Human Responsibility: David Chytraeus (1531-1600) on *Necessitas*." In *Lord Jesus Christ, Will You Not Stay?: Essays in Honor of Ronald Feuerhahn*, edited by J. Bart Day et al., 221-38. Houston: FFC, 2002.

"'A Hammer against Free Choice': Johannes Wigand's Interpretation of Luther's *De servo arbitrio*." In *Vanha ja nuori. Juhlakirja Simo Heinisen tädyttäessä 60 vuotta*, edited by Kaisamari Hintikka, Hanna-Maija Ketola, and Päivi Salmesvuori, 131-46. Helsinki: Luther-Agricola-Seura, 2003.

"Nikolaus Gallus' Critique of Philip Melanchthon's Teaching on the Freedom of the Will." *Archiv für Reformationsgeschichte* 91 (2000): 87-110.

"On Eternal Predestination and God's Election by Grace: The Exegetical Basis of the Lutheran Teaching in Cyriakus Spangenberg's Commentary on Romans 8 and 9." *Lutheran Synod Quarterly* 34 (1994): 32-59.

"Preaching Predestination: Martin Chemnitz's Proclamation of God's Election of Believers." *Concordia Journal* 28 (2002): 23-40.

"Seelsorge und Lehre in der Spätreformation am Beispiel von Nikolaus Selneckers Abhandlung zur Prädestinationslehre." *Lutherische Theologie und Kirche* 25 (2001): 14-34.

The translation of *De Servo Arbitrio* throughout much of this volume is from *Luther's Works, Volume 33 (Career of the Reformer III)* edited by Philip S. Watson, copyright © 1957 Fortress Press. Used by permission of Augsburg Fortress.

"One of the Most Famous Exchanges in Western Intellectual History"

Christian faith is entirely extinguished, the promises of God and the whole gospel are completely destroyed, if we teach and believe that it is not for us to know the necessary foreknowledge of God and the necessity of the things that are to come to pass. For this is the one supreme consolation of Christians in all adversities, to know that God does not lie but does all things immutably, and that his will can neither be resisted nor changed nor hindered.[1]

Since God has taken my salvation out of my hands into his, making it depend on his choice and not mine, and has promised to save me, not by my own work or exertion but by his grace and mercy, I am assured and certain both that he is faithful and will not lie to me, and also that he is too great and powerful for any demons or any adversities to be able to break him or to snatch me from him. "No one," he says, "shall snatch them out of my hand because my father who has given them to me is greater than all" [John 10:28-29]. So it comes about that, if not all, some and indeed many are saved, whereas by the power of free choice none at all would be saved, but all would perish together.[2]

Content and Method in Wittenberg Theology

These assertions can serve as summaries of the argument of the Wittenberg reformer Martin Luther in his classic face-off on the topic of "bound choice" with Desiderius Erasmus of Rotterdam in 1525. Luther's *De servo arbitrio* addressed a broad range of issues related to the capabilities of the human will and God's grace toward his sinful human creatures. The Wittenberg reformers presupposed that the almighty Creator had fashioned his human creatures in his image. As creatures they depend on their Creator, and when they rebel against him they are unable to restore themselves to the fulfillment of their humanity. The Creator must re-create them. These axioms formed the framework of the Wittenberg theology, centered as it was on the person of God and on the fundamental questions regarding what it means to be God's human creature.

Because Luther presupposed that God talks, that he creates and that he concretizes his will by speaking, words — just the right words — were vital for his way of practicing theology. Throughout his life he engaged in ongoing experiments on how best to express his insights into the relationship between God and his human creatures. At times his exegetical work led him to devise new expressions for his biblically based exploration of the teaching of the catholic tradition. As a child of the scholastic system of the medieval university, Luther also resorted to concepts formulated from traditional scholastic philosophical raw material to clarify and defend his teaching. His argument for the absolute necessity of all things, as products of the will of the Creator, is a prime example of this intellectual exercise in *De servo arbitrio*. The two citations above — the first from its early pages, the second from its conclusion — illustrate his expression of the governing concern which dominates this work and all others from the Wittenberg reformer's pen.

Before he wrote *De servo arbitrio* in 1525, Luther had laid down fundamental elements of his understanding of how biblical revelation works in the lives of hearers. In 1518 at Heidelberg, before his Augustinian brothers, he had anchored his theology at the foot of the cross, in a theology that "calls a thing what it is," that is, that squarely faces sin and evil because it trusts that God triumphs over them even though the pious mind cannot always grasp how he is working. Indeed, he works under appearances of "the opposite," by accomplishing his good will through what seems evil, while human beings seeking the good find themselves entrapped in evil.[3] In *On Christian Freedom* (1520) he set forth his conviction that both as creatures and as sinners human beings live within limits, bound to God's design for their humanity, bound in sin and unable to practice that humanity, which centers in trust in the Creator. The reformer sketched his understanding of the doctrine of justification in that treatise and asserted that God frees those in bondage to sin, death, Satan, and the law through Jesus Christ so they might be free to enjoy their humanity — freed to be bound to their neighbor in love.[4] Luther sought to foster trust and dependence on God's promises, for he believed that God's Word of promise restores the reality of the harmonious relationship between God and human creatures designed by the Creator in the beginning. He believed that trust in God, revealed in Jesus Christ, constitutes the core and foundation of true human living. Luther sought above all the consolation of the troubled conscience, and he was certain that such consolation comes only through the forgiveness of sins won by Christ in his death and resurrection. In the passages above the reformer singled out the certainty of God's creative foreknowledge and inalterable decision to save his own chosen people as the basis for his peace. That peace rested firmly on God, specifically on his action in the saving event of Christ's sacrifice and resurrection and on his action in delivering the benefits of Christ through his re-creating Word.

Luther and his adherents in the next generation expressed their definition of the content of theology in a number of ways that pointed toward new methods of searching Scripture and of proclaiming the life its message offers. In part they grew out of what the reformer had labeled a *theologia crucis* in 1518. Luther called "the theology of the cross" "our theology" in the early 1530s;[5] a few years later the distinction between two dimensions of righteousness won that title.[6] The content of Luther's refocusing the theological task to the relationship between God and his human creatures generated its own theological method. This method presumed that God actually effects his will through his Word, expressed in oral, written, and sacramental forms. In contrast to a scholastic search for the pure logical statement of the truth that could be objectively analyzed and proven, Luther's theology of the cross sought ways to bring the seeming foolishness of the message of Christ's death and resurrection to sinners (1 Cor. 1:18–2:16), so that they might be turned in repentance to the Crucified One. For this theology of the cross was not about suffering but about the Word which comes from Christ's cross to kill sinners as sinners and to bring them to new life in Christ.[7] This rhythm of the dying and rising of daily repentance was to be accomplished through proper application and distinction of the law of God, which evaluates the sinner's performance, and the gospel, which bestows forgiveness of sins and life upon the repentant sinner. In contrast to a scholastic presentation of well-argued information, this distinguishing two dimensions of righteousness and two forms of God's Word compels believers to search for the proper way to drown the sinner and raise up a new creation in Christ (Rom. 6:3-11). Luther believed God's Word does things. It executes his will. Its bearers or proclaimers are agents of God's active resolve to restore the relationship with his chosen people that sin has broken. Thus, the practice of the theology forged in Wittenberg under Luther's leadership required a new method for its fresh conception of God's Word and how it works.

The question of whether Luther's Reformation was "conservative" or "radical" is sometimes debated, and the answer reflects the focus and concern of the one who formulates it. As with all paradigm shifts, Luther's view of the church and his understanding of the biblical message contained many older elements. His passing on of the tradition also contained many new perspectives and formulations. Indeed, Luther's new understanding of faith affected his understanding of God's grace. His new perspectives on justification reflected specific understandings of God and what it means to be human that departed from the Aristotelian framework and its questions which shaped much of the medieval scholastic theological deliberation. But however such issues of content are evaluated, the reformer's method of distinguishing law and gospel in order to transform the identity of the sinner into that of a child of God did result in a different constellation to the body of doctrine which he put to use in the life of the church. His understanding of God and of the human creature, as well as his view of sin, required him to hold a series of elements in tension because he believed that to break through those tensions perverted or obscured fundamental components of the biblical message.

Luther, of course, did not think alone. No theologian ever does. He was part of a collegium at the Leucorea, the Graecized name for the university in the town dubbed "white mountain." This group embraced Philipp Melanchthon, Johannes Bugenhagen, Justus Jonas, and a half-dozen others in their more or less immediate vicinity during the last quarter-century of Luther's life.[8] Around them formed a cluster of followers, some of whom had never studied in Wittenberg, that may be called "the Wittenberg circle."[9] It was a group with a common commitment to proclaim the gospel of Jesus Christ and to do so according to a model they adopted and adapted from their mentor. Together they were involved in experimenting with appropriate articulation of the biblical message. They influenced Luther while he lived, and he continued to shape their thought after he had died. But, as is always the case, hearers pass the message on in their own way.

These Wittenberg theologians believed that Christian "doctrine" does not merely report what is on the mind of God. They believed that doctrine functions, as a tool of God, as his act upon the life of its hearers. Because their practice of theology was shaped both by God's Word and by the necessity of using it to bring a new generation of sinners to repentance and to bestow the forgiveness of sins upon the repentant, Luther's adherents formulated new ways of saying what they believed he had passed on to them. Among other means to do this was their use of doctrinal synonyms. Within the body of doctrine, some "members" or topics can be used to accomplish the same goals or perform the same functions as others. In the treatment of God's grace and human performance, both the doctrine of the bondage of human choice and the doctrine of God's unconditional election express the same concern from different angles. In pursuing the goal of assuring believers of their salvation, the promise of God in the means of grace functions somewhat synonymously with the proclamation of God's eternal choice of his own. Because they had no epistemological theory articulating how presuppositions shaped assertions in their own thought, individuals within the Wittenberg circle too often did not recognize that they shared concerns with their opponents but expressed them in a different manner or with a different topic or doctrine. Thus, the debates among Luther's and Melanchthon's followers serve as laboratories for observing how these students had learned to make their theology work. These controversies show the coincidence of the content of the Wittenberg message with its method (for instance, distinguishing law and gospel or formulating the Word to accomplish most effectively on the psychological level what it threatened or promised).

As is always the case, the members of the Wittenberg circle formulated their biblical teaching out of a number of elements, not only Luther's insights. For instance, neither Luther nor his disciples completely escaped medieval habits of the practice of theology. They did abandon certain questions that had occupied medieval thinkers, and they foreswore the use of much scholastic teaching and method. Furthermore, their humanistic training at Wittenberg led them to attempt to convey their ideas in the best rhetorical style possible and to be concerned about effective communication skills for the sake of the gospel. Their theological education cultivated the ability to distinguish law and gospel properly, for the condemnation of sin and the nurturing of faith in Christ. But some old wineskins still had their appeal, and sometimes the followers of Luther tried to shore up their ideas with Aristotelian patches. In spite of them, however, his students did live with the tension that lay at the heart of Luther's interpretation of the biblical message.

Controversies over the proper interpretation and best use of Luther's legacy broke out particularly in the realm of Luther's most daring reassessment of medieval theology. He struggled to tell as much as he could on the basis of Scripture about God and about the human creature without trespassing the limits placed on rational thinking about the mystery of God and the mystery of humanity. Likewise, he tried to hold himself back from too much explanation of the mystery of how evil can exist since God is almighty and absolutely good and the accompanying mystery of why evil continues in the lives of the baptized, reborn children of God. All Christian systems of thought are compelled to come to terms somehow with these mysteries. All Christian theologians slip into some concessions to harmonize and homogenize the biblical data regarding God the Creator and the human creature, who is also sinner. Wittenberg theology attempted to hold in tension the total responsibility for all things that belongs by definition to the Creator with the limited but complete responsibility he has assigned to his human creatures within their own spheres of activity. God is lord of all, and the human creature is morally bound to carry out the Creator's will. Wittenberg theology strove to keep these two assertions in a paradoxical tension, emphasizing one or the other in response to specific agendas imposed by their immediate situations. The practical elaboration and application of these axioms took place under the implicit acknowledgment that the nature of the human creature as a creature remains ever a mystery in part, as does the existence of evil, especially its continuation in the life of the baptized, who must struggle against it in a life in which God's law and his gospel produce daily repentance.

Sorting out those two "total" responsibilities, God's and the human creature's, has led most Christian thinkers to formulations that balance the roles of God and human beings by assigning each a part of an abstract responsibility for order in the universe and peace in human hearts.[10] The Wittenberg theologians had learned from Luther and Melanchthon that trying to find a reasonable balance between God's actions in behalf of sinners and human attempts to reach out to God could only place burdens on troubled consciences. Their disciples instead attempted to continue maintaining the Wittenberg tension between the two responsibilities, each total, as they addressed the vital human questions regarding who God is and what it means to be human. The distinction of law and gospel allowed them to do so in their preaching even if that art is difficult to execute in practice. This study focuses on their attempts to do so, with primary attention aimed at the ways in which they used (or did not use) one of Luther's key works on the tension between the two "responsibilities," his *De servo arbitrio*.

The Reception of *De servo arbitrio* as a Theological Issue

Some individuals have swayed history and shaped cultures by their deeds, others by their words, still others by the contributions of both active careers and persuasive pens. Martin Luther's acts of confessing his theology publicly in themselves altered opinions and decisions of both the powerful and the peasants, but his Reformation is often viewed as a success because the printing press stood at his disposal, and he learned to exploit it effectively. Thus the assessment of his overall impact *(Wirkungsgeschichte)* involves in part the study of the impact of specific works he wrote *(Rezeptionsgeschichte)*.

Great books have histories of their own. Some individual publications make such a revolutionary or controversial impression upon contemporaries and succeeding generations that the study of their influence upon others and their use by others can reveal to the historian much about the circumstances and thought of these later scholars as well as the reasons for the author's significance. John W. O'Malley calls "Erasmus' challenge in 1524 to Luther's teaching on justification and Luther's acrid response the next year" "one of the most famous exchanges in western intellectual history." O'Malley is correct when he observes that "the bibliography on the 'debate' is immense," though in fact he is not so correct when he adds, "almost every book that treats at length of either of the protagonists has something to say about it."[11] That may have been true in the twentieth century but was not in the sixteenth.

Luther himself shared O'Malley's assessment of the importance of his own work.[12] Many of his contemporaries apparently did not, although his first biographer, Johannes Cochlaeus, his arch-foe, did mention it in his polemical study of Luther's life, the first longer bibliographical treatment it received.[13] This fact should have propelled Lutheran biographers to defend *De servo arbitrio* in their biographical apologiae. It did not. Writing in 1565, two decades after his mentor's death, Johannes Mathesius, the reformer's former student and most important sixteenth-century "biographer," commented on Luther's activities in the 1520s and 1530s with but one brief mention of conflict between Luther and Erasmus — and then not on their dispute over the human will. Instead, the relatively less important critique of Erasmus's ecclesiology, which Luther composed in 1534, commanded the biographer's attention: "Meanwhile our Doctor continued to preach faithfully and lecture assiduously at the school; he wrote interpretations of many wonderful psalms, comforted many troubled individuals and cities, and undertook a presentation of his opinion on the explanation of the Creed of Erasmus of Rotterdam, warning everyone of the rude and dangerous man's writings, as his letter to Amsdorf clearly shows."[14] Although Mathesius presented Luther's life in detail, he did not report anything of their dispute in the mid-1520s.

That Luther's colleague and confidant Philipp Melanchthon avoided mention of this conflict in his two biographical sketches soon after Luther's death is quite understandable; neither his preface to the second volume of Luther's Latin works nor his public oration at Luther's death can be categorized as a thorough biographical survey of its subject's life and thought.[15] That Johannes Sleidan's account of "the state of religion and the republic under Charles V" noted only that Luther had reacted to Erasmus's defense of free choice with *De servo arbitrio* and offered no details of their dispute or the contents of their works may be explained by Sleidan's focus on the political events of the entire Reformation.[16] Mathesius was different. His homiletical biography was designed to present the course of events that constituted Luther's life, including his major literary works, and yet its author ignored *De servo arbitrio*.

So had Ludwig Rabus when he composed an overview of Luther's life, particularly of his literary production, a decade earlier (1556). The encounters with Erasmus earned but a very brief mention in Rabus's treatment of 1524-26, none at all in 1534-35.[17] Rabus corrected this omission in 1572, when he prepared the second edition of his accounts of the lives of those who had given witness to the faith, but the dispute over the bondage of the will still received scant attention. His first mention of their strife fell under the year 1526 (the work appeared, according to our reckoning, in the last part of 1525, which some sixteenth-century Germans would have counted as the beginning of 1526). In a throwaway line, introducing other polemical writings, Rabus explained why the reformer had not gotten around to writing against the Sacramentarians in that year: "because he answered the book on the free will by Erasmus of Rotterdam." In 1534, Rabus reported, Luther and Erasmus again exchanged views on the free will, thus failing to note that ecclesiology and not the powers of the will occasioned this exchange.[18] In view of the extensive quotations that fill Rabus's pages, the absence of excerpts from *De servo arbitrio* is telling. Either the book had little or no significance for the martyrologist, or he believed its contents would not edify his readers.

Although different in style and purpose from Mathesius's and Rabus's works, the twenty-one semiannual paeans Cyriakus Spangenberg preached and published between 1562 and 1573 on "the Man of God, Martin Luther" could be expected to contain extensive reference to Luther's dispute with Erasmus, for Spangenberg, a fervent disciple of the reformer, emphasized precisely the positions of *De servo arbitrio* in his own work.[19] But also in Spangenberg's homilies, organized around metaphorical descriptions of his mentor, the dispute was seldom mentioned, and the content or argument of *De servo arbitrio* was not put to use at all.[20]

Two of Luther's disciples wrote guides to aid students and pastors in their reading of Luther. That of his former student Joachim Mörlin failed to mention *De servo arbitrio*. Advising his own readers to peruse Luther's writing diligently, Conrad Porta, pastor in Eisleben, mentioned *De servo arbitrio*, along with his comments on Psalm 51, as the place to look for Luther's treatment of original sin and "bound choice," but Porta did not make further observations about the work.[21]

Compared to many of Luther's works, *De servo arbitrio* initially commanded widespread interest[22] but then utterly disappeared from the market. It appeared in some eight printings within its first year (in influential printing centers, including Nuremberg, Augsburg, Strasbourg, as well as Wittenberg),[23] and thereafter during the sixteenth century, in Lutheran circles, only in the reformer's collected works. The German translation was issued twice in Wittenberg in 1526 and thereafter only in 1554, apart from the Wittenberg edition of Luther's works (1553).[24] Actually, *De servo arbitrio* remained in comparative obscurity for a quarter-millennium. In the late sixteenth and seventeenth centuries Calvinists cited it more prominently and favorably than Lutherans, and Lutherans understood the work in the context of the reformer's own "correction" of his position in his comments on Genesis 26 some fifteen years later.[25]

In marked contrast to its relative neglect in the period after Luther's death stands a modern fascination with the work. In the nineteenth century followers and foes alike rediscovered *De servo arbitrio,* and it became the source of both severe criticism of the reformer's theology and new insights into the nature of his thought. In fact, many of Luther's partisans throughout four centuries have not known what to do with his treatment of the bondage of human choice. This not so much reflects on Luther's argument as it raises at least two other factors. First, many nineteenth- and twentieth-century scholars have not had sufficient understanding of the rhetorical and logical principles of scholastic debate to recognize how Luther was constructing his sophisticated argument; many were also insensitive to the ways in which the Wittenberg professor's pastoral concern for God's people shaped his use of scholastic methods. But even more, the scholarly lack of clarity over *De servo arbitrio* indicates how even great minds find themselves trapped within their own presuppositions — what "cannot be" in their own thought world could not have existed in the context of another, particularly if they admire and make use of a historical figure in ways that contradict that person's own positions. Albrecht Ritschl could not do better than the judgment that *De servo arbitrio* is "a wretched concoction" *(unglückliches Machwerk).*[26] Some interpreters of Luther have indeed tried to save Luther for their own way of thinking and obligingly have provided a "worthy" way out of the reformer's radical statements about God and the human creature in *On Bound Choice,* straying so far from the mark as to provoke Klaus Schwarzwäller to comment on one author's attempt: "What some people don't find in *De servo arbitrio!*"[27]

Since the appearance of Schwarzwäller's survey in 1969, a goodly number of studies have continued the search for the real definition of the significance of *De servo arbitrio,*[28] but no assessment of the earliest influence and use of the work exists. This study endeavors to fill a part of that gap with an investigation of how Luther's own students and their contemporaries in the quarter-century after his death used *De servo arbitrio*, particularly in the course of the "synergistic" controversy within the Wittenberg circle over the freedom of the will and, in the controversy's later stages, over predestination or God's election of his own people. The study begins by suggesting an outline of Luther's views and Melanchthon's positions on the topics that shaped their disciples' teaching on the human will and God's plan for the salvation of sinners. It concludes with an analysis of the solution to these controverted questions attained by the Formula of Concord, the final attempt in the sixteenth century to formulate a definitive definition or interpretation of Luther's theology for the churches that claimed his name. To assess its answers to the critical questions of that age regarding the human will and God's gracious choosing of his own people, readers need an orientation to the debates of that period as they were grounded in the thought of Luther and his colleague, Melanchthon. For students and followers synthesized what they had learned from "Doctor Luther" and "the Preceptor," as they called the younger colleague. This study presumes that these two theologians and their disciples struggled to make clear that God, as the creator of all that is and the moving agent of all that happens, exercises total responsibility for everything in his creation, while at the same time they insisted that God has given every human being responsibility for obedience in his or her own sphere of life.

By focusing on the reception of *De servo arbitrio*, this study will examine the Wittenberg way of practicing theology. The struggles within the Wittenberg circle to express the biblical message regarding the Creator and the human creature illustrate how theologians experiment with expressions for their ideas, employing different terms and doctrinal synonyms in the search for the best way of proclaiming the Christian message, and how they attempt to solve the dilemmas of doing so effectively in different topical locations, sometimes on God's side, sometimes on the human side. How these factors of content and method were held together in a creative tension within the thought of the Wittenberg circle in the sixteenth century is the story that is presented in these pages.

CHAPTER I

"None of My Works Is Worth Anything, Except Perhaps *De servo arbitrio* . . .": Luther and the Bondage of Human Choice

Erasmus and Luther: A Feud Waiting to Happen

When Martin Luther composed the thirty-sixth article in his *Assertion of All Articles* in 1521, summarizing his critique of medieval theology as it had developed in the preceding five years, he repeated and retracted a thesis he had asserted three years earlier in Heidelberg:

> Free choice after [the fall of Adam into] sin is merely a term, and when [such choosing] does what it is able to do [*facit, quod in se est*], it commits moral sin. . . . So it is necessary to retract this article. For I was wrong in saying that free choice before grace is a reality only in name. I should have said simply: free choice is in reality a fiction, or a term without reality. For no one has it in his power to think a good or bad thought, but everything (as Wyclif's article condemned at Constance rightly teaches) happens by absolute necessity.[1]

As early as 1516 the Wittenberg professor had wrestled with the problem of justifying himself in God's sight through the strength of his own will, and that struggle had led him to the conclusion, as he would later comment, that by his own understanding or strength he could not believe in Jesus Christ or come to him.[2] In theses prepared for the promotion of Bernhard Bernardi in 1516, Luther had asserted that apart from the gift of God's grace there can be no freedom for human beings, while at the same time he insisted that grace does not coerce the will.[3] Already at this point he was making every effort to hold to God's total responsibility for the salvation of sinners, to present God as the only agent of human salvation, and at the same time to preserve the integrity of human beings as creatures of God by insisting that they must be obedient creatures, exercising full responsibility for those tasks God entrusts to them.

The junior professor from Wittenberg did not invent the issue of the freedom of the will; it was, in the words of Karl Zickendraht, "in the air"[4] when in 1521 he placed it toward the end of the *Assertion,* his digest of his own public teaching. The forthright simplicity of such radical statements seems to indicate that Luther was already convinced of the importance of the concept of the freedom or bondage of the will for the structure of his entire way of thinking. He could not have realized in 1521, however, that he was giving Desiderius Erasmus of Rotterdam the instrument by which three years later the great humanist would be able to separate himself from the reformer without rejecting his own call for reform.

Erasmus's declaration of distance between himself and his erstwhile confederate in the efforts for reform occurred in those turbulent days when the currents propelling dreams for remedying the ills of Christendom in head and members were swirling in different directions. Clear concepts of what "Reformation" might mean had not yet crystallized in papally dominated Europe. There were reasons enough for people to have thought that the two intellectuals had common interests. The public debate over curing the church's ills had not yet clarified the fundamental antagonisms between Erasmus's program for a traditional reform of morals and institutional life and Luther's conception of change centered on proper teaching and preaching of the biblical message. In fact, many intellectuals and ecclesiastical leaders knew that the two had corresponded,[5] had used each other's materials,[6] and had criticized the same enemies of what each regarded as good order in the household of God. Therefore, the break between the two which Erasmus solemnly pronounced in his *De libero arbitrio diatribe sive collatio,* published in September 1524,[7] came as something of a surprise in some quarters. In fact, it only confirmed the growing recognition by both men that their fundamental concerns and points of view differed radically.

Already in March 1517 the Wittenberg professor had written his friend Johannes Lang that he was "daily losing pleasure over Erasmus" because the great scholar was concerned with the human more than the divine.[8] For his part, Erasmus's pleasure at having in his wider circle this young German instructor in far-off Wittenberg, at the edge of civilization, was fading rapidly. The young monk's brilliance was beginning to overshadow his own radiance, and this irritated the vain and proud prince of learning. In 1519 he made it clear that his abhorrence of controversy was leading him to worry about Luther's modus operandi in seeking reform.[9] He resented the publication of Luther's "collected works" in 1518 and made such a fuss that printers feared his wrath and set aside plans for a second edition.[10] The shift of commitment by his followers who were increasingly caught up in Luther's movement unsettled Erasmus.[11] Furthermore, he saw many of his own ideals threatened by the message and the manners of the Wittenberger. He feared that both Luther's radical ideas and his boisterous advocacy of those ideas would alienate the powers and frustrate true reform, as he understood it.

Erasmus did not appreciate Luther's initial attempt to establish personal contact between the two of them through the mediation of Georg Spalatin, for the younger scholar referred the elder scholar to passages where his *Novum Instrumentum,* which Luther had been using for his lectures, was in error. Luther had hoped to build a mutually profitable exchange of ideas through scholarly critique; in this case humanist flattery would have been better suited for the intended audience. The theologian was insensitive to the philologist's prickly pride.[12] As political pressures grew, Erasmus looked upon Luther with "mounting disquiet" according to Leif Grane.[13] By 1521 Erasmus knew he could never come to Luther's support, and both men began anticipating conflict between them.[14] Having begun to feud publicly with one former ally by responding to Ulrich von Hutten's provocation in 1523[15] and increasingly bitter in his comments on other humanist supporters,[16] Erasmus decided the next year that the time had come when he could not remain on the sidelines in the Luther affair any longer.

Erasmus did not choose the topic of the freedom of choice because it had served as a central point of his theological concern; his modest appraisal of the positive potential of the will was rather a necessary presupposition to his understanding of the practice of the Christian faith through the virtues of the *philosophia Christi.* Ernst-Wilhelm Kohls's classic study of his theology, based largely on earlier writings, reveals how relatively seldom the topic of the free will had emerged in his thinking and how he had subjected the will largely to God's grace, as he would in his *Diatribe.*[17] But it is clear that Luther's intense and adamant emphasis on God's grace had rankled the older scholar and — within his constellation of theological axioms — jeopardized his passionate promotion of the ethical life. Furthermore, Erasmus's English friends King Henry VIII and Bishop John Fisher had recently compared Luther's view of the will to the "Manichaean" — deterministic[18] — views of the English archheretic John Wycliffe; Zickendraht has shown that part of Erasmus's treatise on the will rests upon Fisher's writings.[19] This topic of the freedom of the will enabled the Dutch scholar to address the "Luther question" in a manner that would be faithful to his own principles, would make the desired impression on the Roman Catholics who were pressing him to declare himself on the Luther affair, and would not jeopardize his own call for reform.

When Erasmus dropped the bomb of his *Diatribe [Inquiry] or Discourse concerning Free Choice* in the fall of 1524, Luther did not react publicly at first, in part because he perceived that Erasmus's somewhat maladroit attack upon his ideas was expressed in a fashion that would be difficult to rebut without disparaging and deprecating his older and highly respected antagonist.[20] Luther recognized Erasmus's attack as a scholastic critique, formed within the thought world of the medieval scholastic process of scholarly exchange, similar to the challenges he had received from Jacob Latomus and others. Erasmus actually had little experience in that world, and his fine humanistic rhetorical thrust did not meet the university standards for skillful logical parrying. Therefore, Luther hesitated to enter the lists against a foe he deemed so ineptly armed. It was not only that: the usual distractions of university life — plus marriage and revolting peasants — during the following year also delayed Luther's reply. Under pressure from colleagues, particularly Joachim Camerarius, who worked on Luther through his bride,[21] he finally set pen to paper, and his *De servo arbitrio* appeared in print on December 31, 1525.

It is usually said that with *De servo arbitrio* Luther spoke his "last word" to Erasmus,[22] but that is not true. Apparently Luther did write a letter to his adversary after the appearance of his own work, communicating his reasons for the sharp tone of his criticism, for Erasmus sent an answer on April 11, 1526.[23] The appearance of the *Diatribe* had indeed galled the reformer, but his extant correspondence from 1526 is remarkably free of comment on his own reply to it, in contrast to his mention of other works and his dispatch of them to friends.[24]

Erasmus replied publicly very quickly to Luther's treatise, working day and night to have the first half of his *Protector of the Diatribe [Hyperaspistes diatribae]* available at the spring book fair in Frankfurt am Main.[25] Luther was soon aware of both that work[26] and also Erasmus's attempt to quash Luther's continuation of his attacks, for instance, by trying to enlist Elector John of Saxony for that purpose.[27] When the second half of the *Hyperaspistes* appeared, Melanchthon urged moderation, suggesting that Luther not reply directly to Erasmus but treat the issue of the will and free choice in a detached manner.[28] Indeed, the older Wittenberg colleague had other concerns on his mind as tensions rose with those he called "Sacramentarians" and "Schwärmer"[29] in 1526 and 1527. Although the *Hyperaspistes* aroused his ire, he did not express apprehension about the impact these further assaults from Erasmus might have. But he did react. As often happened in his era, the professor took the battle first to the lecture hall, choosing to lecture on Ecclesiastes in the fall semester 1526 and to use its text as the basis for a further critique of Erasmus's view of "skepticism" and of the freedom of the will. Luther focused in these lectures on the debilitating effect Erasmus's view of the will's freedom would have for the exercise of Christian vocation in daily life. Luther emphasized the need for human creatures to exercise responsibility for the part of the world God had placed in their care, on the basis of a firm faith in Christ, anchoring that faith in the mercy and providence of God. To have to strive to will correctly in order to please God takes the focus of human effort off the neighbor's need and places it on the actor. Trust in God as the giver of righteousness in relationship to him frees those bound in sin to love other people for the sake of those neighbors, not for the sake of attaining one's own salvation. Other matters continued to distract Luther in the period after the completion of the lectures, and they were not prepared for publication until 1532.[30] Whether Erasmus noticed that the discussion was being continued is not clear. The reformer also took pen in hand to challenge Erasmus's suggestion for the restoration of the unity of the church in 1534, and that marked the end of their public exchange.[31]

Whatever he may have thought of Erasmus's effort, Luther certainly did not regard his own *De servo arbitrio* as one book among many. He had had time to consider the matter by 1537, when he wrote to Wolfgang Capito that along with his catechism the treatment of bound choice was his best work: "none of my works is worth anything except" the catechism and *De servo arbitrio*, he said.[32] He thought so a decade after its appearance, undoubtedly for the same reasons for which he thanked Erasmus in the volume itself. His opponent had focused attention on precisely this vital element of his theology. "It is not irreverent, inquisitive, or superfluous, but essentially salutary and necessary for a Christian to find out whether the will does anything or nothing in matters pertaining to eternal salvation. . . . this is the cardinal issue between us, the point on which everything in this controversy turns," he told Erasmus.[33] In concluding the book, he reiterated the point: "You and you alone have seen the question on which everything hinges, and have aimed at the vital spot; for which I sincerely thank you since I am only too glad to give as much attention to this subject as time and leisure permit."[34]

The Nature of *De servo arbitrio*

Several considerations must govern any assessment of this document. Readers must recognize that *De servo arbitrio* is an "occasional" work, a polemical work, a somewhat narrowly focused work set in the larger framework of Luther's thought within its historical development, a work fashioned by Luther's scholastic rhetorical training, and a work that emerged within the engagement of two great thinkers who did not summarize their entire theological point of view even if modern scholarly attention has focused much attention on their debate.

First, *De servo arbitrio* was an "occasional writing" — though certainly not only that.[35] As Schwarzwäller observes, labeling a book "an occasional writing" does not tell us much about its purpose and context;[36] every occasion is unique. The term "occasional writing" does not help identify the literary form or method of argument; it does not designate a certain genre. Such publications are responses to a wide variety of specific occasions and situations. Thus, they take on the character of other genres. In Luther's case, on the basis of his understanding of theology as the proclamation of God's Word, a great deal of his writing and speaking took on the character of a confession or testimony of his faith, as he described his first Galatians commentary when it appeared in print in 1519.[37] Luther followed Erasmus's lead in casting their debate in the form of a scholastic disputation, but in that form Luther was not conducting an academic search for truth. In fact, the opening argument of *De servo arbitrio* points to one fundamental difference between the scholar from Rotterdam and the Wittenberg professor: their understanding of the task of the public teaching of God's Word. Luther was confessing his faith in this polemical confrontation, and he scorned Erasmus's praise of skeptical distance over against difficult questions. When God had spoken in Scripture, Luther could not refrain from bold "assertion," from "a constant adhering, affirming, confessing, maintaining, and an invincible persevering" of and in the faith, as he himself defined assertion.[38] Reinhuber calls attention to the broad range of meaning that *assertio* had gained in late medieval Latin usage and focuses on three aspects that help explain what Luther meant with this term that became so important for his practice of theology. His assertion grew out of and expressed the promise of God, his promise to be at work through the Word that is the Holy Spirit's instrument. Assertion was for Luther, secondly, his own personal confession of faith, a description of the reality God reveals. Thirdly, it stated a commitment to God's Word and his action which is designed to deliver the reality of the Word's working to other people.[39]

Second, to refine the description of this occasional writing, *De servo arbitrio* is, as Schwarzwäller points out, "a polemical occasional writing."[40] That is not merely a judgment regarding its tone but much more regarding its genre. That the assertion of a theological position naturally involves polemic was more obvious to early-sixteenth-century academics than to twenty-first-century readers. In fact, from the Old Testament prophets through the later scholastic theologians, Luther's predecessors and models had practiced the art of condemning false teaching, for they believed that the content of their message could not be properly understood in many cases if readers did not comprehend its setting and significance in the immediate historical context. That required a clear presentation of what was not meant as well as what was meant, a clear distinction of truth from falsehood. To explain what is not meant by a statement in a specific context clarifies the speaker's or writer's point of concern and lessens the possibility of the hearer or reader placing the statement in another context, giving it a different meaning. Conscious of how the minds of their hearers actually functioned, the preachers of the Christian gospel had always provided aids for the assessment of the threats to the proper understanding of their proclamation. Such negative definition of the truth was a necessary completion of Christian confession in the early church, when the differences in the revelation of God in Jesus Christ had to be made clear in relationship both to Judaism and to countless other forms of religiosity that gladly put Christian forms to use in the service of their own spiritual principles. Medieval theologians continued the practice of rejecting false teaching both against contemporary heresies and against the historical objections to the catholic faith.[41]

Throughout his career Luther practiced the art of polemic as he had learned it from his instructors. For they had used polemic not only for purposes of clarifying the truth; they had also used it as a means of testing intellectual skills in the formal academic disputation, the university's version of the princely court's tournaments as the locus for demonstrating the skills of one's trade. From participation in countless such disputations at the universities of Erfurt and Wittenberg, Luther had learned how to marshal evidence to support his views from the Bible and from the tradition of the church with rapier-like logic, and for Luther, always with an eye toward the care of souls, the comforting of consciences. He had already taken these methods into the arena of published exchanges, using direct address of his opponent, careful and extensive exegetical argumentation, traditional scholastic logical-analytical tools and occasional patristic citation in confuting the attacks of Jacob Masson (Latomus) in 1521.[42] In his *Against Latomus* the Wittenberg professor exhibited the same concern for careful definition of terms, based on "the Holy Spirit's usage," that became a major analytical device in *De servo arbitrio*.[43] Such striving for clarity through demarcation from other ideas was also encouraged by his colleague Philipp Melanchthon, with his humanistic concern for proper communication. His dedication to effective rhetoric only strengthened Luther's desire to establish clarity through the rejection of possible perversions of God's Word.[44]

17

Luther's polemic was sharpened by his feeling of betrayal at the hands of the papacy. It is insufficient to say "Luther's natural inclination was to be mild, good, gentle, pure and merciful" (which is probably a doubtful assumption in any case), "but the abuses in the Church and the exploitation of the laity forced him to be outspoken and aggressive."[45] He had presumed that the pope would advocate and advance the gospel of Christ; instead the papal court rejected his message and persecuted his followers. He had counted on reform-minded people, like Erasmus, to join him in working for the improvement of the church, and Erasmus was demonstrating his inability to comprehend the heart of the gospel. Luther wrote, "if I seem to be rather too hard on your Diatribe, you must forgive me; for I do it in no malicious spirit, but out of concern because by your authority you have been seriously damaging the cause of Christ."[46] The reader is struck by Luther's impatience and incredulity that someone so brilliant as Erasmus could not understand the Scripture. His sense of betrayal, coupled with this impatience that fed upon the apocalyptic mood of his age, had become embedded in his own perception of reality. Expectations that fundamental change was about to erupt in the whole of society filled the late medieval air, but Luther was one of those who simply anticipated Christ's imminent return to judge the world and bring it to an end. His eschatological convictions — he was certain that Satan was engaging in the last battle for believers' hearts and minds as the world's close approached — drove him to argue for the message of God's unconditional grace with urgency and passion.[47] Erasmus might be able to delude himself into thinking that a dispassionate, purely academic and reasonable discussion of the bondage or freedom of human choice in relation to God was possible. Luther was certain that their exchange was part of the final combat between God and the devil. The warfare between God and Satan took place throughout human history in the clash of God's truth with the devil's lies, and Luther sensed the end of history at hand, when only an intensification of the conflict could be expected.[48] Polemical use of God's truth could defeat the devil, for only the sword of the Spirit, that is, the Word of God, could triumph over the murderous lies of the Deceiver. In those last times, as Luther viewed his own age, polemic was inevitably the order of the day.

Third, the topics discussed in *De servo arbitrio* were not, for Luther, subchapters in a philosophical disquisition. They were much more like "topics" in the sense of Melanchthon's topoi or *loci communes,* the constituent parts treated by the discipline of theology. Thus, they were not units of thought in a string of equally weighted ideological pearls. They were integral working parts of a "body of teaching," a part of a whole that functions as God's instrument of accomplishing his will. Such a *corpus doctrinae* may be viewed from a number of perspectives, all of which contribute to the functioning of an organic whole. The Wittenberg circle understood its teaching, *doctrina,* as a single rule of faith, a unitary expression of God's description of himself and of his creation, extracted for conveying through preaching and teaching from Scripture. Each of Luther's writings concentrates on one or more aspects or topics from that organic whole but is set within the larger "body of teaching" *(corpus doctrinae)* that he found revealed in the Bible and regarded as ultimately serving the pastoral care of the baptized.[49]

Therefore, *De servo arbitrio* should not be seen as an individual, isolated, or independent piece of work. It stands within the longer, larger stream of the development of Luther's thinking. It contains the Wittenberg professor's reactions to Erasmus at a particular point in the maturation of his thought, a process that continued to the end of his life. *De servo arbitrio* deserves special attention and analysis, to be sure, because Luther thought it an excellent summary of his own proclamation of the biblical message and, to a lesser extent, because recent scholarship has deemed the work important. But all theological expression is always a work in progress. This was particularly true of the Wittenberg theology as it was developing in the 1520s. Throughout the sixteenth century those in the Wittenberg circle continued to experiment with ways of conveying and expressing the insights of Luther, Melanchthon, and their colleagues both in German and in Latin. For the scholastic vocabulary no longer served well, once the old framework for thinking through the biblical message had been splintered. Therefore, the study of the argument of *De servo arbitrio* is of little significance if not placed in the larger context of other works by the reformer in other circumstances. *De servo arbitrio* focuses on a few topics — not just the human will — but reflects and reveals the organic nature of Luther's entire theology. Thus, each topic in this work cannot be considered apart from the larger and long-term development of his theology.

Because he was commenting on an extensive and intricate complex of biblical concepts upon a field of conflict — and one defined by his opponent — and because he was quite scrupulous in meeting Erasmus's argument as he had laid it out in his *Diatribe,* Luther was not completely in control of how he proceeded with his presentation — even though he believed he could present his case effectively on Erasmus's turf. His work is a refutation of Erasmus's argument, and only secondarily a presentation of his own views. On the other hand, it dare not be ignored in cataloguing the topics of *De servo arbitrio* that the work comes to its climax in what Gottfried Wilhelm Leibniz would later label the question of theodicy. Luther did in the end take command and answer his own question on his own terms even if the bulk of the work is a careful, point-by-point response to Erasmus.

On the path to the book's summary on the question of evil, Luther viewed God and his human creatures from a number of angles. Any single formulation will focus on one or another aspect of this many-faceted jewel that was the body of his faith, teaching, and confession, but readers should never ignore the context of his entire theological effort. Obviously, it cannot be overlooked that *De servo arbitrio* announced to its readers that it was responding to Erasmus's challenge to Luther and was doing so on the basis of Augustine's expression "bound choice."[50] Martin Doerne insists that the work's title decisively defines Luther's intention in composing the work. "It is not entitled 'De praedestinatione' or 'De Deo abscondito' but 'De servo arbitrio.'"[51]

In fact, attempting to define precisely the central controlling concept and concern of *De servo arbitrio* is a little like looking into a kaleidoscope, since it has several facets. Its title reveals first of all that Erasmus was providing the reformer the occasion to present his views on the much larger picture of God's saving will. The question regarding bound or free choice is but one facet of a multifaceted way of viewing and defining the complex of ideas which Luther believed stand at the heart of God's revelation of himself for the salvation of his people. His teachings on sin, on Christ, on justification, on faith, on God's choosing his own children are of one piece with his teaching on the human will — one "body of doctrine." This title also reveals that Luther was grasping Augustine as a weapon because it employed the bishop of Hippo's contrast of the "free" and "bound" will.[52] Heiko Oberman suggests "the Majesty of God" as an appropriate alternative for the title[53] (though "the grandeur of the Creator" might better capture this idea). Gottfried Krodel supports this interpretation: "In the final analysis it is the concept of God from which all differences between Erasmus and Luther are derived."[54] Such speculations aside, Bengt Hägglund argues that "free choice" is too narrow a synopsis of the work because it concerns the entire disposition of the human creature toward the Creator and the Creator's disposition toward his sinful human creatures.[55] Schwarzwäller asserts that the critical and abiding hinge of Luther's thought, also as he expressed it in *De servo arbitrio,* is summarized best in his Galatians commentary of 1531/1535: the real subject of theology is "the human creature guilty of sin and condemned, and the God who justifies, the savior of this human sinner. If any other subject apart from this is sought or disputed in theology, it is an error and poison."[56]

From one angle or another, however, Luther returned again and again to the question of the meaning of being human. Alongside his confession of God as the almighty and sovereign Creator stands his determination to confess what it means that the human being is a creature, the creation of a Creator, a Creator who makes things by saying "Let there be" (Gen. 1:3-26). His search for the proper description of humanity cannot be separated from his focus on God — on the nature and disposition of the Creator, upon whom by definition the human creature, as the object and handiwork of the Creator's creativity, is dependent. But he was striving to tell his readers what their own capabilities were as creature, both in relationship to God and in relationship to his creation. Indeed, the advent of sin has complicated the task of contemplating the mystery of humanity immensely. Thus, in *De servo arbitrio* Luther's description of humanity treats both the limitations and the potential God placed in his design for being human and the corruption and potential of humanity bound and captivated by unbelief and the other sins that flow from it. The whole work must be comprehended within its author's redefinition of the mystery of God and the mystery of humanity, the Creator-creature relationship based on God's speaking and human trust, and his exploration of the human inability to explain the mystery of evil.

Alongside these questions of content, Eilert Herms has highlighted the pastoral concern that flows — somewhat deep below the surface perhaps, but with tremendous force — under the entire work by demonstrating how Luther asserts the certainty that believers may have because God is Lord of their lives and the world. Herms shows the many aspects of this confession of the certainty that trust in Christ produces, according to the argument of *De servo arbitrio*.[57]

That pastoral concern demonstrates itself above all in the reformer's concluding summary of his argument, which addresses the question of theodicy. The fact that the human will is bound in its relationship to God — a fact Luther affirmed from his own experience but also concluded from his understanding of the biblical revelation of his Creator — places God's mercy and his justice in question. Luther knew that, and he directed his argument in *De servo arbitrio* to arrive at the confession, "We are also certain and sure that we please God not by the merit of our own action but by the favor of his mercy promised to us, and that if we do less than we should or do it badly, he does not hold this against us but in a fatherly way pardons and corrects us."[58] But he also realized that this does not answer the question of God's mercy and justice in the light of the human experience of evil from within and without. So he concluded his dispute with Erasmus by assessing the problem with the aid of three "lights." The light of nature finds it an insoluble problem how the good can suffer while the evil prosper, but the light of grace presents God's love in its everlasting dimension. The light of grace, however, finds it an insoluble problem how God can condemn those who have no power to turn themselves to him. Thus, the lights of both nature and grace find God unjust.

The light of glory, however, affirms that God's incomprehensible righteousness will be revealed. "In the meantime we can only believe this."[59] For "if his righteousness were such that it could be judged to be righteous by human standards, it would clearly not be divine and would in no way differ from human righteousness. But since he is the one true God, and is wholly incomprehensible and inaccessible to human reason, it is proper and indeed necessary that his righteousness should be incomprehensible," as Paul says in Romans 11:33.[60] On the path to this stance of awe before his Creator and Savior, Martin Luther had paused in the pages of *De servo arbitrio* to examine what the Creator and Savior had revealed about himself from several angles, or topical points of viewing the biblical revelation.

Fourth, alongside differing definitions of the theological task and differing estimations of how to determine truth, Luther and Erasmus were separated by different senses of what they were called to do as intellectuals in the public sphere and how the discipline of theology should best function. They revealed in their writings differing understandings of how theology was supposed to operate and what its goals were. Throughout his career Erasmus had sought public order and intellectual solutions to life's problems (though he previously tried not to couch these solutions in scholastic form, nor did he have much practice in scholastic argumentation). "Where would the normal Christian be if, at the mercy of 'fate,' he were relieved of all responsibility for his own moral improvement!"[61] Luther, on the other hand, had continually sought the peace of the troubled conscience through the proclamation of God's Word of promise in Christ (though his preaching also aimed consistently at the cultivation of the life of repentance and faith, which frees the bound will to serve God and neighbor in true human freedom, which is love [Gal. 5:1, 13]). In this case Luther unfolded his theology within the context of the academic practice he had employed as a budding scholastic thinker.

Heiko Oberman concludes that Erasmus's view of Scripture excluded common Christians from using it; his view of a Bible so full of mysteries placed it only in the hands of a pope given the right to open its seven seals or in the hands of the scholars, the scholastic theologians who had been "consecrated" for deciphering its pages.[62] Heinz Holoczek observes, "Indeed, the difference regarding the will was hardly the real critical point in the conflict between the two. More decisive in their distinctive points of view were their differing concepts of faith and their conflicting ways of relating to Holy Scripture."[63] Holoczek's own explanation of the differences in their concept of the faith, however, misses the mark; false is his judgment that the difference in their definitions of faith rested on Luther's need for detailed definition of the content of that faith (since he had rejected the authority of the church) whereas Erasmus operated with a much looser definition of the content of the church's dogma since he placed his confidence in the tradition and in the authority of ecclesiastical officials.[64] The difference lies rather in Luther's belief, as he made clear in *De servo arbitrio,* that God had made his revealed truth quite clear in Scripture and demanded trust in his Word. In addition, Luther was driven by his concern for terrified consciences. Wrestling with the ultimate question of how a good and omnipotent God can coexist with evil — theodicy — he was certain that the only solution for human arrogance and human despair lay in being grasped by the God who speaks his truth for the comfort of his people.[65] Erasmus, on the other hand, showed less concern for the existential state of believers than for the morality they practiced, and so moral suasion rather than doctrinal proclamation moved his passions. If readers miss the fundamental orientation around issues of daily Christian living that drove these authors, their works will remain as enigmatic as they will if readers fail to grasp the scholastic method that gave them their form.

Thomas Wabel refines the answer given to the question regarding the authors' approaches to Scripture. "The fundamental lack of understanding between Luther and Erasmus is to be traced back to the difference in their fundamentally dissimilar ways of reading Scripture," in Luther's case, based upon the distinction of law and gospel and the use of Christ as the center of biblical revelation.[66] This meant that Luther demanded that theologians were to convey to the church God's truth simply and obviously because it is God's truth, the message that God wants his people to hear, a message that not only describes God's saving will but also effects it. Secondly, they must dedicate themselves above all to the pastoral care of consciences. That meant words of God's condemning law were to be addressed to defiant rebels, and words of gospel were to be applied as balm to threatened, smoldering wicks and broken, terrified reeds. Luther did not intend to compose a philosophical dissertation but rather to expound theology, by which he understood the delivery, proclamation, and confession of God's Word for the good of the church and its members. For the reformer, God's Word was not merely descriptive but also creative; that is, it does what it says to its human hearers. That God's Word occupies such a key position in the divine economy, Luther had learned from his textbooks and instructors from the school of Gabriel Biel, who had placed God's power and authority in his Word.[67] Luther was convinced that readers would be grasped by the Word of God he was asserting and would experience God's address in his rehearsal of the biblical material he was exposing. The message of Luther's work comes clear only when readers also recognize that the author believed that God's Word is at work as his law and his gospel, as his judgment or his forgiveness: the Word creates new life in Christ for sinners.

23

Fifth, Luther and Erasmus use forms of argument defined by scholastic disputation, making it difficult for twenty-first-century readers to follow. Ironically, Erasmus was not an experienced scholastic combatant; he had held himself outside the university enterprise and eschewed what he considered the irrelevant quibblings of the scholastics and their debates. He was trying to assault Luther with a form of academic exercise at which he had far less experience than his opponent. Despite his great intellectual gifts, his aim was not always so precise, his execution sometimes misfired. His choice of the descriptive *Diatribe* ("discussion in a back and forth" fashion) as a title announced his intention to exchange ideas rather than to insist upon or confess a specific viewpoint,[68] but he pursued his argument in the *Diatribe* with the scholastic method of positing definitions and conclusions and then examining them critically.[69] Oberman observed, "It was precisely in his confrontation with Luther . . . that the outstanding Bible scholar was more scholastic and medieval than ever before. His polemical treatise was oriented toward the past; it was extremely conservative in its rejection of public discussion of unauthorized, untried, and hence unacceptable solutions and biblical interpretations."[70] His conservative stance not only expressed itself in its refusal to venture where medieval thinkers had not gone before, but also in its attempt to use scholastic method. Furthermore, his lack of practice at scholastic argument made his presentation lame.

In contrast to Erasmus, Luther's entire academic training had schooled his mind in the art and practice of scholastic argumentation. The young Wittenberg professor possessed first-rate skills in the processes of the disputation. From Luther's use of traditional scholastic method, comments Schwarzwäller, his demonstrations took on clarity, but this also means that his discourse can grow tedious.[71] Schwarzwäller identifies four levels on which Luther pursued his argumentation: He focused simply on the subject matter in a confessional manner at times, at others he pursued rational argument. He refuted Erasmus with earnest discussion of the theological implications of his position and with a logical analysis that sometimes fell into sarcasm.[72] In each of these instances readers must be sensitive to the function and goal of Luther's analysis.

Finally, readers dare not be overwhelmed by the players in this dramatic confrontation, however significant the question Erasmus laid on the table and Luther dissected thoroughly in their exchange. Failing to recognize that their presuppositions and definitions of certain terms differed, they sometimes talked past each other. For instance, Hägglund points out that Erasmus defined the will as a neutral ability to decide, which stands between the judgment of reason and the actual decision. For Luther the will is the inner orientation of human creatures which determines the entire direction of their lives and expresses — in the actions it causes — their very identity.[73] Because they were arguing from different premises, readers cannot presume that these two intellectual titans, the German Hercules and the Prince of Humanists, with their differing but remarkable intellectual aptitudes, presented themselves in this debate at their clearest and best, or in their most mature stage of thinking, on any given topic. Erasmus took on a question that Luther had been trained to answer in sophisticated scholastic form, and Luther's response reveals at many points that he had also become a skilled exegete. Nonetheless, his being drawn onto Erasmus's turf at points worked to his disadvantage at times. His scholastic argumentation, for instance, in the discussion of divine necessity,[74] sometimes obscured his fundamental concern for the integrity of the human being as a rational and volitional creature fashioned by God and for pastoral care of troubled consciences. The fact that Erasmus was a fine philologist, with excellent tools for linguistic analysis, does not mean he was well equipped to elucidate the thought patterns of the biblical writers.[75] Luther made that point in concluding his critique of the *Diatribe*,[76] and scholars with as different perspectives as Anthony Levi, James Tracy, and Klaus Schwarzwäller agree that Erasmus had strayed into a swamp when he ventured into the question of the human will. Whether fair and accurate in his assessment or not, Levi, an Erasmus scholar, reveals the frustration the *Diatribe* produces in readers when he writes, "It is as if, having failed to prevent the schism or to remain neutral in the theological debate it provoked, Erasmus had become dejectedly self-destructive, proclaiming his independence of the sectarian strife into which he had been unwillingly conscripted by annoying both sides before delivering the assault on Luther's position which he knew would be regarded as an inadequate show of goodwill toward the pope." That is due, Levi believes, to the "impossibility of finding an orthodox solution to the problem of reconciling the affirmation of free will with a non-Pelagian theory of grace."[77]

Tracy's analysis of Erasmus's reasoning reveals that he tripped over his own argument at times because he actually held two contradictory views regarding the subject;[78] Luther had suggested that his antagonist held three different estimations of the will's capabilities.[79] The same might be said of Luther as well, but Erasmus did not present a system which enabled him to hold opposing concerns in a practicable tension, as did Luther with his distinction of law and gospel. Erasmus tried to homogenize and harmonize divine and human responsibilities without reference to the specific attitude of the individual at the time of the application of the message. Schwarzwäller observes the difficulties Erasmus had in formulating his position clearly and points out how easily Luther could find contradictions and inconsistencies in it. Finally, for Schwarzwäller, Erasmus failed because he attempted to pursue ontological, ethical, and anthropological questions within a theological framework and thus "in truth he is practicing a philosophy in theological clothing."[80] Bernhard Lohse echoed these judgments: "Indeed, in the *Diatribe* Erasmus did not succeed in conducting a genuine engagement with Luther's position because he had no understanding either for the view of sin, grace, and justification that Luther had gained from Paul or for Luther's concept of the certainty of salvation."[81] Perhaps Erasmus did not recognize that himself; perhaps he would not have cared if he had.

Furthermore, however large for the history of Christian dogma the controversy between the two looms from the perspective of theologians a half-millennium later, it must be noted, as Martin Brecht commented, that "this controversy actually was only a circumscribed episode for Luther."[82] The same can be said for Erasmus. Both men recognized how vital the issue was for the life of the Christian and for the proclamation of the church, but their public confrontation caused neither catastrophe nor new acclaim and support for either. The way in which they posed and argued the vital questions of how to confess God and how to understand what it means to be human continued to command attention in later periods. In their own time these questions remained at the heart of the enterprise of reform within every Christian church, but their own debate receded in significance for their contemporaries.

In addition, Luther may have regarded *De servo arbitrio* highly, but he did not regard it as infallible. He himself offered codicils to what he had bequeathed to his followers in *De servo arbitrio*. He was among the first "receptors" of his own work. The most troublesome part of the book for his followers was his argument from divine necessity. Erasmus had raised the bogeyman of determinism in his *Diatribe*,[83] and Luther rose to the challenge, rejecting the scholastic distinctions that Erasmus had found helpful to make room for a bit of free will. His understanding of the Creator God led him to insist on a doctrine of divine necessity, that God's willing creates an absolute necessity embracing all of his creation. He soon abandoned this particular experiment in expressing his views, but in 1525 it seemed to work. Almost immediately, however, he apparently sensed the difficulty produced by this importation of terminology, often ill-defined, from ancient pagan philosophers into biblical thinking. He strove to deal with it head-on, and only later reconsidered the wisdom of using this line of argumentation. It is not clear whether an addition to the book itself regarding the concept of absolute divinely instituted necessity, written into the Wittenberg and Jena editions of Luther's works, came from his pen or not. Early in Luther's argument in *De servo arbitrio*, in the midst of the discussion of necessity and contingency, Georg Rörer, the editor of the complete works of the reformer, both in the version published in Wittenberg and in the rival version published in Jena, inserted the following paragraph:

> I could wish indeed that another and a better word had been introduced into our discussion than this usual one, "necessity," which is not rightly applied either to the divine or the human will. It has too harsh and incongruous a meaning for this purpose, for it suggests a kind of compulsion, and the very opposite of willingness, although the subject under discussion implies no such thing. For neither the divine nor the human will does what it does, whether good or evil, under any compulsion, but from sheer pleasure or desire, as with true freedom; and yet the will of God is immutable and infallible, and it governs our mutable will, as Boethius sings: "Remaining fixed, you make all things move"; and our will, especially when it is evil, cannot of itself do good. The reader's intelligence must therefore supply what the word "necessity" does not express, by understanding it to mean what you might call the immutability of the will of God and the impotence of our evil will, or what some have called the necessity of immutability though this is not very good either grammatically or theologically.[84]

The authenticity of this addition is impossible to prove or disprove. Rörer knew Luther very well, had conversed with him intensively and extensively for more than twenty years, and since 1537 had the charge from the electoral Saxon court to edit Luther's writings.[85] The second volume of the Wittenberg Latin edition appeared in the year of Luther's death; Rörer was working on it while the reformer was still alive.[86] But whether Luther wrote and/or approved of this addition remains unclear. What must be acknowledged is that Luther was constructing a new theological paradigm, and that effort inevitably drew him into trying out new vocabulary. He learned from such experiments even when they failed to produce satisfactory results.

Whether this addition came from the reformer's own pen or not, he articulated in his lectures on Genesis his concern that his words about absolute necessity in *De servo arbitrio* might have given a false impression. There he digressed from treating the text of chapter 26 to comment on pastoral problems that might arise from a false reading of his work on the bound choice. He expressed his fear that his words concerning an absolute and necessary unfolding of all things would be misunderstood after his death, and so he directed his students to look only to Jesus Christ, the revelation of God. Addressing specifically the problem of the doubt and despair or the arrogant and defiant security that can result from a doctrine of double predestination, he distinguished between sinful speculation and trusting the promise of God in Christ.[87] In commenting soon thereafter on Genesis 27:43-45, he observed that the thoughts of "those who refer everything to predestination and thus do away with all the activities and means God has ordained" and say, "If these things must happen, they will happen of necessity even without work on my part," are "wicked and impious because God wants you to make use of the means you have at your disposal."[88] Luther's second thoughts regarding the terminology of necessity were oft repeated by his students as they strove to deal with the tension between God's total responsibility for all things and human responsibility as God's obedient creature.

Readers of Erasmus's *Diatribe* and Luther's *De servo arbitrio* in the twenty-first century must take all these aspects of the controversy between Erasmus and Luther into consideration in order to understand its course and significance. Recognizing them would certainly have benefited sixteenth-century readers as well. Since these readers came to Luther's and Erasmus's pages without acknowledging the ways in which presupposition and hermeneutic shaped the expression of their varying positions, they did not always sense that the two were sometimes arguing past each other. The ways in which their contemporaries understood and interpreted the two contestants in this exchange and the ways they put particularly Luther's thought to use therefore command attention even as we assess their own teaching, their interpretation of Luther's teaching, and how they passed it on to subsequent generations.

The Roots of Luther's View of Choice

The author of *De servo arbitrio* was casting his ideas into the public arena in the midst of the theological explosion that he had ignited as he introduced a profound paradigm shift in Western Christian theology, in its definition of the focal point of the biblical message, and in its method. Luther was, in Peter Matheson's words, forging "a new universe of discourse in which people could discover anew who they were."[89] The reformer fashioned this new universe out of elements from his own personal experience and from his instruction at the university. His entire life he engaged in a continuing set of experiments in formulating his insights into the biblical message in language that carried it adequately. He phrased his questions regarding human identity in part out of the language of monastic piety, in part from the language of late medieval scholasticism, in part with the biblical language being explored in fresh fashion by those we call humanists, Erasmus and Melanchthon among them. *De servo arbitrio* is one of several important manifestos in which Luther laid out vital elements of this paradigm shift.

When the reformer formulated his views of the bondage of human choice for the *Assertion of All Articles* in 1521, he was still drying off from wrestling with the life-and-death questions of his own righteousness, his own identity, in God's sight. That inner contest had pitted elements of his scholastic learning against each other. But he recorded few hints and no explicit analysis of how he digested the various components of the philosophy and theology he had learned in Erfurt. Luther's Ockhamist[90] instructors did impress upon his mind certain axioms that have left traces of his working presuppositions in his writings. Like all traces, these often elude precise analysis, but substantive remnants of Ockhamist thinking nonetheless do help to explain much about the development of his thought. His revolt against this teaching on grace and works, on sin and salvation, is well known and carefully chronicled.[91] But from the writings of Gabriel Biel and from his Erfurt instructors who had studied under Biel, Luther also assimilated a definition of God as the almighty Creator, who according to his absolute power could do anything he pleased, who conformed to no external standard, who defined the Good by his Word or covenant. In the Old Testament Biel and his intellectual progenitor William of Ockham had discovered a Creator who holds all things in his hands and who has claimed responsibility for all that happens in his creation. Luther's thinking shows clearly the vestiges of their concept of the true and only God, who stands sovereign and supreme over his creation, beyond the grasp of human reason. Luther also never lost Ockham's and Biel's concept of the utter reliability of the Word of this God as his revealed covenants with human creatures; the reformer remained certain that God's Word could be trusted because God does not fail to hold to his promises.[92]

At the same time, Biel and Ockham took human responsibility very seriously, so seriously that they assigned a critical role to the exercise of that responsibility in winning salvation from sin. They approached the central questions of human existence from the starting point of human performance, its role and value, rather than from God's creative activity. Therefore, their blending of the biblical concept of obedience to God's commands with Aristotle's anthropology and ethics led them to insist that human beings must do their best in order to earn God's grace if they are to merit salvation.[93] In contrast, while Luther continued to take human responsibility to obey God's law seriously, he rejected this harmonization and homogenization of God's sovereign, creative activity with human performance. For the reformer had suffered much in his conscience because of this kind of blending of divine grace and human effort. In Luther's view the Ockhamist synthesis had not truly balanced God's gracious exercise of his responsibility for his creatures with the human being's exercise of responsibility in the realm God had created for human performance. By attempting to give each a complementary place alongside the other, the Ockhamists obscured the total unconditionality of God's love for his own human creatures and mitigated his stringent demands for their obedience by ascribing some merit to works that remained insufficient in and of themselves. Whenever the law which demands human performance is simply laid alongside the gospel, which delivers God's gracious love, the command or the condemnation always holds sway over the sinner's attention, as Luther knew from his own experience. Because of this, speaking of God's initiative and God's assumption of responsibility for life and proper living never led him to a philosophical determinism, but rather to the unconditioned love of the living Creator. Not a principle but rather a loving person determined Luther's world and what happened in it. God's promise expressed in the gospel brought comfort to the reformer's conscience and moved his will to act in truly human fashion, that is, in obedience to God's design for human life.[94]

Therefore, he came to assert both the Creator's total responsibility for his creation and the total responsibility of human creatures for the sphere of life entrusted to them, in which the Creator expects and demands their trust and the obedience that flows from it. God alone is the creative agent for all in his creation; at the same time, human beings are the responsible agents in the sphere of life God gives them. Oberman argued that this reflection on the "ultimate problems of God's sovereignty and human responsibility" was anchored in Luther's own biography. This is certainly true, but the actual formulation of the answers to which Luther came arose out of his study of Scripture: under the discipline of his own academic training he placed Scripture in the context of what his own experience had shown him regarding these definitive questions of life.[95] Experience and exegesis together led him to formulate this paradoxical placing of total divine responsibility and total human responsibility alongside each other. Both God's Word and his own spiritual struggles provided him with an understanding of humanity that met the biblical parameters for defining God's relationship to sinners and to believers. Not a synthesis or harmonization of divine and human activity, this paradox did not assign grace and works respective parts within a process of salvation. It instead held in perpetual tension what the biblical writers said about God and what they said about human creatures. The result placed the human conscience fully in the hands of a providential and predestining God and at the same time placed responsibility for the care of God's creatures fully upon that conscience.

Throughout, *De servo arbitrio* reminds its readers of Luther's sense of the Creator's unrestricted power, inherited from his Ockhamist instructors, and thus his total responsibility for all things. But the book also clearly sets forth the reformer's assessment of how to describe the total responsibility of human creatures for the obedience God demands of them even though he rejected the Ockhamist assignment of a merit to human performance that could play a major role in establishing human identity and worth in God's sight.

The Theology of *De servo arbitrio*

Three theological axioms form the foundation of Luther's treatment of Erasmus's argument. First, God is Creator. Second, the human being is a creature, fashioned by and dependent upon the Creator and his design for humanity. Luther regarded the fall into sin as an inescapable corollary of this axiom. Sin meant simply that human creatures had broken their relationship with God; therefore, they are further dependent on his action, as he planned it before the foundation of the world, to be returned to him. Third, restored to trusting in him, his own chosen people, having been given the gift of faith, are engaged in a lifelong struggle against the evil that sin produces in their lives. Even after God reclaims and re-creates them as his own, the presence of sin makes daily repentance necessary for believers — a strange mystery but an incontrovertible fact.[96]

Each of these convictions presupposed and inevitably led back to the concepts of the Creator God's total responsibility and sovereignty over his creation and the total responsibility of human creatures to carry out God's design for their humanity. Ten theses summarizing the reformer's application of these fundamental truths in *De servo arbitrio* (not all treated in equal length or depth in the book) will aid in assessing how Luther's and Melanchthon's students interpreted and employed the work. The topics of election and repentance, not extensively addressed in *De servo arbitrio,* are inseparable in the reformer's thought from the elements upon which Luther concentrated there and played a role in the controversies related to the book's topics.

The message of *De servo arbitrio* in its larger context in Luther's thought may be paraphrased and summarized as follows. (1) God is a person, the almighty Creator of all that exists, the sovereign Lord and sole acting agent over his creation, totally responsible for all that takes place. (2) The Creator is by definition hidden from his creatures but has revealed himself in his incarnation as Jesus Christ and in Holy Scripture. (3) God has chosen from among fallen sinners people to be his own children and has restored them to their full humanity, that is, to trusting in him, through the work of Christ. (4) God acts in his Word, condemning sin through the law and conveying Christ's benefits to his chosen people through the gospel, in oral, written, and sacramental forms, called collectively the means of grace. (5) Human beings are creatures and thus totally dependent on God their Creator. (6) This dependence of the human creature on God can be explained and defended by a doctrine of absolute necessity, that is, that all things happen necessarily as God designs and decides. (7) Human beings are responsible for their own disposition and actions but are sinful, captive to Satan and their own desires, and thus totally dependent on God for liberation from their sinfulness. (8) Human beings are designed by God with active minds and wills that are to be dedicated to carrying out their callings in obedience to God. (9) Believers are engaged in a lifelong struggle against their own abiding sinfulness. Their lives are lives of repentance. (10) God is not responsible for evil. No explanation of the existence of evil and its continuation in the lives of believers is possible.

Let God Be God

God is a person, the almighty Creator of all that exists, the sovereign Lord and sole acting agent over his creation, totally responsible for all that takes place.

Wherever Luther began a specific assertion or confession of biblical teaching, he presumed the person of his God. He always insisted that God be regarded and treated as God, not as an impersonal object that could be manipulated by magical formulas or rites, and not as a person of only something more than mere human power and capability. Though not often found in Luther's own writing, the exhortation "Let God be God"[97] can serve as an apt summary of *De servo arbitrio*.

This God was indeed, for Luther, Creator. Luther's argument in *De servo arbitrio* rests upon the presupposition that God the Creator alone establishes human existence, identity, and righteousness, three words that come close to being synonyms when used to encapsulate Luther's view of humanity. Hans Joachim Iwand noted that Luther's teaching regarding the will's lack of freedom must be viewed in the light of the reformer's belief regarding the nature of the Creator and his relationship to his creation.[98] As Creator he is totally distinct from his creation — wholly other — and is active at the foundation of all that he has made: in, behind, and through all creation. By definition God is beyond and above everything he has shaped with the word of his creative mouth. "He is God, and for his will there is no cause or reason that can be laid down as a rule or measure for it since there is nothing equal or superior to it, but it is itself the measure of all things. For if there were any rule or measure or cause or reason for it, it could no longer be the will of God."[99] Erasmus's assignment of the topic of "free choice" gave Luther the opportunity to affirm this confession of God's Godness in terms of freedom. The Wittenberg professor sharply distinguished two fundamental levels of what "freedom" can mean, for the Creator and for the creature. "Free choice is plainly a term for God and can be properly applied to no one but the Divine Majesty alone; for he alone can do and does (as the psalmist says [Ps. 115:3]) whatever he pleases in heaven and on earth."[100]

The Creator is not subject to human ways of foreknowing. His foreknowledge is creative; it determines the future rather than passively observing it as an already existing object. "God foreknows nothing contingently, but foresees and purposes and does all things by his immutable, eternal, and infallible will."[101] Because this God is the person whose mercy is new every morning and whose love has appeared in Jesus Christ, it "is the one supreme consolation of Christians in all adversities to know that God does not lie, but does all things immutably, and that his will can neither be resisted nor changed nor hindered."[102] Without using the term "predestination" for God's choosing his own children, Luther made it clear that believers can have sure comfort only if their salvation from sin — their identity as children of God — rests upon God's decision alone, apart from any human contribution.[103] For Luther this not only made for effective pastoral care; it reflected the very nature of the Creator as he is revealed in the Bible.

Throughout *De servo arbitrio* Luther strove to make it clear that this God, who as a person spoke through the prophets and, finally, as the incarnate God in Jesus Christ came into a conversation with sinners that transforms them into his new creation, is not a fixed or unmoved and unmoving Ultimate. This free and freely acting God is a person who continues to be engaged with all that he has made. God's "willing" served as a synonym for God's continuing exercise of his providential agency, his responsibility for all creation.

> For the will of God is effectual and cannot be impeded, since it is the power of God's nature itself; moreover, it is wise, so that it cannot do something wrong. Now, if his will is not impeded, there is nothing to prevent the work itself from being done, in the place, time, manner, and measure that he himself both foresees and wills. If the will of God were

such that, when what he was doing was completed, what he had accomplished would remain but the will stopped functioning, as is the case with the human will, which ceases to will when the house it wanted is built, just as it also comes to an end in death, then it could be truly said that things happen contingently and mutably. But the opposite is the case; God completes what he is doing and his will continues to function.[104]

Such a confession, repeated often throughout *De servo arbitrio,* distinguishes Luther's thinking about God, freedom, and human life very clearly from the determinism of philosophical systems that assign to an impersonal fate the liability for all that happens.[105] Luther trusted in God's providence; he did not base that trust in any way on some concept of fate or destiny but simply on the person of God as he has revealed himself on the cross.[106] That person is righteous — has his core identity — in his compassion and love. God's "righteousness" had long been defined as his justice — his fairness — which presumed that he punished wrongdoers and rewarded the good on the basis of their own deeds. That definition arose out of the human tendency to define the world around human performance. It was supported by Aristotle and by the Latin use of the one word, *iustitia,* for both human justice and the more fundamental meaning of righteousness, that which defines or describes the essence or core identity of a person or thing. Luther, too, used *iustitia* and its German equivalent *Gerechtigkeit* in both senses. He defined God's essence not in terms of the Creator's fair treatment of human creatures according to their actions. Rather, he confessed that God is truly God at his most Godly when he shows mercy and bestows his love. Even his wrath betrays his desire to show mercy and goodness to those he wants to bring back to faith in himself, for whom he wants to restore truly human life.[107] That is not obvious to sinful human creatures, for God is hidden from their ability to grasp him. They are dependent on his revealing himself.

Within some six years Luther was lecturing on Galatians for the second time, and in his exposition of the epistle he relied on the affirmation of God's creative activity that Paul made in his teaching on baptism (Rom. 6:3-11; Col. 2:11-15). In baptism, according to the apostle, God kills and buries sinners so that he may raise them up through Christ's resurrection to new life.[108] This depiction of God as the Creator of new life, of new creatures, formed the heart of the reformer's maturing understanding of God's saving work. The topic of dying and rising through the action of the Word in baptism expressed homiletically Luther's view of God as the Creator who re-creates through Christ's death and resurrection when he brings the gospel of Christ to his chosen people.

God Hidden and Revealed

The Creator is by definition hidden from his creatures but has revealed himself in his incarnation as Jesus Christ and in Holy Scripture.

From his Ockhamist instructors Luther had learned to distinguish what God might be in his absolute power, where he is beyond human grasp, from what can be known of him as he exercises the power he has ordered in his covenants.[109] His teachers may have found delight in speculating about the absolute power of God (questions Luther largely placed off-limits for human rationalizing, within the domain of what he called "the hidden God," where reason can only sink into a swamp of dangerous speculation); at least they occasionally turned students loose in disputations to test their mettle in logic on problems posed beyond the context of divine revelation. Luther laid down the principle of avoiding wild God-chases, for he believed that searching for God apart from his Word could only lead to arrogance or despair. This conviction proceeded, to be sure, from his theological education in Erfurt, which had fostered a strong sense of human dependence on God's revelation. From the beginning of his call for the church's return to biblical teaching, his focus had concentrated on the concrete person of God, as he came into conversation with the Old Testament people who heard his prophets (for example, Jer. 1:1-19; Ezek. 1:3; Hos. 1:1; Mic. 1:1; etc.) and above all as he addressed the world in the Word made flesh (John 1:14), as Jesus Christ, God revealed upon the cross.[110]

Schwarzwäller associates Luther's call to let God be God with the reformer's maxim "Christ alone."[111] For letting God be God does not "elevate" him to the level of an abstract eternal principle but trusts what God says about himself, through his prophets and in Christ (Heb. 1:1-2). "Luther stops at the boundary that God's Godness draws; . . . he surrenders himself completely to the God that meets him there. On the other hand, Erasmus is forced by his conclusions to know something *about* God that is not from God . . . but from himself, or more precisely, from a metaphysical principle that gives human beings the possibility of making a judgment about what is God, what belongs to God, what is divine, and what is not."[112]

Luther placed his teaching regarding God within the framework of his fundamental distinction between God Hidden and God Revealed, which he developed in detail first in his theses for his Augustinian brothers assembled at Heidelberg in 1518. This distinction formed a basic part of his "theology of the cross." He differentiated *Deus revelatus* from *Deus absconditus*. The latter term meant, in different contexts, either God as he actually exists beyond the grasp of human conceptualization — particularly when the human mind is darkened by sin — or God as sinners fashion him in their own image, to their own liking. (In addition, it must be noted that the revealed God hides himself in human form in order to show himself to his human creatures.)[113]

Luther took the hidden God seriously for a number of reasons. Without the admission that there is more to God than meets either eye or ear, God could be tamed, measured, managed within the realm of the human ability and possibility to judge. From the human perspective God remains God because human creatures are creatures as well as sinners, and it is not possible for the product of God's creative words to master knowledge of the Creator. "For if his righteousness were such that it could be judged to be righteous by human standards, it would clearly not be divine and would in no way differ from human righteousness. But since he is the one true God, and is wholly incomprehensible and inaccessible to human reason, it is proper and indeed necessary that his righteousness should be incomprehensible" (Rom. 11:33).[114]

Wandering across the boundary into the swamp of trying to plumb the depths of God's inner being meant trouble, even death, for sinners, Luther believed. "The secret will of the Divine Majesty is not a matter for debate, and the human temerity which with continual perversity is always neglecting necessary things in its eagerness to probe this one must be called off and restrained. . . . Let it occupy itself instead with God incarnate, or as Paul puts it, with Jesus crucified, in whom are all the treasures of wisdom and knowledge, though in a hidden manner [Col. 2:3]."[115] In the Heidelberg Disputation Luther had focused first on the blank wall created by the impossibility of the human creature's, to say nothing of sinner's, conceptualizing of God, just to prove that with fallen eyes no one can see God. With fallen human ears no one can return to the Edenic hearing of his Word. Then Luther focused very sharply on God in his revelation of himself (John 1:18): no one has seen God, but Jesus of Nazareth, God in the flesh, has made him known: a God with holes in his hands, feet, and side; the God who has come near to humankind, into the midst of its twisted and ruined existence.

Luther observed that God is to be found precisely where his scholastic predecessors, whom he labeled "theologians of glory," were horrified to find him: as a child in a crib, as a criminal on a cross, as a corpse in a crypt. God reveals himself by hiding himself right in the middle of human existence as it has been bent out of shape by the human fall. Luther's theology of the cross thus intended to depart from the fuzziness of human attempts to focus on God apart from God's pointing out where he is to be found and who he really is. God on the cross reveals the fullness of God's love as well as the inadequacy of all human efforts to patch up life to please him. Christ sufficed for Luther; when he had heard Jesus, he had heard it all.[116]

Schwarzwäller begins his commentary on *De servo arbitrio* with an analysis of the work's conclusion, for, as he rightly notes, the conclusion leads the reader to the book's climax. The orator in Luther brought his presentation together and to an end with the observation, "If we believe that Christ has redeemed human creatures by his blood, we are bound to confess that the whole human being was lost. Otherwise, we should make Christ either superfluous or the redeemer of only the lowest part of humanity [in Aristotelian anthropology the appetites or sensual desires], and that would be blasphemy and sacrilege."[117] Instead, Luther confessed Christ as truly God come in human flesh as true human being, who died and rose again to give new life to God's elect. Christ is the way, the truth, the life, and salvation (John 14:6), Luther affirmed, "and outside of Christ there is nothing but Satan, apart from grace nothing but wrath, apart from light only darkness, apart from the Way only error, apart from the Truth only a lie, apart from Life only death."[118]

This particular issue concerned Luther fifteen years later when he lectured on Genesis. Precisely in an effort to guard against misinterpretations of *De servo arbitrio,* Luther placed in God's mouth the following words:

> "From an unrevealed God I will become a revealed God. Nevertheless, I will remain the same God. I will be made flesh, or send My Son. He shall die for your sins and shall rise again from the dead. And in this way I will fulfill your desire, in order that you may be able to know whether you are predestined or not. Behold, this is my Son; listen to him (cf. Matt. 17:5). Look at him as he lies in the manger and on the lap of his mother, as he hangs on the cross. Observe what he does and what he says. There you will surely take hold of me." For "he who sees me," says Christ, "also sees the Father himself" (cf. John 14:9). If you listen to him, are baptized in his name, and love his Word, then you are certainly predestined and are certain of your salvation.[119]

Luther here goes further. He rejects any discordance between hidden God and revealed God even though the hidden God lies far beyond human grasp.

> If you believe in the revealed God and accept his Word, he will gradually also reveal the hidden God, for "he who sees me also sees the Father," as John 14:9 says. He who rejects the Son also loses the unrevealed God along with the revealed God. But if you cling to the revealed God with a firm faith, so that your heart is so minded that you will not lose Christ even if you are deprived of everything, then you are most assuredly predestined, and you will understand the hidden God. Indeed, you under-

stand him even now if you acknowledge the Son and his will, namely, that he wants to reveal himself to you, that he wants to be your Lord and your Savior. Therefore you are sure that God is also your Lord and Father.[120]

This Lord and Father cannot be captured by human imagination but can be grasped only by human trust. Luther's understanding of what it means that God is Creator compelled him to presume that something of God must be beyond human kenning, and his conviction regarding the deafness and blindness induced by human sinfulness only strengthened this view. But he held firm to the unity of the God who had demonstrated his love on the cross, in the human person the second person of the Trinity had become. Therefore, he did not attempt to draw some abstract principles regarding life's vital questions from the wisdom of the church. He trusted the person of God as he had revealed himself and focused all of human life on the Creator who had become Savior and Sanctifier for sinners.

God Chooses His Own

God has chosen from among fallen sinners people to be his own children and has restored them to their full humanity, that is, to trusting in him, through the work of Christ.

Luther himself later saw that the question of the predestination of God's children to be rescued from their sinfulness and returned to trust in him would be raised in connection with *De servo arbitrio*,[121] and more recent scholars have connected his teaching of the consolation of God's election of the faithful to this work.[122] Almost a decade before its appearance, Luther had recognized the doctrine of predestination as an inherent part of his developing understanding of justification by grace. In his "Disputation against Scholastic Theology" of 1517, he had argued that "the best, infallible preparation for grace, and the only disposing factor for its reception, is God's eternal choosing and predestination." He rejected the scholastic phrase that one who has been predestined could be damned *in sensu diviso* (for the sake of a logical distinction) but not *in composito* (according to plan) and that predestination was necessary by a *necessitas consequentiae* but not by a *necessitas consequentis*.[123] And yet the idea of God's predestining power had troubled him in the course of his spiritual struggles. His monastic superior and spiritual counselor Johannes von Staupitz had directed him away from thoughts of predestination to the wounds of Jesus,[124] and he seemed to follow this advice in *De servo arbitrio.* This treatise treated the predestination of the saints indirectly and seldom, and it totally ignored the fundamental Bible passages on which Wittenberg students later based its comfort, Romans 8:28-39 and Ephesians 1:3-11. Yet it is clear that in his repudiation of the power of the human will to turn itself to God he was crafting his position upon the presupposition of God's predestination of those he had planned to save before the foundations of the world.

When the term "predestination" occurs in *De servo arbitrio,* however, it is mostly used in a more general way than specifically to refer to the salvation of the elect. Pagan peoples had an intuitive notion of God's predestination in the sense of his planning all things, Luther taught, for divine foreknowledge, in the imagination of the peoples of the earth, stands behind all things.[125] He also used the concept as a way of describing the creative foreknowledge that belongs to the Creator; when God knew something in eternity, he was causing it to happen within time.[126] Grace indeed stems from God's purpose or predestination, Luther averred.[127] His view of God Hidden and Revealed led him to anchor God's choice of his own children in the promise found in his revelation of himself in Christ, Scripture, and the use of the Word of the gospel in the means of grace. From the principle of God's immutability that he had learned from Bielist instructors[128] and from the comfort he had received through Staupitz's pastoral care,[129] he fashioned an understanding of God's Word that led him to confess, "when God promises anything, you ought to be certain that he knows and is able and willing to perform what he promises." That means that "the Lord knows those who are his" (2 Tim. 2:19). "Therefore, Christian faith is entirely extinguished, the promises of God and the whole gospel are completely destroyed, if we teach and believe that it is not for us to know the necessary foreknowledge of God and the necessity of the things that are to come to pass. For this is the one supreme consolation of Christians in all adversities, to know that God does not lie, but does all things immutably, and that his will can neither be resisted nor changed nor hindered."[130] Without using the term, it is clear that Luther affirmed God's unconditional predestining of his own people.

Although he had earlier advanced the doctrine of predestination as a weapon against false views of human merit, in the years after 1525 he became more hesitant regarding the use of this term. Indeed, he presumed that God's decision is the ground of his delivery of grace in the gift of faith in Christ. In lecturing on Galatians in 1531, he could put in Paul's mouth a paraphrase of "who had set me apart before I was born" (Gal. 1:15): "Every gift . . . that God intended to give me, and all the good things that I was ever to do at any time in all my life — all this God had predestined even before I was born, when I could not think, wish or do anything good but was a shapeless embryo. Therefore, this gift came to me by the predestination and merciful grace of God even before I was born."[131] Much more often than not, however, he expressed his fears about its potentially negative impact (presuming that the student recollections still extant and recorded in the "Table Talks" represent a fair sampling of his opinions). He observed to the students hearing his lectures on Genesis that "certain ruin" comes "when we soar too high and want to philosophize about predestination."[132] Some nobles and other important people were arguing, "If I am predestined, I shall be saved, whether I do good or evil. If I am not predestined, I shall be condemned regardless of my works." Such "wicked statements" Luther countered by anchoring the believer's knowledge of predestination in Christ and in the promise conveyed in oral, written, and sacramental forms. To have certain knowledge of God and to be able to cling to God's promises, Luther counseled, God's people must be certain that God stands by his promises, and therefore they can "flee for refuge to him who is unchangeable. For in Malachi 3:6 he makes this assertion about himself: 'I the Lord do not change.' And Romans 11:29 states: 'The gifts and the call of God are irrevocable.'"[133] God's immutability was not an abstract principle for Luther but a characteristic of God encountered in Jesus Christ and in the promise of life in him. Only through the Word in the means of grace, where Christ comes to believers, could God's eternal plan for his people be known. At about the same time as his lecture on Genesis 26, if his student Johannes Mathesius's reports are to be believed, he shared with those gathered at his table his concern that pondering and disputing about predestination leads to despair. He anchored his own hope in God's choice of him as God had made it before the foundation of the world, but he relied upon God's revelation of his sovereign will in Christ and in the revealed Word.[134]

About the same time he made the comments cited above to students, Luther composed a letter that appeared in a collection of his devotional writings published after his death. The letter repeated that God's foreknowledge and predestination are known only through God's revelation in Christ and the means of grace. It was addressed to "an important person" in Lower Saxony and dealt with that person's struggles with the idea that God had predestined the saved. Whether Otto Clemen's suggestion that editorial expansion probably altered the original letter, no longer extant, is true or not,[135] the text printed by Caspar Cruciger is consistent with the reformer's views at this time. Luther's answer began with the presupposition that God is almighty and knows all things, every droplet of water in the sea, every star in heaven, every tree's roots, branches, and leaves. This God had counted every human being and knows them all. From this understanding of God, Luther recognized, someone could think that God has predestined all people either to salvation or damnation. But, the reformer added, God wants all to be saved and to participate in his eternal bliss (1 Tim. 2:4).[136] God does not want sinners to die but to be turned to him and live (Ezek. 18:32). Thus, Luther's correspondent should know, God's grace is without limit toward those who trust in him. Luther directed this person to the means of grace, God's Word which delivers Christ, the only way to the Father.

> For the Word is certain, true, and eternal, through which all things and creatures in the whole wide world . . . were created and made, and through which all that lives and moves is wonderfully preserved. You should regard the Word as greater, more important, more powerful, more effective than these fleeting, vain ideas [regarding predestination to damnation] prompted by the devil, for the Word is true and human thoughts are vain and empty. So remember that God the Almighty did not create, predestine, and choose us to perish but to be saved, as Paul gave witness to the Ephesians, and had to begin his discussion not with the law or with reason but with the grace of God and the gospel that is proclaimed to all people.[137]

Luther concluded that it was pointless to torture oneself with thoughts of predestination when God's Word of grace and mercy had been spoken. If God controls the course of nature, then believers may place their own salvation in his hands as well. "If you accept the gospel and God's Word and cling to it and grasp it, and remain faithful to it to the end, then you will be saved, and if not, you will be damned, 2. Timothy 2:[12]."[138]

In a similar letter written August 18, 1545, Luther affirmed that God's predestination is found in Jesus Christ alone,[139] a message he had made clear in 1531 to the sister of his student Hieronymus Weller, Barbara Lißkirchen. His formula for her battle against doubts over predestination consisted in four points. First, she should recognize that doubts about God's having chosen her as his child come from the devil. Second, she should ask herself where God has commanded her to think about these things, and, finding no such command, she should say, "Hey, get out of here, you accursed devil, you want to drive me to worry, but God says everywhere, I should let him take care of my worries and says, 'I am your God, that is, I take care of you. . . .'" Third, she should tell the devil that she does not want to listen to such ideas. Fourth, she should "turn her heart to Christ and rely upon him and his promise alone."[140] For Luther God's commitment to his chosen people was clear, but he did not venture into speculation regarding that plan made before the foundation of the world. He comforted believers with the results of the plan as they had become clear in the death and resurrection of Christ and in the action of the means of grace in their own lives.

In these statements the interplay of doctrinal synonyms is clear. In the organic whole of Luther's body of teaching, different topics could perform much the same function. The solace which comes from Luther's understanding of God's unconditional plan for salvation, including his predestination of individuals, as he executed it in Christ and delivers it through the promise bestowed in the means of grace, could be pronounced by elaborating on any one of these three topics. The relationship of Creator and creature can be described with synonyms which focus either on God or the human being. When Erasmus dictated the focal point of the human will as the issue that had to be discussed, the reformer addressed the problem of God's responsibility and human responsibility on the human side, confessing that sinners cannot but choose Satan's direction apart from God's re-creating power. Luther could also address the same questions on God's side of the equation, however, anchoring comfort and confidence in God's unchanging will to save his chosen people and the promise of that salvation delivered in his promises in absolution, preaching, and the sacraments. His changing composition of these doctrinal synonyms exhibits the organic unity of his entire body of teaching. Luther was applying the gospel in the Wittenberg way. This is how his theology functioned.

De servo arbitrio reveals that Luther had absorbed scholastic training in logic well, and so it is no wonder that scholars have often cited passages to demonstrate that he held a doctrine of double predestination in the work, even if, most concede, he repudiated it later. Doerne correctly observes, however, that "we look in vain in *De servo arbitrio* for sentences in which Luther expressly asserts an election to damnation. He speaks thereof only in the negative and indirectly,"[141] for instance when he wrote,

> It is therefore right to say, "If God does not desire our death, the fact that we perish must be imputed to our own will." It is right, I mean, if you speak of God as preached; for he wills all people to be saved, seeing he comes with the word of salvation to all, and the fault is in the will that does not admit him, as he says in Matthew 23[:37]: "How often would I have gathered your children, and you would not!" But why that majesty of his does not remove or change this defect of our will in all people, since it is not in the human creature's power to do so, or why he imputes this defect to people when they cannot help having it, we have no right to inquire; and though you may do a lot of inquiring, you will never find out.[142]

Two things must be noted. First, Luther's distinguishing of law and gospel comes through clearly in this passage. If the question regards human responsibility, the burden of the law falls squarely upon the creature made to be responsible before God. If the question regards the origin of human life and salvation, that answer must come from the gospel of the love and mercy of the omnipotent God. Second, Luther engaged the question of theodicy here — and retreated from it with the admission and assertion that God's choosing his own and the condemnation of those who reject him together form a mystery that the Bible does not explain and that human speculation cannot decipher. He could not follow a logic that led him to conclude that God creates or effects the evil of human sin and condemnation even when his affirmation of God's total power and responsibility brought him to the brink of such a conclusion.

It is clear that Luther presumed that God had chosen those who would come to faith, but he insisted that this element of biblical teaching could be used only to bring comfort to believers. Any other use of the concept of predestination, whether to provide a license for sinning to the rebellious or to bring the weak in faith to despair, was a false use of this teaching. Therefore, the reformer often made it clear that God's predestination of his people was not a matter of law but only of gospel. This topic, like all others, was to be put to use in good pastoral care for the comfort and assurance of troubled consciences, or it was not to be used at all.

God Saves through the Means of Grace

God acts in his Word, condemning sin through the law and conveying Christ's benefits to his chosen people through the gospel, in oral, written, and sacramental forms, called collectively the means of grace.

Luther's God was a talking God. The "Word of God," in the several senses of the term in which Luther used it, serves as the Creator's instrument for effecting his will and revealing who he is. His word alone discloses how he interacts with the human creatures he created to be in fellowship and communication with himself. "The Word of God comes, whenever it comes, to change and renew the world."[143] The reformer understood the biblical description of God as a revelation in human language which conveyed into his own time God's presentation of himself as an incarnation in human flesh, which the evangelist John had called "Word" (John 1:1-4, 14, 18).[144] In the cross God displayed his wisdom and power, where he presented himself, as he really is, to humankind. "The omnipotence of the Lord of Hosts and the incomprehensibility of his action, no less than the fact that we are fully lost and must come to naught in God's presence are all brought into focus, as is our salvation, in the name of Jesus Christ."[145]

Because Scripture serves as the basis and authority for conveying the benefits of Christ, according to the reformer, he began his treatise on the bondage of the will by insisting upon the clarity of God's communication of himself and his will in Scripture. "The Word of God is for us a 'lamp shining in a dark place' [2 Pet. 1:19]. If part of this lamp does not shine, it will be a part of the dark place rather than of the lamp itself. Christ has not so enlightened us as deliberately to leave some part of his Word obscure."[146] That did not mean for Luther that human reason could grasp the proper meaning of biblical words on its own, apart from the Holy Spirit's aid and power. Luther conceded that "there are many texts in the Scriptures that are obscure and abstruse, not because of the majesty of their subject matter, but because of our ignorance of their vocabulary and grammar." Although he did not state it explicitly, he seems to have attributed that gap sometimes to the fact that creatures cannot grasp all that is to be known about God and sometimes to the desire of sinners to refashion God according to their own likings. But he did not concede that human misunderstanding or bafflement in the face of one or another passages made the knowledge of what God was saying in Scripture uncertain.[147] On the basis of 1 Corinthians 1 and 2, he understood false interpretation to be the nature of a sinful world's reception of God's Word. But the Word remained sure in spite of human doubt and confusion. Indeed, what the world perceived as foolishness and "weak thinking" constituted God's wisdom and power, Luther argued on the basis of Paul's text. Therefore, "it is not due to the weakness of the human mind (as you make out) that the words of God are not understood but, on the contrary, nothing is more fitted for understanding the words of God than such weakness; for it was for the sake of the weak and to the weak that Christ both came and [continues to] send his Word."[148]

Luther believed that God speaks and therefore delivers his message of new life in oral, written, and sacramental forms. The oral forms include preaching, absolution, and Christian conversation. Among the written forms of various genres stands Scripture in the privileged position as the governing authority of all forms of the Word because the Holy Spirit himself spoke directly through its authors. God has also given his Word in sacramental forms, when he joins human language to other elements: the water of baptism and the bread and wine that convey Christ's body and blood.[149]

All other forms of the Word rest upon God's revelation of himself in

Scripture. As the basis of their discussion of bound or free choice, Luther asserted to Erasmus that Scripture is clear to the ears and eyes of faith. His perception of God as both hidden and revealed permitted him to concede that "in God there are many things hidden, of which we are ignorant." But God and God's Word are two different objects of faith. Believers trust in God even though their knowledge of him is limited to what he has revealed of himself. Believers trust his biblical revelation because God's Word is certain, and God speaks clearly in his written Word. Both the external clarity of the Word as it is taken from the biblical page for proclamation and the internal clarity of faith's understanding enlighten the darkened human heart through the power of the Holy Spirit and bring the light of God's truth.[150] Luther connected his understanding of God's communication with his people through his Word to the person of God himself. In his Word believers have the promise of God, and "this is the one supreme consolation of Christians in all adversities, to know that God does not lie but does all things immutably, and that his will can neither be resisted nor changed nor hindered."[151]

In his debate with Erasmus Luther wished to place the focus not on human choosing but on God's life-restoring conversation with sinners, based on his choice of them to be his own. The Wittenberg reformer often made appeals to his hearers or readers to believe, but he was certain that God's Word alone creates faith and reshapes rebels into children.[152] God's communication with those he has chosen to be his own takes place in two forms, one which evaluates the performance of the sinner, another which bespeaks new life to those put to death by that evaluation. Luther presumed that the words of the Creator are to be heard in two forms: the law that prescribes and evaluates human performance and the gospel that restores new life to sinners. These two forms of God's discourse not only describe his disposition toward his human creatures but actually accomplish his will for them.

For the distinction of law and gospel is not only a theoretical hermeneutical principle which aids preachers in proclaiming God's Word. Much more, it is a description of how God as Creator works with human creatures. He eliminates sinners with his word of condemnation. No sinner can survive the appraisal of God's law; it does sinners to death. It was never an instrument of life but only of instruction and evaluation: "The words of the law are spoken not to affirm the power of the will but to enlighten blind reason and make it see that its own light is no light and that the virtue of the will is no virtue."[153] God the Re-creator brings dead sinners to new life through the good news of Jesus Christ, as the Holy Spirit fashions the relationship of trust by coming with his Word of promise to them. Luther regarded Erasmus's chief problem as his failure to distinguish law and gospel.[154]

There was no doubt in Luther's mind that God's law imposes responsibility upon his human creatures and that whether they feel themselves bound or not, the law holds them responsible for fulfilling God's plan for human living. Moses' exposition of God's law "has removed every obstacle to their knowing and keeping clearly before them all the commandments, and left them no room for the excuse that they were unaware or did not possess the commandments, or had to seek them from elsewhere. Hence if they do not keep them, the fault will lie neither with the law nor with the lawgiver, but with themselves."[155] But the exercise of that responsibility had not established human righteousness in Eden. It was rather the result of the gift of that righteousness. And it remains true, Luther asserted, that those who rely on the works of the law are cursed (Gal. 3:10). Attempting to make themselves good by their own works, they demonstrate that their trust is planted in another, not in the true Author of Life. "In the sight of God those who are most devoted to the works of the law are farthest from fulfilling the law because they lack the spirit that is the true fulfiller of the law, and while they may attempt it by their own powers, they achieve nothing."[156]

> It is the task, function, and effect of the law to be a light to the ignorant and blind, but such a light as reveals sickness, sin, evil, death, hell, the wrath of God, though it affords no help and brings no deliverance from them, but is content to have revealed them. Then, when people become aware of the disease of sin, they are troubled, distressed, even in despair. The law is no help, much less can they help themselves. There is need of another light to reveal the remedy. This is the voice of the gospel, revealing Christ as the deliverer from all these things.[157]

God speaks life. His final Word (in the absolution that renews faith in him), just as his first Word (in the creation of Adam and Eve), springs from his mercy and conveys his steadfast love, his creative and creating joy at shaping creatures and children for himself. The gospel is the center of Luther's theological enterprise, for it is a word of new creation and life. God's new covenant or testament "properly consists of promises and exhortations." It is the preaching of this gospel, "which is nothing else but a message in which the Spirit and grace are offered with a view to the remission of sins, which has been obtained for us by Christ crucified; and all this freely, and by the sole mercy of God the Father, whereby favor is shown to us, unworthy as we are and deserving of damnation rather than anything else."[158] God exercises the responsibility to which he has obligated himself simply because he wanted to, and he gives new life to sinners through Christ crucified, the executed and resurrected revelation of God, who has come himself in human flesh with light and life (John 1:1-18).

Luther did not explicitly define the relationship between God's creative Word that brought the world into being as God said "Let there be . . ." and the re-creative Word of the forgiveness of sins. But he often did draw the parallel between the two. The nature of the former remains a mystery; for that matter, so is the working of the latter. But the God who described his own creative activity as speaking in Genesis 1 is a God who continues to work with his people through selected elements of his created order, including human language. He engages believers in his Word, "through which he offers himself to us, and this word is the beauty and glory in which the psalmist celebrates him as being clothed" (e.g., Ps. 21:5).[159] Humanity is grounded and centered in the human creature's relationship with God. The trust that constitutes the human side of that relationship arises in conversation, as God addresses sinners, uses his word of judgment to end their sinful identity in his sight, and gives them new life through his word of forgiveness and life. The language under which he hides his power is ordinary, propositional, communicating human language, in the words of the prophets and apostles in Scripture, in the words of Christians as they proclaim it to one another. This conviction informed not only the reformer's pastoral use of words but also his hermeneutics in the conflict with Erasmus: "We must everywhere stick to the simple, pure, and natural sense of the words that accords with the rules of grammar and the normal use of language as God has created it in human creatures."[160] "Words are always to be used in their ordinary, natural meaning, unless we have proof to the contrary."[161]

This gospel, as a Word of re-creation and restoration, serves God as an instrument for delivering his love to those he has chosen and for doing battle in their behalf against Satan. God is the Lord of life, and Satan is a murderer. The two are in perpetual conflict with each other. God speaks truth, also in the Word made flesh, who is the way, the truth, and the life (John 14:6); Satan lies because that is his nature (John 8:44). The battle over life and death takes place, for Luther, in the confrontation of the two words, the devil's deceit and God's powerful, re-creative Word of life and truth. God discharges his responsibility for his creation through his Word.

In the midst of this struggle God's chosen people remain his children. The creative Word of God has given his people their identity in his creation, as a gift, by pronouncing them his creatures and his children. From that identity flowed expectations for their performance in daily life. The righteousness of their God-given identity vanished as they mysteriously broke their relationship with God and placed their central and guiding faith in creatures rather than the Creator. The performance that flows from unfaith may approximate God's plan for human performance but always falls short. Therefore, when God's law evaluates sinners, it may assign a variety of grades to their activities in terms of their usefulness in human society, but in the case of the central trust, the affirmation of their identity, sinners always fail. God must restore them to faith in him; he must revive their humanity. He does so through his re-creative power in the gospel.

Human Beings Are Dependent Creatures

Human beings are creatures and thus totally dependent on God their Creator.

Acknowledging God as Creator — and as Re-creator — means recognizing that "God and his creatures are never partners of equal rank. . . . God must remain the Creator, that is, the only Lord, not only in the realm of 'nature' but also in the realm of 'grace,'" as Doerne comments; he labels the following passage the most important in *De servo arbitrio*:[162] "Before human creatures are created and become human, they neither do nor attempt to do anything toward becoming creatures, and after they are created, they neither do nor attempt to do anything toward remaining creatures, but both of these are done by the sole will of the omnipotent power and goodness of God, who creates and preserves with our assistance." Nonetheless, God expects human creatures to be his active servants and obedient children. The reformer continued:

> He does not work in us without us, because it is for this he has created and preserved us, that he might work in us and we might cooperate with him, whether outside his own realm in his general omnipotence, or inside his own realm by the special power of this Spirit. In the very same way, before human creatures are born again as new creatures in the realm of the Spirit, they do nothing and attempt nothing to prepare themselves for this new birth and this realm, and when they have been recreated, they do nothing and attempt nothing toward remaining in this realm, but the Spirit alone does both of these things in us, recreating us without our contribution and preserving us without our help as recreated beings.[163]

Seldom does Luther lay out more clearly his understanding of God being God and the human creature acting as human creature. Here he emphasizes both God's omnipotence and human performance, for the "working in us but not without us" — the "cooperation" of the human creature with God — refers to the functioning of the mind and will as a child and conversation partner of the Creator, in conversation with him. And that he found perfectly consistent with the fact that "free choice does many things, but these are nonetheless 'nothing' in the sight of God."[164]

The way Erasmus had shaped the question placed anthropology at the center of their debate. There it was immediately clear that the two scholars were separated by fundamentally different paradigms for defining humanity. Both turned to Holy Writ, Luther to metaphors that enabled him to emphasize the dependence of these creatures upon their Creator: the metaphors of the two riders,[165] the potter and the clay,[166] and new birth in the Holy Spirit.[167] Erasmus's paradigm for defining biblical anthropology sprang from Sirach 15:14-17: "It was he who created humankind in the beginning, and he left them in the power of their own free choice. If you choose, you can keep the commandments, and to act faithfully is a matter of your own choice. He has placed before you fire and water; stretch out your hand for whichever you choose. Before each person are life and death, and whichever one chooses will be given."[168] This paradigm defined sinners as responsible, relatively independent adults who could be helped by God's grace to fulfill their responsibilities — rather than as children brought by new birth into the kingdom of God.

The key to Luther's interpretation of what humanity was, and has become again in Christ, is his distinction between two kinds or dimensions of human righteousness within the unity of the human person. That is, he believed that humanity cannot be defined simply by focusing on obedience to God's commands but rather must be explained in two relationships, as Christ explained God's plan for human living: loving the Lord God with everything the human being has, and loving neighbors as self (Matt. 22:37-40). Luther advanced this anthropological thesis in 1518 and 1519,[169] and refined it over the years to the point where he could call it "our theology" by 1535.[170]

Erasmus's ideas regarding free choice proceeded from the presupposition that there is only one dimension to humanity, and it is all wrapped up in acts of obedience to God's law. Human failing being what it is, sinners need some help — quite a bit, Erasmus argued for the most part — to meet God's expectations for their performance of that law. But their free choice to move in God's direction was critical for fulfilling their humanity. Luther rejected this image of humanity. His reading of Scripture, Romans 3, for instance, compelled him to distinguish God's gift of human identity and the expectations of trust in him from love for the neighbor that flowed from their God-bestowed identity as children of God. God freely and unconditionally gave Adam and Eve their identity, just as he freely and unconditionally restores this identity to those brought into his family by the Holy Spirit. That this identity as his children expresses itself in obedience to God's commands is self-evident for Luther. This distinction between two kinds of righteousness, two dimensions of being human, informed the argument of *De servo arbitrio* as well.

Luther took up the challenge of interpreting Erasmus's prime passage, and he did so on the basis of his distinction of two realms of human righteousness. Sirach 15 teaches

> that human creatures are divided between two realms. In one of them they are directed by their own choice and counsel, apart from any precepts and commandments of God, namely in dealing with things beneath them. There they reign and are lords, having been left in the hand of their own counsel. Not that God so leaves them as not to cooperate with them in everything, but he has granted them the free use of things according to their own choice, and has not restricted them by any laws or injunctions. . . . In the other realm, however, human creatures are not left in the land of their own counsel but are directed and led by the choice and counsel of God, so that just as in their own realm they are directed by their own counsel, without regard to the precepts of another, so in God's realm they are directed by the precepts of another without regard to their own choice.[171]

God bestows the core of human identity in this latter "realm." He created, and he re-creates his human creatures as children of God. He does so as sovereign Creator, out of his mercy, depending on nothing external to his own gracious will toward his chosen children. When Luther spoke of the bondage of choice, according to Hägglund, he was affirming not only that "human creatures are captive under the power of sin, but also that they exercise no control over their lives at all but are totally dependent upon the all-embracing power of God."[172] For "if God is truly God and the creator of heaven and earth, his power must embrace everything that happens, everything that exists. His power is not an abstract characteristic, but" — Hägglund cites Luther — "'the active power by which he potently works all in all.'"[173] For Luther was convinced that even when human creatures revolt against him, God remains Creator, and they cannot evade him. When sinners believe God is far from them, they are in fact experiencing his providential power, even if they have turned it into the power to punish and condemn.[174] To exercise such total power is the nature and therefore the responsibility of the Creator. He has determined the existence of his human creatures, and their relationship to him is the core of human living. In this relationship his children react to his unconditioned mercy by trusting and loving their Creator and Savior above all things. In this realm of the "vertical" (our expression, not Luther's) relationship, God's gracious love defines the humanity of his chosen children and draws forth the faith that governs their lives and determines their state of mind and their actions. "'To become children of God,' John says" (John 1:12), takes place "by a power divinely bestowed on us, not by a power of free choice inherent in us."[175]

If in Eden human creatures were human only because of God's creative grace, then sinners certainly depend alone on the favor of their Maker. Therefore, in arguing that human choice may obediently perform one command or another of God but cannot embrace God himself, Luther emphasized that righteousness in God's sight, being human in relation to God, is manifested apart from the law (Rom. 3:28). "It is as if God said, 'I am obliged to forgive them their sins if I want the law fulfilled by them; I must also put away the law, for I see that they are unable not to sin, especially when they are fighting, that is, when they are laboring to fulfill the law in their own strength.'"[176] Only faith, from the human side, makes human beings righteous; only God can fashion a righteous child of God out of a sinner.

> Paul clearly distinguishes the two righteousnesses, attributing one to the law and the other to grace, maintaining that the latter is given without the former and apart from its works, while the former without the latter does not justify or count for anything. . . . the righteousness of God is revealed and avails for all and upon all who believe in Christ. . . . Paul denies that anything outside this faith is righteous in the sight of God; and if it is not righteous in God's sight, it must necessarily be sin. For with God there is nothing intermediate between righteousness and sin, no neutral ground.[177]

This righteousness of faith "does not depend on any works, but on God's favorable regard and his reckoning on the basis of grace. Notice how Paul dwells on the word 'reckoned,' how he stresses, repeats, and insists on it. . . . Now if righteousness is not reckoned to the one who works, then clearly his works are nothing but sins, evils, and impieties in the sight of God." Not human performance but God's Word of love and grace that elicits and creates trust in him constitutes righteousness, true human identity, in relationship to God. This righteousness is completely God's gift, as John 1:12 demonstrates: God gives the power to become the children of God.[178]

Luther's argument in *De servo arbitrio* rests upon the presupposition that God as creator alone establishes human existence, identity, and righteousness. However, from that gift of identity flows the human performance of God's commands. The human execution of God's plan for human action is not the cause of human worth but the result of receiving the gift of humanity. It must be noted that Luther held that the human will is "bound" not only because of sin. Its powers are limited because of the nature of being a creature as well. Luther's placing the focus in defining humanity on the creaturely dependence of the human being rather than on the creature's faculties, such as willing, and the corresponding responsibilities on the human side gave him a fundamentally different orientation from Erasmus — and from many of his own students as well.

All Things Happen by Necessity

This dependence of the human creature on God can be explained and defended by a doctrine of absolute necessity, that is, that all things happen necessarily as God designs and decides.

Luther tried to make clear what it means that God continues to be Creator with absolute and unconditioned power as befits a Creator with the concept of necessity. In so doing he took a medieval, scholastic term out of its Aristotelian context and attempted to use it to assert the biblical witness to the sovereignty and omnipotence of God. Some medieval theologians had tried to solve the problem of divine determination and human freedom with a distinction between two definitions of necessity. *Necessitas consequentis,* a necessity that rests solely upon what God wills, stands in contrast to *necessitas consequentiae,* which defines the necessity of an act as resting on God's plan but contingent upon certain freely made human decisions. This terminological distinction raised as many problems as it solved, Luther believed, and it solved the critical problems in a deceptive way. His rejection of this distinction in favor of a single and absolute necessity that flows from God's will and foreknowledge raised immediately the specter of a determinism that destroyed human integrity. Luther clearly stated that his use of this language was not intended to do that.

What God wills happens immutably but not through coercion, he insisted. The Creator, a person, determines what happens, not an impersonal necessity, an impersonal fate, apart from God. God does so at the same time his human creature is acting according to God's design for humanity that makes this creature a responsible and willing child of the Almighty. Early in *De servo arbitrio* he struggled to make certain that "necessity" was not to be understood as a "compulsion" that reduced the human creature to an automaton or marionette. Luther insisted that the will continues to act as a will: human beings perform acts of willing — "spontaneously and freely" (Watson: of its own accord and with a ready will). And this readiness or will to act "they cannot by their own powers lay aside, restrain, or change, but they keep on willing . . . even if compelled by external force [the devil] to do something different."[179] The work of the Holy Spirit changes the human will so that it acts "from pure willingness and inclination and of its own accord, not from compulsion." The converted will "cannot be turned another way by any opposition, nor be overcome or compelled even by the gates of hell, but it goes on willing and delighting in and loving the good, just as before it willed and delighted in and loved evil." The Holy Spirit and God's grace continue to bestow the new life of the new creature, and that new life includes the restoration of the proper functioning of the human will.[180]

Troublesome for most of his disciples and many thereafter were those passages in which Luther's affirmation of God's lordship seems to make him responsible for evil. The reformer admitted that he, too, struggled with this mystery of evil. But in his determination to confess the absolute lordship of the Creator, he on occasion gave the impression that God is responsible for evil. Yet he always conditioned such statements to make certain that the underlying trust in God's goodness could stand in spite of the affirmation of his unqualified lordship even over evil. In engaging Erasmus's argument from Origen, that God had raised up an evil Pharaoh but had not created him as evil — had permitted him to do evil but not caused that evil — Luther argued that "although God does not make sin, yet he does not cease to fashion and multiply the nature that has been vitiated by sin through the withdrawal of the Spirit, as a wood-carver might make statues out of rotten wood."[181] Fifteen years later, when asked at supper about the hardening of Pharaoh's heart, Luther averred that God's hardening of the Egyptian should be understood "literally" *(proprie)* rather than "figuratively," but not as if God actively caused the rejection in Pharaoh's heart because "God does not do evil though his omnipotence does all things. God hardened Pharaoh, who was evil, by not sending him his Spirit and his grace. Why such things happen lies beyond proper human inquiry," the professor told his hearers.[182] He remained without an answer, confronting the theodical challenge simply with trust in Christ.

In similar fashion, he argued that the rider of the horse is not responsible for the lameness which gives him a bad ride.

> Here you see that when God works in and through evil men, evil things are done, and yet God cannot act evilly although he does evil through evil

people, because he who is himself good cannot act evilly. Yet he uses evil instruments that cannot escape the sway and motion of his omnipotence. That evil takes place is the fault, therefore, of the instruments, which God does not allow to be idle even though God himself is the one who keeps all things in motion. It is as if a carpenter were cutting badly with a chipped and jagged ax. Hence it comes about that the ungodly cannot but continually err and sin because they are caught up in the movement of divine power and are not allowed to be idle, but rather they will, desire, and act according to the kind of person they are. All this is settled and certain if we believe that God is omnipotent and also that the ungodly are creatures of God although turned away from God. Left to themselves without God's Spirit, they cannot will or do good. The omnipotence of God makes it impossible for the ungodly to evade the motion and action of God, for they are necessarily subject to it and obey it. But their corruption or aversion from God makes it impossible for them to be moved and carried along with good effect. God cannot lay aside his omnipotence because of human aversion, and the ungodly cannot alter their aversion. It thus comes about that they perpetually and necessarily sin and err until they are put right by God's Spirit.[183]

Luther's sense of human responsibility led him to reject the proposition that if God exercises total responsibility over the world, human beings cannot be held responsible for sin. He insisted that human creatures remain fully responsible even though God is the agent of all motion, that is, the cause of all that happens, in his creation. Luther simply stated,

> Let no one suppose when God is said to harden or to work evil in us . . . that he does so by creating evil in us *de novo*. You must not imagine God is like an evil-minded innkeeper, full of wickedness himself, who pours or mixes poison into a vessel that is not bad, which itself does nothing but receive or suffer what is bad from the one who is doing the mixing. . . . In us, that is, through us, God is at work when evil takes place, but he is not at fault. The defect lies in us since we are by nature evil and he is good. But as he carries us along by his own activity in accordance with the nature of his omnipotence, good as he is himself, he cannot help but do evil with an evil instrument though he makes good use of this evil in accordance with his wisdom for his own glory and our salvation.[184]

Luther's understanding of what it means that God is Creator led him to assert that God is the moving Mover, the totally responsible agent, at work throughout his creation. His definition of humanity led him to insist that human beings be held responsible for their evil works. Because he believed that his function as theologian called him to deliver God's Word as law to the unrepentant and as gospel to the faithful, he felt no compulsion to attempt to reconcile the actions of God and those of human creatures in the exercise of their respective responsibilities. He held the various biblical descriptions of God's reality and human experience in tension.

Human Beings Are Sinners

Human beings are responsible for their own disposition and actions but are sinful, captive to Satan and their own desires, and thus totally dependent on God for liberation from their sinfulness.

Luther's focus on the person of the Creator and his definition of humanity in terms of two kinds of righteousness cast a different light than that shed by late medieval scholastic theology on how words like "sin" and "transgression" are to be understood. For abuse of God's name, rejection of his Word, disobedience to parents and other authorities, murder, abuse of sexuality, stealing, and damaging the neighbor's reputation all arose from failing to fear and love God, according to Luther's explanation of the Decalogue. He interpreted the first commandment as ordering and centering human life around "fear, love, and trust in God above all things." He explained all other transgressions of God's commands as the result of not fearing and loving God.[185] "Unbelief is not just one of the grosser passions but sits and holds sway at the pinnacle — the citadel of the will and reason, just like its opposite, faith. To be unbelieving is to deny God and make him a liar" (1 John 1:10), Luther affirmed.[186] He called Erasmus's attention to Paul's description of the sinner as

> ignorant of God, a despiser of God, turned aside from him, and worthless in the sight of God. . . . It is no small matter to say that the human creature is ignorant of God and despises God, for these [attitudes] are the sources of all crimes, the privy of all sins, indeed, the hell of all evils. Could any evil not be there where there is ignorance and contempt of God? In short, the reign of Satan in human creatures could not have been described in fewer or more expressive terms than by his saying that they are ignorant of God and despisers of God. That betokens unbelief, it betokens cruelty and lack of mercy toward our neighbor; it betokens love of self in all matters in relation both to God and to human creatures.[187]

By defining the human responsibility to trust in God as the center of human life, Luther constructed a radically different paradigm from that of his Ockhamist instructors. They had focused on human performance of a wide range of works as the key first to winning God's grace and then to using it effectively in meriting life with him. Luther's definition of humanity as centering in trust in the person of the Creator altered the image of what it means to be human radically. For trust is not an action human creatures can perform in the same way they perform acts of love and refrain from acts of harm to the neighbor. Trust must be created by the one who is trustworthy; human love is a response to something in the Beloved that elicits that love. Human life finds a different framework from that of a performance-centered prescription in Luther's definition of the core of humanity as a passive righteousness which consists on the human side of trust as a gift from God.

In *De servo arbitrio,* where the question under examination addresses not human performance but human inability to produce what God expects, there is little said regarding the activities of sin. The origin of sin and the fallen will's bondage of choice are the critical issues. There Luther is consistent and clear: human beings are not created to sin and God does not want them to sin, but in the mystery of evil they do sin, inevitably and on a much deeper level than mere moral transgressions of God's plan and pattern for life. They sin by failing to fear, love, and trust in their Creator above his creatures. They fashion false gods out of other creatures. They break the relationship God wants to have with them, they ignore him, they twist and contort his image, they try to live apart from him. Scripture depicts this relationship as bondage and captivity, as sickness and death, as deafness or blindness, or as outright revolt against God. Luther described the situation of sinners as one in which they would not remain if they recognized their plight for what it was. They would leave behind Satan's bondage and blindness if they could only perceive the reality of this situation.[188] Thus, the insistence of sinners that they have a freedom to do what they please is a constitutive element of the self-deceiving construction of a world without the Creator. Because freedom without condition is a characteristic of God alone, the claim to such freedom is a natural part of the sinner's attempt to create and constitute a world apart from the limited freedom God gave humankind originally and restores to the faithful in the new creation in Christ.[189]

The human creature, the sinner, for whom Christ came to die and rise is, in Luther's view, the whole human being, the entire creature shaped by God and deceived to death by Satan. "Luther's picture of the human creature differed from Erasmus' not in that it represented another philosophical anthropology" — both men operated with the ancient dichotomous or trichotomous division of human beings, believing that the reason or spirit was the crown of the earthly creature; "decisive was the unity of the human being." Only when human creatures are viewed from God's perspective does it become clear that the differentiation of lower and higher powers means little; human beings are totally creatures of God, and fallen human beings are totally sinners.[190]

Human beings cannot generate themselves, and could not, even apart from sin, before the fall into sin. As creatures, they are always dependent on their Creator. As sinners who have corrupted their humanity, they remain alienated from him and from their own nature as his human creatures. They are truly captives. Apart from this re-creative power of God, sinners remain beasts of burden ridden by Satan. Indeed, Luther appropriated and reshaped a medieval metaphor when he wrote:

> If we are under the god of this world, away from the work and spirit of the true God, we are held captive to his will, as Paul says to Timothy [2 Tim. 2:26], so that we cannot will anything but what he wills. For he is that strong man armed, who guards his own palace in such a way that those whom he possesses are in peace [Luke 11:21], so as to prevent them from stirring up any thought or feeling against him. . . . But if a Stronger One comes who overcomes him and takes us as his spoil, then through his Spirit we are again slaves and captives — though this is a royal freedom — so that we readily will and do what he wills. Thus the human will is placed between the two like a beast of burden. If God rides it, it wills and goes where God wills, as the psalm says, "I was like a brute beast in relationship to you; nevertheless, I am continually with you" [Ps. 73:22-23]. If Satan rides the animal, it wills and goes where Satan wills; nor can it choose to run to either of the two riders or choose one or the other, but the riders themselves contend for the possession and control of the animal.[191]

The reformer was convinced that this metaphor serves to describe the boundness honest sinners experience when they seek to assess their own abilities to decide for or against God. It illuminates the biblical teaching of God and his nature as Creator. It does not assign blame to God. Bound to the Creator by their created nature, bound in sin under Satan's alienating power, creatures have become something wholly other than designed: in bondage to sin and Satan, the creature's freedom to be bound to the neighbor and to God has been destroyed.

Sin has destroyed the righteousness of faith that God gave Adam and Eve at creation (they had no probationary period in which God let them prove their worthiness to be human, Luther was certain).[192] Erasmus had only been trying to preserve a little human dignity in the process of recovery from sin, but Luther believed that sinners must die (Rom. 6:23). He believed that God bestows the gift of death to their identity as sinners so that they may be raised up with Christ to be the children of God (Rom. 6:3-11). Therefore, the Wittenberg professor reacted to Erasmus's pious thoughts by observing:

> On the authority of Erasmus, then, free choice is a power of the will that is able of itself to will and unwill the word and work of God, by which this human choosing is led to those things which exceed both its grasp and its perception. But if it can will and unwill, it can also love and hate, and if it can love and hate, it can also in some small degree do the works of the law and believe the gospel. For if you can will or unwill anything, you must to some extent be able to perform something by that will, even if someone else prevents your completing it. Now in that case, since the works of God which lead to salvation include death, the cross, and all the evils of the world, the human will must be able to will both death and its own perdition.[193]

That does not happen, Luther was convinced. Instead, God justifies; that is, he restores human righteousness and identity as his child, on the basis of his choice, made before the foundation of the world, through the death and resurrection of Christ, and bestows this new identity through the gift of faith, that the Holy Spirit works in the hearts of those God has chosen. In commenting on Isaiah 40:1-2, "Jerusalem's iniquity is pardoned, she has received double for her sins," Luther confessed,

> The Hebrew expression "iniquity is pardoned" means freely given good-will; and it is by this that the iniquity is pardoned, without any merit and indeed with the opposite of merit. And this is the point of what follows: For "she has received from the Lord's hand double for all her sins." This includes . . . not only the forgiveness of sins, but also the end of the warfare; and that means nothing else but that with the removing of the law, which was the power of sin [1 Cor. 15:56], and the pardoning of sin, which was the sting of death, God's people reign in freedom from both sin and death through the victory of Jesus Christ . . . they have not obtained these things by their own powers or merits, but have received them from Christ the conqueror and the giver.[194]

Luther's search for God ended at the cross, where God reveals his power and his wisdom in his own broken body and spilled blood (1 Cor. 1:18–2:16).

Scholars note that Luther stopped using the term "theology of the cross," but his theology remained grounded in the crucifixion and returned always to the cross. There he came, he was certain, carried by the Holy Spirit's power in the Word, as a sinner, whose life was possessed by evil because he failed to fear, love, and trust in his Creator above all else. There he was given forgiveness of sins, life, and salvation.

Human Creatures Are Totally Responsible Agents

Human beings are designed by God with active minds and wills that are to be dedicated to carrying out their callings in obedience to God.

God justifies sinners so that they may be freed to live in willing obedience to God's commands. Indeed, they must recognize that this obedience has worth only on earth. They practice this obedience for the sake of the neighbor, who by God's design is dependent on the love of other human creatures. These acts of obedience to God's plan for life have no redeeming value before the throne of God. Human beings act, and God demands responsible action. But believers' coming into God's kingdom and remaining faithful to him depend on the Holy Spirit alone, who "recreates us without us and preserves us without our help in our recreated state."[195] Out of their identity as children of God believers experience the expectations their Lord has for them, expectations that they will perform his will as his agents in his world, that they will conform to his plan for human living. Human performance results from God's creating the relationship of love and trust between him and his chosen children.[196] Within that relationship, in the realm he has given them as their responsibility, they are not puppets and automatons even though they are creatures who depend on him for their every breath. Judas betrayed Christ willingly even if he did it necessarily because God foreknew he would be a traitor.[197]

This indissoluble tension between God's total responsibility and total human responsibility shimmers through Luther's distinction of God's supreme agency from the human agency that flows from his creation of human creatures as human. "Then follow exhortations, in order to stir up those who are already justified and have obtained mercy, so that they may be active in the fruits of the freely given righteousness and of the Spirit, and may exercise love by good works and bravely bear the cross and all other tribulations of the world." Luther regarded the promise of new life in the Crucified and the exhortation to produce the fruits of faith in him as "the sum of the whole

New Testament."[198] In the mystery of their humanity they are freely willing creatures who exercise and enjoy the responsibility God has given them to care for his world. In this realm they have work to do, neighbors to love, a creation to maintain.[199] They perform God's commands through their will, but the human will is not constitutive of what it means to be human. Iwand captured Luther's intention: "Therefore, we do not want to understand the human being on the basis of the will, but the will on the basis of what it means to be human."[200] In the realm of human performance, in the sphere of the actions governed by God's command to care for his creation, human righteousness consists of acts of love. Indeed, Luther believed in a righteousness of works: "there is the righteousness of works, or moral and civil righteousness" by which Abraham "is righteous in the sight of other human beings."[201] In the realm of human responsibility for the neighbor, "we know there are things free choice does by nature, such as eating, drinking, begetting, ruling."[202] That does not mean free choice or human love had any role in establishing or preserving the core identity of God's reborn children. "The children of God do good with a will that is disinterested, not seeking any reward, but only the glory and will of God, and being ready to do good even if — an impossible supposition — there were neither God's kingdom nor hell."[203] The righteousness of works had value for Luther, but only in the "horizontal" realm, among the creatures of God. He had insisted on this point from his early Reformation preaching to the end of his life, and made it clear in *De servo arbitrio*.[204]

Thus, Heinrich Bornkamm was only half right — or was totally right from only one perspective! — when he commented that "Luther gives human creatures immeasurably less credit than Erasmus does and God immeasurably more."[205] Although it is clear that in this work human action was not his major concern, Luther clearly stated that outside faith in Christ sinners can still perform a certain, often fairly high, measure of good in what he labeled "civil righteousness."[206] His expectations that believers could demonstrate God's love and care were also high. But this was true as an expression of his belief that human creatures are held responsible by God for obedience to his plan for human living. It did nothing to alter the fundamental assertion of *De servo arbitrio* regarding God's claiming and exercising responsibility for recreating his chosen children through Christ's death and resurrection. He liberates his creatures from their bondage to sin so that they may enjoy their freedom as the human creatures he fashioned to trust him and deliver his love to the rest of his world. Recognizing the mysterious coexistence of both God's responsibility and human responsibility is necessary for understanding Luther's teaching on what it means to be human.

Believers Live a Life of Repentance

Believers are engaged in a lifelong struggle against their own abiding sinfulness. Their lives are lives of repentance.

But this exercise of human responsibility is not as simple as it might seem. God and Satan, truth and deceit, faith and false faith are locked in a battle that does not cease on earth. Therefore, Luther soberly assessed the continuing mystery of evil in the lives of God's children and treated this mystery along with the mystery of the nature of created humanity and the paradox of God's total responsibility for his creation and the human creature's total responsibility for his or her own exercise or performance of human life. The saints were not only under attack throughout their lives;[207] they had continued to sin themselves. Luther's foundation for his critique of medieval indulgence theory in the first of his Ninety-five Theses, "the whole life of the Christian is a life of repentance,"[208] was not a focal point of *De servo arbitrio,* but Luther's conviction regarding the necessity of that daily dying and rising, that regular effect of both law and gospel, is reflected in his argument in this work, too. For God's grace must effect the turning of sinners from false gods and false faiths, but in the genuine psychological engagement of the human creature with God and his plan for human living, the law must also reveal the failure of those false objects of trust.[209]

Such sinners must continue to die to their false identity as those who put their trust in one or more creatures even as they come alive to their new identity in Christ as God's restored children. God brings himself out of hiding as he transforms sinners through law and gospel. "When God makes alive, he does it by killing; when he justifies, he does it by making people guilty; when he exalts to heaven, he does it by bringing them down to Hell" (1 Sam. 2:6).[210] Without the law's death knell, the gospel of Jesus Christ has no meaning. Luther observed, "This word, 'I desire not the death of the sinner,' has no other object than the preaching and offering of divine mercy throughout the world, a mercy that only the afflicted and those tormented by the fear of death receive with joy and gratitude, because in them the law has already done what it has to do and produced the knowledge of sin. Those, however, who have not experienced what the law is designed to do and neither recognize sin nor feel death, have no use for the mercy promised by that word."[211] When God speaks in his law, he acts like a father who shows his children how helpless they are, so that they depend on him, or like a physician giving a diagnosis, or like a victor who tramples on enemies to demonstrate their foolishness.[212] This is how Luther envisioned public teaching of the Word of God is to work, how pastoral care functions.

Erasmus tried to salvage at least a bit of the sinner in order to preserve human integrity. Luther took seriously the biblical language which talked of the return of sinners to God in terms of death and resurrection (Rom. 6:3-11; Col. 2:11-15),[213] new birth (John 3:3-5; Titus 3:3-8), and new creation (2 Cor. 5:17; Gal. 6:15). His understanding of the baptismal rhythm of dying and rising, as stated in the fourth question on baptism in the *Small Catechism,* remained the framework of his daily life: "Baptism signifies that the old creature in us with all sins and evil desires is to be drowned and die through daily contrition and repentance, and on the other hand that daily a new person is to come forth and rise up to live before God in righteousness and purity forever."[214]

God Is Not Responsible for Evil

God is not responsible for evil. No explanation of the existence of evil and its continuation in the lives of believers is possible.

Why? — that is the ever present question. For Erasmus, according to Thomas Reinhuber, the critical question in the debate over the freedom of the will concerned God's justice.[215] Schwarzwäller is correct in saying that Luther is not so presumptuous as to attempt to forge a theodicy in *De servo arbitrio* or in any other work: he does not provide a justification for God. Yet he does provide a response — if not an answer — to the question of why evil exists if God is good and almighty. He does so in part because not only daily life but also the Bible imposes the question on its every reader, in part because his burning concern for pastoral care of troubled and afflicted minds and hearts insisted that the gospel of Jesus Christ address also this question that stands at the core of so many pastoral problems. Luther himself had experienced the offense that the clash of God's responsibility and the responsibility of the sinful human creature creates. "I myself experienced this offense more than once, and it brought me to the very depth and abyss of despair, so that I wished I had never been created a human being, before I realized how salutary that despair was, and how near to grace."[216] The existence of evil remained a mystery which Luther refused to try to penetrate.[217] "God must be left to himself in his own majesty, for in that regard we have nothing to do with him, nor has he willed that we should have anything to do with him." Seeking him in his Word is appropriate and sufficient.[218] Instead of probing the secrets of that majesty, impossible to penetrate because the Creator dwells in light inaccessible (1 Tim. 6:16), believers should focus on God incarnate, Jesus crucified.[219] For God is above all creaturely assessment or evaluation.[220]

In Luther's theology of the cross there is something of an answer to the question of God's justice raised by sin and evil. The theology of the cross focuses attention on the God who has come near to humankind in the midst of afflictions, not just with sympathy, as medieval popular piety sometimes emphasized, but with the solution for the evils that afflict sinners. In the cross God has rendered his verdict upon sin: it is evil, and it must be destroyed. On the cross Christ destroyed sin as the factor that determines the identity of the chosen children of God. Luther did not fashion a justification for God's permitting evil or his failure to cope with it adequately. Bound to Scripture, he found no more of an answer to the "why" of evil than that given to Job. He simply wanted to let God be God. He trusted that the God who had come to engage evil at its ugliest on the cross would triumph finally over every evil. Therefore, he did not feel himself compelled to veil any part of the truth about God or about evil. On the basis of his argument in Heidelberg in 1518, Gerhard Forde has described Luther, as a theologian of the cross, in this way: theologians of the cross "are not driven to simplistic theodicies because with Saint Paul they believe that God justifies himself precisely in the cross and resurrection of Jesus. They know that, dying to the old, the believer lives *in* Christ and looks forward to being raised with him."[221] For God "justifies" himself by delivering and restoring us to the fullness of humanity through Christ's self-sacrifice on the cross.

De servo arbitrio reflects the theology of the cross as it moves toward its conclusions, which address human challenges to God's justice. Throughout the book Luther sought above all to confess that God is Lord of all. The work did not shy away from those passages in Scripture in which God seems to be responsible for evil. The reformer can be accused of trying to explain too much in this work, and when that is true he explains God in the manner of the Old Testament prophets who saw God at work in good and evil (Exod. 4:11; Isa. 45:7; Amos 3:6). Furthermore, he confessed that the human will is bound by its nature as the will of a creature, and it is bound by the sinfulness that has afflicted it since the fall into sin in Eden. The means by which that original sin, or root sin, as Luther often called it, was conveyed to the entire human race never interested the Wittenberg theologians. They were concerned with the perversion of all of human life that resulted from it. Luther did not believe that this root sin made every human action virtueless. It simply permeated all of human life with false faith, with the wrong orientation to life, with the failure to fear, love, and trust in God above all things. "The ungodly sin against God whether they eat or drink or whatever they do because they perpetually misuse God's creatures in their impiety and ingratitude and never for a moment give glory to God from their heart."[222] And the fallen creature, dead in trespasses and sins (Eph. 2:1), could not find life apart from the Creator's re-creative power. Human creatures must be resurrected, and they must be resurrected by the Holy Spirit on the basis of the work of Jesus Christ in his death and resurrection.

But, Luther insisted, God is not responsible for evil. That much was clear to him. In treating the hardening of Pharaoh's heart, as noted above, Luther wrestled with maintaining God's Godness and recognizing evil for what it is. "God does not create evil in us *de novo!*" (Watson's translation, "from scratch," is apt), Luther insists. "In us, that is, through us, God is at work when evil takes place, but he is not at fault. The defect lies in us since we are by nature evil and he is good. But as he carries us along by his own activity in accordance with the nature of his omnipotence, good as he is himself, he cannot help but do evil with an evil instrument though he makes good use of this evil in accordance with his wisdom for his own glory and our salvation."[223] The paradox of God's total responsibility and total human responsibility becomes acute, among other commonplaces, under the topic of sin and evil. The tension between the two defies solution, in spite of the best efforts of human reason. Luther's faith simply stopped before pressing for an ultimate answer that his very conception of the relationship between Creator and creature forbade him to pursue.

Luther's deep concern for pastoral care compelled him to return to this question at the end of *De servo arbitrio,* in the section Bernhard Lohse rightly calls "probably decisive for the interpretation of the entire treatise."[224] There he outlined three levels of response, none of which offers an answer satisfying to human reason and its desire to control. Under what he calls "the light of nature" the insoluble problem is posed: How can the good suffer and the evil prosper? The "light of the gospel" answers that the evil suffer everlasting condemnation, but it poses the insoluble problem of how God can condemn those who were born in sin and guilt and have no power of their own to free themselves. The question must be remanded to "the light of glory," which speaks alone of faith and confesses that God's judgment is "one of incomprehensible righteousness," that the Creator is "a God of most perfect and manifest righteousness."[225] For Luther the only possible Christian response to the question that would later be labeled "theodicy" is finally placing oneself in God's hands.

> Now you may well be disturbed by the thought that it is difficult to defend the mercy and justice of God when he condemns the undeserving, that is to say, the ungodly who are what they are because they were born in ungodliness and can in no way help being and remaining ungodly and

worthy of condemnation but are compelled by a necessity of nature to sin and perish (as Paul says: "We were all children of wrath like the rest" [Eph. 2:3] since they are created so by God himself from seed corrupted by the sin of the one man Adam). But the point really is, in fact, God must be honored and revered as supremely merciful toward those whom he justifies and saves, supremely unworthy as they are, and there must be at least some acknowledgement of his divine wisdom so that he may be believed to be righteous where he seems to us to be unjust. For if his righteousness were such that it could be judged to be righteous by human standards, it would clearly not be divine and would in no way differ from human righteousness. But since he is the one true God and is wholly incomprehensible and inaccessible to human reason, it is proper and indeed necessary that his righteousness also should be incomprehensible, as Paul also says where he exclaims, "O the depths of the riches of the wisdom and the knowledge of God! How incomprehensible are his judgments and how unsearchable his ways!" [Rom. 11:33].[226]

This confession of God's total otherness, superiority, and lordship and the total dependence of the human creature upon the Creator is Luther's fundamental response to the question of God's justice. His faith clings to the person of his Creator, and in him, as he revealed himself in Jesus Christ, Luther found sufficient response to the unanswerable question.

*   *   *

Luther himself was among the first "receptors" who commented not only on the topics treated in *De servo arbitrio* but also on two occasions on the book itself. Apart from a letter to Capito in 1537, Luther left no record of his enthusiasm for *De servo arbitrio.* Nor did he quote or argue from it. But then, Luther seldom cited his earlier works, whether as authority or as example. His fears about its misuse, uttered while lecturing on Genesis 26,[227] gave his students a way of dealing with his use of the concept of absolute necessity in the work, as shall be shown below. His insistence on the bondage of the will never wavered but remained a pillar of this proclamation and teaching. Relatively rarely did he treat God's election of his chosen children to be his own, but the presumption of predestination stands behind his every utterance regarding God's grace.

In *De servo arbitrio* Luther addressed the paradox of God's total responsibility and total human responsibility on the divine and on the human side: he affirmed God's total responsibility by positing a simple bondage of human choice in relationship to God but did not deny the human responsibility of total obedience to God; on the divine side he affirmed the absolute necessity of God's decision for all that happens in his creation. In both cases these "solutions" drive his readers to reliance on the goodness of God and to trust in Jesus Christ. His earliest students followed their mentor; the next generation displayed a bit more independence from his formulations as they digested the entire Wittenberg repast. The concerns of *De servo arbitrio* had to be processed along with Melanchthon's as the next generation sought to affirm God's responsibility for all things and their own responsibility for all things God had placed in their domain. Even when they expressed it in other ways, they presumed that sinners were bound to be freed for true human living in trust toward God.

This was Luther's way of practicing theology. Biblical interpretation and application in the Wittenberg way operated within a different framework from its predecessors, specifically focused on pastoral care through proclamation — both admonition and consolation. The Wittenberg way of exercising the office of public teacher of God's Word presumed that this exercise took place within the struggle of the repentant life and that God's disposition as the merciful Father placed the gift of Christ in the gospel at the center of the theological enterprise. Since the Word of God conveys what it says and delivers God's will in the form of a new creation, the Wittenberg way of theology presupposed that what its practitioners were doing actually accomplished God's plan to save those he had chosen to be his own. That took place on the basis of God's discharging his responsibility for all things and of his human creatures executing their responsibilities as God had given these responsibilities to them.

CHAPTER II

Drawing the Spirits in His Path:
De servo arbitrio Wins a (Critical) Following

The Lutheran Humanists and the Bound Will

Despite the fact that his confrontation with Erasmus remained a circum-scribed episode for Luther and did not affect the masses, it "drew the spirits all the more vigorously in his path," as Martin Brecht has noted.[1] While his reply to the *Diatribe* may have cost the young Wittenberg professor sympathy among the humanists of Erasmus's generation, such as Ulrich Zasius,[2] it certainly confirmed the recognition in many of their common younger disciples that the clear delineation of the bondage of the human will was essential for Luther's evangelical theology and thus also for their own teaching. Even before 1525 Luther's views on God's absolute lordship over all things and the freedom or bondage of the will had won the support of many of his advocates. For instance, Melanchthon in his *Loci communes* of 1521 had rejected the concept of free choice when the matter is viewed from the perspective of God's power to determine all things.[3] Luther's and Melanchthon's pastor and colleague Johannes Bugenhagen had grounded his understanding of predestination in God's creative power when he composed his commentary on Ephesians 1 in 1524. There he referred readers to Melanchthon's *Loci* as he explained that, in spite of the offense unbelievers take at the biblical teaching of predestination, believers should confess it, "as all things have been created by God, that they may be ruled by him altogether with his power."[4]

Another Wittenberg colleague, Justus Jonas, an epistolary friend of Erasmus, took pen in hand to translate *De servo arbitrio* into German as soon as it appeared. In 1523 he briefly indicated in his commentary on Acts that he saw God's election as a basis of the doctrine of justification: faith constitutes human righteousness and is based not on human merits or works but "on God's election or predestination and on the freely given mercy of God, on his good will that precedes all that we do."[5] The title of his translation of *De servo arbitrio* did not render Luther's title literally: instead of speaking of "bound choice," it used his earlier expression: "That the free will is nothing." His preface informed Count Albrecht of Mansfeld that Luther's clear answer to Erasmus's little book had to be available to show particularly the papal party that the defense of the free will was an offense and contrary to the gospel.[6]

An interesting aspect to the engagement between Luther and Erasmus is the fact that an enthusiastic supporter of Luther, Nikolaus Hermann, cantor in Joachimsthal, seems to be the person who rather quickly prepared a German translation of Erasmus's *Diatribe*. Hermann's analysis in the preface of the translation identified the heart of the conflict as a difference in giving primary place to God's responsibility or the responsibility of the human creature. His preface explained the dispute by contrasting Luther's concern that faith not be made to rest upon human works and powers with Erasmus's concern that Christians not become presumptuous and lazy. Hans Holeczek has suggested that Hermann's translation was an effort at winning sympathetic understanding for Erasmus's position in Lutheran quarters.[7] This is unlikely, for Hermann also drew the parallel between Luther's dispute with Erasmus and Augustine's with Pelagius. Few readers would have failed to recognize what this comparison of Erasmus and the heretic Pelagius meant.[8] Luther was in the right company. Erasmus was not. More likely is the conjecture of Christopher Brown, that Hermann's extensive marginal annotations from *De servo arbitrio* suggest that the publication provided an avenue for putting the positions of not only Erasmus but also Luther before the reading public in ducal Saxony, where Luther could not be published, so that the readers could come to the judgment regarding Erasmus's Pelagianism to which the preface points.[9]

Indeed, if Erasmus wanted to draw the dividing line between himself and Luther in order to consolidate in his train those who had been supporting both of them, he must have been disappointed. Not only Melanchthon, Bugenhagen, and Jonas remained on Luther's side. So did a cluster of other humanists of their generation who had benefited much from Erasmus's scholarship, inspiration, and commitment to reform. By September 1524 Wolfgang Capito in Strasbourg was confessing his rejection of Erasmus's position and anticipating Luther's response to the *Diatribe*. Four years later, his commentary on Hosea expressed his rejection of the concept of the freedom of the will in Luther-like language.[10]

Urbanus Rhegius matured intellectually in humanist circles at Basel and other universities. He became cathedral preacher in Augsburg in 1520. A correspondent of Erasmus, he had gained a reputation as a learned and progressive young theologian by 1525. He tempered his former enthusiasm for the great humanist scholar's work and criticized both Erasmus's churchmanship and his doctrine of the human will after the appearance of the *Diatribe*.[11] A decade later, as he prepared a homiletical handbook for the pastors under his supervision as superintendent of the churches of Braunschweig-Lüneburg, he gave young preachers instruction on how to speak properly regarding "free choice" and "the mystery of predestination." He distinguished what the will can do "in the sight of this world" from what it can do in relationship to God. In the latter realm it is completely dependent on God's grace to do good. The regenerated will is free, and through the Holy Spirit can do good works with God's grace. Predestination, he concluded, is a decree of God's will, to bring people from infidelity to trust, acceptance of God's commands, and perseverance in faith. He based certainty regarding God's predestining his chosen people to salvation on Ephesians 1:4, Romans 9:10-13, and Malachi 1:2-3. But with a strong sense of the implications for pastoral care, he cautioned that preachers must speak of this mystery with great sensitivity since it is solid food for adults, not milk for children. Paul taught it for the edification of believers; he did not intend to cultivate the attitude that "if you are predestined, you may do what you wish, good or bad; you will be saved anyway." Such an idea Rhegius labeled a blasphemous error. "Those predestined to eternal life believe the gospel and improve their lives." God calls some in their youth, others in old age, but he wants them all to trust in Christ and live in him. Those who persist in evil living have no faith and therefore are not among the elect. Rhegius insisted that the predestined do not follow their own will but God's in their daily lives, as Paul taught in Ephesians 2:8-10. For God is at work in them, enabling them both to will and to work for his good pleasure (Phil. 2:13).[12] Rhegius knew how to distinguish law and gospel in the Wittenberg way.

Johannes Brenz had learned his humanist skills at Heidelberg, where in 1517 he had assisted his instructor Johannes Oecolampadius in composing the index for Erasmus's edition of Jerome. Oecolampadius had registered his objections to Erasmus's defense of the freedom of the will in print before Luther did.[13] Brenz shared the disquiet his teacher had exhibited by bringing patristic evidence against Erasmus's position before the public. In the midst of his introducing the Reformation in Schwäbisch Hall, in 1525, Brenz, like Oecolampadius and Rhegius, let his disapproval of the *Diatribe* be known.[14] In his commentary on John's Gospel, Brenz demonstrated the necessity of speaking both of God's reliability and his faithfulness, based on his unchangeable nature, and of the human being's need to repent and exercise the responsibilities God has given him. These themes, along with Brenz's rejection of the concept of the free will[15] and his linking the predestination of the children of God closely to Christ,[16] reveal how well he understood Luther even if certain shifts of emphasis can be highlighted in their treatment of the problem. The Swabian reformer followed the Wittenberger in connecting the believer's knowledge and use of God's election of his children to the Word and to faith. Indeed, Brenz did move beyond Luther's more ambiguous statements regarding the damned to teach a predestination to damnation, although he clearly rejected any thought that God might be the cause of evil.[17]

The same was true of Nikolaus von Amsdorf, Luther's close friend, former colleague, at the time pastor in Magdeburg. Though not among the humanistically educated in the Wittenberg circle, he agreed with Brenz fully. He represented the teaching of *De servo arbitrio* in his encounters with Roman Catholic priests and canons in Magdeburg, affirming not only the bondage of the will but also its activity under that bondage, as Luther had.[18] Although he never advocated a doctrine of predestination to damnation in his published writings, he did so in private critiques of Melanchthon's rejection of divine necessity in the 1535 *Loci communes*.[19] The sensitivity to the proper application of law and gospel gave way to scholastically cultivated tidy explanations. Preserving the tension of God's total responsibility and the total responsibility demanded of human creatures gave way to the concern to make the former clear.

Some of Luther's followers undoubtedly failed to share — many even to understand fully — the reformer's views of the bondage of the will. He won followers for a variety of reasons and through the appeal of various aspects of his message. Nonetheless, the leading advocates of his message and his cause regarded his views on bound choice as an integral part of the Wittenberg theology.

Pulverizing Free Choice and Seeking a Balance (or Dynamic Tension): Melanchthon on the Freedom of the Will

Humanist and Reformer

Luther began *De servo arbitrio* by observing that he had already refuted the Sophists' arguments for free choice and that "they have been beaten down and completely pulverized in Philipp Melanchthon's *Loci communes,* an irrefutable little book which in my judgment deserves not only to be immortalized but even canonized."[20] Nearly thirty-five years later Melanchthon apparently understood the relationship of their thinking on the subjects treated in *De servo arbitrio* in a more precisely focused way. On the one hand, he insisted that in regard to God's election of his people he had shared the same concern for the consolation of consciences as Luther;[21] on the other hand, he distanced himself from the strict doctrine of divine necessity and similar contentions in *De servo arbitrio*.[22]

As is the case in any movement, the direction and leadership of the Wittenberg Reformation rested upon a partnership of minds, a multiple partnership, to be sure, but one centered in and driven by the two colleagues Martin Luther and Philipp Melanchthon. Each had his own abilities, interests, and concerns, and each thought and wrote on the basis of his own experiences and academic training. For a variety of reasons, from the sixteenth century to the present Melanchthon has often been judged not in his own right but against some measurement fashioned from Luther's life or theology. The expectation that he should have been Luther's clone has often prevented viewing him as a full, contributing partner in the Wittenberg enterprise. From the last years of his life to the present, such skewed expectations have haunted assessments of his teaching regarding freedom of the will and his role in the debates launched by the publication of *De servo arbitrio*. A closer review of Melanchthon's teaching regarding the human will and God's choosing of his own is necessary in any study of the reception and use of *De servo arbitrio* because his and Luther's students turned to that volume and interpreted it against the background of what they had learned from both men. No member of the Wittenberg circle remained outside the magnetic field of the younger colleague, whom they called "the Preceptor," and of his thinking on the subjects treated by *De servo arbitrio,* whether specific Melanchthonian impulses were received positively or negatively.

Although Melanchthon's relationship with Luther on precisely this issue of bound choice and the freedom of the will has been variously interpreted, fiercely debated and disputed for nearly 450 years,[23] the extant documents give a clear picture of the course of Melanchthon's careful crafting of his position as successive developments in his time challenged him to express himself regarding the various aspects of the teaching. His position on the issue is tangentially connected to his relationship with Erasmus. In his first years in Wittenberg the *Praeceptor Germaniae* enjoyed a positive though not intimate epistolary relationship with Erasmus. But when his humanist mentor fell into conflict with his Wittenberg colleague over the bondage of the will, Melanchthon gave Luther his unmitigated, though not completely uncritical, support. His reservations, it must be noted, concerned the vehemence of Luther's contributions to the dispute; in no way did he disagree with Luther's assertions regarding the lordship of the Creator and the bondage of the human will, although he did not share his colleague's enthusiasm for defending these positions with an argument for the absolute necessity of everything. Erasmus himself recognized where Melanchthon stood, as Karl Zickendraht observed a century ago.[24]

Although the common wisdom of previous scholarship still is voiced (for example, "In the controversy over the will, Melanchthon did not in any way follow Luther's extreme position, but rather came close to Erasmus"),[25] Timothy Wengert has illuminated the course of events in the controversy on the basis of various kinds of documents from Melanchthon's own hand. Wengert has shown how Melanchthon in fact promoted Luther's view of the will and defended both his position and person. He did so both in correspondence, with Erasmus and with others, and in his classroom lectures and their subsequent publication.[26] It may be true that later, in the mid to late 1530s, "Melanchthon distanced himself more and more from Luther" in his view of the will,[27] but the distance dare not be exaggerated nor its precise nature obscured. The nature of their differing concerns must be noted if the position of each of them is to be understood.

Melanchthon had expressed both admiration and disagreement when writing of Erasmus's work in the years 1510-19, and the older man made several generous gestures of praise and encouragement toward the budding scholar, whom he termed "a mere youth, scarcely a boy" in 1516. The two began to exchange letters in 1519, sometimes adorned by humanist compliments, sometimes pointed in their concern and criticism.[28] In 1524 Melanchthon lauded Erasmus's accomplishments to Johannes Memminger but then asked, "Can you explain why you now praise [him] so highly to me, when up to this point he still has not clearly shown in any writing what he really thinks piety and 'the righteousness of God' consist in?"[29]

Melanchthon is usually portrayed as the champion of the new humanist movement within the German educational establishment, and that portrayal is not false but is often misfocused. His own education included learning in the *via antiqua* in Heidelberg, in the *via moderna* in Tübingen, and the appropriation of "humanistic" aspects of contemporary instruction at both universities.[30] Paul Oskar Kristeller and Charles Trinkaus have demonstrated that the term "humanist," however, does not designate one particular ideological orientation but rather a methodological approach to learning.[31] Lewis Spitz has shown that "humanist" anthropology had negative and pessimistic assessments of human life as well as positive appraisals;[32] he, with others, has analyzed how Luther, like Melanchthon and through Melanchthon, was deeply influenced by various currents of humanistic learning.[33] The label "humanist" only lays the foundation for describing Philipp Melanchthon, the *Praeceptor Germaniae,* as a thinker. It says something about his method of pursuing learning and his preference for ancient sources, but these he thoroughly integrated into a theological framework he forged for himself from listening to Luther and reading Scripture and the ancient church fathers.

From the time he began assimilating his academic training with Luther's way of thinking, Melanchthon struggled to find appropriate ways to hold God's total responsibility for all things as Creator and Savior in the proper tension with total human responsibility for serving God and neighbor in obedience to God's plan for human life. Toward the end of his life, in a work he labeled his personal "confession," the *Responses to the Articles of the Bavarian Inquisition,*[34] he cited one of his instructors in Tübingen forty years earlier, Franz Kircher of Stadion: "Both propositions must be believed: there is divine determination, and there is contingency, and not every point of contradiction between the two can be explained."[35] Here Melanchthon acknowledged explicitly this tension between God's total responsibility for his creation and human responsibility for obedient service to God. This tension seems to have guided the formulation of his thought implicitly throughout his treatment of these questions since the early 1520s. Even when he attempted to clarify his position on one front or the other with expressions that break that tension, he usually found a way to remind readers of the biblical insistence on the total responsibility of God for all that happens while he held up the biblical insistence on the total responsibility of all human creatures for that which God has placed within their sphere of performance.

To be sure, as was the case with Luther, Melanchthon's changing concerns produced different points of focus over his more than forty years on the Wittenberg faculty. While demonstrating that certain common themes run through the entire expression of the Preceptor's convictions, Wolfgang Matz has identified five phases in the development of Melanchthon's teaching on the will.[36] Other scholars, from different viewpoints, could probably suggest plausible divisions with other foci. However the point of departure, the approach, the central concern of his discussion may have shifted over the years, the Preceptor's interest in and insistence on maintaining both the total divine responsibility of the Creator for his creation and the total human responsibility imposed by the Creator upon individual human creatures always governed his expositions of the topic. Luther's younger colleague, like Luther, suffered criticism in the sixteenth century because of this, sometimes for emphasizing God's responsibility too much (for the most part from Roman Catholic adversaries), but at other times he was attacked for focusing on human responsibility (for the most part from former students who believed he was betraying Christ's gospel and Luther's reform).

Several factors should be remembered in assessing Melanchthon's teaching regarding the will. First, from 1520 on he demonstrated an unwavering concern for the teaching of the justification of sinners by God's Word of grace and mercy, effected through and expressed in Jesus Christ. His consistent preoccupation with the clear confession of the sole efficacy of God's grace and human trust in Christ provided the underpinnings for his exposition of Scripture and the catholic tradition throughout his life. The troubled conscience remained the first audience for which he spoke and wrote, and he never vacillated from his assertion of God's total responsibility for the salvation of the troubled sinner.[37]

At the same time, throughout his career his interest in what makes the human creature human never faded. He came to Wittenberg well schooled in scholastic and humanistic anthropologies, and he naturally posed the questions of the psychological theories of his time. In part, this simply reveals the nature of the scholar his education had shaped; in part, it reflects his professional concern to teach students how to convey and transmit their ideas and God's Word clearly and effectively. As an instructor in rhetoric and dialectic, he had to wrestle with questions about the way human communication works. Such was his calling as a member of the arts faculty. Because Luther's concept of the living and active voice of the gospel placed his colleague's rhetorical thinking in a particular theological framework, Melanchthon's formulation of his understanding of human communication took on a special urgency. Melanchthon shared Luther's belief that the proclamation of God's Word was the Holy Spirit's instrument of saving people from their sins; through the Word the Spirit cultivates faith in human beings, who are created by God to function psychologically, that is, to trust with mind and will on the basis of an understanding of God's love in Christ conveyed by that Word. Searching for the proper understanding of how to bring sinners to faith in Christ was part of God's plan for their salvation.[38]

Furthermore, Melanchthon's instructors had cultivated in him the humanist ideal of the ethical and virtuous life. His reading of Scripture and his listening to Luther's fiery appeals for Christian living from the pulpit in Wittenberg only reinforced this concern for the moral life. Public disorder, for example, in the early days of the Reformation in Wittenberg in 1521 and 1522, or in the Peasants' Revolt in 1525, further strengthened his commitment to teaching the commandments of God for daily life. Perhaps the crowning impetus for these concerns came in 1527 and 1528 when he and Luther were both shocked and deeply distressed by the pitiful state of public behavior in the Saxon villages they inspected during the official visitation of churches in Elector John's principality. At the very same time, one of the inner circle of the Wittenberg reformers, Johann Agricola, called into question the need and propriety of preaching the law to believers.[39] Melanchthon never again could pass up an opportunity to emphasize the life of good works that faith produces.

Melanchthon also lived in a world of more complex personal and professional relationships and obligations than did Luther. As the chief ecclesiastical diplomat for electoral Saxony (and often for other evangelical princes and municipalities), he was forced to engage the arguments and accusations of Roman Catholic opponents and conversation partners personally and directly in a way Luther was not. For the elector's personal ambassador, fulmination was inappropriate and insufficient. He had to make the case for Wittenberg theology plausible to those who did not want to hear it made plausible. That meant he had to be prepared to explain his and Luther's views within the framework set by scholastic theologians who believed that the truth came only in scholastic (Aristotelian) form. Furthermore, upon his explanations rested in part the possibility for a political solution to the problem of the imperial threat to eradicate the Lutheran movement. This situation made him particularly sensitive to misrepresentations of the evangelical position, especially those that seemed to contain a kernel of truth. Such was the attack upon his own *Loci communes theologici* by the Roman Catholic theologian Johannes Cochlaeus in 1525. A master with the polemical rapier, he had accused Melanchthon of treating human beings as stones or beasts, and of making God the cause of evil and author of sin, among other charges. He placed Melanchthon in the same category as the ancient Manichaeans, whom Augustine had opposed.[40] Melanchthon felt compelled to address such criticism of the theology he had learned from and with Luther.

Because Melanchthon's views on the issues raised by Erasmus's attack on Luther and Luther's reply are said to have shifted dramatically over time, the analysis of these views presented in the following pages is set forth not according to the theses outlined above but instead in rough chronological form. This should aid readers to ascertain the continuity and development of the ways the Preceptor shifted emphases in his treatment of three critical topics he formulated as basic building blocks of biblical teaching: the freedom of the will, contingency and necessity, and predestination. The students whose works are discussed in chapters III through VII studied in Wittenberg or began their reading contact with Melanchthon at different times, but the entire second generation of the Wittenberg circle absorbed his theology on a continuing basis as he continued to elaborate it.

As is true of every university instructor at the beginning of his or her career, Melanchthon's new surroundings in Wittenberg immediately began to make an impact on him when he arrived in 1518. The dynamic and excitement of the Wittenberg Reformation and Luther's person and message changed the young scholar in deep and lasting ways from his first months at the university. In 1519 he dedicated his skills to drafting a guide to the epistle to the Romans, his *Theologica institutio,* a practice run for composing the first edition of his *Loci communes theologici* two years later. Both works make several points clear. Melanchthon taught that the will is not free, for two reasons: because of the total responsibility of the Creator for all things — expressed in terms of divine predestination of everything in his creation — and also because of the failure of human responsibility, due to sin — expressed as the inability of sinful human desires to seek the good, to turn themselves to God.[41] Like Luther, Melanchthon laid primary emphasis on the omnipotence and all-competence of the Creator; much more than Luther, he was intrigued by the way the anthropological factors of the mind, will, and emotions function. Therefore, not only the human status as sinner but also sin's perversion of the desires *(affectus),* as the agencies of human action, determined his analysis of the absence of freedom of the will.

The Loci communes *of 1521*

The *Loci communes theologici* of 1521 began its orientation to reading Scripture on the basis of the epistle to the Romans, at the place where the young author envisioned his readers were existentially located, in their sinfulness, with bound wills. His first topic treated "the powers of the human creature, and free choice." Melanchthon discussed the will in terms of anthropological questions regarding the processes of will, reason, and emotions coming together, as he laid the foundation for his assessment of the will's ability to make free choices upon both God's determination of all things and also the uncontrollable and wicked emotions that drive the will. The locus began by recalling that Augustine and Bernard had written on the subject. The selection of these authorities indicates the author's intention to focus on God's gracious exercise of his mercy toward sinners. He concluded this topic with three summary statements. If the human will is considered from the standpoint of God's predestining power, there is freedom neither in the external nor in the internal realm, but all things happen according to divine determination. (It must be noted, according to Hartmut Günther, that Melanchthon's use of the concept of predestination actually stands not as an independent axiom, but in service of his insistence that the human will is bound and that God is the active governor of all his creation.)[42] God is responsible for all things. Second, if the human will is considered from the standpoint of external or earthly works, it seems to have freedom according to human judgment. The integrity of God's human creature as a willing creature is preserved. Third, if the will is considered from the standpoint of human desires or emotions *(affectus)*, it is clear that it has no freedom, according to human judgment. For these desires cannot be tamed.[43] Sin holds sway over them. From the beginning of his published consideration of the question of the human will, Melanchthon recognized explicitly that the question behind the question would shape its own answer regarding the will, an answer different from the answer given when the underlying concern came out of other presuppositions and concerns.

Throughout the *Loci* Melanchthon grounded his argument upon Scripture, and his presentation of the role of God's determining power in assessing human free choice also rested on a number of Bible passages: "From him and through him and to him are all things" (Rom. 11:36), "He accomplishes all things according to his counsel and will" (Eph. 1:11), "Are not two sparrows sold for a penny? Yet not one of them will fall to the ground apart from your Father" (Matt. 10:29), "The Lord has made everything for its purpose, even the wicked for the day of trouble" (Prov. 16:4), "All our steps are ordered by the Lord; how then can we understand our own ways?" (Prov. 20:24), "The human mind plans the way, but the Lord directs the steps" (Prov. 16:9), "I know, O Lord, that the way of human beings is not in their control, that mortals as they walk cannot direct their steps" (Jer. 10:23), and other similar passages. There is no doubt in the reader's mind that Melanchthon affirmed God's total responsibility, lordship, and control over his creation. Yet it is also important to note that he did not expressly develop a doctrine of the predestination to salvation (much less to damnation) of individual believers or sinners. He used the term "predestination" for God's sovereign governance of all things, as Luther would in *De servo arbitrio.* Neither of them applied the term specifically to the salvation of individual believers in 1521 and 1525, although God's lordship over the salvation of his chosen people was certainly implied in his predestining of all things. Melanchthon's later revulsion toward teaching that there are a fixed number of the elect distinguished his understanding of predestination from Luther's. The roots of this rejection of this assertion as a constitutive element of the doctrine of predestination among some of his students seem to have lain in his initial formulation of his doctrine.[44] His *Loci* of 1521 did not consider God's commitment to individual believers but focused on the faith which the Holy Spirit works in believers and on the Word of God that the Spirit uses to create that faith. Important in the assessment of Melanchthon's view is not only the difference between his view and Luther's but also the fact that, whatever some of his students and later adherents may have thought, Luther himself used the doctrine of predestination as such relatively seldom. In the early writings of both colleagues the term rarely refers specifically and explicitly to predestination to salvation; its normal usage refers generally to God's determination of the course of all things.

It is also important to note that in spite of his thoroughly biblical anthropology, centered upon the sinful corruption of the human creature, Melanchthon found it natural to answer certain questions about the mechanisms of human thought and action with recourse to Aristotle, whom he directly cited several times in this locus. Sometimes he explained how Aristotelian and biblical terms function as synonyms; sometimes he implicitly recognized that biblical writers had not addressed certain matters, such as the mechanics of willing, that the philosopher had.[45] Sometimes he acknowledged that Aristotle could not provide answers to some questions posed within a biblical way of thinking.

The Commentary on Colossians

Melanchthon envisaged his *Loci* of 1521 not as a work of systematic theology, or an aid for teaching the whole analogy of faith, but rather as an exegetical tool, an aid for teaching the book of Romans (though by implication, on the basis of Romans, the whole of Christian teaching). The Preceptor's actual classroom teaching of theology was conducted to a significant extent in the form of lectures on biblical books. The development of his presentation of the doctrine of human freedom of choice took place also in those lectures, also in their published form as commentaries. When Luther turned to the text of Ecclesiastes as a field on which to do battle with Erasmus, after the appearance of the *Hyperaspistes* in 1526, Melanchthon turned to Paul's letter to the Colossians, in fact, in the following year. Among other topics, he there presented his views of human responsibility by treating the human will and good works, directing them in part against Erasmus and perhaps Cochlaeus, in part against the "antinomianism" of Johann Agricola. He did not simply repeat his earlier insights. Some revisions may be noted in his treatment as he was revising the *Loci* in 1522, and these shifts continued into the later 1520s. For instance, in 1522 the relationship of reason and will changes with the abandonment of his clear subordination of reason to will that had been present in his earlier comment. That human creatures exercise some (limited!)

freedom in external matters becomes clearer, as does Melanchthon's rejection of any impersonal determinism.[46]

The three versions of his commentary on Colossians that appeared in 1527 and 1528 reveal further modifications in concern and emphasis. In 1527 an excerpt from the lectures appeared under the title *Dissertatio,* followed by a *Scholia,* Melanchthon's own reworking of his lectures. In 1528 he revised the *Scholia,* intensifying his critique of the advocates of the freedom of the will.[47] In his lectures the Preceptor attacked "philosophy" for its denial of God's governance of the world because evil and wrongdoing contradict it. He further criticized philosophy for undermining Christ's justifying work, and for undercutting the Holy Spirit's action in sanctification.[48] Melanchthon's engagement with the intellectual tradition of the West and his Roman Catholic academic colleagues compelled him to address the paradox of God's total responsibility for all in a world in which evil exists. Through the aid of the Holy Spirit God's Word reveals what philosophy cannot learn (1 Cor. 2:14), that God governs all things. At this point Melanchthon had abandoned his use of the term "predestination" for God's determining power, but he asserted the total responsibility of God for the world by speaking of his "governing" *(gubernatio)* or his "general action" in regard to all things *(actio Dei generalis).*[49] Matz also notes that in the first edition of the Colossians *Scholia* Melanchthon adjusted the correlation between his argument against the freedom of the will on the basis of original sin and the argument on the basis of the creaturely nature of human beings in relationship to their Creator in favor of the latter.[50] He further clarified the role of the will by ascribing human righteousness in God's sight to the faith that the Holy Spirit creates, a clear affirmation of his distinction between two kinds of righteousness, that of faith (in the relationship with God) and that of obedience, the performance of God's commands to love (in relationship with other creatures). God bestows the former as a free gift, but human creatures perform the latter in their good works.[51] Melanchthon insisted on the latter, the execution of human responsibility, by explaining how the Holy Spirit produces the Christian life through faith and by affirming the possibility of external compliance with God's plan for human living even apart from the Holy Spirit ("civil righteousness" or "the imitation of the law"). He paid some attention to both the sanctified life and the virtuous life of the unbeliever. God's Word of forgiveness bestows righteousness in God's sight and creates faith, and the Holy Spirit works in the continuing process of repentance through both the mortification of sins and the vivification of obedience. The dying and rising induced by law and gospel continue throughout the Christian life. Melanchthon explicitly rejected the charge that his insistence on God's omnipotent lordship and his movement in all creatures was making God the author of sin and evil.[52] His consistent rejection of the charge that God is the author of sin is a reaction to the charges that his affirmation of God's lordship and providential governance of all his creation was so strong that it could logically lead to the conclusion that God must be held responsible also for evil.

When he revised the *Scholia* in 1528, Melanchthon strengthened his case against the proponents of the concept of freedom of choice. Again asserting the absolute authority of God's Word, particularly against human reason, he argued that the righteousness of faith clings alone to Christ and is created by God's favor through the Holy Spirit's action. Only by setting aside thoughts of human contribution can the troubled conscience find peace, Melanchthon asserted, as always concerned above all about the bruised reed and smoldering wick. Alone, the will has no power to abandon concupiscent desires. Although he avoided referring to God's governing power as much as possible, Melanchthon did venture that God's assistance is necessary even for the performance of civil righteousness. All good proceeds from God; at the same time, Melanchthon wanted to make sure that no one should think that God is the cause or author of evil. Nonetheless, he averred that the will has no power to choose to turn itself to God. The law is able to coerce some external obedience from unbelievers, but this kind of obedience apart from faith is fatally flawed by indwelling, original sin.[53]

Melanchthon was lecturing and writing on Colossians in the midst of his visitation of Saxon parishes. This encounter with the way the Wittenberg message was being received in the countryside and towns of Saxony shocked Luther and Melanchthon. Both of them reacted with increased attention to the preaching of the law even though they framed that preaching in different ways. For both men the earlier concern for the integrity of the human creature in responsible obedience to God's commands came ever more to the fore in the succeeding years. The cultivation of a spirit of repentance and of new obedience also formed part of their conception of the pastoral care of their people, whom God had entrusted to them. Luther used the law more often in its accusatory form, while Melanchthon focused more on the instructional role of the law in the Christian life.[54] This influenced the balance each struck in his public teaching between God's responsibility for all things and human responsibility for the sphere of life entrusted to these creatures of God.

The Development of Melanchthon's Thought, 1530-1559

Melanchthon's Views in Official Statements of Faith

Within months of the appearance of the revised Colossians commentary Melanchthon became caught up in the political maneuvering and theological exchange that climaxed with the presentation of his Confession at Augsburg in June 1530 and the publication of the Apology of the Augsburg Confession the following April. These two documents and his other official writings for the Protestant princes and municipalities reflected his effort to hold God's total responsibility for salvation in tension with the human integrity of human creatures through the exercise of their responsibility to trust and to obey. Two of the key preparatory documents Melanchthon was using, the Schwabach Articles and the Marburg Articles, had not treated the topics of the freedom of the will and the cause of sin, but the attack of John Eck upon the Lutheran churches in his *Four Hundred Four Propositions* demanded an answer to the charge that the Wittenberg theology abandoned the catholic faith.[55] Melanchthon rose to the challenge.

In the Augsburg Confession (1530) he wrote, "Concerning free will [the evangelical churches] teach that the human will has some freedom for producing civil righteousness and for choosing things subject to reason" — securing individual responsibility for public order and moral behavior — but "it does not have the power to produce the righteousness of God or spiritual righteousness without the Holy Spirit" — securing God's grace in the exercise of his re-creative responsibility for the salvation of sinners. He added, securing the Lutheran description of how God works to restore faith to sinners, "this righteousness is worked in the heart when the Holy Spirit is received through the Word." When the Augsburg Confession was published, Melanchthon added a rejection of Pelagian teaching and affirmed the necessity of the Holy Spirit's power in creating faith.[56] His reaction to the guarded acceptance of this article by the Roman Catholic *Confutation of the Augsburg Confession* in his own Apology reaffirmed that the human will has limited freedom to produce good works in the earthly sphere of life but is completely dependent on the Holy Spirit for coming to faith. Even in the saints, faith is retained only with the Spirit's assistance. God is the Lord of his people, and only his grace preserves them as his children.[57]

As the Lutheran governments were preparing to enter into negotiations with Roman Catholic theologians, at the command and invitation of Emperor Charles V, in 1540, the Saxon government asked Melanchthon to strengthen the text of the Lutheran "symbol," the Augsburg Confession, for the colloquy that took place in stages at Worms and Regensburg. Complying with that commission from Elector Johann Friedrich, Melanchthon expanded and changed the text not only in the tenth article (on the Lord's Supper), which made this "Altered Augsburg Confession" notorious at a later point in the sixteenth-century disputes over the Wittenberg legacy, but also in several other articles. Article XIX, on the cause of sin, remained the same, but article XVIII, on freedom of the will, was elaborated. The Preceptor added John 15:5, Christ's words "without me you can do nothing," to fortify the total responsibility of God for salvation.[58] Melanchthon further explained, "spiritual righteousness is effected in us when we are aided by the Holy Spirit. Furthermore, we receive the Holy Spirit when we assent to God's Word as we receive comfort in our terrors by faith, as Paul teaches, 'you receive the promise of the Spirit through faith'" (Gal. 3:14). In addition, the expanded text of the article makes clear the distinction between civil righteousness and spiritual "movements," such as true fear of God, patience, steadfastness, faith, prayer, persistence in the worst of temptations. For this living of the godly life "it is necessary that we be governed and aided by the Holy Spirit, as Paul says, 'the Spirit gives us help in our weakness'" (Rom. 8:26). To the rejection of Pelagianism Melanchthon added a repudiation of "this madness" of any human contribution to salvation because "it obscures the benefits of Christ."[59] It may have been true that the language of "aiding" and "assenting" was more acceptable to the opponents than some alternatives, but Melanchthon understood the former as an expression of the total dependence of the sinner upon the saving action of God and the latter as a defense of the integrity of the human creature's functioning according to God's design, trusting in his promise.

Twenty years after the Augsburg diet of 1530, when the Preceptor was called upon to write a new official presentation of the Wittenberg theology for use at the Council of Trent, he omitted an article on the freedom of the will from his German version of this Repetition of the Augsburg Confession, or, as it was entitled in Latin, Saxon Confession. The Latin version did contain such an article, however, but in a different location than Melanchthon had formerly placed it in his *Loci communes.* Here the topic was not considered in the context of sin and the law that condemns sin but rather following the treatment of justification, before the article on "new obedience." This ordering implies that insofar as the will acts in a God-pleasing way, it does so because God has already re-created it in justification. This article was brief and simply averred that external moral discipline must be distinguished from the renewal of the Spirit, which is the beginning of eternal life. Those who have not been reborn can discipline themselves to perform the demands of the law in external fashion. But fallen human creatures cannot liberate themselves from sin and eternal death by their own natural powers, Melanchthon affirmed. "That liberation, conversion to God, and spiritual renewal take place only through the Son of God, who lives in us through the Holy Spirit." God alone is responsible for salvation. But then the Preceptor added, "And the will is not idle in the acceptance of the Holy Spirit." The integrity of the human being's response as a thinking and willing creature of God could not be abandoned to "Stoic and Manichaean" misinterpretations that would reduce the human creature to something less than the creation God had fashioned in his own image.[60] The phrase admits of two interpretations, one insisting that the Holy Spirit first moves the will, and thus it acts by willingly accepting God's forgiveness in Christ because the Holy Spirit has moved it. The other interpretation suggests that an act of human will is a necessary part of conversion without which the Holy Spirit's power accomplishes nothing.

The following year, 1552, Melanchthon was asked to compose a study guide to prepare candidates for ordination in the duchy of Mecklenburg for their examination. It contained no question regarding freedom of the will, but in 1554 the Latin translation appeared, with such a question. Melanchthon's answer began with the rejection of the "Stoic madness" concerning the necessity of all things, affirmed sufficient freedom in sinners to preserve public order and moral discipline, and then confessed that apart "from the gospel and the Holy Spirit, it is impossible for inner obedience to God's commands to begin, that is, true fear of God, true faith, invocation of God and love for him." Natural human powers can do nothing to initiate faith. Nonetheless, faith is necessary, and the errors of the "Manichaeans and Schwenkfelder" that teach a salvation apart from faith and the working of God's Word must be rejected. For, as Melanchthon taught in the *Loci* of 1535, there are three factors that come together: God's Word, the Holy Spirit, and the will that assents to God's Word and does not resist it. That assent accepts the universal promise of the gospel.[61]

Melanchthon wanted to make clear that God is solely responsible for salvation. At the same time, he felt compelled to repudiate the impression his opponents had taken that the Wittenberg theologians made God responsible for evil as well. He did this in part by insisting that God has promised salvation to all, in part by affirming the activity of the human will, even if the Holy Spirit causes this activity, when it accepts the promise. Melanchthon was also concerned to insure the comfort that Christ brings to forgiven sinners, and so he focused on the promise of the means of grace, which he found tangible in contrast to a vaporous claim about God's predestining will which, independent of the means of grace, could only foster speculation. These official statements of the faith did not contain the detailed treatment that the *Loci com-*

munes offered readers, but in their brevity they demonstrate the central concerns of Melanchthon's teaching.

Melanchthon's Views in the Revisions of His Loci communes

As Melanchthon fashioned his views officially for Lutheran churches and governments in the 1530s, 1540s, and 1550s, he was also revising his textbooks of biblical teaching, his *Loci communes,* in which he developed his position on predestination, contingency and necessity, and the human will. The face-to-face encounter with Roman Catholic negotiators in Augsburg in 1530 began a period of intense reflection for Melanchthon. Among other results, it produced a thoroughgoing reshaping of his *Loci communes,* a reshaping which reflected his rethinking and reworking of his way of treating the freedom of the will. Melanchthon revamped the *Loci* of 1521 completely in 1535. This text was revised substantially in 1543 (under the title *Loci praecipui theologici*) and periodically thereafter, though with fewer changes, until 1559. It is this work that fueled the suspicion and drew the criticism of some of his former students in the 1550s.

The *Loci communes theologici* of 1535 was not only much longer than its precursor of fourteen years earlier. It had also changed in its fundamental organization and purpose. It was no longer a guide to reading Romans and thus an aid for teaching biblical doctrine in general. It was a new way of using the traditional medieval schema for organizing questions regarding the teaching of Scripture, according to the methods Melanchthon had learned to use among the humanists.[62] One result of this is that the topic "on human powers or free choice" did not initiate this new review of biblical teaching, as it had in 1521, when the practical problems of preaching and teaching shaped the author's thinking. In 1535 Melanchthon took the traditional outline for overviews of biblical teaching, based on the ancient creeds as well as on Peter Lombard and John of Damascus, and loosely followed its model, initiating his work with the topic "on God." After the exposition of the doctrine of the Trinity and creation came a locus on the cause of sin and contingency, followed by the topic of "human powers." Predestination to salvation was treated in the context of the topic of justification.

This new work is of inestimable significance for several reasons. First, it reflects what students in Wittenberg learned and studied in the years after its appearance in 1535, both because it indicates what Melanchthon himself taught and also because it served as the basis for lectures by junior instructors. Second, it was read by many preachers and teachers throughout German lands and beyond who never studied in Wittenberg and was incorporated into sermons, instruction, and other printed works written in imitation of it. Furthermore, it reveals Melanchthon's own doctrinal development. It constitutes one of his greatest contributions to the execution of humanist method and the formulation of Lutheran teaching.

Matz has observed that while in the *Loci communes* of 1521 predestination had served as the criterion for determining how to answer the question of the freedom of the will, in the *Loci* of 1535, as in an extant "fragment" or partial draft of the text from 1533, Melanchthon bestowed this criteriological function on obedience to the law.[63] His first concern as a teacher of the discipline of theology had shifted as he perceived his surroundings shifting. In 1521 he was opposing medieval views of the role of human merit in salvation. In 1533 and 1535 his emphasis on the exercise of human responsibility reflects his distress over public immorality and the fragility of the social order which pervaded his thinking after the visitations of 1527/1528, his concern about the antinomian attitudes and convictions of some Wittenberg students, such as Johann Agricola, and his desire to counter Roman Catholics' polemic against what they viewed as the evil influences of the Wittenberg teaching of justification by faith.[64]

In the last quarter-century of his life (1535-60) the Preceptor addressed the believer's obedience to the law in many settings. He always viewed that obedience, which meets the expectations the Creator has built into the life of the human creature he has made responsible in his world, within his fundamental framework for human living, the Spirit-given identity of reborn children of God. God bestows that new identity through his justifying action, as expressed in trust in the Creator, who came to restore human life as Jesus Christ.[65] This can be seen not only in Melanchthon's theological works. When he formulated an analysis of the will on the basis of Aristotelian texts, in his commentaries on the Stagarite's *Ethics* (1538, 1550) and *De anima* (1553), for example, his biblical presuppositions also set the framework of the discussion, for also here he presumed that the human being is a creature, God's creation, and that human life is lived within the framework God has designed.[66] He noted that Aristotle helps readers understand the earthly realm in which human life is lived, but philosophers cannot account for the cause of human weakness.[67] The Greek thinker could not understand sin. He had no God against whose person and commands human activity could be measured. Life in this world cannot be adequately treated, in the final analysis, apart from the biblical revelation regarding God and his human creatures.

Melanchthon's thought on the freedom of the will not only falls under that topic itself but is also treated in his presentations of the topics of predestination and contingency. Therefore his mature positions on all three of these loci impinge on his teaching regarding God's total responsibility and total human responsibility.

Predestination   The 1533 fragment — a working draft for the recasting of the *Loci* — does contain a brief topic "on predestination," which admonishes readers that this locus can be understood neither from human reason nor from the law, but only on the basis of the gospel. This was a fundamental axiom for the Wittenberg conception of good pastoral care. "Predestination" is to be discussed only to highlight God's justification of sinners, which he effects through the Word of the gospel. Two things must be remembered when speaking of the promise of the gospel: it is free, and it is universal. Therefore, no one should abandon hope because of a belief in a fixed number of the elect (among whom believers fear they might not find themselves). Thus, the believer's election can be apprehended only a posteriori, that is, through the hearing of God's Word that produces faith. No speculation is allowed in regard to God's choosing of his people. Melanchthon fended off suggestions that the election of the righteous must connote divine predestination to damnation. Like Luther at this time, he expressed his concern for tender consciences by pointing to the universality of the promise and to the assurance that faith brings by clinging to the mercy and love of God.[68] He never abandoned this foundational disposition toward the proclamation of God's saving work in Christ.

The Preceptor had significantly altered the outline and wording of the locus "on predestination" in the 1543 edition of his great work, although the fundamental ideas of 1535 remained. In 1535 the topic had found its place within the group of topics that proceed from the doctrine of justification, and it began with the insistence that predestination be considered only on the basis of the gospel, not of the law. In 1543 it stood among the miscellaneous topics toward the end of the *Loci praecipui theologici* and began with an ecclesiological focus, the church as a whole rather than individual believers being the object of God's predestination. In both, however, the Preceptor emphasized the universal promise of the gospel, tied any talk of predestination to Christ, to faith in him, and to the means of grace that produce that faith. He also rejected a doctrine of election that offered the promise only to some undefined group of "the elect." God is no respecter of persons (Acts 10:34), and the justification to which his people are predestined comes alone through faith in the promise of the benefits of Christ (Rom. 3:22; 10:12; John 3:15), a promise made to all people (1 Tim. 2:4). Melanchthon explicitly rejected the interpretation of Romans 9:16 which suggested that the promise is directed only to particular people; the passage concerns only the mercy of God and is designed to console the faithful. Teaching that there is a certain number of elect children of God robs the promise of its comfort.[69]

In 1537 the Preceptor prepared theses for disputation on 1 Timothy 2:4, "God wants all people to be saved," with basically the same ideas. Subtle disputations regarding election bring the pious no benefit because they foster doubt that the universal promise applies to them.[70] The 1543 locus warns that trying to decide why Cain and Esau were not elect while Abel and Jacob were can only crush pious thoughts under the weight of the law.[71] Like Luther at the end of *De servo arbitrio,* Melanchthon at this point stopped in awe before questions of a theodical nature. Nonetheless, despite his continuing emphasis on the distinction of law and gospel, he was not able to apply the distinction to the relationship between God's universal promise of salvation and the particular application of the promise to the elect, in the manner in which some of his students, such as Cyriakus Spangenberg and Martin Chemnitz, could and would. Melanchthon believed that the latter excluded the former. These two students held the particular application of the promise in tension with its universal offer and the mystery of the ability of some sinners to reject it.

Contingency and Necessity   That mystery was part of the larger mystery of the existence of evil. The exposition of the cause of sin in the *Loci communes* of 1535 asserted, "God is not the cause of sin, and God does not will sin. The causes of sin are the will of the devil and the will of the human creature." When God "hardened" Pharaoh's heart (Exod. 4:21; 7:3, 13), he did not really harden it but only permitted Pharaoh to harden his own heart, Melanchthon claimed, in contradistinction to Luther but following his own interpretation in his 1532 Romans commentary.[72] In the early draft of his new approach to writing his *Loci,* from 1533, Melanchthon observed that the question regarding the freedom of the will cannot be properly answered because sin so obscures human ability to judge. He objected to the doctrine of the freedom of the will because it abolishes the gospel through its denial of the total corruption of human powers.[73] His repugnance toward Luther's assertion that all things happen by absolute divine necessity began to come out in the open through his treatment of contingency in human affairs within the framework of a *necessitas consequentiae,* which Melanchthon distinguished from the *necessitas consequentis,* the scholastic distinction that Luther had opposed. The Preceptor stated that these questions about necessity were not of great importance, and so he treated them only briefly. In constructing this interpretation, Melanchthon was trying to take seriously human responsibility by rejecting a raw determinism, but at the same time he wanted to place all human action within the sphere of God's governance by positing a necessity ultimately dependent on God. This draft from Melanchthon's pen reveals no other major changes in his position.[74] Since God cannot be the cause of sin, Melanchthon continued, expanding his new understanding of necessity, contingency must exist and there can be no absolute necessity, a repudiation of his position in 1521 as well as Luther's in 1525. Things that happen according to the *necessitas consequentiae* are not by their nature unchangeable or predetermined, but they become so because of God's decree or because of human actions that bear with them natural results. "Stoic fate," an eternally and impersonally fixed necessity, is madness; it is untrue; and its suggestion that human beings sin because they must is abhorrent, Melanchthon asserted.[75]

The Preceptor was not rejecting a position actually held by his contemporaries when he wrote against the belief that God was the author of sin and the creator of evil. No evangelical theologian had contended that. Melanchthon's insistent rejection of that position was designed to counter a potential logical conclusion that might be deduced out of the Wittenberg way of thinking. Encounters with Roman Catholic theologians at the colloquies held under imperial sponsorship at Hagenau, Worms, and Regensburg in 1540 and 1541 — and the failure of those colloquies to create a better situation for the Lutherans — intensified his concern to defend and explain Lutheran teaching, a concern expressed already a decade earlier.[76] Specifically with regard to the charge that the Wittenberg theologians had taught that God is the cause of evil, his student and confidant Martin Chemnitz later recalled that the Roman Catholic negotiator in the colloquies, Johann Eck, had "provoked arguments which lasted whole days with citations from the earliest writings of Luther and Philip."[77] This accusation the Preceptor had wanted to rebut at all costs. Increasingly Melanchthon viewed the articles of the faith regarding the will and predestination from the ecclesiological perspective employed by his Roman Catholic interlocutors.[78]

When the Preceptor revised his *Loci* in 1543, he had a new occasion to make certain that he not be vulnerable to charges of Stoic determinism. He had recently begun a friendly epistolary exchange with John Calvin, but Calvin's doctrine of predestination and the Genevan's attempt to enlist Melanchthon in its defense troubled the Wittenberger and cast a heavy shadow over their correspondence in 1543 (and would again in 1552).[79] Melanchthon's revised locus "on the cause of sin and on contingency" of 1543 repeated the basic arguments of the locus composed eight years earlier, with the same Bible passages and more, but was four times as long. In this third edition of the *Loci* he expanded his comments on the concept of contingency to make certain that God could not be regarded in any way as responsible for evil. He was wrestling with the mystery that a human being created in the image of a willing, thinking God, and necessarily dependent on him, could sin. Because God cannot be the cause of sin or will sin, it follows that there is "contingency, that is, that all things which take place do not take place by necessity," sins of every kind being the best example. "The cause of the contingency of our actions is the freedom of the will." Melanchthon continued to regard God as the one who "determines" contingency, but carefully distinguished between that which he wills, that which depends alone on his will, and that which "he does partly, and the human will does partly." In this sentence Melanchthon fell back into a scholastic-like effort to break through the paradox of two responsibilities by synthesizing God's action with human actions. The example of Saul's sins, which God foresaw but did not will — only permitted — is presented to the reader. "Thus, this foresight does not produce necessity, nor does it alter the mode of acting in the human will, which remains in the [fallen] nature, that, is the liberty which remains there." For God sustains that nature with its ability to make such decisions. It does not, however, have the capacity to make the decision to turn back to God.[80] Melanchthon repeated his interpretation of the concept of necessity, insisting that the evils that happen according to the *necessitas consequentiae* fall within God's "determination" — setting of limits — but are not in accord with his will.[81]

With a passing observation Melanchthon noted that the concept of "necessity" in the discipline of physics was a form of *necessitas consequentiae*, fixed by God's creative act.[82] Indeed, the treatise published in 1549 under his name and that of his student Paul Eber on Aristotle's *Physics* did contain comments on God's providence, contingency, fate, and therefore on the various shades of meaning that the word "necessity" bears. Eber had delivered the lectures on physics that stand behind the volume, but Melanchthon had contributed a great deal to their composition. The definition of providence in the treatise embraces both "the knowledge by which God takes all things into consideration and foresees them, and his governance, by which he preserves the whole of nature." Providence includes his paternal care for the human race, his punishment of evil and his liberation of the innocent. "These things cannot always be assessed in the same way," the text adds, taking into account the question of evil in the presence of a good and almighty God. This question received further treatment without any more of a definitive answer than Luther gave. In the course of a detailed address to the problem, however, Melanchthon rejected the Stoic doctrine which necessarily connects secondary causes to God and makes him a cause of good and evil.[83]

At the introduction to the locus "on contingency" in the *Physics*, Melanchthon and Eber continued their critique of Stoicism. In the interest of providing stability for celestial motion in a system of thought originally conceived without a personal Creator God, the Stoics fostered a doctrine of absolute necessity, which defines necessity in human decision making on the same basis as its definition in nature. Employing the concept of *modus agendi,* the Wittenberg instructors defined the order established by God in nature as the mode of action appropriate for heavenly bodies and earthly movement. Natural causes are established by a *necessitas consequentiae,* that is, by God's ordination. However, the mode of action appropriate for human beings is the exercise of the freedom God bestowed upon these responsible creatures, who must be distinguished from other parts of God's creation.[84] The human will was so created by God that contingencies are a part of human life; the fall into sin is one example of such contingent action that is independent from God. "God is not the cause of sin, that is, he does not will it, he does not approve it, he does not drive the wills of human beings to sin."[85]

Scholastic conceptions of physics demanded a consideration of the concept of fate, *fatum.* It often signifies "a divine decree concerning that which God governs directly, not through secondary causes." It may designate a series of natural causes (Aristotelian fate) or the governance of certain things on earth through the stars (physical fate). But the term was also used by the Stoics to affirm that God governs all things directly and thus is responsible for everything that happens, including evil. This definition Melanchthon and Eber definitively rejected.[86] The integrity of the creature God made to be human was at stake for them, and they felt compelled to defend that integrity through the assertion of the will's freedom to act, even if the Holy Spirit's power was required to turn its actions in God's direction.

The Preceptor had opened his revised topic on the freedom of the will in 1543 by rejecting the opinion regarding the necessity of all things delineated by the fifteenth-century humanistic pioneer Lorenzo Valla,[87] whose larger oeuvre must have contributed to Melanchthon's own study of ancient sources. He did not wish to reject the position of Calvin publicly, it seems. Contemporary Roman Catholic theologians had made Valla a symbol of the view they labeled Stoic or Manichaean determinism, and Melanchthon could use him as a target of criticism to distance himself from such a view. He did associate Valla with the ancient Stoics, the embodiment of a false fatalistic view of necessity. The Italian humanist's denial of contingency and his rejection of the freedom of the will led to impiety, Melanchthon believed. God governs the whole world, he repeated, but in 1543 his concern had shifted to affirming human responsibility. Therefore, more than previously in his writings, the ability of the will to make decisions within the earthly realm came to the fore. At the same time, however, the Preceptor affirmed that the will as it is corrupted by sin is not free to turn itself to God. There is no power in the sinner to trust God on its own. Here Melanchthon ignored the creaturely limits of the will, a natural correlation to his revision of his expression of God's almighty power and lordship, and focused only on the impotence which sin has wrought in the will. Human responsibility had to be maintained. Therefore, Melanchthon found recourse to the church fathers as a better way of explaining such matters and escaping the labyrinth of scholastic questions. The Bible passages that focused on the Holy Spirit's power in creating faith (Rom. 8:9, 14; 1 Cor. 2:14; John 3:3; 6:44; 14:16-17) were interpreted in light of the statement attributed to Basil that God turns human creatures, calls them, moves them, aids them, but they must see to it that they do not resist (μόνον θέλησον, καὶ ὁ θεὸς προαπάντα, *Deus antevertit nos, vocat, movet, adiuvat, sed nos viderimus, ne repugnemus*). Melanchthon added a similar assertion (ὁ δὲ ἕλκων τὸν βουλόμενον ἕλκει, *Id apte dicitur auspicanti a verbo, ne adversetur, ne repugnet verbo*) by Chrysostom.[88] Such an explanation preserved both God's sinlessness and human responsibility. The integrity of God and that of his human creature were saved.

Freedom of the Will   The second and third editions of his *Loci* offer a much broader analysis of the freedom of the human will than that of 1521, with certain shifts of emphasis and expression. In 1543 Melanchthon noted that the vocabulary of the prophets and apostles designates intellect and will as mind and heart or judgment and appetite. He emphasized the distinction between the will and intellect or reason, and he placed within the human will the possibility of freedom of choice *(liberum arbitrium)*. He defined freedom of choice as the faculty of the will for choosing and desiring those things which are excellent and for rejecting those things which are burdensome. When mind and will are bound to each other and act together, they exercise this freedom of choice.[89] Melanchthon rejected the idea that a neutral will exists in and of itself and can be abstractly considered. He wished to deal instead with the activity of the will *(voluntas)* as a mark of human integrity, and he differentiated it from the actual choices *(arbitrium)* the will makes as it acts. Denial of the will's activity therefore threatened the very integrity of the creature God had fashioned as human.[90] The bondage of choice — the restriction of the options for the actions of that will — is a distinct issue.

By 1535 the critical question regarding the human will for Melanchthon had become whether and to what extent it can obey God's law. He discussed this question under three points. The first dealt with civil righteousness; like Luther and all their students at Wittenberg, he affirmed that even in the fallen human creature there is sufficient judgment left to allow sinners to practice the external works of civil righteousness, the "righteousness of the flesh," according to Paul. Misbehaving Saxon peasants were without excuse. This practice of external discipline does not merit remission of sins, and it is not the righteousness through which human creatures become righteous before God. Nonetheless, it is of value for human society. Human weakness and the temptations of the devil do weaken the ability to perform this civil righteousness, but it is sufficiently strong to enable sinners to construct a decent society.[91] Melanchthon's concern for human responsibility is evident in this first point.

The second point in Melanchthon's treatment of freedom of choice concerns the depravity of the human will. He affirms that the fallen human will is not able to satisfy the law of God since this law demands not external discipline and "shadows of works," but instead the whole obedience of the heart. In regard to God this will is captive, not free but depraved and dead, unable to trust God freely, with a joyful heart.[92] Melanchthon presumed that faith in God, the trust commanded by the first commandment, is the center of and key to human existence. When the will's capacity to act on its own in moving itself toward God became the topic under focus, Melanchthon remained totally committed to the Wittenberg teaching that only God's grace and the action of the Holy Spirit can renew the sinful will and mind.

It is in the discussion of his third concern in regard to freedom of choice that Melanchthon employed language which later offended some former students. In this section he discussed the spiritual actions of the will. It is clear that this section confused such students because Melanchthon was trying to preserve a delicate balance between his affirmation of the will (with its freedom of choice) as a necessary part of a functioning human creature and his desire to preserve the emphasis on God's grace which framed and filled his theology. Luther attempted to maintain this balance with pastoral application to specific situations by employing two critical methodological distinctions: between law and gospel and between passive and active righteousness. Melanchthon laid out his exploration of the question in a pedagogical form. That meant laying down general precepts or principles. As a result, he did not always clarify which agendas he was addressing with specific statements.

On the topic of the freedom of the will in his *Loci praecipui theologici*, Melanchthon began, "From the beginning of the world the living members of the church were and are those who are not governed only by human powers and human effort but are those in whom the Holy Spirit causes spiritual movements, in whom he arouses acknowledgment of God, fear, faith, love, and other virtues to a greater extent in some, to a lesser extent in others. . . . It is a great and unspeakable benefit of God that he has promised us the aid of the Holy Spirit, . . . for without that aid we would fall ever more deeply into sinfulness."[93] Melanchthon insisted that the human will is not able to accomplish anything spiritual without the Holy Spirit. All that God demands — true faith, true fear, true trust in his mercy, true love of him, etc. — is accomplished only with the assistance of the Holy Spirit.

However, in commenting on 1 Corinthians 2:14, "the natural human creature is not able to perceive the things of the Spirit of God," Melanchthon explained the difference between those who have this fear and trust and those who do not with reference to something in the human creature. This reflects his concern to combat any hint that God could be responsible for evil and any suggestion which could undercut the exercise of human responsibility. On the one hand, Melanchthon observed that when David — who had already been converted — committed adultery, he did not feel the wrath of God immediately but later, when "moved by the Holy Spirit." Here Melanchthon asserted that the Holy Spirit was necessary for the sinful will of the converted David to repent — or "convert" again. On the other hand, in explaining how sinners receive the promise of the Spirit through faith, Melanchthon brought forth the "three causes of good action," the Word of God, the Holy Spirit, and "the human will which assents to and does not reject the Word of the Lord."[94] This in itself did not necessarily assign an active role to the will. For the "causes" to which Melanchthon referred were in actuality "elements" in the explanation of a phenomenon, as conceived by Aristotle. The material "cause" or element described or defined the object upon which the effective element — the actual cause responsible for the object — worked to produce the phenomenon. A material element thus could be the passive recipient of the action of the effective cause.[95] In describing the three "elements" of good actions, Melanchthon was labeling a normally functioning will as that third, "material," element, theoretically passive in its willing as the Holy Spirit, its effective cause, and the Word of God, his tool, the instrumental cause, bring about the good action of the will.[96]

However, other phrases in Melanchthon's writings seemed to indicate an active, contributory role for the will as the material cause in conversion. He noted that the human creature is able to reject God's Word as Saul did freely of his own will. He insisted that Pharaoh and Saul were not coerced to repudiate God, but freely and voluntarily rejected him. So much Luther said, and all their students agreed. But Melanchthon also used language his colleague did not: "when the mind hears and, holding itself upright, then does not reject nor treat the word with diffidence but assents to that Word with the Holy Spirit giving assistance, the will is not idle in this struggle." Melanchthon cited Basil and Chrysostom to support his position, for example, by using Basil's words, "God turns us, calls, moves, and aids us, but we must look to ourselves that we not reject." Here the mention of the Holy Spirit is not clear enough to assure that the will's activity is actually determined by the Spirit's re-creative action. Some students believed that their preceptor was presuming a commitment of the will before, and thus as a cause of, its regeneration by the Spirit.

Melanchthon continued by repeating his long-standing rejection of a double-predestinarian view that the number of those not able to be converted is fixed; he supported his position with the example of David's conversion. David responded to hearing the promise by exercising a freedom of choice, although Melanchthon refused to separate this exercise of free choice from the Holy Spirit's help: "when there is the attempt [of the will] to sustain itself, the Holy Spirit is already giving aid, as Paul says 'the gospel is the power of God to salvation.'" Yet the will still seems to prepare the way for that aid: "It is the power of God to those who do not reject or have contempt for the promise but to those who assent and believe." Melanchthon labeled "enthusiastic and Manichaean" the expectation that there will be an infusion of good qualities without human action, apart from the proclamation of the gospel.[97]

The Preceptor then cited "certain ancient" authorities: "freedom of choice in the human creature is the faculty for applying itself to grace [*facultas applicandi se ad gratiam*], that is, hearing the promise and trying to assent to it and rejecting sins against conscience." He appealed to this ancient teaching because he wanted to make clear that there are no contradictory wills within God; yet his choice of a device to do so was questionable if not foolish. For this phrase as used by late medieval theologians had frequently raised Luther's strong objections.[98] Erasmus had used it in his *Diatribe* to oppose Luther's view. It thus served as a provocation to his critics. Melanchthon continued, positing that the divine promise is universal, and therefore there must be "in us some reason for the difference [that explains] why Saul is rejected and David is accepted, that is, it is necessary that there be some dissimilar action in these two individuals."[99] Melanchthon saw in the words of Jesus in Luke 11:13, "he gives the Holy Spirit to those who seek him," proof that those who spurn or reject the Word of God or who make no effort to turn from their sins to the Holy Spirit cannot receive him or the gift and power of the Word.[100]

Matz argues that the presence of both the Lutheran teaching of justification by faith apart from works and Aristotle's doctrine of virtue, which had served as the foundation for the medieval doctrine of the necessity of good works for salvation, created an *"Inhomogenität"* and a tension in Melanchthon's theology.[101] That may be, but the tension is present in Luther as well, even though he does not employ the concept of virtue from Aristotle in the manner of his younger colleague. The tension arises out of the Wittenberg hermeneutic that held in tension the total responsibility of the Creator for every aspect of creation and the total responsibility of each individual human creature to perform the tasks God fashioned for humanity in obedience and faithfulness. The difference between the two colleagues lies both in the emphases placed on one side of the equation or the other at specific times and also in the greater inclination on Melanchthon's part to try out formulations that resolved the tension of the paradox of God's and human responsibilities, at least in part.

Reactions to Melanchthon's Teaching in the 1530s and 1540s (or the Curious Lack Thereof)

Noteworthy is the fact that Melanchthon's teaching on these topics went without public critique at the time of the appearance of the *Loci communes.* Scholars have wondered why Luther did not differ with Melanchthon in some form traceable in our day. Neither he nor any of his colleagues registered dissent from the formulation of the new edition of the *Loci.* It elicited private criticism from Nikolaus von Amsdorf, but on only one point, the Preceptor's assessment of necessity. Apart from Amsdorf, apparently no one in the Wittenberg circle raised objections to the *Loci communes* treatment of the freedom of human choice before mutual suspicion and bitterness poisoned the atmosphere within the Wittenberg circle in the 1550s, at the same time that some of Melanchthon's most loyal disciples intensified his teaching of human responsibility through the exercise of the will.

In 1535, in a memorandum structured as a disputation, Amsdorf argued for Luther's concept of absolute necessity against Melanchthon's attempt to preserve logical room for human responsibility through the distinction of *necessitas consequentis* and *necessitas consequentiae.* Amsdorf granted that contingency appears reasonable when daily life is considered. But even in those cases which appear to fall under the control of human choice and human willing, Scripture reveals that God is truly master and lord of the situation, as in the case of King Saul, who went searching for his beast of burden and was anointed king (1 Sam. 9–10), and who lost part of his army (1 Sam. 13), or when Rehoboam tried to assert his own control in Israel (1 Kings 12). Jewish leaders believed they were masters of the situation when they condemned Christ to death, but that also happened according to God's plan. The unsearchable wisdom and simple immutable will of God governs all things (Rom. 11:33), even the sparrow's falling (Matt. 10:29). For Amsdorf this did not mean that human beings did not experience their own decision making. But that experience must be understood as a product of God's direction (Jer. 10:23). Using Luther's analogy of God and Satan as riders of the sinner as donkey, and combining it with Isaiah's and Paul's illustration of the potter who may make pots to whatever purpose he wishes, Amsdorf came to the conclusion that God gives some of his human creatures to Christ and others to Satan. He thus moved beyond Luther's use of the analogy in *De servo arbitrio* and placed God in control of the damnation of evil people, by positing an action of God that placed them in Satan's domain. Amsdorf repeated this point when he wrote another assessment of the *Loci* in 1541; in it he spoke of those vessels of wrath "prepared for destruction" and labeled Esau "one who was by necessity a vessel of wrath, that is, impious, rejected, and condemned." In this memorandum he also rejected Melanchthon's use of 1 Timothy 2:4 to express the concept of the universal atonement, citing Christ's words that his blood was poured out for many, not for all (Matt. 26:28; Luke 22:20), and that many but not all are called, and from them only few chosen (Matt. 20:16), a position Luther had not taken.[102] Whatever Melanchthon's reply, he may not have completely satisfied his former colleague, for in 1544 he expressed concern to other friends that Amsdorf's criticism of a number of issues in the documents prepared by Melanchthon and Martin Bucer for the reformation of the archdiocese of Cologne could be a prelude to an altercation between them over the freedom of the will.[103]

In the affirmation of the biblical message as a revelation that God is creator and that the human creature is both creature and human, the Wittenberg circle struggled to give appropriate and proper emphasis to God's total responsibility for all in his creation and to the responsibility of human creatures for the sphere in which God has made them his servants and called them to carry out his will. The Wittenberg reformers and their followers felt compelled sometimes to emphasize the *creature*liness of the human creature, and sometimes to emphasize the *human*ness of the human creature. When they wanted to make it clear that God creates without conditions met or contributions rendered from the human side, they focused on the creaturely status of human beings. When they wanted to confess that the child of God trusts and obeys as psychological and social being designed according to the image of the speaking God, they focused on those elements that express the human elements of thinking and willing, of hoping or despairing. The followers of Luther and Melanchthon needed sometimes to emphasize the creative power of the merciful God that makes sinners new creatures and sometimes to emphasize his gracious will that they be his obedient children. They labeled the discussion of what the Creator and Savior does "gospel," and the description of what trusting and obedient children of the Creator and Savior do "law," as they sought to maintain the paradox of God's total responsibility for all things and the human responsibility to trust in God and care for his world. It was the Wittenberg way to practice theology, using God's Word to produce a life of repentance through the forgiveness of sins and the promise of Christ.

Melanchthon's Last Word on the Freedom of the Will

Less than two years before his death Melanchthon found occasion to compose a sort of "doctrinal last will and testament," his *Responses to the Articles of the Bavarian Inquisition* of 1558/1559. Although his response was chiefly a critique of Roman Catholic theology as expressed in newly published visitation articles in Bavaria, he also used it to reiterate his views on the freedom of the will and God's predestination, against the views of some of his students. This work does not introduce new elements into the Preceptor's public teaching. It was written in the midst of a heated battle in which some of his students defended, and others attacked, his positions on several issues. Therefore, this document figures in the unfolding of the controversies which led to the Formula of Concord and plays a role in the story told in chapter III of this book.[104] The collapse of negotiations between Catholic theologians and the Lutherans at the Colloquy of Worms in 1557 primed Melanchthon's desire to make a clear public statement against Roman Catholic teaching. Visitation articles composed to examine parish priests in Bavaria provided the occasion to do so. Because his health was failing, he decided to make a final statement of his theology with this treatise and therefore to include in it a repudiation of the "Stoic, Manichaean" understanding of the bondage of the will that had troubled him for more than two decades. This work repeats his conviction that God is totally responsible for all things, including the salvation of sinners, and that his human creatures have been created with complete responsibility for the sphere of life given to them, for their obedience to God's will. But his concern for defending total human responsibility dominates his treatment of the human will in his answer to the Bavarians' question, "Whether they [the local priests] believe that there is free choice in human beings." Three axioms guided his argument. First, God is not the cause of sin. Second, human beings can exercise freedom in external actions, which Paul calls the righteousness of the flesh. Third, God wants to maintain discipline among all people. This discipline is not a fulfillment of God's law, which demands perfect conformity to his will, both internal and external obedience. It is not even the beginning of inner obedience, the obedience of faith, and therefore is not to be counted as righteousness in God's sight. Believers must maintain these axioms or they will fall into Pyrrhonian doubts that lead to hatred of God and his teachings.[105]

Melanchthon's answer to the question regarding the free will in the *Responsiones* began with the assertion, "In human beings who are not reborn there is some freedom of the will which is able to perform external works. Achilles was able to control his hands, so that they would strike Agamemnon, and he could compel them not to strike him. Alexander was able to restrain his actions so that he did not lay a hand on the wife and daughters of Darius."[106] It was God's will that this much freedom remain in all people so that they might recognize the difference between acting freely and not being able to act freely, and so might be governed by the discipline that comes through their obedience to moral commands. This external discipline creates external works that conform to God's law and respond to his threats against those who break that law. God's punishment of those who break his laws is testimony to his providence, for he wants all people to know the difference between righteousness and unrighteousness.[107] These fundamental assertions reflect Melanchthon's concern to assert human responsibility, both so that obedience to God's law be practiced and also so that the sinner, not God, be held responsible for evil.

Two impediments horribly obstruct the freedom of external actions: human weakness and the devil's impulses. From birth human beings possess both a small spark of knowledge of God's law and a large torch of evil desires, created by original sin. Melanchthon defined original sin in his usual fashion as "a heart devoid of the fear of God and true trust in God, a heart without God, which burns with love of self, craves what God has forbidden, is restless, rages, hates God, fights against laws and other people."[108] These human desires are made worse by the impulses of the devil. The failure to trust God and the impulses of the devil cause the horrible evils that beset the human race, such as the atrocities of Nero and of unjust wars, and the presumptuousness of false teaching, for example, of Muhammad or other heretics.[109] Melanchthon also explicitly condemned the "Pelagians," all who claim that original sin does not exist and that human beings can satisfy God's law through natural human powers without the Holy Spirit. This is blasphemy against the Son of God and the Holy Spirit and destroys true teaching regarding the law, sin, grace, and God's benefits. But it is vital for Christian obedience to recognize the freedom that the reborn have to serve God. To make this clear Melanchthon mentioned the difference between the chastity of the patriarch Joseph (Gen. 39:1-18) and that of the noble Roman Publius Cornelius Scipio

Africanus. Reflecting his psychological theory of human *affectus* (emotions, passions), he insisted that the Holy Spirit does not violate the powers that God created in human beings; freedom to determine their external actions remains in the saints. The Spirit comes to the aid of this freedom, and thus consideration of God's Word was stronger in Joseph because the Son of God was strengthening his understanding and the Holy Spirit was arousing his heart. When Scipio considered the divine command, "do not commit adultery," the love of God was not burning in his heart. When Achilles restrained his own hand from evil, he was still filled with anger, whereas when David spared Saul, God was creating genuine sympathy within him. Apart from the Holy Spirit's power, no God-pleasing activity is possible.

Having repeated his basic conviction regarding human powers under sin, Melanchthon turned to the foes among his own students. He undertook his combat with a caricature of their position, reflecting his own fears of where their way of teaching God's sovereign grace could lead. "I reject and detest the madness of the Stoics and Manichaeans, who affirm that everything happens by necessity, both good and evil actions. . . . I beg the young to flee these monstrous opinions, which insult God and are harmful to public morality. For if all things happen by necessity, there is no need to reflect on our actions and take care in making decisions, as Paul admonished, 'be careful how you live' (Eph. 5,15)." Implicit in the background of his position lies his fear of being associated with Luther's doctrine of absolute necessity[110] and Calvin's doctrine of double predestination.[111] He wrote, "it is the most certain truth that God does not will sin, nor does he drive the human will to sin, nor does he support or approve of sin, but truly turns his anger against sins."[112] From this premise Melanchthon drew the conclusion that the wills of human beings and the devil were not coerced to do evil, but both misused their freedom to turn themselves away from God. "There is contingency, and the source of contingency in our actions is the freedom of the will."[113] Melanchthon conceded that, as his onetime instructor in Tübingen, Franz Kircher, had said four decades earlier, "Both propositions must be believed: there is divine determination, and there is contingency, and not every point of contradiction between the two can be explained."[114] He steadfastly held to the Wittenberg assertion of total divine responsibility for salvation and total human responsibility for obedience to God's command.

The respective actions of the Holy Spirit and of believers themselves in daily life could not be treated without discussing the struggle of the believer against the remnants of sin in the baptized. Melanchthon shared Luther's approach to the mystery of continuing evil in the lives of believers and constructed an interpretation of what it means that the whole life of the believer is a life of repentance. The reborn continue to experience sorrow over sin and punishment alongside the consolation of the gospel, faith, prayer, joy in God, the beginning of love for God, filial fear, and patience.[115] In this struggle the believer, like David, acts according to his will without coercion but with the Holy Spirit's support and power. David's will was acting also when he rejected the Holy Spirit and committed adultery. Without God's immense assistance the saints would not be able to do his will, but with his help they can "present their members to God as weapons of righteousness" (Rom. 6:13). Melanchthon strove to make clear how human beings as creatures of God function: God wants a correct understanding of his teaching to fill the minds of believers; it is his will that their doubts be overcome and their assent to the truth be confirmed. He wants their minds to be taught by God's Son and carried and led by the Holy Spirit. Here, as throughout this treatise in his repeated allusions to justification by faith, Melanchthon was trying to emphasize that God alone is responsible for the sanctified life of believers, whom he has created anew by converting them to faith in Christ. Furthermore, he showed that he adhered to Luther's distinction of the two kinds of human righteousness. He not only insisted on the necessity of the obedience of converted minds and hearts; he also averred that it was not the performance itself that pleased God, but rather the "righteousness of a good conscience," that is, the righteousness of faith that clings to Christ.[116]

Melanchthon treated the doctrine of God's election of his chosen children to grace in passing in this work. As throughout his career, so throughout the *Responsiones,* Melanchthon's first concern about this topic was the comfort of the believer. That comfort did not come, he was convinced, by anchoring the believer's assurance in God's choice of his own children before the foundation of the world. He had always avoided the concept of particularity — that God had chosen a particular number of the elect — because he believed that it implied predestination to damnation, and thus deprived believers of the comfort of God's promise. He attributed the despair and death of Francesco Spiera, an Italian evangelical, to his belief that God had predestined a specific number for salvation. Spiera had abandoned the evangelical faith under threat of Roman Catholic persecution, and according to the report of his friend Matthaeus Gribaldi of Padua, he died convinced he could not return to faith.[117] Melanchthon altered the story somewhat to fit his purposes here. He added a story regarding an unnamed person who almost fell back into adultery when he presumed false assurance from the doctrine of election. Melanchthon's alternative to offering believers comfort through the assurance of God's unconditioned choice of believers to be his own was the comfort offered in the promise of the Word of God in the means of grace. The

Preceptor told how his colleague and pastor Johannes Bugenhagen had dealt with a person who had raised the possibility that he might not be among the elect even though he was sorry for sin, sought absolution, and believed the gospel. He received Bugenhagen's confirmation that he truly was accepted by God through his grace because of his Son. "The pastor commanded him to believe the promise, leaving aside that dispute [regarding particularity]." Believers trust the promise of the gospel. The gospel alone is the source of true consolation.[118]

Melanchthon displayed in this treatise the same concerns that had guided his teaching for forty years, albeit with different points of emphasis than his readers encountered at the beginning of his career. In the course of the 1520s and 1530s the world around him changed. He did not abandon his belief that as the Lord of creation, God saves his people alone through his grace, and alone through his initiative. But he had also become aware of the need to proclaim human responsibility clearly among followers of the Wittenberg Reformation, and he had had pressed upon him the necessity of explaining why his and Luther's ascription of all power to God does not make God the author of sin and evil. He insisted that God's predestining plan is accessible to believers only through God's Word, in its oral, sacramental, and written forms, and that Christ's followers should turn only to these means of grace for their comfort. Living the Christian life meant for Melanchthon listening to and trusting the promise delivered through the means of grace in the daily struggle against sin, and it meant responsible obedience to the commands of the God whose Spirit empowered the response of faith to God's will for this life of love. Melanchthon's affirmation of the believer's obligation of response and obedience led him to use certain phrases that some of his former students had to find suspicious because they came to the questions of God's and human responsibility with different concerns and perspectives. The potential for turmoil that these differences could cause did not become apparent while Luther lived. Events not connected with the older colleague's death — the defeat of Lutheran princes by Emperor Charles V and the resulting struggle over his religious policy for Germany — created a situation in which these expressions of Melanchthon evoked intensive struggles to find the proper way of teaching and confessing God's total responsibility for all things and total human responsibility for hearkening to the Word of God. As a person whose life unfolded in the lecture hall and in diplomatic negotiations, Melanchthon faced a different challenge than did Luther, who remained preacher even before his students, in striking the delicate balance between holding God's and human responsibility in tension, on the one hand, and on the other, attempting clear explanations for curious learners or hostile negotiators for the other side. Melanchthon strove his entire life to reach this balance through the Wittenberg way of practicing theology as he sought to divide the Word of truth in Wittenberg or Augsburg, Regensburg, and Worms.

CHAPTER III

Luther's and Melanchthon's Students Debate the Doctrine of the Freedom of the Will

The Outbreak of Controversy: The Struggle to Define Wittenberg Theology

Every movement that challenges existing ideas and institutions and alters or replaces them enters a period of self-examination and redefinition, sometimes even before its initial leaders pass from the scene. This was also the case with the Wittenberg Reformation. The most severe time of such testing came for the followers of Luther and Melanchthon in the period immediately following the former's death, even though tensions and disagreements had arisen earlier out of their students' differing interpretations of Luther's and Melanchthon's theology.[1] Within months of Luther's death, other events ignited and impelled the process of rethinking and reformulating his message in new situations. The war against the Wittenberg Reformation which Emperor Charles V had declared with the Edict of Worms in 1521 had been in the stage of intense planning at the imperial court for some two years before hostilities erupted in June 1546 in the so-called Smalcald War. Its conclusion came with the defeat of the evangelical armies under Elector Johann Friedrich of Saxony and Landgrave Philip of Hesse on April 24, 1547. The two Protestant princes were led in chains from the battlefield and sentenced to death (although the sentences were not executed).

Charles created a commission to formulate a temporary religious settlement for the evangelical lands within his German empire that would serve as a bridge to normal religious life under the papacy once the Council of Trent had defined that normality anew. This policy, forged at the Diet of Augsburg in 1547-48, was dubbed "the Augsburg Interim" by its critics.[2] It endeavored to return the followers of Luther to the Roman obedience and to doctrine and practice that conformed to the core of the medieval church's standards but reflected the desire for reform that Charles had learned in the Erasmian circles responsible for his education. The plan was rejected and condemned almost unanimously by evangelical theologians and church leaders, including Melanchthon.[3]

However, Melanchthon found himself in a difficult situation after his prince's defeat. The emperor handed over Wittenberg and its university, along with the title and powers of "elector" and a large portion of Johann Friedrich's territory, to the former elector's cousin, the son-in-law of Philip of Hesse, Moritz, duke of Saxony, a Lutheran prince who had supported Charles and his brother Ferdinand in the Smalcald War. Melanchthon committed himself above all else to saving the University of Wittenberg and its confession of the faith. Thus, he quickly became a servant of Wittenberg's new overlord. Moritz believed he had received guarantees from the Habsburg princes, Charles and Ferdinand, that he would not have to alter the religious life of his lands after the war, but the emperor could not remember granting such a guarantee. Moritz, therefore, was caught between the rock of Habsburg determination to bring their German realm into submission to both emperor and pope and the defiant convictions and strong commitment to Luther's reform of nobility, townspeople, peasantry, and university professors. The emperor who had bestowed lands and power could take them away with a single command, enforced as necessary by the Spanish and imperial occupation troops that were imposing his new religious policy in parts of southern Germany, driving Lutheran pastors into exile and reclaiming churches for Rome. The new elector turned to his counselors to find a way out of his dilemma.

Moritz's counselors began drafting an alternative policy for his realm. Melanchthon and his Wittenberg colleagues were drawn into the process. They fought against concessions to papal teaching proposed by Moritz's secular counselors and Roman Catholic theologians within the committee that finally drafted a policy labeled "the Leipzig Interim" by its foes.[4] But Melanchthon, Bugenhagen, and others also believed it was vital for the continuation of Lutheran preaching in Saxon pulpits to reach some kind of accommodation with Charles and Ferdinand. Therefore, they believed that in this policy draft they had reached a reasonable solution to a very difficult problem. The most important principle they worked with was "adiaphora," neutral matters regarding which God has given neither command nor prohibition. Melanchthon had insisted in the Augsburg Confession (article XV) that ecclesiastical practices and customs in this category could not be required or imposed upon the people of God as requirements for salvation because only faith and obedience to God's commands constitute the true Christian way of life. Nonetheless, in the situation of 1548 he was convinced that Moritz's imposition of concessions in ceremonial and liturgical matters could be used to buy time and breathing room for the evangelical confession of the faith in Saxony. The so-called Leipzig Interim presented a Lutheran understanding of justification by faith in some detail, with an extensive expression of Melanchthon's concern for the new obedience that faith produces, and it prescribed a number of conservative practices that would make the Saxon church appear in some regards as if it were in compliance with the Augsburg Interim. The electoral government presented it to the territorial diet at Christmas 1548. The diet rejected it, and Moritz could do no better than to introduce its ceremonial prescriptions by edict, and then not in every corner of his domain.

Melanchthon had struggled vigorously against Moritz's secular counselors to achieve a religious policy for the newly reconstituted electoral Saxony that was as faithful to the Wittenberg theology as possible. He regarded the work he and his colleagues had invested in the draft for this new Saxon religious policy a good-faith effort to save the Lutheran cause. A significant group of former associates, led by his old friend Nikolaus von Amsdorf, his former junior colleague Matthias Flacius Illyricus, and his former students Joachim Westphal and Nikolaus Gallus, reacted with horror to this proposal they branded "the Leipzig Interim." They deemed Moritz a "Judas" because he had betrayed Johann Friedrich and stolen his lands and title. They considered Melanchthon and his colleagues who were cooperating with Moritz traitors to the cause of Luther and even apostates from the gospel of Christ. Initial critical exchanges led quickly to a deep and abiding bitterness on both sides.[5] Amsdorf and Flacius could not understand how Melanchthon could abandon the Word of God and Luther's teaching. Melanchthon had never suffered fools or critics among his own disciples gladly, and he could not understand how his former students, colleagues, and friends could not recognize the necessity of temporary concession in order to preserve the faith. Acrimony and rancor gave rise to more acrimony and rancor. The inevitable exchange among Luther's heirs regarding the precise definition of his message took place in the midst of mistrust, resentment, and ever deepening suspicion.

Since the end of the eighteenth century the two chief "parties" within the Wittenberg circle have been called "Gnesio-Lutherans" and "Philippists." As anachronistic and imprecise as these terms are, and as problematic as the division of Luther's and Melanchthon's followers can be in regard to specific aspects of their thought and activities, these terms will be used to designate the two groups within the Lutheran churches that respectively interpreted

Luther's theology more radically (the Gnesio-Lutherans) or, from a medieval perspective, more conservatively (the Philippists).[6] Readers must remember that despite the sharpness of their clashes over the proper interpretation of the Wittenberg legacy, more united them than divided them. This was precisely what made their conflicts so intense.

The Synergistic Controversy

The Origins of the Controversy

At first, Luther's and Melanchthon's students and followers divided over questions related to the nature and necessity of confessing the faith in a time of persecution, focusing on the use of adiaphora in relation to public confession. The text of the Leipzig Interim led them also into controversy over the proposition that "good works are necessary for salvation." The dispute regarding adiaphora erupted immediately after the bootlegged printing of the policy draft dubbed "the Leipzig Interim" in 1549. The debate over the "necessity of good works for salvation," a phrase employed by Melanchthon's colleague Georg Major though repudiated by Melanchthon himself, broke out in 1551/1552. The conflict over the role of the human will in salvation was related to the latter disagreement, for both had to do with the definition of human responsibility. But this conflict did not begin to win public attention until 1558, although it was foreshadowed earlier. For instance, the single passage that the Leipzig Interim cited word for word from the Augsburg Interim concerned the will: "Since God does not justify human beings on the basis of the works of righteousness that they do, but gratuitously, that is, without their merit, if they want to glory, let them glory in Christ alone, by whose merit alone they are redeemed from sin and justified. Yet the merciful God does not deal with such people as with a dead block of wood, but draws them through acts of will, if they are of the age of reason. For such people do not receive those benefits of Christ, unless their minds and wills are moved by the prevenient grace of God to detest sin."[7] In the context of the effort to present an official Saxon policy that seemed to comply with the catholicizing Augsburg Interim, such words appeared to be a perfidious betrayal to those who could not understand why Melanchthon had decided to seek accommodation with the emperor rather than boldly confess the faith as they believed he had in Augsburg nearly twenty years before.

Melanchthon was deeply hurt by the criticism that his best-faith efforts to save the church had earned him from his students. He did not take their criticism lightly or easily. Among his early responses to the betrayal of Flacius, who had left the Wittenberg faculty, resigning his professorship in Hebrew in protest against the Leipzig policy draft, was an attack on the Croatian's understanding of the freedom of the will. In his preface to Caspar Cruciger's Latin translation of Luther's *Last Words of David,* dated May 1, 1550, Melanchthon attacked "Stoic ravings about necessity and fate," noting that the "Stoics'" honoring of God's wisdom, beneficence, and ordering of the world commends their fine words, but they eradicate the need for prayer with their teaching and undermine knowledge of the true God.[8] Five months later, in an oration written for delivery by his colleague Georg Major at a doctoral promotion, Melanchthon further attacked the "fatalism" of those who did not want to rely on the words of the gospel but instead chose to dispute about election, probably a caricatured reference to the position of Flacius and Gallus.[9] Melanchthon was driven by the concern to stave off the criticism that Wittenberg theology taught that God was the cause of evil and to maintain the integrity of human obedience to God. He took God's responsibility for all things for granted. His students were driven by the concern to confess God's total responsibility particularly for the salvation of sinners in the face of the renewed Roman Catholic use of military might aimed at stamping out the Lutheran confession of the faith. They presumed that God was not responsible for evil and found no difficulty insisting on human responsibility while making it clear that God alone is the agent of salvation.

In the turbulent, threatening atmosphere of the immediate postwar period, several bastions of resistance to the threat of imperial suppression emerged in northern Germany. Alongside leaders in several Hansa towns, the city council and ministerium of Magdeburg defied pope and emperor — and the new Wittenberg establishment as well — in the months following the Smalcald League's defeat. In the *Confession, Instruction, and Admonition of the Christian Church at Magdeburg,* composed for the ministerium of that city in 1550 by Nikolaus Gallus, the nascent Gnesio-Lutheran movement that had gathered around Amsdorf and Flacius issued its programmatic declaration of independence from Melanchthon's school.

Gallus had come to Wittenberg at age fourteen in 1530 and studied there for a decade, earning Melanchthon's praise for his learning.[10] Called as a deacon to Regensburg in 1543, he was driven into exile by the enforcement of the Augsburg Interim in the city, and fled back to Wittenberg. He assumed a pastorate in Magdeburg in 1548. There he became the leader of the city's ministerium, which stood under the influence of Amsdorf and Flacius. The *Confession* Gallus composed for the ministerium echoed earlier Lutheran positions on the central biblical teachings. It affirmed, for example, that the human will and that of the devil are the cause of evil; God is not. In its exposition of "the gospel and justification," the *Confession* stated that human beings cannot call upon the Holy Spirit and come to faith by their own natural powers or free will.[11] But Gallus did not pursue the matter in his public writings for most of the following decade. Instead, his published polemic against his former preceptor and other former professors or student colleagues in electoral Saxon service focused on adiaphora and good works. He first shared his reservations on these topics in correspondence with Melanchthon and his Wittenberg colleagues Johannes Bugenhagen and Georg Major regarding his objections to the Leipzig Interim as early as May 1549,[12] and then in tracts.[13]

Within a few years Gallus also began to express his reservations regarding Melanchthon's views on the freedom of the will. On April 23, 1556, the Preceptor reported to Albert Hardenberg that Gallus was preparing "books against me concerning Stoic necessity."[14] On May 1 he wrote to Johann Mathesius that Gallus wanted to do battle against him;[15] a letter of June 30 informed Mathesius that "the pugnacious Gallus" had written that he, Melanchthon, did not approve Luther's *De servo arbitrio*.[16] On December 1, 1556, Melanchthon wrote Gallus himself. The agony caused by the alienation from his former students did not overcome his suspicions; he did not try to reach accord with Gallus. Instead, he oversimplified the matter with the question "Do you defend Stoic necessity?" and thus reduced the disagreement between Gallus and himself to the question of whether the human creature is no more than a block of wood in conversion, the critical phrase in the Leipzig Interim.[17] Gallus replied with a long letter the next month. Here it is clear that concerns about Roman Catholic accusations concerning Stoic determinism and licentiousness among the Lutherans did not dominate Gallus's thinking or dictate his formulations of his teaching. He wanted to counter the tendencies to assign some role to the human creature in conversion and salvation, a concern reflecting his suspicions of the Roman party — he and Flacius were engaged in polemic against the Council of Trent at the time[18] — as well as his fears regarding the compromising spirit of some of his colleagues from student days in Wittenberg.

His letter of January 12, 1557, stated simply that he did not believe in some kind of general "Stoic" necessity but was speaking only of the freedom of the will as a power for conversion to God when he taught that the fallen will is bound, not free. In other actions and after regeneration Gallus believed that the will was free to make choices appropriately. Nor did he accept a description of his position which suggested that he compared the human will to a block of wood. A block of wood cannot be in rebellion as is the human will before its conversion. He also very specifically rejected the charge that he assigned to some hidden cause the reason why some are reborn and others are not.[19] In this epistolary exchange it is clear that, no matter how similar the Preceptor's and the student's understanding of God's grace and human response were, they were posing different questions to express their central concerns and points of departure. Furthermore, two different models of describing the fallen human creature were at work. Although he could clearly confess that the will was bound and unable to come to God without grace, Melanchthon's desire to avoid the "Manichaean" position attributed to the Wittenberg theologians by Roman Catholic opponents determined his approach to the issues at hand.

Gallus rejected Melanchthon's charge of Manichaeanism without trying to refute it; he focused only on the ever active human will which was always acting in accord with its allegiance of ultimate trust, whether that trust was placed in God or an ungodly object. When he wrote Melanchthon on April 19, 1557, Gallus did not touch upon the freedom of the will, but he pleaded with his former teacher, whom he addressed as a "wise and good man," to seek true reconciliation regarding the issues plaguing the church.[20] Melanchthon, however, expected only new aggravation from Gallus, as he related to a former student, the Nuremberg civic leader Hieronymus Baumgartner, some weeks later.[21] In fact, Gallus waited for two years and the outbreak of a more general public controversy before he presented his case against Melanchthon's views on the freedom of the will in print.

In the midst of this private discussion the Preceptor published a third edition of his commentary on Ecclesiastes. Here "Melanchthon certainly had opportunity to deal with the disputed doctrines, especially the matter of the will and its capabilities, but he steered clear of the controversy. . . . [he] scrupulously avoided discussion of free will in conversion,"[22] and instead concentrated on God's providence and the human obligation to fulfill God's commands in the context of daily callings. His remarks on Ecclesiastes emphasize that human beings are "completely dependent upon God for whatever results from the effort put forth in daily life."[23] The Preceptor remained the exegete in this work, this time resisting the temptation to use the lecture hall to advance his concerns for public teaching. He believed that God had revealed himself as the Lord of creation, had revealed that his human creatures are totally dependent on him, and that sufficed for his message at this point.

Because he and his followers also defended the integrity of the human creature whom God made to respond in trust and obedience, greater contention erupted within the Wittenberg circle over God's responsibility and human responsibility. In fact, on the question of the freedom of the will, "erupt" is not quite accurate. It took some time before this issue simmered over into public disagreement. It was Gallus's mentor Nikolaus von Amsdorf who began the public dispute with comments on theses composed by Leipzig professor and superintendent Johannes Pfeffinger. The theses had originally served as the basis of a university disputation in 1555. The most crucial thesis stated, "If the will is inactive, and conducts itself in a purely passive manner, there is no difference between the pious and the impious, the elect and the damned, as between Saul and David, between Judas and Peter. Then God is acting as a respecter of persons and the author of resistance in the impious and damned. That constitutes teaching contradictory wills in God, and that assertion conflicts with all of Scripture."[24] These theses aroused a critical reaction from the ducal Saxon theologians led by Amsdorf in early 1556,[25] and finally became the occasion for public controversy when Amsdorf reacted in his *Public Confession of the Pure Teaching of the Gospel and Confutation of Contemporary Ravers*[26] to Pfeffinger's republication of the theses in 1558.[27] Pfeffinger and Amsdorf exchanged charges in tracts without mentioning *De servo arbitrio,* although Amsdorf's allusion to Luther's analysis of John 15:5, "apart from me [Christ] you can do nothing," reproduces Luther's exegesis of the verse in that work.[28] Pfeffinger insisted that he denied any human contribution to salvation, affirming his faithfulness to both of his "Preceptors," Luther and Melanchthon.[29] Amsdorf believed that Pfeffinger's position on free choice was an attempt to subvert Luther's teaching. He freely conceded that the human will remains "a living and real power that is always at work and acting," but he also insisted that when the devil is in control, this will cannot act at all to liberate itself.[30]

Amsdorf quickly gained support for his criticism of Pfeffinger's view of the will in a publication which offered readers the opinions of three of his associates in the service of the "young lords" of ducal Saxony, Johann Friedrich the Middler and Johann Wilhelm, the sons of the former elector Johann Friedrich the Elder. They were Johannes Stoltz and Johannes Aurifaber, court preachers for the young dukes, and Matthias Flacius, professor of theology at the ducal university in Jena. Before his death in 1556, Stoltz had composed a critique of Pfeffinger's position; he did not refer to *De servo arbitrio* in his theses against Pfeffinger, but the editor of the piece, Aurifaber, did, in the preface prepared in October 1558 for its publication. In it he noted that Stoltz had done nothing but defend Luther's position in *De servo arbitrio.*[31] Flacius referred to Luther's work several times in his "Refutation of Pfeffinger's Propositions regarding Free Choice," which appeared in this volume as well.[32] The reformer's work commanded sufficient respect to serve as a symbol for a position even if its text was not cited.

This exchange came before the public eye against the background of a struggle within ducal Saxony over a new statement of faith being prepared under the supervision of Dukes Johann Friedrich the Middler and Johann Wilhelm. It was a reaction in general to the turmoil that had plagued Lutheran church life for nearly a decade and specifically to the scandal caused by evangelical disunity at the colloquy in Worms called in 1557 by Emperor Ferdinand.[33] There the ducal Saxon theologians, led by Viktorin Strigel, professor of theology at the dukes' university in Jena, and reinforced by two Gnesio-Lutheran delegates, Joachim Mörlin of Braunschweig and Erasmus Sarcerius of Mansfeld, had called on Melanchthon and his colleagues to reject their positions on adiaphora, good works, and other issues (though the dispute on the freedom of the will had not yet broken out, it was later reported that Mörlin had confronted Melanchthon regarding his description of the free will as the capability of turning oneself toward grace in his *Loci*).[34] The collapse of the colloquy because of evangelical disunity had intensified efforts at resolving the doctrinal differences dividing the Wittenberg circle. The contribution of ducal Saxony to that process was a *Book of Confutation,* constructed in a cauldron of intensely personal and political antagonisms within the principality during the course of 1558. The principle behind this effort at theological agreement was to define controverted issues by confuting false positions, since the ducal Saxon theologians believed that wandering away from the theology of Luther and the Augsburg Confession lay at the root of the discussions, difficulties, and disputes.

The initial draft of the *Book of Confutation* was prepared by Strigel and colleagues in his circle, all of whom felt a strong affinity for Melanchthon. Strigel was locked in a power struggle within the Jena faculty which had broken out when Matthias Flacius had become his colleague in 1557. The ducal government turned the draft over to Flacius and several of his adherents, including the brothers Joachim and Maximilian Mörlin, Erasmus Sarcerius, and Johann Aurifaber. The final version of the book reflected the convictions of Amsdorf, Flacius, and their comrades. Its locus on the freedom of the will made no reference to *De servo arbitrio;* it only mentioned that "the holy Man of God Luther" had triumphed over the defenders of the free will. It rejected three errors: that after the fall, before the renewal effected by the Holy Spirit, the natural powers of the sinner's free will can keep God's law perfectly; that with the help of grace the natural powers are able to turn a person to God; and that through renewal in this life the human creature can become perfect and receive the image of God and original righteousness again. Against these positions it presented a series of theses: All the imagination and invention *(tichten und trachten)* of the human heart is evil (Gen. 6:5; 8:21). "I have sinned against you alone" (Ps. 51:4), and all that is born of the flesh is flesh and requires new birth (John 3:6). The heart of every human being is by nature stony and must be created anew (Jer. 24:7; 31:33; 32:40; Ezek. 11:19; 36:26). No one comes to the Father but through Christ (John 14:6). By nature no one can receive anything from God's Spirit (1 Cor. 2:14). God must effect the believer's willing and doing (Phil. 2:13).[35] These rather simple statements of the Wittenberg tradition reveal that the public discussion of the topic of the human will had not yet reached proportions that required extensive definition or exploration. It is difficult to identify elements in these statements to which Strigel might have objected. He did see, however, that the issues that had most troubled his preceptor, the questions of God's responsibility for evil and human responsibility for trust and obedience, were not addressed.

Melanchthon himself took issue with the teaching of the *Book of Confutation* in a memorandum to his prince, Elector August, written on March 9, 1559. There he recalled that he had rejected the "Stoic and Manichaean madness" already while Luther lived and had written that all human works, good and evil, take place by necessity. "This way of speaking is against God's Word, harmful for public discipline, and blasphemous." He affirmed his conviction that apart from the Holy Spirit the human will can exercise a measure of freedom in the performance of works that maintain public order and virtue. The Holy Spirit also restores this freedom to those who are reborn. He cast Gallus and the Weimar theologians into the same category as the strident spiritualist critic of Wittenberg theology Caspar von Schwenkfeld, claiming that they, like him, taught that God effects conversion without means, or that God forces human beings to repent whether they pay attention to his Word or not. The action of the Holy Spirit in and through his Word, functioning as law and gospel, stood at the heart of Melanchthon's discussion of conversion. This assertion of God's working through the Word was the Preceptor's way of affirming that God does not work magically (his reaction against medieval superstitious use of the sacraments *ex opere operato*), and that he does work with human creatures as the human reflections of his own image that he created (Melanchthon's confession of the biblical understanding of human responsibility and of human trust in the God who speaks in his Word). "Grace precedes, but the will moves along with it," he insisted. "If the will can turn itself away from this comfort, it must be understood that it does something and follows the Holy Spirit when it accepts this comfort." When human creatures reject the Word of God, they reject with the will; thus, Melanchthon argued, when the will is putting up total resistance, there is no conversion. Flacius and Schwenkfeld speak of God's forcing conversion and new birth, Melanchthon reported, in contrast to his own position that those who are in sin should consider the promise of grace in remorse and terror. God works through this promise, gives the Holy Spirit, draws the human being, bestowing a spark of faith, to initiate the comfort of the gospel and the struggle against sin. Flacius, Stoltz, and Gallus wanted to speak to the terrified sinner of God's gracious election, but Melanchthon found no comfort there. Comfort lay for him in the universal promise, not in speculation about God's contrary wills.[36] In a poignant historical note the Preceptor recalled that he had written a letter of consolation in 1545 to Flacius's friends in Venice,[37] in which he had conveyed the consolation of the gospel in just this way. Luther had also at that time and often at other times affirmed his trust in the universal promise of Christ and the assurance it brings. For faith comes by hearing (Rom. 10:17). Melanchthon wrote that he knew many who had fallen into despair because they could not be certain that they were numbered among the elect. Therefore, he had always directed people to the promise, in which they had found joy. For God does not effect faith apart from the consideration of his Word. Therefore, and with these words, Melanchthon concluded his reaction to the doctrine of the will in the *Book of Confutation:* "grace precedes, but the will goes along with it, and God draws, but he draws the person whose will is functioning."[38]

In this memorandum Melanchthon clearly revealed the concerns that shaped his view of the freedom of the will. He wanted to make certain that the integrity of the human creature and of faith as a trust that clings to God's promise be maintained. He feared the abandonment of the understanding of the relationship between God and the human being as a relationship based on conversation, the conversation of God in his grace and human faith. He saw no other way of understanding election apart from a double predestination that could only destroy the comfort of the gospel; the antidote for the hopelessness that discussion of election would engender lay in the universal promise of forgiveness through Christ for all. Some of his students, on the other hand, could not eradicate their fears that his description of the action of the human will compromised his insistence on the exclusivity of God's grace and his gift of faith. Likewise, their preceptor could not listen carefully enough to them to respond to their concerns, instead caricaturing their position so that he could dismiss it without engaging it.

Melanchthon versus Gallus

Melanchthon's fears of a public attack from Gallus[39] prompted him to plan something of a preemptive strike. By the time he composed his critique of the *Book of Confutation,* this defense against the Flacians had already appeared, as one section of his *Responsiones ad impios articulos Bavaricae inquisitionis*. On December 21, 1558, he had informed his former student, the ducal counselor in Braunschweig-Lüneburg, Joachim Moller, that his new attack on the Counter-Reformational measures of the Bavarian government also addressed Flacius's description of the sinner before conversion as a block of wood.[40] In composing the preface for his Latin *corpus doctrinae* in February 1560, he noted that his *Responsiones* had dealt with the calumnies woven together from excerpts from his writings by "the synagogue of Flacius and Gallus' battalion concerning divine necessity."[41]

Melanchthon's reaction to the Bavarian visitors' question for parish priests regarding the free will defended God's sole responsibility for salvation with statements regarding the exclusive nature of God's grace and the gift of faith he gives his people. This topic dominated his attack on the theology and practice that the articles were written to preserve and perpetuate. His treatment of the free will also asserted clearly the believer's reliance on God's grace alone, taught that God's Word creates saving faith, and rejected Pelagian opinions. But his answer to the question regarding the human will was most concerned with clarifying the teaching regarding human integrity and human responsibility, so that no magical view of the working of God's Word would be possible and so that none would be confused and believe God might be responsible for evil.[42] Gallus remained suspicious of his preceptor's way of describing the action of the human being in conversion, fearing that he was leaving room for a contribution of the human will to this process apart from the Holy Spirit's empowerment. Therefore he finally rose to the challenge of the *Responsiones* and engaged Melanchthon openly in print regarding the bondage of the will. He chose a two-pronged defense of his own teaching, with negative critiques of Melanchthon's position, especially as formulated in his *Loci praecipui theologici*,[43] and with a positive exposition through the reprinting of Luther's *De servo arbitrio*.[44]

For the first time since 1526, Justus Jonas's translation of Luther's work appeared in a separate printing; it had been republished in the Wittenberg German edition of Luther's works in 1553.[45] Gallus pointedly explained why he believed the text should be available for all to read. Erasmus had defined the free will as "a power of the human will through which human beings could so dispose and direct themselves toward the things that serve salvation, or turn themselves away from these things," Gallus contended. This definition was also the student's translation of his preceptor's description of the will as having a "facultas applicandi se ad gratiam."[46] Melanchthon had written precisely this phrase from Luther's arch-opponent into his *Loci* after Luther's death, Gallus lamented. At the same time, the Preceptor had abandoned Luther's description of the will as "purely passive," adopted the Interim's rejection of the will as comparable to a block of wood apart from the Holy Spirit's action, and ascribed a kind of cooperation, or synergy, to the will alongside the Holy Spirit. All of this contradicted Luther's teaching.[47] Gallus summarily rejected the false rumor that Luther had abandoned the position of *De servo arbitrio*.[48] The elder reformer's position had remained the same as he had expressed it in his *Confession concerning Christ's Supper* of 1528, and Melanchthon had incorporated this position into the Augsburg Confession.[49] Gallus did not hesitate to use Luther's concept of necessity and the doctrine of predestination to reinforce this presentation of biblical teaching. The reformer himself had demonstrated that his concept of necessity was not that of the Stoics but rather of the prophets and apostles.[50]

Gallus's exchange with Melanchthon embraced both his attempt to counter what he regarded as a false representation of his and his comrades' teaching and his analysis of the deviation of Melanchthon's own teaching from theirs and Luther's. Gallus began by making it clear that all in the Wittenberg circle, adherents of the Preceptor and his critics alike, agreed on six fundamental principles regarding human freedom of choice and related questions. First, after the fall human creatures have some freedom of choice, sufficient to live in outward discipline and respectability. They even can hear the Word of God, learn it, and think about it as sinners, apart from the Holy Spirit, before conversion. Second, when they are converted, believers can perform God-pleasing works of new obedience. Third, through the grace, assistance, and support of the Holy Spirit, on the basis of their new spiritual will, they can remain with God in grace and live a God-pleasing life or, on the other hand, they can fall once again into godless practices through the will of the old flesh. The proper distinction of law and gospel is necessary for the proper cultivation of the life of repentance, Gallus believed. Fourth, God's decision to predestine the elect to faith lies in his hidden will and therefore can and must be ascertained and considered only out of God's revealed will and his activity in his use of the means of grace.[51] Fifth, those who live in faith and repentance must be reminded that they are among the elect to strengthen their faith and give them consolation; the unbelieving and unrepentant must be told that they are not among the elect as a warning, to call them to repentance. Gallus used the topic of God's choosing his own only within the proper distinction of law and gospel. Sixth, God neither wills nor causes sin. He does not wish that sinners die but rather that they be converted and live. Indeed, he wants all to be saved just as he wants all to repent. However, God does not give his gifts in all places in the same manner. Nonetheless he remains eternally faithful, wise, and just.[52] Without mentioning *De servo arbitrio*, Gallus followed its path to a stance of awe before the mystery of why some are saved and not others.

This summary of the teaching on which Gallus believed all followers of Luther and Melanchthon could agree reflects the Wittenberg concerns to hold God's responsibility for all and total human responsibility in tension. For Gallus was correct in maintaining that all Wittenberg theologians preserved a concept of civil righteousness and freedom of choice in earthly matters, even to the point of being able to hear the Word of God with an unbelieving heart. All insisted on new obedience through a will renewed by the Holy Spirit. All insisted that God's bestowal of grace according to his plan could be known only through the means of grace, in oral, written, and sacramental forms. All insisted that God is in no way the cause of sin and evil. All tried to distinguish law and gospel, so that believers would hear God's condemnation when they were defying his Word and flee to his mercy in repentance. But Gallus's fears regarding his preceptor's altered expressions of his teaching remained, as did the Preceptor's suspicions of those he viewed as unfaithful progeny.

After omitting Melanchthon's name in some of his critiques, Gallus finally printed the allegation that his mentor's use of the language of the medieval theologians regarding the ability of the sinful heart to "make an effort in the direction of grace" was in direct opposition to Luther's refutation of that position in Erasmus and was indeed a rejection of Melanchthon's own position in the Augsburg Confession and its Apology.[53] Gallus had heard his professor's concerns regarding the trap of determinism but dismissed such fears in regard to his student's position as an unjustified concern: people ought not be tarred with certain labels simply because they may agree with certain other parties on one point or another, a rejoinder to Melanchthon's facile use of the epithets "Stoic" and "Manichaean" for Flacius and Gallus. That would make all who support some understanding of freedom of the will papists, he stated, arguing that indeed Melanchthon's opinion did agree with Erasmus's and that the Preceptor's rejection of his own opinion as Stoic also fit into the pattern of polemic against Luther practiced by Erasmus and the papal party. In some detail Gallus showed the difference between a Stoic doctrine of necessity and the biblical teaching regarding the actions of God the creator in relationship to his human creatures. He affirmed that the fallen human will should not be compared to a block of wood since it is active in rejecting God's Word until the Holy Spirit has changed it into a new creature.[54] The relationship between the Creator who was restoring his fallen creatures through the re-creating Word of Jesus Christ and those creatures could not be comprehended within the Stoic philosophical framework. For it presumed no such

Creator God and could only pose the alternative images of a freely willing being or an automaton when treating the functioning of the will. Gallus, in marked contrast, regarded the relationship between God and human creature as comparable to that of parent and child, and that presuppositional framework set the discussion of the will for Gallus on a different basis. He insisted that even though the sinful human nature can listen to and meditate upon the Word apart from God's grace, in true penitence the will makes no contribution to its own transformation but is purely passive. Indeed, it functions but is dependent upon the assistance of the Holy Spirit, who enacts the changes in the human mind, will, and heart which bestow upon the repentant person a new way of thinking, willing, and acting.

In Gallus's exposition of his understanding of the will, it becomes clear that he and his preceptor were separated by differing emphases and concerns in their proclamation of God's total responsibility for the salvation of sinners and their total responsibility to repent and trust God's promise. These differing emphases stemmed from a significant difference in the presuppositional framework which determined the expression of their anthropology and soteriology. Gallus's apprehension about the spirit of Pelagianism in every sinner's heart led him to find Melanchthon's affirmation of God's grace insufficient in the light of the expressions the Preceptor chose for defending human integrity with his affirmations of the will's activity. For Gallus, coming to faith could best be described with the biblical concepts of regeneration, conversion, and repentance, all of which express the nature of this change wrought by the Holy Spirit. Gallus insisted that the word "regeneration" itself indicates that conversion can be accomplished only by the Holy Spirit, since birth is a gift from parents, not the result of the child's own effort or performance. Believers become new spiritual creatures when the Holy Spirit effects this new creation through the regenerating power of his Word.[55] Melanchthon certainly used these same terms and expressed these same concepts, but his first concern remained clarity regarding human responsibility, so that God could not be held responsible for evil and believers would act as God had made and called them to act. Gallus was arguing on the basis of the difference in paradigm between his own view and that of Melanchthon, for Gallus viewed conversion as new birth or new creation and Melanchthon viewed it as an adult reaction to the promise of God. Further clarification may well have been impossible given the bitterness that had turned professor and student against each other in the preceding decade. Clarification slipped beyond reach in any case when death removed Melanchthon from the polemic of his time the following spring, on April 19, 1560.

Flacius versus Strigel

Less than four months later a confrontation similar to that between Gallus and Melanchthon took place within ducal Saxony, this time face-to-face, as Viktorin Strigel and Matthias Flacius met in a formal academic disputation. The two combatants shared a common education in Wittenberg; Flacius began his studies there in 1541, Strigel in 1542. But they had come to the Leucorea for strikingly different reasons. The young Illyrian came in search of peace of conscience, to which Luther guided him. Viktorin, physician's son from Kaufbeuren, came in search of good learning, at the direction of a professor at Freiburg in Breisgau, who wanted this prize pupil to study with Melanchthon. Melanchthon sent Strigel to Jena to help Johann Friedrich's sons Johann Friedrich the Middler and Johann Wilhelm organize a new institution of higher learning when they lost Wittenberg in 1548. The two young dukes had called Flacius to Jena in 1557 to strengthen its theological faculty. It was Flacius's first academic appointment since he left his post as instructor of Hebrew at Wittenberg in 1549. The two were equally indebted to Melanchthon's instruction, and both had supported the ducal Saxon policy, which was not always in accord with Melanchthon's opinions. But Strigel did not share Flacius's feeling that the Preceptor had betrayed Luther and Christ. Furthermore, Strigel felt threatened by Flacius's arrival on the faculty, and he had made life as difficult as possible for his new colleague.[56] But the duke reinforced Flacius's position by bringing his supporters to Jena — among them Johannes Wigand and Simon Musaeus — and this group won the battle over the *Book of Confutation*. In fact, Strigel briefly went to jail because of his opposition to it.

For Flacius the role of the will in the creation of faith was a topic that urgently needed public clarification because of the doubts raised about the Wittenberg teaching by Melanchthon and others. In November 1559 he conducted a public disputation at the university on the subject, in which he was clearly more concerned about affirming God's responsibility for salvation than for clarifying the believer's responsibility to respond to God's giving of new life. He made token historical reference to the dispute between Luther and Erasmus as the classical confrontation over the issue but made no use of *De servo arbitrio* in his argumentation.[57]

After Strigel's release from prison in September 1559, after more than five months of confinement, and in view of his at least partial rehabilitation, Johann Friedrich urgently sought a settlement of the feud between his two leading theologians. In accord with Flacius's wishes, and against Strigel's political instincts, Johann Friedrich arranged a formal academic disputation to provide a forum for clearing the air. Flacius, his colleague Simon Musaeus, and the superintendent in Jena, Balthasar Winter, drafted theses for debate: seven on the freedom of the will, eight on the distinction of law and gospel, four on good works, four on adiaphora, and three on academic method, specifically addressing the possibility of "objective" theological pronouncements. Johann Stössel of ducal Saxony and Joachim Mörlin of Braunschweig reviewed and approved the text; the ducal court arranged for the disputation to begin on August 2, 1560.

The freedom of the will was the only topic that came under discussion before the duke saw that a solution to his difficulties was slipping ever further away and canceled the contest in the thirteenth session of the disputation. Flacius had focused his attention on God's responsibility for the salvation of sinners; he wanted to discuss justification and God's exclusive responsibility for it. Strigel defined his concern as the ongoing life of repentance, and human responsibility as a newborn child of God. He had insisted on discussing the psychological factors of the exercise of the freedom of the will and was especially concerned to identify its *"modus agendi."* He conducted his argument in terms of Aristotelian psychology. He was determined to represent Melanchthon's concern that human responsibility be maintained and to repudiate the idea that God could be the cause of evil.

Flacius accepted the Aristotelian bait as he strove to defend God's total responsibility for salvation with every weapon at his disposal. His failure to lay Aristotelian terminology completely aside forced him, as the only alternative to Strigel's identification of original sin as an "accident," to define it as the substance of the fallen human creature.[58] He adopted Luther's description of the sinner as being in the image of Satan to reinforce his point. Strigel countered, using Luther quotations — among other works, from *De servo arbitrio* — in his argument as well (although neither disputant relied extensively on Luther; both rather tried to ground their case biblically). In the end Flacius's use of radical expressions alienated his prince even though he had borrowed them from Luther's writings or based them upon similar expressions from his mentor's pen. Ekkehard Muehlenberg concludes that Strigel confronted Flacius "only in a stammering way, with hesitation, and in clumsy and ambiguous formulations. That the outcome was not a total disaster for Strigel but rather favorable for him" lay not in "Strigel's clarity in the formulation of his ideas" but in Flacius's pursuing his idiosyncratic definition of original sin.[59]

Immediately following the disputation Flacius issued a collection of citations from Luther's writings to support his key contentions. In it several quotations from *De servo arbitrio* appeared, both as hermeneutical orientation and as a source of correct teaching regarding humanity.[60] Although his allies did not immediately break with him over his use of terms such as "substance" for original sin and "image of the devil" for the sinner, the disputation marked the point at which this approach to defining fallen humanity became prominent in his public teaching. It led to tensions with some of his closest friends, and then to complete rupture in relationships with all but a few faithful followers, who continued to defend his doctrine of original sin to their deaths.[61] This clash over this terminology was to a large extent a conflict over the proper interpretation of Luther and over the propriety of using Aristotelian categories to clarify the reformer's insights. It was also a struggle within the Gnesio-Lutheran party to express Luther's anthropology properly. The divergent expositions of his writings treated many passages, but they came chiefly from his published comments on Genesis and selected psalms as well as the *Church Postil,* not from *De servo arbitrio.*[62]

Their confrontation in Weimar was decisive for both its chief participants. Strigel won the battle but was weary of the war. He moved to Leipzig in electoral Saxony in 1563, and although he lectured in its theological faculty, he was not given a professor's chair there. In 1567 his changing understanding of the Lord's Supper provoked his colleague Johannes Pfeffinger to have him barred from lecturing, and he moved to Heidelberg. In correspondence in these last years his propensity for defending the activity of the human will led him to defend the proposition that God gives the gift of faith only to those who hear God's promise and incline toward it. At the same time, he rejected the "horrid opinion regarding the bondage of the will" and the doctrine of predestination it carried with it.[63]

The Weimar Disputation caused Flacius to lose the confidence of his duke. When they had differences of opinion over Johann Friedrich's plans for a more tightly controlled consistory to govern the church, the protests from Flacius and his colleagues earned them all exile, with Flacius and his friend and colleague Johannes Wigand leaving town in December 1561.[64] The record of the disputation was composed by Wigand, edited by Musaeus, and published at least three times in 1562 and 1563.[65]

The Public Polemic Continues

Within ducal Saxony Johann Friedrich the Middler proceeded with the consolidation of his own power over his church. Flacius and his followers had been removed from the scene, Strigel was still under loose confinement because he refused to accept the *Book of Confutation.* He did not commit his views to print, and so the controversy stalled momentarily. The faculty of the

University of Rostock, with David Chytraeus at its head, registered its reactions to the disputation, and even though Johann Friedrich the Middler had close connections to the dukes of Mecklenburg, the Rostock reaction did not serve him well. It came down largely on Flacius's side. For the Rostock theologians made three points on the free will (they also commented on the other items on the original agenda for the disputation). First, they affirmed the will's ability, even in its sinfulness, to practice civil righteousness. Second, they confessed that original sin has fully "corrupted the will and permeated it with the poison of sin," so that it can accomplish nothing in regard to God on its own. Third, God converts sinners into his children. In elaborating this last thesis, the Rostock professors used the three causes Melanchthon had advanced in discussing "conversion": the Holy Spirit, God's Word, and the human will. That Musaeus was willing to print this memorandum suggests that the concept of three causes could still be understood by people of his Gnesio-Lutheran persuasion as a proper description of an active, though bound, will. In elaborating this point the Rostock memorandum cited Scripture, including Philippians 2:13, "It is God who is at work in you, enabling you both to will and to work for his good pleasure," and a passage from *De servo arbitrio*. Luther, they reminded readers, spoke of "the very renewal and transformation of the old creature, who is a child of the devil, into the new creature who is a child of God. This person is simply passive and does nothing, but becomes something without qualification. It is 'becoming' that John is speaking of: 'To become children of God,' he says, by a power divinely bestowed on us, not by a power of free choice inherent in us."[66]

The court in Weimar turned to Duke Christoph of Württemberg for aid in finding a resolution to the problem. Two of his ecclesiastical diplomats, Jacob Andreae and Christoph Binder, came to Weimar to formulate a solution to the dispute over the human will. The resulting "Declaration of Viktorin" confessed that sinners cannot in any way bring themselves to God but that they do possess a *modus agendi*, the capacity or aptitude which makes them able to receive the Word of God. The Holy Spirit must restore freedom of choice to the human mind before faith in Christ is possible.[67] Protests rocked ducal Saxony from those who feared that a human "mode of acting" necessarily meant a human contribution to new birth.[68] The ducal government launched a visitation to procure subscriptions to the new declaration, and resistance among the pastors led to the composition of a "superdeclaration," which defined the *modus agendi* as the external hearing of God's Word and a passive potential or aptitude for hearing, with a sharp rejection of any human contribution to salvation.[69] Remonstrations within ducal Saxony continued,[70] and the Württemberg representatives voiced newly found suspicions concerning Strigel the following summer.[71] Political resolve at court settled the controversy inside Duke Johann Friedrich's domains about as well as political resolve ever can, but it could not stop the theological discussion. Exiled critics continued to broadcast their opinions. Indeed, even the restoration of the Gnesio-Lutherans to positions of influence when Johann Friedrich's brother Johann Wilhelm assumed power after Emperor Maximilian's arrest of the older brother in 1567[72] did not bring the wider controversy to an end.

The band of loyal disciples that Melanchthon had left behind, centered in electoral Saxony, especially at the universities in Wittenberg and Leipzig, avoided public confrontation as much as possible. Neither Pfeffinger nor Strigel sought further strife, although in their exegetical and occasional writings they continued to insist on the integrity of the human creature by affirming the activity of the sinful will as the Holy Spirit turns it to Christ.[73] Only a relatively minor member of the Philippist party, Christoph Lasius, at the time superintendent in Cottbus in Brandenburg,[74] fired significant published salvos in the fray for the Philippists.

But from several who took a radical view of Luther's thought against the Philippists — both those who had studied in Wittenberg from the late 1530s to the early 1550s and those who had not — came a number of treatises that amassed biblical evidence and theological argument against "synergism" in any form. Flacius and Gallus provided leadership initially for this informal grouping of Wittenberg students and their allies, but by the 1560s several others were assuming leadership roles as well. They issued a series of expositions of their teaching in the 1560s, largely retracing the line of argument that Gallus had set down in his first critiques of Melanchthon's views. As was typical in the Wittenberg circle, they used several genres to wage their battles. In addition to the straightforward polemical examination of the opponents' position in brief treatises, they composed lengthy disquisitions with Melanchthonian rhetorical-dialectical tools, and also sermons, as well as florilegia with citations from Luther above all.

From exile in Regensburg, where Gallus had welcomed him, Flacius, with Gallus at his side, responded to Strigel,[75] but the chief criticisms of the Philippist teaching on the freedom of the will came from their colleagues, from some who had been driven from ducal Saxony and from other sympathizers as well. The assault on the "synergists" began in earnest in 1562, with publications by Wigand and several of his comrades.

Johannes Wigand fled from Jena to his former home in Magdeburg before accepting a call to head the church in the Mecklenburg town of Wismar, where he wrote against his opponents on the freedom of the will. The most important of his treatises on the subject was entitled *On Human Freedom of*

Choice.[76] This 350-octavo-page disquisition consisted of four sections, each labeled a "Methodus" — Melanchthon's designation for a topic that gives structure to thought — along with four brief appendices which offer exposition of the differences between Luther and Erasmus, and a concluding oration Wigand had delivered at Jena on the "reasons why the dogma of the cooperation of the Old Adam, before rebirth, in spiritual matters, should be shunned." The four topics treated in this work follow the pattern of analysis handed down from Augustine: "intact human choice before the fall," "corrupt human choice after the fall, in external matters," "the bound or captive choice in things spiritual and divine in all who are not reborn," and "free choice in the reborn or restored."[77] Throughout Wigand used the Melanchthonian method he practiced in much of his writing, carefully crafting his analysis on the basis of questions prescribed by his preceptor's revision of Aristotle's rhetoric and dialectic. These questions concerned vocabulary, fundamental definitions, various aspects or forms of the matter under consideration, its purposes, and similar elements of delineation.[78] The third section, on bound choice, included a number of citations from Luther's works, intended to demonstrate the proper teaching on the subject.[79] Wigand did not define what kind of authority he was assigning his mentor here, but in other writings it is clear that he regarded Luther as a secondary authority, under Scripture, a replacement for popes, bishops, and councils, for adjudicating questions of biblical interpretation.[80]

The five parts of Wigand's exposition of *De servo arbitrio* follow the fourth section of his treatise, on the free choice exercised by the reborn. Wigand did not compose a digest of Luther's book. Instead, each part presents citations or paraphrases from the work, never in excerpts longer than 500 words, sometimes very brief, sometimes weaving together sentences from a longer section of the volume. These excerpts supported the case Wigand had made for rejecting "synergism." The first part offers thirty-one "arguments of Erasmus, or the papal church, from his *Diatribe,* and Luther's solid and unshakable responses from *De servo arbitrio*"; the second, fifteen demonstrations of "how Erasmus tried to evade rather than refute Luther's objections, and Luther's refutation of Erasmus' evasions." In the third, Luther's treatment of selected Bible passages is compared with Erasmus's exegesis; the fourth presents "proofs or arguments which Luther lays down against free choice." Finally, Wigand provided thirty-seven "guidelines" or "rules" (*regulae seu* κριτήρια) from *De servo arbitrio* for presenting biblical teaching on human choice in matters of faith, thus summarizing Luther's work.[81] He believed that his rules could be easily committed to memory and used as axioms that would solve the basic questions posed by the controversy over freedom of the will.

The preceding parts of Wigand's summary of *De servo arbitrio* focus almost exclusively on the will's lack of ability to choose to trust in God and obey him. The "rules" offer a broader view of Luther's entire argument, focusing also on questions of biblical authority, the use of reason, and the fundamental hermeneutical principles that guided Luther's examination of Erasmus's exegesis in behalf of his defense of some freedom for the will in matters relating to God. In view of Luther's extensive, incisive, penetrating analysis of Erasmus's doctrine of the freedom of the will in *De servo arbitrio,* Wigand's rules offer readers good hermeneutical orientation but do not provide a dramatic or sophisticated argument against the position of his foes within the Wittenberg circle. They function instead as a reinforcement of arguments he had already made and, above all, an appeal to the reformer's authority in settling theological questions.

In Magdeburg Wigand's friend Tilemann Heshusius was superintendent, and he joined the fray with his own critique of synergism, written as an extensive analytical essay. Heshusius had not arrived in Wittenberg during Luther's lifetime and had been close to Melanchthon until alienated from the Preceptor by Melanchthon's opposition to Heshusius's defense of Luther's view of the Lord's Supper.[82] In his work on the bondage of choice, Heshusius praised Luther's destruction of the arguments of the "semi-Pelagian Erasmus," who, Heshusius alleged, had become the patron of his opponents within the Wittenberg circle. He placed Luther in the line of defenders of God's truth that included Augustine, while he numbered Erasmus and Melanchthon in the line of those who opposed divine truth regarding the freedom of the will.[83] But Heshusius's argument rested upon biblical grounds. He seldom called Luther to the lists in his combat against the false teaching of Strigel and his comrades.

Wigand and his fellow Saxon exiles had allies in other quarters, particularly the stronghold of the Gnesio-Lutherans, Mansfeld County. Christoph Irenaeus, pastor in Eisleben, examined the freedom of the will in his lengthy treatment of the Apostles' Creed, composed in 1562, with occasional use of *De servo arbitrio.*[84] Cyriakus Spangenberg, court and town preacher in Mansfeld, published a sermon emphasizing that God alone is responsible for converting sinners but that he works their conversion through the preaching of the gospel, which produces new birth and faith.[85] The entire Mansfeld ministerium also issued a brief, formal critique of synergist views.[86] Two years later the superintendent of the churches in the county, Hieronymus Menzel, also criticized Strigel for being at odds with Luther's position in his debate with Erasmus.[87] None of these publications made use of Luther's *De servo arbitrio,* however.

The most massive assault on synergism came from the pen of a deacon in Chemnitz, Georg Herbst (Autumnus), who assembled a long collection of Luther citations to guide readers through the dispute over the free will. After his university studies Herbst entered the ministry, about 1552, and became deacon in Chemnitz in 1556. Under the protective leadership of his superintendent, Johannes Tetelbach, Herbst survived a decade in electoral Saxony, but his Gnesio-Lutheran views finally led to his ouster and exile two years after he published this work because he refused to accept the *Corpus doctrinae Philippicum* as his doctrinal standard.[88] In his preface he appealed to Luther's affirmation in the *Small Catechism*, "I believe that I cannot by my own reason or strength believe in Jesus Christ or come to him," as the basis of his presentation of Luther's teaching on the subject.[89] He also pointed out to his readers that Luther had commented on the freedom of the will in many other writings, above all *De servo arbitrio*,[90] a work to which he indeed referred somewhat frequently, though less often than to the Genesis lectures and the reformer's treatment of Psalm 51.

Herbst divided his bouquet of blossoms from Luther's garden of insights into two parts. The second brought Luther's comments to bear on a series of Bible passages. The first treated fifteen topics, including the definition of "free will" and "conversion," the nature of the sinner's disposition toward God, the reasons why sinners cannot come to God on their own, the means God uses for conversion, the role of the distinction of law and gospel and of the means of grace in that process, the hidden will of God regarding the condemned and its inaccessibility to human reason, and God's faithfulness to his promise of salvation. With this volume readers had a thorough and detailed argument against the synergists, digested from Luther's writings.

Timotheus Kirchner lost his position as pastor in the village of Herbsleben in Johann Friedrich's purge. The thirty-year-old had studied in Wittenberg and Jena. As an exile he was called to be court preacher for the count of Asseburg in Ampfurth.[91] There he began work on his thesaurus of Luther's theology, two volumes, one in German, one in Latin, which arranged citations from Luther according to Melanchthon's topics in his *Loci communes*. The human will and its capability for making choices, of course, were among the topics Kirchner had to treat. His German volume contained material only from Luther's German works, and therefore its discussion of the will did not rely upon *De servo arbitrio*,[92] but in his Latin thesaurus the work against Erasmus provided the bulk of the presentation on the free will, 80 percent of the fifty-two citations.[93]

Kirchner's training in Melanchthonian rhetoric guided the construction of his topics. That on free choice began by focusing on the theological question at hand with a page of citations on "choice, or human powers in matters external," which addressed "to what extent" there is free choice in external behavior and "sound free choice in civil and external affairs." Kirchner came to the central question regarding "bound choice in spiritual matters, in the person who is not reborn," with a section "on the word 'free choice,'" then continued "on the definition of free choice," and proceeded to treat "the status of the controversy over this subject," "the material or subject, that is, the human being in conversion: that he does or attempts nothing but holds himself *purely* passive in conversion," and "that the conversion of the impious human being is purely God's work." Kirchner produced eleven statements from Luther's concluding argument in *De servo arbitrio* as "confirmation" of these last two propositions and laid six objections to rest, also with citations from *De servo arbitrio*. The analysis came to its formal conclusion with the final cause, the purpose or function, of the teaching on the bondage of the will. Kirchner added, however, seven folio pages on vexing questions or expressions under discussion in connection with the topic: the concept of immutable necessity among them. In the manner of the medieval disputation and in conformity with Melanchthon's rhetorical principles, Kirchner continued with "confirmations" of his position that sinners are converted "by God's action alone apart from our cooperation or any *modus agendi* in us," the last phrase a direct rejection of Strigel's position. The first argument was Luther's statement of the principle of logic that a positive assertion must be proved, a negative must not. Luther's rhetorical play with his opponent had added little to his case, but Kirchner cited it nonetheless, for it called for a precise focus on the doctrinal issues rather than on argumentative skill.[94] In his massive reference work, Kirchner's extensive citation of *De servo arbitrio* conveyed much of the work's content to Kirchner's intended audience, the pastors who could not afford to have Luther's works in their libraries.

As the controversy continued to simmer on the wider stage, a pastor from Flacius's circle, Christoph Obenhin, superintendent in Ursel in the county of Königstein, entered the lists for the Gnesio-Lutheran position with *Report on the Free Will*, which called on Melanchthon's earlier writings as well as Luther's for support.[95] Obenhin and his fellow Gnesio-Lutherans were battling for the minds and mouths of the pastors of Lutheran churches and for the faith of the laity. Most of their works appeared in but one edition; the controversy commanded a real but limited market. These works reflect their concerns to preserve what they believed to be the proper balance and tension between God's total responsibility for the salvation of sinners and the responsibility of God's human creatures to trust and obey him. Without denying the latter, they found it necessary in the world of their parishioners to emphasize

God's work in turning human wills from active resistance to trust in Christ's atoning death and his resurrection and to obedience to God.

In the midst of the conflict in print, local ministeria were also divided over the role of the will in conversion, for example, in Göttingen, where in 1566 the arrival of a new ecclesiastical superintendent, Philip Keyser, from the Gnesio-Lutheran ministerium of Erfurt, became the occasion for a disagreement with school rector Joachim Meister, a student of Melanchthon. Maneuvering for power over the school added to the controversy, to be sure, but the chief issue centered on the rector's accusations that Keyser was a "Flacian heretic" because of his views of the passivity of the will in conversion.[96] In a position statement prepared for the city council in the midst of the discussions, Keyser averred that he affirmed the psychological activity of the will but that in relationship to God, having lost the image of God, and because of the influence of the devil, the will must be described as purely passive and resistant to God. The Word of God can be heard by the Old Adam but cannot be grasped apart from the Holy Spirit. The will, according to Keyser, can be said to cooperate with the Holy Spirit once the Spirit has come to dwell and work in the believer. Nonetheless, Keyser did insist on the description of the sinner as a block of wood or a beast in relationship to God's Word apart from the Holy Spirit, for the sinner remains blind, ignorant of God, immersed in diabolic depravity, a captive and slave of Satan until the Spirit effects conversion.[97] The controversy was laid to rest in January 1570 by a commission consisting of Martin Chemnitz of Braunschweig, Rudolf Möller of Hameln, Friedrich Dedekind of Neustadt am Rübenberge, and Bartholomaeus Sporckhof of Wunstorf. In a letter written six years later, Chemnitz recalled that the commissioners found equally dangerous both the proposition that the Holy Spirit is given to those still resisting him and the proposition that he is given to those who stop resisting and ask or try to assent and obey. Each proposition needed explanation within a larger context which made clear what concerns were being addressed.[98] The commissioners forged a declaration consisting of eight articles. First, sin has corrupted the human nature but the human being is not a stone or irrational beast. Indeed, the free will continues to function even though it is hostile to God. Second, in spiritual matters the will hates God's judgment and is dead as far as doing good is concerned. Third, the Holy Spirit converts sinners from their hostility; in spite of the resistance of their wills against God, the Spirit draws them to him through the means of grace. Fourth, the Holy Spirit effects rebirth, renewal, or conversion not through coercion but by making those who will not trust in God into people who do trust in God. Fifth, the gift of renewal does not produce perfect obedience, but the struggle of repentance continues in the Christian's life. Sixth, human understanding of the Spirit's work proceeds from God's Word, not from human feelings. Seventh, the Holy Spirit wages the battle against the old Adam in every believer. Eighth, the conversion of sinners does not alter their substance but gives them new birth or renewal.[99] It is clear that the commission wished to avoid Flacius's view of original sin as the substance of the fallen sinner, but in general its position matched that of Keyser.

The commission recognized that both sides had valid concerns, and its settlement tried to honor the concerns of the Philippist Meister, who had actually left Göttingen by the time of the commission's visit, by rejecting the images of the fallen sinner as stone or block of wood. The Gnesio-Lutheran Keyser, of course, also affirmed the activity of the bound and sinful human will. The commission insisted with him that only the action of the Holy Spirit turns the hearts and minds of sinners away from unbelief to trust in God. As both sides had taught, the settlement focused on the means of grace as God's instrument for regeneration, renewal, and conversion.

The Altenburg Colloquy

The festering controversy over the freedom of the will contributed to the general unrest among theologians of the Wittenberg circle and the evangelical princes and municipalities of the empire in the mid-1560s, and so it joined other issues on the agenda of controversy that had propelled Lutheran princes and theologians to seek concord and agreement since 1553. In that year Duke Christoph of Württemberg first launched a diplomatic initiative seeking an end to the incipient disputes that already were clouding the Lutheran horizon. A decade and a half later, neither political nor ecclesiastical leaders had succeeded in finding the path to harmony, but the urgency to do so had only mounted. When in 1567 Johann Wilhelm succeeded his brother, Johann Friedrich the Middler, to the throne in ducal Saxony, after the latter's arrest, the new ruler opened negotiations with his cousin, Elector August, to restore religious harmony between the churches of their domains. This led to a colloquy held at Altenburg in a series of sessions between October 28, 1568, and March 9, 1569. The electoral Saxon side was represented by only one Wittenberg instructor, Paul Eber — the theological faculty was in a state of rebuilding at the time. Eber was accompanied by two theologians from Leipzig, Heinrich Salmuth and Andreas Freyhub. The ducal Saxon theologians came from the reconstituted ecclesiastical establishment, which Johann Wilhelm had returned to the Gnesio-Lutheran orbit in 1567; they were Johannes

Wigand and Timotheus Kirchner from the faculty in Jena and Christoph Irenaeus, Johann Wilhelm's newly appointed court preacher.

In the last session the electoral Saxon contingent abandoned the colloquy because the Philippist theologians believed that the ducal Saxon party was not negotiating in good faith. The plan for the colloquy had envisioned discussion of differences regarding justification by faith, good works, the freedom of the will, and adiaphora. However, the dialogue on justification continued throughout the sessions that were held, and so the freedom of the will was not treated in Altenburg. However, the ducal Saxon Gnesio-Lutherans published extensive protocols of the sessions,[100] and the electoral Saxon Philippists responded with their own rendering of the exchange.[101] The colloquy's collapse also elicited several other treatises.[102] These publications provide a penultimate chapter to more than a decade of debate on the freedom of the will. The last chapter was to come in the efforts to compose the Formula of Concord.

As the title of the ducal Saxon account of the colloquy announced, Wigand, Kirchner, and associates added to the report on the actual discussions in Altenburg the statement regarding the free will that they had hoped to discuss there along with justification and good works. The theologians from Jena reinforced their biblical argument for the bondage of human choice in relationship to God with citations from a number of Luther's works. Among them *De servo arbitrio* played a relatively modest role in providing support for the Gnesio-Lutheran position. This ducal Saxon statement rejected seven "corruptions" of biblical teaching in their opponents' teaching on the human will, documented with citations from a variety of their writings. The electoral Saxon response did not reply to this challenge in its protocol but rather in the *Final Report*, also issued in 1570, as a broader rejoinder to a series of accusations from the Gnesio-Lutheran party. This document analyzed the individual criticisms of the Gnesio-Lutheran agenda in its protocol from Altenburg on the free will and rejected each of its condemnations, using *De servo arbitrio* in one case to support the defense of electoral Saxon teaching.

The first assertion of the Jena theologians charged that the electoral Saxons taught that before their rebirth sinners have the power to meditate upon spiritual matters relating to God and their salvation, to understand and grasp them, and to accept them.[103] The electoral Saxon theologians responded by reiterating their belief that by nature sinners cannot receive anything spiritual but are completely dependent on the Holy Spirit (1 Cor. 2:14); that is clear from their commitment to the Augsburg Confession, they stated. But they also strove to defend the integrity of the human creature as God had shaped humanity with functioning mind and will. They insisted that God does not work on human beings as if they were blocks of wood, but rather he draws them in such a way that their wills cooperate with him if they are old enough to reason and make decisions. If Gregory of Nazianzus could use such language as "God draws those whose wills are working," they asserted, so could they.[104] It was precisely this phrase from the ancient father that had aroused Gnesio-Lutheran fears of a false representation of how God works in sinners.

Secondly, the Jena theologians accused their foes of rejecting the proposition that there is nothing in believers or in their powers that moves them to assent to the promise of grace and their acceptance of it with faith.[105] The Wittenberg faculty response quoted Paul, "It depends not on human will or exertion, but on God who shows mercy" (Rom. 9:16), to demonstrate their conviction that God is alone responsible for salvation. But their concern for the integrity of the human creature's humanity drove them to argue that if the promise is universal and there are not mutually contradictory wills in God, there must be some reason in Saul and David that explains why the former rejected God and the latter trusted, why Saul was rejected and David accepted. While Luther lived, Melanchthon had taught in his locus on predestination that the cause of the rejection of sinners lies in human sinfulness that does not accept the gospel and refuses to trust in God. The reason for David's faith and Saul's unbelief dare not be assigned to a secret choice by God, but must be placed in the realm of God's Word and the acceptance or rejection of its universal promise. For the electoral Saxon theologians there was more than sufficient biblical proof that human responsibility plays a role in coming to faith: "Strive to enter through the narrow door" (Luke 13:24), "O that you would listen to his voice! Do not harden your hearts" (Ps. 95:7b-8a), "Listen! I am standing at the door, knocking; if you hear my voice and open the door, I will come in to you and eat with you, and you with me" (Rev. 3:20). Believers should not be perplexed through strange and confusing disputations about eternal election but should be pointed to the universal promise of the gospel.[106] The polarity of human and divine responsibility expressed itself in the tension the electoral Saxon theologians reflected in this statement, but not clearly. Their deep concern that God not be seen as the cause of evil and that believers exercise new obedience tipped the balance in the direction of human responsibility, and that provoked the apprehensions of their opponents in the ducal Saxon camp.

Third, the ducal Saxons objected to the language of *"causa"* — factor or element understood as cause — in the Melanchthonian treatment of the will.[107] The Philippist defense repeated the definition of the third *causa* of conversion as the "will that responds to the Word with its assent and accepts it." Such a definition was used in lectures in Wittenberg during Luther's life and appeared in print in 1545, while he was still alive, without his protest, the electoral Saxons contended. The *Final Report* defined the will as an instrumental cause of election, that is, that which grasps and accepts the promise. Luther himself had said the same, it claimed, in his lectures on Genesis 26.[108] This use of the Aristotelian terminology, however, shifted from Melanchthon's definition of the will as the material factor in conversion or repentance, a passive factor acted upon by the Holy Spirit through the Word. By assigning the will a role as an instrumental factor which "grasps and accepts" God's Word in coming to faith, this Philippist formulation at Altenburg indeed seemed to imply an active role for the human will in actions performed apart from the Holy Spirit's aid.

Fourth, the Jena theologians condemned the description of the action of the Holy Spirit in conversion as "the first part," the "second part" being the power and ability of the sinful will.[109] For the electoral Saxons the alternative to stating that the will responds to the promise would be to teach — as Flacius did, they alleged — that the human creature is nothing more than a block of wood.[110]

Fifth, the Gnesio-Lutherans repudiated the use of the description of the will as a "capability of applying itself to obtaining or preparing for the reception of grace."[111] The Wittenberg theologians responded that such a definition is necessary to avoid the false conclusion that God coerces people into faith. Such a phrase does not claim that this power is present in sinners apart from the working of the Holy Spirit, they insisted.[112] The phrase could not, of course, escape its tradition, and the ducal Saxons could not help but understand it in the context of its use by Gabriel Biel and Erasmus to convey quite a different intent. It was impossible for Wigand and his colleagues to believe that the electoral Saxon theologians were not well aware of that tradition.

Sixth, the electoral Saxons erred, their counterparts in Jena claimed, in rejecting the description of the natural will in conversion as passive. Seventh, the Jena theologians rejected the Wittenberg and Leipzig dismissal of the idea that the natural will resists God's work of conversion until the Holy Spirit has actually effected that conversion.[113] From Wittenberg and Leipzig came the reply to these two charges in one argument. Their adversaries, they charged, were trying to use certain phrases from *De servo arbitrio* to stir up controversy. They rejected the proposition that the will resists God without interruption until God coerces it through an act of new creation, as if God's almighty power was working on a block or stick of wood that can only suffer his action. That, they believed, Luther himself had rejected as he lectured on Genesis, when he warned his students against the concept of absolute necessity, which he had employed in *De servo arbitrio*.[114] *De servo arbitrio* served also as a rhetorical symbol for this one concept in Luther that the electoral Saxons believed had to be repudiated. Their endeavor to get beyond the tension between God's responsibility for salvation and the human responsibility to trust and obey by fortifying their clear confession of human integrity did raise reasonable doubt about their holding to a confession of deliverance from sin by grace alone. They did confess that God alone is responsible for forgiving sins and granting new life, but they also created suspicions by the way they defended the necessity of the will's role in human trust and obedience.

When the Jena theologians replied, they restated their objections to the electoral Saxon use of the definition of the will as an "ability to apply itself to obtaining grace," to listing the will among the "causes" or factors in the conversion of sinners to God, and to claiming that there must be a reason for God's acceptance of believers within the believers themselves.[115] Then, in the course of 1570, they also issued a *Confession on the Free Will,* a statement of what they would have liked to be able to say at Altenburg, according to its title page.[116] Using Augustine's division of the question into four parts — defining the powers of the free will before the fall, after the fall in sin, after conversion, and after death in eternal life[117] — and appealing to Luther's teaching in *De servo arbitrio* and in his Genesis lectures, the ducal Saxons set forth their view of the capabilities and incapabilities of human willing. They insisted that the corrupted will can achieve a large measure of the "external righteousness of the flesh" in the affairs of the community and the household in spite of the darkening of reason that sin has brought. Sinners can practice virtue but they tend to choose evil, even in earthly affairs. But the Jena theologians completely excluded any movement of the will in God's direction, any positive action in spiritual affairs, on the basis of the corrupted will's own powers. Thus, they rejected the "Pelagians and Sophists" who teach that the sinful will can cooperate with God, and also those who teach that the sinful will can contribute even a little bit to conversion, as Erasmus had contended. The ducal Saxon theologians made it clear that they also rejected the ravers and Schwenkfelders who believed that God converts people apart from his Word. Then they distinguished their views from their Philippist adversaries by rejecting those who held that the human mind must respond to God's Word and accept it, as the electoral Saxons had asserted in the *Final Report,* and those who did not believe that unrepentant sinners continue to resist God's Word and the Holy Spirit "furiously and rabidly" until they are converted and born again. The Jena theologians wished to remain with Luther and simply confess that the entire illumination or renewal of sinners rests in the power of the Holy Spirit, in no way in human powers.[118] Again, the difference in conceptual framework, assuming rebirth as a child, or responsible adult action, divided the two sides and made it difficult for them to understand each other.

The confession continued with an explanation of the capabilities of the free will in the reborn children of God. After the resurrection of the dead, the human will will function in a completely perfect manner, but in this life it depends on the Holy Spirit in its battle against the sinful flesh. Nonetheless, the Bible speaks of the cooperation of the reborn and renewed human will with the Holy Spirit, the ducal Saxons taught. For the Word of God creates faith in the believer's heart that leads to new obedience.[119]

At the same time as the dispute unleashed by the Altenburg colloquy was playing itself out, Jacob Andreae was pursuing a mission for the government of Württemberg in search of Lutheran concord, with five brief articles designed to create a basis for agreement among the warring factions within the churches of the Augsburg Confession. The Jena theologians found his solutions woefully inadequate, in part because of their brevity, in part because of the resulting generality and vagueness. The faculty in Jena prepared a critique, which reiterated the position they were defining against Wittenberg and Leipzig, but did so without recourse to citations from *De servo arbitrio*.[120]

Thus, by late 1570 the two sides had reinforced their public stances without coming nearer to a solution of their dispute. Their exchange in the wake of the Altenburg Colloquy demonstrates again that presuppositions regarding the nature of the relationship between Creator and human creature separated the two sides. That they could not clearly identify these presuppositions and engage each other at the level of conceptual framework doomed them to talking past each other to a certain extent. Both sides indeed sought to affirm that God is totally responsible for salvation and that human creatures must exercise responsibility in obedience to God's commands for human life. At the same time, their differing concerns and emphases did lead them to different conclusions regarding certain critical aspects of soteriology. In some cases the false teaching they wished to avoid determined more of the way they presented their thought than did the biblical basis for it or the pastoral need they wished to address. This led both sides to misunderstand and misrepresent the other.

The Gnesio-Lutherans from ducal Saxony placed primary focus on God's responsibility for salvation and were thus suspicious of every Philippist attempt to affirm the activity of the will as a part of what it means to be a human creature of God. The Philippist theologians from electoral Saxony were so concerned that they not sacrifice their affirmation of that human integrity that they avoided the biblical language of new creation. The Jena theologians presumed that conversion involves new birth or new creation; their model for understanding the newly converted believer was a newborn child. The Wittenberg and Leipzig theologians presumed that the thinking and willing convert is functioning in relationship to God as would two adults, albeit one something less than the equal of the other. The Gnesio-Lutherans were concerned that laypeople would understand the Philippist language in such a way that placed the burden on the believers and their ability to perform an act of willing acceptance, and so their fears collided with the Philippist concern that their hearers and readers could think that the Word of God works magically and coercively. Although both operated with the distinction of law and gospel as the primary guide for their proclamation, the two sides were not able to use the distinction to break through their impasse and maintain the irreducible tension within the biblical witness to the total responsibility of God for all things in creation, including the salvation of sinners, and the total responsibility of human creatures to trust and on the basis of that trust to obey.

Until the lone voice of Cyriakus Spangenberg suggested addressing the tension between total divine responsibility and total human responsibility on the divine side in 1567, by affirming God's sovereign choice of his own people in the teaching of predestination, both sides sought to address the relationship between God's responsibility and human responsibility on the human side of the equation. The Philippists solved the question of evil and asserted the integrity of the human creature by emphasizing human action of the will. Flacius and his Gnesio-Lutheran comrades secured their belief in God as the sole acting agent in all the world on the human side as well, by confessing that the human will is bound while insisting on human integrity as a matter that could be taken for granted. With his radical view of original sin as the substance of the sinner, Flacius reinforced his position on the bondage of the will with another solution on the human side. In doing so he and a few others put *De servo arbitrio* to use in a limited way. Their citations from Luther's great work reveal that they understood his fundamental points in his dispute with Erasmus and were attempting to confess them in their address of the issues of their own day.

CHAPTER IV

Luther's Students Use *De servo arbitrio* in Teaching on the Freedom of the Will

The tendency of Luther's students to pass over *De servo arbitrio* in their accounts of his life exhibits itself to a great extent in their theological writings as well. In the generation after the deaths of Luther and Erasmus, the linking of their names remained a slogan, a verbal symbol for a body of thought, at least in the Wittenberg circle; Matthias Flacius and Nikolaus Gallus called *De servo arbitrio* "one of Luther's best books," because it offered the "basis for a proper doctrine of our justification."[1] The work was reprinted in both the Wittenberg and Jena editions of Luther's works.[2] In accord with Jena's principle of not publishing translations, the German rendition of Justus Jonas did not appear in the Jena edition, but it did in the Wittenberg. Marginal annotations help guide the readers through the work in all these versions, but they do not reveal the orientation of the editor to its content. These annotations call attention to the content of paragraphs but offer no interpretation. The "Gnesio-Lutheran" Jena edition provides the very same annotations as the "Philippist" Wittenberg Latin edition, probably because both were edited by Georg Rörer. He did not hesitate to point the reader to the places in which Luther discussed necessity and the hardening of Pharaoh's heart, passages the Philippists would rather have ignored.[3] Georg Major was at the helm when the German translation was published in the Wittenberg edition; although his marginal annotations differ substantially from Rörer's, they also advise the reader of the discussions of necessity and the hardening of Pharaoh's heart.[4]

Indeed, *De servo arbitrio* was relatively seldom employed in actual argument or exposition of biblical texts even when the activity of the will was debated. There are sufficiently significant exceptions to this general observation, however, to make an appraisal of the reception of the book useful for assessing both the public teaching of the late Reformation Lutheran churches and also the ways Luther continued to shape the life of the churches that bore his name. Eight of the roughly twenty publicists in the synergistic controversy made significant use of *De servo arbitrio,* and in some of the statements of the half-dozen groups of theologians — ministeria or faculties — that issued formal opinions in the dispute, the work was also occasionally cited. It must be noted that they all read Luther to a greater or lesser extent through Melanchthonian lenses, incorporating the insights they had learned and/or read from him into their efforts to pass on Luther's message. When they departed from an element of his argument in *De servo arbitrio* — for instance, his argument regarding the absolute necessity of the unfolding of God's will — it was often to present more clearly what they regarded as the core of his thought.

The Use of *De servo arbitrio* apart from the Synergistic Controversy

That *De servo arbitrio* was not suitable for use in some kinds of writings in the next generation is clear. Much of its argument would have been difficult to incorporate directly into devotional literature. But Luther's rich exegetical insights in *De servo arbitrio* could have been put to use in a variety of exegetical works. A brief survey of selected texts suggests this was not the case.[5]

De servo arbitrio offered a wealth of hermeneutical insights along with its argument for Luther's view of God and human nature. In the generation after Luther's death some of his followers explored the principles and means of biblical interpretation; as a source for hermeneutical discussion, *De servo arbitrio* occasionally served to reinforce an axiom or observation, but rarely. Matthias Flacius revered the work but cited it seldom in the hermeneutical essays of his *Key to the Sacred Scriptures.*[6] Georg Herbst used one citation from it to place the authority of the ancient fathers in proper perspective, that is, as subject to the truth of Scripture.[7] Timotheus Kirchner treated a number of issues of biblical authority and interpretation in the exposition of the topic "Word of God" in his *Thesaurus of Explanations of All Articles and Chapters of Catholic, Orthodox, True, and Godly Christian Teaching,* but he cited *De servo arbitrio* only once, in a folio page and a half against "the sophists' statement that Scripture is obscure."[8] In this passage Luther argued against Erasmus's contention that Scripture contains many difficult and dark concepts. He insisted that human ignorance may veil parts of its message for sinful readers, but that God brings out and openly displays matters of the highest majesty and the profoundest mysteries in its pages, and Christ opens the reader's mind so that the gospel may be preached to all creation.

As a summary of the rules for the practice of theology that Luther had set forth in *De servo arbitrio,* Johannes Wigand appended a series of guidelines which focused on questions of biblical authority, the use of reason, and the fundamental hermeneutical principles that guided Luther's examination of Erasmus's exegesis in behalf of his own defense of some freedom for the will in matters relating to God. These "rules" are presented in the order found in Luther's text and thus begin with the statement that a Christian "must delight in assertions or he will be no Christian" (§1), the reformer's claim that theology must boldly profess biblical truth apart from rational disputation.[9] His insistence on the clarity of Scripture, which means that all its teachings should be proclaimed to the common people, earned a place in Wigand's orientation to *De servo arbitrio* (§3, 4),[10] before he went on to lay down grammatical, rhetorical, and theological rules for interpreting Scripture properly. Under the rubric of properly distinguishing law and gospel (§10),[11] and with the skills for linguistic analysis he had learned at Wittenberg, Wigand cited Luther to affirm that the words of the law, the imperatives of God's commands, do not describe what sinners are actually able to do but rather what are God's expectations for the exercise of human responsibility (§6-9).[12] Wigand also counseled readers to follow Luther's interpretative principles: "words are always to be used in their ordinary, natural meaning, unless we have proof to the contrary" (§29), or "words are to be defined according to their subject matter or the intention of the speaker" (§30).[13] Wigand also repeated definitions of key terms that Luther had posited during the course of his argument: "merit" (§15), "flesh" (§25), and "new birth" (§27). But these few references only place in sharper relief the lack of interest among Luther's students in grounding their exegesis and hermeneutics on material from *De servo arbitrio.*

The Synergistic Controversy as Setting for the Use of *De servo arbitrio*

Luther's and Melanchthon's students conducted the theological enterprise fundamentally on the basis of their reading of Scripture. For the most part they did not display an awareness of the role that presuppositions play in human communication. In the interpretive process they presumed that their hearers, parishioners, fellow pastors and teachers, or opponents in other theological camps operated with the same foundations and same perceptions of the truth that they did. This permitted them to proceed freely with the presentation of their ideas. All members of the Wittenberg circle took for granted that they must begin with Scripture. Nonetheless, they ascribed a limited authority to the ancient fathers of the church, and they also accorded something more than merely a limited authority to Martin Luther and sometimes also to Philipp Melanchthon.[14] Thus, as they found it appropriate, their writings called upon one or both of these mentors to reinforce or complete — or even occasionally to present — their own argumentation. So it was in their use of *De servo arbitrio.*

In the synergistic controversy Luther's writing provided support for the argument primarily of the Gnesio-Lutherans, although occasionally Philippist theologians also cited the work in their own defense. Kirchner, Obenhin, and Herbst piled up their excerpts from the work, since excerpting served as the chief vehicle of conveying the message in the genre of the florilegium, which they chose for their respective contributions to the synergistic controversy. Flacius, Gallus, Irenaeus, and Wigand (both in his own treatise and in the Jena faculty publications, which he certainly helped compose) found the occasional extract from *De servo arbitrio* to be of help. With Cyriakus Spangenberg's name added to the list of those who made use of the work in this controversy (in his sermons on predestination), it appears that some of the leading thinkers of the period found this book significant. To be sure, Obenhin, Herbst, and Irenaeus did not play large roles in shaping Lutheran thought at the time, but Flacius, Gallus, Wigand, Spangenberg, and also Kirchner made substantial contributions to the development of Wittenberg theology in the third quarter of the sixteenth century.

In this regard the reformer's own "favorite" writing obtained a small but significant role in the continued development of the Wittenberg understanding of the important theological topic of the human will and the related topic of God's predestination of his own people to salvation. As such a source for authoritative pronouncement for some of the Wittenberg disciples, and as a good resource or colorful expression for sound argument, *De servo arbitrio* differed little if at all from many of Luther's published texts.[15] However, among the many works of the reformer that were often cited by his students, *De servo arbitrio* also commands interest because its argument for God's sovereign determination of all things relied for support on the hypothesis of the absolute necessity of all things. Some of his students rejected this idea — with or without mention of their teacher's name. Most of them regarded *De servo arbitrio,* if they cited it all, as a good expression of their mentor's views.

Let God Be God

All theologians of the Wittenberg circle in the 1550s and 1560s — Philippist, Gnesio-Lutheran, and others — affirmed God's lordship over the creation he had fashioned by his own Word. The ducal Saxon theologians made particular efforts to ground their defense of the bondage of the will in this biblical presupposition. Kirchner employed a long passage from *De servo arbitrio* to set in place his fundamental definition of the term "free choice" within theological discourse. It can properly be applied only to God, Luther had insisted, reflecting his understanding of what it means that God is Creator. Kirchner took this passage to analyze the term *liberum arbitrium;* he reproduced an even longer passage to define its essence, a passage which had initiated Luther's refutation of Erasmus's concept of free choice. Luther had argued that "if you can will or unwill anything, you must to some extent be able to perform something by that will, even if someone else prevents your completing it." That would mean also being able to love and hate and being able to will death for oneself, but all these are works of God. Indeed, Luther repeated, "free choice is a divine term and signifies a divine power."[16]

In applying this fundamental conviction regarding God's nature as Creator to the matter of overcoming the sin of unbelievers through their conversion to faith in Christ, Kirchner strove to help his readers understand that the biblical language describing believers as "new creatures" means that God creates human creatures anew in his sight when he brings them to faith. For him, as for Luther, the conversion of sinners was purely and simply a re-creative act of God. Kirchner affirmed this cardinal principle of Luther's theology with one extended citation, which placed the question in the realm of the biblical understanding of creation and the relationship between Creator and human creature before it applied the principle to the sinner.

> Before human beings are created and are human beings, they do not attempt to do anything toward becoming a creature, and after they are created, they neither do nor attempt to do anything toward remaining a creature, but both of these are done by the sole will of the omnipotent power and goodness of God. . . . In just the same way before a human creature is changed into a new creature of the Kingdom of the Spirit, he does nothing and attempts nothing to prepare himself for this renewal. . . . The Spirit alone does these two things in us, recreating us apart from us and preserving us as recreated human beings.[17]

Strigel alluded to this same passage to demonstrate that he shared Flacius's commitment to God's total responsibility for the new creation or new birth of believers;[18] both Heshusius and the professors of Jena used the passage in the same way a few years later.[19]

His students repeated Luther's use of John 1:12-13, "To all who received him, who believed in his name, he gave power to become children of God, who were born not of blood or of the will of the flesh or of the human will, but of God," to affirm that God alone has the power to make sinners into his children. Erasmus had argued that these words of the evangelist suggest cooperation between the free will and God's grace. Wigand cited a longer passage from *De servo arbitrio* against this interpretation. He began with Luther's observation that this passage "is a hammer against free choice, as almost the whole of John's Gospel is." The human creature's work is not under discussion, argued Luther; but rather the "very renewal and transformation" of the sinner, "who is a child of the devil," and "is simply passive (as they say) and does nothing, but becomes a whole human being . . . by a power divinely bestowed on us, not by a power of free choice inherent in us." The Rostock faculty had used this passage in its reaction to Flacius's theses for disputation in Weimar.[20] Wigand concluded with Luther's judgment: "John is preaching the riches of the Kingdom of God which are offered to the world through the gospel, and not the virtues of free choice; and at the same time he indicates how few there are who accept them. This is due, of course, to the antipathy of free choice, which has no power while Satan rules over it but to spurn grace and the Spirit that fulfills the law, so splendidly effective are its endeavor and desire as regards the fulfilling of the law."[21] Kirchner shared Wigand's and Luther's belief that this passage affirmed God's total responsibility for the rebirth of God's people; he quoted his mentor, "by his division John rejects everything that is not born of God, inasmuch as he says we do not become children of God except by being born of God; and this takes place, as he himself explains, by believing in the name of Christ. This rejection, moreover, includes the human will, or free choice, since it is neither a birth from God nor faith. But if free choice were worth anything, the human will should not be rejected by John, nor should people be drawn away from it and directed to faith and new birth alone."[22]

Wigand, Herbst, Kirchner, and others claimed Luther's exegesis for their own affirmation of God's total responsibility for salvation, for instance, in citing his interpretation of passages comparing the human creature to a pot fashioned by a potter (Isa. 45:9; Jer. 18:6; Rom. 9:20-24). This metaphor had challenged Erasmus's interpretive skills. Wigand summarized the venerable humanist's argument, "Here the subject is [temporal] punishments, to which we ought to submit. Second, admonition to repentance follows. Third, it is written in 2 Timothy 2 [:21], 'All who cleanse themselves . . . will become special utensils.'" Quoting Luther, Wigand first discounted the argument that Erasmus had eradicated bondage of choice by his application of the metaphor of human creatures as clay in God's hands to cases of temporal afflictions. Even that argument would be clear evidence that God's will prevails over the human will, the reformer had taught. Wigand shared Luther's conviction that the master prepares the vessels; they do not prepare themselves. God remains creator and lord.²³ Herbst cited another treatment of the metaphor to insist that God is lord and his grace alone causes sinners to pursue righteousness.²⁴ With a long segment from Luther's contention that medieval concepts of human merit destroyed Paul's affirmation of God's graciousness and his responsibility for salvation, Herbst averred that arguments for cooperation between God and human creatures in salvation cannot stand.²⁵

The statement of Malachi 1:2-3, "I have loved Jacob, but I have hated Esau," cited by Paul in Romans 9:13, was critical for the debate over God's lordship and human dependence upon him. The passage had of course required comment from Erasmus. Wigand introduced Luther's "refutation of the Erasmian interpretation" with his synopsis of the Malachi passage: "first, God does not love and hate in the manner we do; second, this speaks of temporal afflictions, not eternal; third, it restrains the arrogance of Jews and gentiles." Among Wigand's longest excerpts from *De servo arbitrio*, this passage wove together three discrete but interrelated segments of Luther's extensive examination, about one-fourth of the reformer's treatment of the verse. In one sentence Wigand repeated Luther's more detailed assessment that Jerome, on whom Erasmus depended for his exposition, had not understood this passage. Then Wigand offered a longer passage from Luther that began, "Paul is discussing whether it was by the virtue or merits of free choice that [Jacob and Esau] attained to what is said of them, and he proves it was not, but it was solely by the grace of 'him who calls' that Jacob attained to what Esau did not." Luther posed the critical question, "What help was free choice to Jacob, and what hindrance was it to Esau, when before either of them was born or had done any thing, it had already been settled by the foreknowledge and determination of God what should be the lot of each . . . ?" Ignoring more technical arguments in the reformer's text, Wigand continued with a description of Paul's intention in using Malachi in Romans 9: "God called Jacob before he was born because he loved him, not because he was first loved by Jacob or moved by any merit of his." Wigand concluded by demonstrating that the interpretation of the passage as a reference to temporal misfortune cannot stand.²⁶ But he did not venture into speculation about God's predestining power in Jacob's life. He focused only on the issue of human merit.

The report of Exodus 4:21 and 7:3 regarding God's hardening of Pharaoh's heart presented his lordship in particularly stark form. For the most part, Luther's students tried to avoid confronting the problems this passage poses. When the text of Romans forced them to do so, most of them retreated to Melanchthon's exegesis, avoiding the difficult theodical question and finding that God had done no more than permit Pharaoh to harden his own heart.[27] Luther had rejected this interpretation. After a protracted analysis of Erasmus's argument for such a construal of the text, he stated simply that human creatures dare not "seek to measure God by human reason and make excuses for him," but should instead "reverence the secrets of his majesty but [not] pry into them."[28] He did not attempt an explanation but let the mystery of God's sovereign actions stand.

Wigand provided his readers with an overview of this debate. Erasmus explained God's hardening of Pharaoh's heart (Exod. 9:7, 12; Rom. 9:18), according to Wigand's summary, with an appeal to Origen, who had stated that God gave the occasion for the hardening but that Pharaoh bore the guilt; thus "hardening the impenitent" is "a trope, a manner of speaking, not a theological truth." Luther's rebuttal, according to Wigand's synopsis, contained four points. First, Erasmus had promised to combat Luther only on the basis of Scripture but then had turned to Origen and Jerome as authorities for this passage. Second, "hardly any of the ecclesiastical writers have handled divine Scripture more ineptly and absurdly than Origen and Jerome." Third, "it is dangerous, and indeed impious, to twist the word of God without necessity and without authority." Fourth, God "hardens Pharaoh when he presents to his ungodly and evil will a word and work which that will hates — owing of course to its inborn defect and natural corruption. And since God does not change it inwardly by his Spirit . . . , the result is that Pharaoh is puffed up and exalted by his own imagined greatness . . . and is thus hardened and then more and more provoked and exasperated the more Moses presses and threatens him."[29] Wigand used Luther's words to emphasize Pharaoh's responsibility for his own defiance of God while at the same time affirming God's responsibility for changing hearts. To this citation Wigand added Luther's judgment, "You see here that Pharaoh is hardened precisely in order that he may resist God and delay his redemption, so that occasion may be given for many signs and for a declaration of the power of God."[30] Wigand concluded, "Why God does not change evil wills is a matter of the mystery of his majesty, where his judgments are incomprehensible."[31] Wigand recognized that Luther's approach to questions of God's unconditioned choice of his elect and the freedom or bondage of the human will's exercise of choice in spiritual matters remained a mystery, coupled to the paradox of full divine and complete human responsibility.

Kirchner underscored the lordship of the Creator by maintaining that to concede free choice to the human being undermines the biblical affirmation of God's grace. He repeated Luther's contention that if Erasmus were right regarding free choice, the biblical concept of God's redemption of sinners by grace alone would lose its meaning. For "if Christ is the Lamb of God that takes away the world's sin [John 1:29], then it follows that the whole world is subject to sin, damnation, and the devil."[32] Likewise, Paul's understanding of justification by faith in Romans 3 and 4 permits no exercise of free choice, a human work.[33] Jesus' words in John 14:6, "I am the way, the truth, and the life," further substantiate God's total responsibility for human salvation, for if Christ is the way, truth, and life, what is not Christ or in Christ is "included in error, deceit, and death."[34] Of John 6:44, "no one comes to me unless my Father draws him," Luther asked, "What does this leave to free choice? . . . He plainly teaches here, not only that the works and efforts of free choice are fruitless, but that even the message of the gospel itself (which is what this passage is about) is heard in vain unless the Father himself speaks, teaches, and draws inwardly."[35] Luther continued by treating John 16:8-9, "the Spirit will convince the world of sin because they have not believed in me." "When he makes the whole world guilty of this sin, this experience shows that the world is as ignorant as it is of Christ until the convicting Spirit reveals it, then it is evident that in the sight of God free choice, with its will and its reason alike, is reckoned as a captive of this sin and as damned by it. . . . we are compelled to serve in the kingdom of Satan unless we are delivered by the power of God."[36] With these passages Luther, and thus Kirchner, placed the sinful human creature totally in God's hands. Gallus observed that in *De servo arbitrio* Luther was striving above all to preserve the believer's trust which rests upon God's will and his power against the devil,[37] and Kirchner strove to strengthen his readers' trust in God in a similar way. This was the goal of practicing theology in the Wittenberg way.

In the works of Luther's disciples who put material from *De servo arbitrio* to use, the confession of God's total responsibility for salvation from sin is reinforced and made crystal clear through citations from Luther's work. Unlike some of their contemporaries, who often repeated "grace alone" but did not elaborate on their axiom that God is the only active agent in salvation, Wigand, Kirchner, and Herbst used the paradigm of God's creation of the universe through his Word to explain his action and his responsibility for the re-creation of the sinner into a child of God. These devotees of *De servo arbitrio* did not always confront the theodical mystery as openly and fully as Luther had at the end of *De servo arbitrio*. However, when they raised the question of evil's existence or the conflict of God's goodness and omnipotence with sin and rebellion against God, most conceded that the human mind cannot solve that theodical mystery. Nonetheless, they affirmed both his power and his mercy as limitless — and they did so with the aid of *De servo arbitrio.*

God Hidden and Revealed

Particularly important for Luther's presentation of the biblical representation of God's lordship was his distinction between the hidden God and the revealed God. Although Melanchthon could describe God in somewhat similar ways,[38] this distinction did not find its way explicitly into his topical summary of the teaching of Scripture and so did not become a constitutive element in the public teaching of his students, as did the topics that organized his presentation. Gallus, however, recognized the value of the distinction and used it to warn against trying to plumb the depths of God's wisdom with the temerity of human wisdom. As he introduced his edition of the German translation of *De servo arbitrio,* he cited Luther's admonition to turn only to Jesus Christ the crucified.[39] In his comments on the dispute over the human will, Martin Chemnitz cited Luther's comments on Genesis 17 regarding the necessity of turning alone to the God who had revealed himself in his Word, as the Braunschweig theologian joined Luther in cautioning against speculation regarding the hidden God.[40] Heshusius, too, put the distinction to use in his criticism of synergism, explaining that with this distinction Luther had shown that God does not deceive and does not contradict himself. Instead, the mystery of his wisdom is to be found only through faith in the Mediator.[41] Heshusius's comrade Wigand also found this distinction between God's hidden and revealed will, or God preached and God hidden, or God and God's Scripture[42] — Wigand rendered these expressions with "God's Word and God himself" — to be a fundamental axiom of orientation for theology (Wigand's rules from *De servo arbitrio* §11-12). This led to the conclusion, in Luther's words, that hearers of God's Word are to deal with questions of predestination and bondage of human choice on the basis of the premise that "God is righteous even when he seems to us to be unjust," a judgment Wigand found worthy as the conclusion of his rules (§37).[43] He had understood his mentor's conclusion: the student "justified" God by freeing him from submission to human judgment. Like his instructor, Wigand simply let God be God.

In his summary of Luther's teaching on the freedom of the will, Herbst explicitly treated this distinction in two of his fifteen theses, fully aware of the place of the "theodicy question" in Luther's thinking. The first was entitled "on the hidden and secret counsel and will of God, and how it relates to the conversion and salvation of one person, and the hardening of another"; the second repeated the reformer's warnings against probing God's hidden will. Herbst cited a series of passages from Luther in establishing these theses. His comments on Ezekiel 18:23, "Have I any pleasure in the death of the wicked, says the Lord God, and not rather that they should turn from their ways and live?" provided instruction on the distinction between God as he is to be proclaimed and God as he is in his hiddenness. The Ezekiel passage

> is speaking of God's mercy, which is proclaimed and offered to us, not of that hidden and awesome will of God whereby he ordains by his own counsel which and what sort of persons he wills to be recipients and partakers of this mercy that is proclaimed and offered. This will is not to be the object of our inquiry but is to be reverently adored, as by far the most awe-inspiring secret of the Divine Majesty, reserved for himself alone and forbidden to us. . . . To the extent that God hides himself and wills to be unknown to us, it is no business of ours. . . . God must therefore be left to himself in his own majesty, for in this regard we have nothing to do with him insofar as he is clothed and set forth in his Word.[44]

For, Herbst pointed out, Luther believed that God must remain God, not the plaything of human imagination. To ask why God does not stop the "motion of his omnipotence" that sustains the evil human will, even as it becomes worse, is to want "God to cease to be God on account of the ungodly." This, Luther stated, "belongs to the secrets of his majesty, where his judgments are incomprehensible. It is not our business to ask this question, but we are rather to adore these mysteries. And if flesh and blood is offended here and murmurs, by all means let it murmur; but it will achieve nothing. God will not change on that account."[45] Luther refused to weaken his affirmation of God's total control of all things, Herbst reminded readers: "God does not will the death of a sinner, according to his Word, but he wills this death according to that inscrutable will of his." But the reformer refused to pursue that path and move to the logical conclusion that God has two contradictory wills. He turned from the hidden God to the revealed God, continuing, "It is our business, however, to pay attention to the Word and leave that inscrutable will alone, for we must be guided by the Word and not by that inscrutable will. After all, who can be directed by a will completely inscrutable and unknowable? It is enough to know simply that there is a certain inscrutable will in God, and as to what, why, and how far it wills, that is something we have no right whatever to inquire into, hanker after, care about, or meddle with, but only to fear and adore."[46] Herbst quoted Luther again, declaring once more that the secret will of God's majesty is not a matter for debate; God's majesty is impenetrable (1 Tim. 6:16). Human impertinence must turn away from its own questions and "occupy itself with God incarnate, or as Paul puts it, with Jesus crucified . . . for through him it is furnished abundantly with what it ought to know and ought not to know." For the incarnate God weeps, wails, and groans over the perdition of the ungodly, "when the will of the Divine Majesty purposely abandons and reprobates some to perish. And it is not for us to ask why he does so, but to stand in awe of God who both can do and wills to do such things."[47] Herbst led his readers without hesitation to face the paradox of God's power and goodness alongside the existence of evil through Luther's eyes. To those who were charging that the concept of the hidden God was merely a way out of an uncomfortable argument, Herbst cited Luther, "This is not our invention but a precept firmly based on the divine Scriptures," and added Paul's words from Romans 9:19-24.[48] Herbst used Luther's discussion of God's actions in relationship to fallen humanity from the perspectives of "the lights" of nature, grace, and glory at the end of *De servo arbitrio* to assert that the human being, who cannot always understand God's ways on earth, must bow before his majesty in matters spiritual.[49] As the conclusion to his recitation of Luther's warnings against the pursuit of answers regarding the hidden God, Herbst set before the readers one of the longest excerpts from Luther's writings in his entire collection, his caution to his students in the Genesis lecture on chapter 26 regarding the perversions of his argument in *De servo arbitrio* that he anticipated would arise after his death. In this passage he counseled clearly and fervently that believers should trust in God's promise as conveyed in the means of grace when they turned to the comfort that God's predestining love in Christ offered them.[50]

Herbst understood the importance of Luther's distinction of God Hidden and God Revealed for his confession of God as Creator and as Savior and for his definition of humanity as the creature of God, resting totally in his hands. Wigand, Chemnitz, and Heshusius recognized that this insight played a key role in the argument of *De servo arbitrio*. All four of them paused before the mystery of evil and resisted trying to dissolve the paradox of the coexistence of God's absolute goodness and might with the existence of evil. Although the distinction of God Hidden and God Revealed did not occupy a central place in their thought, it gave them aid at critical points in dealing with the tension of God's responsibility and that of the human creature as well as the mysteries related to the existence of evil. It also provided vital assistance in bringing the consolation of God's Word to troubled consciences, a crucial element in the Wittenberg way of practicing theology.

God Chooses His Own

The disciples of Luther and Melanchthon also largely ignored God's election of his people as a doctrinal topic in the 1550s and 1560s. Before Cyriakus Spangenberg placed this locus squarely before the reading public in 1567,[51] it remained one form of expressing the gospel's comfort that Philippists intentionally refused to adopt and that Gnesio-Lutherans seldom felt compelled to take in hand. It is true that Luther had given them relatively little reason to do so in his own writings. Gallus and Kirchner, as well as Wigand and Judex in their *Syntagma,* mentioned God's predestination of his chosen children. Gallus's references in his preface to the German translation of *De servo arbitrio* took for granted that justification could not be understood apart from its foundation in God's predestination of believers. But until Spangenberg brought this teaching to the public agenda, it was not treated in detail. Likewise, the topic of the universality of God's salvific promise did not loom large in the Gnesio-Lutheran writings on the freedom of the will. The Wittenberg *Final Report* of 1570 called upon Luther in *De servo arbitrio* to affirm that God wants all to be saved. For "he comes with the word of salvation to all, and the fault is in the will that does not admit him, as he says in Matthew 23, 'How often did I not want to gather your children, and you did not want that.'"[52] Most Gnesio-Lutherans also affirmed and repeated the universality of the promise of salvation for fallen sinners. They presumed this teaching just as they presumed that salvation rested on God's predestining plan. But the former teaching seemed obvious without repeating it, from their point of view, and predestination seemed too likely to distract tender consciences into speculation and despair or to impel arrogant consciences into disobedience and defiance of God. Therefore, they failed to emphasize these doctrinal synonyms. The former was lodged as a presupposition in their proclamation of God's grace; the latter was an unavoidable constitutive part of their use of the means of grace.

God Saves through the Means of Grace

All of Luther's and Melanchthon's disciples shared their mentors' common emphasis on the means of grace, the proclamation of the promise of salvation in Christ conveyed by God's Word in oral, written, and sacramental forms. Because their Philippist opponents in the synergistic controversy emphasized the use of the means of grace, the Gnesio-Lutherans had no reason or grounds to use Luther's discussion of how God's Word works in *De servo arbitrio* for polemical counterpoint. This was a topic on which there were genuine agreement and a large degree of similarity of expression among all within the Wittenberg circle, at least up to the late 1560s, when at the University of Wittenberg itself spiritualizing tendencies influenced the teaching on the means of grace. All were nonetheless conscious of the key place in the body of Luther's teaching held by the article on God's Word as means of grace.

Both Gnesio-Lutheran and Philippist writings sometimes reproduced Luther's understanding of the nature of God's Word as a seemingly weak and foolish word for the world and as the power of God to kill and make alive, to judge and to save.[53] But they did not often call upon Luther's rich treatment of this topic in *De servo arbitrio* to reinforce this vital element of their transmission of biblical teaching. Herbst was an exception. He met the objection that the human mind is too weak to understand such lofty matters as the freedom of the will with Luther's epistemology of the cross. "Nothing is more fitted for understanding the words of God than such weakness; for it was for the sake of the weak and to the weak that Christ both came and sent his Word. It is due to the malice of Satan, who sits enthroned in our weakness, resisting the Word of God. If Satan were not at work, the whole human world would be converted by a single Word of God heard but once, and there would be no need of more."[54]

Herbst's readers then received instruction regarding how the power of God's Word as the instrument and vehicle of the Holy Spirit converts them to trust in him. In John 6:44, Jesus' words that only those can come to him whom his Father draws, Luther found the claim "that even the message of the gospel itself (which is what this passage is about) is heard in vain unless the Father himself speaks, teaches, and draws inwardly. . . . The ungodly do not come even when they hear the Word unless the Father draws and teaches them inwardly, which he does by pouring out the Spirit."[55] "It has pleased God to impart the Spirit, not without the Word but through the Word, so as to have us working in cooperation with him when we sound forth outwardly what he himself alone breathes inwardly wherever he wills."[56]

This latter allusion to John 3:8 was important for Herbst because he wanted to make clear to readers that the Word of God does not work magically but effects faith, and it does so as the Holy Spirit's tool. He clearly understood God to be a speaking God, and he understood the relationship between God and his human creatures as a mutual conversation. Among a number of Luther's treatises, he turned to *De servo arbitrio* to affirm this element of his teaching, applying generally what Luther had written regarding the need for the Spirit's guidance in his discussion with Erasmus: "This requires also the

Spirit of God to give the growth and to be a living teacher of living things inwardly . . . yet . . . the Spirit is free and blows not where we will but where he wills."[57]

Like the Philippists, the Gnesio-Lutheran theologians all recognized that the means of grace in Luther's theology operate within the framework of the distinction of law and gospel. Without making clear that questions regarding God's total responsibility and the total responsibility of the human creature depended on the distinction, Wigand placed it among his fundamental rules for theology that readers should gain from *De servo arbitrio* (his "rule" 10).[58] He also insisted, with Luther, that the words of God's law, the imperatives of his commands, do not describe what sinners are actually able to do but rather what are God's expectations for the exercise of human responsibility (§6-9).[59]

Kirchner, too, wanted his readers to recognize the importance of the distinction of law and gospel and quoted Luther in such a way that they might see its role in understanding what Scripture says about God's mercy and human obedience. In treating Ezekiel's words, "I desire not the death of the sinner but rather that he may turn and live" (Ezek. 18:23, 32), Luther had elucidated this distinction, and Kirchner reprinted a long passage, filled with the themes of hope and pardon as well as the necessity of the sinner's feeling God's wrath. Luther had explained that this passage from the prophet

> has no other object than the preaching and offering of divine mercy throughout the world, a mercy that only the afflicted and those tormented by the fear of death receive with joy and gratitude because in them the law has already fulfilled its assignment and brought the knowledge of sin. Those, however, who have not yet experienced the function of the law, and neither recognize sin nor feel death, have no use for the mercy promised by that word. But why some are touched by the law and others are not, so that the former accept and the latter despise the offered grace, is another question and one not dealt with by Ezekiel in this passage. For he is here speaking of the preached and offered mercy of God, not of that hidden and awful will of God whereby he ordains by his own counsel which and what sort of persons he wills to be recipients and partners of his preached and offered mercy.[60]

In defining the "final cause," the goal of the church's teaching about the freedom of the will, Kirchner cited Luther's wrestling with the problems produced by examining it. The reason this doctrine must be taught, apart from the fact that God had revealed it, concerned the effective application of law and gospel, and the use God makes of each in creating faith. There were "two considerations which demand that such things should be preached. The first is the humbling of our pride, and the knowledge of the grace of God; and the second is the nature of Christian faith itself." For proclaiming the bondage of the will is done for the sake of God's chosen children, "that being humbled and brought back to nothingness by this means they may be saved." Furthermore, faith rests upon what God has hidden. "Thus, when God makes alive, he does it by killing; when he justifies, he does it by making people guilty; when he exalts to heaven, he does it by bringing down to hell. . . . Thus, God hides his eternal goodness and mercy under eternal wrath, his righteousness under iniquity."[61]

Herbst also called upon Luther to testify regarding the necessity of distinguishing law and gospel in proclaiming God's Word. From the end of a section of *De servo arbitrio* in which Luther criticized Erasmus's failure to practice this distinction, Herbst reminded his readers that a doctrine of free choice brings sinners to despair when they recognize their sin and try to bring about their own conversion to God: the free will of the sinner under the impact of the law could do "nothing but fall into a worse state and add despair and impenitence to its sins, if God did not quickly come to its aid and call it back and raise it up by a word of promise."[62] Herbst also addressed one practical problem in the distinguishing of law and gospel that Luther had confronted. Against the charge that Luther's teaching on the bondage of the will would make people secure in their sin and lead them to neglect doing good, he quoted the reformer: "The elect and godly will be corrected by the Holy Spirit while the rest perish uncorrected."[63] Herbst was reaffirming that the whole life of the Christian is a life of repentance.

Luther placed his entire discussion of the bondage of the will in the context of the proper distinction of law and gospel. Melanchthon had reminded readers that predestination could not be understood at all apart from the proper application of this distinction. Herbst and Kirchner followed their example, recognizing that the boundness of the will certainly could not be properly comprehended outside this hermeneutical framework. Effective proclamation of God's Word depends on the assessment of which word from God is needed for the hearer or reader in the specific situation in which God's message is delivered. In general, their contemporaries from all corners of Wittenberg's world presumed that was true. The group including Kirchner, Herbst, and Wigand enunciated the principle clearly in their use of *De servo arbitrio*. They also insisted that the effective use of the gospel in its oral, written, and sacramental forms was the key to delivering the forgiveness of sins, life, and salvation, and to assuring believers of God's inalterable love for them in Christ. That proclamation stood at the heart of the cultivation of life lived in the rhythm of law and gospel, the life of repentance and freedom in Christ.

Human Beings Are Dependent Creatures

God, the speaking Creator, brought his human creatures into existence through his Word, and he re-creates them through his Word. In *De servo arbitrio* Luther wished to elucidate not only who God is but also what it means to be human. Erasmus had sought to delineate the meaning of the humanity God had wrought by insisting that the definition should center on the performance of human responsibilities toward God as well as other creatures through a limited freedom of choice, exercised by a will that thus had to be called "free." Luther, too, insisted on the exercise of human responsibility but held that responsibility in tension with God's responsibility for creation and re-creation. His definition of humanity began with the relation of faith and trust that binds every human creature to the Creator. In a number of ways and passages the reformer demonstrated that the human will does not enjoy a "freedom" that entails some kind of control over life. Not only because of the bondage of sin but also because of the nature of creatureliness, Luther taught, is the will unable to master its own world.

Luther's disciples placed this question of the freedom or bondage of the will at the heart of their debate over what it means to be human in the synergistic controversy. The concept of human freedom of the will was simply not to be found in the Bible, Herbst avowed in a paraphrase of the reformer's dialogue with Erasmus.[64] But neither he nor most of his contemporaries framed the definition of the will's bondage in terms of human creatureliness, as Luther had done. They concentrated upon the bondage imposed on human choosing by the fall into sin. This enabled them to avoid the possibility that the integrity of human responsibility would be discarded and the human creature would be so defined as to be incapable of responsible choice and thus responsible obedience. Kirchner was one exception. As he initiated his discussion of "free choice," he fashioned a definition from Luther's words regarding the difference between God's freedom and human freedom that at least implicitly touched upon the limits of human creatureliness. He cited Luther's comment on Genesis 2:7, that God gave human creatures free choice in matters *infra nos* ("beneath us," that is, within the human sphere of responsibility) when he made them lords of other creatures (Gen. 1:26). By drawing this contrast within the context of the Garden of Eden before the fall into sin, Luther limited the freedom the human creature was able to exercise in relationship to God as a creature, apart from consideration of the invasion of sin into its competence.[65] Kirchner immediately repeated this distinction from *De servo arbitrio* with words that reminded the reader of the respective places of Creator and creature: if the term "free choice" is to be used at all regarding human creatures, Luther wrote, it should be allowed "only in respect to what is beneath them and not what is above them. That is to say, they should know that with regard to their faculties and possessions they have the right to choose, to do, or to leave undone, according to their own free choice, though even this is controlled by God's free choice alone, who acts in whatever way he pleases."[66]

As he elaborated the core of his definition of the will's bondage, Kirchner defined the point at issue in the dispute over free choice by using Luther's description of what was at stake in his debate with Erasmus. Also from that perspective Kirchner focused on the creatureliness of human beings. Kirchner quoted his mentor:

> it is not irreverent, inquisitive, or superfluous, but essentially salutary and necessary for a Christian to find out whether the will does anything or nothing in matters pertaining to eternal salvation . . . this is the cardinal issue between us, the point on which everything in this controversy turns. . . . For if I am ignorant of what, how far, and how much I can and may do in relation to God, it will be equally uncertain and unknown to me, what, how far, and how much God can and may do in me although it is God who works everything in everyone [1 Cor. 12:6]. But when the works and power of God are unknown, I do not know God himself, and when God is unknown, I cannot worship, praise, thank, and serve God, since I do not know how much I ought to attribute to myself and how much to God. We are therefore obligated to be very certain about the distinction between God's power and our own, God's work and our own, if we want to live a godly life.[67]

Thus, Kirchner's Luther concluded, "We are not discussing what we can do through God's working but what we can do of ourselves; that is to say, whether, created as we are out of nothing, we do or attempt to do anything under the general motion of omnipotence to prepare ourselves to be the new creature of the Spirit."[68] Kirchner felt compelled to select extracts from this and others of Luther's works which made it clear that the fundamental point regarding human choosing lay in the nature of humanity, in the relationship between Creator and human creature, and not only in the effects of sin upon that nature and relationship.

That point was reinforced by Kirchner's citations that defined the *materia* or *subiectum* under discussion. He made it explicit that human beings in the process of being converted can do or attempt nothing, but remain purely passive. Theses 35-39 of Luther's "Disputation concerning the Human Creature" of 1536 established that human creatures are *pura materia Dei,* fashioned by the Creator, in this (sinful) life on the way to being restored as the image of God.[69] On the basis of Luther's words on Genesis 2, in the *Leipzig Resolutions,* and on Psalm 5, Kirchner emphasized the purely passive posture of the human creature. From *De servo arbitrio* he took up John 1:12, "He gave them power to become children of God," Luther's "cudgel against free choice," to remind readers that sinners, who are children of the devil, are renewed and transformed into the new creature who is a child of God. They are "purely passive (as is said) and do nothing but become complete."[70]

The word "passive" provided Luther with his key description of the nature of human creatureliness and its dependence on God in what he called the distinction of two kinds of righteousness: what makes human beings righteous, or truly human, in relationship to God and in relationship to his other creatures. In general, Luther's and Melanchthon's disciples did not adopt his way of talking about this distinction. They tended more toward Melanchthon's language, speaking of the "righteousness of faith" and the "righteousness of works," the former in relationship to God, the latter in relationship to other human creatures and the rest of God's world. Luther and Melanchthon had made it clear that both are necessary constitutive elements of humanity: the former expressed in trust in God, the latter in love for the neighbor. In their use of *De servo arbitrio,* members of the second Wittenberg generation generally failed to cite the passages in which Luther used precisely this formulation to define the two dimensions of humanity, as he understood God had created them. Kirchner and Herbst were exceptions. Among the Bible passages Kirchner presented to help explicate Luther's view of the will was Romans 3:21-25, which had provided the reformer with

> absolute thunderbolts against free choice. First: "The righteousness of God is manifested apart from the law." . . . it is very clearly evident that all the devoted endeavors of free choice are worth absolutely nothing. For if the righteousness of God exists apart from the law and the works of law, must it not much more exist apart from free choice? Especially as the highest aspiration of free choice is to practice moral righteousness, or the works of the law, with the help afforded by the law to its own blindness and ignorance. . . . Paul clearly distinguishes the two righteousnesses, attributing one to the law and the other to grace, maintaining that the latter

is given without the former and apart from its works, while the former without the latter does not justify or count for anything.[71]

Herbst cited a lengthy passage from Luther's discussion of Erasmus's key passage in defense of his own view, Sirach 15:14-17, which included the words,

> We thus learn from Sirach that human creatures are divided between two realms, in one of which they are directed by their own choice and counsel, apart from any precepts and commandments of God, namely in their dealings with that which is under their control. Here they reign and are lords, as having been left in the hand of their own counsel. God has not surrendered control to them in such a way that they do not have to work together with him in everything and are not restricted by any laws and injunctions. . . . In the other kingdom, however, human creatures are not left in the hand of their own counsel but are directed and led by the choice and counsel of God so that just as . . . in the kingdom of God they are directed by the precepts of another [God] without regard to their own choice.[72]

Herbst elucidated this distinction with Luther's interpretation of the Hebrew concept of "return." Returning to the Lord, repentance, does not take place apart from God's turning to his people.[73]

Apart from speaking of two realms in human life, the writings of the 1550s and 1560s from the Wittenberg circle reveal that Kirchner and others among Luther's students did operate with the presupposition of the distinction of two kinds of righteousness in their evaluation of concepts of human merit. For Luther's definition of righteousness in God's sight as a gift from God that elicits trust in the believer eliminated any kind of merit based on human performance from a discussion of salvation. Against Erasmus's contention that all Bible passages which speak of merit and reward prove that the will is free to choose, Kirchner cited a longer passage from *De servo arbitrio* which argued that "it is God alone who by his Spirit works in us both merit and reward, though he discloses and proclaims them both to the whole world by his external Word, in order that his power and glory and our impotence and ignominy may be proclaimed even among the ungodly and unbelieving and ignorant."[74] Kirchner continued with another passage designed to reveal the emptiness of the concept of merit by way of Luther's analysis of the medieval concept of congruent and condign merit. Luther insisted that Paul's entire argument for salvation by grace, apart from the works of the law, allowed no place for any human merit in salvation. Granting only a little merit is no different from granting much merit to human works, he argued.[75] The Jena professors used this passage to demonstrate the impossibility of any human merit as well.[76]

Luther's distinction of the righteousness of faith from the righteousness of works contributed to his understanding of the ways in which God's law functions for human beings. Its expectations did not set forth for him a series of requirements that had to be attained or maintained to win or preserve the human creature's relationship with God. The law served rather to measure the performance of works that God wished to flow from the gift of identity as his child. He freely bestowed the identity itself on human beings, first as creatures and then, after their rebellion, as sinners forgiven and refashioned as new creatures in Christ. Kirchner chose two brief excerpts from Luther's rather long treatment of Sirach 15:14-17. Regarding Sirach's words "If you will observe the commandments and keep acceptable fidelity forever, they shall preserve you," Luther replied, "I do not see how free choice is proved by these words. For the verb is in the subjunctive mood ('if you will'), which asserts nothing."[77] Typical of Luther's treatment of Erasmus's argument that imperatives directed at human beings prove that they must be able to choose the good, is his analysis of the imperative mood in Deuteronomy 30:15, 19: "I have set before your face the way of life and of death. Choose what is good." Luther responded, "The words of the law are spoken not to affirm the power of the will but to enlighten blind reason and make it see that its own light is no light and that the virtue of the will is no virtue. . . . Heap up, therefore, all the imperative verbs (from the bigger concordances if you like) into one chaotic mass, and provided they are not words of promise, but of demand and law, I shall say at once that what is signified by them is always what people ought to do and not what they do or can do."[78] This argument was repeated by Flacius in the Weimar Disputation,[79] by Wigand,[80] Irenaeus,[81] the Jena faculty,[82] and Herbst. Herbst called upon Luther from a number of passages in *De servo arbitrio* to explicate this principle, including his words: "that inference, 'If you will, you can,' is inadmissible, and instead it must be understood that by this and similar expressions human creatures are warned of their impotence, which in their ignorance and pride, without these divine warnings, they would neither acknowledge nor be aware of."[83]

Luther's avowal of the human being's complete dependence on God was vital for his anthropology. But the need of some of his disciples to affirm the integrity of the human being led them to mention this dependence less often and less explicitly than Luther had. Kirchner, however, demonstrated that he had absorbed Luther's drawing the parallel between God's original creation and his new creation through the means of grace as he transformed sinners through his creative Word into his children. That these children find their identity in trust in God through his re-creative Word of God and not in any human action, performance, or obedience (their own or Christ's) was the foundation of Luther's theology, he claimed. Like Kirchner, Herbst clearly enunciated this distinction of two kinds of righteousness in a way few of their contemporaries did. Both used *De servo arbitrio* to do so. Others, including Wigand and Irenaeus, recognized that the righteous actions demanded by the law cannot be performed by sinners, and therefore cannot constitute human righteousness before God: they thus captured part but not all of this critical and central insight of Luther's thought. Most others were content to focus on the bondage imposed by sin, without making clear what constituted original human righteousness.

Human Creatures Fallen into Sin

For the most part the students of Luther and Melanchthon maintained that the human will does not function "freely" in relationship to God because it is bound in sin. This conclusion not only repeated Luther's insights into the deep corruption of human nature, a corruption which stems from not fearing, loving, and trusting in God above all things. It also permitted a Melanchthonian defense of the integrity of the human creature as a responsible and obedient agent of God's will in the world of sinners. The second Wittenberg generation taught quite unanimously that the Holy Spirit frees the will through the forgiveness of sins to serve God in cooperation with the Spirit.

Although he emphasized more than most of his contemporaries that as creatures human beings are totally dependent on the Creator, Kirchner also led his readers to recognize that sin had placed the will in bondage. His definition of humanity rested on the nature of the human being in relationship to the Creator: human life could not exist apart from another in the driver's seat. "In relation to God, or in matters pertaining to salvation or damnation, human beings have no free choice, but are captive, subjects, and slaves either of the will of God or the will of Satan."[84] Free choice "has no power while Satan rules over it but to spurn grace."[85] It is "nothing else than the supreme enemy of righteousness and human salvation."[86] That meant that the captive human will is trapped in the total warfare between God and Satan. It allowed no middle ground, Luther insisted. If Erasmus imagined that some "willing in the absolute sense, without reference either to good or evil" exists, "a kind of willing which, while it cannot indeed turn toward the good without grace, yet even without grace does not forthwith will only evil, but is a willing pure and simple, which by grace can be turned upward to the good, by sin downward to evil," he was mistaken, "for the power of applying itself to salvation cannot be a merely abstract willing . . . since desire must strive and endeavor in some direction." Luther concluded that it is "a mere dialectical fiction that there is in the human creature a neutral and unqualified willing." Such abstractions transform the discussion into a philosophical inquiry into the nature of humanity. Luther was dealing pastorally with the problems and pains of real life. Into that picture no abstract will could fit. Luther's world dealt with the reality of willing and willing badly. Kirchner deemed this point an important reinforcement and clarification of Luther's position, a necessary element in fostering the life of repentance.[87]

Kirchner and others (such as Flacius) understood that there can be no neutral or middle position between God and Satan. One or the other is in charge of human lives, and when one is absent the other is present. Flacius argued, with Luther's words, "Neither God nor Satan permits sheer unqualified willing in us, but as you [Erasmus] have rightly said, having lost our liberty, we are forced to serve sin, that is, we desire sin and evil, we speak sin and evil, we do sin and evil."[88] Flacius pursued the matter of "compulsion" to sin which Strigel had criticized in their disputation further by repeating Luther's address of Erasmus: "Indeed, you say . . . that the human will since the Fall is so depraved that having lost its liberty, it is compelled to serve sin and cannot restore itself to any better result. . . . You make out that the Pelagians were of this opinion. I think Proteus [Erasmus] has now no way of escape here; he is caught and held fast by the plain statement that the will, having lost its liberty, is compelled and held captive to sin. What an exquisitely free choice, which has lost its liberty and is called by Erasmus himself a slave of sin!"[89]

Flacius proceeded to the conclusion that this means that the sinner has become the image of Satan, a term he had lifted from Luther's Genesis commentary.[90] Kirchner rejected Flacius's use of the term "image of Satan," but he agreed with his appraisal of the reality of the rule and activity of Satan: it confirms the bondage of the will, he said, citing Luther's observation that because God and the devil are not mere observers of human life, watching from far away, but rather deeply involved in daily life, and in conflict with each other on the field of human life, the human being experiences the bondage of the will.[91] Luther's metaphor of the beast of burden demonstrated this observation as well.[92] Herbst also described the human creature before conversion as a captive in the devil's kingdom and cited *De servo arbitrio*, among other passages, to describe what that meant.

Scripture represents the human creature as one who is not only bound, wretched, captive, sick, and dead, but in addition to his other miseries is afflicted, through the agency of Satan his prince, with this misery of blindness, so that he believes himself to be free, happy, unfettered, able, well and alive. For Satan knows that if people were aware of their misery, he would not be able to retain a single one of them in his kingdom because God could not but at once pity and aid them in the wretchedness which they recognize and therefore cry for help. For God is extolled highly throughout Scripture as being near to the contrite in heart, as Christ declares regarding himself according to Isaiah 61, that he has been sent to preach the gospel to the poor and to bind up the brokenhearted. Accordingly, it is Satan's work to prevent people from recognizing their plight and to keep them presuming that they can do everything they are told.[93]

The Jena faculty concluded with Luther simply that "free choice is nothing but a slave of sin, death, and Satan, not doing and not capable of doing or attempting to do anything but evil."[94]

Although Satan appeared in these writings as the one who imprisons and tyrannizes helpless sinners, that portrayal of the archenemy of believers is not so prominent in the period after Luther's death as it had been for the reformer in *De servo arbitrio*. That was not because in general an eschatological framework had disappeared from Wittenberg thinking. On the contrary![95] But in a discussion in which the responsibility of sinners for their defiance of God commanded attention, images of being imprisoned or being ridden were potentially confusing. The reformer himself had recognized that, and often depicted the human dilemma not only in terms of captivity to Satan but also as the result of the breakdown of trust in God, that is, original sin. His disciples repeated this judgment. All people were included under sin and condemnation by Adam's transgression (Rom. 5:12), Kirchner wrote, and therefore, he avowed with a quotation from *De servo arbitrio*, "original sin itself leaves free choice with no capacity to do anything but sin and be damned."[96]

Furthermore, Luther had concluded that to affirm the freedom of the will meant to denigrate, demean, and depreciate the work of Christ and God's grace. In supporting his basic definition of original sin as the complete perversion and poisoning *(vergifftung)* of the human creature, Herbst cited Luther's closing words of *De servo arbitrio:* "In summary, if we believe that Christ has redeemed human creatures by his blood, we are bound to confess that the whole person has been lost; otherwise, we should make Christ either superfluous or the redeemer of only the lowest part of the human creature, which would be blasphemy and sacrilege."[97] Kirchner reminded readers that Luther regarded Paul's use of the universal terms "all," "none," "nowhere," "apart from" as proof that no human effort can contribute to salvation but that only God-given faith can restore the broken relationship between sinner and Creator. This demonstrated that the sinner cannot choose God but is bound to choose evil.[98] Wigand cited one of his generation's favorite passages from *De servo arbitrio:* Luther's contention that the argument that human choice can accomplish a little really proves that "free choice can do everything" (Wigand's rule 16).[99] He held the contrary position: "However many passages there are in the Divine Scriptures that speak of [God's] help, they all abolish free choice" (§33), and "the prophets include both actuality and potentiality [in passages speaking of human sin], and to say that one does not seek for God is the same as saying that he cannot seek for God" (§34).[100] Thus, Wigand paraphrased Luther, "The propagators of free choice deny in what they speak and write, but affirm in fact and in their hearts, that they are worse than the Pelagians on two counts" (§35), and "the propagators of free choice deny Christ" (§36).[101] With his colleagues in Jena Wigand asserted, in Luther's words, "What the grace of God does not do is not good. Hence it follows that free choice without the grace of God is not free at all, but immutably the captive and slave of evil since it cannot of itself turn to the good."[102]

Herbst turned several times to *De servo arbitrio,* among other works, to aver that sin has bound the human will so that it cannot turn to God. That many spurn the gospel "is due, of course, to the antipathy of free choice, which has no power while Satan rules over it but to spurn grace and the Spirit that fulfills the law."[103] Irenaeus used this passage to speak of the Holy Spirit's fashioning a new creature out of the sinner, who resembles clay in the Spirit's re-creative work.[104]

The Gnesio-Lutheran defenders of the bondage of choice repeated Luther's criticism of Erasmus's description of the will as a "faculty of applying itself to grace" *(facultas sese applicandi ad gratiam),* the phrase Melanchthon had also adopted in the later revisions of his *Loci.*[105] Gallus had initiated the critique of the Preceptor's representation of the will's powers,[106] and his comrades continued it by citing Luther's own rejection of Erasmus's use of the phrase.[107] No sooner had Luther died, Flacius asserted in his initial critique of Pfeffinger, than "the leader of the Adiaphorists" began to use this expression, which the reformer had rejected in *De servo arbitrio.*[108] In the Weimar Disputation Flacius explicitly rejected a Melanchthonian formulation regarding the freedom of the will at only one point in the debate. He mentioned that at the colloquy in Worms three years earlier Joachim Mörlin had repudiated the "false definition of free choice by Erasmus that was inserted [into Philipp's

Loci] after Luther's death, that 'free choice' meant the capability of turning oneself toward grace."[109] Luther had rejected this opinion in *De servo arbitrio*, Flacius rightly asserted, adding that when Tilemann Heshusius had lectured at Wittenberg on the *Loci communes* (at Melanchthon's instigation, in 1552-53), he had affirmed that "this definition is not correct."[110]

One of the most interesting cases of the rejection of this definition comes in an overview of Christian teaching gleaned from the works of both Melanchthon and Luther by Georg Walther, a deacon at Saint Ulrich's church in Halle. He had not become involved in the controversies of the time and tended to be favorable to Melanchthon. In formulating his locus on the will, he relied chiefly on Melanchthon but also selected quotations that assert the will's lack of capacity to turn itself to God; yet he did include Luther material as well, including Luther's warnings against Erasmus's teaching on the free will as the ability to apply itself to grace.[111]

Several of Luther's most pointed expressions found their way into the argument of his students as they defended his understanding of the bondage of the will. Both in his earlier tracts and in the Weimar Disputation Flacius cited Luther's assertion that the human creature is simply passive *(merē passivē)* in relationship to God because God alone gives human beings power to become his children (John 1:12).[112] The Jena faculty cited the same passage in its rejection of those who refused to speak of the purely passive stance of the sinner in conversion, as did Herbst.[113] Herbst also defended Luther's assertion that the will is purely passive with his comments on Paul's simile of the potter and the clay in Romans 9:19-24; the reformer commented that "the whole purpose of his epistle is to show that we can do nothing."[114]

Luther's disciples largely avoided his metaphor of the block of stone or wood as a description of the sinner in the process of conversion, an expression he had not taken in hand in his combat with Erasmus. Flacius did employ it frequently but not with reference to *De servo arbitrio;*[115] Herbst defended the propriety of the comparison with a citation from the work, equating it with Luther's description of the fallen will as "a captive, subject, and slave either of the will of God or the will of Satan."[116] Likewise, the reformer's image of the will as a beast of burden ridden either by God or Satan attracted little attention from his disciples, although Flacius found it helpful and defended it against Strigel in the Weimar Disputation.[117]

In their attempt to explain the paradox of the responsibility of God and the responsibility of his human creatures on the human side of the equation, the bondage of the will under sin and Satan played a critical role. These students of Luther had grasped the reasons why their mentor had confessed that the human will is bound by sin, even if they had avoided to a large extent his ideas regarding the natural limitations of creatures as creatures. Thus, they were able to capture his way of expressing what it means to be bound by sin. That prepared them to call for repentance and to deliver the forgiveness of sins.

All Things Happen by Necessity

In connection with the bondage of the sinner, Strigel had raised the issue of Luther's use of the concept of absolute necessity to defend the lordship of the Creator and his total responsibility for all things. Strigel forthrightly called it a "horrid way of speaking,"[118] but he also maintained that Luther's comments on the will demonstrated that the reformer had not meant that everything happens by an absolute necessity which invalidates all human activity and responsibility. He summarized a passage from *De servo arbitrio* to prove his point: "We cannot will anything but what [the god of this world] wills. . . . And this we do readily and willingly, according to the nature of the will, which would not be a will if it were compelled; for compulsion is (so to say) 'no will.'"[119] Flacius made an effort to explain Luther's concept of necessity to Strigel, who, Flacius was sure, misunderstood and misinterpreted it. In reaction to Strigel's accusation that he, Flacius, was advocating a Stoic and Manichaean view, based upon his teaching regarding necessity, Flacius repeated Luther's distinction of the necessity of coercion and the necessity of immutability. Strigel told Flacius that what he meant was *necessitas consequentiae,* and Flacius told him he was not going to use dialectical distinctions that are open to a variety of interpretations. Strigel stated that Luther's opinion that "all things happen by necessity" was open to misinterpretation as an assertion that God is responsible for evil. Flacius accused him of exaggerating what Luther had said, since the reformer had insisted that God remains good as the governor of all things, reminding his hearers of Luther's use of the metaphor of a good artisan making use of a bad tool. The exchange continued over the propriety of Strigel's use of dialectic, with Flacius citing Luther's comment that it is miserable when dialectic is used to judge ecclesiastical matters. Flacius's indignation echoes throughout the debate, up to the conclusion of his case with its affirmation that the concept of "necessity" describes and clarifies the human experience of God's will but imposes no limit or condition on God.[120] This exchange illustrates the difficulty of breaking through presupposition and prejudice to a satisfactory explanation.

In the years following the disputation some prominent followers of Luther and Melanchthon would publicly repudiate this teaching regarding necessity: David Chytraeus had no scruples about identifying Luther as an advocate of this terminology, while Nikolaus Selnecker attached no name to the idea he rejected.[121] In an unpublished manuscript of 1561, Martin Chemnitz excused Luther from his formulation of a doctrine of absolute divine necessity in *De servo arbitrio* by quoting the reformer's own warning to his students in his Genesis lectures that they should not misunderstand his words about absolute, immutable necessity but should instead look to the revealed God in the means of grace for an address to questions regarding the free will and God's election of his own.[122] The electoral Saxon *Final Report* did the same.[123] His students tried to read Luther in the full context of his life and work, and they turned in this case to his later point of view, his mature reflection on an earlier expression of his theology.

Still others had no hesitation to acknowledge or even repeat Luther's argument from necessity. Nikolaus Gallus simply rejected the claim that Luther's words on necessity in *De servo arbitrio* should be interpreted in a manner that would make them deterministic and thus deny human responsibility. Luther himself had rejected that accusation, Gallus wrote.[124] Wigand captured Luther's approach quite competently in his treatment of Erasmus's use of Origen to get God off the hook with a theory of his permissive will. According to Wigand, God "hardens Pharaoh when he presents to his ungodly and evil will a word and work which that will hates — owing of course to its inborn defect and natural corruption. And since God does not change it inwardly by his Spirit . . . , the result is that Pharaoh is puffed up and exalted by his own imagined greatness . . . and is thus hardened and then more and more provoked and exasperated the more Moses presses and threatens him."[125] Wigand used Luther's words to emphasize Pharaoh's responsibility while at the same time affirming God's responsibility for changing hearts. To this citation Wigand added Luther's judgment, "You see here that Pharaoh is hardened precisely in order that he may resist God and delay his redemption, so that occasion may be given for many signs and for a declaration of the power of God."[126] Wigand concluded, "Why God does not change evil wills is a matter of the mystery of his majesty, where his judgments are incomprehensible."[127] Wigand recognized that Luther's approach to questions of God's unconditioned choice of his elect and the freedom or bondage of the human will's exercise of choice in spiritual matters remained a mystery, coupled with the paradox of full divine and complete human responsibility. Kirchner, too, did not hesitate to present and defend Luther's use of his own particular concept of necessity. It was part of the initial, foundational definition of the (lack of) freedom of the will. The reformer had posited three possible positions regarding human choice: first, that the human being cannot will anything good but does retain a desire to do good — even though that desire does not really belong to the person who has it; second, that free choice can accomplish nothing that is not sinful, Augustine's position; and third, that "free choice is an empty name and all that we do comes about by sheer necessity." Kirchner must have thought discretion in order here; he omitted Luther's own identification of the third alternative as that "of Wyclif and Luther."[128] Luther equated the last two and then demonstrated how the first, which Erasmus was trying to defend so that he not be placed among the Pelagians, did not essentially differ from the other two. All that this kind of argumentation produces are "verbal monstrosities," an "abuse of language."[129]

Kirchner returned to the topic of necessity when discussing the "final cause" or purpose of the topic on the bondage of choice. There, too, he did not shy away from letting Luther speak from his own pages on the "necessity of immutability." Luther insisted that he rejected an explanation of sin that posited any kind of coercion, Kirchner demonstrated. Sinners' readiness or will to act cannot be set aside, restrained, or changed by their own powers, but "keeps on willing and being ready; and even if compelled by external force to do something different, the will remains averse and is resentful against whatever compels or resists it." This is the necessity of immutability:

> the will cannot change itself and turn in a different direction but is rather the more provoked into willing by being resisted, as its resentment shows. . . . By contrast, if God works in us, the will is changed, and being gently breathed upon by the Spirit of God, it again wills and acts from pure willingness and inclination and of its own accord, not from compulsion, so that it cannot be turned another way by any opposition, nor be overcome or compelled even by the gates of hell, but it goes on willing and delighting in and loving the good, just as before it willed and delighted in and loved evil.

The passage continues with Luther's analogy of the beast of burden being ridden by God or Satan,[130] a passage cited by Herbst[131] and the Jena professors as well.[132] Kirchner added Luther's interpretation of Jeremiah 10:23, "I know, O Lord, that the way of the human being is not in himself; that it is not in anyone to walk and direct his own steps," to his discussion of free choice. Erasmus had granted that God controls all things according to this passage, and Luther had highlighted this contradiction in his opponent's position in order to reiterate that all human life (matters temporal, for which the human creature has been given governance, as well as matters spiritual) lay in God's hands under an inalterable necessity. Again, the editor cut his citation short just before Luther placed his position in the company of Wycliffe's view of necessity.[133]

Strigel, Selnecker, Chemnitz, and Chytraeus repudiated Luther's view of necessity in *De servo arbitrio* in the 1560s. Not all their contemporaries were so disposed, even though all recognized a certain difficulty in the concept. But even Gallus, Wigand, and Kirchner strove to make clear that neither Luther nor they fell into a deterministic view that did not take into account the person of the Creator and his personal love for his human creatures. Nonetheless, it is clear that Luther's experiment with the scholastic terminology of necessity was an experiment that failed.

Human Beings Are Totally Responsible Agents

If on the one hand Luther had secured his convictions regarding God's total and sovereign responsibility for everything in his creation, he did not on the other hand ignore human responsibility, even in his defense of the bondage of the will. Herbst instructed his readers regarding the proper interpretation of the claims made for the human will by the ancient fathers of the church. Luther affirmed that the Holy Spirit works with human creatures who think and will, for human beings were so created by their Maker, just as he created plants and animals with their own natures. "If we define the power of free choice to be that by which a person is capable of being taken hold of by the Spirit and imbued with God's grace, as a creature made for eternal life or death, that is a correct definition. For we grant this power or aptitude, or as the Sophists say, this disposing quality or passive aptitude, and who does not know that it is not found in trees or animals? For heaven, as the saying goes, 'heaven was not made for geese.'"[134]

But the Gnesio-Lutherans tended to take this point for granted, as Gallus had pointed out.[135] Viktorin Strigel, however, focused precisely on this point in his debate with Flacius and made effective use of Luther's affirmation that the human will functions and must function if human beings are to remain human beings. The Gnesio-Lutheran authors tended to include Luther's affirmation that the will is active — even though bound in its inability to choose God — within a larger passage regarding necessity and the activity of the will. In connection with the discussion of the ancient phrase "God draws, but he draws the willing," Christoph Irenaeus commented, "God draws those to whom he gives [the ability] to will."[136] Kirchner, Herbst, and the Jena theologians cited the words upon which Strigel had focused at Weimar: "We cannot will anything but what [the god of this world] wills. . . . And this we do readily and willingly, according to the nature of the will, which would not be a will if it were compelled; for compulsion is (so to say) 'no will.'"[137] These Gnesio-Lutherans did not wish to sacrifice the reformer's view of human responsibility in any way, even if in the midst of controversy it was not their major concern.

All disciples of Luther and Melanchthon agreed that a deep-seated corruption had permeated the human creature through the fall into sin. This conviction pervaded the writings of all involved in the synergistic controversy and expressed itself in their assessment of the will. For in their writings, as noted above, they did not often ascribe the bondage of the will to the creaturely nature of humanity, as Luther did in part, but rather followed him in focusing on the ravages of sin and the power of Satan. Flacius referred to *De servo arbitrio* without a specific citation or reference in defining "bound choice" in his *Key to the Sacred Scriptures.* There he recalled that Luther had equated the sin that governs the fallen human creature with Satan as the rider of a horse [*sic*].[138] Early in the synergistic controversy Flacius turned to Luther's language regarding the transformation of the fallen human creature from God's image to the image of the devil, referring the reader to *De servo arbitrio* even though the reformer had not used the term there but rather in his Genesis lectures.[139] In 1559 the characterization of the sinner as being in "Satan's image" meant, for Flacius, that "even though the free will could be used in a limited way in external, earthly matters, in spiritual matters, whatever it undertakes — going to church, hearing and reading God's Word, leading an upright life, wanting to serve God — is nothing but outward show and hypocrisy, for none of it takes place with a heartfelt desire, out of true fear and love of God."[140] Flacius distinguished the question of the integrity of human functioning as creature from the Creator's control of salvation.

Throughout their writings the Gnesio-Lutheran critics of Strigel and Pfeffinger insisted on the obligations of new obedience. They strove to make clear to hearers and readers that God had created human beings to function responsibly according to his divine definition of what it means to be human. Like Luther, when engaged in the defense of God's total responsibility for all things, they expressed his sovereign control of his creation with an emphasis on the bondage of the will. That did not mean that they wished to sacrifice their avowal of the integrity of the human creature and of the active nature of the human will in the midst of its captivity to Satan. They sought to proclaim both law and gospel and hold them in tension.

Believers Live a Life of Repentance

Christ's redemption, however, has freed the sinner from this captivity. Nonetheless, Luther recognized, believers spend their lives battling the devil, the world, and their own desires to live life apart from God. In fact, this was his "Achillean argument" against the freedom of the will: that those who have been brought to faith in Christ still have to struggle against their own sinful impulses and are powerless to overcome them without the Holy Spirit. This passage from *De servo arbitrio* was often repeated by the reformer's followers.[141] The mystery of the continuation of evil in the lives of God's faithful people could not be solved. It could only be taken into account, and that through the life of daily repentance.

On the basis of *De servo arbitrio,* Nikolaus Gallus rejected the idea that the free will apart from God's aid has any power to repent and practice the Christian life, even as he acknowledged the necessity of this life of repentance and obedience.[142] Such a recognition permeated the preaching and teaching of Gallus and his contemporaries. They had indeed grasped that God repeats and renews the baptismal death and resurrection he had given sinners throughout life because, for some mysterious and hidden reason, believers still must struggle against their own sinfulness. That struggle found treatment in proclamation and writings of all sorts in the late Reformation without being connected specifically to *De servo arbitrio.* Like Luther, they believed that God had bound his human creatures to trust and the obedience it produces in his shaping of their humanity. They proclaimed Christ's liberation from the bondage to sin and Satan into which these human creatures had fallen. They sought to cultivate a life of love, that is, true human freedom, by binding their hearers once again to God's promise in Christ.

God Is Not Responsible for Evil

The students of Luther and Melanchthon had all learned from the latter that they must take care not to suggest to either papalist adversaries or hearers in their parishes that God is responsible for evil. They had no trouble repeating that axiom, but most of them avoided the deeper questions of the mystery of the existence of evil that the acknowledgment of the bondage of the will poses. Wigand avoided all details in affirming as the last of his rules gleaned from *De servo arbitrio* (§37): "God is righteous even when he seems to us to be unjust."[143] Chemnitz's summary of the controversy over free choice was largely dedicated to affirming that "God is not the author of the cause of sin. . . . God did not create sin in the beginning, and he does not now will sin. He does not approve it. He does not support it. He does not effect it. He does not drive anyone into sinning." Luther's comments on Genesis 17 supported his caveat against any suggestion that God is responsible for evil.[144] Herbst quoted from Luther's explication of the hardening of Pharaoh's heart to demonstrate that his position did not lead to the conclusion that God is a cause of sin. "Although God does not make sin, yet he does not cease to fashion and multiply the nature that has been vitiated by sin through the withdrawal of the Spirit, as a wood-carver might make statues out of rotten wood. Thus as is human nature, so are human creatures made; God creates and fashions them out of the nature they have."[145] Herbst continued the citation of the section some lines later: "Since, then, God moves and actuates all in all, he necessarily moves and acts also in Satan and ungodly people. But he acts in them as they are and as he finds them; that is to say, since they are hostile to him and evil, and caught up in the movement of this divine omnipotence, they do nothing but hostile and evil things."[146] Likewise, Herbst met the apprehension of Melanchthon and his followers that God could be seen as a "respecter of persons" (Acts 10:34) with the rejoinder, "only blind reasoning regards God as unjust; he alone is just at every time."

Luther regarded it as inevitable that eventually human reason would have to acknowledge the absurdity of every solution it invents to the problem of God's free choice and the bondage of human choice.[147] Herbst let Luther continue his argument with a subsequent passage from *De servo arbitrio:* "it gives the greatest possible offense to common sense or natural reason that God by his own sheer will should abandon, harden, and damn people as if he enjoyed the sins and the unending, eternal torments of his wretched creatures, when he is preached as a God of such great mercy and goodness, etc." For this reason theologians had invented distinctions between the ordained and absolute will of God, between the necessity of consequence and the necessity of the consequent, as the reformer recalled from his own scholastic training. "Nothing has been achieved by these distinctions except that the ignorant have been imposed upon by empty talk. . . . Nevertheless, there has always remained deeply implanted in the hearts of ignorant and learned alike, whenever they have taken things seriously, the painful awareness that we are under necessity if the foreknowledge and omnipotence of God are accepted. Even natural reason herself, who is offended by this necessity and makes such efforts to get rid of it, is compelled to admit it by the force of her own judgment, even if there were no Scripture at all."[148]

This refusal to delve more deeply into the question later labeled "theodicy" reveals that at least some of Luther's and Melanchthon's students and followers comprehended Luther's fundamental "answer" to the mystery of evil. Herbst continued, counseling his readers that they join Luther in bowing before the majesty of God, as he had done at the end of *De servo arbitrio* with his discussion of the difficulty of defending the mercy and justice of

God.[149] Kirchner met a similar "objection" to his position regarding the scandal of teaching the bondage of human choice with the same long citation that Herbst placed at the disposal of his readers. Luther had pointed Erasmus and his other readers away from the mystery of the perishing who are compelled by a necessity of nature (since all were children of wrath according to Paul in Eph. 2:3). He directed them instead to the mercy of God "toward those whom he justifies and saves, supremely unworthy as they are." God's ways are indeed "incomprehensible and inaccessible to human reason," and so believers must confess with Paul (Rom. 11:33) that his ways are unsearchable. Finally, Kirchner concluded with Luther that ultimate questions of human existence, regarding God's righteousness over against sinners, are incomprehensible in a fallen world.[150]

Wrestling with new ways of posing the questions that Luther had used to frame his call for reform, his students often put his words and works to use. Among the works they wove into their writings was *De servo arbitrio*. They captured aspects of its message in varying degrees. Luther's view of the bondage of the will under Satan's control and sin's hegemony shaped the fundamental concern of the Gnesio-Lutherans in the synergistic controversy. Luther's acknowledgment of the activity of the human will, even while it was held in bondage, was repeated, and sometimes perhaps taken for granted, by the Gnesio-Lutherans, while the Philippists reaffirmed it as they repeated Melanchthon's concern for defending the integrity of the human creature even in sin. Both groups emphasized that God's promise in the means of grace constitutes the only instrument by which the Holy Spirit effects saving faith and the foundation of the assurance of believers that they are children of God. The second and third generations of the Wittenberg circle did not however need *De servo arbitrio* to affirm their mentor's teaching on the promise and the means of grace. It was cited to support that view, but not frequently or decisively. Neither group formulated an active and explicit doctrine of predestination before 1567; in this regard they differed from neither Luther, in *De servo arbitrio* and most other writings, nor Melanchthon after 1521.

Perhaps the critical question regarding the reception and use of *De servo arbitrio* in the years following Luther's death centers on his view of the relationship between Creator and human creature. For Luther the mystery of that relationship led him, particularly in *De servo arbitrio*, from his recognition of his own inability to turn himself to God to his acknowledgment of his own total dependence as creature, not only as sinner, upon his Creator. With the exceptions of Timotheus Kirchner, Georg Herbst, and Johannes Wigand, his students did not capture and reiterate Luther's sense of creaturely dependence alongside their convictions regarding the ravages of human sinfulness.

Nor did most of them wrestle with the theodical question that Luther addressed at several points in his *De servo arbitrio* and employed as the final, definitive focus for the work in its conclusion. Precisely this tendency to avoid wrestling directly with the question of theodicy had prevented them from using the topic of God's election of his own to salvation. Nonetheless, it is clear that they continued to craft their message in the Wittenberg way. With different emphases and methods they were aiming at using the law's condemnation to produce repentance and the gospel's gift of new life to foster faith in Christ and the new obedience that flows from it.

CHAPTER V

"Pious Explanations of Necessity": Predestination as Problem in the Wittenberg Circle

Although Luther had found deep comfort for troubled consciences in God's unconditional and immutable choice of them as his children, he had not developed the topic of God's predestation of his chosen people in detail in his writings. It is present as a presupposition and on occasion addressed explicitly. Indeed, he could combine God's spiritual predestation with his temporal providence and paraphrase Paul's words "being set apart before I was born" (Gal. 1:15): "Every gift — whether great or small, whether physical or spiritual — that God intended to give me, and all the good things that I was ever to do at any time in all my life — all this God had predestined even before I was born, when I could not think, wish, or do anything good but was a shapeless embryo. Therefore this gift came to me by the mere predestination and merciful grant of God even before I was born."[1] More common were comments such as "the sophists engage in a debate about an election made according to God's purpose, but I have often warned that one must refrain from speculations about the uncovered Majesty. For just as they cannot possibly be true, so they are also useless for our salvation. Let us rather think about God in the manner in which he presents himself in the Word and in the sacraments."[2]

Many a modern reader who comes to the text of De servo arbitrio with the image of the work shaped by casual references in textbooks, biographies, and even monographic studies is astonished to find that the book contains no detailed treatment of God's gracious election of those he planned to bring to faith through his promise in Christ. The work certainly does overflow with Luther's dogged avowal of God's total responsibility for all things, and particularly for the salvation of his people, but the reformer focused on expressing that idea by asserting, on the divine side, that God's creative will is certain because his willing creates an inalterable necessity for his decisions, also his decision to save the elect, and on the human side by affirming the human will's inability to choose God over Satan. Others of his works contain traces of the doctrine of election, although Luther generally connected God's planning the salvation of individual believers before the foundation of the world closely with the delivery of God's promise through his Word, in oral, written, and sacramental forms. To be sure, Luther and Melanchthon reveal different accents in their teaching of this topic. But they fully shared a deep and abiding concern about the despair that a false use of the thought of predestination could bring, even if Melanchthon's horror of "Stoicism" was more vigorously and frequently expressed.

It is therefore not surprising that the students of Luther and Melanchthon avoided the teaching to a large extent in their expositions of the gospel. When they first turned special attention to the subject, they often did so with special caution, above all distancing themselves from a doctrine of double predestination. Melanchthon's reaction against Calvin's teaching on predestination in the 1540s seems to have haunted them. Since the outline of his *Loci communes* compelled those who formulated their own replications of that textbook to treat the topic, it does appear in that genre in the late Reformation. Not until 1567, however, with the appearance of Cyriakus Spangenberg's *Seven Sermons on Predestination,* did the topic receive positive treatment on the public agenda of teaching within the Wittenberg circle. He brought the topic to the public with an appeal to Luther's *De servo arbitrio,* but that helped little; his sermons evoked sharp criticism from the "synergists" of electoral Saxony. Their disagreement stands behind the treatment of the teaching of election in article XI of the Formula of Concord.

Initial Treatments of Predestination

The Topic in Loci communes

As was the case with the failure of Wittenberg students to use the exegetical insights of *De servo arbitrio* in interpretations of passages related to the freedom or bondage of the will,[3] so its use in passages relating to the election of the children of God was negligible.[4] Nor did Luther's great work find a place in dogmatic discussions of the topic of election. Melanchthon himself had firmly fixed the place of the topic "on predestination" among the *loci communes,* even if he found it necessary over the course of the years to reframe his presentation of God's providential governing in his exercise of his will to save sinners.[5] Thus, those who composed similar textbooks treated it as well. When Johannes Wigand and his colleague Matthaeus Judex constructed their summary of biblical theology for the first century of their history of the church, the so-called Magdeburg Centuries, published separately as the *Syntagma or Corpus doctrinae of Christ, Assembled from the Entire New Testament,* in 1559, they provided readers with a collage of passages from the New Testament on predestination in a comparatively brief locus.[6] The Old Testament offered more material when they produced a similar summary of its theology as an independent work five years later.[7]

Their introduction to the topic surveyed the biblical vocabulary in the typical fashion the two authors had learned from Melanchthon, assembling a half-dozen synonyms for God's act of choosing his own. The decree of God, issued in his secret counsel before the foundation of the world, they asserted, was grounded in Jesus Christ and his obedience, passion, death, and resurrection (above all, an exposition of Eph. 1:3-14). This decree sets forth his will that through the hearing of the Word human hearts be converted to faith in Christ. This faith produces sanctified living in incipient new obedience that produces the fruits of righteousness. This faith also leads to persecution of the faithful on earth and to their final liberation at Christ's return. Wigand and Judex specifically refused to answer the question they posed: Why are some saved and not others? They insisted on remaining focused on and faithful to the revealed Word of God alone.[8] As good students of both their mentors, they affirmed that God's promise in Christ applies to all people.[9] Wigand and Judex did not turn to *De servo arbitrio;* they were inventing a new genre in their fashioning such a summary of the thought of the biblical authors, and they employed their writings alone. They did reflect Luther's chief concerns in that work, but did so without a doctrine of absolute necessity — though with a strong emphasis on God's total responsibility for salvation and with reference as well to human contrition. The elements of Wittenberg theology that Cyriakus Spangenberg and Martin Chemnitz would later employ to construct a doctrine of election were present in Wigand and Judex's exposition of the biblical material. But this topic in their *Syntagma* won neither critique nor praise at the time it was published.

Timotheus Kirchner used Melanchthon's loci form to organize Luther texts into a presentation of the reformer's thought. Although Kirchner had written his Latin locus on "free choice" largely out of citations from *De servo arbitrio,* he ignored the work as he constructed his topic on "predestination" in his *Thesaurus* of Luther's thought, organized by topics.[10] Georg Walther, deacon in Halle, in contrast, did use the reformer's comments from his rejection of Erasmus in constructing his treatment of predestination in his similar

collection of citations from Luther and Melanchthon. He defined predestination *(Versehung)* as God's election *(Erwelung)*. His discussion of the subject
relied heavily on Melanchthon's commentary on Romans of 1540 and his *Loci
communes,* but employed treatises by Luther as well, including *De servo
arbitrio.* After proffering biblical references, he began his treatment by citing
Luther's argument that believers must know that God's predestination is intended only for their comfort.[11] He distinguished God's secret predestination, which he did not discuss, from God's revealed predestination, which he
defined with the aid of Luther's admonition to turn to the revealed Word of
God, for it demonstrates and delivers his mercy in Christ.[12] Regarding the
purpose of God's predestination, Walther again turned to Luther as well as
Scripture to demonstrate that the doctrine is designed and given for the comfort of believers.[13]

"On Predestination" had occupied a place in Melanchthon's original
Loci communes of 1521 because the concept performed an important function
in securing the gospel for the Wittenberg theologians at the time. As
Melanchthon fell under attack from Roman Catholic theologians because of
his and Luther's alleged Stoic determinism, he shifted the position of the
topic and treated it differently than he had at the beginning of his career. His
students who continued to treat the topic in their *Loci communes* filled it with
its gospel content, as Luther and Melanchthon had taught them. But none of
them made the topic into a critical locus.

Marbach versus Zanchi

John Calvin had provoked Melanchthon's apprehensions regarding the teaching of a predestination to damnation. However, it was not Calvin himself but
a faithful disciple of the Genevan reformer, Hieronymus Zanchi, who trig-
gered the first public discussion of predestination in the Lutheran churches.
An Italian exile who had found in Calvin's exposition of the gospel his new
life, Zanchi reluctantly challenged the Lutheran approach to teaching God's
eternal plan to save his people.

Zanchi had fled Italy in the footsteps of his mentor, Peter Martyr
Vermigli, after his reading had brought him to Calvinism. Thomist in orientation and training, Zanchi had left his native Alzano for the Augustinian
monastery in Bergamo and then went on to Lucca. His abbot there, Vermigli,
had him read not only Aristotle and Aquinas but also Luther and
Melanchthon, the reformer of Strasbourg Martin Bucer, and Calvin. Richard
Muller sees "a strong voluntaristic as opposed to an intellectualistic, an

Augustian [*sic*], perhaps Scotist rather than a Thomist leaning"[14] in his development of his doctrine of predestination; in other words, he was a somewhat creative user of the rich traditions that lay at his disposal. In 1552, at age thirty-six, with the Inquisition at his heels, Zanchi fled to Geneva, studied under Calvin, and the next year followed his former abbot to Strasbourg, assuming Vermigli's position in the Strasbourg Academy when the older man left for Oxford. After a stormy ten years in Strasbourg and a brief pastorate in Switzerland, Zanchi settled into the service of the Reformed establishment in the Palatinate, teaching at Heidelberg and then Neustadt an der Haardt until his death more than a quarter-century later. He must be counted as one of the foremost theologians of incipient Calvinist orthodoxy.[15]

He came to Strasbourg after imperial pressure had forced the city's leading reformer, Martin Bucer, to move to England (in 1549), and after death had removed others in the Reformation's first generation of leaders, including Wolfgang Capito, Caspar Hedio, and Matthias Zell. Bucer's successor at the head of the city's churches was Johann Marbach, who came as a student to Wittenberg from Strasbourg's academy in 1536, sent there by the Strasbourg ministerium in the days when the Wittenberg Concord of that year was drawing the theologians of the two towns closer together. Marbach returned to the city in 1546 after serving in several other places. While in Wittenberg he had become a devoted adherent of Melanchthon, who composed the theses for his doctoral promotion; he also learned to revere Luther. The elder reformer had presided at his doctoral disputation in 1543.[16] After Bucer's departure from Strasbourg, Marbach slowly but deliberately carried out a "second Reformation" of the city's ecclesiastical life that Bucer had positioned between the plan for reform of his friends in Wittenberg and that of his friends in Geneva and German Switzerland. Marbach's "Lutheranizing" of the public teaching and the political policies of Strasbourg involved no little conflict, above all between him and the longtime head of the Strasbourg Academy, Johannes Sturm. The municipal government kept a firm hand on the church and school system of the city as well, and played a considerable role in the maneuvering between the forces loyal to Sturm with his own vision of the Bucerian Reformation and the growing number of Lutheran pastors gathered around Marbach.[17] Zanchi's nuanced and somewhat detached, if not outright aloof, appraisal of Luther had aroused Marbach's uneasiness upon the new instructor's arrival at the academy in 1553, even though Zanchi cited Luther in his own defense on the teaching of predestination. The relationship between the pastor and the professor did not improve over the subsequent eight years, as Zanchi's commitment to Calvin's teaching on the Lord's Supper and also his particular doctrine of predestination and reprobation became clear.[18] When the nearby Palatinate began drifting toward Calvinism after the accession of Elector Friedrich III in 1559, the context of the struggle with Calvinist thought became more charged, for it involved new political realities alongside the theological issues. Marbach's acquaintance Tilemann Heshusius was dismissed from his leadership posts in the Palatine church and at the University of Heidelberg, chiefly over his defense of the true presence of Christ's body and blood in the Lord's Supper. But Heshusius had also criticized the doctrine of double predestination that accompanied a denial of that presence in Genevan theology.[19]

In fact, Zanchi had a warm appreciation for Luther's exposition of God's sovereign control of all things including salvation in *De servo arbitrio*. His study in Geneva had convinced him of the verity of Bucer's conviction, "Christians ought to believe that they are predestined, for otherwise they cannot believe that they are justified."[20] Zanchi had no problem with Luther's views of necessity, as formulated in 1525. He embraced them and quoted Luther in his teaching, distinguishing coercive necessity from immutable necessity on the basis of the Wittenberg professor. He further cited Luther's preface to Romans and his commentary on Genesis 26 to explain his own soteriological view of necessity.[21] He sought help from Calvin because he assumed that in the Genevan's correspondence with Melanchthon he must have remonstrated with his friend in Wittenberg regarding the latter's apostasy from his original position on predestination and the free will.[22]

Although he later formulated his understanding of predestination in a much fuller form, Zanchi already knew what he believed regarding the choice God made in determining his elect in and through Christ.[23] With Thomist principles of theological argument and without a sense of Marbach's insistence that God works through the means of grace within the distinction of his condemning work and his saving work — law and gospel — Zanchi's mind was unable to meet Marbach's. Without Zanchi's concern to resolve the tensions of divine and human responsibility on the divine side, where they must ultimately lie, according to his way of thinking, Marbach's mind could not meet Zanchi's.

Marbach was, of course, fully committed to his own understanding of Luther as well. He placed Luther's affirmations regarding God's lordship over his world and his total responsibility for the salvation of sinners in the context of two important pillars of Wittenberg theology that he had absorbed from both Luther and Melanchthon.[24] First, he understood that law and gospel must be held in perpetual tension and properly applied to the situation of specific hearers; that meant that he found Zanchi's exposition of Luther lacking in the understanding of life in the midst of sin that he had learned from the reformer. (James Kittelson observes that he had learned his abiding concern for the proper pastoral care of his people not only in Wittenberg but also from his Strasbourg mentor, Bucer.)[25] Second, Marbach believed that the oral, written, and sacramental forms of the Word of God are God's means of grace, his instruments for accomplishing his task of re-creating sinners, and as God's own tools they deliver God's saving promise to his people. Believers dare not seek God's plan apart from his revelation of it in the promise actually delivered and effected in proclamation and the sacraments.[26] His lectures on the Gospel according to John in 1546 had used Luther's distinction of the hidden God and the revealed God to direct the believer's trust to the means of grace.[27] When Zanchi insisted on anchoring Christian knowledge in the "a priori" of God's plan before the foundation of the world itself, Marbach saw that as an invitation, or condemnation, to despair. He contended that election must be known only from the "a posteriori" of God's promise in the Word.[28]

The antagonism between Marbach and Zanchi, with its roots in their personal relationship, their theological views, and their institutional commitments to the Company of Pastors or to the academy respectively, came to a head in early 1563. The municipal government decided to call in a commission of theologians and political counselors from outside the city to resolve the conflict. The theologians represented the Palatinate duchy of Zweibrücken (Cunmann Flinsbach), the duchy of Württemberg (Jakob Andreae), and the city of Basel (Simon Sultzer and Ulrich Coccius); the secular advisers included Wolfgang von Köteritz of Zweibrücken, who, like Andreae and Sultzer, had corresponded frequently with Marbach. It was clear for all to see who the city fathers wanted to win.[29]

The theologians composed a "Consensus among the Theologians and Professors in Church and School at Strasbourg," dated March 18, 1563. Flinsbach, who like Marbach had studied in Strasbourg and Wittenberg, probably drafted the section on predestination, with input from the others. He had come to Strasbourg from his native Bergzabern for his secondary education, and proceeded from there to Wittenberg in the spring of 1546. He had studied under Melanchthon and won his master's degree in 1548. In 1551 he assumed office in Zweibrücken, in the Palatinate, and soon became superintendent of the church there.[30]

The Consensus that was designed to reconcile Zanchi and Marbach stated briefly that the city's teaching on the Lord's Supper conformed to the Augsburg Confession presented to the emperor in 1530.[31] In addition, it embraced the Wittenberg Concord of 1536, in which Luther and Bucer had enunciated a common expression of the doctrine of the Lord's Supper.[32]

The document's treatment of predestination began on a note of pastoral concern, with Romans 15:4: "For whatever was written was written for our instruction, so that by steadfastness and by the consolation of the Scriptures we might have hope." That meant, according to the Consensus, that the purpose and goal of all teaching dare not conflict with the apostolic teaching on repentance and dare not deprive troubled consciences of their consolation and hope. With this passage the pastoral concern of Marbach and Flinsbach laid down the fundamental hermeneutical direction of the statement. It was to exposit biblical truth for the sake of God's people, applying God's Word to their lives through the distinction of the law that works repentance and the gospel that consoles and bestows hope. This was the way they had learned to practice theology at Wittenberg.

The document proceeds with the confession that God knows all things eternally (Ps. 139), including the predestination of the elect (Rom. 8 and 9; Eph. 1). However, this teaching is "an abyss and apart from Christ leads people astray and casts them into the void, unless it is sought in Christ, for God chose us in Christ before the foundations of the world were laid, Ephesians 1[:4]." Therefore, believers must contemplate predestination in such a way that they are turned to Christ (Matt. 11:25-30). The gospel of Jesus Christ reveals what God has decided in his eternal decree (John 3:16; 6:37-40). This means that God's promise excludes not a single sinner. For God has said, "As I live, I do not desire the death of the sinner. Be turned, and repent from all your sins, and your evildoing will not be your ruin, Ezekiel 18 [:23, 30, 32]," and Christ invites all people to lay their burdens on him (Matt. 11:28). God gives faith freely, apart from human works and merit, so that sinners can receive the grace he promises in Christ (Phil. 1:29). Not all answer God's call, however. Why that is remains a secret beyond human reason's ability to investigate. The very contemplation of the question inspires fear and adoration (Rom. 11:33; Matt. 11:25). Because of this, afflicted consciences should not try to look to God's hidden will but to his will revealed in Christ. As a student in Wittenberg in 1542, Marbach may have actually heard Luther's lecture on Genesis 26, in which he warned against misunderstanding predestination. The Consensus reproduces quite precisely the reformer's reflections on God's choosing his own people from the mass of sinful humanity.

The document continues with its rehearsal of the concerns students heard expressed in Wittenberg while Flinsbach and Marbach studied there. First, God's permitting sin may not be interpreted as an indication that he wills sin. He hates sin; the devil, who does not remain in the truth, is sin's author (John 8:44-47). God forbids sin and reveals his wrath against it (Ps. 5:4-5). He reveals his goodness by putting evil to use in the service of his own purposes (Rom. 9:17; Exod. 9:16) and in his punishment of sin (Rom. 1:18). But in no way can God be said to be responsible for evil. Every evil opposes his will.

Therefore, none should consider themselves vessels of wrath (Rom. 9:22-24) but rather should listen to Paul when he urges, "All who cleanse themselves will become special utensils, dedicated and useful to the Lord, ready for every good work" (2 Tim. 2:21). This concern for the dominance of the gospel in considering God's choosing of his own is balanced in the Consensus by the insistence that believers should not deceive themselves into thinking that God's election gives a license to sin. Living according to the flesh brings death (Rom. 8:6; 1 Cor. 6:9-10; Gal. 5:19-21). The law must also continue to call sinners to repentance. For faith produces repentance and frees believers from the tyranny of sin.

Finally, the Consensus taught that the doctrine and discussion of predestination has two purposes or goals: to reject the idea that human powers or freedom of choice can play a role in the justification of sinners, as Augustine, Luther, and Bucer had clearly taught, and to give consciences the firm consolation of the gospel in their daily struggle against sin, based on the confidence that no one will tear Christ's sheep out of his hand (John 10:28). Thus, to avoid both the Pelagianism that places trust in human works and powers and an Epicureanism that looks to God's election as a license to sin, believers must look to God's revealed will, set forth in Christ. Without citing Luther but in agreement with his comments on Genesis 26, the document concludes by saying that this revealed will is not contrary to the hidden will but must be sought in Christ.[33]

Zanchi balked at subscribing to the Consensus, then gave in with a qualified subscription, thereafter attempted to publish his views in Basel and thus became embroiled in a legal hassle with the Strasbourg council, and finally left the city for Chiavenni, having accepted a call to be pastor of a congregation there.[34]

The challenge of the Calvinist Hieronymus Zanchi had elicited from Luther's and Melanchthon's students a formal statement on God's predestining of his own people for salvation. In the rather brief and simple statement prepared by the team of negotiators, the leader Cunmann Flinsbach, probably in consultation with Marbach, crafted a confession that repeated fundamental concerns expressed by their mentors in Wittenberg. God's total responsibility for salvation was clearly confessed, but the necessity of repentance, and thus of human responsibility — and through it the integrity of human creatures as God had made them — was also expressly maintained. Their approach was shaped by the desire to distinguish law and gospel, to preserve the call to Christians to repent because they remain in the struggle between sinful desires and the Holy Spirit, and at the same time to preserve the gospel that the doctrine of predestination offers without any use of it in the proclamation of the law. The Strasbourg Consensus insists, as had Melanchthon and Luther, that God is not the cause of evil in any way. It warns against using election as an excuse for sin, thus upholding the effective application of the law to sinners. It emphasizes the consolation of the gospel in Christ that is based on God's eternal plan and — more importantly, as is clear from the document — is revealed in Christ and the Word that delivers him to sinners. These alumni of the Leucorea were putting into practice the art of biblical application learned from their instructors.

Predestination as Problem in the Wittenberg Late Reformation

In the following two years the topic of predestination elicited critical examination from a parish pastor in Erfurt, Leonhardt Palhöfer, and two other theologians who would a decade later become authors of the Formula of Concord, David Chytraeus and Nikolaus Selnecker. Independent of one another and for different reasons, these three addressed pastoral problems connected with a doctrine of double predestination, the latter two without attending to the positive use of this teaching. Palhöfer had learned theology at the University of Erfurt, from the Gnesio-Lutheran ministerium that held lectures in the arts faculty there. The other two had studied at Wittenberg, Chytraeus from 1544 to 1550, Selnecker from 1549 to 1557. Both had enjoyed a particular measure of Melanchthon's favor. All three shared his concern that predestination could be misconstrued and found special occasions to treat the topic in 1564 and 1565, in the middle of the synergistic controversy but probably not primarily because of it.

Leonhardt Palhöfer's Rejection of Particular Predestination

Precisely what brought the Erfurt Gnesio-Lutheran pastor Leonhardt Palhöfer to compose two attacks on double predestinarian thinking in 1564 is not clear. Palhöfer was a close associate of the resolute defender of Luther's legacy in a radical, Gnesio-Lutheran form, the senior of the Erfurt ministerium, Andreas Poach. Since 1540 active as a servant of the church in the city, Palhöfer assumed the pastorate of the Preachers' (Dominican) church in 1556 and, with several of his pastoral colleagues, taught in the adjunct evangelical theological faculty at the city's university. According to his student Johannes Dinckel, who published his writings on predestination nearly thirty years later, Palhöfer had lodged the protest against the concept of "particular election," the idea that God had determined in his plan wrought before creation the specific individuals he would save on the basis of Christ's work. Palhöfer brought this protest, first voiced by his colleagues Poach and Georg Silberschlag, into written form in 1564, two years before his death. He did so to help their students at the university avoid the errors of thinking that God had predestined some to damnation and that Christ had not died for all.[35]

Palhöfer's unnamed opponent had taught that predestination *(Vorsehung)* should be understood as the election *(Erwelung)* of particular individuals to salvation. Without the model for the position that Spangenberg would develop three years later regarding God's choosing individual believers by name before the world's foundations, Palhöfer proceeded in somewhat awkward fashion to posit that predestination must be "universal"; that is, that God's election applies to all since his promises are universal. Concerns that individual believers not lose comfort through speculation about their own election drove the Erfurt pastor's concern.

Palhöfer first made clear that he rejected synergism.[36] To deny God's responsibility for predestination to salvation is a disparagement of his saving activity. Human creatures "have not elected or ordained that they receive eternal life on the basis of their own will, plan, powers, works, or worthiness. God has done that out of his free will, out of pure grace and mercy, in Christ Jesus, before the world was created" (22). He concluded that God is totally responsible for the salvation of sinners. He defined predestination as God's activity, his choosing of those who through faith in Christ come to eternal life. But he wished to clarify the matter of universal or particular predestination. Palhöfer's logic bound promise and predestination together in a manner that Spangenberg and Chemnitz later rejected. He insisted that if there is a predestination of particular individuals, then the promise of salvation in Christ cannot be universal. "This predestination of God is not particular in respect to God's will and mercy but rather universal. In respect to his foreknowledge and providence it is particular" (33). Therefore, he consistently and repeatedly rejected "particular predestination" while affirming God's general predestination.

Palhöfer knew that the question would be posed: Why do not all people who have God's Word believe? If God wants all to be saved, why do some have the ability to reject him? He adamantly maintained his opposition to searching for the hidden will of God apart from the Word and anchored the comfort of believers in the Word that comes through proclamation of the biblical message. Dependent alone on God's revealed Word, believers must simply hold to saying with Paul, "Faith comes by hearing, and hearing through the Word of God" (Rom. 10:17), that is, through the Holy Spirit's work in bringing them to faith (27-28, 34-45, 76-91). "Therefore, although all people are predestined by God in Christ to salvation, that not all are saved is not due to predestination but to the devil and human beings, to the devil in that he holds people back from God's Word or hinders faith in some other way, and to human beings, in that they have contempt for God's Word and do not hold to the activity of the Holy Spirit" (45). At some length Palhöfer developed his charge that the preachers of the Word and the hearers are equally at fault for unbelief (48-50). If the promise in Christ would be made unsure by teaching a particular predestination, the ministry of Word and sacrament would become useless, he argued (58-65). God does act apart from his revelation, and his actions are both wondrous and fearful. But believers cling only to the revelation of what God has planned, without speculation, sharply distinguishing what is hidden from what is revealed (68-79).

Luther agreed with his position, Palhöfer contended, quoting Poach's new edition of the *House Postil* and repeating short quotations from *De servo arbitrio* in both of the brief treatises in this book: "Satan knows that if people were aware of their misery, he would not be able to retain a single one of them in his kingdom because God could not but at once pity and aid them in their wretchedness."[37]

Leonhardt Palhöfer's opinions were not developed in a rigidly disciplined way, as were those of Selnecker, Chytraeus, Marbach, Flinsbach, Chemnitz, and Spangenberg. His ideas were entered into the public discussion thirty years after he wrote them, in the 1590s, perhaps in connection with the debate between Samuel Huber and Aegidius Hunnius in Wittenberg.[38] They do indicate how one pastor, apparently representing several of his brother pastors in Erfurt, attempted to sort out the problems associated with the doctrine of predestination in the Wittenberg circle of the time. He clearly rejected any contribution of the human will to conversion or salvation. He desired to make clear that God is not the cause of evil. He was particularly concerned to rest faith upon the means of grace, the public promise of salvation. Thus, he came to defend a universal predestination of all people. Distinguishing the hidden will of God, which governed such questions, from the revealed will that brought assurance of salvation to the faithful, he simply retreated before the question raised by the failure of God's Word to bring about the desired result, conversion, in some instances.

Nikolaus Selnecker's Rejection of
Predestination to Damnation

Nikolaus Selnecker's involvement in the public controversy over the freedom of the will had been minimal before he wrote his treatise *On Predestination* in 1565. After his completion of studies in Wittenberg in 1557, he served the government of Elector August of Saxony, always a part of the Philippist establishment there but always somewhat in tension with colleagues for a variety of reasons. When Duke Johann Friedrich the Middler needed help reconstituting his devastated theological faculty in Jena in 1565 after Viktorin Strigel's departure, he turned to his cousin, August, for aid. The elector sent Selnecker, along with two colleagues, Andreas Freyhub and Heinrich Salmuth, to rebuild the faculty. Selnecker remained in Jena as professor. Without doubt he supported the position enunciated in the Strigelian *Declaratio*. With the imprisonment of Johann Friedrich by Emperor Maximilian II in 1567 and the assumption of power by his brother, Johann Wilhelm, the Philippistic interlude in ducal Saxony came to an end. The younger brother restored Gnesio-Lutherans to the faculty, and Selnecker returned to Leipzig,[39] without having been drawn into the public debate over freedom of the will.

However, at the same time he assumed responsibilities in Jena, he did comment in print on predestination, the first Lutheran tract so entitled: his *Doctrina de praedestinatione*, a modest tract of ten quarto leaves. A little more than half the treatise contained a second essay, on the topic of fate.[40] Both parts are also found word for word as the only appendix to Selnecker's extensive treatment of the five chief parts of doctrine in Luther's catechism, his *Paedagogia christiana*, also first published in 1565.[41] The author did not explain what caused him to treat the subject in this tract itself, but a comment fourteen years later, in 1579 — a treatment of predestination in his textbook of Christian teaching, the *Institutio Christianae Religionis* — sheds light on his approach to the topic in 1565. There he recorded the suicide note of "the rector of a certain school" with the initials P. I., who had taken his own life on July 22, 1562, because of his despair, rooted in his conviction that God had predestined him to damnation. This "P. I." was identified as "Petrus Ilesuanus" in a contemporary report.[42]

Suicide haunted Selnecker's world, as it has most societies, as a particularly grievous sin, and it provoked sharp reactions from theologians. Taking one's own life, according to the Brandenburg ecclesiastical superintendent Andreas Celichius, contradicted the natural love implanted by God in human hearts; it broke the fifth commandment; it revealed instability, ingratitude, or an epicurean heart; it upset angels, ministers of the Word, and other Christians. It also insulted God by making him a "cruel tyrant," by denying his grace, and by regarding the gospel as impotent.[43] For Selnecker the case of P. I. was simply "blasphemia,"[44] because his belief that God could have predestined him to damnation denied God's grace and the gospel's power. Selnecker's treatment of predestination in his treatise of 1565 in fact aimed at repudiating misbelief of the sort expressed by P. I. Against this background Selnecker did not feel compelled in this case to assert God's sovereign power as had Luther in combating late medieval views of grace and works forty years earlier. He focused on God's promise to the faithful through the means of grace in order to give believers the comfort of God's grace.

It is particularly striking that this treatise on predestination lacks a discussion of predestination in any positive sense. God's act of choosing believers to be his children forever is not mentioned. The Bible passages which form the basis for Selnecker's later treatment of this teaching, such as Romans 8:28-39 and Ephesians 1:3-14, are ignored. Selnecker's first concern was to prevent misunderstanding of the doctrine which might lead to despair. He repeatedly emphasized the promise of the gospel without setting it in the eternal plan of God and without describing the unconditional nature of God's choice of believers to be members of his people. For he intended to reject the belief expressed by P. I. that God has planned the damnation of some people. Thus, he dedicated most of his brief tract to repudiating any suggestion that God could be responsible for evil and especially for the evil of damnation visited upon a human creature arbitrarily, apart from that person's sinfulness. In so doing he demonstrated that he was Melanchthon's disciple, for he repeated the central elements found in Melanchthon's revision of this topic in the third edition of his *Loci communes theologici,* following his mentor in responding to a false understanding of the doctrine as an occasion for fatalism and the despair it produces. In no way could God be responsible for sin or evil.

Selnecker began his little book with the citation of a poem which sets forth several principles that should guide the consideration of this teaching. These principles lay a foundation for his entire presentation, anchored in the gospel of Jesus Christ, rejecting any hint of the idea that God can be responsible for evil or acts in arbitrary ways toward his human creatures. The poem consisted of six theses: God's Word is a Word of promise. He treats all people equally. His will is not contradictory. His goodness is greater than human sinfulness. The fall of Adam doomed the human race. God is a God of life and salvation.[45]

On the basis of these principles Selnecker developed seven rules for the discussion of predestination. First, believers ought not form ideas concerning God's essence and will apart from God's Word. Selnecker presumed the distinction between *Deus absconditus* and *Deus revelatus*. Second, God's promise of grace is universal. Third, God is no respecter of persons. Fourth, in God there are not contrary wills; his will is that all people be saved and that none be condemned. Fifth, grace overwhelms sin. Sixth, as in Adam all died, so in Christ all will arise, all according to their proper destinations, believers to eternal life and salvation, the impious to eternal death. Selnecker explained, "for believers receive grace, but the impious guilt and wrath. There can be no middle ground." His seventh point, developed at some length, reveals his foremost concern. God has not created any creature for sin or death. He does not will sin. He does not effect sin. He does not assist sin. He does not approve of sin. He hates it, punishes it, and wants all to be converted and be saved. If they do not wish to come to their senses, they are subject to the punishments they deserve. But God is in no way responsible for sin, and he does not reject human creatures for any other reason than their refusal to hear his Word and trust in him, Selnecker insisted, supporting his argument with several Bible passages. "I bring those who do not listen to Christ's voice to ruin" (his paraphrase of Nah. 2:13). "Israel, you bring misfortune upon yourself, for your salvation is in me alone" (Hos. 13:9). "You are not a God who delights in wickedness" (Ps. 5:4). "Sin is of the devil" (perhaps a paraphrase of 1 John 3:8).[46] Nowhere in this discussion is there a mention of God's plan for saving those he chose to be his own before the foundation of the world.

Selnecker then considered objections that "secure people" *(obiectiones hominum securorum)* might pose to his position in defense of a fatalistic view of predestination. Each of these arguments presented a picture of an arbitrary and angry God, the picture of God that stood behind the school rector's suicide note. Selnecker did not speak of the "permissive will of God" in regard to evil, but instead addressed arguments he formulated in opposition to the idea that God might will evil.

First, Selnecker noted, some argue that God's foreknowledge *(praevisio)* is immutable and that what he foreknows happens by necessity, whether it is good or evil. Selnecker replied that God's foreknowledge does not coerce the human will to sin, for, in line with his seventh rule, God neither wills nor assists human sinfulness. He instead sets the limits of the sinfulness of tyrants like Nero, Pharaoh, Saul, Sennacherib, and others. Just as the mathematician's foreknowledge of an eclipse is not a cause of the eclipse, so God's foreknowledge of sin does not cause it. Selnecker posited that the concept of absolute necessity cannot be drawn from the concept of God's foreknowledge.[47] He did not support this claim with biblical or logical argument. It was an indisputable presupposition. The possibility of God's foreknowledge being creative, that is, a foreknowing that creates rather than observes the "future" reality, was not an option for Selnecker.

The second objection he refuted was the assertion that because no one can say "Jesus is Lord except by the Holy Spirit" (1 Cor. 12:3), what human creatures do and attempt in relationship to their salvation helps not at all, for all depends on predestination. Selnecker conceded that the Holy Spirit brings people to faith, but he bound the work of the Holy Spirit inseparably to the means of grace. His readers were to remember that God gives his Word and his Holy Spirit through the Word, and he calls them to hear that Word so that they receive the Holy Spirit. When those who hear the gospel notice the first spark of faith, they may be certain that the Holy Spirit is present, moving them and comforting them, for the gospel is the power of God unto salvation for all who believe (Rom. 1:16). God is at work in the faithful, enabling them both to will and to work for his good pleasure (Phil. 2:13), and no one can come to Christ unless drawn by the Father and taught by him (John 6:44-45). Melanchthon's disciple expressed his concern for the exercise of human responsibility by affirming simultaneously that the human will is not coerced but receives grace by being drawn as an acting will; in the words of Clement and Chrysostom, "God draws the one whose will is acting." This idea was confirmed for Selnecker by the words of Jeremiah, "Turn me, and I will want to be turned" (31:18), and of David, "Deal with your servant according to your steadfast love, and teach me your righteousness" (Ps. 119:124).[48] With the exception of these last two passages, Selnecker had taken his biblical material from Melanchthon's approach in the *Loci*.

Selnecker quickly set aside false interpretations of two other Bible passages. That "many are called but few are chosen" (Matt. 22:14) is true, not because of divine predestination but because of human guilt. For God wants all to be saved (1 Tim. 2:4),[49] and salvation comes from God. Human ruin can be blamed only upon sinners themselves (Hos. 13:9). Selnecker's answer to those who wished to use the passage "even the hairs of your head are all counted" (Matt. 10:30) to support a concept of inevitable divine necessity was based on rhetorical analysis. He rejected such an interpretation because these words were intended to be a statement of consolation, not a "Stoic axiom."[50]

Melanchthon had provided his students with a grammatical analysis of the passage regarding God's hardening of Pharaoh's heart (Exod. 4:21), and Selnecker was not the only student of Melanchthon who employed an insight from their preceptor to help readers understand that the Hebrew verb form here meant that God permitted — but did not cause — Pharaoh to sink ever deeper into resisting God's will.[51] The Lord withdrew his supporting hand from the Egyptian monarch just as a human father disinherits a disobedient and contemptuous son. Selnecker attempted to explain the hardening of Pharaoh's heart with biblical testimony regarding God's use of Satan and of evil to carry out his own will indirectly. First, he cited the example of the parallel reports in 2 Samuel 24:1, where the Lord became angry with the Israelites and commanded David to count them, and 1 Chronicles 21:1, where Satan became angry with the Israelites and commanded David to count them. Selnecker believed that God gave Satan permission to command David to take the census and thus used Satan to effect his own purposes. To this example he added the testimony of the first verses of Psalm 79, in which God uses the pagan peoples to visit his judgment on Israel. Selnecker summarized: "you punish us through your enemies." Assyria was also called the servant of God when it delivered his punishment, and in his own time, Selnecker believed, the Turks, Muscovites, and pope were serving as God's whips, his servants for the punishment of the "ungrateful and stubborn Germans." The parallel to Pharaoh's resisting God's will and thus bringing himself into damnation is not made clear, but for Selnecker it apparently sufficed to establish that God is lord of the actions even of his adversaries, as Luther had done in *De servo arbitrio*. God rules even in situations where evil takes place, but that does not make him the author of evil, Selnecker insisted.[52]

That God wills evil, some argue, can be seen in the crosses he sends, for instance, in his visitation upon Job. They conclude that many evils come from God. Selnecker's "easy" answer to this false interpretation of Job was that the crosses in the lives of the pious are God's will because he wants to lead them to the good. Such crosses would not exist if sin did not exist. It is necessary to distinguish the evil that guilt has brought upon a person from the evil that delivers punishment. For God gives permission for evils of punishment to fall upon believers. In reference to this form of evil Amos said, "Does disaster befall a city unless the Lord has done it?" (3:6), and Jeremiah wrote, "Is it not from the mouth of the Most High that good and bad come?" (Lam. 3:38). Selnecker admonished readers in such situations not to grumble against God, but against their own sin, turning to him. For every cross has its root in sin even if it is not imposed because of a specific sinful act.[53]

Another argument for the proposition that God wills evil was based upon his punishment of sins through the law of retribution. Selnecker refuted this with the simple axiom that God punishes sin and wills its punishment, but he does not will sin itself. When he punishes mediately through the Turk, he is not responsible for the sins of marauding armies. He is the judge who rightly punishes sin.[54]

The final *obiectio* against which Selnecker argued was that if someone foresees that evil is going to happen and has the power to stop it and does not, he certainly seems to take pleasure in that evil. Therefore, since God could stop evil and does not, he must act unjustly. Selnecker's rejoinder illustrates how he strove to defend the integrity of the human creature, solving the problem on the human side. He responded that God created human creatures with a free will and never forces them to obedience or conversion. He demands a "spontaneous spirit," that is, the response of a free will. God receives those who obey him. Having strayed into synergistic language, Selnecker then apparently tried to correct a false impression he feared he might have given. Beyond this answer Christians can only repeat Paul's words, "But who indeed are you, a human being, to argue with God?" (Rom. 9:20) and "O the depth of the riches and wisdom and knowledge of God!" (Rom. 11:33). Selnecker found that his brief arguments had proved that God does not will sin nor does he want any of his human creatures to be condemned. He had predestined no one to eternal damnation. He wants all to be saved (1 Tim. 2:4); for that purpose he sent his Son into the world (John 3:17).[55] With these arguments Selnecker countered thoughts like those of the despairing school rector. He strove to solve the problems posed with as rational explanations as possible, but in the end he also used Romans 11 to recognize that God stands above such human solutions.

For the comfort of such people who have doubts about God's gracious will for them, Selnecker then offered four *causae* from which they could gain consolation. The first is their call into the congregation of those God had called to faith and salvation, "the church of Christ, which holds to sound teaching and the pure and correct use of the sacraments, baptism and the Lord's Supper." As the place where the means of grace are found, the church conveys God's comfort to believers. Secondly, Selnecker turned to the internal effects of God's Word to convey comfort. Believers find consolation in the movement of the Holy Spirit in their hearts as they hear and embrace the teaching of the gospel. "The Holy Ghost marks them with his seal" in the Word of truth and "is the pledge of our inheritance" of freedom (!) (Eph. 1:13-14). The third "cause" of the Christian's comfort is the new life in Christ which arises when believers avoid sin and pray to God that they may be ruled by him, remaining his temple instead of falling into error and sin. Finally, believers find comfort in the use of the sacraments as seals of their righteousness and of God's grace. These four *regulae* of comfort should prevent dangerous questions and speculation in believers' minds, of the sort that brought the rector's life to an end. In the succession of God's actions in the process of salvation, as Paul presented it in Romans 8:29-30, the key action was his calling. Selnecker insisted upon the principle of all Lutheran theologians of his generation, that the means of grace, the promise of God, his "Word of truth," was the key to the proper understanding of God's love for sinners as he expressed it in Jesus Christ.[56]

Melanchthon, too, had offered consolations to readers of his locus on predestination.[57] However, in addition to Melanchthon's insistence that to assure the believer's comfort election always be connected to the means of grace and membership in the church, Selnecker turned attention to believers' own perception of the Holy Spirit's action in their lives and to the good works produced in their lives by God's choosing them to be his own. Thus, Selnecker searched for confirmation of the believer's election within that person's own experience as well as in the Word of God. He was focusing his readers' attention not only on objective and external sources of assurance but also on the subjective, internal perception of the Spirit's work.

Selnecker also found impetus for treating the Stoic concept of fate in Melanchthon's *Loci,* for the Preceptor had insisted that Stoic presuppositions dare not be employed in interpreting Paul.[58] Particularly in his disagreement with Calvin regarding predestination Melanchthon had repudiated any kind of "Stoic fatalism." The term "fate" was, however, so deeply embedded in the intellectual structures of the time, particularly in the new humanistic learning, that Selnecker wanted to appropriate it for use in teaching the faith. His treatment of *fatum* began with a definition: its root is in the Latin verb *fore* (to be or become). Its participle, *fando,* was the equivalent of the Greek πεπρωμένη or εἱμαρμένη, "determined by fate." Properly, however, in Christian theology the concept signifies God's providence or the divine decree concerning that which God's will governs as the immediate cause, not as a secondary cause, of something that happens. Selnecker repeated Melanchthon's schema. Four uses of the word must be distinguished, *fatum historicum, seu poeticum; fatum physicum seu astrologicum; fatum Aristotelicum, seu peripateticum;* and *fatum Stoicum.* Three of these definitions can be used to express aspects of God's providence, but *fatum Stoicum* contradicts biblical teaching because it posits an absolute necessity determined by divine decision and thus robs human beings of their responsibility and makes God responsible for evil, according to Selnecker.

Fatum Aristotelicum refers simply to the order of natural causes which God has established in his creation; for instance, cows produce cows and human creatures produce human creatures.

Fatum historicum designates the divine decree or divine providence that determines the good, for example, that Daniel would be preserved from harm among the lions (Dan. 6) or that God's just judgment must fall upon transgressors, such as the Roman emperor Julian. The ancient poets gave many other examples, Selnecker noted. He also further distinguished three kinds of *fatum historicum: praeuisio, praesensio et scientia rerum futurarum* (πρόγνωσις); *decretum* (πρόχεσις); and *prouidentia* (πρόνοια). "Foreknowledge" means that God foresees everything in the future and places limits on the evil he foresees.[59] The "decree" refers to the action of God's will which determines what is going to happen, sometimes contingently, with a *necessitas consequentiae*. Selnecker explained that such events take place only because God wills them even though they take place within the unfolding of human history. Examples include his decision to send his Son into the flesh, to raise the dead and to reveal what he plans. At this point Selnecker might have set forth the teaching of Paul in Romans 8 and Ephesians 1 regarding the doctrine of election, but he did not. He continued to avoid the subject. "Providence" is the action of the divine will by which God preserves and governs the natural order he has already established. He continues to give light, motion, and life to his creatures.

Fatum physicum describes the course of natural causes, for instance in the position of the stars and their association with human temperament and decision making as well as with natural happenings. Although he was not an active practitioner of astrological arts, Selnecker agreed with his preceptor and other humanists on their usefulness.[60]

The only definition of *fatum* Selnecker rejected was that of the Stoics, for it contradicts Christian teaching at several key points. For the Stoics had connected first causes and secondary causes in such a way that they taught an absolute and inevitable necessity (ἀνάγκη) which, according to widespread Christian opinion, made God the author of evil and denied human responsibility.[61] Selnecker dedicated the last ten pages of his tract to analyzing arguments for absolute necessity and dismissing them.[62] A citation from Epiphanius concludes his discussion; it states that if Stoic fatalism is true, law and learning must vanish. In rejecting fatalism on these grounds, Selnecker also dismissed the possibility that God could have predetermined the damnation of those who reject him.

Selnecker's entire treatise presented to the reading public an argument against the misconception that the biblical teaching on predestination could mean that anyone who knows the gospel has been created by God for condemnation. He wrote to contradict the belief represented in the suicide note of P. I. Against such doubt and despair Selnecker's proclamation of God's love for sinners in Jesus Christ and his emphasis on the promise of God in the means of grace repeated and represented Melanchthon's approach to the doctrine of predestination. His tract was designed to reinforce the unspoken ban on use of the consolation of God's eternal election among Lutheran theologians. Only in this way, he believed, could he bring law and gospel properly to those who were entangled in doubts like those that had plagued Peter Ilesuanus, and that was the task to which he had been called.

David Chytraeus's Rejection of Absolute Necessity

A decade later Selnecker would be appointed to a team constituted by the electoral Saxon government to formulate a statement of faith that would bring the disputes plaguing the Wittenberg circle to an end. One of his colleagues in that team of six was David Chytraeus, whom Melanchthon, according to later reports, had embraced as a son when he arrived in Wittenberg at age thirteen in 1544.[63] Melanchthon sent him to a professorial post at the University of Rostock in 1550, where he remained for a half-century, shaping the life of the church of Mecklenburg and lands far beyond, above all, in Austria and throughout the Baltic region. It is true that Chytraeus opposed Melanchthon's ecclesiastical policies quite decisively at certain points; e.g., he found an attempt to end Lutheran doctrinal disagreement, the Frankfurt Recess of 1558, insufficient if not incorrect. But he also remained faithful to his preceptor's memory and defended his image of his preceptor after his death.[64] In attempting to use the insights of both his mentors, Chytraeus was one of the majority of their students who believed that Luther and Melanchthon had conveyed the same teaching, a point he made most emphatically against those who believed that Philipp had advanced beyond — or deviated from — Doctor Luther's theology.[65] He was a natural candidate to aid in the search for the proper formulation of Lutheran agreement in 1576 and 1577.

Throughout his career Chytraeus continued to demonstrate how important both mentors' theology had been for him as he endeavored to proclaim and teach the gospel in his own situation. One of his often-exhibited sensitivities concerned the integrity of the human creature, and he occasionally came close to synergistic expressions in representing Melanchthon's concerns for human responsibility. But by 1561 he had expressly rejected such usage, and in 1567 approved the position of the Weimar *Confutationsbuch* of 1559 on the absence of any freedom of the will in choosing God apart from the Holy Spirit.[66] Lowell C. Green has clarified his position in a careful analysis of his use of Melanchthonian language.[67]

In early 1565, in the midst of other ecclesiastical and literary activities, as a well-established professor of theology at Rostock, with contacts throughout the Baltic region, Chytraeus composed a short treatise on a series of related words, "necessity, divine determination, fate, contingency, human powers, and free choice."[68] It was dedicated to Martin Olai Helsing, a Swedish churchman, with whom Chytraeus had studied in Wittenberg in the late 1540s.[69] His preface expressed his desire to share with the Swedish church this discussion of the terms he labeled useful for both philosophy and the doctrine of the church. He urged Helsing to share his analysis, taken from lectures prepared for his students in Rostock, with his archbishop, Laurentius Petri. Petri was involved at just this time in a dispute with Calvinists who had come to Sweden, two of them to serve as tutors to the sons of King Gustav. The archbishop's attack on the Calvinists had begun with a treatise issued in 1562. His campaign was meeting with some success at the time when Chytraeus wrote, for in 1565 King Erik XIV prohibited the propagation of Calvinist theology, reversing an earlier policy which had opened the doors to the Calvinists.[70] Helsing had joined in the anti-Calvinist campaign with a tract of his own.[71] Given Melanchthon's opposition to Calvin's doctrine of double predestination, it is possible that his disciple in Rostock was assisting the Lutheran cause against the Calvinists in Sweden with this publication.[72] In the preface Chytraeus singled out the term *necessitas* as a particularly troublesome concept because of its ambiguity and the many ways philosophers and Christians had used it. Augustine, he observed to Helsing, studiously avoided the term.[73]

Twenty percent of his treatise addresses the concept of necessity. Chytraeus began in good Melanchthonian fashion with a careful definition of the concept. Necessity is a word that describes a relationship, based upon an effective "cause" which produces some consequence or result. Its formal "cause," that which gives it its form and definition, is the order or binding factor which immutably establishes what this necessity ordains. Chytraeus's readers then review the many shades of meaning and the grand variety of usages the term has, beginning with "absolute necessity," things which are by their very nature immutable. Since God has power over everything he has made, only his own essence possesses the characteristic of absolute necessity. Chytraeus employed "necessity" as a synonym for an abstract absolute immutability. He ignored the fact that Luther had used the term to assert the total sovereignty of the person of the Creator. Therefore, unlike Luther, he inevitably attacked an impersonal determinism under this term. At this point he issued his first of several warnings against extending the definition of absolute necessity in a direction which could lead to the Stoic opinion that attributes immutable necessity to human evils, crimes, and vices (A2a-A4b). At the same time, he affirmed a biblical doctrine of Creator and creation and excluded the possibility that God is responsible for evil.

Parallel to Selnecker's description of *fatum*, Chytraeus went on to define *necessitas physica* in the order of natural causes as the *modus agendi* which God had installed in nature. He expanded Melanchthon's definition with biblical references and examples, and illustrated how God can operate within the natural order apart from this necessity, that is, the normal mode of action that the Creator had built into his creation. Fire, for instance, did not consume the men in the Babylonian furnace (Dan. 3:8-30). Water behaves in the way it did when God divided the Red Sea and the Jordan only at his command (Exod. 14:21-31; Josh. 3:7-13). Philosophers may argue for an unshakable and immutable stability of the natural order, but the church affirms that God can change all things. In no way does that mean, however, Chytraeus quickly added, that "Chrysippus, the prince of the Stoic sect," should be believed when he characterizes human evil and vice as products caused by God or a necessity determined by fate! That point concerned Chytraeus above all (A4b-A6a). With skillful and sensitive care he crafted his definition in order to convey the biblical concept of the Creator that he had learned from both his Wittenberg mentors.

The Rostock professor examined necessity in more detail. Commands carry with them a certain necessity, particularly when they come from God (A6a-A7a). Necessity can imply coercion, but not in every case; such coercion contradicts the freedom of the will and free choice, as God created them in the human creature.

Chytraeus addressed the thorny subject of Luther's concept of necessity in *De servo arbitrio* with no little historical sensitivity. He conceded that "at the beginning of his battles" the reformer had used the phrase "all things happen by necessity." Then he cited as genuine the passage Georg Rörer had inserted into the text of *De servo arbitrio* in the Wittenberg and Jena editions of Luther's works (at the time Chytraeus was studying in Wittenberg). In it Luther had expressed his wish to find a better word than "necessity," since "it has too harsh and incongruous a meaning for this purpose, for it suggests a kind of compulsion, and the very opposite of willingness. For neither the divine nor the human will does what it does, whether good or evil, under any compulsion, but from sheer pleasure or desire, as if truly acting freely" (B1a-b).[74] Later Chytraeus addressed Luther's rejection of the distinction between *necessitas consequentiae* and *necessitas consequentis;* he was quite sure that even though the reformer seems to reject the distinction, he in fact employed it. This served Chytraeus as a reason to avoid the discussion of necessity, in line with Augustine's insistence that God's foreknowledge never be used to argue for an abolition of the choice exercised by the human will (C2b-C3b). Such comments exhibit Chytraeus's aversion, inherited from Melanchthon, to the concept of necessity. He completed his discussion of the word by noting three more definitions: "necessity" can refer to (1) the things that happen according to God's established order, (2) the calamities and hardships which hold people in bondage, and (3) the things in life that are theoretically mutable but cannot be changed because God's decree has made them necessary (B2b-B5b).

Chytraeus moved from the concept of necessity to that of "divine determination." He defined it, in a codification of Melanchthon's usage of the term, as "an action of the divine mind, by which God knows all things and foresees all future events, whether good or evil, and promotes the good while permitting what is evil, establishing its limits and boundaries, further than which it will not be permitted" (B5b-B6a). Synonyms for "divine determination" include "wisdom," "foreknowledge" or "foreseeing," "providence," the "disposition of God" or "decree of God," "predestination" or "election," which pertains to those who are to be saved, the future heirs of eternal life. *Sapientia seu Scientia Dei* refers to God's knowing all things, eternal and temporal, past, present, and future, good and bad. *Praescientia seu Praeuisio Dei* refers to the action of the divine mind by which he foreknows and foresees all future good and evil, both necessary and contingent. *Providentia* is the action of the divine mind that not only knows all things and foresees the future, but also preserves the nature of things and provides the human race with what it needs, aiding and defending the good, punishing the unrighteous. *Dispositio seu Decretum Dei* is the action of the divine mind that actually arranges and orders future events according to God's good pleasure. Some of these decrees take place inevitably, simply on the basis of his will, such as the creation of the world, the sending of his Son, the establishment of the church, the resurrection of the dead, and the last judgment. Others are conditional, such as his decrees regarding punishment, which can be withdrawn for the penitent. This was the case in Jeremiah 18:8, Jonah 3:10, 2 Kings 20:1-6, and Isaiah 38:1-8. Chytraeus found that these instances proved his fundamental assertion regarding God's power and human responsibility: "These examples clearly show that foreknowledge and divine arrangement or decrees are not a matter of Stoic fate, nor are all things that are foreseen and foretold by God simply and absolutely immutable and necessary" (B6a-B7a).

Chytraeus explained that "predestination" — understood properly — can be used to explain what the divine decree and arrangement actually mean for the pious, who have been chosen for eternal life because of Christ. Prosper of Aquitaine had distinguished between foreknowledge and predestination.[75] Chytraeus found the distinction useful because it preserved God's foreknowledge without making him responsible for evil, yet it affirmed that God has chosen those who believe apart from any merit. That enabled the Rostock professor to counter the argument attributed to Boethius, Lorenzo Valla, and Luther in *De servo arbitrio,* which contended for an absolute necessity that made both good and evil equally immutable results of God's will. What God foreknows embraces his predestination in grace, but his foreknowledge of evil does not predestine evil people to damnation, as his message of judgment upon Jerusalem in Isaiah 37 shows. In the case of the good works of the reborn, both God's will and the human will are at work.[76] Noteworthy in Chytraeus's discussion of predestination is the absence of any explicit development of the teaching of consolation based on the unconditional nature of God's choice of those in whom the means of grace have worked faith, the heart of Luther's teaching. Like Selnecker, and Melanchthon before him, he exhibited more than a little reluctance in using the topic.[77]

"Closely related to divine providence and determination is the word fate," Chytraeus reminded readers familiar with the complex of terms that Latin and Greek philosophy had imposed upon Christian discussion of God's exercise of the responsibility he undertakes as Creator and Savior. Like Selnecker, Chytraeus followed Melanchthon's discussion of "fate" closely, presenting four definitions of the word: "the will and decree of God, or providence and divine ordering," "the power and mode of action that God uses to govern nature," "the way in which the stars govern certain actions on earth,"[78] and Stoic fate that moves from the assertion of the stability of heavenly bodies and causes of natural relationships to the assertion of an absolute necessity which binds God himself.[79] The first three definitions could stand, Chytraeus believed, sharing Selnecker's viewpoint, but the last, in which secondary causes as well as primary causes are immutably determined, violates God's Word, which teaches that human integrity depends on the exercise of human responsibility, that is, the freedom to choose, as described in Sirach 15:14-17. This freedom was largely lost in the fall, but sinners are able to exercise it to a very limited extent. To deny this is to make God the cause and author of all evils, and the fault for them actually lies with the devils and human beings (C8b-D2b).

Chytraeus reinforced his rejection of absolute necessity with an explanation of the concept of contingency that aimed at asserting human responsibility and repudiating any suggestion that God is responsible for sin. The fall of Adam and Eve into sin was contingent; it did not take place by absolute necessity, not by God's initiative or coercion. Contingency has three sources or causes: human freedom of the will, the ability by which human beings are able to choose and reject alternatives; the various forces at work in nature; and above all, God's free will, the expression of his omnipotence (D2b-D6b). The treatise concludes with a lengthy discussion of "human powers" and "free choice," which also consciously are turned into an antidote for a doctrine of absolute necessity that would make God a cause of evil. Five human powers determine the shape of humanity, Chytraeus asserted, reflecting Melanchthon's use of Aristotle: *Vegetans, Sentiens, Appetens, Locomotiva, Rationalis seu Mens*. The highest of these powers is the mind, knowledge, or reason, which enables the human creature to know God and his will and direct life toward loving and obeying God. The mind has been given the power to reject or accept the law of God. Chytraeus recognized that Scripture never uses the term "free choice," and it does not define the human will as the substance of the soul or as a part of the human creature, as is the case with the philosophical definition of the word. Nonetheless, he found it necessary to retain the term, for it expresses the biblical concept of the will describing the action of the will, its willing, its loving and approving, as in Psalm 1:2, or Matthew 6:1 (D6b-E1a).

He defined "free choice" in part by its opposite, Luther's term "bound choice," although he addressed different subject matter with his definition. For Chytraeus it referred to the power and right to make decisions in general, not restricted to the human relationship with God. In its purest sense only God has complete free choice; it belongs to no human being. Just as political freedom does not release people from obligation to keep the law, Christian freedom is enjoyed in the liberation from sin, death, and the power of the devil, and in the practice of righteousness to which believers are bound when they receive the gift of the Holy Spirit by grace through Christ their mediator (reflecting Luther's exposition of Christian freedom in his famous tract of 1520).[80] Thus, "free choice" refers to the ability placed in the human will by God, by which, without being coerced to do something against their own will, people are able to will or not to will spontaneously, to choose or not to choose, to do a specific action. Only vestiges of this free choice remain after the fall. For the devils and fallen human beings are not able not to sin because of the tyranny of sin and death. They have lost Adam's ability to obey God with integrity and perfection apart from any impediment. This inability to avoid sin is in no way due to God's determination; in no way can sin be said to take place because of an immutable and absolute necessity. Chytraeus reinforced his claims with a number of quotations from Augustine (E1b-F2a).

Chytraeus clarified his position by considering free choice in God, the angels, and in human creatures before and after the fall. Not bound by any "fatal necessity" or any order of secondary causes, or nature apart from his creative act, God is Creator, and his will is dependent on nothing else but his own willing. The angels' free choice is limited by God's created boundaries, and since they were not forced to serve God, they could exercise a measure of free choice that brought some to irreversible eternal condemnation. Before the fall human creatures exercised free choice as the ability of the mind and will in the first parents, by which they were able to recognize God's essence and will as creator without error, to distinguish good from evil, and with God's help to practice the life of true righteousness and holiness for which they were created. After the fall, those who are not reborn can still exercise choice and discern good and evil, but apart from God's grace they cannot do anything in spiritual matters. Here Chytraeus specifically affirmed Luther's statement that "free choice" is an empty phrase, a label without substance,[81] since the will cannot make even the smallest move in God's direction, cannot kindle faith in Christ, cannot begin to worship God. In spiritual matters human choice is bound, captive to sin and death, impotent and defective. When through water and the Spirit (John 3:5-8) mind and will are reborn through the Holy Spirit, then they are able under the Spirit's power to trust God and his mercy, to fear and love him, and to exercise patience. Chytraeus also looked forward to the perfect exercise of obedience to the Creator that comes after life on earth in blessedness (F2a-G1a).

Chytraeus proved himself a true student of Wittenberg when he assessed the several sides of the topic of God's responsibility for the salvation of sinners and the human responsibility of obedience to God from the several aspects provided by the philosophical and theological terminology associated with these articles of faith. He reflected the concern of both Luther and Melanchthon to affirm God's total responsibility for everything that happens under his creative hand, and at the same time he endeavored above all else to recapitulate Melanchthon's utter rejection of any hint that God could be the author of evil, a concept Luther certainly did not advocate but occasionally could be understood to have implied in his defense of the utter sovereignty of the Creator in *De servo arbitrio*. The Rostock professor insisted on full human responsibility and the integrity of human creatures as God had fashioned them, with mind and will, but he also maintained unequivocally that the action of the will could not bring sinners to God or faith in Christ in any way apart from the re-creative action of the Holy Spirit. In affirming the two poles of this tension, Chytraeus felt free to criticize a position on necessity ascribed to Luther on the basis of passages in his *De servo arbitrio* that seemed to undercut the integrity of the human creature. Chytraeus could not tolerate a concept of divine necessity that he believed made it necessary to define God as the, or a, cause of evil. That contradicted the fundamental definition of God that he had learned at Wittenberg. He contended that it is impossible for sinners properly to exercise the freedom of the will, while reminding readers again and again that God could not be the cause of evil. Unlike Selnecker, Chytraeus left the door open for teaching predestination, but like Selnecker, he did not develop it in his treatise. He highly respected both Luther and

Melanchthon, but he felt compelled to develop his own position on this most critical issue for Wittenberg theology. In this regard he exhibited the same caution and fear as Palhöfer and Selnecker, although he came closer than they to the evangelical spirit of Marbach and Flinsbach as they created a pastoral tool from the topic of God's inalterable choice of his own people. Their ideas found echo and extension in the work of Cyriakus Spangenberg and Martin Chemnitz.

CHAPTER VI

"God Has Predestined Those Who Cannot Be Lost": The Formulation of the Lutheran Doctrine of Predestination

Cyriakus Spangenberg

Not all their contemporaries shared Palhöfer's, Selnecker's, and Chytraeus's apprehension of teaching and proclaiming God's gracious choice of individual believers. Chytraeus's fellow student in Wittenberg, Cyriakus Spangenberg, produced seven sermons on the subject two years after the treatises of Selnecker and Chytraeus appeared.[1] In these sermons, composed as a critique of the "synergism" of the theologians of electoral Saxony, Spangenberg strove to demonstrate the usefulness and significance of preaching on God's unconditional choice of his children for the clear elucidation of the gospel. In so doing he was convinced that he was faithfully conveying what he had learned from Luther and read in the reformer's writings, above all in *De servo arbitrio*. In his sermons he actually laid the foundations anew for a formulation of the topic of predestination that drew the teaching of many Lutherans on God's election of his own in the direction of Luther's definition of God's relationship to his human creatures in *De servo arbitrio*. In the two decades since the reformer's death, Wittenberg colleagues had rarely expressed the position Spangenberg advanced, although the *Syntagma* of Johannes Wigand and Matthaeus Judex did develop the topic in brief form in a way similar to Spangenberg. The Strasbourg Consensus also had summarized this position. Nonetheless, Spangenberg's published treatise aroused a small controversy, which led to the addition of predestination to the agenda of controversy among German Lutherans around 1570.

Spangenberg was born in the parsonage at Nordhausen, son of one of Luther's most fervent supporters in his own generation. Johann Spangenberg, born less than a year after the reformer, had studied in Erfurt at the same time as Luther. In 1524 he became pastor in Nordhausen and remained there until called to be superintendent of the churches of Mansfeld County in 1546. By that time his oldest son, Cyriakus, had been studying for four years in Wittenberg, having commenced his university program before his fourteenth birthday. He had learned to appreciate Luther's person and his theology at his parents' table, and his own personal experiences hearing the reformer and getting to know him confirmed for the young man that God had sent Germany a prophet with special authority in Martin Luther.[2] The Smalcald War drove Cyriakus out of Wittenberg in late 1546, and his father appointed him teacher in the Latin school in Mansfeld. Following a brief return to Wittenberg, during which he received his master's degree, he assumed a position as preacher in Eisleben, shortly after his father's death in June 1550. A letter of condolence at his father's death from Melanchthon reveals a good relationship between student and preceptor at that time.[3]

In 1553 the younger Spangenberg became both the town preacher and also the court preacher in Mansfeld; in 1559 he was named general-dean for the county. He worked closely with the superintendents of Mansfeld's churches, Johannes Wigand, Erasmus Sarcerius, and Hieronymus Menzel, until he and Menzel divided over the issue of Flacius's doctrine of original sin as the substance of the fallen creature.[4] In November 1566 Spangenberg received leave from the counts of Mansfeld to assist in the organization of the Lutheran church in Antwerp, and there he worked closely with Flacius for three months.[5] Spangenberg's intervention in defense of Flacius's view of original sin caused him to be wanted for criminal apprehension by neighboring electoral Saxony and electoral Brandenburg. In 1575 the Brandenburg prince Joachim Friedrich sent troops to arrest him. He escaped, although his pregnant wife was assaulted in the raid and a number of his supporters in the community were jailed. As exile and pilgrim, he continued to play a role in the public discussion, particularly of original sin, and sought out Jakob Andreae to register his objections to the treatment of the topic in the Formula of Concord. No reconciliation occurred between the two; Spangenberg felt Andreae was willing to make gestures of accommodation but did not come to the heart of the matter.[6] From 1580 to 1590 he served as pastor in Schlitzsee in Hessen,[7] and spent the last fourteen years of his life in Strasbourg, chiefly engaged in literary work.

He wrote feverishly and well, displaying a broad knowledge with depth in many areas. Melanchthon's loci method led his student to produce surveys of human knowledge and wisdom on a variety of topics, including the nobility, music, and the plague, and the Preceptor's interest in history strengthened the foundations that his father had laid for Cyriakus's research on the history of his region.[8] He edited and expanded his father's postil-like collection of funeral sermons[9] and provided pastors with model sermons regarding marriage and other subjects. Among many works of biblical exegesis, his homiletical commentaries on seven of the Pauline epistles stand out, in the words of Miriam Chrisman, as "the most important biblical commentaries of the period."[10] Spangenberg's contemporaries recognized him as one of the leading scholars and thinkers among Luther's and Melanchthon's students, a fact obscured by his later tenacious defense of Flacius's understanding of original sin as the formal substance of the sinner, which alienated him from most of his contemporaries.

Spangenberg's Biblical Commentaries

In his biblical commentaries Spangenberg had already laid a basis for his consideration of God's election of his own as he preached on it as a dogmatic topic in 1567.[11] In 1557 the Mansfeld preacher had issued the first of his sermonic expositions of Pauline texts, on the two epistles to the Thessalonians. His comments on 2 Thessalonians 2:13-17 presented a primer on predestination. It emphasized the role of the means of grace in the practical use of a Lutheran understanding of election. In treating the Thessalonians passage Spangenberg cited 2 Timothy 2:13, "If we are faithless, he remains faithful, for he cannot deny himself," revealing his fundamental orientation: "For we have a certain comfort since we know with certainty that God loves us. We do not doubt it at all, for we know that he has chosen us for salvation, and it is undeniable that he daily calls us through the outward Word, through the gospel, to life everlasting. Through this call we become certain of our election. What more could our faithful God do than that?" Spangenberg outlined how God shows his mercy to his people. He began with baptism, but the ultimate roots of God's baptismal promise lay, for Spangenberg, in God's choosing of his own. He defined God's election as "nothing other than his choice of a special people, many individuals, for himself. Out of his own free will and its good inclination he chose them to be his church and his congregation, that they might recognize and praise him. He graciously gave them righteousness, forgiveness of sins, and eternal life, and he wants to share his eternal glory with them after this life. . . ."[12]

The text of Romans 8 looms behind this description of God's election. The elect include all who have received comfort through faith in the Lord and have not fallen from the faith. Sin causes people to be rejected; Christ is the only cause for their election. In addition to Romans 8, Spangenberg cited John 6:44-46: "No one comes to me unless the Father calls him." Those who hear and learn the gospel and do not arrogantly discard it but find comfort in it and remain in it, even if they experience weakness, are the elect. Spangenberg consistently put the emphasis on God's love and mercy and on the power of the gospel, all the while acknowledging that believers will often experience weakness of faith. Spangenberg's primer continued by answering the fundamental questions (25b-26b):

> *Who elects?*
> God.
> *When did he make the choice?*
> Before the creation of the world (Eph. 1:3-14).
> *Why did he elect?*
> So believers would not have to worry about his providential care, which he had resolved in his divine counsel from the very beginning.

Believers are thus freed from the concern over whether God has intended them to be saved. For in Spangenberg's sermons on 2 Thessalonians 2:13-14 the preacher assured his readers that they have three guarantees of their status as the elect children of God. First, the sanctifying power of the Holy Spirit assures them of salvation. Second, their faith in the truth, in Christ himself, provides such a guarantee. For Christ is the holiness of his own elect people. Third, the call through which God has called them in the preaching of the gospel gives certain assurance to believers. Again, Spangenberg felt compelled to note that there is great comfort in weakness itself, for God's act of choosing his own assures his children of salvation and their election is confirmed in the call of the gospel (25a-27b). He understood how to use doctrinal synonyms effectively in pursuit of this goal of consolation.

Nine years later, the year before the appearance of his sermons on predestination, 1566, Spangenberg published his commentary on the first eight chapters of Romans. In his exposition of the eighth chapter he followed Melanchthon's lead in reveling in the comfort of the gospel which the apostle had outlined in the chapter's closing verses.[13] The student echoed and expanded his preceptor's comment by setting forth fourteen "magnificent, beautiful, comforting reasons why Christians should be neither ashamed nor terrified by the cross and suffering in daily life." Beginning in verse 17, Spangenberg rehearsed these reasons for Christian consolation and comfort in the midst of the cross. Christ also suffered (8:17). Their suffering does not imply in any way that believers will not enjoy the future glory which Christ has prepared for them (8:18). All of creation suffers as it hopes for this future glory (8:19). If the rest of creation will be freed from suffering, certainly believers will be liberated from it as well (8:20-21). The saints and apostles, such as Saint Paul himself, were not free of suffering, but they did not turn away from their eternal hope because of it (8:23). It is the very nature of hope that we do not see that which gives us comfort, but nevertheless we await that for which we hope in patience (8:24-25). Hope will bring us an improvement in our lot, for hope will not let itself be shamed. The Holy Spirit provides us with his aid in the midst of suffering (8:26-27).

The ninth reason for comfort in the midst of adversity begins Spangenberg's treatment of God's election of his own children. God has predestined and foreseen what will befall his chosen children, and so they can willingly experience whatever pleases him (8:28-30). God is mightier than everything which opposes his own, and he will help them (8:28). In any case, God is determined that believers will not doubt his good pleasure toward them (8:31-37). He has chosen them with his firm and certain choice, and no cross or suffering can change this choice. They know they have a mediator, Jesus Christ, whose intercessions to God in behalf of his people will not fail (8:34). It is impossible for them to be separated or cut off from Christ (8:38-39).[14]

Spangenberg's discussion of Romans 8:28-30 begins with his reiteration of Paul's words that all things work together for the good of those who love God. Spangenberg recalled the promise of the psalmists that "in all that they do, they prosper" (Ps. 1:3b), and that God will act in behalf of those who trust in him (Ps. 37:5). Biblical examples of his promise abound, in the lives of Abraham, Jacob, Joseph, David, and Daniel, for instance. Spangenberg added his own experiences to theirs to demonstrate God's faithfulness in caring for his own. He also made certain that his readers understood that "those who love God" are those whom God loved first, those who keep God's Word (John 14:23a). His readers were also given to understand that God's love serves the needs of believers in the best possible fashion, even when they are in the midst of persecution, suffering, anxiety, peril, and death.[15]

Believers have such assurance because they know that God has intentionally chosen them as his own. The doctrine of election serves to counter two mistaken opinions, Spangenberg observed. First, it rejects the error that God has saving love for some who remain outside the remnant of his people whom he has called to be his children. Like Melanchthon, Spangenberg bound his doctrine of election to the doctrine of the church. There are no heathen who will be saved; there is no salvation apart from the gospel's promises. For no one comes to the Father except through Christ (John 14:6). Two fundamental components of Spangenberg's theology — God's mercy in

Christ and his power which works through the Word — are expressed here. Second, the doctrine of election renders any pretense of righteousness through one's own performance of works impossible. For Paul links God's love with the believer's trust which relies on him alone, and not on works.[16]

Both these points formed keystones for Spangenberg's understanding of God's unconditional election of those he would call to be his children. In both he was repeating fundamental principles which had guided Melanchthon's interpretation of these passages in Romans 8–11.[17] Also in his treatment of Paul's comments on election in Romans 11, Spangenberg made it clear that God chose his people in Christ, saved them through Christ, and justified them through faith in Christ alone. "The teaching on God's predestination is certain and can never be altered. For God has predestined and chosen for himself, before the world began, in his Son Christ Jesus those who cannot be lost. What has not been chosen in Christ Jesus has no part in the Kingdom of God. Who is elect and who is not elect can be seen in faith or unfaith."[18]

Spangenberg based his understanding of God's election of his own children upon Paul's word "purpose" in 8:28: "those who are called according to his purpose." He defined God's purpose as "his eternal plan, resolved according to his good pleasure, which no creature can frustrate or change." Peter had mentioned this "definite plan and foreknowledge of God" as the basis for the crucifixion of Christ in Acts 2:23; Paul had elaborated upon it in Ephesians 1 (especially v. 11). This was the purpose of God which has been revealed through Christ's appearance (2 Tim. 1:9-10). Spangenberg added a comment from Bernard of Clairvaux: this teaching does not terrify because it deals not with what believers have merited but with what God has put in place; not with the way believers feel but with God's intention to call them holy.[19]

As he had emphasized, in chorus with Luther, Melanchthon, and all other Wittenberg contemporaries, already in his Thessalonians commentary of 1557, Spangenberg insisted that God's dealing with his own had to be understood through the means of grace. Commenting on Paul's reassurance that "God has not rejected his people whom he foreknew" (Rom. 11:2), Spangenberg wrote that the elect dare never forget "the covenant God has made with us in baptism. . . . For his reliable promise and assurance in his word, in absolution, and in the sacraments (which cannot lie or deceive) give us comfort. We can boldly and firmly rely upon the means of grace, as God's unchangeable word. Even when we think that our faith is not so strong, we can hold to this word." For — Spangenberg again cited 2 Timothy 2:13 — "even if we are faithless, he remains faithful."[20] Indeed, God had ordained the proclamation of the gospel for the benefit and salvation of his elect, and he guided the elect among the Jewish people to faith through that Word.[21] Spangenberg distinguished the inward call from the outward call, which God effects through the means of grace. That inward sense of being called as God's child is completely dependent upon the outer call through the Word. Spangenberg posed the question, "How can I be sure that I am a called child of God?" Through God's Word alone, was his only answer. There is no other way to know what God's purpose for us is; there is no access to any secret counsel of God. Those who are troubled should know that God has called them through his gracious purpose; they could not have come to Christ on their own.[22]

Spangenberg used Romans 8:29 and 30 to sketch a description of God's saving work in behalf of sinners. Like his Lutheran contemporaries, he did not construct a fixed dogma of an *ordo salutis,* as did the Calvinist defenders of predestination when they battled the Arminians in their midst a generation later. Nonetheless, Spangenberg did follow the text of Romans 8:29-30 in setting forth a description of God's plan as he understood it. He presented his "order of salvation" three times in treating Romans 8 and 9, each time developing the steps in God's plan in a slightly different fashion. This suggests that he was not creating a dogmatic locus in his mind but rather responding to the text itself.

In the first instance, his comment on Romans 8:29 and 30, the text began to lay out God's purpose with God's foreseeing his own as his children. Before they were born, before the foundations of the world were laid, Spangenberg reminded his readers, God knew and determined that they would be his elect children. Adam's fall could not destroy the Creator's purpose for his elect. Spangenberg understood this foreknowing, through which God wrote the names of the elect in the Book of Life apart from any human merit, as a re-creative foreknowing. It simply pleased God to cast his favor and grace upon the elect and grasp them in his love.

Secondly, God predestined them to be his own. That meant that God ensured them of the glory of eternal life with him, but it also meant that he would submit them to the cross and suffering. It furthermore assures believers that all things will work together for their good and that they will be conformed to the image of his Son in their good works. They will not reflect the image of Satan (a statement which reflects Spangenberg's commitment to Flacius's doctrine of original sin).

Thirdly, God has called his own through the means of grace. Spangenberg used Paul's concept of calling to reject the inner spiritualism of the "Ravers" of his day who refused to recognize how God works through the various forms of his word (2 Thess. 2:13b-14).

Fourthly, God justifies his own through the imputation of the forgiveness of sins and the righteousness of Christ. This justification, Spangenberg insisted, is solely God's work.

Finally, God will glorify his own. To explain this Pauline phrase Spangenberg cited Bernard of Clairvaux once again. In his sermons on the book of Wisdom, Bernard had written that the kingdom of God is planned, promised, presented, and perceived. It is planned in predestination, promised in the call of the means of grace, presented in justification, and perceived in glorification. In predestination is God's grace, Bernard taught; in the call of the means of grace, his power; in justification his joy; in glorification his glory.[23]

Spangenberg had not used Paul's text in Romans 8 as the basis of an extensive treatment of predestination. Instead, he had incorporated the concept of election somewhat directly but simply into his proclamation of the comfort which God bestows upon his chosen children in the midst of suffering and the cross of daily life. In his commentary he was pursuing an argument or explanation of Paul's message for his readers, not composing a doctrinal essay. He offered the pastors who would read his sermons suggestions for their own proclamation of the comfort of the gospel of Jesus Christ to their people. Spangenberg's pastoral concern treated the doctrine of election as it stood in the text, and he did not make a special issue of it.

On the other hand, the comfort of God's eternal choice of his own continued to help Spangenberg explicate Paul's message of the gospel's comfort in the interpretation of the remaining verses of Romans 8. The emphasis in his sermon on Romans 8:31-34 fell upon God's power as it exhibits itself in the saving work of Jesus Christ and in the Word of God that conveys the love God bestows through Christ's death and resurrection.[24] But in his sermon on what he called the "rhetorical masterpiece" of Romans 8:35-37, he emphasized two reasons why nothing can separate believers from God. First, he loves them. Second, he has set their lives in order through his purpose and plan.[25] Nevertheless, it is striking how little Spangenberg did say about election here, the year before he issued seven sermons on the topic, given the rich material on election in Romans 8. As Luther's disciple, he had not learned to think automatically of the topic of election.

Spangenberg's Sermons on Predestination of 1567

The Reasons for Spangenberg's Preaching on Predestination

Apparently no one found Spangenberg's exposition of God's election of his own children offensive when it appeared in the pages of biblical commentary.

In sharp contrast, when he expanded his thoughts on predestination in sermons dedicated to expounding on the doctrine's significance for disputes over the freedom of the will, a storm broke out. A year after his *Seven Sermons on Predestination* appeared in 1567, he felt compelled to issue a defense of his views.[26] In this apology the author explained why he had thought it necessary to address the topic for the reading public. One of his reasons arose from the repute that Luther's *De servo arbitrio* "enjoyed" among his contemporaries. Not without a touch of irony Spangenberg wrote,

> It was no secret how highly the Blessed Luther's book *De servo arbitrio* was regarded by those of our time, by the world's most prominent people. Since my book's position agrees completely with that of Luther's work, and was taken in part from it, I could presume that it would be judged no more graciously than his. If I had wanted to attain honor with the world and its best people and win their thanks, I should have stayed home with my sermons. However I might have wanted to make a special name for myself, I in fact produced nothing new, nothing of my own, but rather repeated the same thing that the great prophet of God, Doctor Luther, had powerfully and magnificently treated in his *De servo arbitrio.*[27]

The confusion wrought by the synergistic controversies indeed had pressed Spangenberg to reassert Luther's teaching on God's gracious election of his people, he informed the readers of his apology. For he feared that the synergists' attacks on the foundation and basis of the faith had caused some to think they could take their salvation in their own hands. Doing so could only lead to a loss of the comfort Saint Paul had given through his presentation of the election of God's people in Christ Jesus. At the same time, the opinions of the "Anabaptists and Sacramentarians" had threatened to lead his people astray.

Behind these impulses from the controversies of the 1550s and 1560s stood a number of theological reasons for proclaiming the gospel through the confession of God's unconditional grace in predestination. These the preacher listed as he began this series of homiletical discourses on his subject.[28] God's command, Paul's example, and the dependence of people whose reason cannot grasp this message when they hear it all commend such preaching. So do the benefits and profit it brings. Spangenberg began by turning the theodical question to theological advantage. First, preaching on election humiliates reason and turns the believer to God's Word. Indeed, it produced in Luther himself a salutary despair, as he had reported in *De servo arbitrio:* "I myself was offended [at the idea of God's cruelty in abandoning sinners to eternal torment] more than once and brought to the very depth and abyss of despair, so that I wished I had never been created a human being, before I realized how salutary that despair was, and how near to grace." Otherwise, Spangenberg added, "we go around and think ourselves as wise as God himself, and that is the greatest foolishness."[29]

Second, preaching on election strengthens faith, for it leads believers to depend completely on Christ (Eph. 1:4-6). Third, such preaching assures believers that they will remain God's children because their salvation rests alone on God's counsel and plan. This firm foundation of God's mercy is sealed with the words "The Lord knows those who are his" (2 Tim. 2:19), as Christ also said, "Those whom you gave me, I have preserved and none of them has been lost" (John 17:12). (It must be noted that Spangenberg omitted the reference to Judas that follows these words immediately: "except the one doomed to destruction so that Scripture would be fulfilled." He avoided incorporating a doctrine of double predestination into his teaching at a point where he might have.) Finally, predestination should be proclaimed because it cultivates true humility and gives believers magnificent comfort, such as that which enabled David to say in the midst of various afflictions, "I will be silent and not open my mouth. You will take care of it" (Ps. 39:9).[30]

The sermons on predestination had arisen out of his preaching on the book of Romans, he noted, and contained nothing other than a careful treatment of what he had found in its first eight chapters, which come to a climax in Paul's proclamation of God's unconditional, electing love in the last verses of chapter 8 and in chapter 9.[31] As he began preaching on Romans in his series of homiletical treatments of Pauline epistles, some in Mansfeld and in other places had urged him to consider election in detail when he came to the eighth and ninth chapters of the book, both to correct those who treated the topic in a frivolous manner and also to provide comfort for troubled consciences. His own conscience drove Spangenberg to honor this request, for he knew "how terribly difficult, obscure, and confusing this article can be, not in itself but because the ideas of human flesh and the cleverness of our reason make it so when we do not make our minds captive to obedience to Christ and subject them to God's Word" (A4b-A6b). Because he had been about to leave for "Brabant" (Antwerp), he had decided to give his congregation a written guide to the biblical teaching regarding election (B3a-b; on synergism, cf. B7b). Differing opinions regarding this article of faith and how to explain it had resulted in sharp disputations even among his friends (he had studied with Chytraeus and Palhöfer's mentor Poach) (B6b-B7a). Certainly, Spangenberg realized that some who had attacked his *On Predestination* as "heretical, blasphemous, and deceptive" had done so in good faith because they had honest concerns — even though he was also convinced that others had used its publication as a pretext to assail him publicly, from the pulpit or at the princely court, because they were jealous, resentful, and opposed his theology in general (A2b-A4b).

The charge that these sermons had brought readers to depression and despair particularly disturbed the author, for he had intended to bring them comfort through the anchoring of God's grace and mercy in his own will and his favor apart from every human influence. The book could be misread only when a reader concentrated on words and phrases out of their context. However, other charges revealed the mistaken notions of his critics in Spangenberg's eyes. For instance, those who denied that God's grace "makes a difference between the elect and others" failed to understand God's grace and the seriousness of sin. Those who are predestined to be his children (Rom. 8:29) are different from those who remain under his wrath. He insisted against his opponents that the number of the elect is indeed fixed; otherwise no individual believer could gain comfort from this teaching (C3b-C7b). He knew he was being accused of capitulating to the Calvinist position, "that God is in part a cause of sin," a charge that can be traced back to Melanchthon's concern over Calvin's doctrine, which concern had stereotyped the entire topic of election among many of his students. The Mansfeld preacher insisted that he had done nothing but repeat the teaching of Paul, Augustine, and Luther on this, and had striven to avoid that false teaching (B6a). In a letter to Hartmann Beyer in Frankfurt am Main of August 21, 1567, Spangenberg asserted that he had simply presented the thoughts of Scripture, Augustine, Luther, Urbanus Rhegius, and Johannes Brenz in the book.[32] His sermons grew out of three years of work on a collection of citations from "the Fathers, particularly Augustine, Prosper, and Fulgentius, and also the dear man of God Luther and a few others," in preparation for preaching on the topic. (As noted above, Spangenberg had often gathered such collections as he put Melanchthon's loci method to use in a number of scholarly activities.) Those who had heard the sermons he had prepared from these patristic citations and the Bible had all been strengthened in the faith and had received comfort from them, he claimed, for they had been directed to trust in God alone and rely only on the merit of Christ Jesus (B1a-B2a). The method the preacher followed in these topical sermons differed necessarily in certain ways from his exposition of biblical texts, in which he proceeded through the words and phrases with observations about the grammar, syntax, and vocabulary as well as the theological content of the material. But in general his method remained the same, weaving together specific biblical texts with his own judgments and observations, reinforced with citations from the Fathers, including the three he mentioned in his *Apology*.[33]

The Hermeneutical Basis of Spangenberg's
Preaching on Predestination

In Spangenberg's biblical comment he occasionally gave some attention to hermeneutical questions. He prefaced his Romans commentary with an extensive examination of the principles of interpretation to be employed in reading the biblical text.[34] Likewise, in his sermons on predestination he wanted readers to recognize the principles and presuppositions that must govern proclamation of God's unconditional choice of his people. The first of these sermons outlined seven guiding premises for the presentation of the doctrine of predestination.

The first principle turns the preacher and teacher exclusively to "God's Word and the Holy Scripture," and thus away from human reason and thinking. In expanding on this point in his sixth sermon, Spangenberg turned to Luther's distinction between the hidden and revealed God, planting all consideration of predestination exclusively within God's revelation of himself in Christ. God's refusal to let Moses see his face (Exod. 33:20) signifies that believers may not peer "into the secret counsel of God and interpret and delve into the profound and hidden reasons for God's will with their own ingenious ideas." To "view God from the rear" (Exod. 33:23) meant "to recognize God's will from his Word and his gracious miracles that took place with his Word." Only in this way can people learn the will of their Creator. God has covered himself with the veil of the body of Christ (Heb. 10:20). Through him alone believers can see into the Father's heart and know his eternal thoughts. For those who see Christ see the Father (John 14:9). Human reason cannot deliver such knowledge, for those who do not have the Holy Spirit cannot apprehend God's message (1 Cor. 2:14). Only God's Word can govern human thinking about God's choice of sinners to be his own children.[35] Spangenberg had captured Luther's understanding of the importance of stopping in awe before the hidden God and trusting completely in his revelation of himself in Christ.

Second, predestination cannot be treated without careful attention to the distinction of law and gospel, for it can be understood properly only as gospel, a principle Spangenberg reiterated in his *Apologia*.[36] Whenever preachers fail to use God's election of his children as comfort and encouragement, they misrepresent this teaching. If one tries to assess God's gracious election from the standpoint of the law, that is, from the evaluation of human performance, it is necessary to assert that God knew what individuals would do, which good works they would produce, so that he could lift the burden of sin and condemnation from them on the basis of their performance. Only despair results from honest confrontation with God's law. Therefore, believers must hear the gospel of Christ, to whom all judgment over life and death has been given (John 5:27), when they think of predestination. Spangenberg cited Paul: God has revealed his plan, forged before the foundation of the world, only through Christ (Eph. 1:3-11). "God is faithful and has called you into fellowship with his Son, Jesus Christ, our Lord" (1 Cor. 1:9). The apostle thanked God for the Thessalonians, whom God had chosen to be saved from the beginning through the Holy Spirit's sanctifying work and through faith in the truth, to which he had called them by Paul's proclamation of the gospel to be the holy property of Christ (2 Thess. 2:13-14).[37]

Third, biblical language should be used to present the topic of God's election of his own; philosophical expressions must be avoided. Apart from his use of Melanchthon's principles of organizing all learning by topic, Spangenberg had shied away from Melanchthon's rhetorical-dialectical way of teaching more than other Gnesio-Lutherans like Wigand and Heshusius. He counseled in this case that preachers must approach this article of faith in true humility and not put on airs in proclaiming it. He sensed that attempts to domesticate Aristotle for use within the church could have a reverse effect. He feared it inevitable that foolish philosophical opinions try to limit God and explain everything with secondary causes. He had tried to master the art of answering questions the Bible poses and resisting the temptation to force biblical material into Aristotelian categories. The result is that all human beings are supposed to forge their own fortunes, and such ideas are even applied to salvation by some. Believers can rely only on the Word of God itself.[38]

Fourth, predestination cannot be understood apart from its context within the exposition of faith in Jesus Christ and the righteousness of faith. Apart from this focus on Christ, any mention of predestination will be dangerous.[39] Spangenberg quoted Luther's letter to an "important person from Lower Saxony" struggling with doubts about predestination, which pointed to Christ alone, specifically to the Father's command to listen to Christ (Matt. 17:5). Even when the human heart is so despairing and hardened that it cannot listen to the Father, Christ stands in its way and says, "Come! Come!" All are to come to him (Matt. 11:28). For God's promise in Christ assures all people of his love for them and his desire to give them life (John 3:16). This promise is a general promise, made to all who believe, and no one is to be excluded as one of the elect who looks in faith to God's grace in Christ. None who trust in him should believe that they are unworthy because of some sin. Their names are written in the Book of Life, which is Christ himself.[40]

Fifth, the proclamation and use of this teaching must serve the honor of God, praising his wisdom, grace, goodness, love, faithfulness, and mercy, and must serve to comfort and edify the faithful, strengthening them in faith, anchoring them in patience and hope, and building them up for every cross and trouble.[41] Finally, teaching predestination should arouse Christians to live according to God's will in their relationships with other people.[42] Spangenberg believed that confidence in God's love for them would move believers to good works. They had been freed from bondage to be free to love those to whom God had bound them.

Spangenberg intended to reproduce Luther's chief concerns and his approach to the teaching of God's gracious election of his own with this hermeneutical orientation. God's total responsibility for salvation did not mean he is responsible for the condemnation of those who had failed to exercise their responsibility as human beings. God hid from humankind the answers to the questions posed by the tension between these two responsibilities. Spangenberg preached to his people, and they needed to hear the law and the gospel that produce the repentance and trust of daily Christian life.

Spangenberg's Definition of God's Choosing His Children

After framing his discussion of predestination with his hermeneutical ground rules, Spangenberg put forward his definition of the term in his second sermon. Divine predestination is "an eternal, certain, inalterable, powerful counsel and conclusion of God to make a considerable group from among the entire human race righteous, to save these people, and to glorify them."[43] He expanded the definition immediately:

> It is a certain, conclusive counsel of God concerning future matters, as he wills either to create, continue, and preserve the good, or, on the contrary, to punish, repulse, obstruct, or destroy evil, as he has expressly explained in his Word. From this can be recognized his unmerited grace and goodness toward those who are to be saved and on the other hand his strict and stringent righteousness against those who are to be condemned, and thus his omnipotence and immeasurable power appear everywhere in his gracious benefits and his righteous punishments. It is the final and unshakable decision of God through which he separates his elect from the others to be with him, and those whom he has not included in this decision will not take part with the elect. For God has the free, unbound, uncoerced choice, that he may choose whom he wishes and give these chosen ones to his Son Jesus Christ, to bring them to eternal life. No one can tear from his hand these people who have been given to the Lord Christ. On the other hand, eternal condemnation and the fire of hell has

been prepared for those who are not elect, according to divine righteousness, as Christ himself says in Matthew 25[:41].[44]

Like Marbach, Flinsbach, Palhöfer, Chytraeus, and Selnecker, Spangenberg strove to preserve God's word of judgment that drives sinners to repentance while maintaining the tension with the gospel that alone creates and renews new life through trust in Christ.

In subsequent sermons the preacher fortified his definition of the unconditional nature of God's choice of the saints with several homiletical excursions. He asked the question of the time of God's choice to reinforce his point that God's mercy alone determines the salvation of believers, using Ephesians 1:4, "before the creation of the world," to make that clear.[45] Several alternate explanations that reason might raise were reviewed and dismissed in the third sermon. God did not choose the elect simply so that he might have a following so large that it could not be numbered, like the stars in the heaven (Gen. 15:5), although that does describe the people of God. Rather, God chose his own people quite apart from their numbers (Deut. 7:6-9) (G4b-G5a).

Nor is "papal teaching" correct when it claims that God predestines those who God foresaw would do good works; that undermines the entire biblical teaching of salvation. When papal theologians argue that Paul's speaking of cleansing oneself to be prepared for proper use (2 Tim. 2:20-21) places the burden of salvation on the human agent, readers should note that Paul was doing no more than admonishing believers to rely on God's grace and his calling, avoiding false teaching and godless living, for the apostle himself insisted on salvation through Christ alone in this passage (2:19). This "papal teaching" makes good works the cause of salvation and election, makes Paul's awe of God's wisdom (Rom. 11:33-36) look silly, confuses the temporal with the eternal, deprives believers of their assurance and casts them into despair, takes away God's power, and makes individual believers idols, who do God's work by saving themselves. It does not help to base predestination on foreseen faith or on personal devotion. Both are gifts of God and the result, not the cause, of his choosing (G5b-H3a). Such arguments amount to nothing more than a reversion to putting the power to save in the provenance of the human will, and against that Spangenberg appealed to Luther's position in *De servo arbitrio*. He quoted his mentor:

> In that case God elects no one, nor is there any room left for election, but only the freedom of choice that accepts or rejects his forbearance and wrath. But if God is robbed of the power and wisdom to choose, what will

he be but the false idol, Fortune, at whose nod everything happens at random? And in the end it will come to this, that people are saved and condemned without God's knowledge since he has not determined by his certain choice who are to be saved and who condemned, but after offering to all people in general the forbearance that tolerates and hardens, then the mercy that corrects and punishes, he has left it to them to decide whether they want to be saved or condemned, and in the meantime he has himself, perhaps, gone off to the banquet of the Ethiopians, as Homer says. It is such a god that Aristotle, too, depicts for us, that is to say, one who falls asleep and lets all sorts of people use and abuse his kindness and his condemnation. (H3a-b)[46]

Spangenberg's fifth sermon offered a further explanation by discussing two important characteristics of God's act of planning or predestining the salvation of his people. Here the preacher emphasized the unalterable nature of God's predestination, using Luther's comments on Romans 9 from his preface to the epistle to present the assurance against the devil's doubts that God's unconditioned choice of his people gives them in times of weakness and uncertainty.[47] Augustine, the example of Joseph (Gen. 50:20-21), Samuel's and Balaam's admonitions (1 Sam. 15:29; Num. 23:19), and the Lord's own words through the prophets and Solomon (Mal. 3:6; Isa. 14:24; Eccles. 3:14) all confirm Paul's conclusion that nothing can separate God's people from him (Rom. 8:38-39) (K7b-L2a).

Spangenberg placed his understanding of God's predestination of his children within a larger schema of the Creator's activities. In this way he explicitly affirmed the connection implicit in *De servo arbitrio* between God's choice of his own people and his general providential care that began at creation. That is where Spangenberg's "order of God's activity" began. First, he created all things; second, he created angels and human creatures, who all received a "free, unbound, uncoerced will to desire and do what is good." But sin entered the creation through the misuse of this free will, the third act in the drama of God's creation. Fourthly, in his righteousness God resolved to condemn this evil and apostasy, and fifthly, his omnipotence banned the evil angels forever. The sixth stage of the story, however, presents God's mercy toward his chosen people among the fallen human creatures. Seventh, his truth demanded that punishment be executed, and so he resolved to send Christ to suffer in the place of sinners to satisfy his righteousness. Eighth, God called his chosen children through the Word and through the Holy Spirit, giving them faith, converting, awaking, enlightening, vivifying and justifying them, giving them life and salvation through faith apart from any contribution or action on their part. He then, ninth, governs and preserves them in faith, love, hope, patience, and all virtues against the devil, the world, death, and hell. At the same time, tenth, he has resolved to let those who are not elect be sent to hell; Spangenberg carefully avoided assigning God responsibility for their condemnation, imitating in his own way Melanchthon's use of the concept of God's permissive will. Indeed, he has placed limits on the evil they can do, point eleven (D7b-E2b).[48] Luther had stated, "God foreknows nothing contingently, but he foresees and purposes and does all things by his immutable, eternal, and infallible will." That was the basis of Spangenberg's assertion that God's promise in Christ cannot be changed and that believers thus have sure comfort from the teaching of God's predestining love for them in Christ (E2b-E4b).[49]

Spangenberg did employ Prosper's distinction of *praescientia* from *electio* and *praedestinatio* that, in simplified form, Chytraeus had also used.[50] The former, foreknowledge, is God's seeing of things before they exist or happen. It is a special form of his omniscience, which lies beyond the ability of human reason to grasp. It is a part of his hidden and incomprehensible wisdom, his eternal view of what would take place: the good, which he effects through his willing, and the evil, which he allows to happen. God promotes and is pleased with the good (e.g., Gen. 18:16-19), and he distinguishes it completely from the evil, which he does not support or further and with which he is displeased (Exod. 3:19-20; 14:3-4; Josh. 11:20). Election, in contrast, is God's freely made choice of his own people from among the whole human race, which he knew would fall before it did. God chose in his secret and hidden counsel those who would constitute his church (Deut. 7:6-9; 10:14-15; Pss. 65:4; 106:4-5). This election depends purely upon God's love and mercy; he is in no way bound to choose any fallen human being. God's election of his people became concrete in predestination, which is

> nothing other than the wise and well-considered plan and conclusion of the divine majesty by which he undertook from eternity in his holy counsel to resolve to call those whom he had loved and selected in his only begotten Son Jesus Christ to be his children through the gospel; to enlighten them with the Holy Spirit; to give them faith and through it righteousness, making them new creatures, who with the grace given through the Holy Spirit serve Christ his Son in faith and all godliness, confess the gospel, suffer persecution, bear the cross with patience and finally experience delivery from all evil and inherit eternal salvation. (J3a-b)

This predestination is a spiritual expression of God's love parallel to the providence through which he imparts every temporal blessing (H7b-J6a). Though he did not cite *De servo arbitrio* in this section, Spangenberg reproduced Luther's concerns effectively. Furthermore, it is a characteristic of God's unchangeable plan that it does not coerce the godless to commit sin and do evil. God is not unjust. He justly punishes those who reject his Word, but he does not cause sin or evil. Just as the sun shines and does not cause darkness, but does not give light to the bad eye, so God lets his Word shine, and those who reject his Word bear total responsibility for their unbelief (L2a-L3b).

Spangenberg presumed that only people who had been brought to faith should be contemplating God's predestining love, and he further presumed that the Holy Spirit produces faith in the chosen children of God only through the means of grace. God executes his plan for the salvation of the elect through an outward and an inward call, the preacher explained in his fourth sermon. The outward call comes to all who hear the gospel; many are called but few are chosen (Matt. 22:14). For the number of the elect is small. They also receive and accept the inner call wrought by the Holy Spirit. This inner call helps explain why not all who hear the gospel come to faith, and it also guards against a magical view of the means of grace. God's call through the gospel is "a revelation and proclamation of divine predestination, for through it we understand God's attitude toward us, what his will and attitude toward us is," as disclosed in Matthew 11:28, John 3:16, Isaiah 53:4-5, and Ezekiel 33:11. Those who want to cast doubt on this message must be told that human wisdom cannot comprehend how God works (1 Cor. 2:6-7, 9-10). In Christ the elect learn that God is calling them, and his call produces faith (J6b-K3b).

An underlying pastoral concern for the comfort of afflicted consciences exhibited itself throughout Spangenberg's *De praedestinatione*. Knowing that God has resolved to save believers reminds them of the riches of God's grace and goodness, as Paul had announced when he wrote that God had prepared vessels of mercy for glory (Rom. 9:23). For God has planned from eternity to conform them to the image of his Son (Rom. 8:29). Hearing God's promise that salvation rests alone upon his decision strengthens faith in Christ (Rom. 8:29-39), for none given to him will be lost or torn from his hand (John 6:39; 10:29). In this vein Paul, in Ephesians 1:18, prayed that the Ephesians might enjoy the hope and the riches of God's inheritance for them that he had just told them of at the beginning of the first chapter of his epistle. The elect experience such blessings from God as a witness to his love. They also should turn to the promises of God in Scripture for assurance of his choice of them (Isa. 49:15). In addition, they can be certain that their names have been written in the Book of Life. Spangenberg first demonstrated that God maintains a "Book of Life," although in doing so he cited passages of little comfort since they speak of eradicating sinners from that book (Exod. 32:32-33; Ps. 69:28) as well as those designed to comfort the elect (Dan. 12:1; Luke 10:20; Phil. 4:3; Rev. 20:12-15; 21:27) (L7b-M3b). In the next sermon he defined the Book of Life as Christ, who inscribes the names of believers in himself. "If you do what God has commanded, go to hear the sermon, listen to the gospel which Jesus Christ tells you, and embrace the treasure of grace he offers in your heart, take comfort and rejoice in Christ and his merits, do not let your unworthiness scare you away, call upon grace, and desire to serve God in gratitude with fitting obedience, then you are certainly one of the elect, and nothing can prevent your election, for your name is written before your eyes in the Book of Life since true faith gives the name Christian to those whom Christ calls a child of the living God from the Book of Life" (O8b-P1a). Election produces faith. God's choosing does not work magically, but according to the order he has ordained in establishing the power of his Word in the means of grace, in preaching, absolution, and the sacraments. Spangenberg sought to give guidance to questions which might arise in parishioners' and readers' minds as they sought comfort in God's plan behind his promise. In that process he, like Selnecker, turned to the internal spiritual experiences of his hearers and readers to find confirmation of their election. This was only a supplement, to be sure, but demonstrated his recourse to the subjective side of faith for a part of his consolation of the believer.

Spangenberg then addressed questions related to the comfort God's election gives the troubled sinner. The first asked whether the elect can fall into sin and lose the faith. Some argued that the elect cannot sin or that, once they have sinned, they cannot be brought back to God's grace, Spangenberg noted. Although he did not explicitly instruct his readers to treat such questions only through the distinction of law and gospel, his answers reveal something of the way in which he used the distinction to deal with concrete instances of pastoral care in this manner. Experience teaches, he began, that some who have confessed the faith do become apostates and *mammelukes*.[51] That indicates that they were not among the elect. Many are called but few are chosen, Christ had said (Matt. 22:14), but only those who endure until the end will be saved (Matt. 10:22; 24:13). The elect will be brought back to faith, as were David, Peter, Thomas, and others of the elect, for it is impossible for the elect to be lost, as both the Venerable Bede and Augustine had taught. Spangenberg refused to make light of any sin, including those of the elect, for God is truly displeased with every sin but wants to set aside his wrath and truly desires to give life to sinners. Good performance is no excuse for former sins; the elect must repent of their sins (Ezek. 33:12-13). Believers must trust in God's unconditional grace but at the same time guard against a false security and presumption, Spangenberg stated, distinguishing law and gospel without labeling what he was doing. He enlisted comments to that effect on Psalm 1 from the sixth-century church father Remigius to make the point.[52] Sinners dare not use election as a license to sin. Such sinners belong to those of whom Saint Paul said, "Their condemnation is deserved" (Rom. 3:8).[53] Spangenberg put the law to work, maintaining its necessary tension with the gospel.

The second question asked whether the specific number of the elect had been determined by God's counsel before the foundation of the world. This question had engaged students of Luther and Melanchthon because it seemed a good test of the intention of their teaching regarding predestination. Spangenberg believed that if believers were to have confidence that they were among the elect, they had to trust that their names, and thus their number, lay explicitly in God's plan. He granted that the number is unknown among human creatures, but it rests certainly in the heart of God. Specific names among the local congregation cannot be distinguished from other names of people in the congregation and put on a list of the elect. But it is certain that not all are elect. God based his choice purely on his mercy, and he is a God who orders everything by its measure, number, and weight (Wisd. of Sol. 11:20).[54]

Question 3 addressed the objections of those who held predestination to be a dangerous teaching that causes believers to stumble. Spangenberg cited Augustine against them, pointing out that God's Word is always to be proclaimed. Epictetus's advice, "There is nothing which cannot be used in beneficial fashion if it is grasped at the right place," must be heeded also in the proclamation of God's election, Spangenberg counseled. He further rejected the charge that the doctrine leads to despair. To those who maintained that Luther had warned against teaching predestination, Spangenberg cited Luther, who, he insisted, had warned against false presentations of God's election, not against all presentations of it.[55] Spangenberg also used Luther's words to counsel against speculation regarding predestination, citing his letter to Caspar Aquila of 1530 and the letter to the troubled person, 1545.[56] The reformer had not said that meditation on God's predestination was wrong, but rather that the temptations to know more than God has revealed must be avoided. Spangenberg cited Luther's reminder to look only to the means of grace for assurance of salvation, but he also pointed out that the reformer wanted to avoid abuse of the teaching on predestination, not the teaching itself.[57]

In concluding this sermon he offered again a brief definition of predestination and reprobation.

> The gracious predestination is God's inalterable plan to call those whom
> he has chosen and loved in Christ Jesus his Son, to make them righteous,

to sanctify them, to govern them, and finally to lift them to glory, and thereby make them participants in the riches of his great goodness and glory. Harsh rejection and reprobation is also God's inalterable plan, to permit the others, whom he has not chosen, to be as they are and to punish them with everlasting torment because of their unrighteousness, and thereby to manifest his righteous wrath and his power.[58]

In the fifth sermon this summary is repeated: "In his election God has ordained the means, creates, uses, and exercises them so that the elect may come to righteousness and then move on to glory. In his rejection he has decided that he will punish the godless with everlasting condemnation at last, but he has not ordained sin, nor has he ordained that they must commit sin; much less has he created, used, or exercised this sin through them."[59] It is not hard to imagine, on the basis of such passages, why those who suspected Spangenberg of some sort of deterministic tendencies could accuse him of a doctrine of double predestination. However, he had carefully crafted his words so that he posited God's rejection and punishment of the godless while avoiding the claim that God causes them to sin or determines their fate with a decision or decree that bound them to damnation. Like others in the Wittenberg circle, this preacher was striving to hold the paradox of God's total responsibility and total human responsibility in the Wittenberg tension.

In fact, Spangenberg usually tried meticulously to avoid teaching that God had predestined some to reprobation, but in his attempt to work out in somewhat consistent fashion an answer to questions raised by the tension between divine and human responsibility, he had indeed sometimes backed away from affirming the universality of God's promise in Christ while affirming it at other times. In 1559 he preached on the beginning of John's Gospel. There he stated categorically: "God wants to help all and to bring them to a knowledge of the truth" (Luther's translation of 1 Tim. 2:4), "and that not all believe is their own fault. It is in no way God's failing, for he has the gospel preached to them so that they should believe it and through faith be saved."[60] In his sermon on the 1 Timothy passage, published in 1564, he affirmed that God wants to help all people in every way, but he is also the Savior of all, especially believers, as Paul wrote of "the living God, who is the Savior of all people, especially of those who believe (1 Tim. 4:10b)." For God's help comes to all, but the best help he gives is "when he lets them come to the truth."[61] Regarding 1 Timothy 2:5, "There is one mediator between God and humankind, Christ Jesus," Spangenberg told his hearers and readers, "he gave himself for all, for the upright and the evildoers, and that the evildoers and obstinate do not make use of this gift is their own fault because they do not receive it in faith."[62]

But in his exposition of John 1:9, "The true light, which enlightens everyone, was coming into the world," he explained that "faith is not everyone's thing, and few are chosen." Therefore, Spangenberg concluded, "he enlightens all people who come into the world, that is, all people who are enlightened in the world are enlightened by this light, and no human being comes to earth who can be enlightened by another light." So he also interpreted the word "all" in Romans 11:32, "for God has imprisoned all in disobedience so that he may be merciful to all," and Romans 5:18, "just as one man's trespass led to condemnation for all, so one man's act of righteousness leads to justification and life for all," as referring to "all who receive justification and life in faith, for we see that not all people in fact become righteous through Christ. But those who do become righteous become righteous through him."[63]

Spangenberg distinguished between God's secret predestination and his revealed predestination. God has reserved some knowledge for himself, such as the date of Christ's return, the years of individual lives, the means he will use to overthrow the church's enemies, and other such topics. What God has revealed is that according to his inalterable will and plan he saves sinners through the obedience, merit, suffering, death, and resurrection of Christ (Acts 2:23; 3:20; 10:41; 1 Cor. 15:3-4; Eph. 1:3-11). Furthermore, he has revealed that will to both Jews and Gentiles (Acts 2:5; 10:1-48; 15:1-29; Rom. 9:24; 10:12; 11:11-14; 15:8-13). God also resolved in his plan for humankind to convert human hearts to faith through the preaching and hearing of his Word, but at the same time he wished to condemn those who reject his proclamation and become hardened in their rejection of it (Rom. 9:17-18; 10:19-21; 11:7-8). He has committed himself to sanctifying those who come to faith through his Holy Spirit and to dwelling in their hearts (1 Pet. 1:12-16; 2 Cor. 6:16). His plan also lays crosses upon the saints, who are caught in the battle between Christ and the devil, between true and false teachers; the life of the elect is filled with suffering, trouble, persecution, and opposition, as foretold in Genesis 3:15.[64]

Spangenberg crafted his topic "predestination" from many of the perspectives that shaped Luther's presentation of God and humanity in *De servo arbitrio*. He intended thereby to clarify an important element in the Wittenberg construction of the gospel of Jesus Christ for terrified consciences. This topic brought him into opposition with Melanchthon's concerns regarding the implications of predestination for the question of God's responsibility for evil and for the questions of human irresponsibility and despair that could be generated by false perceptions regarding God's eternal plan for the salvation of his people. Spangenberg's commentaries and his seven sermons on predestination focus primarily on God's nature as the Creator who in his love has fashioned human creatures and has chosen from among fallen humankind a new people, new children, for himself. Although Spangenberg did not repeat in detail Luther's argument for God's sovereign control of all things, including salvation, he accentuated God's total responsibility for saving sinners, whose wills are bound in disobedience and rebellion against their Creator. At the same time, the Mansfeld preacher could not present his conception of the biblical message without distinguishing law and gospel, for (like Marbach, Flinsbach, Selnecker, Chytraeus, and all his closer Gnesio-Lutheran colleagues) he knew that the whole life of the believer had to be a life of repentance, of daily dying as sinner and rising as child of God. On occasion his language drifted into expressions that upheld God's absolute responsibility for everything in a manner that invited criticism. It is not surprising that Philippist sensitivities, rubbed raw by fifteen years of clashing, did not try to put the best construction on his words. Nonetheless, it is clear that Spangenberg was striving to maintain the proper tension and balance of law and gospel, the equilibrium of God's responsibility and human responsibility.

Opposition to Spangenberg

The *Seven Sermons on Predestination* appeared in early 1567; Spangenberg sent a copy to Duke Johann Albrecht of Mecklenburg on February 25.[65] The work aroused discussion immediately; the author informed Duke Johann Albrecht that his former fellow student, Luther's last amanuensis, Johann Aurifaber, pastor in Erfurt, was hard put to defend him there,[66] although the ministerium there was dominated by Gnesio-Lutherans. Apparently Palhöfer, Poach, and Silberschlag raised questions about Spangenberg's work. Like others in their generation, they apparently had serious reservations regarding the topic.

Furthermore, the *Seven Sermons* quickly became a political issue. The electoral Saxon theological leadership had long suffered the attacks of its foes, particularly from the Flacian circle, with relatively little public defense. After Melanchthon's death in 1560, the dean of the faculty was his faithful student and colleague Georg Major, who hated controversy more than his preceptor did.[67] But by 1567 a group of younger men, led by Melanchthon's son-in-law Caspar Peucer, a member of the Wittenberg medical faculty, and his colleagues in the theological faculty, especially Paul Eber and Major's son-in-law Paul Krell, were taking the leadership within the electoral Saxon church into their own hands. They were much less hesitant to engage in public controversy, at the political level as well as the theological. Thus, Elector August's government summoned Spangenberg and his superintendent and friend

Hieronymus Menzel to appear in Dresden in January 1568 to answer charges in connection with the sermons on predestination. After some vacillation and in consultation with their counts, the Mansfeld theologians decided not to go,[68] but the antagonists in electoral Saxony were not to be shaken from the pursuit. Most immediate among the political consequences was the decision to place the *Seven Sermons,* along with a number of other "Flacian" works, on a list of "forbidden books," that is, books that Saxon booksellers were not to offer and students at the universities of Wittenberg and Leipzig were not to possess or read.[69]

Theologically, August's theologians engaged Spangenberg's work in their *Final Report* on the colloquy at Altenburg, published in 1570,[70] and more briefly in their *Foundation of the True Christian Church,* issued in 1571.[71] In these works the electoral Saxon ecclesiastical establishment came out fighting, turning the tables on their opponents by accusing them of a series of heresies, among them what they held to be the false view of predestination found in Spangenberg's *Seven Sermons.* It is clear that the electoral Saxon critique was driven by two concerns: theologically to uphold human responsibility without denying God's responsibility for salvation, and pastorally to prevent the licentiousness or the despair of those who would find in a theology of predestination either permission to sin or the hopelessness of the reprobate. The examination of Spangenberg's ideas began with the charge that he was teaching a "brand-new, never before heard of gospel" *(gantz nagel neu vnerhorte Euangelium),* a "special paragon of the flacian spirit."[72] (The Wittenberg faculty associated as many of its opponents as possible with the foreigner Flacius, who had antagonized most of his friends as well as his longer-term foes.) Against this heresy the Wittenberg and Leipzig faculties argued that believers should not seek answers regarding their salvation in the secret, hidden, and inscrutable counsel of God, but in God's clear and incontrovertible Word and command. The invention of contradictory wills in God, choosing some for salvation and others for damnation, conflicts with John 3:16 and makes God a "respecter of persons," who treats some people in one way and others in another (against Acts 10:34). For Spangenberg taught, the Saxons posited, that not all have been included in God's promises of salvation. His fabrication of the "particularity of election" fit well with the Flacian view of the human creature as a block of wood or stone, they concluded, labeling it a terrible and harmful confusion of law and gospel that eradicates the entire gospel by abolishing the "universality" of the promise that comforts every troubled heart (186a-187b). Thus, the electoral Saxon theologians found Spangenberg's *Seven Sermons on Predestination* a "godless, harmful, damnable book," closer to Xenophon's view of the gods, who show partiality to some, arbitrarily and randomly refusing to support others. Flacius had been the first to give this damnable devilish answer that God does not owe anyone anything, so no one can accuse him of being unfair. Such an answer takes away the universality of God's promises and leaves only this false idea of particularity. Therefore, the Saxon theologians claimed, Flacius and Spangenberg abolished the means of grace and the office of preaching, the promise of the Holy Spirit, and God's pledge of salvation (195a-197b).

Precisely the agony of doubt whether they were among a specific number of God's chosen people, whether their names were written in the Book of Life, had caused Cain, Saul, Ahithophel, Judas, Francisco Spiera, and Peter Ilesuanus to despair. Others use such a teaching as an excuse for living in a "wild, dissolute, defiant security." Both these ungodly consequences can be prevented by listening to God's Word (187b-189a). Two questions confront people in their greatest and most difficult spiritual struggles. The first concerns their own merit and unworthiness because of their sins. The second questions the universality of the promise that is offered in Christ. In such struggles the promise that Christ has died for all is the only message of comfort. If the promise is valid only for those whom God chose and predestined in his eternal counsel, then there is no hope. Comfort, on the contrary, is found only in God's Word, in the proclamation of his wrath upon all and in the proclamation of his grace and mercy for all. Believers dare not turn to this secret counsel, but only to the Word that reveals what God has decided (189a-192b). For those whom God rejects and condemns are not rejected and condemned because of his gracious counsel and decision. The fault lies alone with the world's wickedness and its terrible contempt for his Word, his Son, his eternal grace (192b-193a).

The electoral Saxons did not shy away from addressing Bible passages regarding God's sovereign choice of believers, passages they knew could be used to contradict their position. They mentioned Romans 9:16, "So it depends not on human will or exertion but on God who shows mercy," and Ephesians 1:3-11, or 2 Timothy 1:9, "God has saved and called us with a holy calling, not according to our works but according to his own purpose and grace. This grace was given to us in Christ Jesus before the ages began." Following Melanchthon's disposition of the doctrine of predestination in 1543, they applied these passages not to individuals but to the entire church (194b-195a).[73] Finally, the electoral Saxons brought their readers back to Luther's comments on Genesis 26, where Luther repudiated the harmful doctrine of Spangenberg, this "blind man, audacious, insolent, and impudent" (198a-b). Whatever political factors swayed the electoral Saxon engagement with Spangenberg's person, and whatever pent-up psychological frustrations with

Gnesio-Lutheran criticism burst out in the Wittenberg and Leipzig reaction to him, it cannot be denied that honest and significant theological concerns also moved Melanchthon's loyal followers to defend the integrity of the human creature whom God made to trust and obey even though they misrepresented their opponents' positions. Like all theological disputes, this debate exhibited a mixture of politics and personality with genuine theological principles.

About this time a popular exposition of *God's Election and Eternal Predestination* appeared from the presses of Jakob Bärwald's heirs in Leipzig under the names of Luther and Melanchthon. The electoral Saxon ecclesiastical establishment used the Bärwald press as one of its mouthpieces. The booklet was published in what seems to be a series of devotional tracts. In fact, there were no citations from Luther in the work, and only one from his colleague, but its authors apparently believed they were reliably and faithfully representing the reformers' understanding of the teaching that a few years earlier would not have earned any public treatment. It begins with the passage "Many are called, but few are chosen" (Matt. 22:14). Believers are not to pose questions that concern God in his majesty. They should avoid thinking about his predetermination, lest they fall into despair. They should look to Christ alone. Only the preaching of the gospel reveals God's disposition toward sinners, and in its presentation of Christ alone is comfort to be found.[74] The Wittenberg theologians were not merely using the doctrine of predestination in their polemic. They worried that the public discussion of this teaching could lead to despair among the people.

Spangenberg replied to the *Final Report* in a volume prepared by his fellow pastors in Mansfeld in 1570. Their attacks on the theology of electoral Saxony[75] had won them mention in the *Final Report,* and Spangenberg added his own appendix to their reply.[76] He began by citing Chrysostom: Christians should diligently strive for a good conscience and a good name. He had a good conscience; he wished to defend his name against the charges lodged against him "out of pure hatred, without basis and truth." Christ, the prophets, and the apostles had experienced this cross, and he was prepared to bear it as well.[77] In fact, Spangenberg was capable of even sharper personal exchange. He knew he had not departed from Luther's teaching and regretted that the electoral Saxon theologians had decided to disagree with his teaching in public, since Paul had spoken so clearly in Romans and Ephesians on the subject of predestination. He rejected the charge that his teaching was "brand-new"; Luther had taught it, in accord with Romans 8–11 and Ephesians 1, as had Augustine, Melanchthon (in his first *Loci communes,* his annotations on Romans, and his commentary on John, works, it must be noted, that had been published in 1522-23), Urbanus Rhegius, and Johannes Brenz. Indeed, in a deft move against the electoral Saxon theologians, who already were being labeled "crypto-Calvinists" because of their sacramental teaching, Spangenberg asked rhetorically if John Calvin, Heinrich Bullinger, Peter Martyr Vermigli, Andreas Hyperius, (Andreas) Fricius (Modrzewski), and others had not written on the topic. But above all, Luther had taught precisely what Spangenberg was teaching, in *De servo arbitrio* and in his comments on Genesis 26. For what Luther had written in *De servo arbitrio* he did not repudiate in his Genesis lecture — he simply clarified his intention in the earlier work.[78] His own father, Spangenberg recalled, had also taught that God's choice of the elect, made before the beginning of the world, stands firm and cannot fail.[79] Spangenberg concluded that he was teaching no "brand-new" doctrine.

He further spurned the accusation that he had exhibited a poisonous spirit and the charges that his teaching would lead to dissolute living. He denied having taught that people should try to ascertain God's will and plan for their lives apart from the Word of God. In large print he wrote, "The entire teaching of predestination is rooted in Christ, stems from him, and returns to him. As soon as Christ is excluded for a moment from predestination, the doctrine is nothing, and is false and incorrect." Since Christ had set forth this teaching, the electoral Saxons should refrain from their blasphemy.[80]

He then addressed the charge that he taught that Christ was not the savior of all but only of some human beings. He used Urbanus Rhegius's words from his work "on the perfection and fruit of Christ's sufferings."[81] Rhegius had written that Christ had merited the abolition of guilt and the bestowal of grace and glory for all people. That not all are saved is not due to limits of his suffering but to the world that does not want to receive his merits and trust in him. Rhegius had continued by addressing a series of questions: "Who are those who believe in him? And why do not all believe? Why does he give faith to one person and not to another?" His answer rested upon his understanding of God's choosing his own. He referred readers to Acts 13:48, "as many as had been destined for eternal life became believers," and to Romans 8:30, "those whom he predestined, he called."[82] To that Spangenberg added Luther's comments on Romans 9–11 in his preface to the epistle to the Romans: there the reformer had taught "God's eternal predestination, from which flows who is to believe and who is not to believe, who will be freed from sin and who will not be freed from sin, so that it is not a matter that rests in our hands but alone in God's hands. That is absolutely necessary, for we are so weak and uncertain, that if it depended upon us, no one would be saved. The devil certainly overpowers us all. But God is certain and his predestination does not fail." For Spangenberg this was decisive. To support this position he cited

Melanchthon's annotations on Romans 8 from 1522.[83] Like many of his contemporaries, Spangenberg believed there had once been essential agreement between Luther and Melanchthon, whatever he may have thought about later divergences, and he wished to save his preceptor for the tradition of Wittenberg theology when he could.

Spangenberg further rejected the charge that he had concocted a doctrine of two contradictory wills in God. God's will is one, and this will had resolved to choose people in Christ before the world was created. On the basis of God's choice and the calling to faith in Christ that follows from it, God gives salvation. Those who are not chosen and do not believe in Christ are condemned, as Mark 16:16 states. God indeed loved the whole world, but those who believe are those who are saved (John 3:16). Spangenberg called it absurd to believe that this makes God a "respecter of persons."[84] His teaching simply repeats the biblical writers' insistence that God saves sinners apart from any conditions that they must fulfill.[85]

In reacting to the accusation that he denied the universality of the promises of God, he affirmed only that the promises apply to all who believe. By defining the promise of Christ precisely in this way, Spangenberg seemed to limit its validity for all sinners and justify his opponents' attack. Because he elsewhere speaks of God's will to save all people, it is more likely that this is an example of the general Wittenberg tendency to focus on the concrete application of the promise and its realization through the gift of faith. Here his goal was to assure every believer of the sure comfort found in God's choice of him or her. The elect constitute a large and glorious number. He emphasized that he shared the electoral Saxon desire to comfort the troubled conscience through the Word. Only through the means of grace can those in spiritual struggles find consolation. But the promise of the gospel of Christ rests upon God's plan for saving his own, completely apart from human merit. This also is necessary for the full consolation of the troubled.[86]

In the end both sides had repeated their suspicions of the other and their own chief concerns. Uniting them, as students of Wittenberg, was the belief in God's total responsibility for salvation and the human creature's total responsibility for trust and obedience to the Creator. Dividing them were deeply felt concerns that the other side in their dispute was sacrificing the pure and proper expression of their own fundamental concern. The Wittenberg and Leipzig theologians were convinced that Spangenberg was making God responsible for evil and sacrificing the integrity of the human being by not taking seriously the need for responsible human response to God in trusting in Christ with heart, soul, and mind, and obeying his commands. Spangenberg and the Mansfeld ministerium were certain that the electoral Saxon ministerium had returned to medieval teaching by denying God's sole responsibility for the salvation of sinners. The bitterness and rancor of a decade and a half of dispute and the deeply held persuasions of each side made a breakthrough to concord in teaching most difficult.

Martin Chemnitz

Spangenberg's sermons commanded the attention of the entire Wittenberg circle, including that of Martin Chemnitz, the superintendent of the church in Braunschweig. He wrote to a Wittenberg student, Conrad Schlüsselburg, shortly after the appearance of Spangenberg's sermons:

> I have read Spangenberg's little book on predestination, and I do not see that it teaches anything false or any newly invented formulations. It repeats what Augustine, Luther, and Brenz have taught regarding the question on the basis of God's Word and does so in the same words for the most part. I would like, however, not to arouse controversy, especially in this embattled time, which offers more than enough other disputes. For I see what a long web of insoluble and dangerous questions hang from this argument. Certain things are not explicated sufficiently in Spangenberg's book, and they could give occasion for arguments that it would be better not to stir up.[87]

Chemnitz, one of Melanchthon's few prized pupils who had lectured on the *Loci communes,* had succeeded Joachim Mörlin, his longtime friend and fellow combatant in the disputes over the Wittenberg legacy, as superintendent of the city's churches on October 15, 1567.[88] Brief periods of study in Wittenberg combined with a strict and extensive program of private study, which included intensive engagement with Luther's works and wide-ranging reading of the ancient fathers of the church, had shaped Chemnitz into a leading voice within north German Lutheran churches. Together with Mörlin, he had claimed a prominent role in defining the public confession of the ministeria of Lower Saxony on several issues, above all, the Lord's Supper. In 1565 he had begun to publish what would become a four-volume critique of the Council of Trent, and in its first volume the depth of his understanding of Luther's and Melanchthon's teaching on justification by grace through faith in Christ became readily apparent. The appearance of Spangenberg's treatise and discussions of God's election of the faithful within the duchy of Braunschweig-Wolfenbüttel propelled Chemnitz into the middle of the development of the Lutheran doctrine of predestination. The student was imbued with Melanchthon's strong concern for the clear proclamation of human responsibility and his neuralgic reaction against any hint that God might be responsible for evil, and so he was cautious and wary when confronted by the unambiguous proclamation of God's predestining love set forth by Spangenberg. As mentioned above, when Chemnitz had summarized his views of the freedom of choice in 1561, his chief concern was the assertion that God is not the cause of sin and evil. Then he had used Luther's comments in his Genesis lectures on *De servo arbitrio* to warn against interpreting it in a deterministic way with a doctrine of absolute necessity that would undercut human responsibility for sin.[89]

Chemnitz's letter to Schlüsselburg did not immediately lead to taking a public stance on the issue in print, although in 1570 he did guide the ministerium in Göttingen to its settlement of related issues regarding the freedom of the will.[90] The controversy that Spangenberg's book evoked, however, certainly lies in the background of his addressing the biblical teaching of God's election in the autumn of 1572. At that time some "misunderstandings" regarding divine election did elicit a request from his prince, Duke Julius of Braunschweig-Wolfenbüttel, that the superintendent preach on the subject "for the sake of Christian unity" and agreement on the subject.[91] Chemnitz complied with a sermon in the ducal chapel in Wolfenbüttel on the Gospel lesson for the twenty-second Sunday after Trinity, Matthew 22:1-14, the parable of the wedding feast, which includes the words "Many are called but few are chosen" (v. 14). It was published the following year. When Chemnitz's fellow pastor Melchior Neukirch (ca. 1540-97) organized selected sermons from Chemnitz's pen into a postil in 1594, he chose this sermon for the twenty-second Sunday after Trinity.[92]

In 1569, three years before he preached on Matthew 22, Chemnitz prepared a handbook for pastors and preachers in Braunschweig-Wolfenbüttel to use in preparation for their doctrinal examinations during the official visitation of the churches. That work had constituted an important part of the Reformation of Duke Julius's lands. Julius had acceded to the throne the previous year and began immediately to introduce the Lutheran faith that his father, Duke Heinrich, had tried so hard to stamp out. In the first edition of this little booklet, Chemnitz did not treat the doctrine of election at all, but the second edition, issued in the autumn of 1574, contained a fairly extensive examination of predestination, repeating elements from the sermon on Matthew 22 of two years earlier.[93] The explication in this enchiridion of the doctrine aimed at a more technical theological treatment of the biblical material and how to convey it than readers found in his sermon, but its goal remained fixed upon preaching and teaching the truth about God's unconditional choice of his children before the foundation of the world. Chemnitz intended also in this discussion of election to prepare pastoral candidates for the tasks of warning and comforting pious members of congregations. As similar as the treatments of election are in the sermon and the textbook, the brief interval between his delivery of the sermon and his revision of the handbook did witness developments in his teaching.

Chemnitz preached the sermon for people he called "common, simple hearers." He described it as a "plain, elementary sermon on the level of children," specifically designed to explain this deep secret of God's promise in a simple manner suitable for little children learning the catechism, for he was nothing more than a preacher of the catechism himself.[94] At this level he hoped to set forth fundamental guidelines for the use of the biblical teaching on God's choosing of his own children in a way that did not give rise to despair or arrogant security.

The preacher first laid down a hermeneutical rule to guide consideration of the text since it took form in a parable. Parables are not stories that can be interpreted in one way by one person, in another by another, as might be thought from their genre, Chemnitz reminded the congregation. Christ always gave his hearers the key to the meaning of the parable either preceding or following the story. In this case he indicated that the parable concerned "the difficult article of faith on the great mystery of God's predestination, how God predestined, elected, and ordained the elect in Christ Jesus to eternal life." Christ placed this mystery before his hearers in parable form to remind preachers not to try to soar too high with their thoughts and to remind hearers to grasp this article of faith in all simplicity.[95]

The pastoral care expressed here was echoed in a letter written four years later regarding a controversy over predestination in the town of Osterode. There Chemnitz refused to "give a categorical answer to naked, abbreviated, dangerous questions" apart from their context in proclamation or teaching.[96] Chemnitz's caution expressed itself also in his handbook, as he introduced pastors to the mystery of election. He rejected his preceptor's idea that the proclamation of God's choosing the elect in Christ for salvation before the world began was not useful or necessary, was offensive and harmful.[97] Chemnitz proceeded directly to the pastoral problems encountered in proclaiming God's election: presumption and despair. He argued that election, like all biblical teaching, is designed to lead to repentance and faith. It should assure believers of salvation.[98] In his own sermon on Matthew 22 he had indeed done this. Chemnitz further explained to his hearers that in his fatherly and faithful love God has given his people his Word to bring them hope through patience and comfort (Rom. 15:4), to warn them (1 Cor. 10:11), to provide teaching, reproof, correction, and improvement in righteousness (2 Tim. 3:16). For the Holy Spirit works through the Word as it is proclaimed, heard, and meditated upon (2 Cor. 3:3); it is a living seed through which they receive new birth (1 Pet. 1:23) and God's power to save (Rom. 1:16).[99] Chemnitz's belief that God's Word is his means of granting grace and that it actually conveys saving power, bringing about new life and salvation in its hearers, provided the foundation of his entire comprehension of how God reveals his electing will to believers. He sketched the proper way to present God's election of his own within the framework of the proper distinction of law and gospel.[100]

Having laid the groundwork for pastoral care and application of his message to his hearers' lives, Chemnitz turned to the theological framework of his analysis of the biblical material. He reiterated Prosper's distinction between God's foreknowledge of all things, including evil, and his electing or predestining knowledge. The former embraces what he knew about human deeds that would oppose his will; in no way has God caused them, even though he sets limits upon them (Acts 14:16; 17:26). God's predestination and election are an expression of his gracious will and good pleasure; in this case God is the cause of everything good. He creates the good. In proffering guidelines for preaching on election, Chemnitz set forth the distinction between thinking of the doctrine *blos* (in isolation or simply in and of itself as a philosophical concept, which could lead logically to a doctrine of double predestination) and thinking of it in Christ, the true Book of Life. (In fact, for Chemnitz, no doctrine should be thought of apart from Christ.) The former casts the preacher into speculation about the secret counsel of God, the latter onto the biblical revelation in Matthew 22, Romans 8, and Ephesians 1. The latter focuses on the call God gives through the means of grace, on justification and glorification, not on the mystery of how God chose his own.

In his sermon on Matthew 22 Chemnitz had traced God's design for human salvation and execution of this plan in seven stages;[101] the handbook presented God's saving action in eight points, offered to guide the preacher's meditation upon the redemption of sinners. (1) God resolved and planned to redeem humankind through pure grace in Christ. Chemnitz's interest in Christology expressed itself here, in the sermon in two distinct points, the decision of God the Father to have his Son assume human nature, allegorically compared to the king's giving up his offspring for marriage in the parable, and God's placing his Son under the law as a sacrifice for sin. (2) This grace in Christ's merits and blessings was to be presented to human creatures through the revealed Word and the sacraments God would place alongside it. The sermon distinguished in two stages God's decision to select the believers who would be the brides of his Son and to call them through the means of grace. (3) God works effectively in human hearts, enlightening them through the Holy Spirit, effecting true repentance in them, kindling, increasing, strengthening, and preserving faith in them through the preaching, hearing, and meditation on the Word. This constituted the sermon's fifth event in salvation. (4) God justifies the repentant believers and condemns those who resisted his Word. (5) Through the Holy Spirit God sanctifies and renews the justified and brings them to new obedience. (6) God preserves his people in the face of all evil, against sin, death, devil, the world, and their flesh, in the midst of temptation, cross, spiritual struggles, and suffering — the sermon's sixth point. (7) God preserves those who rely firmly on his Word, pray diligently, and remain faithful, and he pours out his wrath on those who show contempt for his Word. (8) God planned the eternal salvation of those he had called and justified, when they have endured to the end, for that is why he predestined his own — that they might be saved. The sermon concluded with an assertion not contained in the handbook: because God knew that the evil in human nature would not follow this call from God and the efforts of the Holy Spirit, but would resist and refuse God's grace, he resolved to condemn all who showed contempt for his call. All these aspects of God's gracious interaction with his people are included in his predestining resolution or plan, according to Chemnitz.[102]

Spangenberg had also used Romans 8 to construct steps in God's execution of his plan of salvation: God formulated a purpose and plan; he predestined; he called his own through the means of grace; he justified the elect whom he called; and he will glorify his chosen children. As with Spangenberg, the list functions in a rather limited way for Chemnitz. It is not an effort to identify precisely how God operates from his perspective, but rather it describes the human experience of God's saving action. Chemnitz took as the core of his description of God's saving action the description of Romans 8:29-30, but he did not suggest that a strict progression of certain experiences is necessary for salvation.

A definite homiletical structure determined the way Chemnitz's sermon unfolded, and the preacher informed his hearers what they should listen for. His sermon was to begin with an exposition of the article of faith presented in the parable. It would then provide reproof and correction (2 Tim. 3:16). It would conclude with comfort for its hearers. First, Chemnitz affirmed that God's Word clearly teaches that "God predestined, chose, and ordained those who would inherit eternal life before the foundation of the world was laid" (Eph. 1:3-4). He reinforced this fundamental assertion with a bevy of Bible passages, as was his wont in his homiletical method (2 Tim. 1:9; John 13:18a; Rom. 9:11b-12; 8:29; 2 Tim. 2:19a; Phil. 4:3c). However, hearers must remember that human reason cannot grasp this mystery. Because God's choice cannot be changed (Rom. 11:29; Isa. 46:10), some fall into ungodly security and vice, arguing that they can neglect Word, sacrament, repentance, faith, and improvement of life because they are elect in any case. Others fall into despair because they do not know whether their names are in the Book of Life despite their practice of repentance, faith, and the beginnings of new life, saying all that is in vain if they were not chosen before the foundation of the world. Such difficulties make it necessary to consider the mystery of election through a parable.[103] Chemnitz was apprising his hearers that considering the doctrine of election would confront them with the tension inherent in the paradox of total divine responsibility and total human responsibility.

He continued with a reflection of his longtime concern: that God not be held responsible for evil. God did not muster his troops before the beginning of the world and say, "This one I am writing into the Book of Life, that one I am writing into the Book of Death. This one is to be saved, that one is to be rejected and damned," Chemnitz assured his hearers. He recalled a metaphor from Jean Gerson (1363-1429), the Parisian theologian whose work Luther had also frequently cited: "Some dream up ideas, such as if the manager of the kitchen had a cage full of pigeons and told the cook, 'slaughter these, let those go free and fly away.'" Such ideas confuse the matter completely. In this parable Christ teaches instead that "God's predestination or choosing consists of and encompasses the fact that God saw ahead of time that the human race would fall away from him through sin and because of this fall be under God's wrath and the devil's power unto eternal ruin and damnation; because of this before the foundation of the world God considered, resolved, and determined how he could save the human race from its ruin." Here Chemnitz avoided specific mention of God's choice of individual believers. It appears that he was delicately treading the path of presenting the doctrine in a way that would safeguard human responsibility and prevent any implication of divine responsibility for evil by abstracting the doctrine of election out of the realm of application to individual believers.[104]

The caution Chemnitz initially exhibited in his 1572 sermon regarding the specific number of the elect and the direct application of God's election to individual believers had been abandoned by August 1574. In direct confrontation with the ideas attributed to the Philippist establishment in Leipzig and Wittenberg, recently discredited, he wrote, "There is no basis for the opinion that God prepared no more than salvation in general and that the persons who are supposed to be saved are able to work out their own salvation with their own powers and abilities and must do so. Rather, in his eternal plan, according to his gracious resolution, God thought of each and every person among the elect who is supposed to be saved through Christ, and he predestined and chose them for salvation, and he ordained how he would bring them to faith, support and preserve them, through his grace, gifts, and activity." In no way can people prepare themselves to be eligible for God's election. He chose his people before the foundation of the world, and their interaction with God's Word, effected by the Holy Spirit, results from that unconditioned choice of God.[105]

The critical question for pastoral care came from yet another angle: How can I know that I am among the elect? Chemnitz's answer in the handbook echoed that of the two sermons he had preached on the subject; he used both parables, from Matthew 22 and Matthew 20, in his answer. The means of grace bring this comfort to those who believe. The promise of God in the Word confirms that they are children of God. Chemnitz insisted that the call of God never ceases to be his earnest intention for those who hear his Word. Those who turn away from the voice of God in his Word will perish, but those who live in repentance and faith can be certain that God will remain faithful as well.[106]

The summary of the treatment of this doctrine expresses itself in pastoral terms: "What is the proper use of this teaching? What is its purpose? What is it good for?" Pastors were to keep six points in mind when using the teaching regarding election. (1) This teaching confirms God's unconditional grace by resting it upon God's decision before he created the world. (2) It powerfully refutes all opinions that want to ascribe some power to the human will in spiritual and divine matters. (3) It brings the comfort of knowing that God resolved and ordained salvation for his people before the foundation of the world. (4) It gives hope in the face of all of Satan's attacks. (5) It offers comfort in the midst of all suffering and every cross, for it conveys Paul's certainty that such things cannot separate God's people from him (Rom. 8:38-39). (6) Finally, it also provides a warning against showing contempt for God's Word.[107] This last point changes the focus from God's gift of new life in Christ to the actions of the believers, from the gospel to the law, from the Lord's responsibility to human responsibility.

The final section of Chemnitz's treatment in his handbook poses a series of objections, in good Melanchthonian rhetorical style, to what had been presented: If there is a definite number of elect, then why should I bother? Why is God's Word preached in some places and not in others? Why are some hardened in their hearts and others converted? Why are some who fall raised up again and others given over to a reprobate mind? Chemnitz refused to fall into the trap of pushing either side of the paradox of responsibilities so far that "logical" answers could be produced to these questions. In Söderlund's phrase, he adhered to the "broken" or "asymmetrical" — law/gospel — approach to election. These things, he stated, must be left as mysteries, a part of God's secret counsel. That God knows all things is clear, but the faithful dare never transgress the limits of their knowledge imposed by God's revelation and by what he has not revealed there. The treatment of election ends with a passage Chemnitz and many of his Wittenberg contemporaries cited often, following Luther in his concluding remarks of *De servo arbitrio:*[108] "O the depth of the riches of the wisdom and knowledge of God; how unsearchable are his judgments, and how past finding out are his ways, for who has known the mind of the Lord? Or who has been a counselor to him? that is, beyond and above that which he has revealed to those using his Word" (Rom. 11:33-34).[109]

In his sermon Chemnitz had preferred talking about the two natures of Christ and the incarnation as God's means of procuring the salvation of believers, and so he used the parable's motif of marriage as the occasion to burst into a coda of praise to God for bringing human and divine natures together in the one person of Christ. Chemnitz found a glorious guarantee of human redemption and salvation in the personal union of the two natures. With recent attacks from the Wittenberg crypto-Philippists on the position he had developed in his *On the Two Natures of Christ* clearly in mind, he added, "Not that the human nature becomes equal to the divinity, but that through the personal union it is placed in fellowship with the honor and worthiness of God's Son and with all that belongs to him."[110]

With this discussion of the relationship between bridegroom, bride, and guests in the parable, Chemnitz led his hearers into a lengthy consideration of the invitation or call which the king extended through his servants. The use of the means of grace was key to Chemnitz's discussion of election. All knowledge of believers' election had to be dependent on the promise of the forgiveness of sins, which was the operative factor in realizing what God intended in his eternal choice. Chemnitz turned only to the revealed God. For Paul praises God for revealing his secret, hidden counsel through the proclamation of the gospel. "When I want to know what God decided in his grace in regard to me and my salvation, I dare not climb up to heaven. That is too high for me. I can only receive the report through the call which is presented to me in the proclamation of the Gospel and is sealed and confirmed for me through the sacraments."[111]

This sufficed for the first part of Chemnitz's sermon. The second part — the warning hearers should heed in the parable — rested upon the experience of the Old Testament Jews, who found in their chosenness a ground for ungodly security. Like Luther, Melanchthon, and all his Wittenberg contemporaries, Chemnitz believed that the whole life of the believer is a life of repentance; those bound in sin were to be liberated to be free to serve the neighbor, not to be bound to new sins. To avoid this kind of self-deception among his own hearers, Chemnitz cautioned the congregation, "God the heavenly king did not, in his divine counsel before the world began, ordain or resolve his election or choice so that the guests, when they had been called to the wedding, might show contempt for that Word, refuse to follow it, mock and kill the servants that brought it to them, or appear externally to be elect but without true repentance and conversion." No, God chose his elect that they might "hear the Word through which they are called, accept it through God's power and blessing, follow it, shed the old creature through true repentance, and put on the Lord Christ through true faith, let the Holy Spirit reign in their lives and lead them on God's paths." Those who resist the Word that calls them will, according to God's eternal plan, be damned (C2a-b). With rhetorical flourish the preacher marveled that invited guests could reject such a wonderful invitation. Did God invite people to trouble and torture them? No! He invited them to give them eternal life. Do the guests have to do some kind of hard work or give gifts to attend? No! He has prepared everything. Will the guests lie under the table or be hounded by dogs? No! They will sit at the high table of eternal salvation. Human nature is so miserably perverted by sin that sinners want salvation without heeding God's call. Sinners do not want to repent! The parable demonstrates to both preachers and hearers the necessity of the proclamation of repentance. For preachers in particular, that means they pay careful attention to their message, proclaiming no false teaching but faithfully administering Word and sacrament (C2b-D2b).[112]

The parable compelled the preacher to add one more warning. One guest did not try to kill the servants who were issuing the invitation. He sat down at the table, confessed God's Word, boasted in the gospel, continually had the Word on his lips, and put the gospel first, but he kept wearing the "fur coat of the Pharisees" and did not dress in the wedding garment. The king threw him into outer darkness because he did not want to discard the old creature but rather desired to remain in sin without true repentance. God's forgiveness comes to sinners again and again, but refusal to repent earns condemnation. Similarly, reliance on works earns condemnation (D2b-D4a). With this Chemnitz had laid down the law with a strong admonition to respond to God's Word. The burden of the human responsibility to obey the first commandment crushes the sinner.

The third part of the sermon aimed at comforting troubled consciences. Chemnitz directed those with questions about their own standing before God to the means of grace. As God had repeatedly stated (Rom. 10:8; 8:30; Eph. 1:13; 1 Cor. 2:10), the call of his Word in the means of grace gives assurance to individual believers. "I know that his general call refers to my person specifically because in Absolution and in the sacrament the general promise is applied to me, for my person, specifically, and is sealed and made certain" (D4b-E1a). Acceptance of the promise rests in no way upon human power, Chemnitz reminded his hearers. It is contrary to the entire Scripture to teach that "the natural free will of the unregenerate human being has the power and ability to accept God's grace" (1 Cor. 2:14-16; 2 Cor. 3:4-6; Rom. 8:14; etc.) (E1b). At this point in the sermon Chemnitz clearly expressed the trust that individual believers can have that they are elect:

> My salvation meant so much to our Lord God that he planned it before the foundation of the world, and because I have been ordained for salvation, I have the strong and sure assurance of it in the face of the weakness of my flesh, the world's anger, and the deceit and might of all the gates of hell. I know from this that God will not change his disposition and will toward me, for Paul said in Romans 11[:29], "God's gifts and call are unchangeable." This article gives believers the comfort that their own salvation does not rest upon their works or worthiness but that grace was given to them in Christ Jesus before the beginning of the world, when they did not yet exist. . . . "If God is for us, who can be against us! Who will separate us from God's love, for I am certain that neither death nor life, nor what is present nor what is in the future, can separate us from God's love, which is in Christ Jesus our Lord" [Rom. 8:31, 35-38]. (E2a-b)

Here Chemnitz clearly affirmed the total responsibility of God for the salvation of sinners.

With pastoral sensitivity Chemnitz faced the hard question: What about those who have begun in faith but have fallen away? For only those who endure to the end will be saved. "This article of faith gives those who have been called according to God's counsel through the Word a comforting answer." Christ's sheep hear his voice and will not perish nor be torn from his hand (John 10:27-28). God will hold fast to those he has called unto the end (1 Cor. 1:8-9). For "he who has begun a good work in you will fulfill it on the day of Jesus Christ" (Phil. 1:6). Adam had received all the gifts and properties of the perfect, pure human nature, but had lost them. Through the redemption accomplished when God united human nature with the divine nature in the one person of his Son, God has restored the blessedness of humanity (E2b-E3b).[113] Here Chemnitz let the gospel rule.

Chemnitz ended his sermon by expanding upon the comfort offered by the text with a discussion of the wedding garment. With verses that described the sinner's clothing (Isa. 64:6) and that pictured God's children in the dress of glory (2 Cor. 5:2-4; Ps. 45:8-10; Gal. 3:27; Isa. 61:10), he brought the assurance to his hearers that the king will recognize his own when he comes, even though their appearance in this world may be lowly. Because the renewal of the believer is not complete, only Christ will serve as the wedding garment of the believer before God's judgment throne (E3b-E4a). In this manner Chemnitz was attempting to draw the balance between human and divine responsibility within the dialectic between law and gospel.

Chemnitz reflected concern for upholding God's sovereign grace and his unconditional mercy for his chosen children while at the same time rejecting the slightest hint that the Creator could be responsible for evil. His homiletic and instructional treatments of election never strayed from the context of the proper distinction of law and gospel, with the call for repentance and the insistence on full human responsibility for obedience to God sensitively woven together with the pronouncement of the work of Christ and the steadfast love of God for his children. His preaching had prepared him to formulate a means of bringing concord to his church. His preaching had prepared a text that could present the Wittenberg teaching on predestination well.

Jakob Andreae

Chemnitz's partners in composing concord included Nikolaus Selnecker, David Chytraeus, and Jakob Andreae. Andreae had studied theology at the University of Tübingen, not far from his birthplace in Waiblingen in Swabia, in the principality of Württemberg. He had come to Tübingen at age thirteen after preparatory school in Stuttgart, at a time when the theology faculty of the university was weak, and his professors exercised less influence on his thinking than did his colleague in the service of the Württemberg church, Johannes Brenz. In spite of his less than brilliant theological capabilities, he advanced in the ecclesiastical service of Duke Christoph of Württemberg after the Smalcald War as something of an understudy to Brenz. Andreae and his prince dedicated Andreae's life to the cause of establishing harmony and unity within the church. As pastor in Göppingen and then professor in Tübingen, Andreae served the duke and his son Ulrich as a local administrator, both in the town and later at the university, but above all he became their most effective diplomatic ambassador to other churches. His missions to ducal Saxony in 1562 and to Strasbourg in 1563 are but two examples. The crowning event of his career was his leadership of the efforts that resulted in the Formula of Concord.

If Andreae had not been involved in what became the successful search for concord among the Lutheran churches, his disputation on predestination from 1574 might well go unnoticed. However, the thoughts he fashioned for an academic exercise in December of that year reflect his mature consideration of the teaching less than a year after he had drafted the Swabian Concord as a proposal for Lutheran agreement on the divisive issues besetting the churches of the Augsburg Confession. With his colleagues at the University of Tübingen, Theodor Schnepf and Jakob Heerbrand, Andreae had begun a series of disputations on the topics of Melanchthon's *Loci communes*. Between 1571 and 1574 students had defended theses in nearly forty such disputations.

Andreae had composed the series' treatment of the freedom of the human will in 1571. These theses reflect his engagement with the chief issues of the day, including Flacius's doctrine of original sin; three months before the disputation he had conducted a dialogue with Flacius in an attempt to reconcile him to the mainstream of Lutheran thinking.[114] In his theses Andreae asserted that God had created the will with the capacity to choose perfectly. That ability was part of what God made the human creature to be. This ability to choose remained in the fallen human being, but sinners can only choose evil. They are not forced to choose evil but willingly sin and willingly become a slave of sin and Satan's property. Although will and intellect can produce a more virtuous or less virtuous life in relation to other people, the will remains God's enemy, hating God's law, not wanting to act according to it and not able to do so. It is different from a block of wood or stone in that it is active even if it cannot be active in a good, that is, God-pleasing, manner. When Luther debated the scholastics, Andreae argued, he had not disputed the fact that sinners perform acts of willing; he had denied that they can will the good. Thus, the will remains the "substantial power" of the soul even in sinners (perhaps an attempt to come to terms with Flacius's definition of the original sin as the substance of the fallen sinner). It is clear that the Tübingen professor was dealing with the critical issues under debate in the wider Wittenberg circle.

In the conversion of the sinner to faith in Christ, however, the soul's power remains turned against God until the Holy Spirit moves it to conversion. Sinners cannot will their own turning to God but must receive it as a gift of his mercy. But the Holy Spirit moves the will but does not force or coerce it. That means that the will stops rejecting the Spirit as he makes it into a "willing will." Andreae was still threading his way through the debates into which he had intervened in ducal Saxony seven years earlier. This conversion takes place through God's Word, through preaching and hearing it, for it is God's tool and instrument which changes the will. This topic brought Andreae at that point to aver the universality of the gospel's promises against those who would argue that because they might not be in the predestined number of the elect, they were hearing the Word in vain. No secret will excludes anyone, for Christ did not say "come to me, you who are predestined," but "come to me, you who are weary and bear a heavy load" (Matt. 11:28). For God wants all to be saved and to come to the knowledge of the truth (1 Tim. 2:4). Andreae associated false ideas about predestination with Flacius's view of original sin in these theses. His theses presented the view that the disciples of Melanchthon advocated on the necessity of the Holy Spirit's moving the enslaved will in conversion and the necessity of the means of grace in conversion. He also insisted that the universal promise of the gospel of Christ gives believers full assurance of their salvation, and he acknowledged that the human will is actively willing as the Holy Spirit changes it.[115] In 1571 he was still hoping to attain reconciliation among the Lutheran churches through the active support of the electoral Saxon theologians. Although he had never studied in Wittenberg, he had read, learned, and digested the Wittenberg way of thinking.

It fell to Andreae to preside in the disputation on predestination three years later as well. He had treated human powers and the freedom of choice in 51 theses; he required 181 to present his teaching on "the predestination of the elect to eternal life." He had added the topic to the formal agenda of controversy in 1574 as he wrote it into his Swabian Concord, probably in response to the Wittenberg criticism of Spangenberg. Echoes of the accord Flinsbach had worked out for Strasbourg with Andreae's assistance can be heard in the theses he composed. Brenz's doctrine of predestination to damnation and Andreae's own experiment with Strigel's *modus agendi* leave no traces in the disputation. Andreae framed the discussion with the apostolic assurance that had introduced the Strasbourg Consensus more than a decade earlier: "Whatever was written in former days was written for our instruction, so that by steadfastness and by the encouragement of the scriptures we might have hope" (Rom. 15:4), the hope that Satan continually seeks to destroy. Andreae laid down the fundamental rule for considering predestination: it is a matter of the gospel that creates hope, not of the law that terrifies, accuses, and condemns. He continued with Prosper's distinction between foreknowledge, which he deemed a synonym of providence, and predestination, which is God's act of choosing those to whom he would give the gift of faith. Providence teaches that God governs the whole world, and it speaks of his relationship to all creatures. Predestination is his decree in eternity concerning the salvation of all who repent and trust in Christ their Savior. Against "the scholastic theologians" Andreae argued that the only cause for this choice is God's mercy and Christ's merit, for "it depends not on human willing or exertion but on God who shows mercy" (Rom. 9:16). This mercy is known only through Christ; human reason cannot grasp it, for it is blind in spiritual matters.[116]

Andreae rejected speculation about an "absolute decree" that God had made which would necessarily send some to damnation. He repudiated two "absurd" ideas: that the faithful should be driven to question God's love for them because they do not know if by some absolute necessity they are numbered among the condemned, and that in "Epicurean" fashion people can live as they wish since their eternal destiny stands inalterable in God's plan whatever they do. The faithful must lay aside these abuses of God's teaching regarding predestination. Indeed, many are called and few are chosen (Matt. 22:14), and the Lord knows who are his (2 Tim. 2:19), namely, those who have been destined for eternal life and brought to faith (Acts 13:48). This predestination is revealed in Christ, who is the Book of Life, in whom the names of the elect are recorded. Those who desire to inquire about God's choice of his people for eternal life must listen to Christ (Matt. 17:5). For "it is not the will of the Father in heaven that one of these little children be lost" (Matt. 18:14). God does not desire the death of the impious, but rather their conversion to life (Ezek. 33:11). God wants all to be saved and come to a knowledge of the truth (1 Tim. 2:4).[117]

God does not will sin. He hates and despises it. Andreae alleged that Calvin had asserted that God is the cause of the fall into sin, in his commentary on Genesis 3;[118] such a thought must be banned from the church of God as blasphemy, he insisted. This error arises from a confusion of God's foreknowledge with his election of the faithful and a false conclusion that his foreknowledge creates some kind of necessity that forces people to sin. Such an opinion is false and nullifies the universal promises of God that he desires that all be turned to life. Scripture clearly reveals that responsibility for sin rests solely upon human sinners (Hos. 13:9 in the Vulgate: "your ruin comes from you, O Israel, but in me is your help"; and Isa. 59:2). Thus, it is blasphemous to conclude that those who do not believe cannot believe because God does not want them to believe or that God does not call everyone to repentance and faith. Christ has revealed that the opposite is true. All who listen to him find rest (Matt. 11:28). Those who hear the gospel should never wonder if they are among the number of the elect. For God promises in his Word that those who trust in Christ shall be saved. No absolute decree of God annuls the promise they hear there. Andreae likewise rejected any form of predetermined reprobation by God. He kept in tension the assignment of responsibility for sin, with the resulting condemnation borne by human sinners, and the assignment of responsibility for life and salvation to God.[119]

The theses on predestination concluded with brief discussions of related problems. Andreae considered the problem posed by Malachi 1:2-3, "I have loved Jacob, but I have hated Esau." Luther used the passage to establish that God is absolute sovereign, unchanging in his exercise of his divine power;[120] Andreae used it to assert the continuing condemning power of God's law upon those who reject him and his grace and mercy to those who believe. God's hatred for Esau arose out of the older brother's contempt for God's promise, contempt God did not cause by his will. God loved Jacob and gave him the gift of faith through the Holy Spirit. Those who claim that some infants who are baptized are not among the regenerate because they were not included in God's secret decree of salvation are wrong. For baptism is the washing of regeneration which brings them to Christ. If some who are baptized reject Christ, that is not due to God's will but to their own wickedness, Andreae averred, practicing the distinction of law and gospel that had determined the approach he and his fellow negotiators took in Strasbourg a decade earlier. This led him also to affirm, without trying to dissolve the tension, that it is false to conclude that because God's gifts are irrevocable, those who sin against conscience can believe that they are immune from condemnation. David lost the Holy Spirit by committing adultery and had to hear Nathan's proclamation of repentance (2 Sam. 12:1-14), as Luther had taught in the Smalcald Articles.[121] God's nature is unchanging and therefore his gifts are irrevocable, but human sinfulness flees from God. His will is unchangeable: he wants all to believe the gospel and he wills that all who believe shall be saved. His will condemns those who do not believe. This contradicts neither the universality of the promise nor the particularity of election. Finally, Andreae concluded, believers must turn to the proclaimed Word of God and hear there that their names have been inscribed in the Book of Life, that is, in Christ.[122] Andreae kept the tension of God's total responsibility and full human responsibility without specifically mentioning it.

These theses echoed what Andreae had proposed in his Swabian Binding Summary a few months earlier. There readers found his solution to the disputes over election that he feared could erupt in the wider Wittenberg circle, probably as a result of the antagonism between Spangenberg and his critics in electoral Saxony. Foundational for his treatment of God's "eternal predestination or election" is Prosper's distinction between God's eternal foreknowledge, which embraces all of creation, good and evil alike, and his eternal election, which involves only those he chooses to be his children for eternal life. This act of choosing he executed in Christ. It assures his chosen people of salvation. Unlike God's foreknowledge, which also involves his hidden and unsearchable will, God's choice of his own is revealed through Christ in the proclamation of God's revealed will. Although Luther's contrast between the hidden and the revealed God is not explicitly repeated, it was shaping Andreae's presentation. God is not a cause of sin or damnation. He wants all to be saved, and he has prepared the gift of salvation for all (Ezek. 33:11; 1 Tim. 2:4). But he has also chosen those whom he makes his own before the foundation of the world (Eph. 1:3-14), and through the preaching of the Word and through baptism he brings them to life in trusting him, as a loving Father. The salvation he gives rests upon Christ's merit alone.[123]

Andreae addressed several specific problems connected with the public discussion of the topic of election in this document. He interpreted Paul's statements regarding the vessels of wrath in Romans 9:19-23 with a focus on God's forbearance, emphasizing that he did not make them as vessels of wrath according to the apostolic description — in contrast to the vessels of mercy, which the Creator clearly fashioned himself according to the text. He explained God's hardening of Pharaoh's heart as divine punishment for the Egyptian ruler's continued rejection of the Lord. The Swabian Binding Summary concludes its positive presentation of predestination with the declaration that the proper teaching of this topic gives God glory because of his mercy, and it comforts those who are troubled about their salvation while giving no encouragement for disobedience, for the insolence that asserts that a person can sin freely because he or she is among the elect.[124]

As in each of the twelve articles of his binding summary, Andreae also rejected false views, in this case four regarding God's election: that his unchangeable but hidden will impels people into sin and the transgression of his commandments; that God has predestined some to damnation in his eternal, secret, hidden plan; that Christ did not mean "all" when he extended his promise of rest in himself; and that those who recognize that they are living as vessels of dishonor and vessels of God's wrath may never become vessels of God's honor and be saved. Each of these rendered true pastoral care of troubled consciences impossible, and Andreae rejected them all.[125] Close to reaching the formula for concord that he had been seeking for twenty years, Andreae was constructing his position on every issue out of biblical raw materials within the framework of proper pastoral care.

*   *   *

The raw materials for deliberation on God's choice of his own children out of the mass of fallen humanity lie strewn throughout the writings of Martin Luther, even though he often cautioned against letting reason try to plumb the depths of either the mystery of evil or the mystery of God's predestining his own to be his people. Luther's caution was strengthened by the deep concerns of Philipp Melanchthon for the proper understanding of the integrity and responsibility of the human creature and of God's not being in any way the cause of evil. The mainstream of Lutheran teaching could have continued to flow in the direction set by Melanchthon's cautious locus on predestination in his *Loci communes*. It did not, however. Between 1559 and 1567 several members of the Wittenberg circle attempted to formulate the topic in a manner which, without dismissing Melanchthon's concerns, laid his caution aside. In their *Syntagma* of New Testament teaching (1559), Johannes Wigand and Matthaeus Judex turned to Ephesians 1 and Romans 8 to confess that God chose individual believers before the foundation of the world to be the ones he would call through the means of grace to be justified and glorified as his children. Timotheus Kirchner used Luther's own words to reinforce this teaching, although he did so from other sources than *De servo arbitrio* (since little was to be found there). In Strasbourg four years later Johann Marbach and Cunmann Flinsbach, assisted by Jakob Andreae and Simon Sultzer, clearly expressed their concern for the integrity and responsibility of the human creature by insisting that believers need to repent of their sins. They did so by teaching that believers can fall from grace. But they anchored the faith of their parishioners in God's conditionless election of his own, apart from any consideration of any foreseen merit of their own. In the following years Leonhardt Palhöfer, Nikolaus Selnecker, and David Chytraeus, all faithful theologians of the Wittenberg circle, expressed their reservations about a doctrine of particular predestination, for both pastoral and dogmatic reasons.

But in 1567 Cyriakus Spangenberg turned to the doctrine of predestination as a means to repudiate synergistic teaching regarding the contribution of the human will to salvation. With his decision to enter into the discussion of the contribution of the human will to salvation with an argument from the divine side, regarding God's unconditional choice of his own people, Spangenberg had shifted the direction of the debate. He focused on God's action in predestining the faithful to salvation instead of continuing the dispute on the human side, with evaluations of human action in willing and choosing. He aroused a storm of controversy as electoral Saxon theologians added his defense of predestination to their list of Gnesio-Lutheran errors. But Spangenberg also thereby drew other leading Lutheran thinkers, above all Martin Chemnitz and Jakob Andreae, into the process of framing and forging the topic of predestination in a Lutheran way. In the years immediately before and during their common work on the Formula of Concord, these two attempted in academic and pastoral forums to represent Luther's and Melanchthon's understanding of how God has saved his people in Christ, taking God's eternal plan for their salvation into account. The fruits of their labors and the thinking of their colleagues, including Selnecker and Chytraeus, appear in the second and eleventh articles of the Formula of Concord.

CHAPTER VII

The Formula of Concord

The Roads toward Concord

Within months of the outbreak of controversy over the Leipzig Interim and related theological issues within the Lutheran churches, efforts to resolve differences and establish harmony and concord began. Two groups pursued a program of reconciliation: the princely and municipal governments responsible for public order and the proper practice of the Christian faith, and theologians working independently or together with political authorities. In 1553 Duke Christoph of Württemberg called a meeting of evangelical governments to discuss ways of ending other controversies before the freedom or bondage of the will had even become an issue; the princes met again in 1554 at Naumburg for the same purpose, but without results. Flacius himself floated "Gentle Proposals" for reconciliation and common confession in 1556 and called for a synod of theologians to resolve the disputed issues with a petition circulated in 1560, to no avail.[1] Further attempts in the late 1550s and early 1560s included the effort of the princes, assisted by Melanchthon and other theologians, to formulate harmony in the Frankfurt Recess[2] and the ducal Saxon proposal, from the pen of a group of Gnesio-Lutheran theologians, *The Book of Confutation*.[3] The approach of this volume governed the efforts of the ducal Saxon government to reach accord through the colloquy at Altenburg in 1568-69. The collapse of those negotiations in March 1569 seemed to presage a continued confrontation that had no hope of conclusion.[4] No endeavor for resolution and reconciliation had produced progress toward the reconciliation of the camps and the formulation of the controverted teachings in a way satisfactory to all or even most of those involved.

The bitterness and suspicion that prevailed on all sides prevented significant movement toward concord.

But the determination to find a path toward concord remained. The accession of Duke Julius to the throne of his father Duke Heinrich, in Braunschweig-Wolfenbüttel in 1568, provided the occasion for three prominent theologians to be loaned to the duchy for the introduction of the Reformation. Martin Chemnitz, Jacob Andreae, and Nikolaus Selnecker did not always see eye to eye, but in the cauldron of their common work in bringing Luther's and Melanchthon's message to Braunschweig-Wolfenbüttel, they learned, in spite of their differences, to work together and to a certain extent to think together as well.

Just months before his death, Duke Christoph launched his final attempt to bring theological harmony to the Lutheran churches of Germany. He sent Andreae north with a double assignment, to aid Julius in reforming his principality and to visit princely courts and town halls with proposals for Lutheran concord. Andreae did so with his "Confession and Explanation" of five disputed articles of faith, an effort that in the end came to naught. He created only more suspicion of his own motives and modus operandi in the process. For he had followed the Philippist paradigm for seeking an end to the disputes, through a princely imposed settlement that condemned no false teaching or teachers and affirmed the truth in only the most general of terms.[5]

Not to be deterred, Andreae proceeded to try another approach. He turned to the form of the sermon, with a simple argument from the catechism, and he used the condemnation of false teachings and false teachers to set forth positions designed to reconcile the alienated theologians of the Lutheran churches. In so doing he had moved from the Philippist method of establishing agreement to that of the Gnesio-Lutherans when he published six Christian sermons on the divisions among the theologians of the Augsburg Confession in 1573.[6] Andreae had not yet added the topic of election to his agenda of controversy, and he treated the human will in his third sermon, which focused on the doctrine of original sin and Flacius's interpretation of it. In line with the catechetical argumentation he employed throughout this treatise, Andreae employed the catechism to answer the chief question in the controversy, "in what way is human nature corrupted through original sin, and what kind of powers have survived in it; to what extent do they remain, especially in spiritual matters . . . ?" He quoted Luther's explanation to the third article, pleading that he could not by his own reason or strength believe in Jesus Christ or come to him.[7] The common layperson, for whom Andreae claimed to be writing these sermons, thinks Scripture contradicts itself on this question, Andreae admitted, implicitly recognizing the question of theodicy and the tension that lay behind the appearance of the contradiction involved. Not so, Andreae insisted, conceding that the mystery of humanity and of the believers' relationship to God seems to present the human mind with incongruities. This is simply part of God's way of working. He converts through the preaching of his Word. In this process of the Spirit's creating faith through the proclamation of the gospel, the human being "is not a stick of wood or a block in conversion but indeed much worse than a stick or a block." Sinners may strive for salvation and even come to hear God's Word by their own volition, "but they remain forever unconverted on the strength of their nature and powers. Therefore, human nature is absolutely nothing in its conversion and is capable of absolutely nothing for its conversion on the basis of its own powers." The Holy Spirit must change the human heart, create a new will, bestow a new spirit. This transformed will can then accept the Word as it is preached.[8] In line with the Strasbourg Consensus he had helped draft a decade earlier, Andreae guarded against a doctrine of predestination to damnation by insisting that the promise of the gospel is universal and that those who hear it must know that God is directing it to them.[9] In the book's marginal notations alongside this discussion, Andreae identified the party he was rejecting as that of Viktorin Strigel, the position he supported that of "Illyricus, Dr. Heshusius, Dr. Wigand, Nikolaus Gallus, and D. Musaeus." It was clear that he intended to approach, if not adopt, the Gnesio-Lutheran position.

Whatever they thought of the content of the sermons, the north German theologians to whom Andreae appealed for support had two reservations. First, the sermonic form reduced the controversies to a level too simple to be taken seriously as a resolution of complex theological questions. In addition, the sermons came as a personal appeal from a man who elicited more suspicion than respect from those who needed to be drawn together. Therefore, Chemnitz and others advised Andreae to have his faculty recast his ideas in a more scholarly form. Andreae did prepare such a document but ignored the request to involve his colleagues. In 1574 he composed the accord now labeled the Swabian Concord. Its text was bogged down in revision by Chemnitz, David Chytraeus, and the ministeria of north Germany when events in electoral Saxony changed the Lutheran political landscape decisively.

Elector August had discovered that some of his most trusted counselors, ecclesiastical and secular, had been consciously and deliberately proceeding with the introduction of a spiritualizing view of the Lord's Supper and related positions that endangered the legal status of Saxony under the terms of the Religious Peace of Augsburg of 1555. August felt betrayed. With the support of his wife, Electress Anna, a Danish princess, he jailed or exiled those he considered duplicitous plotters against the public peace. Labeled "crypto-Calvinists" at the time, they should be identified more accurately as "crypto-Philippists."[10] The elector then began to reconstruct the ecclesiastical establishment of his electorate. To do so he borrowed Andreae from Württemberg, as other governments had in the past, to aid his own theologians who had remained loyal to him and to Luther.

Prince and professor quickly formed a team to reestablish what they considered the true Wittenberg legacy, creating a public theology from the elements of Reformation thought they believed had come from the pens of both Luther and Melanchthon.[11] Although those theologians who remained in August's service did not share the spiritualizing views of the Lord's Supper held by the crypto-Philippists, they had faithfully represented Melanchthon's views of the activities of the human will and had rejected Spangenberg's revival of Luther's thought on predestination. But August and (to a certain extent) Andreae were prepared to turn to other theologians to use the Saxon crisis as the opportunity to forge a settlement for all the churches in the larger Wittenberg circle. To do so they created a working core group to supplement — and in fact to direct and shape — the work of the electoral Saxon commission charged with the reconstruction of the church in August's lands.

In part over Andreae's objections, August put together this working group, choosing two from his own staff (Andreae and his longtime faithful servant Nikolaus Selnecker), receiving two representatives from electoral Brandenburg (Andreas Musculus and Christoph Körner), and inviting two of the most prominent theologians in the Lutheran churches (Martin Chemnitz and David Chytraeus) to join the group. In a conference with electoral Saxon representatives at Torgau in May 1576, this committee combined and edited passages from three documents: Andreae's Swabian Concord, the Swabian-Saxon Concord (as the revisions to Andreae's text by Chemnitz and Chytraeus are called), and the Maulbronn Formula, a separate attempt to formulate a solution to the controversies by theologians from Württemberg, Baden, and Henneberg a few months before the Torgau meeting. They then sent their document to all the evangelical ministeria in Germany for responses. From these efforts a consensus on proper Lutheran teaching emerged.

When the court in Dresden received the responses from these ministeria, it asked Andreae, Selnecker, and Chemnitz to assess and digest them. In a two-week-long session in the first half of March 1577 at Bergen abbey near Magdeburg, the three hammered out a revision of the Torgau book, trying to take objections from the ministeria into account. They were joined by Chytraeus, Musculus, and Körner at Bergen abbey from May 19 to 28, and the group made its final revisions. Their statement seemed to their princely patrons too long, so Andreae took their work in hand and composed an epitome of this Solid Declaration, as the book prepared at Bergen has come to be called. An extensive effort to win more support brought even the elector of the Palatinate, Ludwig VI, into the settlement,[12] and in 1580 this Formula of Concord was published with other Lutheran confessional writings in the *Book of Concord.* In spite of harsh criticism, particularly from Calvinist lands,[13] and formal rejection in some Lutheran territories where some believed the document slighted Melanchthon's thought and authority, the Formula of Concord laid the basis for the public teaching of Lutheran churches from that time on. Therefore, its treatment of the questions raised by Luther's *De servo arbitrio,* especially in its articles on the free will and on predestination, helps assess the balance sheet of a quarter-century of public debate over these topics.

The Formula of Concord on Bound Choice and the Freedom of the Will

Scholars differ on the degree to which the Formula of Concord repeated or diverged from Luther's views in its articles on the freedom of the will and election.[14] F. H. R. Frank focused on those points at which the Formula faithfully echoed the reformer's chief concerns.[15] Ekkehard Muehlenberg, who interpreted the Formula's treatment of the freedom of the will as a repudiation of "Melanchthon's Reformation doctrine and humanism" and "an affirmation of the perspective of the Flacians,"[16] believed this treatment to be riddled with "unavoidable but also intentional" contradictions.[17] On the other hand, some interpreters have found the Formula of Concord guilty of "rationalizing tendencies" because of its assertion of the human ability to hear God's Word apart from the Holy Spirit's activity in the human heart and mind. Even Rune Söderlund, who insists that the Formula continues to reproduce Luther's "broken" or "asymmetrical" understanding of predestination and thus of the freedom and bondage of human choosing, holds this view because of the concordists' assertion that "serious and diligent" hearing of God's Word will be accompanied by God's grace, an effort he regards as an attempt to fathom how God's Word actually works on human hearts and minds.[18]

Two observations must be made in order to assess the Formula's teaching on the freedom of the will and predestination and its relationship to Luther's teaching historically. First, Friedrich Hübner reminds readers that the doctrinal formulations of 1577 inevitably were different from those of 1525, and that is particularly true given the fact that not the Luther of 1525 but rather the Luther of the 1530s and 1540s along with Melanchthon had instructed the generation that constructed the Formula. With the concerns of the later Luther and Melanchthon ringing in their ears, it was impossible for Wittenberg students simply to repeat Luther's position against Erasmus from 1525, ignoring what they had heard directly from his lips. Hübner therefore rejects critics who believe that the Formula of Concord's position represents a degeneration from Luther's lofty teaching in *De servo arbitrio*. Hübner argues, too, that the Formula "decisively veers away from Philippism and returns to Luther's line of thought."[19] That judgment is partially correct, but it needs refinement. Second, Söderlund's elaboration of Bengt Hägglund's designation of the Formula's teaching on the freedom of the will and election perceives the "broken" or "asymmetrical" nature of its insistence that God alone is responsible for sinners' salvation and that human beings are responsible for their own damnation.[20] This teaching is also asymmetrical in its confession of the responsibility of God for salvation — its application of the gospel to the sinner crushed by the law — and its appraisal on the basis of the law of the sinner's responsibility to trust God above all things and of the integrity of human beings as thinking, willing creatures of God. The intention of the authors of the Formula of Concord on the freedom of the will and election cannot be understood apart from the proper distinction of law and gospel, an important element in their pastoral concern for the proper preaching of God's Word.

What came to be known as the Solid Declaration of the Formula of Concord assumed its fundamental shape at the Torgau meeting in May 1576, even though extensive revisions altered its treatment of the freedom of the will the next year in Bergen abbey. Around the table in Torgau sat some of the leading lights of Lutheran Germany. They represented a variety of positions in the various controversies they were to resolve. The text the theologians in Torgau constructed included above all material from the pen of David Chytraeus, from his contributions to the reworking of Andreae's Swabian Concord. His Torgau colleagues supplemented his thoughts with paragraphs from the Maulbronn Formula, above all its use of citations from Luther and Melanchthon. At Bergen, however, suggestions from ministeria that had reviewed the "Torgau Book" led to extensive revisions by the group of three. Most critical in advocating alterations in the Torgau text on the freedom of the will was the memorandum prepared by the theologians of the dukedom of Prussia, led by Johannes Wigand and Tilemann Heshusius; they offered no suggestions for improving the book's article on God's election of his own.[21] These revisions, adopted by the committee of six in its May meeting in

Bergen, left Chytraeus less than pleased, although he was present as part of the group.[22] The changes in fact did little to alter the substance of his argument. Half the final version indeed does come from his draft. Although Chytraeus's definition of the "chief question" of the controversy was not used as he had proposed it, its concern remained in the final text. Chytraeus had defined it as the question

> whether we human creatures (since after the fall we are not sticks of wood or blocks of stone or irrational animals but rather reasonable creatures of God, who have been given understanding and a certain measure of free will in outward matters and temporal affairs) also still retain these powers and the capability in spiritual things regarding our conversion to God, so that we acknowledge God truly, understand and believe the gospel, and turn ourselves to God with pure hearts and ardently desire and accept the benefits of Christ and eternal salvation, fear, love, and trust God from our hearts and are obedient to God's law and satisfy it.

He paraphrased his question by asking whether unconverted sinners can dispose themselves by their own powers and abilities to receive and follow the Holy Spirit's call (his text eventually answered the question negatively).[23] Chytraeus was striving to preserve the focus on the integrity of the human creature that had remained his chief concern in this issue. In addressing the Prussian critique, the committee of three refashioned the introduction of the Solid Declaration, stating the central issue more simply as the question "what the mind and will of the unregenerated human being are able to do in conversion and rebirth on the basis of their own powers that remain after the fall, when God's Word is proclaimed and God's grace is offered to us."[24]

Chytraeus thought it necessary to explain that if the teaching regarding the freedom of the will was not properly understood, a number of other biblical teachings would be affected. Like his Wittenberg mentors, he understood the teaching of the Bible to be a "body," that is, to consist of organically interrelated parts, which function together in describing God and the human creature. The definition of humanity through a description of the will as bound or free had immediate implications for the way other elements of the Bible's message are proclaimed. Among the topics affected by the formulation of the teaching on the will, according to Chytraeus, are creation and anthropology, original sin, redemption in Christ, conversion and justification, new obedience and the demands of God's law, order and discipline in society, and the relationship between the righteousness of human performance in society and the righteousness that God gives in relationship to him. To bring controversy over the will to an end, Chytraeus thought it necessary to discuss six issues. First, the free will should be defined, both in regard to its powers before the fall into sin and also in regard to its capability after the fall. Second, it must be clear what the will in sin cannot do. Third, the necessity of the Holy Spirit's action in bestowing renewal and new birth must be maintained. Fourth, the ways and means by which God converts must be specified. Fifth, the role of the will that has been freed by Christ's work in the performance of virtues and good works in the reborn children of God must be discussed. Sixth, false teachings that would weaken or destroy this teaching must be rejected.[25] Throughout, pastoral concern, expressed in the commitment to distinguishing law and gospel properly, governed the author's thinking.

Chytraeus began by insisting on the integrity of the human creature. He believed that without a clear statement regarding human understanding, heart and will, with all the associated powers that constitute a human being, the nature of humanity as a creation of God cannot be properly understood. For to possess these powers defines what it means to have been created in God's image. In their original condition human creatures had been able to acknowledge God and obey him through their free will.[26] The fall into sin corrupted and perverted the will's powers. It did not eliminate them. Sinners possess a certain measure of freedom in temporal matters that are within the domain of reason, in external discipline and temporal government, in the avoidance of crimes and major offenses, in temporal government and the conduct of the household, in the arts and crafts, etc., as is shown in Romans 2:14, Titus 3:5, 1 Timothy 1:9, and Matthew 5:20, according to Chytraeus. Teaching that sinners retain this much power in their wills is important because it enables sinners to take God's commands seriously, the Rostock professor explained; it also helps avoid the terrible temporal punishments that evil deeds draw down upon people. It offers others the example of a virtuous life, thus preserving them from vice and evil deeds, and it points sinners to Christ. Chytraeus's assertion of the integrity of the human creature insured the potential for sinners to be restored to the fullness of their humanity and thus met one of Melanchthon's basic concerns.

But, he also insisted, it is not possible for this use of the will's freedom or power to contribute in any way at all to human salvation.[27] The Prussian theologians agreed with that point fully, but Chytraeus's equation of the freedom exercised by the will with the very heart and mind of the human being they found worse than sloppy. They feared that it repeated, from another perspective, the confusion of substance and accidents which had brought them into conflict with Flacius.[28] They also took exception to Chytraeus's definition of Paul's concept of the law as pedagogue as a reference to its ability to elicit civil righteousness from the unconverted. They believed Paul meant that the law functions as the pedagogue who leads to Christ when it accuses and condemns sinners, moving them to repentance.[29] They found the Torgau Book's analogy of eyes that are blinded when they look at the sun even though they can see clearly when they look at things on the earth more than inadequate; it implied capabilities that the sinful will, "totally blind and dead in terms of that which pertains to God," does not have.[30] Their appeal for clarity in this regard produced revisions in Chytraeus's text.

The committee at Bergen extended Chytraeus's comments on the powers of the sinful will with the words and phrases "blind," "completely dead," "without a spark of spiritual power," "not capable of acting in their own behalf or of applying this grace to themselves or of preparing themselves for it." The text defined sinners as slaves of sin (John 8:34) and prisoners of the devil, who drives them (Eph. 2:2; 2 Tim. 2:26).[31] These claims found elaboration in Chytraeus's original draft. Even though sinners still have a "dim spark of knowledge that a god exists," they are "ignorant, blind, and perverted, so that when the most skillful and learned people on earth read or hear the gospel of God's Son and the promise of eternal salvation, they still cannot comprehend, grasp, understand, or believe it on the basis of their own powers." "They regard it as foolishness and fables until the Holy Spirit enlightens and teaches them" (1 Cor. 2:14; 1:21; Eph. 2:1, 5; 4:17-18; 5:8; Matt. 13:13, 11; Rom. 3:11-12; Acts 26:18; John 1:5; Col. 2:13).[32] In the midst of defining the sinner as dead and without a glimmer of true faith, Chytraeus made the pastoral observation that even the tiniest glimmer of faith is very comforting for believers because they know that God ignited it or it would not be there. The prayers of the saints for God's instruction, illumination, and sanctification also demonstrate that, apart from God's intervention and initiation, that kind of turning to him in faith is not possible (Ps. 119; Eph. 1:17-18; Col. 1:9-11; Phil. 1:9-10).[33]

Chytraeus continued by noting that the dilemma of sinners consists not only in their lack of power or strength to turn themselves toward God. They are "perverted and turned toward evil and against God" (Gen. 8:21; Jer. 17:9; Gal. 5:17; Rom. 7:14, 18, 22-23; 8:7). Chytraeus reinforced this point with Luther's "Achillean argument" in *De servo arbitrio*[34] from the struggle against sin that still takes place in the children of God: "if in Saint Paul and other reborn people the natural or fleshly free will resists God's law even after rebirth, how much more is it rebellious and hostile toward God's law and will before rebirth." It is hard as stone (Ezek. 36:26; Jer. 5:3) or an unhewn block of wood (Hos. 6:5), or as antagonistic as a wild, ferocious beast (Ps. 73:22), comparisons used by Luther in *De servo arbitrio,* though not in this way.[35] Nonetheless, Chytraeus had wanted to make certain that this description of the sinner's lack of ability to come to faith did not undercut the proper understanding of human integrity and responsibility. Therefore, following a line of argument enunciated by Nikolaus Gallus in 1559,[36] he pointed out that sinners "behave in this case worse than a block of wood, for they are rebellious against God's will and hostile to it" until the Holy Spirit creates faith in them. Only he can and does "effect new birth and the inner reception of another heart, mind, and disposition" through the Word that initiates trust in Christ (Deut. 29:4; 30:6; Ps. 51:10, 12; Ezek. 11:19; 36:26; Matt. 11:27; 13:15; Luke 24:45; John 15:5; 6:29, 44; Acts 5:31; 16:14; 1 Cor. 4:7; 12:3; 2 Cor 3:5 [in Vulgate]; 5:17; Gal. 6:15; Eph. 2:8; Phil. 1:29; 2:13; 2 Tim. 2:25; Titus 3:5; James 1:17).[37]

To reinforce these points the committee at Torgau lifted a series of citations assembled in the Maulbronn Formula from the Augsburg Confession, the Apology of the Augsburg Confession, the Smalcald Articles, Luther's catechisms, and his *Confession on the Holy Supper* of 1528, where in his concluding summary of his teaching he had rejected the notion that the will can exercise freedom apart from Christ and the Holy Spirit.[38] Finally, the Maulbronn task force had referred to Luther's discussion of God's giving new birth by drawing sinful hearts to himself "in his book against Erasmus, *On the Bondage of the Will*, where he represented and supported his position thoroughly and in detail." By this time, however, no mention of *De servo arbitrio* sufficed without the supplement of a reference to Luther's Genesis commentary, specifically chapter 26.[39]

Having firmly asserted total divine responsibility for the conversion and salvation of sinners, the text of the Solid Declaration picked up again the thread of Chytraeus's argument. He had made a series of claims regarding the aspects of the understanding of the bondage and freedom of the will that affected pastoral care, carefully weaving together elements of law and of gospel. In upholding human responsibility he brought the law into action against "Enthusiasts and Epicureans" who misuse this teaching as an excuse for a "dissolute and disorderly as well as indolent and sluggish" life. The teaching of the impotence of the will in regard to creating faith may not be used to justify continuing in rebellion against God or waiting for God to convert through "his brute power."

On the other hand, Chytraeus wanted to bring the comfort of the gospel of God's responsibility for salvation to timid hearts with troubling thoughts and doubts. To do that he made a number of points that had become regular elements in his contemporaries' confession of the topic of the human will. First, he insisted on the universality of the promise that God has made in Christ. God wants no one to perish and so sent his Son to die for the whole world (Ezek. 33:11; John 3:16). God furthermore provides for the public proclamation of law and gospel and desires that all who hear should be saved. Even those who have not been converted can hear and read God's Word. The Holy Spirit must come to draw them to himself by breaking their sinful hearts through the law and the terror, regret, and sorrow over their sins that it produces. The preaching of forgiveness of sins in Christ ignites faith in them through the Spirit's power. Not the preacher but the Spirit effects faith. So preachers should proclaim the Word and leave the conversion to God.[40] In this section Chytraeus asserted that the preacher and the hearer "should be certain that when the Word of God is preached purely and clearly according to God's command and will and people listen to it seriously and diligently and meditate upon it, God will certainly be present with his grace and give, as has been said, what human beings otherwise could neither receive nor take on the basis of their own powers."[41] Certainly, as it stands in the Formula, these words are not an attempt to "rationalize" or tame the tension between God's responsibility for salvation and human integrity. The last words cited were adopted from Andreae's Swabian Concord, and Chemnitz added to them a reminder that the Holy Spirit's presence cannot be assessed by human feelings.[42] The issue under discussion is the ability of human beings as creatures so fashioned by God to function as thinking, feeling persons. That their reading and hearing of God's Word is not an efficacious act that carries them in Christ's direction is clear. The Holy Spirit remains the creator of the new mind and heart.

The Torgau committee then drew upon Andreae's Swabian Concord to remind readers that those who reject the Word of God and disdain the tools of the Holy Spirit bring judgment upon themselves. God is not at fault! The concordists wanted to make clear that God is not responsible for evil. The Bergen committee reworked and reinforced Chytraeus's insistence on the exercise of human responsibility by laying the blame for rejecting God upon the sinner. The practice of distinguishing law and gospel was at work as the law was addressed to the unconverted listeners of the Word.[43]

The distinction also shaped the Formula's treatment of the converted will as it lives out the life the Holy Spirit bestows in conversion. Material threaded together from Chytraeus, Chemnitz, and the Bergen committee emphasized Luther's and Melanchthon's concern for the continuing life of repentance that puts to death the disobedient spirit and carries out new obedience responsibly. This, too, reflects the desire to protect the concept of human integrity that included the responsibility of God's creatures to be the people God made them to be. God comes to us first, Chemnitz had written in his supplement to Andreae's comments in the Swabian Concord, but "in a true conversion there must be a change — new impulses and movements in mind, will, and heart."[44]

The Bergen committee addressed the confusion surrounding the terminology that in part was to blame for the synergistic controversies. This endeavor reveals something of the struggle for the proper terminology that could convey the new framework for thinking of God and the human creature that went on throughout sixteenth-century Lutheran thought. A brief reference to Luther's attempt to help readers "understand certain other particular, subsidiary points in his dispute" raised the topic of *de absoluta necessitate* but rendered no judgment, surprisingly. This neutral stance stems from a passage in the Maulbronn Formula, from the southern theologians less dominated by Melanchthon's concerns than their counterparts in the north.[45] The explicit rejection of that element of Luther's teaching by Chytraeus, Selnecker, Andreae, and Chemnitz found no echo here.

The Bergen committee reiterated its contention that the sinful human being cannot simply be compared to a stone or block of wood since that could imply that the sinner does not have responsibility for responding to God's Word.[46] To be sure, throughout and even after conversion, sinful resistance to the Word of God remains in those whom the Holy Spirit converts, but it dare not be said that the will only resists the Word or does so completely, for the Holy Spirit converts human beings as human beings, with functioning minds and wills. No Gnesio-Lutheran would have disagreed. Such statements arose from the desire to reject any concept of divine necessity that might obscure the obligation of the human creature to trust in God with heart and mind.[47]

On the other hand, the concordists refused to accept Viktorin Strigel's term *modus agendi* as a description for the will apart from sin. They heard in that term the ascription of some positive power to sinful human creatures, and so they turned the term over to God, speaking of his *modus agendi* of working with rational creatures (thus, the Solid Declaration invalidated the very point that Strigel had tried to make with his use of this term).[48] The Bergen committee balanced this point with a similar rejection of any compulsion. The Holy Spirit moves mind and heart in a natural way, corresponding to God's design of the creature and the human integrity it produced. That in turn meant that the converted will does work together with the Holy Spirit in struggling against temptation and in producing the fruits of faith and rebirth.[49]

Thus, the concordists also warned against misunderstanding what Luther meant when he said the will is "purely passive" in conversion. It is not that sinners only endure what God effects in them. Luther believed, they explained, that God engenders faith through the proclamation and hearing of God's Word. Conversion takes place totally and completely as "a product, gift, present and activity of the Holy Spirit alone . . . working through the Word in the mind, will, and heart of the human being." This is not comparable to a picture being etched in stone or a seal being pressed in wax. Human beings know and feel and will as the Holy Spirit changes their mind and emotions and decision-making powers.[50] Alongside the passivity of the sinful mind and heart lie their functions as a part of the human creature as God fashioned humanity in Eden.

Chytraeus attempted to rescue Melanchthon's controversial term *facultas applicandi se ad gratiam* by using it to affirm the created gifts of rationality and willing. However, his Gnesio-Lutheran critics understood this phrase as an avowal that the sinful will had the capability to apply itself to the task of winning grace for itself. Therefore, it aroused the ire of Wigand, Heshusius, and their colleagues in Prussia.[51] With slight revisions the committee of three retained Chytraeus's limited use of the term, and therefore did not fully accede to the Prussians. The committee at Bergen wrote that any such human exercise of this faculty arises "not out of our own natural powers but alone through the activity of the Holy Spirit."[52] Why this expression could be properly interpreted but *modus agendi* could not be, may be due to the fact that a *modus* was more likely understood to express a *causa efficiens,* a *facultas* more likely a *causa instrumentalis* or *materialis* and could thus be understood passively.[53]

Even more clearly the concordists at Bergen distanced themselves from Melanchthon's use of the phrases from Chrysostom and Pseudo-Basil: "the human will is not idle in conversion but also does something," or "God draws [those who come to him], but he draws those who will it." Such expressions could hardly be understood other than as an affirmation that the natural free will can do something in conversion, they argued in accord with their Prussian correspondents.[54] That is as impossible as a corpse contributing to its own resuscitation. "God makes willing people out of rebellious and unwilling people through the drawing power of the Holy Spirit."[55]

Finally, the concordists also refused to acknowledge any possibility of a proper interpretation of the "three causes" of conversion, a list that for Melanchthon had included the human will along with God's Word and the Holy Spirit. The committee interpreted *causae* as effective causes rather than as the "factors" Aristotle and Melanchthon had described in this "causal" way of composing explanations for almost everything. In this way the Bergen theologians agreed with the Prussian critique,[56] concluding that the mind and will of the unreborn are nothing other than an object of God's action. Indeed, Melanchthon's assignment of the will to the category of material cause had also made the human will the object of the activity of the effective cause, the Holy Spirit, through the instrumental cause, the Word. But the language was too likely to be misunderstood, and so the concordists rejected it.[57]

Friedrich Hübner provides an accurate assessment of the second article of the Formula of Concord when he writes that it enables Christians to announce that God is Lord and alone has the power to save, that humanness shrinks to nothing in his sight. But at the same time, according to Hübner, the article demands that this insight dare not permit a theological skepticism regarding human creatures. Instead it binds them to their responsibility as receivers of the gospel.[58] The article's explanation of the relationship between God and the human creature reveals in part the paths Wittenberg theology had trod since 1525. The very title of the article portends a treatment not of the will's bondage — the question of God's lordship in calling forth new creatures in Christ — but of the will's freedom — the question of human integrity and responsibility as the creature God fashioned for trusting and, because that is the direction in which trust impels, obeying. In fact, however, article II of the Formula of Concord does dwell long and hard on the will's bondage, insisting on human integrity but also confessing its absolute impotence and corruption in its ability to turn to God and trust in him. Article I, on original sin, conceded the corruption but insisted, against Flacius's equation of the very essence of the sinner with original sin, that even in the fall the integrity of the human creature as God's creature remains. Article II teaches that the will remains active but has been programmed with the disabling virus of false faith and the incapacity to do the slightest to get rid of it. To confess the need for a Creator's creative act of rebirth, the concordists marshaled a number of metaphors and descriptors on the human side for the will: ignorance, blindness, death, perversion, corruption, to name but some. Yet the description of the will as dead had to be qualified, for the will captive to the law, sin, and Satan was defined as active in its revolt and resistance against God. Furthermore, the human creature remained creature and thus rational and volitional, an assertion necessary to make against Flacius's definition of the fallen human being as substantially original sin and against Roman Catholic charges of Stoicism and Manichaeanism.

This definition of humanity as a rational and volitional creature of God was also important because it was necessary for the Lutheran teaching of the means of grace; that is, it made clear something of the mystery of what it means to be a human conversation partner with God. If God's creative initiative and lordship was to be confessed properly, his approach from outside the human believer through his Word had to be maintained. Against those who denied that God works effectively through the oral, written, and sacramental forms of his Word, the concordists insisted on the necessity of God's restoring conversation with his human creatures through the gospel, which exercises its re-creating power through the message of Christ, through its delivery of his benefits in the Word. God's lordship, God's continuing conversing with his chosen children through the means of grace and through his law, and God's having fashioned a rational and volitional human creature are also necessary components of the Lutheran understanding of the repentant life. All in the Wittenberg circle recognized as one of their chief assignments the equipping of the baptized children of God to carry on the struggle of daily repentance in the face of the mystery of the persisting presence of sin and evil in their lives.

Article II hones in on the specific phrases that had caused most debate among the Wittenberg disciples. It left Luther's *de absoluta necessitate* stand without comment (SD II:44), even though most of his followers had joined him in warning against the misunderstanding of the phrase; it reserved more caution for his more widely defended expression "purely passive" out of concern that it could undercut the necessity of using the means of grace (SD II:89). Furthermore, it repudiated any suggestion that the Holy Spirit forces or compels the human will (SD II:64), as Flacius was thought to have sometimes implied. On the other hand, it rejected the analysis of the will based on Aristotle's three causes (SD II:90), the ancient fathers' expressions implying independent activity of the will (SD II:86), and the description of the activity of the will while it is still captive to sin as a *modus agendi* (SD II:61). However, it found characterizing the will as a *facultas applicandi se ad gratiam* appropriate so long as it is clear that it "does not arise out of our own natural powers but alone through the activity of the Holy Spirit, etc." (SD II:78).

The concordists endeavored to pass on the confession of the faith that Luther and Melanchthon had bequeathed them, as they understood it. The common concerns of Philippists and Gnesio-Lutherans for the practice of distinguishing law and gospel in the repentant life, for the ascription of all power to God while avoiding blaming him for evil, and for maintaining the integrity and responsibility of the human creature are presented in article II. Without ignoring the Philippist emphasis on human responsibility and without sacrificing the clear insistence that believers practice the life of trust and obedience with heart, soul, strength, and mind, the concordists did confess God's total responsibility for salvation in a manner shaped by Gnesio-Lutherans such as Chemnitz, Wigand, and Heshusius. What emerged in this text reflects the theological thinking that emerged in Wittenberg in the 1520s, as that thinking had developed over a half-century.

On God's Eternal Foreknowledge and Election

The Torgau commission had taken Chytraeus's draft in the Swabian-Saxon Concord as the basis of its discussion of the human will, set aside large portions of his text, and added to the locus a series of citations from the early Lutheran confessional documents gathered in the Maulbronn Formula. The Prussian critique made it necessary to alter the article in Bergen. The eleventh article, on "the eternal election of the children of God," on the contrary, remained in the form it took in Torgau, a form created by placing Andreae's views in the Swabian Concord alongside Chemnitz's in the Swabian-Saxon Concord. The result was that the locus contained some repetition in its two distinct treatments of its topic. It opened with Andreae's observation that no serious conflicts had arisen publicly among the theologians of the Augsburg Confession regarding election, but that some theologians in the Lutheran churches had "not always used the same language."[59] That was a very mild assessment of the tensions between the Wittenberg faculty and Cyriakus Spangenberg; it reveals how cautiously Andreae approached this subject. He strove to avoid opening public discussion of the topic. He concluded his introductory word by observing that "it is not by chance that Holy Scripture does not treat this article in just one place but rather carefully treats and emphasizes this topic in many places."[60] The theologians at Torgau concluded therefore that the abuse and misunderstanding that had sometimes accompanied discussion of this element of biblical teaching dare not be ignored.

They had in fact not had an easy time coming to a conclusion themselves. Chemnitz reported a few months later that they had struggled with the question of whether to call God's election of his own "particular." They had wanted to avoid stating that predestination is universal, as if all people were predestined to salvation. Chemnitz reported that the Strasbourg Consensus had influenced the committee decisively. Its rejection of universal predestination and support for particular election carried the day. But the Torgau committee had also wanted to avoid the impression that the word "particular" could convey, as if God's intention was not to save all sinners, Chemnitz observed.[61] Their careful formulation affirmed that "in his counsel, intention, and preordination God did not only prepare salvation in general, but he also graciously considered each and every one of the elect, that is, those who would be saved through Christ, and he chose them for salvation," but it went on to focus the attention of believers on the promise delivered in the means of grace rather than permitting them to speculate on their election apart from the expression of the promise in preaching, absolution, and the sacraments.[62]

The argument proposed at Torgau began by establishing what the teaching of God's unconditional choice of his children does not mean. Chemnitz's handbook provided most of the material, which he had written into his Swabian-Saxon Concord. But the organization of the argument changed somewhat. It began with the distinction of God's foreknowledge, which applies to all creatures, and election or predestination, which does not apply to those who remain in sin but only to the children of God whom he chose and predestined to eternal life before the foundation of the world (Eph. 1:4-5). This distinction, which Spangenberg and Chytraeus used and which can be traced back at least to Prosper of Aquitaine in the sixth century,[63] does not confront the tension between God's responsibility and human responsibility as directly as Luther's understanding of the creative foreknowledge of God. But it does preserve both human responsibility and human dependence for life upon God as well as maintain both God's innocence, on the one hand, and his unlimited power in the act of salvation, on the other. For God alone is responsible for choosing his children; sinners are responsible for their own rebellion and condemnation.[64] This is precisely that law/gospel distinction that Söderlund labels broken or asymmetrical. Chemnitz's pastoral concern flowed immediately from this distinction, or better said, stood behind it. God did not choose his children in the manner of a military muster: "this one shall be saved, that one shall be damned; this one will remain faithful, that one will not remain faithful!" — as he had already stated in 1573.[65] God's willing the salvation of his people is a mystery, but it is not a "secret, inscrutable will or counsel." Chemnitz distinguishes God's unexplainable mercy from the conundrum of evil in a reality for which God is totally responsible. Believers have no reason either for a false security and a life of impenitence or for faint-heartedness and despair. God has revealed his "counsel, intention, and preordination" in Jesus Christ, the true Book of Life, and through the preaching of his Word.[66] Toward the conclusion of his treatment of God's choosing his own, Chemnitz reiterated his pastoral concern that this teaching of election be understood as "beautiful, wonderful comfort" for those who know they are weak and sinful. They can know that against the very gates of hell (Matt. 16:18) Christ's church will stand as the place where God offers his unconditional promise.[67]

Chemnitz used material from his handbook to present his understanding of God's salvation of sinners from the perspective of his preordaining choice of the elect. Before the foundation of the world God had determined that he would redeem and reconcile the human race to himself through Christ and his meriting of righteousness and eternal life. Christ's merits and benefits were to be distributed through Word and sacraments. God determined that the Holy Spirit would be active in human creatures through the Word as it is preached, converting them to true repentance, enlightening them in true faith. His will established that he would make those righteous who repent and accept Christ by faith, and these righteous people will be sanctified in love. God determined that he would protect them in the midst of their struggle against evil, lead and guide them, and increase their faith and obedience, preserving them to the end, and giving them eternal life. In the larger context of his work, it is clear that when Chemnitz wrote that God had planned to justify those who repent and trust in him, he also believed that God gives the ability to repent and trust through the Holy Spirit. His concern for human integrity and responsibility led him, however, to express what God does in justification in terms of these results, and thus the tension between God's responsibility and human responsibility is embedded in his formulations.[68] The concordists expanded on this concern when they included Andreae's sketch of the results of election as a child of God in the good works of new obedience.[69]

Chemnitz reinforced his convictions regarding God's total responsibility for salvation by clearly stating that God's choice of those he would save applies to the individuals he has brought to faith. Individual believers should have confidence that the Word of God that they have experienced assures them personally of God's love — no matter how difficult that is for human reason to grasp.[70] Chemnitz tied his affirmation of individual election to the means of grace, thus meeting one concern of the Wittenberg faculty directly while supporting Spangenberg's interpretation of Luther. This emphasis on the means of grace as God's instrument for drawing people to Christ and the only source for knowing about God's choosing of his people occurs in Andreae's section of article XI as well.[71] At the same time, Chemnitz insisted with the Wittenberg theologians on the universality of God's promise (Matt. 11:28; Luke 24:47; John 1:29; 3:16; 6:39, 40, 51; Rom. 3:22; 10:12; 11:32; 2 Pet. 3:9; 1 John 1:7; 2:2). God's Word does not deceive; all who hear its call to faith and its offer of salvation may be certain that the promise is meant for them. The elect are indeed those who hear Christ's voice and follow him (John 10:27-28). Even if the signs of faith — prayer, thanksgiving, sanctification in love, hope, patience, comfort in crosses (Rom. 8:25) — are very weak, believers still know that in their hunger and thirst for righteousness (Matt. 5:6), the promise of their God is sure. For the God who has begun his good work of salvation has assured us that he will complete it — and at that point Chemnitz's concern for insuring human responsibility asserted itself — "if we do not turn away from him but 'remain steadfast to the end in that which he has begun' (Matt. 20:22, 24:13; Phil. 1:6)."[72] Chemnitz devoted several paragraphs to buttressing his assurance that God's Word can be trusted. Some might ask why many are called but few are chosen (Matt. 22:14), and so he warned against thinking that God has two contradictory wills, one expressed in his calling all sinners to faith, another in his sending some to damnation and choosing only a few. Human rebellion or rejection of God is the only cause of condemnation;

God's foreknowledge certainly does not cause their rejection. This point was repeated again in Andreae's contribution to article XI.[73] God wanted all his human creatures; some of them rejected him (Matt. 23:37). Christ offers his promise of life through Word and through the sacraments, which confirm the promise individually to all believers.[74]

In the Strasbourg dispute over predestination in 1563, Hieronymus Zanchi had insisted that God gives the gift of perseverance to all the elect. Chemnitz felt compelled to comment on the possibility of believers falling from faith. His commitment to the continuing distinction of law and gospel in believers' lives formed a vital part of his vision of pastoral care, and to hold strictly to the perseverance of the saints would deprive the law of its power against resurgent sin in the lives of the baptized. He soberly recognized the reality of the mystery of the continuation of evil in believers' lives, of the never ending struggle against genuine temptation and real sin. Therefore, to preserve the law's threat against sin, he insisted on proclaiming condemnation to rebellious sinners within the church, maintaining the theological logic of the distinction of law and gospel. Here he revealed that he, like Marbach, followed Melanchthon in focusing initially on the need to call for the exercise of human responsibility in the Christian life. Those who accept the Word with joy but then fall away (Luke 8:13) have willfully turned themselves from God to "grieve and embitter the Holy Spirit; they entangle themselves once again in the defilements of the world and redecorate their hearts as a haven for the devil" (2 Pet. 2:10, 20; Luke 11:24-25; Heb. 10:26).[75]

In the Swabian-Saxon Concord Chemnitz had repeated his conviction that the teaching of the doctrine of election brings with it "powerful admonitions and warnings" against rejecting God's promise and against foolish speculation about what might stand behind his revealed will in the Word. This seems to place him at odds with the frequent Wittenberg observation that this teaching is of use only in the realm of the gospel. This illustrates how there may be disjunction between the content of a teaching — in this case, its assurance of God's inalterable commitment to his chosen children — and its function — when it psychologically focuses the hearer's attention on his or her rebellion against God. Here Chemnitz condemned the kind of inquiry that seeks to plumb the depths of God's planning. Believers dare not conjecture regarding the time of the conversion of themselves or others, nor should they try to guess why he favors some lands at one time and then lets the Word and the church grow weak there while they gain strength in other places. God does send a famine of the Word to lands and peoples as a call to repentance and an expression of his judgment. But sinners have no claim on God. They justly receive the wages of sin. They can only rejoice in his "unmerited, sheer grace and mercy." For, as God told Israel, "that you have gone to ruin is your own fault; that you have been helped rests alone on my grace" (Hos. 13:9, in the Vulgate translation that Chemnitz and his Lutheran contemporaries consistently used). The last word from Chemnitz in the Solid Declaration confessed with Paul, "How unsearchable are his judgments and how inscrutable his ways! Who has known the mind of the Lord?" (Rom. 11:34).[76] Thus, he echoed Luther's concluding confession at the end of *De servo arbitrio* as the proper response to the theodical question.

Andreae's draft also began where Luther had anchored his consideration of such questions: with the reminder that "the eternal election of God should be considered in Christ and not apart from or outside of Christ," an axiom Chemnitz had apparently found discussed in sufficient detail in Andreae's treatment. As Chemnitz had done, Andreae tied his lengthier presentation of Christ's place in the doctrine of election to the proclamation of God's Word. Like Chemnitz, he admonished his readers against torturing themselves with thoughts about God's secret counsel and directed them to Christ and to Word and sacrament.[77] Throughout his presentation in the Swabian Concord, Andreae had returned to this focus on Christ, and those elements of his earlier draft remained in the Solid Declaration.[78]

By adding Andreae's material to Chemnitz's the concordists provided their readers with treatments of two critical Bible passages on God's sovereign exercise of responsibility that could be interpreted as making him responsible for evil as well as good. Andreae repeated the Lutheran distinction between God's making "vessels for honor" and the making of the "vessels of dishonor," an activity of the devil and human beings (Rom. 9:22-23). God endures the vessels of dishonor, according to the apostolic text, but he actually creates the vessels of honor.[79] In the hardening of Pharaoh's heart (Exod. 9:12; Rom. 9:17), God cannot be accused of responsibility for evil because this hardening simply confirmed what Pharaoh wanted for himself. His desire to rebel against God brought the judgment of God's hardening his heart upon him; the responsibility for that judgment rested with Pharaoh alone. "In no way should this be interpreted or understood as if God did not want to grant Pharaoh or other people salvation but instead had preordained them to eternal condemnation in his secret counsel, so that they could not or would not be saved."[80] Söderlund points out that in its exegesis the Formula of Concord makes clear that its authors used this passage differently than Luther had.[81] This is indeed an affirmation of Melanchthon's concern that God in no way be held responsible for evil. Nonetheless, the concordists' dogmatic conclusion strives to repeat Luther's attempt to keep in tension God's total responsibility and that of the human creature.

Finally, Andreae also took on his role as comforting and consoling pastor. The topic of God's choosing his children comforts believers by reminding them that their salvation lies totally in God's hand, and yet it is to not strengthen the impenitent in their impudence. It is, like every part of God's teaching, "written for our instruction, that by steadfastness and by the encouragement of the Scriptures we might have hope" (Rom. 15:4).[82]

In the attempt to provide guidelines for the proper use of the recently revived topic of the eternal foreknowledge and election of God — Andreae used the term "predestination" in the title of his summary in the epitome — the concordists tried to preserve the tension between law and gospel, between God's responsibility for salvation and the mystery of the human ability to reject God's grace.[83] The fundamental shape of the article was determined in part by Andreae's experience in Strasbourg some thirteen years earlier, where the chief concern moving him, Marbach, and Flinsbach had been the preservation of an active use of both law and gospel in the struggle of the repenting believer, against a view of the perseverance of the saints which they feared would undercut the life of repentance. Article XI was also in part shaped by Spangenberg's repudiation of synergism and his assertion of God's total responsibility for the salvation of sinners, as Chemnitz developed this viewpoint further.

Like Spangenberg, Chemnitz seized upon the distinction attributed to Prosper of Aquitaine between God's foreknowledge, which embraces all that happens, and his election of his own children from the mass of sinners, which applies only to the faithful. Both Spangenberg and Chemnitz strove to avoid any suggestion that God could be responsible for evil (although Spangenberg's echoing of Luther occasionally elicited from his pen ambiguous expressions regarding the reprobation of the unfaithful). Therefore, neither of these disciples of Luther explicitly recognized that God's foreknowing does not merely observe the future but actually creates it. For Luther God did not foresee what would happen independent of his creative activity, objectively discerning from a distance what happens apart from his involvement, but rather God's creative foreknowing actively determined what the future would be. But through their way of distinguishing *praescientia* from *praedestinatio*, Spangenberg, Chemnitz, and colleagues hoped in formulating concord to prevent God from being blamed for sin and evil.

With that presupposition the concordists did proceed to preserve the law's condemnation of unfaith, reminding readers that confidence in God's choice of them as his children dare never lead to licentiousness or despair (SD XI:10-12). The article assures individual believers that God singled them out as those he would save in Christ (SD XI:23); that is, it affirms particular election, against the Philippist fears that this would cause doubt among the people of God. Chemnitz and Andreae counterbalanced those fears by focusing the faith of the elect firmly upon Jesus Christ, who died for all, and upon the means of grace that deliver personal assurance to believers in the regular practice of repentance. Thus, article XI embraced both the Philippist and Gnesio-Lutheran confession of the universality of Christ's atoning work, and it reiterates the insistence of both groups that the blessing of God's election is delivered to individual believers in the oral, written, and sacramental forms of the Word.

Chemnitz returned to Luther's concluding citation from Romans 11:33 at the end of the section of article XI taken from his handbook. His last word on election is that of the reformer and the apostle: "O the depth of the riches and wisdom and knowledge of God! . . . Who has known the mind of the Lord?" (SD XI:55, 64). Andreae's last word was the first word of the Strasbourg Consensus: "Whatever was written in former days was written for our instruction, so that by steadfastness and by the encouragement of the Scriptures we might have hope" (Rom. 15:4) (SD XI:92). In formulating their guidelines for the use of the topic of election in pastoral care and preaching, the concordists endeavored to explain as much as they could, but they recognized that the mystery of evil and the mystery of what it means to be the human creature of the sovereign Creator remained. In the end they recognized that in Christ the Creator had given his people the hope that endures.

Continuing the Struggle with the Tension between God's Responsibility and Human Responsibility

The Formula of Concord did not lay to rest all the questions raised by the paradox of God's total responsibility for everything and the human creature's total responsibility in his or her sphere of life. A little more than a decade later another theologian entwined in the Calvinist debate over the issue of double predestination once again placed the issue on the agenda of the theological faculty at the University of Wittenberg. Samuel Huber joined the faculty in 1593. Son of a Lutheran-minded pastor in central Switzerland, having studied in Basel, Marburg, and Heidelberg, he brought with him from his previous service in several Swiss congregations his personal challenge to the double predestinarian thought that Theodore Beza had argued against Jakob Andreae at the Colloquy of Montbeliard in 1586.[84] Huber solved the problem of God's implicit responsibility for evil that is inherent in the concept of divine reprobation in much the same manner as Leonhardt Palhöfer had. He taught that God had predestined all sinners to salvation. Equating the promise of salvation with God's decree of predestination, Huber did no more than move the point at which believers confronted the mystery or the tension behind the question of why some are saved and not others. His unanswerable question concerned why some sinners reject God's gift of predestination and are alienated from God forever.

His opponent, his new colleague in Wittenberg, Aegidius Hunnius, distinguished the promise of salvation from predestination to salvation. In an attempt to clarify the nature of God's interaction with sinners, Hunnius tied God's choice of his own to the faith that the Holy Spirit would create in their minds and hearts. On the basis of this foreseen faith *(ex praevisa fide)*, God wrote the names of those he would make believers into the Book of Life. Söderlund finds that Hunnius's position avoided the synergism of the less precisely defined interpretations of conversion by Pfeffinger and Strigel a generation earlier because the faith that is foreseen is a product of the Holy Spirit, excluding any human effort or movement in God's direction.[85] To deal with the impression that God arbitrarily chooses his own, Hunnius posited that his choice is bound up not only with Christ but also with faith. He presumed apparently that his assertion of God's responsibility for salvation in this work of the Holy Spirit sufficed. Nonetheless, the search for a better explanation continued. Some of Hunnius's successors in seventeenth-century Lutheran theological faculties spoke of predestination in view of faith *(intuitu fidei)*, at least implying human contribution at the key point of admitting the Holy Spirit to the human heart and mind so that he might create the faith.[86] In the tension between God's total responsibility for all and human creatures' responsibility for their own lives of trust in God and obedience to him, in the tension between attempts at good explanation and good pastoral care, Lutherans, like all other Christians, continued to strive to formulate "better," "clearer" ways of proclaiming both God's love for his human creatures and human faithfulness to the Creator.

As a benchmark in the reception of Luther's *De servo arbitrio,* the Formula of Concord reflects the thinking of four of the significant participants in the trek of Lutheran theology through the landscape of Luther's legacy in the third of a century following his death. Jakob Andreae had helped shape the Strasbourg Consensus of 1563, an important digest of Lutheran thinking on God's election of his chosen people, and Martin Chemnitz had processed ideas generated by Cyriakus Spangenberg in fuller form as the Lutheran teaching on predestination. David Chytraeus and Nikolaus Selnecker had both published reservations about aspects of public treatment of predestination. These four had also participated in the debates over the bondage and freedom of the human will, as had Johannes Wigand and Tilemann Heshusius, whose common voice in the Prussian Declaration had also contributed to the final construction of the Formula's definition of the freedom of the will. Thus, not only because the Formula of Concord helped mold future Lutheran teaching on these topics but also because its words expressed the synthesis of the thinking of major contributors to the public discussion of these issues, it serves as a point of reference from which can be seen some indication of how Luther's disciples had "received" the message of *De servo arbitrio*.

The Formula of Concord referred readers to Luther's treatise (SD II:44), but not without the codicil from the reformer's lectures on Genesis, namely, his warning against the potential misuse of the book's treatment of absolute necessity. The Formula's articulation of its own teaching regarding the topics of the freedom of the will and predestination indicates that its authors were trying to adhere closely to their mentor's teaching of God's total responsibility for all things. At the same time, they repeated his belief that even sinners possess a remnant of the integrity of their humanity as the creature God fashioned human beings to be; that means that the corrupted will is active even if its choice is bound.

Both its article on the human will and its article on election emphasize God's lordship in setting forth the salvation of sinners. This sovereign act of redemption in Christ's incarnation, death, and resurrection is not explicitly elucidated with the help of the larger framework of God's omnipotence and omnicompetence, as is the case in *De servo arbitrio*. It would not be fair to say that the Formula's God is smaller than Luther's, but its focus on him is more limited. The Formula does focus specifically on God's saving actions in Jesus Christ. Its authors had learned from Luther and Melanchthon that talk of salvation centers on and is permeated by talk of Christ, his suffering, death, and resurrection. In speaking of God's responsibility, the Formula does not differ from Luther in ascribing to God alone every aspect of the fallen human being's rescue from sin and restoration to the fullness of humanity, which is faith in God. Even more extensively than *De servo arbitrio*, the Formula identifies this God as the God who has revealed himself in his incarnation as Jesus of Nazareth. The Formula's presentation of God does not distinguish the hidden and revealed God explicitly, but it operates with the concept. For the attention of believers is directed in both article II and article XI repeatedly to the God who has revealed himself in the means of grace, in the promise of the gospel of Jesus Christ. The effective revelation of God in the oral, written, and sacramental forms of his Word (which is at the heart of Luther's understanding of how God rescues those who suffer under the bondage of their wills to Satan) remains a supporting pillar in the construction of the Lutheran body of teaching according to the Formula. All believers are called to recognize that the Holy Spirit has given them faith through God's effective Word and that he sustains their trust in Christ through that Word. Nonetheless, the Formula does not follow Luther in addressing the mystery of evil and sin. It simply halts before venturing onto the territory trod by the reformer in the last paragraphs of *De servo arbitrio*. Into the realm of the hidden God the concordists refused to peer; they did not want even to glance in that direction. The Formula cites Romans 11:33 to warn against speculation about God's choice of his own (SD XI:55, 64), but leaves related questions aside. Theodical discussion found no place in its text.

But theodicy did lurk in the background. Ignoring Luther's exposition of God's foreknowledge as creative, the concordists instead repeated the distinction of Prosper of Aquitaine, which Spangenberg and Chytraeus, among others, had used, between God's foreknowledge of all things and his predestination of his chosen children to salvation (SD XI:4-27). This distinction does not solve the theodical problem. It only asserts that God is not responsible for the evil he foresees. It thus also evades the issue of God's lordship over all that leads to questions about the origin of evil. Where Luther specifically admitted that the human mind could not grasp the ways of God, the Formula sidesteps the question. It seems content to get God off the hook. It returns to the position of Augsburg Confession article XIX: only the human creature and Satan are responsible for evil.[87] It is precisely at this point, as Söderlund observes, that the Formula diverges most from *De servo arbitrio* in its exegesis of specific Bible passages, such as Romans 9:14-28 (SD XI:84).[88]

Although Satan is certainly a topic in the preaching of the period, he does not appear as an important figure in the Formula's assessment of the state of the human creature under sin, as he had in *De servo arbitrio*. That reflects in part the biblical conviction that no sinner may claim a "way out" by saying, "The devil made me do it." Human responsibility is the chief concern of the biblical writers in this regard, and it was certainly the focal point of the concordists. However, by failing to consider the devil in any meaningful way in its anthropology, the Formula does fail to deal with one aspect of the depth of evil that was a preoccupation of Luther. This fact parallels the Formula's avoidance of what it means to be a dependent creature of an almighty Creator. By so doing it skirted one aspect of the tension between God's total responsibility for all things and total human responsibility for the sphere of life given each individual human creature by God.

It did so in part by focusing on the freedom rather than the bondage of the human will as a topic. There is no doubt in article II, and in other related articles, that the human will is captive to sin and Satan, that it is bound to choose false gods rather than the true God. But the assertion of the sinner's inability to come to faith apart from the Holy Spirit did not automatically lead to exploring the underlying structures of that bondage. By restricting its treatment of the will's bondage to its captivity to sin, the Formula ignores one important aspect of the teaching of *De servo arbitrio,* its presumption that human creatures are dependent on God for their continued existence as creatures even before they are dependent on him for rescue because they have misbelieved themselves into slavery to Satan. Creatures are by definition, as products of the Creator's creative will, dependent, bound within the boundaries set by their Maker, according to Luther. Although he did not label the topic a mystery, he wrestled with the mystery of humanity, what it means to be the human creature of the God who made human beings in his own image to be his conversation partners. The students of Luther and Melanchthon focused only on the challenge of sin to the proper functioning of human life, without probing the deeper questions of the mystery of being a human creature. The concordists invested their energies in insuring that human integrity as a thinking and willing creature be made clear. That effort was congruent with the Formula's repeating Melanchthon's insistence that God is not responsible for evil. Luther did not concede that God could be responsible for evil, but he did acknowledge that God's omnipotence leads human minds in the direction of ascribing what is wicked as well as what is good to the almighty Creator. The Formula stands by its axiom that God is totally good and rejects the lure of theodicy by repeating Hosea 13:9, "Israel, that you have gone to ruin is your own fault; that you have been helped rests alone on my grace" (according to the Vulgate), and Romans 9:20, "Who indeed are you, a human being, to argue with God?" (SD XI:62, 63). The Wittenberg way proclaimed law unambiguously so that it might call sinners to repentance, and it proclaimed gospel unequivocally so that it might deliver the comfort of Christ's death and resurrection to the repentant.

Luther believed that it is the will of God that those bound to be human are bound in order that they might be freed from the burden of aspiring to be more or other than human. They are bound to be freed from all that threatens their humanity and freed to serve God and all of creation, particularly other human creatures, by being the loving human beings who reflect God's image, as God made them to be. Because of the mystery of the continuation of sin and evil in the lives of believers, their whole life must be a life of repentance, a life of dying to sin and rising to the life of trust in God each day, a life of liberation from bondage to sin and Satan. The Formula treats that struggle in some detail, not only in articles II and XI. The assessment of how the document uses Luther's and Melanchthon's thoughts on this topic, one only lightly touched in *De servo arbitrio,* is the subject of a study in itself.

Those who carry on a tradition are called to apply it to their own time, not to reproduce it word for word. Changing circumstances change the ways the original words of the great works of the masters function in a new era. The Formula of Concord demonstrates the same desire to confess both God's total responsibility for all things and the human creature's responsibility for trusting God and the obedience that flows from that trust, which guided Luther as he wrote against Erasmus's conception of the freedom of the will. It also demonstrates that the concerns for human integrity and God's holiness that governed the thought of Philipp Melanchthon, concerns shared by his older colleague, had become important for their students. Like Melanchthon, the concordists strove to insist that God is not responsible for evil and that human beings are responsible for their own lives, but they avoided some of the expressions he and his closest adherents in the 1550s and 1560s had used to secure these points. They did so with clear pastoral concern, anchored in the proper distinction of the law that effects repentance and the gospel that bestows forgiveness of sins, life, and salvation. In so doing, they preserved the tension between God's responsibility and human responsibility that marked the Wittenberg way of thinking from its beginning.

The Wittenberg Circle's Practice of Theology

God exercises total lordship over his creation. Human beings are creatures bound by their very created nature to trust God and hearken to his Word. Sin and evil have invaded God's world and alienated his human creatures from him and bound them to Satan. In his *De servo arbitrio* Luther addressed the enigma produced by these biblical teachings. In doing so he elevated an anthropological question, that regarding the capabilities of the sinful human will, to a special focal point for Lutheran theology. Although he also cautioned against possible misinterpretations of *De servo arbitrio,* the reformer found this treatment of Scripture's content one of his very best works, and that opinion is shared by some modern scholars. Martin Brecht judges the work "Luther's theology in condensed form," addressing "an immense question" "magnificently and deeply."[1] Not all his own students agreed, although some did indeed treasure the position the reformer took in that work. They all regarded a proper estimate of the powers of the human will vital to effective application of the biblical message in the lives of their parishioners. This study has shown that in seeking to affirm both God's responsibility for all things and the human responsibility to believe God and obey him, Luther and Melanchthon strove to reproduce the biblical view of Creator and creature faithfully. Instead of homogenizing and harmonizing what God does and what human beings have been created to do, as many Christian theologians have done, the Wittenberg circle endeavored to hold the two seemingly exclusive propositions in tension, to treat them as a true paradox. In so doing they acknowledged God's lordship by affirming human bondage, in sin but also as creature of God; they acknowledged human integrity in the freedom to exercise proper human responsibility in trusting God and loving the neighbor

(Gal. 5:1, 13); and they rejected both God's responsibility for evil and also human responsibility for even the slightest contribution to liberation from sin. In assessing how these students passed on the ideas Luther expressed in *De servo arbitrio* and blended them with the tradition of the church and their own pastoral concerns, the intricate connection between message and method in the Wittenberg theological enterprise becomes clearer.

Researching Reception

"Reception" describes the extent and manner of later generations' use and interpretation of the thought or writings of a figure of influence. When scholars stake out the parameters for studying the influence of an author and his or her work, they enter into a conversation, a conversation that goes back centuries in the case of that over the bondage of the will. In such studies modern investigators often reveal more about themselves than about either the great book and great thinker of the bygone, or the so-called epigones who tried to draw upon and apply the insights of the past to their own age. From their third vantage point scholars identify critical elements in both the giant's breakthrough and the ways the dwarfs on his or her shoulders handed down the new worldview. Scholars engage in this operation, however, as children of their own time and in conversation with their contemporaries, and so they can hardly escape some anachronistic refashioning of the tradition. Historians feel obliged to represent the past and the tradition it gives in their own terms, but in a manner intelligible and, if possible, meaningful to new generations.

Tradition is a living organism, and students of "reception" become a part of the tradition even as they attempt to assess it "objectively." As the twenty-first-century students of the Reformation focus on texts from a current frame of reference to evaluate the impact of Luther's or Melanchthon's way of thinking, they must offer standards for evaluating both the content of the message and also the process of handing that content to new generations. Evaluating the process, they suggest that the glass was half-full or half-empty, that the epigones understood or did not understand, that they enhanced the potter's vessel through fresh decoration or cracked it by inept handling. In addition, assessments such as this study can suggest what elements of the content of the reformers' teaching are useful for the church's confession or society's pondering in a later time, and also reveal something of the method Christians employ in every time as they evaluate and absorb the legacy of the past.

This study has focused on the explicit use and interpretation of one work of Martin Luther within the larger context of the practice of theology among his disciples. Their use of the entire corpus of their mentor's writings and their memories of him took place as they constructed the message they believed their hearers and readers needed for life and salvation. However, they did much more than simply repeat Luther, Melanchthon, and their other instructors. Their reading in the whole heritage of theology they received from ancient and medieval theologians contributed to their passing on and reshaping the Christian tradition. Nonetheless, their explicit employment of *De servo arbitrio,* at limited but significant points in the discussion of the Wittenberg legacy, demonstrates how the second generation of Wittenberg thinkers critically engaged the theology they had learned from their masters.

This study attempts to clarify for twenty-first-century readers how the Wittenberg understanding of God and the human creature unfolded out of Luther's discussion of the bondage of human choice in his great opus *De servo arbitrio.* Luther's text is available in translation for English-speaking readers, but most of the texts putting it to use in the third quarter of the sixteenth century are not. Furthermore, many readers have some sense of what the debate between Erasmus and Luther was about, but relatively few have thought about how Luther's students and disciples used that debate to address their own critical issues. Therefore, this study has proposed to sort out both his concerns and theirs. This presupposes a peculiar intertwining of the message and method that developed out of Luther's confidence in God's action in the Word made flesh (John 1:14) and the Word as means of grace. It addresses the concerns of the Wittenberg theologians within an analytic framework not employed in the sixteenth century, speaking of God's lordship in terms of his total responsibility for all things and describing what it means to be human according to God's creative plan in terms of the human creature's total responsibility for what God has placed in his or her sphere of life. This framework posits a tension between these two "total responsibilities," even if the responsibility of the creature is limited by God's design while that of the Creator is limited only by the promises and pledges the Creator himself has made in his revelation.

Any assessment of Luther's writings must take into consideration how the adherents of his reform movement treated his words. The role of *De servo arbitrio* in the theological discussion and deliberation of the students of Luther and Melanchthon offers a significant example of this. First, even though many of them accorded Luther great authority,[2] all of them believed that their theology rested ultimately on Scripture. Therefore, they sought to argue first of all from biblical texts and claimed always to be representing proper biblical interpretation, whoever among the ancient or more recent teachers of the church might agree or disagree. The exclusive nature of biblical authority is readily apparent in the polemical writings of all Lutheran theologians of the later sixteenth century. In some treatises issued in the synergistic controversies, absolutely no sixteenth-century authorities were brought to bear on the questions under discussion; Bible passages alone dictated public teaching. In others patristic authorities were cited, more in fact to provide historical context than to confirm the case made with the words of the apostles and prophets, but always as a supplement to those words. Some of these writings on the freedom of the will did cite other works by Luther, including his Genesis commentary and his treatment of Psalm 51. And in certain printed works of the controversy, *De servo arbitrio* took on importance as a symbol of proper teaching and/or as a source for exegetical and doctrinal judgments — though always because it was viewed as a clear expression of biblical teaching. But many students of Luther and Melanchthon used other works by each of them to support their scriptural arguments.

The "reception" of Luther's *De servo arbitrio* has played a central role in this investigation of the Wittenberg theology he initiated. The historical and literary reception and use of this work by the reformer's own students pose some enigmatic questions of a lesser kind. Why was one of Luther's favorite books barely mentioned in early biographies of the reformer? Why was it so little used by his students even though he and many of his students praised it highly? Why did the reformer himself feel compelled to warn against its possible misuse? What elements of its message shaped the thinking of the next generation, and which of its insights slipped from the agenda of Lutheran theology?

Second, the reception of the teaching and argument of *De servo arbitrio* cannot be appraised in precisely the same way the impact of a modern book might be gauged. Sixteenth-century authors did quote others — most often ancient authors, but also medieval scholars and to a lesser extent even living contemporaries. Such references occurred in the text or sometimes in marginal notations, the equivalent of footnotes. Through such citations authors appealed to those they regarded as authorities, or they entered into the historical conversation, frequently taking issue with the opinions of those who had written before them, critiquing their arguments. Often sixteenth-century theologians also incorporated ideas from respected authorities without specific reference to a passage in their works, or they did battle against unnamed opponents. That Luther himself almost never cited *De servo arbitrio* in his later works (and when he did, only to caution against its misuse) says as little about his own opinion of the book as does his one glowing reflection on its worth. The fact that after 1525 he abandoned the concept of divine necessity for the most part stands alongside the fact that he continued to insist on the sinful corruption of the human will and the total dependence of sinners upon God's gracious activity for salvation.

Those convictions resonated through the writings of his followers on both sides of the controversy. Whether they cited *De servo arbitrio* or not, they reflected its affirmation of God's lordship, and some emphasized even more than the work itself its avowal of human responsibility. Therefore, Luther's argument in this particular work may have shaped the way his students thought in a manner impossible to ferret out by reading extant sources. Nonetheless, from the explicit use and interpretation of *De servo arbitrio* something can be learned about the process of tradition and reception in the Reformation era.

The Members of the Wittenberg Circle

This study has attempted to assess the further development of various aspects of Luther's understanding of God the Creator and his human creatures with special focus on the reception of *De servo arbitrio* within the "Wittenberg circle." That loosely defined group of instructors, students, and other adherents claimed Luther's and Melanchthon's theology as their own. This study has not focused on the first generation of the Wittenberg circle, those approximately the same age as Luther or Melanchthon, who echoed his call to reform in the 1520s but had not studied at the Leucorea. Several of them did indeed repeat or even anticipate ideas regarding predestination and the bondage of the will central to *De servo arbitrio*. Instead, under consideration here is the second set of receptors of Luther's work, those who taught and wrote in the third quarter of the sixteenth century. They filtered Luther's lectures and writings through the instruction they received from his most influential colleague, Melanchthon, as well as other elements in their instruction and reading. The practice of theology always takes place as a community project. In their continuing experiments in the search for the appropriate ways of delivering God's Word in their ever changing contexts, theologians engage in conversation with a rich past as well as with contemporaries who include personal friends and fierce foes. The conversation sometimes involves repetition and expansion or fresh applications of the insights of others, but it can also include sharp criticism. The challenges from a range of conversation partners always are raising new questions and fresh provocations, shifting perspectives and distinctive accents.

Luther and Melanchthon developed their own thinking in conversation with each other as well as with the embedded scholastic thought and the fresh approaches of biblical humanism that shaped the world in which they had studied. Their colleagues and students, their opponents and supporters prompted and prodded their formation of a distinctive theology at Wittenberg. Luther's "evangelical breakthrough," however it may be defined in particular, reshaped the fundamental questions discussed in the Western church, with its foci on God's active and living Word, on the justification of the sinner as the center of the biblical message, and on its anthropology of the two dimensions of human righteousness. Throughout their lives the two Wittenberg professors and their followers as well were engaged in linguistic experiments to find the proper vocabulary for articulating this new paradigm of interpreting Scripture. This experimentation is evident in *De servo arbitrio,* and it continued into the synergistic controversies.

The initial group of conversation partners in this enterprise formed around Luther in the second and third decades of the sixteenth century, including above all his colleagues in the theological faculty. Along with Melanchthon, they include Bugenhagen, Jonas, and Cruciger, as well as Nikolaus von Amsdorf, who left town but not the association when called to supervise the Reformation of Magdeburg in 1524.[3] The circle expanded rapidly. Several thousand students passed through Wittenberg during Luther's career; the exact number that studied theology is uncertain. In addition, distant readers absorbed Luther's ideas from his publications and began to participate in the conversation as well. About 125 of Luther's and Melanchthon's students became publishing theologians; some 50 or 60 who did not attend Wittenberg also contributed to published Lutheran theology in the third quarter of the sixteenth century. Some two dozen authors within these groups entered the synergistic controversies in print. This dispute and the parallel debates over good works, justification, law and gospel, and related topics were aspects of a family feud. The heirs were sorting out the legacy of a new way of thinking passed down from the father of their way of thinking. They were deciding how to carry further this new way of thinking about the most vital issues of human existence, about the core and the structure of the biblical message.

The Students of Luther and Melanchthon

The works of these disciples indicate how the Lutheran tradition began to shape itself, around living memories and more or less direct impressions of the man whose words they treasured. It must be noted, however, that almost all of those discussed in these chapters did not know Luther in 1525 (some of them had not yet been born), and therefore their memories of the man came from a later period in his own development as well as from others. In the minds of some in the generation of Wittenberg theologians that succeeded Luther and Melanchthon, not only had the older colleague and his younger partner offered differing views of the teachings treated in *De servo arbitrio,* but the younger and older Luther and the younger and older Melanchthon could be cited against each other on elements of its teaching. That alone does not account for the vehemence of the battles to define this legacy, but it certainly did not impede polemical spirits, fired by the political situation following the Smalcald War and the assaults of theological opponents from several sides.

Most participants in the synergistic controversies had known each other from the time of their university studies, and they naturally presumed that their colleagues had understood their instructors just as they themselves had. Thus, these disputes were battles in a civil war, a *Bruderkrieg;* the participants had gotten acquainted as they listened to Luther and Melanchthon lecture at the Leucorea. Flacius, Gallus, Irenaeus, Pfeffinger, Strigel, Wigand, Marbach, Flinsbach, Spangenberg, and Chytraeus had studied in Wittenberg at roughly the same time, in the early 1540s; Selnecker, Kirchner, Chemnitz, Heshusius a decade later. Contemporaries of this latter group, Friedrich Widebram, Heinrich Moller, Johannes Bugenhagen, Jr., and Caspar Cruciger, Jr., constituted the Wittenberg theological faculty in the late 1560s, when they attacked Spangenberg. They looked for leadership to a colleague in medicine, Melanchthon's son-in-law, Caspar Peucer, who had also studied with Spangenberg, Flacius, and others in the early 1540s. The most prominent exception to this observation was Jakob Andreae, whose acquaintance with his Wittenberg contemporaries came through their writings and meetings of one sort or another. In agreement on many fundamental points of teaching, the members of this constellation struggled in the 1550s and 1560s to define Luther's and Melanchthon's legacy on a series of issues, on which this next generation had varying perspectives. They battled so passionately for their own interpretation of the Wittenberg legacy because they believed that Luther's appearance on the stage of church history had eschatological significance. They believed that the proper tradition of his teaching was vital to the health of the church and the salvation of sinners. For varying reasons they all felt betrayed by some of their compatriots within the Wittenberg school. This provided the spark for fierce but not always enlightened exchanges of views.

United by many common convictions regarding God, his human creatures, and their relationships, they fell into dispute because they correlated members of their respective bodies of doctrine in different ways or put emphasis on different articles of faith. This led some to avoid certain elements of the Wittenberg legacy in particular cases, and caused others to express their commonly held concerns in conflicting ways. None of those under study here intended to deny God's total responsibility for all things, especially for the salvation of the sinner. None wanted to be "Stoic" and deny the integrity of the human creature as a being who wills and thinks, and who exercises the Holy Spirit's gift of faith by willing and thinking. All vehemently rejected the idea that God could be responsible for evil, and all affirmed the responsibility of disbelieving sinners for their own condemnation. But as they attempted to make their chief concerns clear, these disciples of Luther and Melanchthon fell into controversy. In those disputes Luther's *De servo arbitrio* played an important though not decisive role, in part because Melanchthon expressed deep reservations regarding its spirit, to say nothing of its assertion concerning absolute necessity. Thus, *De servo arbitrio* was one factor in the ongoing attempt to hold the total responsibility of the Creator and total human responsibility in tension, so that God's message could function properly among his people.

Luther and Melanchthon

The relationship between these two Wittenberg colleagues is intertwined throughout the background of the synergistic controversies, as are their convictions regarding various aspects of the doctrinal substance of the debates. The nature of the relationship between Melanchthon and Luther has aroused controversy since the mid-sixteenth century. Evaluations have usually tended to discredit the younger colleague, for a variety of reasons, sometimes simply for not reduplicating Luther's thought pure and simple. In fact, the original observer of their relationship, Luther himself, did not record discomfort with Melanchthon's positions on the topics of predestination and the freedom of the will. Melanchthon's comments on Luther's views of absolute necessity did illustrate that he, at least, realized that the two colleagues had differed, but Luther had not regarded their differences as so significant that he criticized Melanchthon's divergent viewpoints in writing.

Recently Reinhard Flogaus carefully examined the allegations that Luther and Melanchthon had significantly different understandings of justification by faith. He found these allegations false since both held that God's justifying action takes place by his Word (forensically) and effects genuine change in the believer (effectively).[4] Flogaus did conclude, however, that the two diverged in their teachings on the role of the will in justification, though he marvels at the absence of any word of condemnation from Luther regarding his colleague's open espousal of the will's activities.[5] As convincing as Flogaus's argument regarding justification is, his comment on the divergence in their positions regarding the human will glosses over the different vantage points from which each advocated his own perspective on the topic. In his study of Melanchthon's teaching on the will, Hartmut Günther concluded forty years ago: "Melanchthon remained rooted in Luther's fundamental point of view his entire life, or better, he found it ever again confirmed anew." The Preceptor never abandoned his understanding of the human creature as God's dependent creature, who, at the same time, in spite of the fall into sin, was capable of outwardly and partially obeying God's law apart from grace and whose will never ceased to act even when it lay outside the sway of the Holy Spirit.[6]

This study has shown that some of their students agreed with Günther, while others tended to perceive differences between the two. What seems clear upon closer examination of texts from both men is that they shared a common belief in God's total responsibility for all things, including the salvation of sinners, and in the total responsibility of every human creature to be the person God created each to be. Both maintained that human beings were made to fear, love, and trust in God above all things and to obey God's plan for human life in accord with their identity as the children of God that their Creator freely and without condition bestowed upon them. In his dispute with Erasmus in 1525, Luther emphasized God's responsibility more than human responsibility, but that is not the case in many of his sermons, both before 1525 and after, to people he regarded as carelessly disobedient in their daily lives. Melanchthon's insistence on the integrity and responsibility of human creatures fashioned to trust God with heart and mind did not alter his insistence that sinners are delivered from their sinfulness only by God's grace in Christ alone, through the faith that the Holy Spirit gives. At the same time, the Preceptor avowed that faith is given to and through a will that is not made of wood or stone but is the acting will that God made an integral part of the human creature at creation. Melanchthon maintained that this remained true even though the will has corrupted itself in its rebellion against God and its doubt of his Word, and is thus unable to move toward God without the Holy Spirit's aid.

Historical circumstances determined the specific emphases that each of the men expressed when treating this topic. The changing contexts of the public discussion of the responsibilities of God and human beings in the next generation shaped the formulation of the Wittenberg legacy on the basis of the various raw materials mined from lectures and publications of the

Wittenberg leadership. Luther was a preacher, proclaiming God's love and his demands directly to his people from the pulpit, and altering his style but little when he lectured to students on biblical texts. Melanchthon was a teacher, concerned to explain ideas and the connections between ideas to students. As a teacher of rhetoric, specifically, he was assigned the task of developing communication skills, and that required attention to the psychological factors of human interaction that did not command Luther's attention or interest, at least not at the same level of intensity. Luther had struggled with his own crushing burden of guilt and his conviction that he had to pave the way for his own justification and to work to preserve it with his own obedience to God's every command. Melanchthon received the gift of Luther's concept of grace, as far as records show, before he had intensely engaged the questions of God's wrath and mercy that shaped Luther's mind.

Both men experienced the disquieting, indeed profoundly disturbing, dissonance between the message their followers were preaching in the Saxon countryside and the behavior of the people, especially during the visitation of 1527-28, and both reacted to it with increased emphasis in their preaching on God's law. For both perceived the necessity of believers recognizing how sin bound them in rebellion against their Creator and how God's creative design also bound them to obedience to his plan for life. Both men strove to free believers from sin through the proclamation of the gospel so that they could be free to exercise their inborn human responsibility. Luther focused more (though not exclusively) on confronting hearers with the accusations of the law, whereas Melanchthon strove more intentionally to use it to instruct and guide sanctified conduct that sprang from faith in Christ.

One other significant difference in the context in which the two lived revolved around the restrictions on Luther's movements imposed by his being a wanted outlaw. He was deprived of the direct contact with his opponents and never filled the role of a representative of the Lutheran princes and cities that commissioned Melanchthon to pursue their interests in negotiations of both theological and political importance. Luther could ignore Roman Catholic misinterpretation of his views or simply fire a dismissive salvo in return. Melanchthon was charged with the formal responsibility of winning a peace for the Lutheran churches through conversation aimed at conciliation with enemies both ecclesiastical and political. He faced the fury and the fire of theologians such as Johann Eck and Johann Cochlaeus. His answers to the challenges they threw in his face had to be reasoned and responsible. For all these reasons Luther and Melanchthon focused on different aspects of the questions set forth in *De servo arbitrio* and emphasized different facets of the rich fare of teaching found there.

Therefore, it is little wonder that their students came to this work, as one among many they had from their mentor's hand, with some ambiguity. Indeed, from the perspective of many in the next generation, *De servo arbitrio* served to symbolize Luther's emphasis on God's lordship and the exclusive nature of his grace, but it still remained only one among many of Luther's books that they used. Those other texts also provided what they needed to insist on God's total responsibility for all things, particularly for the salvation of sinners. In addition, these disciples were concerned above all about cultivating the life of repentance, and other materials from Luther's pen helped them present the topic of total human responsibility more clearly than his reply to Erasmus seemed to. In his Genesis lectures, which some of these disciples had actually heard and all had read, Luther had refocused the message of *De servo arbitrio* upon the promise of God to believers in the means of grace. That focus addressed the everyday situations of their parishioners in a more helpful fashion and could be delivered through many other writings from his pen. Luther knew that he had argued mightily for an important component of his understanding of God and the human creature in *De servo arbitrio*, but both he and his students recognized that this message and other aspects of biblical teaching could be proclaimed from many other texts.

Receiving and Handing Down the Reformers' Message

Assessing how a school of thought functions can be approached from a number of vantage points, including the reception of one particular literary work. For questions regarding reception cannot be answered apart from the larger context of theological discussion. Precisely questions about the use of a key book provide orientation to the larger inquiry regarding theological message and method, for both method and message helped determine which elements of Luther's argument in *De servo arbitrio* remained prominent in the thinking of the next generation, whatever texts they might have used to convey them, and which of its insights slipped from the agenda of Lutheran theology.

The highly significant role of a theologian's own education also becomes clear in this study. Like all students, Luther never escaped the agendas introduced into his mind by his instructors. Teachers teach both negatively and positively. Luther rejected the orientation on human merit and performance of the school of Gabriel Biel. His instructors determined his central concern decisively when they taught him that grace comes to those who do their best. Positively, on the other hand, their proclamation of the lordship of the almighty Creator and human dependence on his revelation gave him the raw materials to place that central concern, the justification of the sinner through faith in Christ, in the context of the understanding of God and his Word that developed out of his biblical lectures and his own experience. On a more focused level, in 1525 Luther thought an argument from absolute necessity both necessary and effective because of his own scholastic training; it seemed like an effective way to confess God's total lordship. For the next generation their Wittenberg experience bequeathed to all of his and Melanchthon's students not only the abiding concern to make clear that God's grace alone saves but also the need to defend human integrity by holding fast to human responsibility to trust and obey through acts of mind and will.

The experience of Luther's and Melanchthon's students demonstrates clearly that the Wittenberg way of practicing theology (as indeed for all theological systems) was a finely tuned synergy of what are often too facilely distinguished as content and method. In Luther's own work and in the debates of his students, it becomes obvious how important it is to determine which are the controlling concerns and concepts for theological formulation and what the ordering and relationship of the topics is to be in the construction of the body of doctrine. The way in which biblical teaching as a whole is conceived, organized, and presented profoundly influences the way its presentation of individual doctrinal topics is formulated and their content is conveyed and comprehended. Alongside such factors internal to a theologian's system are the external factors, particularly both the teacher's opponents and audience. Luther himself preached to people in whom he wanted to cultivate a life of repentance in a different way than he engaged Erasmus on the bondage of the will because his people were wrestling with the temptations of daily life, and Erasmus was threatening the clear proclamation of God's unconditional love toward sinners. His students wrestled with this problem in the context of the charges that their view of grace made God responsible for evil and made human beings puppets or automatons. Their body of doctrine took on a slightly different shape because of that. The foes changed, the issues under debate shifted, and the preaching, teaching, and writing of the individual members of the Wittenberg circle took on a different cast even if the same elements remained within the doctrinal skeleton. For both the subject matter he was arguing against and the manner of argumentation employed by his opponents helped set Luther's agenda and shaped his articulation of his message. The same is true, in their respective contexts, of his followers.

The mold into which Luther and Melanchthon taught their students to pour their message for transmission to their parishioners, a matter of method, too, arose out of Luther's conception of both the purpose and the content of theology. He presupposed that God's Word in human language, whether in oral, written, or sacramental form, serves as an instrument of his power and actually accomplishes what it says, in condemnation but above all in restoring true human life through the forgiveness of sins. Upon that doctrinal definition of "the Word of God" Luther cultivated the ability to distinguish law and gospel, to proclaim total human responsibility to those created by God to trust him and to obey him — to those who needed to hear that message — and to proclaim God's total responsibility for salvation, as he accomplished the restoration of human creatures to their humanity in Christ — to those who needed to hear the gospel of new life. Because the actual goal of their teaching the biblical message strove to end sinful identity and to bestow identity as children of God through trust in Christ, Luther and Melanchthon presumed in their formulation of their teaching that the words their hearers and readers would convey to others had to be fashioned as instruments of God's purpose and power. That led them to hone their language and their conceptualization as finely as possible to make the points they wished to make in specific situations. Sometimes those points lay in the realm of law, or human responsibility, sometimes in the realm of gospel, or God's responsibility. When their students focused on different points of concern, they fell into dispute.

The question that divided the spirits in the 1550s and 1560s was not the question Luther had posed in 1525 regarding the relationship of the sinful human creature to the Creator. He was battling against a medieval compromise of the proclamation of God's grace. The inevitability of sinners trying to limit God because they reject God's being God lured Luther into his doctrine of absolute necessity. "Necessity" prevented sinners from putting a rein on God. The God who controls everything through his unchangeable will cannot be tamed or reduced to someone with whom sinners can negotiate. It must be remembered that for Luther this God was the God who had revealed his love in the self-sacrifice of Christ, true God in human flesh.

In addition, Luther was convinced that without taking the person of God seriously, human beings cannot take their own humanity fully seriously, for they will always make compromises with what they know is the best of humanity in order to be satisfied with the way things are in a fallen world. The mystery of how human creatures exercise their responsibility along with God's exercise of his total responsibility may plague human beings, but even more are they troubled by the mystery of sin and evil existing in the face of the almighty and good God. The conflict between their ideals and their actuality creates a deep discontent in perceptive people. The only way out of that discontent is to return to acknowledging the relationship between the Creator and his human creatures and the reality of sin and evil: true peace and consolation lie only in calling things what they are and clinging to Christ for deliverance.

Luther's eschatological conviction regarding the ongoing warfare between God and Satan set the framework for his efforts to penetrate as far as possible into the fundamental questions of who God is and what it means to be human. There he found himself thrown completely upon God's Word, which established reality according to Genesis 1. God's creative Word is the root of Luther's ontology, and continues to establish the fundamental reality of human life through the promise of new life in Christ. Because trust in that promise cannot be created by human reason or effort, God works through the ministry of his Word to accomplish his saving will. That Word kills and makes alive in the process of daily repentance, Luther insisted. Luther's heirs did not abandon an eschatological perspective, but they did refocus it somewhat. They experienced Satan's battle to deceive believers all around them, and they encountered his temptations in the life of dying and rising in repentance. But they dwelt relatively little on the topic of bondage to Satan that had been so central to Luther's argument in 1525. For them the devil was the deceiver more than the jailer or the rider. As deceiver, he appeared as an opponent to be resisted and thus fit into their defense of human integrity. It required a willing sinner.

It might be said that the disciples of Luther and Melanchthon never differed essentially regarding the bondage of human choice, over the commonly held perception that sinners cannot make a free choice and turn themselves to God. All agreed in principle that this was the case, although — in part in defensive reaction to Gnesio-Lutheran criticism — some Philippists used expressions that gave the impression that they were sacrificing total divine control of salvation. Their compulsion to affirm human integrity and responsibility impelled them to formulate descriptions of the will's activities that their Gnesio-Lutheran colleagues believed compromised the exclusive nature of the Holy Spirit's re-creative action. Apart from a description of the human will as *modus agendi*, Viktorin Strigel found no way to make clear that human beings are responsible creatures of God. At Altenburg the Philippist theologians from electoral Saxony seemed to go even further in trying to emphasize that human responsibility. Nonetheless, their affirmation that the Holy Spirit must turn human hearts and minds to faith in Christ stands alongside their attempts to defend the integrity of the human creature in sin by treating the role of the freedom of the will, even in conversion. Likewise, even when their insistence on God's grace gave Philippist foes reason to accuse them of Stoic determinism, Flacius, Gallus, and Spangenberg were also insisting on the integrity of the human creature and taking the activity of the bound will for granted.

Indeed, all the heirs of Luther and Melanchthon were involved in cultivating the repentant life with attention to a broader range of questions. God's total responsibility for salvation shared center stage with human responsibility in a way not present in 1521 or 1525. Particularly in the minds of Melanchthon, Pfeffinger, Strigel, and their comrades in arms, the topics of God's not being responsible for evil and of the integrity of the human creature, even when caught in sin, commanded serious attention, and the topic of God's sovereign lordship and grace was taken for granted, placed in the shadow of the immediate problems of congregational life and dialogue with Roman Catholic opponents. Luther was addressing the relationship between God and the sinful human creature on the human side, with a focus on the total incapacity of the will to turn to God, and on the divine side with an affirmation of the absolute necessity of God's will coming to pass. The later Melanchthon and his associates were seeking to clarify the nature of God and the nature of his human creatures as well, but on different terrain. They treated God's nature by asserting that he could not be responsible for evil. They treated human nature with a focus on the activity that was necessary to preserve the integrity of human beings as the creatures God had made them to be. They simply presumed that God must convert those who do not trust in Christ. But in pursuing the agenda of human integrity, the force of their own logic carried some of the Philippists into descriptions of the activity of the sinful will that sounded as if a minimal human contribution to the process of conversion is necessary.

The warfare over these issues raged so fiercely because each side saw critical elements of the biblical message and of Wittenberg theology threatened by the positions of the other — and because each side felt betrayed by the other in the aftermath of the Smalcald War. The exclusive nature of God's gracious act of salvation in Christ was threatened by the Philippist positions, the Gnesio-Lutherans believed. The ability of the believer to be a responsible believer, willing and thinking as the creature God had fashioned, was endangered by the Gnesio-Lutheran way of defending God's grace, the Philippists thought. Therefore, the Philippists tried to teach about human willing in a way that preserved the integrity and responsibility of the human creature. In 1559, as the synergistic controversy flared into public discussion, Nikolaus Gallus noted that there was a widespread agreement among both sides in the dispute. All granted that the fall into sin did not deprive human creatures of all freedom of choice. Both sides shared a belief in "civic righteousness," that is, the capability of those outside the Christian faith to make moral choices that corresponded to God's law. Even Matthias Flacius claimed that non-Christians could bring themselves to hear and read God's Word apart from the Holy Spirit's direction.[7] Second, all affirmed that believers can perform acts of willing that produce obedience to God's commands. Third, Gnesio-Lutherans and Philippists shared the conviction that the Holy Spirit supports the converted will in its remaining faithful to God in faith and life but that it is also possible for believers to abandon their faith and their God. This position flowed naturally from the Wittenberg understanding that the whole life of the believer is a life of repentance and the distinction of law and gospel behind it. Fourth, Luther and Melanchthon had both warned against false speculation in regard to God's predestination of his chosen people. Thus, all their disciples naturally insisted on looking to the means of grace, in which God speaks his promise to individual believers, for comfort and assurance that they were truly children of God. Fifth, Wittenberg theologians all confessed that the promise of the gospel must be repeated to believers to reinforce their assurance of God's love for them, while unbelievers and unrepentant people must be reminded of the law's warning that they stand outside God's people and must repent. Finally, all the heirs of Wittenberg firmly rejected the proposition that God wills or causes sin or evil; all taught that he does not want sinners to die but rather to be turned to him and live. All proclaimed the universal promise. Yet all recognized that not every sinner comes to saving faith, and therefore they acknowledged the everlasting faithfulness, wisdom, and righteousness of the Creator without venturing to try to solve the mystery of evil.[8]

Certainly, differences in emphasis and focus did separate the two parties. The Philippists tended to avoid the language of re-creation for God's act of salvation and "new creature" for the one who comes to faith. This fact strengthens the observation that a profound difference in fundamental paradigm for the discussion of conversion governed that discussion. The Gnesio-Lutherans believed that God makes sinners new (2 Cor. 5:17), that entry into the kingdom of God means being born again from on high (John 3:3), that unbelievers must become like very little children to enter God's realm (Matt. 18:3). Philippists turned to other passages to set their more fundamental concern in place, insisting, for example, that God is no respecter of persons and therefore not responsible for evil (Acts 10:34) and that God gives the Holy Spirit to those who seek him (Luke 11:13). Authors on each side took for granted the chief concern of the other and subordinated it to their own chief concern, often without recognizing the mechanics of their disagreement. This difference in presupposition or paradigm prevented people already suspicious of each other from perceiving where the root of their opposition to each other lay.

In the disputes a range of questions posed in *De servo arbitrio* was addressed, including topics about God and his human creatures. On the human side there was agreement that God had so fashioned his creatures that they had wills which never ceased to function. An active will belonged to the common Wittenberg definition of what it means to be human. On the human side there was also agreement that sinners cannot convert themselves into children of God. All sinners rely on God's grace and power to do that. On the divine side, no one in the Wittenberg circle conceded that God was in any way responsible for sin and evil, and all ascribed to him the responsibility for the salvation of sinners. In a rather bold stroke Cyriakus Spangenberg followed the move made subtly in the *Syntagma* of New Testament teaching by Johannes Wigand and Matthaeus Judex and forced onto the Lutheran agenda in Strasbourg by the Calvinist Hieronymus Zanchi. He set out to treat the questions of the synergistic controversies on the divine side with the topic of election or predestination. This maneuver tried to use the strategy of *De servo arbitrio* regarding God's grace on the divine side even though treating predestination to salvation was not a tactic the reformer had employed in the work. Spangenberg attracted Philippist attack; the move to the divine side brought no resolution. But it opened Wittenberg theology to a positive treatment of God's election of his own that had not been attempted in a larger way in the first decades of the Wittenberg Reformation. Martin Chemnitz followed Spangenberg's lead, at princely behest but with no little exegetical and pastoral skill and some theological imagination. He found ways to emphasize human responsibility for trusting God and for obeying him while at the same time affirming God's lordship, no longer with a doctrine of absolute necessity but instead by teaching God's unconditional and particular election of his own children. He continued to press the concern of his earliest years as a theologian: that God not be held responsible for evil. In so doing he did not compromise at all in his asserting the necessity of repentance and full human responsibility. He did so through his distinction of law and gospel, a hermeneutical guide which all members of the Wittenberg circle employed, some more consistently than others. And he preserved the sovereignty of God in the salvation of sinners by resting it ultimately on God's plan to save his children through Christ, made before the foundations of the world.

In the midst of such efforts to balance and maintain all the elements in the tension of the two responsibilities, the discussion of proper terminology to articulate the new Wittenberg paradigm of Christian teaching continued. In the heat of battle, however, the Philippists remained convinced that the Gnesio-Lutherans were Stoic and Manichaean in their insistence that the human will actively opposes God until the Holy Spirit overcomes that opposition, and the Gnesio-Lutherans could not lay aside their suspicions that the Philippist insistence on human integrity led to expressions that placed a controlling role in coming to faith into the powers of the will to make some move, be it ever so tiny, in God's direction. The Formula of Concord produced a settlement that pleased most Gnesio-Lutherans, apart from Flacius's most devoted disciples, and also a majority of the Philippists. Its text reflects Chemnitz's and Chytraeus's attempt to honor the chief concerns of both Luther and Melanchthon while distinguishing usable expressions of each from those that could bring confusion to the church. Luther's "absolute necessity" is mentioned without comment, his "purely passive" is found unusable. Melanchthon's "three causes" and the *"modus agendi"* used by some of his closest supporters ought not be employed, but his description of the will as having a "faculty for applying itself to grace" must only be correctly defined to be cited. In differing measure and in different ways, God's total responsibility for salvation found clear articulation in articles II and XI, and complete human responsibility was expressed in article II as well as treatments of new obedience, e.g., in article VI.

That is not to say that any of the heirs of the Leucorea repeated all the elements in *De servo arbitrio* precisely and completely. Some of those elements are not found, or at least not highlighted, in the publications of the Wittenberg circle in the third quarter of the sixteenth century. The God of awe and mystery whom Luther presented to his readers in 1525 and the human creature's utter dependence on him as a creature, apart from sin, lost prominence, although authors such as Spangenberg and Chemnitz revert frequently enough to Romans 11:33-36 to acclaim the God whose wondrous person is beyond human grasp. They and most of their contemporaries in the Wittenberg circle were trying to cultivate in a practical, pastoral way the connection and conversation between the God who is the only Lord, who expresses his lordship in deliverance and redemption through Christ, and the human creature whom the Creator holds responsible for trusting in him and, out of that trust, obeying him. From the starker side of Luther's picture of God in *De servo arbitrio* his disciples have crossed over to the work's focus on God's mercy, an element that also dare not be overlooked in that work, for he never separated the omnipotence of the Creator from his mercy, love, and faithfulness. The reformer taught his students that God did make human beings to converse with him, to hear his Word and to respond in trust and the prayer and obedience that flow from faith in Christ. The students of Luther and Melanchthon joined the two of them in bringing God down to earth. While they may not have confronted theodical questions as forthrightly as Luther did in concluding *De servo arbitrio,* they did convey to their hearers and readers their two mentors' uncompromising condemnation of sin, and they did call for repentance as directly as Luther and Melanchthon had. They conveyed the comfort of Christ's death and resurrection to their congregations as straightforwardly and simply as their mentors had. In their own way they strove to let God be God, but they were also intent on letting human creatures be truly human. That meant, among other things, relying on God alone. It also meant exercising the responsibility God gave his human creatures. It, therefore, meant that faith involved thinking and willing, under the re-creative power of the Holy Spirit, to be sure, as a part of the human activity God had written into the human design.

All Christian thinkers have wrestled with the tension inherent in the biblical teachings regarding God and his human creatures. For the biblical writers assert that God, as creator, is totally responsible for all things and is therefore totally responsible for the salvation of those who have fallen from his favor. At the same time, they hold human beings responsible for performing as the creatures God created them to be, creatures who fear, love, and trust in God above all else and who care for their neighbors with acts of love in conformity with God's plan for human living. The Wittenberg theologians of the 1520s held these assertions in tension, Melanchthon, for example, in his *Loci communes* of 1521, and Luther, for example, in his *De servo arbitrio* of 1525. Neither man abandoned professing that salvation takes place by God's grace alone through the trust that the Holy Spirit creates to bind human beings to their Creator, a trust based upon what Christ has done for sinners in his death and resurrection. Both men continued to insist that all people owe God obedience, in the performance of the works he commands, and as the source of that obedience, in hearkening to his Word and trusting in his promise, grounded in Christ.

Most Christian theologians have tried to harmonize and homogenize the two responsibilities, God's and the human creature's. Luther and Melanchthon strove throughout their lives to maintain the tension, insisting equally on both the full responsibility of God and the complete responsibility of his human creatures — sometimes more clearly, sometimes less. Because they believed that God's Word always addresses the concrete situations of human life, they sometimes emphasized one or the other to obtain a specific goal, but they never stopped anchoring their proclamation and teaching in the two responsibilities. Their followers caught this basic orientation. They continued to express it in terms of the distinction of law and gospel, while making less use of corollaries such as the distinction of the two realms and the two kinds of righteousness. Their reception of *De servo arbitrio* and the disputes which swirled around the force field that its line of thinking had created within the Wittenberg circle illustrate that the disciples of Luther and Melanchthon did not lose the fundamental orientation which their partnership had set down as the foundation of the Wittenberg Reformation.

As Melanchthon himself wrote late in life, "apart from the Holy Spirit the human will is not able to create the spiritual feelings which God requires, that is, true fear of God, true trust in God's mercy, obedience, and patience in afflictions, the love of God, and similar emotions."[9] Or, as Luther had written more than thirty years earlier, "God does not work in us without us, because it is for this he has created and preserved us, that he might work in us and we might cooperate with him, whether outside his own realm in his general omnipotence, or inside his own realm by the special power of his Spirit."[10] The two men shared a common understanding that God wills that his human creatures, bound by their Creator's design for their humanity, and now bound in sinfulness to Satan, be liberated from their sinfulness so that they might freely exercise the humanity God had created. Both Wittenberg theologians proclaimed that through the incarnation, death, and resurrection of Jesus Christ God has liberated his people to trust in him and out of that trust to obey him. Their students continued to deliver the essential elements of what they had learned from the Wittenberg team as they shaped the gospel of Christ for their own hearers and readers in a new generation.

Notes

Notes to the Introduction

1. WA 18:619.16-21; *LW* 33:43.

2. WA 18:783.28-36; *LW* 33:289.

3. WA 1:353-74; *LW* 31:39-70.

4. WA 7:20-73; *LW* 31:333-77.

5. *In XV Psalmos graduum*, 1532/33 (1540); WA 40.III:193.6-7 and 19-20.

6. Preface to the lectures on Galatians, 1535; WA 40.I:45.24-27; *LW* 26:7.

7. Heidelberg Disputation, WA 1: 350-74; *LW* 31: 39-70.

8. See Timothy J. Wengert, "Melanchthon and Luther/Luther and Melanchthon," *LuJ* 66 (1999): 55-88; Hans-Günter Leder, "Luthers Beziehungen zu seinen Wittenberger Freunden," in *Leben und Werk Martin Luthers von 1526 bis 1546, Festgabe zu seinem 500. Geburtstag*, ed. Helmar Junghans (Berlin: Evangelische Verlagsanstalt, 1983), 1:419 (419-40).

9. I am using the term "Wittenberg circle" for all those who demonstrated allegiance to the theology advanced by Luther and Melanchthon as well as their colleagues and successors that grew out of the partnership of these two and their immediate associates in the 1520s-1540s. It includes all those later identified as Gnesio-Lutherans or Philippists as well as some that do not fit into this categorization. These terms themselves, in use since the late eighteenth century for two clearly identifiable but less easily definable parties within the Wittenberg circle, should not lead students of the period to conclude that there were firmly fixed opposing parties. All in the Wittenberg circle stood under the influence of both Luther and Melanchthon. Although the Gnesio-Lutherans opposed some of Melanchthon's positions, they were all more or less under the influence of his method and many of his teachings. The positions of both parties developed during the quarter-century after Luther's death. The Philippists underwent significant change around 1570 as the Wittenberg theological faculty turned to Christoph Pezel for leadership, a man who had studied for but one semester with Melanchthon and had never known Luther at all.

10. I have chosen to apply the term "responsibility" to both God and human creatures

to emphasize the tension within the thought of Luther, Melanchthon, and their students and followers. For the paradox with which they wrestled as they confessed the mystery of God and the mystery of humanity involved the assumption of responsibility for all within his creation that God assumed as he created and thus became the Lord of his creation, as well as the responsibility for the care of his creation that he made an integral part of what it means to be human. Thus, the integrity or wholeness or coherence of human life depends on the exercise of the responsibilities that God has made an integral part of human life.

11. John W. O'Malley, "Erasmus and Luther, Continuity and Discontinuity as Key to Their Conflict," *SCJ* 5, no. 2 (1974): 47.

12. WA Br 8:99.7-8 (#3162).

13. Cochlaeus, *Commentaria de actis et scriptis Martini Lvtheri Saxonis, Chronographice, Ex ordine ab Anno Domini M.D.XVII. usque ad Annum M.D.XLVI . . .* (Mainz: Franz Behem, 1549), 140-43, 158.

14. Johannes Mathesius, *Historien/Von des Ehrwirdigen in Gott Seligen thewren Manns Gottes/Doctoris Martini Luthers/anfang/lehr/leben vnd sterben . . .* (Nuremberg: Heirs of Johann vom Berg and Ulrich Neuber, 1566), CXIXb. Cf. his sermon on the years 1522-25, XXXVIIIb-La, and on 1525, Lb-LXVIIa, which contain no mention of the dispute over the bondage or freedom of choice. See Luther's letter of Mar. 11, 1534, which Nikolaus von Amsdorf had printed as a brief treatise shortly after Luther had written it to him: WA Br 7:27-40 (#2093). In it Luther critically engaged Erasmus's *De sarcienda ecclesiae Concordia deque sedandis opinionum dissidiis* (Basel: Hieronymus Froben and Nicolaus Episcopius, 1533).

15. The texts are found respectively in *CR* 6:155-70, in which Melanchthon does mention Erasmus's admiration for Luther along with his wish that the Wittenberger not express himself so sharply (163), and *CR* 11:726-34, in which Melanchthon cited Erasmus's praise of Luther (729-30).

16. Johann Sleidan, *De statv religionis et reipvblicae, Carolo Qvinto, Caesare, Commentarij* (Strasbourg: Wendelin Rihel, 1555), 59a. Sleidan noted also Erasmus's earlier appreciation of Luther's efforts at reform (17a).

17. Ludwig Rabus, *Historien. Der Heyligen Außerwo[e]lten Gottes Zeügen/Bekennern vnnd Martyrern . . . Der vierdte Theyl* (Strassburg: Samuel Emmel, 1556), cxlixb-cla; cf. clxxxv.

18. Ludwig Rabus, *Historien der Martyrer/Ander Theil . . .* (Strassburg: Johann Rihel, 1572), 167a, 183a.

19. See chap. VI, pp. 198-220, below.

20. The sermons were initially printed soon after they were preached, but were all gathered together and published as *Theander Lutherus. Von des werthen Gottes Manne Doctor Martin Luthers Geistlicher Haushaltung vnd Ritterschafft . . .* (Ursel: Nicolaus Heinrich, 1589). *De servo arbitrio* is mentioned as the source for Luther's teaching on "the false idea of the free will," 17a, and Erasmus as one of those whom Luther conquered as a "spiritual knight," 34b. Erasmus's praise for Luther's exegesis of Scripture was cited in the sermon on Luther as an "outstanding theologian," 152b.

21. Porta, *Oratio continens adhortationem, ad assidvam Lectionem scriptorum Reuerendi Patris & Praeceptoris nostri D. Martini Lvtheri, vltimi Eliae & Prophetae Germaniae* (Jena: Donatus Richtzenhan, 1571), B1b. Cf. Mörlin, *Wie die Bu[e]cher vnd Schrifften/des tewren vnd Seligen Manns Gottes D. Martini Lutheri nu[e]tzlich zu lesen . . .* (Eisleben: Andreas Petri, 1565). Cf. a similar list in the orientation to learning from Luther presented in the pref-

ace of Timotheus Kirchner's collection of Luther citations arranged by doctrinal topic, *Deudscher Thesaurus. Des Hochgelerten weit berumbten vnd thewren Mans D. Mart. Luthers/ Darinnen alle Heubtartickel/Christlicher/Catholischer vnd Apostolischer Lere vnd glaubens erklert vnd ausgelegt* . . . (Frankfurt am Main: Peter Schmidt and Hieronymus Feierabent, 1568), A2a-A6a, where *De servo arbitrio* is recommended along with the Galatians and Genesis commentaries, the sermons on John 14–17, *On the Councils and the Church,* and *Against Hans Wurst.*

22. In the years before his death, a more prominent treatise by Luther might be published between three and fifteen times; certain works, such as his catechisms and postils, won far wider circulation; see Robert Kolb, *Martin Luther as Prophet, Teacher, and Hero: Images of the Reformer, 1520-1620* (Grand Rapids: Baker, 1999), 156-59.

23. WA 18:597-99.

24. See chap. III below, p. 114.

25. See his comments on *De servo arbitrio* in his Genesis lectures, WA 43:457.33–463.17; LW 5:42-50. See Gottfried Adam, *Der Streit um die Prädestination im ausgehenden 16. Jahrhundert, eine Untersuchung zu den Entwürfen vom Samuel Huber und Aegidius Hunnius* (Neukirchen: Neukirchener Verlag, 1970), 178-79; cf. 40-43, 92-93, 184-85. The very helpful study of Rune Söderlund on the understanding of predestination in Lutheran Orthodoxy, *Ex praevisa Fide. Zum Verständnis der Prädestinationslehre in der lutherischen Orthodoxie* (Hannover: Lutherisches Verlagshaus, 1983), also reveals no dependence of late-sixteenth- and seventeenth-century Lutheran theologians on the work; for example, Johann Gerhard, *Loci Theologici,* ed. Eduard Preuss (Berlin: Schlawitz, 1863), 2:257 ("De libero arbitrio," sec. III), worked to excuse Luther for his doctrine of absolute necessity. The Strasbourg Orthodox Lutheran theologian Sebastian Schmidt edited a commentary on *De servo arbitrio* to lead readers away from a "Calvinist" interpretation of the work: *Beati Patris Martini Lutheri Liber De servo arbitrio, contra Desid. Erasmum Roterdamum: Cum brevibus Annotationibus, Quibus B. Vir ab accusatione, quasi absolutum Calviniorum, vel durius aliquod Dei decretum in libro ipso statuerit* . . . (Strasbourg: Nagel, 1664).

Calvinists in the Palatinate republished the work, *De servo arbitrio Martini Lvtheri, ad D. Erasmvm Roterodamvm* . . . (Neustadt: Matthaeus Harnisch, 1591), with a preface by Jacob Kimedoncius, professor of theology in Heidelberg. The Calvinist polemicist Abraham Scultetus cited *De servo arbitrio* as proof that the Calvinists were right and the Lutherans were wrong in his *Vitalia, das ist ein christlich und freundlich Reyß-Gespräch* . . . (Hanau: Aubrius and Clement, 1618), 77-80. I am grateful to Herman Selderhuis for this reference. Seventy years later, the French theologian resident in the Netherlands, Pierre Jurieau, also cited *De servo arbitrio* in support of his doctrine of predestination in his *De pace inter Protestantes ineunde consultatio. Sive disquisitio Circa quaestiones de gratia quae remorantur unionem Protestantium utriusque confessionis Augustanae & Reformatae* . . . (Utrecht: Franciscus Halma, 1688), esp. 208-20. His Lutheran opponent, Samuel von Pufendorf, in his reply to Jurieau, *Heiliges Religions-Recht/Darinnen angezeiget wird/in welchen Lehr-Puncten die Protestanten einig sind oder nicht* . . . (Frankfurt an der Oder: Johann Völcker, 1696), did not discuss Luther's work but did remark in passing that "we are not pledged to Luther's words or those of any other teacher" (456). I am grateful to Irene Dingel for these references.

26. Albrecht Ritschl, *Die christliche Lehre von der Rechtfertigung und Versöhnung, Bd. 1* (Bonn: Marcus, 1870), 221.

27. Klaus Schwarzwäller, *sibboleth. Die Interpretation von Luthers Schrift de servo arbitrio seit Theodosius Harnack. Ein systematisch-kritischer Überblick* (Munich: Kaiser, 1969), 27: "Was man nicht alles in Dsa. finden kann."

28. A bibliography that lists many recent studies is found in Thomas Reinhuber, *Kämpfender Glaube. Studien zu Luthers Bekenntnis am Ende von De servo arbitrio* (Berlin: De Gruyter, 2000), 244-59.

Notes to Chapter I

1. "Assertio omnium articulorum M. Lutheri per bullam Leonis X. etc., 1520," WA 7:142; cf. the English translation of the German version of this work, *LW* 32: 92-94; based on a paraphrase of the fourteenth of the Heidelberg Theses of 1518; WA 1:354; *LW* 31:40.

2. *SC,* creed, third article, *BSLK,* 511-12; *Book of Concord,* 355.

3. WA 1:147. See Bengt Hägglund, "Die Frage der Willensfreiheit in der Auseinandersetzung zwischen Erasmus und Luther," in *Renaissance — Reformation. Gegensätze und Gemeinsamkeiten,* ed. August Buck (Wiesbaden: Harrassowitz, 1984), 182-83.

4. Karl Zickendraht, *Der Streit zwischen Erasmus und Luther über die Willensfreiheit* (Leipzig: Hinrichs, 1909), 1-3; he refers to the discussion of Lorenzo Valla's rejection of the freedom of the will as well as to Johann Eck, *Chrysopassus praedestinationis* (Augsburg: Miller, 1514); Konrad Wimpina, *De divina providentia* (Frankfurt an der Oder: Johannes Hanau, 1516); and Johannes von Staupitz, *De executione aeternae praedestinationis* (Nuremberg: Friedrich Peypus, 1517).

5. See Martin Brecht, *Martin Luther. Zweiter Band. Ordnung und Abgrenzung der Reformation, 1521-1532* (Stuttgart: Calwer Verlag, 1986), 210-20; ET, *Martin Luther, Shaping and Defining the Reformation, 1521-1532,* trans. James L. Schaaf (Minneapolis: Fortress, 1990), 213-24; see also Heinz Holeczek, "Erasmus' Stellung zur Reformation: Studia humanitatis und Kirchenreform," in *Renaissance — Reformation,* 136-45, and Gottfried G. Krodel, "Erasmus — Luther: One Theology, One Method, Two Results," *Concordia Theological Monthly* 41 (1970): 648-67.

6. Luther's debts to Erasmus are often discussed, e.g., in Johannes Kunze, *Erasmus und Luther. Der Einfluss des Erasmus auf die Kommentierung des Galaterbriefes und der Psalmen durch Luther 1519-1521* (Münster: LIT, 2000); Erasmus's use of Luther texts is not so well known and not so extensive, but at the same time not inconsiderable; see Robert G. Kleinhans, "Luther and Erasmus, Another Perspective," *Church History* 39 (1970): 459-69, and John B. Payne, "The Significance of Lutheranizing Changes in Erasmus' Interpretation of Paul's Letters to the Romans and the Galatians in His Annotations (1527) and Paraphrases (1532)," in *Histoire de l'exégèse au XVIe siècle. Textes du Colloque International tenu à Genève en 1976* (Geneva: Droz, 1978), 312-30.

7. Erasmus, *De libero arbitrio DIATRIBH; siue Collectae . . .* (Augsburg: Simprecht Ruff and Sigmund Grimm, 1524), edited in *Desiderii Erasmi Roterodami Opera Omnia . . . ,* ed. J. Clericus, 10 vols. (Leiden, 1703-6), 9:1215-48; *Collected Works of Erasmus 76, Controversies,* ed. Charles Trinkaus (Toronto: University of Toronto Press, 1999), 5-89. The word "diatribe" took on its current English meaning nearly three centuries later. Erasmus used it, according to the normal usage of the time, to designate an inquiry or academic study of the topic.

8. WA Br 1:90.14-16 (#35).

9. Erasmus, *Opvs epistolarvm Des. Erasmi Roterodami*, ed. P. S. Allen, vol. 3 (Oxford: Clarendon, 1913), 605-7, a letter to Luther of May 30, 1519. See Holeczek, "Erasmus' Stellung zur Reformation," 131.

10. Erasmus, *Opvs epistolarvm Des. Erasmi Roterodami*, 3:445-46, a letter to Lambert Hollonius, Dec. 5, 1518.

11. Heinrich Bornkamm, "Erasmus und Luther," *LuJ* 25 (1958): 13. Cf. Holeczek, "Erasmus' Stellung zur Reformation," 142-43.

12. Holeczek, "Erasmus' Stellung zur Reformation," 136. Cf. Leif Grane, "Erasmus und Luther vor dem Streit 1524/25," in *Widerspruch. Luthers Auseinandersetzung mit Erasmus von Rotterdam,* ed. Kari Kopperi (Helsinki: Luther-Agricola-Gesellschaft, 1997), 9-25.

13. Grane, "Erasmus und Luther," 13.

14. See Luther's letter to Spalatin of Sept. 9, 1521; WA Br 2:387-90.

15. Brecht, *Martin Luther* (German), 2:213-16; (English), 2:216-20.

16. Grane, "Erasmus und Luther," 21.

17. Ernst-Wilhelm Kohls, *Die Theologie des Erasmus,* 2 vols. (Basel: Reinhardt, 1966).

18. The term "Manichaean" refers to a worldview that divides divine power more or less equally between two gods or forces, one good, one evil, but it also was used as a designation for a strict and absolute determinism.

19. Zickendraht, *Streit,* 15-17, 43-44; Erasmus sent a prepublication copy of the *Diatribe* to Henry VIII (50-51). The Roman Catholic association of Luther and Wycliffe became a commonplace in polemic against the former; cf. Peter Canisius, *Commentariorvm de Verbi Dei corrvptelis liber primis . . . contra nouos Ecclesiasticae historiae consarcinatores siue Centuriatores pertractatur* (Dillingen: Sebald Mayer, 1581), c2b.

20. Letter to Spalatin, Nov. 1, 1524; WA Br 3:368.

21. WA TR 4:641, #5069. The observation of Ernst Kroker, cited by Friedrich Stählin, *Humanismus und Reformation im bürgerlichen Raum* (Leipzig: Heinsius, 1936), 3, that Camerarius had hardly expected or desired the "Schärfe und Rücksichtslosigkeit" of Luther's answer to Erasmus reflects more twentieth-century preconceptions of sixteenth-century "humanism" than the reality of the situation within the Wittenberg circle in the mid-1520s. I am grateful to Cornelia Niekhus-Moore for this reference.

22. E.g., Thomas Reinhuber, *Kämpfender Glaube. Studien zu Luthers Bekenntnis am Ende von De servo arbitrio* (Berlin: De Gruyter, 2000), 1, repeats the common wisdom that Luther did not answer Erasmus's *Hyperaspistes* I.

23. WA Br 4:46-48, #992.

24. One exception is his expression of delight that *De servo arbitrio* had pleased Nikolaus Hausmann, in a letter of Jan. 20, 1526, WA Br 4:19.

25. *Hyperaspistes Diatribae Aduersus Seruum Arbitrium Martini Lutheri . . .* (Cologne: Peter Quentel, 1526), and *Hyperaspistae liber secundus aduersus librum Martini Lutheri, cui titulem fecit, Seruum arbitrium* (Nuremberg: Johann Petreius, 1527). A total of seven editions of part 1 and four of part 2 appeared by 1528. See Brecht, *Martin Luther* (German), 2:232-34; (English), 2:236-39.

26. See his letters to Georg Spalatin, Mar. 27, 1526, WA Br 4:42, #989, and May 2, 1526, WA Br 4:69-70, #1007, in which he mentioned that Landgrave Philip of Hesse had sent him a copy of the new publication.

27. See Erasmus's letter to Elector John of Mar. 1, 1526; the elector's comments on this letter to Luther, Apr. 21, 1526; and Luther's counsel to the elector to avoid involvement in the matter, Apr. 23, 1526, WA Br 4:57-60, #1000. See also Robert Rosin, *Reformers, the Preacher, and Skepticism: Luther, Brenz, Melanchthon, and Ecclesiastes* (Mainz: Zabern, 1997), 100-102.

28. In a letter of Oct. 2, 1527; WA Br 4:256-57, #1152. Luther responded Oct. 27, 1527, that he was so ill he had not been able to read the second half of *Hyperaspistes,* to say nothing of doing something about it; WA Br 4:271-72, #1162.

29. In the Wittenberg terminology, "Sacramentarians" designated those who denied that Christ's body and blood were truly in the Lord's Supper, and "Schwärmer" referred to those who "swarmed" or "raved" because they believed themselves filled with the Holy Spirit, apart from any external means of conveying God's Word.

30. WA 20:7-203. See Rosin, *Reformers,* 89-150. It is interesting to note that in the Jena edition of Luther's works, which, in contrast to the Wittenberg edition, aimed to present them in chronological order, *De servo arbitrio* of 1525 is followed by the Ecclesiastes commentary, dated in the Jena edition 1532; Luther, *Tomvs tertivs omnivm opervm Reverendi patris, Viri Dei, D. M. L. . . .* (Jena: Donatus Ritzenhan and Thomas Rhebart, 1567), 230a. The chronology proceeds from 1532 to 1537 in the remainder of the volume.

31. WA Br 7:27-40, #2093; cf. his preface to Anton Corvinus, *Qvatenvs expedit aeditam recens Erasmi de sarcienda Ecclesiae concordia Rationem sequi, tantisper dum adparatur Synodus, Iuditium* (Wittenberg: Nicolaus Schirlentz, 1534), in WA 38:276-79. Erasmus's proposals had been presented the previous year in *De sarcienda ecclesiae Concordia deque sedandis opinionum dissidiis* (Basel: Hieronymus Froben and Nicolaus Episcopius, 1533). Cf. Bornkamm, "Erasmus und Luther," 19-20; Martin Brecht, *Martin Luther. Dritter Band. Die Erhaltung der Kirche 1532-1546* (Stuttgart: Calwer, 1987), 88-91; ET, *Martin Luther: The Preservation of the Church, 1532-1546,* trans. James L. Schaaf (Minneapolis: Fortress, 1993), 78-84; and Holoczek, "Erasmus' Stellung zur Reformation," 148-50.

32. WA Br 8:99.7-8.

33. WA 18:614.3-6; *LW* 33:35. Cf. similar passages, WA 18:602.22-32; *LW* 33:18; and WA 18:786.39-40; *LW* 33:294-95.

34. WA 18:786.26-35; *LW* 33:294.

35. As Martin Doerne insisted: "Gottes Ehre am gebundenen Willen. Evangelische Grundlagen und theologische Spitzensätze in *De servo arbitrio,*" *LuJ* 20 (1938): 47.

36. Klaus Schwarzwäller, *Theologia crucis. Luthers Lehre von Prädestination nach De servo arbitrio, 1525* (Munich: Kaiser, 1970), 38.

37. WA 2:449.16-19; *LW* 27:159.

38. WA 18:603.12-14; *LW* 33:20.

39. Reinhuber, *Kämpfender Glaube,* 17, see 12-17; cf. Thomas Wabel, *Sprache als Grenze in Luthers theologischer Hermeneutik und Wittgensteins Sprachphilosophie* (Berlin: De Gruyter, 1998), 232-35, and Ulrich Asendorf, *Luther und Hegel: Untersuchungen zur Grundlegung einer neuen systematischen Theologie* (Wiesbaden: Steiner, 1982), 106.

40. Schwarzwäller, *Theologia crucis,* 38-39.

41. Hans-Werner Gensichen, *We Condemn: How Luther and Sixteenth Century Lutheranism Condemned False Doctrine,* trans. Herbert J. A. Bouman (Saint Louis: Concordia, 1967), 1-28.

42. WA 8:43-128; *LW* 32:137-260.

43. Wabel, *Sprache als Grenze*, 204-11, 219-20.

44. Cf. the comments of Martin Greschat, *Luther neben Melanchthon. Studien zur Gestalt der Rechtfertigungslehre zwischen 1528 und 1537* (Witten: Luther-Verlag, 1965), 89-109, 166-85, on the mutual influences of the two colleagues on their concept of doctrine.

45. Peter Matheson, *The Rhetoric of the Reformation* (Edinburgh: T. & T. Clark, 1998), 11-12. Matheson's admirable attempt to assess the positive purpose and practice of polemic in the Reformation founders on just such shallow grounds.

46. WA 18:756.15-18; *LW* 33:246.

47. Ulrich Asendorf, *Eschatologie bei Luther* (Göttingen: Vandenhoeck & Ruprecht, 1967), 280-85; John M. Headley, *Luther's View of Church History* (New Haven: Yale University Press, 1963), 181-265.

48. Asendorf, *Eschatologie,* 207-42. It is interesting, in view of the intense eschatological consciousness displayed in Luther's writings on the Peasants' Revolt at about this time (Martin Greschat, "Luthers Haltung im Bauernkrieg," *ARG* 57 [1965]: 31-47), that there is not more explicit eschatological reference in *De servo arbitrio.* That may be due to what Luther considered its inappropriateness in a theological disputation.

49. On the Wittenberg usage of this term for the analogy of faith, see Irene Dingel, "Melanchthon und die Normierung des Bekenntnisses," in *Der Theologe Melanchthon,* ed. Günter Frank (Stuttgart: Thorbecke, 2000), 196-99; cf. also Robert Kolb, *Confessing the Faith: Reformers Define the Church, 1530-1580* (Saint Louis: Concordia, 1991), 20-25. *Corpus doctrinae* came to refer to a collection of writings that summarized all of biblical teaching in a way that guided and evaluated all public teaching, as Dingel shows.

50. *Contra Iulianum* 2.8.23; PL 44:689; see Harry J. McSorley, *Luther: Right or Wrong? An Ecumenical-Theological Study of Luther's Major Work, "The Bondage of the Will"* (New York: Newman; Minneapolis: Augsburg, 1969), 63-110, esp. 90-93.

51. Doerne, "Gottes Ehre," 46.

52. Zickendraht, *Streit,* 58.

53. Heiko A. Oberman, *Luther, Man between God and the Devil,* trans. Eileen Walliser-Schwarzbart (New Haven: Yale University Press, 1989), 212.

54. Krodel, "Erasmus — Luther," 664.

55. Hägglund, "Willensfreiheit," 190, 193.

56. Schwarzwäller, *Theologia crucis,* 47; cf. WA 40.II:328.17-20. Gerhard O. Forde, *The Captivation of the Will* (Grand Rapids: Eerdmans, 2005), reinforces this claim with observations in his fourth chapter.

57. Herms, "Gewißheit in Martin Luthers 'De servo arbitrio,'" *LuJ* 67 (2000): 23-50.

58. WA 18:783.36-40; *LW* 33:289.

59. WA 18:785.26-38; *LW* 33:292.

60. WA 18:784.9-20; *LW* 33:290.

61. Oberman, *Luther,* 213.

62. Oberman, *Luther,* 215.

63. Holeczek, "Erasmus' Stellung zur Reformation," 145.

64. Holeczek, "Erasmus' Stellung zur Reformation," 153.

65. WA 18:784.1–785.38; *LW* 33:289-92.

66. Wabel, *Sprache als Grenze,* 205-6, 213.

67. Heiko A. Oberman, *The Harvest of Medieval Theology: Gabriel Biel and Late Medieval Nominalism* (Durham: Labyrinth, 1983), 217-35, 361-412.

68. Reinhuber, *Kämpfender Glaube*, 5-8.

69. See Béatrice Périgot, "La *disputatio* comme méthode dans la confrontation sur le libre-arbitre d'Erasme et de Luther," *Université de Genève Institut d'Histoire de la Reformation Bulletin Annuel* 23 (2001-2): 31-52, on Erasmus's use of the form of the scholastic disputation and related topics, including Luther's use of the same form along with "humanistic" rhetorical devices to criticize Erasmus's argument. The rhetorical analysis of Marjorie O'Rourke Boyle, for example in her *Rhetoric and Reform: Erasmus' Civil Dispute with Luther* (Cambridge: Harvard University Press, 1983), has occasioned lively scholarly debate.

70. Oberman, *Luther*, 216.

71. Schwarzwäller, *Theologia crucis*, 128.

72. Schwarzwäller, *Theologia crucis*, 104-5.

73. Häggland, "Willensfreiheit," 188-89, 193-94.

74. WA 18:634.23–638.11; *LW* 33:64-70.

75. Bornkamm sketched the differences between the two at the level of background and skills; see his "Erasmus und Luther," 3-22.

76. WA 18:786.35–787.11; *LW* 33:294-95.

77. Anthony Levi, *Renaissance and Reformation: The Intellectual Genesis* (New Haven: Yale University Press, 2002), 299. On p. 300 Levi identifies Luther's denial of free will as "merely the corollary of his abandonment of any attempt to solve the problem within the traditional parameters." Levi's seriously flawed study cannot explain how Luther in fact did that by holding fast to the paradox of total divine responsibility and total human responsibility, but Levi is correct in his general sense of the problem in Erasmus's struggles to formulate his position.

78. James D. Tracy, "Two Erasmuses, Two Luthers: Erasmus' Strategy in Defense of *De libero arbitrio*," *ARG* 78 (1987): 37-60. Schwarzwäller, *Theologia crucis*, 86-87, 108-10, also notes the tensions within Erasmus's own argument.

79. WA 18:667-71; *LW* 33:112-17.

80. Schwarzwäller, *Theologia crucis*, 111; cf. 86-87.

81. Lohse, "Dogma und Bekenntnis in der Reformation: Von Luther bis zum Konkordienbuch," in *Handbuch der Dogmen- und Theologiegeschichte, Zweiter Band: Die Lehrentwicklung im Rahmen der Konfessionalität,* ed. Carl Andresen (Göttingen: Vandenhoeck & Ruprecht, 1980), 36.

82. Brecht, *Martin Luther* (German), 2:210; (English), 2:213.

83. Erasmus, *Opera omnia*, 9:1232-35; *Collected Works*, 76:46-56.

84. In his edition of *De servo arbitrio* in WA 18:616, A. Freitag identified this as a change in the second edition of the Jena edition. In fact, though not found in any of the 1525-26 printings of the work, it was present when the treatise was next printed, in the collected works, already a decade earlier in the first printing of the Jena edition (1557), and even before that in the Wittenberg edition (1546). See Luther, *Tomvs secvndvs omnivm opervm Reverendi Domini Martini Lvtheri . . .* , 2nd printing (Wittenberg: Seitz, 1552), 426a; *Tomvs tertivs omnivm opervm Reverendi Patris Viri Dei, D.M.L. . . .* (Jena: Rödinger, 1557), 171; it remained in the second edition, *Tomvs tertivs omnivm opervm . . .* (Jena: Ritzenhan/Rebart, 1567), 171; cf. WA 18:616; *LW* 33:39. This addition was not present in Justus Jonas's German translation, *Das*

der freie Wille nichts sey/Antwort D. Martini Luther an Erasmum Roterdamum. Verdeutscht durch D. Justum Jonam (Wittenberg: Lufft, 1526), E1a, nor in Nikolaus Gallus's republication of the translation, *Das der freie Wille nichts sey . . .* (Regensburg: Geißler, 1559), F2a.

85. *RE* 24:426-32.

86. According to Christopher Walther, later assisting managing editor of the Wittenberg edition, this volume was printed during Luther's life and with his knowledge and approval; *Bericht von den Wittembergischen Tomis der Bücher des Ehrnwirdigen Herrn Doctoris Martini Lutheri. Wider Matthes Flacium Illyricum* (Wittenberg: Hans Lufft, 1558), A4a.

87. WA 43:458.35–459.6 and 463.3-17; *LW* 5:45-46, 50.

88. WA 43:547.34–548.3; *LW* 5:173.

89. Matheson, *Rhetoric*, 248.

90. Increasingly, scholars of late medieval thought are recognizing the difficulties in using the traditional terms "nominalism" and "Ockhamism" to describe a major but mixed group of theologians and philosophers. Here the terms are used to denote those thinkers whose intellectual roots can in some way be traced back to William of Ockham, represented in Luther's life by figures as varied as Gabriel Biel and Gregory of Rimini.

91. Cf. the summary overview of much twentieth-century scholarly study of Luther's evangelical breakthrough in two works edited by Bernhard Lohse: *Der Durchbruch der reformatorischen Erkenntnis bei Luther* (Darmstadt: Wissenschaftliche Buchgesellschaft, 1968) and *Der Durchbruch der reformatorischen Erkenntnis bei Luther, Neue Untersuchungen* (Stuttgart: Steiner, 1988).

92. Bernhard Lohse, *Martin Luther's Theology, Its Historical and Systematic Development,* trans. Roy A. Harrisville (Minneapolis: Fortress, 1999), 165-66; Oberman, *Harvest,* 30-47. See also the finely focused study of Antti Raunio, "Das liberum arbitrium als göttliche Eigenschaft in Luthers De servo arbitrio," in *Widerspruch. Luthers Auseinandersetzung mit Erasmus von Rotterdam,* ed. Kari Kopperi (Helsinki: Luther-Agricola-Gesellschaft, 1997), esp. 66-70, a study of the concept of *liberum arbitrium* in Luther's Erfurt instructors, Jodocus Trutvetter and Bartholomaeus Arnoldi von Usingen, who brought together elements of Ockhamist and Thomist thought on the subject. These two professors held in slightly different forms that human reason, which controls the will, has freedom in regard to the created order. They also taught that reason directs the will inevitably to seek God, and thus they could teach Biel's view that grace is given to those who do their best *(facere quod in se est).* Unfortunately, the essay moves from this helpful analysis to broader speculation regarding Luther's metaphysic. Cf. also Volker Leppin, *Geglaubte Wahrheit, Das Theologieverständnis Wilhelms von Ockham* (Göttingen: Vandenhoeck & Ruprecht, 1995); Helmar Junghans, *Ockham im Lichte der neuen Forschung* (Berlin: Lutherisches Verlagshaus, 1968); and Bengt Hägglund, *Theologie und Philosophie bei Luther und in der Occamistischen Tradition, Luthers Stellung zur Theorie von der doppelten Wahrheit* (Lund: Gleerup, 1955).

93. On the tension within Biel's system of salvation, see Bengt Hägglund, *The Background of Luther's Doctrine of Justification in Late Medieval Theology* (Philadelphia: Fortress, 1971), 18-34, and Oberman, *Harvest,* 120-84.

94. Hägglund, "Willensfreiheit," 184, 191-93.

95. Oberman, *Luther,* 212.

96. For an overview of the theology of *De servo arbitrio,* see Lohse, *Theology,* 160-68.

97. See Forde, *Captivation of the Will,* chap. 2. Philip S. Watson made this expression

the central point of his summary of Luther's theology in his *Let God Be God! An Interpretation of the Theology of Martin Luther* (Philadelphia: Muhlenberg, 1947). Watson's reference to the reformer's words, "to let God rule and be God," 64, is unclear; the phrase is found in the Kirchenpostille, WA 10.I.1:24.4-11; *Luther's Epistle Sermons, Advent and Christmas Season,* trans. John Nicolaus Lenker, I, in *Luther's Complete Works* VII (Minneapolis: Luther Press, 1908), 117. Cf. Eeva Martikainen, "Der Begriff 'Gott' in *De servo arbitrio*," in *Widerspruch,* 26-45.

98. Iwand, *Um den rechten Glauben, Gesammelte Aufsätze,* ed. Karl Gerhard Steck (Munich: Kaiser, 1959), 26-30.

99. WA 18:712.32-38; *LW* 33:181.

100. WA 18:636.27-30; *LW* 33:68. Cf. WA 18:662.7-26; *LW* 33:103. See Lohse, *Theology,* 165-66, 214-15, 242, and Paul Althaus, *The Theology of Martin Luther,* trans. Robert C. Schultz (Philadelphia: Fortress, 1966), 274-86. Althaus tends to underrate Luther's limits on God's freedom which the Creator has imposed upon himself through his promise of salvation in the gospel.

101. WA 18:615.11-14; *LW* 33:37.

102. WA 18:619.19-21; *LW* 33:43.

103. Luther did not have at his disposal a term that directly corresponds to the twentieth-century concept of identity, but his theology focused upon what is now termed the identity of the human creature, that is, what constitutes humanity. His definition of the human creature posited that human beings are creatures of God, made to be faithful to their Creator and to live out of their trust in him. Rune Söderlund, *Ex praevisa fide. Zum Verständnis der Prädestinationslehre in der lutherischen Orthodoxie* (Hannover: Lutherisches Verlagshaus, 1983), 25, correctly observes that "Luther uses the word *praedestinatio* for everything that God does in his omnipotence, while the Formula of Concord uses *praedestinatio* as a synonym for *electio*." There may be other differences in perspective or emphasis between *De servo arbitrio* and the Formula of Concord, but that difference in definition is clear.

104. WA 18:615.33–616.6; *LW* 33:38. It has been necessary to sharpen the Watson translation at points.

105. Iwand, *Um den rechten Glauben,* 34-37.

106. Schwarzwäller, *Theologia crucis,* 130; cf. Gerhard O. Forde, *On Being a Theologian of the Cross: Reflections on Luther's Heidelberg Disputation, 1518* (Grand Rapids: Eerdmans, 1997), esp. 1-22.

107. Luther spoke of God hiding himself in opposites; cf. WA 18:633.9-23; *LW* 33:62-63.

108. Robert Kolb, "God Kills to Make Alive: Romans 6 and Luther's Understanding of Justification (1535)," *LQ* 12, no. 1 (1998): 33-56.

109. Lohse, *Theology,* 210-15; Oberman, *Harvest,* 30-38; and Marilyn McCord Adams, "Ockham on Will, Nature and Morality," in *Cambridge Companion to Ockham,* ed. Paul Vincent Spade (Cambridge: Cambridge University Press, 1999), 245-72. It must be noted that speaking of God's absolute power and his ordained power in the manner of Ockhamist thinkers is quite different from Luther's distinction of the hidden and revealed God, even though the former complex of ideas probably functioned as the springboard for this distinction in Luther.

110. Especially in the Heidelberg Disputation, WA 1:353-74; *LW* 31:39-70. See Forde, *On Being a Theologian of the Cross.* Lohse, *Theology,* 217, states that Luther's distinction of the

Deus absconditus from the *Deus revelatus* "may be Luther's most important contribution to the tradition of the Christian doctrine of God." Cf. Althaus, *Theology,* 274-86, and David C. Steinmetz, *Luther in Context* (Bloomington: Indiana University Press, 1986), 23-32.

111. Schwarzwäller, *Theologia crucis,* 109. On the soteriological and pastoral concern that shaped Luther's focus on God's omnipotence or his total effectiveness throughout creation, see the analysis of Paul Althaus's view by Christine Kress, *Gottes Allmacht angesichts von Leiden, Zur Interpretation der Gotteslehre in den systematisch-theologischen Entwürfen von Paul Althaus, Paul Tillich und Karl Barth* (Neukirchen-Vluyn: Neukirchener Verlag, 1999), 65-70.

112. Schwarzwäller, *Theologia crucis,* 160.

113. Forde, *Theologian of the Cross,* 77-81, 91-95.

114. WA 18:784.9-13; *LW* 33:290.

115. WA 18:689.18-23; *LW* 33:145-46.

116. For a development of Luther's *theologia crucis* for twenty-first-century anthropology and theodicy, see Robert Kolb, "Luther on the Theology of the Cross," *LQ* 16 (2002): 443-66, a revision of "Deus revelatus — Homo revelatus. Luthers theologia crucis für das 21. Jahrhundert," in Robert Kolb and Christian Neddens, *Gottes Wort vom Kreuz, Lutherische Theologie als kritische Theologie,* Oberurseler Hefte 40 (Oberursel: Lutherische Theologische Hochschule, 2001), 13-34. See also in the same work Neddens's essay, "Kreuzestheologie als kritische Theologie, Aspekte und Positionen der Kreuzestheologie im 20. Jahrhundert," 35-66.

117. WA 18:786.18-20; *LW* 33:293.

118. WA 18:778.38–779.21; *LW* 33:281-82.

119. WA 43:459.24-32; *LW* 5:45.

120. WA 43:460.26-35; *LW* 5:46.

121. WA 43:463.3-17; *LW* 5:50.

122. See F. H. R. Frank, *Die Theologie der Concordienformel* 1 (Erlangen: Blaesing, 1858), 125, and Gerhard Rost, *Der Prädestinationsgedanke in der Theologie Martin Luthers* (Berlin: Evangelische Verlagsanstalt, 1966), 114-31.

123. WA 1:225.27-34, theses 29-32. *Necessitas consequentiae* is a necessity that is contingent upon certain presuppositions, in this context, human actions that create a situation out of which a specific result must flow, whereas *necessitas consequentis* is an absolute necessity, necessity by definition, with no contingency based upon human action. Luther thought this distinction had been invented only to get God off the hook, but in so doing denied his complete lordship and complete responsibility for all things; WA 18:719.4-35; *LW* 33:190.

124. WA TR 2:227-28, #1820.

125. WA 18:618.12-15; *LW* 33:41.

126. WA 18:716.11-15; *LW* 33:186.

127. WA 18:772.38-40; *LW* 33:272.

128. Oberman, *Harvest,* 43-47.

129. David C. Steinmetz, *Luther and Staupitz: An Essay in the Intellectual Origin of the Protestant Reformation* (Durham, N.C.: Duke University Press, 1980); Markus Wriedt, *Gnade und Erwählung, eine Untersuchung zu Johann von Staupitz und Martin Luther* (Mainz: Zabern, 1991).

130. WA 18:619.3-21; *LW* 33:42-43.

131. WA 40.I:130.31–140.17; *LW* 26:71-72.

132. WA 42:670.26-28; *LW* 3:171.

133. WA 43:457.33-40, 458.31-35; *LW* 5:42-43. Luther lectured on Gen. 26 in Dec. 1541; on Feb. 18, 1542, he made comments recorded by an unknown scribe that repeated the content of this section of his lecture on Gen. 26 to a large extent, very similar in detail; WA TR 5:293-96, #5658a from Feb. 18, 1542.

134. WA TR 4:642, #5070. This focus on the means of grace instead of God's predestination can also be found in other *Tischreden:* WA TR 1:427-29, #865; 1:506, #1009; 1:512-13, #1017; 1:514-15, #1019; and 1:602, #1208, all from the early 1530s; 2:561-62, #2631a, b and 2:583-84, #2654a, b, both from Sept. 1532; 4:420, #4656, from mid-June 1539; 5:388-89, #5886.

135. WA Br 10:488. As editor of the text, Clemen found that the letter's verbosity *(Weitschweifigkeit)* and the fact that its treatment of Matt. 11:28 seems to be an insertion must lead to the conclusion that Cruciger altered the text. Certainly, Luther's sixteenth-century editors did polish their raw material from his pen on many occasions, though not as often as the presuppositions of modern scholars have driven them to conclude. But in this particular case verbosity and an exegetical excursus do not seem convincing arguments against a text's being authentic Luther. The repetition of Wittenberg edition editor Christoph Walther's criticism of Johann Aurifaber's dating of the letter to 1528, mentioned in 13:324, does not argue against its fundamental authenticity.

136. Luther's translation of 1 Tim. 2:4, with its restriction to God's providence within this life, does not indicate that he held a view of universal atonement; see the argument of Lowell C. Green, "Luther's Understanding of the Freedom of God and the Salvation of Man: His Interpretation of 1 Timothy 2:4," *ARG* 87 (1996): 57-73. Nonetheless, Luther's use of 1 Tim. 2:4 to assert that God wants all to be saved in *De servo arbitrio* confirms that he did teach this (WA 18:686.1-13; *LW* 33:140), and other comments on the text indicate that at times Luther did see this passage as support for his belief that God indeed wants all to be saved, as he more often argued on the basis of Ezek. 33:11. Green demonstrates that Luther's treatments of 1 Tim. 2:4 illustrate how he struggled in different contexts to make clear both God's total responsibility and the human creature's total responsibility, each within their respective spheres of agency. Cf. Anton Lauterbach's report from June 1539 on Luther's affirmation that God's promises are universal and that the blame for damnation falls upon the human creature, WA TR 4:423, #4665. If this report seems to reflect a student's presupposition more than the professor's position, it must be remembered that while all students place what they hear their instructors say within their own framework of thought, Luther's students, in their awe of him, tried to record and convey his words correctly.

137. WA Br 10:492.128-39 (#3956).

138. WA Br 10:492-94, 494.214-18.

139. WA Br 11:165-66 (#4144).

140. WA Br 12:134-36 (#4244a); cf. the earlier edition of a copy, WA Br 6:86-88 (#1811). See Ute Mennecke-Haustein, *Luthers Trostbriefe* (Gütersloh: Mohn, 1989), 195-206. The words Luther wrote to Caspar Aquila in 1530 on the topic agree with the contents of this letter; WA TR 6:39-41.

141. Doerne, "Gottes Ehre," 72. Cf. also Reinhuber, *Kämpfender Glaube,* 210-14.

142. WA 18:686.4-10; *LW* 33:140. Problematic is the passage "It is likewise the part of this incarnate God to weep, wail, and groan over the perdition of the ungodly when the will

of the Divine Majesty purposely abandons and reprobates some to perish. And it is not for us to ask why he does so, but to stand in awe of God who both can do and wills to do such things." WA 18:689.17–690.8; *LW* 33:145-46. Luther fell into conflict with his own logic and finally beat a hasty and not particularly satisfying retreat. Compare his assessment of the offense that comes when it is thought that God "by his own sheer will should abandon, harden, and damn" people; WA 18:719.7-8; *LW* 33:190.

143. WA 18:626.26-27; *LW* 33:52. On Luther's use of Scripture in the work, see the first chapter of Forde, *The Captivation of the Will.*

144. Wabel, *Sprache als Grenze,* 215-20.

145. Schwarzwäller, *Theologia crucis,* 168.

146. WA 18:656.16-19; *LW* 33:94-95.

147. WA 18:606.10–607.17; *LW* 33:25-27.

148. WA 18:659.27-30; *LW* 33:99-100.

149. Smalcald Articles III:iv; *BSLK,* 449; *Book of Concord,* 319.

150. WA 18:609.4-14; *LW* 33:28.

151. WA 18:619.16-22; *LW* 33:43.

152. WA 18:757.35–758.36; *LW* 33:248-49.

153. WA 18:677.7-9; *LW* 33:127.

154. WA 18:680.23-32; *LW* 33:132.

155. WA 18:687.37–688.2; *LW* 33:143.

156. WA 18:765.14-17; *LW* 33:259-60.

157. WA 18:766.25-31; *LW* 33:261-62.

158. WA 18:692.19–693.1; *LW* 33:150.

159. WA 18:685.14-17; *LW* 33:139.

160. WA 18:700.32-35; *LW* 33:162.

161. WA 18:750.29-30; *LW* 33:237.

162. Doerne, "Gottes Ehre," 63.

163. WA 18:754.1-12; *LW* 33:242-43. It has been necessary to sharpen the Watson translation at points.

164. WA 18:751.22-24; *LW* 33:239.

165. WA 18:635.7-22; *LW* 33:65-66.

166. WA 18:727.3–729.19; *LW* 33:203-6. This metaphor continued to serve Luther; cf. Johannes Mathesius's report from table conversation on Sept. 2, 1540, WA TR 1-2, #5189.

167. WA 18:740.19–749.19; *LW* 33:222-29.

168. Erasmus, *Opera Omnia,* 9:1220-21; *Collected Works,* 76:21-23.

169. "Sermo de triplici iustitia, 1518," WA 2:41-47; "Sermo de duplici iustitia, 1519," WA 2:143-52.

170. WA 40.I:45.24-27; *LW* 26:7. See Robert Kolb, "Luther on the Two Kinds of Righteousness: Reflections on His Two-Dimensional Definition of Humanity at the Heart of His Theology," *LQ* 13 (1999): 449-66, which also appears in *Harvesting Martin Luther's Reflections on Theology, Ethics, and the Church,* ed. Timothy J. Wengert (Grand Rapids: Eerdmans, 2003), 38-55.

171. WA 18:672.7-19; *LW* 33:118-19.

172. Hägglund, "Willensfreiheit," 184.

173. Hägglund, "Willensfreiheit," 191; WA 18:718.28-31; *LW* 33:189.

174. WA 18:710.3-30; *LW* 33:175-76.

175. WA 18:697.29-30; *LW* 33:157.

176. WA 18:6-8; *LW* 33:218.

177. WA 18:768.5-8, 10-11, 15-18; *LW* 33:264.

178. WA 18:697.31–698.24; *LW* 33:157-58.

179. WA 18:634.23-29; *LW* 33:64.

180. WA 18:634.37–635.7; *LW* 33:65. Luther elaborates this point at WA 18:714.38–722.29.

181. WA 18:708.31-33; *LW* 33:174-75.

182. WA TR 4:642-43, #5071.

183. WA 18:709.28–710.8; *LW* 33:176-77.

184. WA 18:710.31–711.7; *LW* 33:178-79.

185. Cf. the *Small Catechism* explanations of the Ten Commandments, *BSLK,* 507-10; *Book of Concord,* 351-54; see Charles P. Arand, *That I May Be His Own: An Overview of Luther's Catechisms* (Saint Louis: Concordia, 2000), 152-60; Robert Kolb, *Teaching God's Children His Teaching: A Guide for the Study of Luther's Catechism* (Hutchinson, Minn.: Crown, 1992), chaps. 2 and 3.

186. WA 18:780.18-20; *LW* 33:283. Forde, *Captivation of the Will,* chap. 4, treats the topic with great insight.

187. WA 18:762.30–763.4; *LW* 33:255-56.

188. WA 18:679.23-29; *LW* 33:130.

189. Iwand, *Um den rechten Glauben,* 260-63.

190. Bornkamm, "Erasmus und Luther," 16.

191. WA 18:635.7-22; *LW* 33:65-66. See Luther's "On Christian Liberty," WA 7:42-73; *LW* 31:333-77.

192. Although Luther did not explicitly distinguish the two kinds of righteousness in his description of creation in the Genesis lectures, it is clear by his rejection of the free will in regard to spiritual matters in his treatment of the book's opening chapters that he presumed that framework; see WA 42:45.18–48.16, 63.15–65.8; *LW* 1:60-65, 83-85. See his comments on Gen. 3, especially WA 42:106.1–117.14; *LW* 1:141-55.

193. WA 18:664.1-9; *LW* 33:106.

194. WA 18:738.9-17; *LW* 33:218-19.

195. WA 18:754.3-15; *LW* 33:243.

196. See Luther's extensive arguments on merit, WA 18:690.31–696.11; *LW* 33:147-55.

197. WA 18:715.20; *LW* 33:185.

198. WA 18:693.1-5; *LW* 33:150.

199. WA 18:672.7-12; *LW* 33:118-19.

200. Iwand, *Um den rechten Glauben,* 56.

201. WA 18:771.38-40; *LW* 33:270.

202. WA 18:752.7-8; *LW* 33:240.

203. WA 18:694.17-20; *LW* 33:153.

204. The nature of Luther's early preaching, as witnessed in his postils, has become clear to me through the work of Makito Masaki, "Luther's Two Kinds of Righteousness and His Wartburg Postil (1522): How Luther Exhorted People to Live Christian Lives" (Ph.D. diss., Concordia Seminary, Saint Louis, forthcoming).

205. Bornkamm, "Erasmus und Luther," 16.

206. WA 18:767.40-42; *LW* 33:264.

207. WA 18:649.26–651.7; *LW* 33:85-87.

208. WA 1:233.10-11; *LW* 31:25. It must be noted that Luther's understanding of this medieval expression developed over the years following 1517. It is used here in the sense of Luther's law/gospel interpretation of the life of repentance in the *Small Catechism*, fourth question on baptism, *BSLK*, 516-17; *Book of Concord*, 360.

209. E.g., in his interpretation of Jer. 15:19 and Zech. 1:3, WA 18:680.32–682.25; *LW* 33:132-35; in his argument regarding this struggle as proof that the will is not free, WA 18:783.3-15; *LW* 33:288.

210. WA 18:633.9-12; *LW* 33:62.

211. WA 18:684.26-32; *LW* 33:138.

212. WA 18:673.34-38; *LW* 33:121.

213. Particularly in baptism; see Robert Kolb, "'What Benefit Does the Soul Receive from a Handful of Water?' Luther's Preaching on Baptism, 1528-1539," *Concordia Journal* 25 (1999): 346-63, and Kolb, "God Kills to Make Alive."

214. *BSLK*, 516-17; *Book of Concord*, 360.

215. Reinhuber, *Kämpfender Glaube*, 9.

216. WA 18:719.9-12; *LW* 33:190.

217. WA 18:717.25-39; *LW* 33:188. As he treated Matt. 23:37, Luther insisted that human creatures dare not pry into the secret will of God (see n. 60 above: WA 18:689.18-24; *LW* 33:145), and in his later comments on Genesis he did provide a corrective to misimpressions he might have caused in his response to Erasmus by warning against trying to learn about the hidden God. Such inquisitiveness is original sin itself (WA 43:458.35–459.15; *LW* 5:43-44; see pp. 37-38 above).

218. WA 18:685.14-15; *LW* 33:139.

219. WA 18:689.18-25; *LW* 33:145.

220. WA 18:712.31-35; *LW* 33:181.

221. Forde, *Theologian of the Cross*, 13.

222. WA 18:768.23-26; *LW* 33:264.

223. WA 18:710.31–711.7; *LW* 33:178.

224. Lohse, *Theology*, 167.

225. WA 18:784.35–785.38; *LW* 33:291-92.

226. WA 18:784.1-15; *LW* 33:289-90.

227. WA 43:457.33–463.17; *LW* 5:42-50.

Notes to Chapter II

1. Martin Brecht, *Martin Luther. Zweiter Band. Ordnung und Abgrenzung der Reformation, 1521-1532* (Stuttgart: Calwer Verlag, 1986), 210; ET, *Martin Luther, Shaping and Defining the Reformation, 1521-1532*, trans. James L. Schaaf (Minneapolis: Fortress, 1990), 213. A separate study of the teaching on the human will and God's election of the saved in the writings of Luther's early followers who did not study in Wittenberg would be a welcome contribution to our understanding of the impact of Luther on his contemporaries.

2. Karl Zickendraht, *Der Streit zwischen Erasmus und Luther über die Willensfreiheit* (Leipzig: Hinrichs, 1909), 50-52.

3. See below, pp. 76-78.

4. Bugenhagen, *Ain kurtze/wolgegründte Außlegung uber die Zehen nachgeenden Episteln S. Pauli* (n.p., 1524), A1b.

5. Jonas, *Annotationes Ivsti Ionae, in acta apostolorvm* (Wittenberg, 1524), E7b; translation: *Annotationes oder Anzaygungen/Justi Jone zu Wittemberg/v[e]ber das Buch der Aposteln Geschicht . . .* (Wittenberg, 1525).

6. Luther, *Das der freie Wille nichts sey/Antwort D. Martini Luther an Erasmum Roterdam. Verdeutscht durch Justum Jonam* (Wittenberg: Hans Lufft, 1526), A1b.

7. Heinz Holeczek, "Erasmus' Stellung zur Reformation: Studia humanitatis und Kirchenreform," in *Renaissance — Reformation. Gegensätze und Gemeinsamkeiten,* ed. August Buck (Wiesbaden: Harrassowitz, 1984), 147.

8. Erasmus, *Eyn Vergleychung oder Zusamenhaltung der spruche vom freyen wyllen/ Erasmi von Roterodam/durch Nicolaum Herman von Altdorff yns teutsch gebracht/von ersten ließ/darnach vrteyls* (Leipzig: Jacob Thanner, 1525), A2a: "Gleych dis getzenck/wie vor tzeyten ist geweßen/tzwischen Augustino vnd Pelagio/Vom Freyen wyllenn/ist ytzt wyderumb tzwischen dem Martino vnnd Erasmu/als mich duncket/eben umb der selbigenn vrsach wyllenn. Denn der Luther/so her sihett/was on her Gottes darauß komptt/so man sich auff eygene werck vnnd kreffte verlast/hat denn Freyen wyllenn gar vmb gestossen/Der Roterodam/so her sihett/was vermessenheyt tzum vbel/vnd faulheyßt tzum dienst gottes entstehett/vnter den bo[e]ßen/so man yhn gar weg nympt hatt sich dar wydder gelegt/yhn tzu erhalten. . . ."

9. Christopher B. Brown, *Singing the Gospel: Lutheran Hymns and the Success of the Reformation in Joachimsthal* (Cambridge: Harvard University Press, 2005), 36.

10. See James M. Kittelson, *Wolfgang Capito: From Humanist to Reformer* (Leiden: Brill, 1975), 78-80, 110-11, 221. Cf. Capito's *In Hoseam prophetam V. F. Capitonis Commentarius . . .* (Strasbourg: Ioannes Hervagius, 1528), 57a, 94b (=104b), 197b.

11. Hellmut Zschoch, *Reformatorische Existenz und konfessionelle Identität. Urbanus Rhegius als evangelischer Theologe in den Jahren 1520 bis 1530* (Tübingen: Mohr [Siebeck], 1995), 154-57; Maximilian Liebmann, *Urbanus Rhegius und die Anfänge der Reformation. Beiträge zu seinem Leben, seiner Lehre und seinem Wirken bis zum Augsburger Reichstag von 1530* (Münster: Aschendorff, 1980), 190.

12. Rhegius, *Formvlae qvaedam cavte et citra Scandalum loquendi de praecipuis Christianae doctrinae locis, pro iunioribus Verbi Ministris in Ducatu Luneburgensi* (Wittenberg: Hans Lufft, 1535), C7a-C8b, "de libero arbitrio"; C8b-D3a, "de Praedestinationis mysterio," translated in *Preaching the Reformation: The Homiletical Handbook of Urbanus Rhegius,* trans. and ed. Scott Hendrix (Milwaukee: Marquette University Press, 2003), 62-69. See also Hendrix, "Urbanus Rhegius, Frontline Reformer," *LQ* 18 (2004): 76-87.

13. Oecolampadius, *De libero arbitrio Divorum Prosperi, Augustini et Ambrosii opuscula perquam erudita* (Basel: Wolff, 1524).

14. Martin Brecht, *Die frühe Theologie des Johannes Brenz* (Tübingen: Mohr [Siebeck], 1966), 9, 10.

15. Brenz, *In D. Iohannis Evangelion . . . Exegesis* (Hagenau: Johannes Secer, 1527), 106b, on John 6:29; 255a, on John 14:17; 268a-b, on John 15:5.

16. Brenz, *In D. Iohannis Evangelion*, 195a, on John 10:14-15; 244b, on John 14:2; 265a-266b, on John 15:2; 274a-275a, on John 15:16. Cf. Brecht, *Die frühe Theologie*, 169-70, 199-201, 213-14, 238.

17. Brecht, *Die frühe Theologie*, 169-70, 199-201, 213-14, 238.

18. See Amsdorf's theses of 1527, reprinted in "Nicolai Amsdorfii Conclusiones," in *Abhandlungen Alexander von Oettingen zum siebzigsten Geburtstag* (Munich: Beck, 1898), 260.

19. See below, pp. 95-97.

20. WA 18:600.21–601.7; *LW* 33:16.

21. In a letter to Johann Mathesius, Apr. 17, 1559, *CR* 9:804, #6734; *MBW*, #8925.

22. In a letter to Landgrave Philip of Hesse on the ducal Saxon Confutationsbuch, Nov. 4, 1558, in B. Spiegel, "Zwei ungedruckte Briefe Philipp Melanchthon's," *Zeitschrift für wissenschaftliche Theologie* 11 (1868): 457; *MBW*, #8769: Melanchthon cited as evidence that the Saxon dukes had abandoned the Augsburg Confession "dass der schwere Streit vom pure passive oder vom Trunco und von adiaphoris neue Gezänke sind wider die [Augsburg] Confession oder ja ausser der Confession, denn ich mit gutem rath, welche rauhe disputationes Lutheri de Necessitate Stoica er ausgelassen in der Confession. Wiewohl auch Luther den Truncum eingesetzt, dass ein Mensch sei wie ein Pflock und noch ärger. . . ." See also a memorandum on the same subject addressed to Elector August of Saxony, Mar. 9, 1559, *CR* 9:377, #6705; *MBW*, #8886: "Ich hab bei Leben Lutheri und hernach diese Stoica und Manichaea deliria verworfen, daß Luther und andre geschrieben haben: alle Werk, gut und bo[e]ß, in allen Menschen, guten und bo[e]ßen, mu[e]ßten geschehen. Nun ist offentlich, daß diese Rede wider Gottes Wort ist, und ist scha[e]dlich wider alle Zucht, und la[e]sterlich wider Gott."

23. For an overview of twentieth-century interpretation, see Timothy J. Wengert, "Philip Melanchthon's Contribution to Luther's Debate with Erasmus over the Bondage of the Will," in *By Faith Alone: Essays on Justification in Honor of Gerhard O. Forde*, ed. Joseph A. Burgess and Marc Kolden (Grand Rapids: Eerdmans, 2004), 112-14.

24. Zickendraht, *Streit*, 44-45, observes that in *Hyperaspistes II*, in *Desiderii Erasmi Roterodami Opera Omnia . . .* , ed. J. Clericus, 10 vols. (Leiden, 1703-6), 9:1458E, Erasmus took exception to Melanchthon's position in the 1521 *Loci*; *CR* 21:99-115; *StA* 2.1:21-40.

25. Holeczek, "Erasmus' Stellung zur Reformation," 147.

26. Timothy J. Wengert, *Human Freedom, Christian Righteousness: Philip Melanchthon's Exegetical Dispute with Erasmus of Rotterdam* (New York and Oxford: Oxford University Press, 1998), and Wengert, "Philip Melanchthon's Contribution to Luther's Debate with Erasmus over the Bondage of the Will."

27. Hans Joachim Iwand, *Um den rechten Glauben, Gesammelte Aufsätze*, ed. Karl Gerhard Steck (Munich: Kaiser, 1959), 16.

28. Wengert, *Human Freedom*, 6-7, 21-27.

29. *Supplementa Melanchthonia* 6/1 (*Melanchthons Briefwechsel* 1) (1926; Frankfurt am Main: Minerva, 1968), 246-49; *MBW* 1:165, #332. Translation Wengert, *Human Freedom*, 27.

30. John R. Schneider, *Philip Melanchthon's Rhetorical Construal of Biblical Authority: Oratio Sacra* (Lewiston, N.Y.: Mellen, 1990), 13-50.

31. Paul O. Kristeller, *Renaissance Thought and Its Sources* (New York: Columbia University Press, 1979), and Charles Trinkaus, *The Scope of Renaissance Humanism* (Ann Arbor: University of Michigan Press, 1983).

32. Lewis W. Spitz, "Man on This Isthmus," in *Luther for an Ecumenical Age,* ed. Carl S. Meyer (Saint Louis: Concordia, 1967), 23-66; cf. also the essays in Robert S. Kinsman, ed., *The Darker Vision of the Renaissance: Beyond the Fields of Reason* (Berkeley: University of California Press, 1974).

33. Lewis W. Spitz, *The Religious Renaissance of the German Humanists* (Cambridge: Harvard University Press, 1963). Cf. Leif Grane, *Martinus Noster: Luther in the German Reform Movement, 1518-1521* (Mainz: Zabern, 1994); Helmar Junghans, *Der junge Luther und die Humanisten* (Weimar: Böhlau, 1984); and Lowell C. Green, *How Melanchthon Helped Luther Discover the Gospel: The Doctrine of Justification in the Reformation* (Fallbrook, Calif.: Verdict, 1980).

34. Melanchthon, *Responsiones scriptae a Philippo Melanthone ad impios articvlos bavaricae inqvisitionis* (Wittenberg: Georg Rhau, 1558). See Robert Kolb, "Melanchthon's Doctrinal Last Will and Testament: The *Responsiones ad articulos Bavaricae inquisitionis* as His Final Confession of Faith," *SCJ* 35 (2004): 97-114.

35. *StA* 6:313.16-22.

36. Matz, *Der befreite Mensch. Die Willenslehre in der Theologie Philipp Melanchthons* (Göttingen: Vandenhoeck & Ruprecht, 2001), 232-38.

37. The way in which the doctrine of justification by faith governed Melanchthon's theology is illustrated in his paraphrases of the Augsburg Confession for the French government in 1534 and the English government in 1536; see Irene Dingel, "Melanchthon und Westeuropa," in *Philipp Melanchthon als Politiker zwischen Reich, Reichsständen und Konfessionsparteien,* ed. Günther Wartenberg and Matthias Zenter (Wittenberg: Drei Kastanien Verlag, 1998), 105-22.

38. On the role of good communication skills in teaching the faith, see, among many other discussions, Melanchthon's letter to the reader and preface in the *Loci theologici praecipui* (1543), *StA* 2.1:165-72.

39. On these developments see Timothy J. Wengert, *Law and Gospel: Philip Melanchthon's Debate with John Agricola of Eisleben over Poenitentia* (Grand Rapids: Baker, 1997), 77-175.

40. Cochlaeus, *De libero arbitrio hominis adversvs locos communes Philippi Melanchthonis, libri duo* (Tübingen: Morhart, 1525). See Wengert, *Human Freedom,* 80-86.

41. *CR* 21:52. See Matz, *Der befreite Mensch,* 27-38.

42. Hartmut Oskar Günther, "Die Entwicklung der Willenslehre Melanchthons in der Auseinandersetzung mit Luther und Erasmus" (Th.D. diss., University of Erlangen, 1963), 37, 39, 42.

43. *StA* 2.1:30-31 (*CR* 21:93): "Si ad praedestinationem referas humanam voluntatem, nec in externis nec in internis operibus ulla est libertas, sed eveniunt omnia iuxta destinationem divinam. Si ad opera externa referas voluntatem, quaedam videtur esse iudicio naturae libertas. Si ad affectus referas voluntatem, nulla plane libertas est, etiam naturae iudicio. Iam ubi affectus coeperit furere et aestuare, cohiberi non potest, quin erumpat."

44. Hans-Georg Geyer, "Zur Rolle der Prädestinationslehre Augustins beim jungen Melanchthon," in *Studien zur Geschichte und Theologie der Reformation. Festschrift für Ernst Bizer,* ed. Luise Abramowski and J. F. Gerhard Goeters (Neukirchen: Neukirchener Verlag, 1969), 175-87, and Rolf Schäfer, "Zur Prädestinationslehre beim jungen Melanchthon," *ZKG*

63 (1966): 352-78. See also Günter Frank, *Die theologische Philosophie Philipp Melanchthons (1497-1560)* (Leipzig: Benno, 1995), 284-90.

45. On the entire treatment of the free will in the 1521 *Loci,* see Matz, *Der befreite Mensch,* 39-78.

46. Matz, *Der befreite Mensch,* 80-87.

47. Wengert, *Human Freedom,* 14-20, reviews the printing history of these three versions, the German translations, and a 1534 revision. Luther warmly approved Melanchthon's commentary in a preface written for its German translation, 1529; WA 30.II:68-69.

48. In addition to Wengert's discussion in *Human Freedom, Christian Righteousness,* see his summary in *By Faith Alone,* 115-23. Melanchthon rejected Erasmus's argument in the *Diatribe* because of his theology, his style, and his behavior, which lacked the *epeikeia* expected from scholars.

49. Wengert, *Human Freedom,* 84, 159-61; Matz, *Der befreite Mensch,* 98-99. Cf., e.g., *StA* 4:222.5 and 224.36.

50. Matz, *Der befreite Mensch,* 100.

51. Charles P. Arand, "Two Kinds of Righteousness as a Framework for Law and Gospel in the Apology," *LQ* 15 (2001): 417-39.

52. Wengert, *Human Freedom,* 84-92. Cf. Matz, *Der befreite Mensch,* 96-107. *StA* 4:220.25–225.33.

53. Wengert, *Human Freedom,* 96-99; *StA* 4:228-43; *CR* 15:1247-52. Matz does not discuss this revision of the commentary.

54. See Wengert, *Law and Gospel,* 177-210. Günther calls the visitation articles that Melanchthon prepared the expression of his transition to a different emphasis in his understanding of the human will; "Entwicklung," 68.

55. The Schwabach and the Marburg articles are found in *BSLK,* 52-72, translation in *Sources and Contexts,* 83-87, 88-92. Eck's work is edited in *D. Johann Ecks Vierhundertundvier Artikel zum Reichstag von Augsburg 1530,* ed. Wilhelm Gussmann (Kassel: Picardy, 1930), translated in *Sources and Contexts,* 31-82. He directly addressed the freedom of the will in his articles 36 and 331 (332). Cf. Wengert, *By Faith Alone,* 113-14.

56. *BSLK,* 73; *Book of Concord,* 50-51 (cited from the Latin version of the Confession). The German reads in translation: "Concerning free will it is taught that a human being has some measure of free will, so as to live an externally honorable life and to choose among the things reason comprehends. However, without the grace, help, and operation of the Holy Spirit a human being cannot become pleasing to God, fear or believe in God with the whole heart, or expel innate evil lusts from the heart. Instead, this happens through the Holy Spirit, who is given through the Word of God."

57. *BSLK,* 311-13; *Book of Concord,* 233-34.

58. See also Augsburg Confession XX,36-40; *BSLK,* 81; *Book of Concord,* 56-57.

59. *StA* 6:23-25.

60. *StA* 6:106; cf. *CR* 28:392-93. The German "Repetition" is found in *CR* 28:481-569.

61. *CR* 23:14-16. The German version is found in *StA* 6:168-259 and *CR* 23:xxxv-cx.

62. Robert Kolb, "The Ordering of the *Loci Communes Theologici:* The Structuring of the Melanchthonian Dogmatic Tradition," *Concordia Journal* 23 (1997): 317-37.

63. Matz, *Der befreite Mensch,* 141; cf. 141-47.

64. See Wengert, *Law and Gospel,* 177-210.

65. Matz, *Der befreite Mensch*, 147-50.

66. Matz, *Der befreite Mensch*, 195.

67. Matz, *Der befreite Mensch*, 199.

68. *CR* 21:330-32.

69. *Loci communes theologici*, 1535: *CR* 21:450-53; *Loci praecipui theologici*, 1543: *CR* 21:912-20; *StA* 2.2:628-38. On the role of Calvin's writings in his formulation of this teaching, see n. 79 below.

70. "Alia disputatio, de sententia: Deus vult omnes homines salvos fieri," *CR* 12:480-81.

71. *StA* 2.2:630.

72. Cf. Luther in *De servo arbitrio*, WA 18:702.1–720.27; *LW* 33:164-84. See also Melanchthon's Romans commentary of 1532, *StA* 5:257-58.

73. *CR* 21:274-81.

74. Matz, *Der befreite Mensch*, 110-38.

75. *CR* 21:371-73.

76. See his comments in the preface to the 1543 edition, *StA* 2.1:165; *CR* 21:601.

77. Chemnitz, *De Controversiis quibusdam, quae superiori tempore circa quosdam Augustanae Confessionis articulos motae et agitatae sunt, Iudicium d. Martini Chemnitii*, ed. Polycarp Leyser (Wittenberg, 1594), 23, translated in *Sources and Contexts*, 205.

78. Although he had begun to treat predestination from that perspective already in 1532; cf. his shift in the interpretation of Rom. 9, Robert Kolb, "Melanchthon's Influence on the Exegesis of His Students: The Case of Romans 9," in *Philip Melanchthon (1497-1560) and the Commentary*, ed. M. Patrick Graham and Timothy J. Wengert (Sheffield: Sheffield Academic Press, 1997), 199-201. Matz, *Der befreite Mensch*, 161, is correct in rejecting the suggestion that the doctrine of the church became the article on which the church stands or falls for Melanchthon; indeed, as he states, doctrinal differences in other articles affected his doctrine of the church.

79. Timothy J. Wengert, "'We Will Feast Together in Heaven Forever': The Epistolary Friendship of John Calvin and Philip Melanchthon," in *Melanchthon in Europe: His Work and Influence beyond Wittenberg*, ed. Karin Maag, Texts and Studies in Reformation and Post-Reformation Thought (Grand Rapids: Baker, 1999), 26-33. The critical issue separating them was the secret will of God; Calvin's position on this topic had occasioned Melanchthon's critique of the Genevan's doctrine of predestination, as it had been developed, for example, in his polemical exchange with the Roman Catholic theologian Albert Pighius. See *MBW* 3:359 (Calvin's dedication of his work to Melanchthon from early 1543), and 407, #3273, Melanchthon's reservations regarding Calvin's position in a letter to him of July 12, 1543. Cf. Anthony N. S. Lane, "The Influence upon Calvin of His Debate with Pighius," in *Auctoritas Patrum II. Neue Beiträge zur Rezeption der Kirchenväter im 15. und 16. Jahrhundert*, ed. Leif Grane, Alfred Schindler, and Markus Wriedt (Mainz: Zabern, 1998), 125-39.

80. *CR* 21:647-48; cf. 643-49.

81. *CR* 21:649-50.

82. *CR* 21:650.

83. *Initia doctrinae Phisicae*, 1549, *CR* 13:203-6.

84. *Initia doctrinae Phisicae*, 1549, *CR* 13:206-8.

85. *CR* 13:209-10. The section continues to col. 213.

86. *CR* 13:329-35.

87. On Valla's role in the development of humanist biblical scholarship, see Jerry Bentley, *Humanists and Holy Writ: New Testament Scholarship in the Renaissance* (Princeton: Princeton University Press, 1983), 32-69. The assessment of Valla's relationship to Luther by Jan Lindhardt, "Valla and Luther on the Free Will," in *Widerspruch. Luthers Auseinandersetzung mit Erasmus von Rotterdam,* ed. Kari Kopperi (Helsinki: Luther-Agricola-Gesellschaft, 1997), 46-53, does not analyze the theological elements they hold in common and the contrasts between the positions of the two adequately.

88. *CR* 21:373-78.

89. *StA* 2.1:263-64.

90. Note Ekkehard Muehlenberg's argument that both Melanchthon and his disciple Martin Chemnitz trapped themselves in an inadequate analysis of the will because they followed Augustine's definition of will as an act distinct from cognition but also not identical with affection or emotion. According to Muehlenberg, Melanchthon identified the Aristotelian *proairesis* with Augustine's concept of the will when it actually refers to reason-governed affection. Muehlenberg attributes confusion in the argument of later sixteenth-century Lutherans to this confusion in Melanchthon; see "Synergia and Justification by Faith," in *Discord, Dialogue, and Concord: Studies in the Lutheran Reformation's Formula of Concord,* ed. Lewis W. Spitz and Wenzel Lohff (Philadelphia: Fortress, 1977), 32-37.

91. *StA* 2.1:238-40.

92. *StA* 2.1:240-41.

93. *StA* 2.1:241.

94. *StA* 2.1:243.

95. On Melanchthon's treatment of the Aristotelian "causae," see "Erotematum Dialectices" (1547), 1580, *CR* 13:673-85. There he defines the material cause: "Materia est, ex qua aliquid fit, ut ex farina fit panis. . . . Hanc praecipue nominamus materiam, quae usitate dicitur Materia ex qua" (679).

96. Lowell C. Green, "The Three Causes of Conversion in Philipp Melanchthon, Martin Chemnitz, David Chytraeus, and the Formula of Concord," *LuJ* 47 (1980): 89-114.

97. *StA* 2.1:244-45.

98. See Joannes Altenstaig and Joannes Tytz, *Lexicon Theologicum* (Cologne, 1619; Hildesheim: Olms, 1974), 595-96, where several late medieval theologians are cited who spoke of the *facultas* of will and reason to choose the good, etc.

99. *StA* 2.1:245-46.

100. *StA* 2.1:246-47.

101. Matz, *Der befreite Mensch,* 232.

102. The manuscript from 1536: "De contingentia. Disputatione prima pars," Dresden: Sächsische Landesbibliothek, Ms. Dres. A180, 752-770; that of 1541: "Annotationes quibus indicatur paucis quae in locis communibus Philippi Melanchthonis displicent per N.A.," Weimar, Goethe-Schiller Archiv der Nationale Forschungs- und Gedenkstätten der klassischen deutschen Literatur, Ehemalige Thüringische Landesbibliothek folio Band XL: 301-309. See Robert Kolb, "Nikolaus von Amsdorf on Vessels of Wrath and Vessels of Mercy: A Lutheran's Doctrine of Double Predestination," *Harvard Theological Review* 69 (1976): 325-43; reprinted in *Luther's Heirs,* chap. 2.

103. See Melanchthon's expressions of concern over Amsdorf's criticisms in letters of Aug. 1544 to Veit Dietrich (*CR* 5:459, #3006; *MBW* 4:112, #3646); to Joachim Camerarius (*CR*

5:462, #3009; *MBW* 4:114, #3652); and to Friedrich Myconius, Oct. 10, 1544 (*CR* 5: 98-99 #3049; *MBW* 4: 135-36, #3705).

104. See below. This work was included in the collection of Melanchthon's writings, the *Corpus doctrinae Philippicum*. See also Heinz Scheible, *Melanchthon, eine Biographie* (Munich: Beck, 1997), 241-50.

105. *StA* 6:313-14.

106. *StA* 6:310.

107. *StA* 6:311.

108. *StA* 6:311: "Quia untrunque nascentes afferimus, et exiguam lucem, quae est aliqua legis noticia, et ingens incendium malorum affectuum, quos gignit peccatum originis, quia corda vacua timore DEI et vera fiducia DEI, seu vacua DEO, ardent amore, appetunt res prohibitas, dolent, fremunt, oderunt DEUM, leges et homines impedientes, quo minus possint vagari, ut cupiunt." This definition reflects the position of the Augsburg Confession, article II, *BSLK*, 53; *Book of Concord*, 37-38. The devil and human weakness as restraints to human freedom entered Melanchthon's usage in the *Scholia* on Colossians of 1527/1528. I am grateful to Timothy J. Wengert for this reference.

109. *StA* 6:311-12.

110. WA 18:614.27–620.37; *LW* 33:36-44. Cf. also Luther's concluding comments, WA 18:784.1–785.38; *LW* 33:289-92.

111. See pp. 88-89, above.

112. *StA* 6:312: "Firmissa veritas est, Deum nec velle peccata, nec impellere voluntates ad peccandum, nec adiuvare nec approbare peccata, sed vere et horribiliter irasci peccatis."

113. *StA* 6:312-13. "Est igitur contingentia, et contingentiae nostrarum actionum fons est libertas voluntatis."

114. *StA* 6:313.16-22.

115. *StA* 6:317-18.

116. *StA* 6:314-16.

117. Matthaeus Gribaldi, *Epistola . . . de tremendo diuini iudicij exemplo super eum, qui nominum metu pulsus, Christum & cognitam ueritatem abnegat . . .* (Basel, 1549); in German also, in several editions, e.g., *Ein Epistel oder sendtbrieff . . . von einem erschrockenlichen exempel Go[e]ttliches gerichts/über einen gelerten man/welcher vß forcht der menschen getrungen/Christum vnd die erkante warheit verleügnet hat* (n.p., 1549).

118. *StA* 6:318-19.

Notes to Chapter III

1. Timothy J. Wengert, *Law and Gospel: Philip Melanchthon's Debate with John Agricola of Eisleben over Poenitentia* (Grand Rapids: Baker, 1997), 77-175; Robert Kolb, "Dynamics of Party Conflict in the Saxon Late Reformation, Gnesio-Lutherans vs. Philippists," *Journal of Modern History* 49 (1977): D1289-1305.

2. *Das Augsburger Interim von 1548*, ed. Joachim Mehlhausen, 2nd ed. (Neukirchen: Neukirchener Verlag, 1996), translated in *Sources and Contexts*, 144-82.

3. Günther Wartenberg, "Philipp Melanchthon und die sächsisch-albertinische Interimspolitik," *LuJ* 55 (1988): 60-80; Irene Dingel, "'Der rechten Lehre zuwider,' Die

Beurteilung des Interims in ausgewählten theologischen Reaktionen," in *Das Interim 1548/50, Herrschaftskrise und Glaubenskonflikt. Symposion des Verein für Reformationsgeschichte in der Leucorea, Wittenberg, 3.10–6.10.2001,* ed. Luise Schorn-Schütte (Gütersloh: Gütersloher Verlagshaus, forthcoming).

4. The text is found in *CR* 7:258-64, with sections from earlier documents 7:51-64 and 217, 219-20; *Sources and Contexts,* 183-96.

5. Oliver K. Olson, *Matthias Flacius and the Survival of Luther's Reform* (Wiesbaden: Harrassowitz, 2002), passim, and Hans Christoph von Hase, *Die Gestalt der Kirche Luthers. Der casus confessionis im Kampf des Matthias Flacius gegen das Interim von 1548* (Göttingen: Vandenhoeck & Ruprecht, 1940).

6. See Kolb, "Dynamics of Party Conflict in the Saxon Late Reformation, Gnesio-Lutherans vs. Philippists."

7. *Das Augsburger Interim,* 48-49; *Sources and Contexts,* 152; cf. the text of the Leipzig Interim, *CR* 7:51; *Sources and Contexts,* 185: "Wiewol Got den mentschen gerecht macht nit auß den werken der gerechtigkait, die der mentsch thuet, sonder nach seiner barmhertzigkait, und das lautter umbsunst, das ist, one seine verdienst, also wo er sich ruemen will, das er sich allain in Christo ruemen sole, durch welches verdiensts allain er von den sunden erlöst und gerecht gemacht wirdet, doch handlet der barmhertzig Gott nit mit eim mentschen wie mit einem todten plock, sonder zeucht ine mit seinem willen wann er zu seinenn jaren khombt. Dann ein solcher emphehet dieselben wolthaten Christi nit, es sei dann, das durch die vorgeendt gnad Gottes sein hertz und will bewegt werde, den sünden vheindt zu werden." This section was composed in Pegau in early July 1548.

8. *CR* 7:581-85, esp. 582-83; *MBW* 6:47-48, #5787.

9. *CR* 11:898. I am grateful to Timothy J. Wengert for these references.

10. *CR* 3:500-501; *MBW* 2:357, #2005.

11. Magdeburg Ministerium, *Bekentnis Vnterricht vnd vermanung/der Pfarrhern vnd Prediger/der Christlichen Kirchen zu Magdeburgk. Anno 1550. Den 13. Aprilis . . .* (Magdeburg: Michael Lotther, 1550), C2a-C3a, D3a-34a; *Confessio et Apologia pastorum & reliquorum ministrorum Ecclesiae Magdeburgensis. Anno 1550. Idibus Aprilis . . .* (Magdeburg: Michael Lotther, 1550), B1b-B2b, B4b-C1b. See David Mark Whitford, *Tyranny and Resistance: The Magdeburg Confession and the Lutheran Tradition* (Saint Louis: Concordia, 2001).

12. *MBW* 5:478-79, #5549. Hartmut Voit, *Nikolaus Gallus, Ein Beitrag zur Reformations-geschichte der nachlutherischen Zeit* (Neustadt an der Aisch: Degener, 1977), comments on Gallus's letter: "Throughout his formulation he was conciliatory but for all that presented the matter all the more decisively and clearly" (132).

13. E.g., Nikolaus Gallus, *Auff des Herrn D. Maiors verantwortung vnd Declaration der Leiptzigischen Proposition/wie gute werck zur seligkeit no[e]tig sind . . .* (Magdeburg: Michael Lotther, 1552), and *Auff die newe subtile verfelschung des Euangelij Christi/in Doctor Maiors Comment vber seine Antichristische Proposition . . .* (Magdeburg: Michael Lotther, 1553).

14. *CR* 8:736, #5968; *MBW* 7:420, #7793.

15. *CR* 8:747, #5976; *MBW* 7:426, #7807.

16. *CR* 8:789, #6022; *MBW* 7:450, #7873.

17. *CR* 8:916, #6127; *MBW* 7:517-18, #8042.

18. Robert Kolb, "The German Lutheran Reaction to the Third Period of the Council of Trent," *LuJ* 51 (1984): 63-95; and *Luther's Heirs,* chap. 5.

19. Dated Dec. 25, 1556, in *CR* 8:933-34, #6137; Jan. 12, 1557, in *MBW* 8:22-23, #8089, on the basis of the original.

20. *CR* 9:142-43, #6232; *MBW* 8:63, #8199.

21. Dated July 30, 1557, in *CR* 9:190, #6292; June 16, 1557, in *MBW* 8:84, #8259.

22. Robert Rosin, *Reformers, the Preacher, and Skepticism: Luther, Brenz, Melanchthon, and Ecclesiastes* (Mainz: Zabern, 1997), 216. The commentary's third edition is found in *CR* 14:89-160.

23. Rosin, *Reformers*, 220; see his treatment of providence, 263-66, and his entire discussion of the commentary, 215-84.

24. Pfeffinger published them originally under the title *De Libertate Voluntatis humanae Quaestiones quinque* (Leipzig: Georg Hantsch, 1555), and republished them with other disputations three years later: *In hoc Libello continentvr vtiles dispvtationes de praecipuis capitibus doctrinae Christianae, quae propositae fuerunt in academia Lipsica* (Frankfurt am Main: Peter Brubach, 1558), 52a-61b. Thesis XVII reads, 55a, "Voluntas si otiosa esset, seu haberet se purē passiuē, nullum esset discrimen inter pios & impios, seu electos & damnatos, ut inter Saulem & Dauidem, inter Iudam & Petrum. Et Deus fieret acceptor personarum, & autor contumacieae in impijs ac damnatis. Et constituerentur in Deo contradictoriae uoluntates, id quod pugnat cum uniuersa scriptura: Sequitur ergo in nobis esse aliquam causam, cur alij assentiantur, alij non assentiantur."

25. Wilhelm Preger, *Matthias Flacius Illyricus und seine Zeit*, 2 vols. (Erlangen: Blaesing, 1859-61), 2:114-15.

26. Amsdorf, *Offentliche Bekentnis der reinen Lehre des Euangelij/Vnd Confutatio der jtzigen Schwermer* (Jena: Thomas Rhebart, 1558), D4a-E1b.

27. Pfeffinger, *Vtiles dispvtationes*, 52a-61b. On Pfeffinger see Friedrich Hübner, "Über den freien Willen. Artikel II: 'De libero arbitrio' aus seinen historischen Grundlagen heraus interpretiert," in *Widerspruch, Dialog und Einigung. Studien zur Konkordienformel der Lutherischen Reformation* (Stuttgart: Calwer Verlag, 1977), 139-42. Hübner unfortunately documents part of his analysis of Pfeffinger with quotations from Flacius, not from Pfeffinger himself.

28. Amsdorf, *Das D. Pfeffinger seine missethat bo[e]slich vnd felschlicht leugnet/vnd gewaltiglich vberzeugt wird/das er die Kirchen Christi zusto[e]rt vnd zuru[e]ttet/vnd die Schrifft verfelschet vnd verkert hab* (1559), D4b-E1a; cf. *WA* 18:748.7–753.11; *LW* 33:234-41.

29. Pfeffinger, *Nochmals gru[e]ndlicher/klarer/warhafftiger Bericht vnd Bekentnis/der bittern lautern Warheit/reiner Lere/vnd strefflichen Handlungen/vnd vnuermeidliche notwendige Verantwortunge Johannis Pfeffingers Doctoris . . .* (Wittenberg: Lorentz Schwenck, 1559), J2a; see also his initial defense, *Antwort: D. Johan Pfeffingers/Pastoris der Kirchen zu Leiptzig. Auff die Offentliche Bekentnis der reinen Lare des Euangelij/vnd Confutation der jtzigen Schwermerey/Niclasen von Ambsdorff* (Wittenberg, 1558), and his *Demonstratio manifesti mendacii, qvo infamare conatvr Doctorem Iohannem Pfeff. Libellvs qvidam maledicus & Sycophanticus germanicē editus titulo Nicolai ab Amsdorff, Necessaria propter Veritatis assertionem & auersionem Scandali, & tuendam existimationem sincereae doctrinae* (Wittenberg, 1558).

30. Amsdorf, *Das D. Pfeffinger*, B2b-C2b.

31. Stoltz, *Refutatio propositionum Pfeffingeri de Libero arbitrio . . .* , ed. Johannes Aurifaber (n.p., 1558), A2b-A3a. In 1566 Aurifaber edited Luther's "Table Talk," *Tischreden oder Colloquia doct. Mart. Luthers . . .* (Eisleben: Urban Gaubisch, 1566), and arranged his subject matter by topic, including one which treated Luther's statements on the free will.

32. Stoltz, *Refutatio propositionum Pfeffingeri*, D4b-L4a. References to *De servo arbitrio* are found on E3b-E4a, G4a-b, L1b-L2a. Flacius did refer to Luther's Genesis commentary in this work as well.

33. On the colloquy itself, see Benno Bundschuh, *Das Wormser Religionsgespräch von 1557, unter besonderer Berücksichtigung der kaiserlichen Religionspolitik* (Münster: Aschendorff, 1988). Melanchthon himself dismissed the idea that evangelical disunity had caused the collapse of the colloquy. In a memorandum prepared for Elector August in early December 1558, he charged that the negotiations had come to naught because the Roman Catholics had insisted on using tradition as well as Scripture as a standard for determining doctrine; *MWB* 8:295, #8802.

34. Matthias Flacius reported this in the Weimar Disputation, *Disputatio de originali peccato et libero arbitrio, inter Matthiam Flacium Illyricum & Victorinum Strigelium* (n.p., 1562; n.p., 1563; Eisleben, 1563), 222. Cf. Melanchthon's *Loci communes theologici*, 1559, StA 2.1:245-46.

35. Saxony, ducal government, *Des Durchleuchtigen . . . Herrn Johans Friderichen des Mittlern . . . in Gottes wort/Prophetischer vnd Apostolischer schrifft/gegru[e]ndete Confutationes/Widerlegungen vnd verdammung etlicher . . . Corruptelen/Secten vnd Irrthumen . . .* (Jena: Thomas Rebart, 1559), 43b-49b; *Illvstrissimi principis . . . Iohannis Friderici secvndi . . . Confutatio & condemnatio praecipuarum Corruptelarum, Sectarum, & errorum . . .* (Jena: Thomas Rebart, 1559), 32b-37a.

36. *CR* 9:766-69, in "Bedenken Herrn Philippi Melanthonis auf das Weimarische Confutations-Buch," Mar. 9, 1559. Melanchthon had expressed his concerns over Flacius's view of the will in a letter to August, Oct. 31, 1558; *MBW* 8:281, #8765.

37. *CR* 6:761-63, #4108; *MBW* 3:405, #3268, dated June 26, 1543.

38. *CR* 9:769. On Flacius's harsh criticism of Schwenkfeld, see Rudolf Keller, *Der Schlüssel zur Schrift, Die Lehre vom Wort Gottes bei Matthias Flacius Illyricus* (Hannover: Lutherisches Verlagshaus, 1984).

39. Letter to Albert Hardenberg, Apr. 23, 1556, *CR* 8:736, #5968; *MBW* 7:420, #7793; letters to Johannes Mathesius, May 1, 1556, *CR* 8:747, #5976; *MBW* 7:426, #7807; and June 30, 1556, *CR* 8:789, #6022; *MBW* 7:450, #7873.

40. *CR* 9:669-70, #6648; *MBW* 8:296, #8806, dated Dec. 21, 1558: "Nam ibi et de Flacii Trunco dixi. . . ."

41. *CR* 9:1054, #6932; *MBW* 8:447-48, #9236.

42. In fact, Melanchthon's Flacian opponents agreed with him at nearly every point, as Gallus had made clear in a letter of Jan. 12, 1557, *MWB* 8:22-23, #8089, and in *Erklerung der Religions streite/zu nottu[e]rfftigem vnterricht der Kirche/vnd ablenung falscher Calumnien. Wider die verfelscher der waren Augspurgischen Confession* (Regensburg: Heinrich Geissler, 1559), A2b-B1b.

43. First, Gallus criticized Melanchthon's position, sometimes explicitly, sometimes implicitly, in a series of small tracts aimed at presenting a summary of the controversies of the time at a popular level: *Erklerung der Religions streite*, Aij b–B b; *Wa[e]chterstimme/Nic. Galli. Wo vnd in was Stücken/vnter dem Namen Lutheri/der Augspurgischen Confession vnd H. Schrift/Wider Lutherum/wider die Augspur. Conf. vnd H. Schrift jtzo gelehret wird* (Regensburg: Heinrich Geissler, n.d.), Aiija-Aiiija; *Religion streite vnd Einigkeit* (Regensburg: Heinrich Geissler, 1560), Aiija; *Tafel der verkerten/vnd gleich vmbgekerten etlicher Lere/bey der*

wahren Christlichen Augsp. Conf. (Regensburg: Heinrich Geissler, 1560). Gallus also dedicated a treatise to a more technical discussion of the questions: *Qvaestio libero arbitrio, qvatenvs illa qvibvsdam nunc disceptatur in Ecclesijs Augustanae Confessionis. Cvm adsertione ex perpetva propheticae et apostolicae scripturae sententia, & ex sententia Lutheri instauratoris doctrinae, authoris & interprecis Augustanae Confessionis* (Regensburg: Heinrich Geissler, 1559); and *Erklerung vnd Consens vieler Christlichen Kirchen/der Augspurgischen Confession/auff die newe verfelschung der Lehre vom Freyen willen/wie die aus dem INTERIM von etlichen noch gefu[e]rt vnd verteidigt wird* (Regensburg: Heinrich Geissler, 1559). See Robert Kolb, "Nikolaus Gallus' Critique of Philip Melanchthon's Teaching on the Freedom of the Will," *ARG* 91 (2000): 87-110.

44. *Das der freie Wille nichts sey/Antwort/D. Martini Lutheri/an Erasmum Roterodamum/Verdeudscht durch D. Justum Jonam/Zuuor niemals allein im Druck ausgangen* (Regensburg: Heinrich Geissler, 1559).

45. Witt A Dt 6:462a-568b. The Latin original had not been reissued since 1526 apart from the Witt A Lat, 2:457a-526a, and the Jena A Latin, 3:165b-238a.

46. On Erasmus's use of the phrase, see Karl Zickendraht, *Der Streit zwischen Erasmus und Luther über die Willensfreiheit* (Leipzig: Hinrichs, 1909), 36-38.

47. *Das der freie Wille nichts sey,* 1559, 2a.

48. *Das der freie Wille nichts sey,* 1559, 2b-3a.

49. In *Vom Abendmahl Christi Bekenntnis,* Luther had "repudiate(d) and condemn(ed) as vain error all teachings that praise the free will as completely opposed to the aid and grace of our savior Jesus Christ"; WA 26:502.35–503.6; *LW* 37:362-63. Cf. *BSLK,* 73-74; *Book of Concord,* 50-53, for Augsburg Confession, article XVIII, on the freedom of the will.

50. *Das der freie Wille nichts sey,* 1554, A1a-b.

51. See chap. II, pp. 88-89, above, on Melanchthon's reaction to Calvin's doctrine of predestination, which seems to have played a significant role in shaping his public teaching on the subject.

52. Gallus, *Erklerung der religions streite,* A2b-B1b.

53. Gallus, *Wa[e]chterstimme,* Aiij a–Aiiij b; Gallus, *Religion streite,* Aiij a; Gallus, *Tafel der verkerten Lere,* Aij a–Aiij a. Cf. *BSLK,* 73-74, 311-13.

54. Gallus, *Qvaestio,* C b–Ciij a.

55. Gallus, *Qvaestio,* A2 b–[B4] b.

56. Olson, *Matthias Flacius,* 307.

57. For example, in Matthias Flacius Illyricus, *Dispvtatio de originali peccato, et libero arbitrio, contra praesentes errores* (n.p., 1559), B6a.

58. On Melanchthon's use of the Aristotelian concept of substance and its impact on his understanding of the human will, see Walter Matthias, "Über die Lehre von der Willensfreiheit in der altlutherischen Theologie," *ZKG* 74 (1963): 109-33.

59. Ekkehard Muehlenberg, "Synergia and Justification by Faith," in *Discord, Dialogue, and Concord: Studies in the Lutheran Reformation's Formula of Concord,* ed. Lewis W. Spitz and Wenzel Lohff (Philadelphia: Fortress, 1977), 18.

60. Flacius, *Warhafftige vnd bestendiger meinung vnd zeugnis/Von der Erbsu[e]nde vnd dem freien willen Des Ehrwirdigen tewren Mans Gottes D. Martin Luthers Aus allen seinen schrifften trewliche vnd mit vleis zusamen gezogen . . .* (Jena: Thomas Rhebart, 1560).

61. Irene Dingel, *Concordia controversa, Die öffentlichen Diskussionen um das luther-*

ische Konkordienwerk am Ende des 16. Jahrhunderts (Gütersloh: Gütersloher Verlagshaus, 1996), 467-541.

62. See, e.g., Johannes Wigand, *Von der Erbs[e]nde/Lere aus Gottes wort/aus dem Du[e]ringischen Corpore Doctrinae/vnd aus D. Luthers Bu[e]chern . . .* (Jena: Donatus Richtzenhan, 1571). Andreas Schoppe, *Rettung Des Heiligen Catechismi wider den Schwarm der newen Manicheer vnd Substantijsten* (Jena: Donatus Richtzenhan, 1572).

63. Matthias Wesenbeck, *Papianus* (Wittenberg, 1567), P5b, as cited in Gustav Kawerau, *RE* 19:101, s.v. "Strigel."

64. Preger, *Matthias Flacius Illyricus und seine Zeit*, 2:157-80; Martin Kruse, *Speners Kritik am landesherrlichen Kirchenregiment und ihre Vorgeschichte* (Witten: Luther-Verlag, 1971), 57-63; and Robert Kolb, "Matthaeus Judex's Condemnation of Princely Censorship of Theologians' Publications," *Church History* 50 (1981): 401-14.

65. *Disputatio de originali peccato et libero arbitrio, inter Matthiam Flacium Illyricum & Victorinum Strigelium;* cf. Preger, *Matthias Flacius Illyricus und seine Zeit*, 2:127-28. See Hans Kropatscheck, "Das Problem theologischer Anthropologie auf dem Weimarer Gespräch von 1560 zwischen Matthias Flacius Illyricus und Viktorin Strigel" (Licentiate diss., University of Göttingen, 1943), who summarizes and analyzes each session of the disputation, 22-39, the position of Strigel, 39-63, and that of Flacius, 64-103. Cf. Albert Pommerien, *Viktorin Strigels Lehre von dem Peccatum originis* (Hannover: Stephanusstift, 1917), 12-17; August Beck, *Johann Friedrich der Mittlere, Herzog zu Sachsen* (Weimar: Böhlau, 1858), 1:319; and Hübner, "Über den freien Willen," 142-47.

66. The text of the memorandum, "Rostokiensivm ivdicivm de controversia inter Illyricum & Victorinum," was printed by Musaeus in *Disputatio*, 393-402, this passage on 393-96. Cf. WA 18:697.26-30; LW 33:157. The memorandum is significant because Chytraeus remained concerned, as a devoted disciple of Melanchthon, to preserve a clear focus on the activity of the human will and thus on the integrity of the human creature. However, in spite of expressions in his writings that sound "synergistic," he strove to emphasize God's grace at the same time. See Lowell C. Green, "The Three Causes of Conversion in Philipp Melanchthon, Martin Chemnitz, David Chytraeus, and the Formula of Concord," *LuJ* 47 (1980): 89-114.

67. The text is printed in Conrad Schlüsselburg, *Haereticorum Catalogus* (Frankfurt am Main: Saurius, 1597-99), 5:88-91.

68. Saxony, ducal pastors, *Warhafftiger vnnd Gru[e]ndtlicher Summarien Bericht Etlicher Predicanten Wie vnd Worumb sie in LXII. Vnd LXIII. Jare in Thu[e]ringen seind jres Ampts entsetzt vnd zum theil verjagt worden . . .* (n.p., 1564).

69. Christian F. Paullini, *Historia Isenacensis* (Frankfurt am Main: Bauer, 1698), 192-94.

70. Among others, Amsdorf attempted a public critique of the Declaration of Viktorin in 1564, without mentioning *De servo arbitrio: Wider die Synergia Victorini. Nemlich Das der Mensch in seiner Bekerung/kein Synergiam noch modum agendi, habe noch haben kan/das ist/ allerding nichts mit wircke in seiner Bekerung/Sondern sey Gottes gnedige wirckung allein* (n.p., 1564). See Robert Kolb, *Nikolaus von Amsdorf (1483-1565): Popular Polemics in the Preservation of Luther's Legacy* (Nieuwkoop: De Graaf, 1978), 214-24.

71. In a memorandum dated July 10, 1563, in Schlüsselburg, *Haereticorum Catalogus*, 5:452-59.

72. The new leaders of the church issued *Confutation. Gru[e]ndlicher vnd ausfu[e]hr-licher Beweis/aus Gottes Wort/der Veter schrifften . . . Das Victorini Strigelij Declaration . . .*

falsch verfu[e]risch vnd verwerfflich. Auf . . . verordnung . . . Herrn Johans Wilhelmen/ Hertzogen zu Sachssen . . . gestellet (Jena: Thomas Rebart, 1567).

73. See Schlüsselburg, *Haereticorum Catalogus*, 5:51-88, "Locus de humanis viribus, seu libero arbitrio Victorini Strigelij dictata Lypsiae, anno 1564 . . . ," and 110-14.

74. Lasius, *Fundament Warer vnd Christlicher Bekerung/Wider die Flacianische Klotzbus/aus vier Irrthumen widers Fundament ersetzt/Klerlich erwisen/vnd gru[e]ndlich widerlegt* (Frankfurt an der Oder: Johann Eichorn; Wittenberg: Peter Seitz, 1568), and *Praelibatio Flaciani dogmatis de prodigiosa conversione hominis, ad gustum totius controversiae proposita* (Wittenberg: Peter Seitz, 1568). Hübner notes Lasius's "ausnehmend scharfe Polemik, eindringendes Denken und bewunderswerte deutsche Ausdrucksfähigkeit" in his expression of Philippist concerns "in unanstößiger Form"; Hübner, "Über den freien Willen," 146-47.

75. Flacius, *Censura de V. Strigilii apostatae declaratione s. potius errorum occultatione* (Regensburg: Heinrich Geissler, 1562).

76. Wigand, *De Libero arbitrio Hominis, INTEGRO. CORRVPTO in rebus externis. MORTVO in rebus spiritualibus. RENATO. Doctrina solidē ac Methodicē Verbo Dei tradita & explicata* . . . (Ursel: Nicolaus Heinrich, 1562). As part of the background of Wigand's disquisition, his work, together with Matthaeus Judex, on the fourth locus of the first century of the *Magdeburg Centuries*, "De Doctrina," must be noted. Judex altered the original plan to treat "On the human creature" *(De homine)* and then "On free choice" *(De libero arbitrio)* by substituting for these two topics the following: *De lapsu hominis, De homine ante lapsum, De homine post lapsum, De homine renato*, with the result that "the free will no longer appears as a title in itself but is considered exclusively from the standpoint of the specific relationship of the human being with God," as Heinz Scheible observes: *Die Entstehung der Magdeburger Zenturien* (Gütersloh: Mohn, 1966), 52.

77. Augustine presented this in his *Expositio quarundam propositionum ex epistola ad Romanos* 13-18; PL 35:2065; and his *Enchiridion ad Laurentium* 118; PL 40:287. Lombard used this analysis in *Sententia* II d 25 e 6; PL 192:707.

78. Wigand followed Melanchthon's description of "Method," in *Erotemata dialectices, CR* 13:573-78. See Robert Kolb, "The Advance of Dialectic in Lutheran Theology: The Role of Johannes Wigand (1523-1587)," in *Regnum, Religio et Ratio: Essays Presented to Robert M. Kingdon*, ed. Jerome Friedman (Kirksville, Mo.: Sixteenth Century Journal, 1987), 93-102.

79. Wigand, *De Libero arbitrio*, 171-74, 182, 190-91. Works cited include the Leipzig Disputation, Luther's comments on several psalms, *De servo arbitrio*, the disputation "De Homine," and commentaries on Micah, Galatians, and Genesis.

80. Seven years later Wigand placed the entire corpus of Luther's writings in a list of secondary authorities for determining public teaching: "Palam & ingenue coram Deo, & vniuerso mundo testamur, nos totis pectoribus amplecti & profiteri, verbum Dei in authenticis libris Prophetarum & Apostolorum traditum & compraehensum, tria Symbola, Apostolicum, Nicaenum & Athanasianum, Augustanam Confesionem, quae Anno Domini 1530, Carolo quinto totiusque Imperio Romano est exhibita, eiusque Apologiam, Smalcaldicos articulos, & scripta Lutheri, & Confutationes Illustrissimorum Ducum Saxoniae," *De confessione in doctrina divina, & necessarijs factis* (Jena: Rödinger, 1569), C5b-[C6]a. Cf. Robert Kolb, *Martin Luther as Prophet, Teacher, and Hero: Images of the Reformer, 1520-1620* (Grand Rapids: Baker, 1999), 68-70.

81. Wigand, *De Libero arbitrio,* 308-12.

82. In 1559, when Heshusius battled against Calvinist views in Heidelberg; see Peter F. Barton, *Um Luthers Erbe. Studien und Texte zur Spätreformation, Tilemann Heshusius (1527-1559)* (Witten: Luther-Verlag, 1972), 196-225.

83. Heshusius, *De servo hominis arbitrio: et conversione eivs per Dei gratiam aduersus Synergiae adsertores* (Magdeburg: Wolfgang Kirchner, 1562), A3a, B2a, R3a-b, Y3a-b.

84. Irenaeus, *Symbolvm Apostolicvm. Das ist. Die Artickel vnsers Christlichen Glaubens/ ausgelegt . . .* (Eisleben: Urban Gaubisch, 1562), with an attached section with its own title page, *Der dritte Artickel Vnsers Christlichen Glaubens/von der Heiligung/Ausgelegt. Mit Vermeldung vnd widerlegung allerley Irthumb vnd Ketzereyen/beide alt vnd new/so dawider entstanden* (Eisleben: Urban Gaubisch, 1562).

85. Spangenberg, *Wider den vermeinten Freyen Willen des Menschen/vnd mitwirckung desselben/in bekerung sein selbst. Eine Predigt vber das Euangelium Marci VII* (Frankfurt am Main: Nicolaus Basse, 1562).

86. Mansfeld Ministerium, *Sententia ministrorvm verbi in comitatv Mansfeldiensi de formvla declarationis Victorini Strigelii in qvestione de libro hominis arbitrio* (n.p., 1562). The efforts of the Mansfeld ministerium against Strigel won the commendation of Joachim Mörlin of Braunschweig in a letter to Menzel and Spangenberg, Feb. 25, 1563; see *Der Briefwechsel des M. Cyriacus Spangenberg,* ed. Heinrich Rembe (Dresden: Naumann, 1887), 1:5-6. As the controversy in ducal Saxony continued, the Mansfeld ministerium issued a protest against the activities of the leading reconciler in the Saxon ministerium, Johann Stössel: *Responsio Ministrorum verbi in Comitatu Mansfeldensi. Ad Apologiam D. Johannis Stosselii . . .* (Eisleben: Urban Gaubisch, 1566).

87. Menzel, *Vom Freyenn willen des Menschen. Eine Predigt vber den Spruch Christi/ Matth. 23 . . .* (Eisleben: Urban Gaubisch, 1564), A6a-b, B2a-B3b, B7b. In the last passage Menzel criticized Strigel for appealing to Luther's writings but misinterpreting them, probably a reference to the Weimar Disputation.

88. He then went to Greiz as superintendent, served as pastor in Tondorf, and then as superintendent in Eisleben, where he died in 1598; see O. Meusel, "Die Reussische oder Reussisch-Schönburgische Konfession," *Beiträge zur sächsischen Kirchengeschichte* 14 (1899): 158.

89. Herbst, *Vom Freien Willen vnd Bekerung des Menschen zu Gott. Warhafftige/ bestendige/vnd in Gottes wort wolgegru[e]ndte Lehr vnd meinung/des tewren vnd Seligen Mannes D. Martini Lvtheri . . .* (Eisleben: Andreas Petri, 1565), B1b. Herbst referred to the location of his citations from *De servo arbitrio* in the Latin Jena edition but gave references to the Jonas translation found in the German Wittenberg edition in the margins. His citations, with minor, largely orthographical variations, largely follow the text found in the Wittenberg edition, vol. 6.

90. Herbst, *Vom Freien Willen,* B3a.

91. Kirchner later served as professor in Jena, Heidelberg, and Helmstedt, and as a leading ecclesiastical official in Braunschweig-Wolfenbüttel, the Palatinate, and ducal Saxony. On his later activities see Dingel, *Concordia controversa,* 400-413 and passim; Inge Mager, *Die Konkordienformel im Fürstentum Braunschweig-Wolfenbüttel, Entstehungsbeitrag — Rezeption — Geltung* (Göttingen: Vandenhoeck & Ruprecht, 1993), 155-60 and passim.

92. Kirchner, *Deudscher Thesavrvs. Des Hochgelerten weitberu[e]mbten vnd theuren*

Mans D. Mart. Luthers/Darinnen alle Heubtartickel/Christlicher/Catholischer vnd Apostolischer Lere vnd Glaubens erklert vnd ausgelegt . . . (Frankfurt am Main: Hieronymus Feierabent and Thomas Rebart, 1570), on the "natural powers of human creatures," and "free will," 75b-87b; on "eternal election or predestination," 125b-127a.

93. Kirchner, *Thesavrvs: explicationvm omnivm articvlorvm ac capitvm, catholicae, orthodoxae, verae, ac piae doctrinae Christianae, quae hac aetate controuersa sunt, ex reuerendi, vereque Dei viri, ac summi Theologi D. Martini Lutheri . . . operibus . . .* (Frankfurt am Main: Thomas Rhebart and Sigismund Feierabend, 1566), 240-70.

94. Kirchner, *Thesavrvs*, 250-51; WA 18:642.21–644.16; *LW* 33:74-77.

95. Obenhin, *Einfa[e]ltiger vnd wahrhaftiger bericht/von dem Freyen Willen vnd bekerung des Menschen/aus heiliger Go[e]ttlicher Schrift/vnnd bewerten alten Kirchenlerern genomen/in diesen letzten vnd betru[e]bten Zeiten . . . wider etliche Ferber vnd Verfelscher der reinen religion. Sampt zugethanen lateinischen Zeugnissen/aus den ersten ausgegangenen Schrifften/des E. W. H. Philippi Melanchtonis/seliger Gedechtnis/trewlich gezogen/zu erklerung dieses Tractats . . .* (n.p., 1569). On Obenhin, see August Korf, *Geschichte der evangelischen Gemeinde in Oberursel a. Taunus* (Oberursel: Evang. Pfarramt, 1902), 51-65, and Ferdinand Neuroth, *Geschichte der Stadt Oberursel und der Hohemark* (Oberursel: Altkönig-Verlag, 1955), 128-29. I am grateful to Volker Stolle for these references.

96. Kurt Dietrich Schmidt, "Der Göttinger Bekehrungsstreit," *Zeitschrift der Gesellschaft für niedersächsische Kirchengeschichte* 34/35 (1929): 66-121.

97. Schmidt, "Bekehrungsstreit," 71-72. Schmidt believes that Keyser's position makes him strictly speaking a follower of Flacius, but his position does not differ from that held in general in the 1560s by the Gnesio-Lutherans of Erfurt, who did not support Flacius's peculiar definition of original sin.

98. Philipp Julius Rehtmeyer, *Historiae ecclesiasticae inclytae urbis Brunsvigae Pars III. Oder: Der beru[e]hmten Stadt Braunschweig Kirchen-Historie Dritter Theil . . .* (Brunswick: Zilliger, 1710), supplement #38, 242-43.

99. Schmidt, "Bekehrungsstreit," 87, 96-98.

100. Jena Faculty, *Colloqvivm zu Altenburgk in Meissen/Vom Artikel der Rechtfertigung vor Gott. Zwischen Den Churfu[e]rstlichen vnd Fu[e]rstlichen zu Sachsen etc. Theologen gehalten. Vom 20. Octobris Anno 1568. bis auff den 9. Martij/Anno 1569. Es ist auch von den zweien hinderstelligen Artikeln/Nemlich vom Freien Willen/vnd von den Mitteldingen/was da ferner im Colloquio/von Fu[e]rstlichen Sechsischen Theologen/hette sollen vorbracht werden/ hinzu gedruckt* (Jena, 1569).

101. Saxony, electoral theologians *Gantze vnd Vnuerfelschete Acta vnd handlung des Colloquij/zwischen den Churfu[e]rstlichen vnd Fu[e]rstlichen zu Sachsen etc. Theologen/vom artickel der Gerechtigkeit des Menschen fur Gott/vnd von guten Wercken/zu Aldenburgk in Meissen gehalten. Vom 20. Octobris Anno 1568. bis auff den 9. Martij/Anno 1569* (Wittenberg: Hans Lufft, 1570).

102. The Jena theologians published the final statements of both sides, *Der Chur vnd Fu[e]rstlichen Sa[e]shsischen Theologen schrifft vnd Gegenschrifft/vom Aldenburgischen Colloquio/durch wen/aus was vrsachen/vnnd welcher gestalt dasselbige zerschlagen vnnd zergangen* (n.p., 1569), and they issued a complaint regarding the electoral theologians' behavior and tactics, *Wie das Aldenburgisch Colloquium zergangen* (n.p., 1569). The electoral Saxon side sought to set the record straight also with *Warhafftiger bericht vnd kurtze*

Warnung der Theologen/beider Vniuersitet Leiptzig vnd Wittemberg Von Den newlich zu Jhena im Druck ausgangenen Acten des Colloquij/so zu Aldenburg in Meissen gehalten (n.p., 1570), and with an extensive attack on a series of Gnesio-Lutheran positions in *Endlicher Bericht vnd Erklerung der Theologen beider Vniuersiteten/Leipzig vnd Wittemberg Auch der Superintendenten der Kirchen in des Churfu[e]rsten zu Sachsen Landen/belangend die Lere/so gemelte Vniuersiteten vnd Kirchen von anfang der Augspurgischen Confession bis auff diese zeit/ laut vnd vermu[e]ge derselben/zu allen Artickeln gleichfo[e]rmig/eintrechtig vnd bestendig gefu[e]ret haben/vber der sie auch durch hu[e]lff des allmechtigen Gottes gedencken fest zu halten* (Wittenberg: Hans Lufft, 1570), the section on the freedom of the will, Rr2a-Vv1a. The Jena reply came in *Bericht Vom Colloquio zu Altenburgk. Auff den endlichen Bericht/etc.* (Jena, 1570).

103. Jena faculty, *Colloqvivm zu Altenburgk*, 498a-502b.

104. Saxony electoral theologians, *Endlicher Bericht*, Rr2a-Rr3b.

105. Jena faculty, *Colloqvivm zu Altenburgk*, 502b-503b.

106. Saxony electoral theologians, *Endlicher Bericht*, Rr3b-Ss1b.

107. Jena faculty, *Colloqvivm zu Altenburgk*, 503b-505b.

108. Saxony electoral theologians, *Endlicher Bericht*, Ss1b-Ss3b. The report is referring to the oft-cited passage WA 43:457.32–463.17; *LW* 5:42-50.

109. Jena faculty, *Colloqvivm zu Altenburgk*, 505b.

110. Saxony electoral theologians, *Endlicher Bericht*, SS3b-Ss4a.

111. Jena faculty, *Colloqvivm zu Altenburgk*, 505b-507a.

112. Saxony electoral theologians, *Endlicher Bericht*, Ss4a-Tt3a.

113. Jena faculty, *Colloqvivm zu Altenburgk*, 507a-510b.

114. Saxony electoral theologians, *Endlicher Bericht*, Tt3a-Vv1a.

115. Jena faculty, *Bericht Vom Colloquio*, Hh1a.

116. Jena faculty, *Bekentnis Vom Freien Willen. So im Colloquio zu Altenburg/hat sollen vorbracht werden/von Fu[e]rstlichen Sechsischen Theologen* (Jena, 1570).

117. See his *Expositio . . . ex epistola ad Romanos*, PL 35:2069, or his *Enchiridion ad Laurentium* 118, PL 40:287.

118. Jena faculty, *Bekentnis Vom Freien Willen*, A3a-B3b. These points are reinforced with biblical argument and with references to Luther's *De servo arbitrio*, B3b-E3a.

119. Jena faculty, *Bekentnis Vom Freien Willen*, E3a-E4a. After a series of contrary teachings, the confession reprints the seven objections to what was being taught in electoral Saxony that had been included in the protocol published the previous year, E4a-F4a and F4a-N4a.

120. Jena faculty, *Bekentnis Von Fu[e]nff Streittigen Religions Artickeln* (Jena, 1570).

Notes to Chapter IV

1. Matthias Flacius and Nikolaus Gallus, *Apologia . . . Das die Adiaphoristen/vnd nit sie/trennung in vnsern Kirchen der Augspurgischen Confession/vnd vneinigkeit angericht . . .* (Regensburg: Hans Kohl, n.d.), C1b-C2a; cf. Andreas Schoppe, *Rettung Des Heiligen Catechismi wider den Schwarm der newen Manicheer vnd Substantisten* (Jena: Donatus Richtzenhan, 1572), A2b; and Mansfeld Ministerium, *Kurtzer Bericht/Wes sich die Prediger/Jn*

der Graff vnd Herrschafft Mansfelt . . . der fur zweien jaren in Deutscher vnd Lateinischer sprach/ausgegangenen Confession halben wider alle Secten/erklerungs weise/vnd sonst in aldern no[e]tigen stu[e]cken/einhellig vergliechen haben (Eisleben: Urban Gaubisch, 1563), D4a-b.

2. Luther, *Tomvs secvndvs omnivm opervm Reverendi Domini Martini Lutheri . . . Continens monumenta, quae de multis grauissimis controuersijs ab anno XX. usque ad XXVII. annum edita* (Wittenberg: Johannes Lufft, 1546), 457a-526a (the marginal notations are reproduced with almost no changes in later printings, e.g., *Tomvs secvndvs omnivm opervum . . .* [Wittenberg: Lorenz Schwenck, 1562], 424a-486b); cf. *Tomvs tertivs omnivm opervm Reverendi patris, Viri Dei, D. M. L. continens quae aedita sunt ab Anno XXIIII. vsque ad Annum XXXVIII . . .* (Jena: Donatus Ritzenhain and Thomas Rebart, 1567), 160a-230a.

3. On the two editions, see WA 60:464-543; on the editors, esp. 465, 481, 501-5. For annotations on necessity, see *Tomvs secvndvs,* Wittenberg, 468a, 499b-500a; on the hardening of Pharaoh's heart, 491a, 492a-493a, 495b-497a.

4. Luther, *Der Sechste teil der Bu[e]cher des Ehrnwirdigen Herrn Doctoris Martini Lutheri . . .* (Wittenberg: Hans Lufft, 1553), 462a-568b (on necessity, 471a; on Pharaoh, 523b-525a), with annotations unchanged later; cf. *Der Sechste Teil der Bu[e]cher des Ehrnwirdigen Herrn Doctoris Martini Lutheri . . .* (Wittenberg: Lorenz Schwenck, 1570), 441a-543a (on necessity, 449b; on Pharaoh, 500a-502a).

5. Obviously, an argument from silence is an open door to false conclusions, but Luther's comments on John 1:12, 3:6, and 15:5 in *De servo arbitrio* could have been used but were not, e.g., in Johannes Wigand, *In evangelivm S. Johannis explicationes* (Königsberg: Johannes Daubmann, 1575), and David Chytraeus, *Jn evangelion Ioannis, Scholia* (Frankfurt am Main: Johannes Spies, 1588). In his *In D. Iohannis evangelion, Iohannis Brentij Exegesis . . .* (1527; Frankfurt am Main, 1542), Johannes Brenz took the occasion to reject the freedom of the will, but without reference to Luther; see on John 1:9-13, 8a-9a; on 3:6, 43a-b; on 15:1-5, 267b-270b, where he treats predestination as well.

Also in commentaries on those passages Luther had treated extensively in *De servo arbitrio,* his students did not make use of that work, nor did they criticize it when they presented differing interpretations. For instance, David Chytraeus said, in commenting on the hardening of Pharaoh's heart in Exod. 4 and 7, that God is not the cause of evil in general and of the rejection of his Word specifically. God neither impels nor effects such rejection in unbelievers, and his permissive will (which permitted but did not cause the hardness of Pharaoh's heart) dare not be so interpreted. See his *In Exodvm Enarratio* (Wittenberg: Johannes Crato, 1561), 222-28. Likewise, in treating Mal. 1:2-3, "Jacob have I loved, Esau have I hated," Chytraeus neither mentioned Luther's interpretation nor followed it strictly (*Explicatio Malachiae prophetae . . .* [Rostock: Jacob Transylvanus, 1568], 8-17), although he told his readers to find the topic of predestination in the chapter. He interpreted God's hatred toward Esau as applying to temporal curses and asserted that God had predestined salvation for the church and that no one should speculate about predestination apart from the means of grace. Cf. Johannes Wigand, *In XII. Prophetas minores explicationes svccinctae . . .* (Frankfurt am Main: Johannes Wolf, 1569), 605-7, with a similar interpretation.

6. He does cite *De servo arbitrio* in his definition of the term *liberum arbitrium* in the work's extensive dictionary of terms; *Clavis Scriptvrae S. seu de Sermone Sacrarum literarum . . .* (Basel: Herwagen, 1580), pt. 1, pp. 571-72.

7. Herbst, *Vom Freien Willen vnd Bekerung des Menschen zu Gott. Warhafftige/bestendige/ vnd in Gottes wort wolgegru[e]ndte Lehr vnd meinung/des tewren vnd Seligen Mannes D. Martini Lvtheri* . . . (Eisleben: Andreas Petri, 1565), Ee3b-Ee4a; WA 18:652.11-32; *LW* 33:88-89.

8. Kirchner, *Thesavrus: explicationvm omnivm articvlorvm ac capitvm, catholicae, orthodoxae, verae, ac piae doctrinae Christianae, quae hac aetate controuersa sunt, ex reuerendi, vereque Dei viri, ac summi Theologi D. Martini Lutheri* . . . *operibus* . . . (Frankfurt am Main: Thomas Rhebart and Sigismund Feierabend, 1566), 27-28; WA 18:606.16–609.14; *LW* 33:25-27.

9. Wigand, *De Libero arbitrio Hominis, INTEGRO. CORRVPTO in rebus externis. MORTVO in rebus spiritualibus. RENATO. Doctrina solidē ac Methodicē Verbo Dei tradita & explicata* . . . (Ursel: Nicolaus Heinrich, 1562), 308-12. WA 18:603.11-12; *LW* 33:20. The section numbers in the following text refer to Wigand's work.

10. WA 18:606.22-24, 621.5-6; *LW* 33:25, 45. Herbst also quoted Luther to establish the clarity of the biblical message, a clarity wrought internally by the Holy Spirit, *Vom Freien Willen*, d3a-b; WA 18:609.4-14; *LW* 33:28.

11. WA 18:680.23-25, 683.228-29, 684.26-32; *LW* 33:132, 137, 138; cf. §17, restating the need to distinguish law and gospel or promises; WA 18:698.16-20; *LW* 33:158-59.

12. WA 18:661.29–666.13, 676.4–680.22; *LW* 33:102-10, 125-31.

13. WA 18:750.25-31, 751.32-33; *LW* 33:237, 239.

14. Robert Kolb, *Martin Luther as Prophet, Teacher, and Hero: Images of the Reformer, 1520-1620* (Grand Rapids: Baker, 1999), 39-74.

15. See Kolb, *Martin Luther,* 39-74, for the use of Luther material in the writings of his students, and on the formal secondary authority he commanded among some, but not all, of his followers.

16. Kirchner, *Thesavrvs: explicationvm omnivm articvlorvm,* 243-46; WA 18:661.30–666.12; *LW* 33:102-10. The specific quotations in our text are taken from WA 18:664.1-3, 15-16; *LW* 33:106, 107.

17. Kirchner, *Thesavrvs,* 249-50; WA 18:753.36–755.18; *LW* 33:242-45; cited also in part by Herbst, *Vom Freien Willen,* K3a-b, and Bb3b-Bb4a.

18. Flacius, *Disputatio de originali peccato et libero arbitrio, inter Matthiam Flacium Illyricum & Victorinum Strigelium* (1562; 1563; Eisleben, 1563), 228.

19. Heshusius, *De servo hominis arbitrio: et conversione eivs per Dei gratiam aduersus Synergiae adsertores* (Magdeburg: Wolfgang Kirchner, 1562), I3a-b, and the Jena theological faculty, *Colloqvivm zu Aldenburgk in Meissen/Vom Artikel der Rechtfertigung vor Gott. Zwischen Den Churfu[e]rstlichen vnd Fu[e]rstlichen zu Sachsen etc. Theologen gehalten. Vom 20. Octobris Anno 1568. bis auff den 9. Martij/Anno 1569. Es ist auch von den zweien hinderstelligen Artikeln/Nemlich vom Freien Willen/vnd von den Mitteldingen/was da ferner im Colloquio/von Fu[e]rstlichen Sechsischen Theologen/hette sollen vorbracht werden/hinzu gedruckt* (Jena, 1569), 503b, and *Bekentnis Vom Freien Willen. So im Colloquio zu Altenburg/ hat sollen vorbracht werden/von Fu[e]rstlichen Sechsischen Theologen* (Jena, 1570), K2b.

20. See pp. 120-21 above.

21. Wigand, *De Libero arbitrio,* 274-75; J. Clericus, ed., *Desiderii Erasmi Roterodami Opera Omnia* . . . , 10 vols. (Leiden, 1703-6), 9:1228; *Collected Works of Erasmus 76, Controversies,* ed. Charles Trinkaus (Toronto: University of Toronto Press, 1999), 41; WA 18:697.23–698.14;

LW 33:157-58. Cf. Herbst's use of this passage in the same manner, *Vom Freien Willen*, E4b-F1b, K2b, and Aa2a-b; and that of the Jena theologians, *Colloqvivm zu Altenburgk*, 508b.

22. Kirchner, *Thesavrvs*, 253; WA 18:777.9-20; *LW* 33:278-79.

23. Wigand, *De Libero arbitrio*, 284-86; Erasmus, *Opera omnia*, 9:1229; *Collected Works*, 76:44; WA 18:727.17-24, 728.19–729.3, 733.18-20; *LW* 33:203-5, 212. Into these citations Wigand inserted a summary of a section on the nature of exhortation.

24. Herbst, *Vom Freien Willen*, K2b-K3a; WA 18:719.36–720.7; *LW* 33:191.

25. Herbst, *Vom Freien Willen*, Hh4a-Ji2a; WA 18:769.38–771.33; *LW* 33:267-70. Cf. similar arguments, *Vom Freien Willen*, Ji3a-b, with a citation from WA 18:669.14-19; *LW* 33:114; and Ji3b; WA 18:771.5-13; *LW* 33:269.

26. Wigand, *De Libero arbitrio*, 282-84; Erasmus, *Opera omnia*, 9:1232; *Collected Works*, 76:46; WA 18:723.23–724.2, 725.12-15, 725.28–726.13; *LW* 33:197-201.

27. Robert Kolb, "Melanchthon's Influence on the Exegesis of His Students: The Case of Romans 9," in *Philip Melanchthon (1497-1560) and the Commentary*, ed. M. Patrick Graham and Timothy J. Wengert (Sheffield: Sheffield Academic Press, 1997), 204-5, 210.

28. WA 18:702.9–709.4; *LW* 33:164-75; these words are found in WA 18:706.28-29; *LW* 33:172.

29. WA 18:705.13-14, 711.20-27; *LW* 33:169, 179. On Erasmus's use of Origen, see Karl Zickendraht, *Der Streit zwischen Erasmus und Luther über die Willensfreiheit* (Leipzig: Hinrichs, 1909), 39-41.

30. WA 18:714.4-6; *LW* 33:183.

31. Cf. WA 18:717.25–719.3; *LW* 33:188-90.

32. Kirchner, *Thesavrvs*, 252; WA 18:744.6-29; *LW* 33:227-28.

33. Kirchner, *Thesavrvs*, 252; WA 18:772.20-35; *LW* 33:271-72.

34. Kirchner, *Thesavrvs*, 253-54; WA 18:779.11–780.9; *LW* 33:281-83.

35. Kirchner, *Thesavrvs*, 254-55; WA 18:781.29–782.11; *LW* 33:285-86.

36. Kirchner, *Thesavrvs*, 255; WA 18:782.12–783.2; *LW* 33:286-88.

37. *Das der freie Wille nichts sey. Antwort/D. Martini Lutheri/an Erasmum Roterodamum/Verdeudscht durch D. Justum Jonam/Zuuor niemals allein im Druck ausgangen*, ed. Nikolaus Gallus (Regensburg: Heinrich Geissler, 1559), A3a-b.

38. See, for instance, his contrast between the God of the law, similar to the God Not Preached of Luther, and the God of the proclaimed gospel, parallel to God Preached, in the Apology of the Augsburg Confession, XII:31ff.; *BSLK*, 257-58; *Book of Concord*, 192.

39. *Das der freie Wille nichts sey*, A2a-b; WA 18:689.17–690.2; *LW* 33:145-46.

40. Chemnitz, *De Controversiis quibusdam, quae superiori tempore circa quosdam Augustanae Confessionis articulos motae et agitatae sunt, Iudicium D. Martini Chemnitii*, ed. Polycarp Leyser (Wittenberg: Gronenberg, 1594), 23-24; *Sources and Contexts*, 205.

41. Heshusius, *De servo hominis arbitrio*, b3b; cf. WA 18:684.26–688.26; *LW* 33:138-44.

42. WA 18:606.11; *LW* 33:25.

43. WA 18:784.9; *LW* 33:290.

44. Herbst, *Vom Freien Willen*, l4a, and m1a-b; WA 18:684.32-40, 685.3-7, 14-16; *LW* 33:139.

45. Herbst, *Vom Freien Willen*, l4b; WA 18:712.19-29; *LW* 33:180.

46. Herbst, *Vom Freien Willen*, m1b-m2a; WA 18:685.28–686.[3] 13; *LW* 33:140.

47. Herbst, *Vom Freien Willen*, m1a-b; WA 18:689.17–690.2; *LW* 33:145-46. Cf. a sum-

mary and quotations from this section in *Vom Freien Willen,* z1b-z3a; WA 18:688.32–690.8; *LW* 33:145-46.

48. Herbst, *Vom Freien Willen,* Hh3b-Hh4a; WA 18:690.13-29; *LW* 33:146-47.

49. Herbst, *Vom Freien Willen,* Hh1a-Hh3b; WA 18:784.1–785.38; *LW* 33:289-92.

50. Herbst, *Vom Freien Willen,* o1a-p3b; WA 43:457.32–463.17; *LW* 5:42-50.

51. See chap. V, pp. 205-20.

52. Saxony electoral theologians, *Endlicher Bericht vnd Erklerung der Theologen beider Vniuersiteten/Leipzig vnd Wittemberg Auch der Superintendenten der Kirchen in des Churfu[e]rsten zu Sachsen Landen/belangend die Lere/so gemelte Vniuersiteten vnd Kirchen von anfang der Augspurgischen Confession bis auff diese zeit/laut vnd vermu[e]ge derselben/zu allen Artickeln gleichfo[e]rmig/eintrechtig vnd bestendig gefu[e]ret haben/vber der sie auch durch hu[e]lff des allmechtigen Gottes gedencken fest zu halten* (Wittenberg: Hans Lufft, 1570), Rr4a; WA 18:686.5-8; *LW* 33:140.

53. E.g., Saxony, electoral theologians, *Endlicher Bericht,* Rr4b-Ss1a.

54. Herbst, *Vom Freien Willen,* d3b-e1a; WA 18:658.17–659.33, here 659.27-33; *LW* 33:98-100, here 99-100.

55. Herbst, *Vom Freien Willen,* e1a-e2a; WA 18:781.29–782.11; *LW* 33:285-86.

56. Herbst, *Vom Freien Willen,* i3b; WA 18:695.28-31; *LW* 33:155.

57. Herbst, *Vom Freien Willen,* k2b; WA 18:602.7-18; *LW* 33:18.

58. WA 18:680.23-25, 683.228-29, 684.26-32; *LW* 33:132, 137, 138; cf. §17, restating the need to distinguish law and gospel or promises; WA 18:698.16-20; *LW* 33:158-59.

59. WA 18:661.29–666.13, 676.4–680.22; *LW* 33:102-10, 125-31.

60. Kirchner, *Thesavrvs,* 257-59; WA 18:683.11–686.12; *LW* 33:136-40.

61. Kirchner, *Thesavrvs,* 263-64; WA 18:632.21–633.15; *LW* 33:61-62.

62. Herbst, *Vom Freien Willen,* x2b; WA 18:684.14-26; *LW* 33:138.

63. Herbst, *Vom Freien Willen,* Gg1a; WA 18:632.3-8; *LW* 33:60-61.

64. Herbst, *Vom Freien Willen,* Q2b, a paraphrase of WA 18:602.22-32; *LW* 33:18-19.

65. Kirchner, *Thesavrvs,* 240; WA 42:64.28-31; *LW* 1:84-85.

66. Kirchner, *Thesavrvs,* 240; WA 18:638.4-9; *LW* 33:70.

67. Kirchner, *Thesavrvs,* 247-48; WA 18:614.1-16; *LW* 33:35.

68. Kirchner, *Thesavrvs,* 248; WA 18:753.36-39; *LW* 33:223.

69. WA 39.I:177.3-12; *LW* 34:139-40.

70. Kirchner, *Thesavrvs,* 248; WA 18:697.21-30; *LW* 33:157. The Jena professors used this passage as well in their *Bekentnis Vom Freien Willen. So im Colloquio zu Altenburg/hat sollen vorbracht werden/von Fu[e]rstlichen Sechsischen Theologen* (Jena, 1570), M2a-b, to argue against the expression that the will has a faculty for applying itself to grace.

71. Kirchner, *Thesavrvs,* 255-56; WA 18:767.25–768.9; *LW* 33:263-64.

72. Herbst, *Vom Freien Willen,* y3b-y4a; WA 18:672.7-23; *LW* 33:118-19.

73. Herbst, *Vom Freien Willen,* z1b; WA 18:682.9-25; *LW* 33:134-35.

74. Kirchner, *Thesavrvs,* 259-60; WA 18:694.34–696.11; *LW* 33:153-55.

75. Kirchner, *Thesavrvs,* 261-62; WA 18:769.32–771.13; *LW* 33:267-69.

76. Jena faculty, *Bekentnis Vom Freien Willen,* J3a-b.

77. Kirchner, *Thesavrvs,* 256; WA 18:672.31–673.7, 675.20-25; *LW* 33:119-20, 125.

78. Kirchner, *Thesavrvs,* 256-57; WA 18:667.7-36; *LW* 33:126-27.

79. Flacius, *Disputatio,* 249. WA 18:676.4–680.22; *LW* 33:125-32. Cf. Flacius's use of this

principle from *De servo arbitrio* in *Clavis Scriptvrae S. seu de Sermone Sacrarum literarum . . . Altera pars* (Basel: Herwagen, 1580), 321-22, tractate VI, "Aliquot theologici libelli etiam ex sermone sacro pendentes, ad eum illustrandum non parum utiles."

80. Wigand, *De Libero arbitrio*, 277.

81. Irenaeus, *Symbolvm Apostolicvm. Das ist. Die Artickel vnsers Christlichen Glaubens/ ausgelegt . . .* (Eisleben: Urban Gaubisch, 1562), T2b-T3b.

82. Jena faculty, *Bekentnis Vom Freien Willen*, F2a.

83. Herbst, *Vom Freien Willen*, y2a; WA 18:675.20-25; *LW* 33:124, in a longer section that includes WA 18:675.37–676.3 and 675.13-19; *LW* 33:123-24 and 124-25; cf. *Vom Freien Willen*, v4a-x1a; WA 18:677.7-36; *LW* 33:127-28; *Vom Freien Willen*, x2a; WA 18:672.32-35; *LW* 33:119-20.

84. Kirchner, *Thesavrvs*, 241-42; WA 18:636.27–638.11; *LW* 33:68-70. This passage was also used for the same purpose by Herbst, *Vom Freien Willen*, A1b.

85. Kirchner, *Thesavrvs*, 267; WA 18:698.10-13; *LW* 33:158. The Jena professors used this passage as well in their *Bekentnis Vom Freien Willen*, E1a.

86. Kirchner, *Thesavrvs*, 267; WA 18:759.19-28; *LW* 33:250-51. Cf. the further reference in *Thesavrvs*, 267-68; WA 18:775.19–776.3; *LW* 33:276-77. The Jena professors used this passage as well in their *Bekentnis Vom Freien Willen*, E1a.

87. Kirchner, *Thesavrvs*, 265-66; WA 18:669.20–670.11; *LW* 33:114-15.

88. Flacius, *Warhafftige vnd bestendige meinung vnd zeugnis/Von der Erbsu[e]nde vnd dem freien willen Des Ehrwirdigen tewren Mans Gottes D. Martin Luthers Aus allen seinen schrifften trewliche vnd mit vleis zusamen gezogen . . .* (Jena: Thomas Rhebart, 1560), *3a (preface), repeated on R3b; WA 18:670.1-11; *LW* 33:115.

89. Flacius, *Warhafftige vnd bestendige meinung*, R3b; WA 18:668.11-20; *LW* 33:113.

90. WA 42:47.14-22; *LW* 1:63.

91. Kirchner, *Thesavrvs*, 253; WA 18:750.10-15; *LW* 33:237.

92. See its use by the Jena faculty, *Colloqvivm zu Aldenburgk*, 501a-b, and *Bekentnis Vom Freien Willen*, H3a; WA 18:635.7-22; *LW* 33:65-66.

93. Herbst, *Vom Freien Willen*, E4a; WA 18:679.23-33; *LW* 33:130; cf. similar citations, *Vom Freien Willen*, P3a and E4b-F1b; WA 18:743.27-35, 749.30–750.39, 782.27–783.2; *LW* 33:227, 236-38, 287.

94. Jena faculty, *Colloqvivm zu Aldenburgk*, 505b; WA 18:775.16-18; *LW* 33:275.

95. See Volker Leppin, *Antichrist und Jüngster Tag. Das Profil apokalyptischer Flugschriftenpublizistik im deutschen Luthertum 1548-1618* (Gütersloh: Gütersloher Verlagshaus, 1999).

96. Kirchner, *Thesavrvs*, 252-53; WA 18:773.8-18; *LW* 33:272.

97. Herbst, *Vom Freien Willen*, B3a; WA 18:786.17-20; *LW* 33:293.

98. Kirchner, *Thesavrvs*, 253; WA 18:773.31–774.16; *LW* 33:273-74.

99. WA 18:698.39; *LW* 33:158.

100. WA 18:755.11-12, 762.18-20; *LW* 33:244 and 255.

101. WA 18:770.21-24 and 777.33-34; *LW* 33:268 and 279.

102. Jena faculty, *Colloqvivm zu Altenburgk*, 505b-506b; WA 18:636.4-10; *LW* 33:66-67. This same section was cited in *Bekentnis Vom Freien Willen*, L1b.

103. Herbst, *Vom Freien Willen*, Aa2b-Aa3a; WA 18:698.3-16; *LW* 33:158. Herbst reinforced this point with Luther's observations on John 15:5-6, Aa4b-Bb1a; WA 18:748.14-19; *LW* 33:234; and WA 18:750.38–751.11; *LW* 33:238.

104. Irenaeus, *Symbolvm Apostolicvm*, P3a-b.

105. On Melanchthon, see above. Cf. WA 18:662.40–663.7; *LW* 33:105.

106. *Das der freie Wille nichts sey*, 1554, (2a).

107. E.g., the Jena faculty in *Colloqvivm zu Aldenburgk*, 506b, citing WA 18:664.27-31; *LW* 33:107.

108. Stoltz, *Refutatio propositionum Pfeffingeri de Libero arbitrio . . .* (n.p., 1558), E3b-E4a.

109. Melanchthon, *Loci communes theologici*, 1559, StA 2.1:245-46.

110. Flacius, *Disputatio*, 222. On Heshusius's lectures in Wittenberg, see Peter F. Barton, *Um Luthers Erbe. Studien und Texte zur Spätreformation, Tilemann Heshusius (1527-1559)* (Witten: Luther-Verlag, 1972), 34-39.

111. Walther's work was an attempt to demonstrate that Luther and Melanchthon had taught the same doctrine: *Erste [-Sechste] Theil der Heubtartickel/Christlicher Lere. In Fragstu[e]cken verfasset/vnd mit Gottes Wort/vnd fu[e]rnamen Spru[e]chen D. Lutheri/vnd D. Melanthonis erkleret vnd bekrefftiget . . .* (Magdeburg: Matthaeus Gieseke, 1573), I: p3b; WA 18:662.40–663.7; *LW* 33:105. On the same page he also cited WA 18:664.15-24; *LW* 33:107.

112. Stoltz, *Refutatio propositionum Pfeffingeri*, G4a-b; cf. WA 18:697.18-30; *LW* 33:157. Flacius repeated this argument in *Bericht M. Fla. Illyrici/Von etlichen Artikeln der Christlichen Lehr/vnd von seinem Leben . . .* (n.p., 1559), C2a-b, and in the disputation, *Disputatio*, 166, with reference to *De servo arbitrio*.

113. Jena faculty, *Colloqvivm zu Altenburgk*, 507b; *Bekentnis Vom Freien Willen*, M1a-b; cf. Herbst, *Vom Freien Willen*, Aa2a-b; cf. his defense of the phrase, Gg2b-Gg3a, with a citation from WA 18:707.21-31; *LW* 33:173.

114. Herbst, *Vom Freien Willen*, O4a; WA 18:719.36–720.7; *LW* 33:191.

115. Flacius, *Bericht M. Fla. Illyrici*, E4a; he referred as well to Luther's calling the sinner a block of wood. He also repeated it in *Warhafftige vnd bestendige meinung*, R4b-S1a.

116. Herbst, *Vom Freien Willen*, Ff2a; WA 18:638.4-11; *LW* 33:70.

117. Flacius, *Disputatio*, 201-5.

118. Flacius, *Disputatio*, 32.

119. Flacius, *Disputatio*, 32, 201-2; WA 18:635.9, 12-14; *LW* 33:65.

120. Flacius, *Disputatio*, 112-15. Cf. Flacius's earlier reference to this passage, *Disputatio*, 33, and WA 18:634.14–636.22; *LW* 33:64-66. Flacius also used this reference in *Clavis Scriptvrae S.*, 415, tractate VII, "Norma seu Regula coelestis veritatis."

121. See chap. V, pp. 184-96.

122. Chemnitz, *De Controversiis quibusdam, quae superiori tempore circa quosdam Augustanae Confessionis articulos motae et agitatae sunt, Iudicium D. Martini Chemnitii*, ed. Polycarp Leyser (Wittenberg: Gronenberg, 1594); the chaper on the freedom of the will is found on 20-30, translated in *Sources and Contexts*, 204-8. Also in his exposition of Melanchthon's *Loci communes*, which remained in oral and manuscript form during his lifetime, Chemnitz strove to affirm God's total responsibility for all that happens while insisting that he was not the cause of evil; see Bengt Hägglund, "Wie hat Martin Chemnitz zu Luthers *De servo arbitrio* Stellung genommen?" in *Der zweite Martin der Lutherischen Kirche, Festschrift zum 400. Todestag von Martin Chemnitz*, ed. W. A. Jünke (Brunswick: Ev. Luth. Stadtkirchenverband und Propstei Braunschweig, 1986), 48-59, reprinted in Hägglund,

Chemnitz — Gerhard — Arndt — Rudbeckius. Aufsätze zum Studium der altlutherischen Theologie, ed. Alexander Bitzel and Johann Anselm Steiger (Waltrop: Spenner, 2003), 65-76.

123. Saxony, electoral theologians, *Endlicher Bericht*, Tt4a-Vv1a.

124. *Das der freie Wille nichts sey*, A1a, A2a-b, A4a. Cf. Gallus, *Qvaestio libero arbitrio, qvatenvs illa qvibvsdam nunc disceptatur in Ecclesijs Augustanae Confessionis. Cvm adsertione ex perpetva propheticae et apostolicae scripturae sententia, & ex sententia Lutheri instauratoris doctrinae, authoris & interprecis Augustanae Confessionis* (Regensburg: Heinrich Geissler, 1559), C1b-C3a.

125. WA 18:705.13-14, 711.20-27; *LW* 33:169, 179.

126. WA 18:714.4-6; *LW* 33:183.

127. Cf. WA 18:717.25–719.3; *LW* 33:188-90.

128. Wycliffe disappeared largely from Lutheran use even though late medieval "saints" or "prereformers" such as John Hus and Jerome Savonarola were heralded in the late Reformation as reformers who had paved the way for Luther; see Robert Kolb, "'Saint John Hus' and 'Jerome Savonarola, Confessor of God': The Lutheran 'Canonization' of Late Medieval Martyrs," *Concordia Journal* 17 (1991): 404-18.

129. Kirchner, *Thesavrvs*, 246-47; WA 18:670.19–671.18; *LW* 33:115-17.

130. Kirchner, *Thesavrvs*, 264-65; WA 18:634.14–635.22; *LW* 33:64-66.

131. Herbst, *Vom Freien Willen*, Ll3b-Mm1a. Herbst argued that Luther here made it clear that he did not teach a doctrine of divine coercion of the will.

132. Jena faculty, *Bekentnis Vom Freien Willen*, D3a-b; WA 18:635.7-22; *LW* 33:65-66.

133. Kirchner, *Thesavrvs*, 270; WA 18:745.20–746.12; *LW* 33:229-31.

134. Herbst, *Vom Freien Willen*, Ff2a; WA 18:636.16-21; *LW* 33:67.

135. Gallus, *Erklerung der Religions streite/zu nottu[e]rfftigem vnterricht der Kirche/vnd ablenung falscher Calumnien. Wider die verfelscher der waren Augspurgischen Confession* (Regensburg: Heinrich Geissler, 1559), A2b-B1b.

136. Irenaeus, *Symbolicum Apostolicum*, a2b.

137. Flacius, *Disputatio*, 201-2; WA 18:635.9, 12-14; *LW* 33:65; cf. Kirchner, *Thesavrvs*, 264-65; the Jena faculty, *Bekentnis Vom Freien Willen;* Herbst, *Vom Freien Willen*, Ll3b-Mm1a.

138. Flacius, *Clavis Scriptvrae S.*, pt. 1, p. 571.

139. Comments on Gen. 1:26; WA 42:47.14-22; *LW* 1:63.

140. Flacius, *Bericht M. Fla. Illyrici*, C1a-b.

141. E.g., by Flacius, *Disputatio*, 233; Kirchner, *Thesavrvs*, 255; Herbst, *Vom Freien Willen*, R2b. The Jena theologians mentioned the "Achillean argument" without referring to *De servo arbitrio: Colloqvivm zu Altenburgk*, 491b. See WA 18:783.3-39; *LW* 33:288-89.

142. *Das der freie Wille nichts sey*, A3b-A4a.

143. WA 18:784.9; *LW* 33:290.

144. Chemnitz, *De Controversiis*, 22-25; *Sources and Contexts*, 204-5; cf. WA 42:647; *LW* 3:139.

145. Herbst, *Vom Freien Willen*, Gg3a-b; WA 18:708.31-34; *LW* 33:174-75.

146. Herbst, *Vom Freien Willen*, Gg3b; WA 18:709.21-24; *LW* 33:176.

147. Herbst, *Vom Freien Willen*, Gg3b-Ggb4a; WA 18:707.32–708.13; *LW* 33:173-74.

148. Herbst, *Vom Freien Willen*, Gg4a-Gg4b; WA 18:719.4-22; *LW* 33:190.

149. Herbst, *Vom Freien Willen*, Hh1a-Hh3b; WA 18:784.1–785.38; *LW* 33:289-92.

150. Kirchner, *Thesavrvs*, 262-63; WA 18:784.1–785.38; *LW* 33:289-92.

Notes to Chapter V

1. WA 40.I:139.30–140.7; *LW* 26:71-72.

2. WA 42:313.20-24; *LW* 2:72. Cf. chap. I, pp. 38-43.

3. See chap. IV, n. 5.

4. Indeed, Luther had not used the chief passages which provided the basis for the later Lutheran teaching on God's election of his own people, Rom. 8:28-39 and Eph. 1:3-11, in *De servo arbitrio*, but his argument there could have been employed in examining these passages. It was not. For example, Nikolaus Selnecker avoided any mention of the work in his comments on Rom. 8 and 9 and Eph. 1, even though they formed the basis of the teaching he had helped draft in article XI of the Formula of Concord by the time of their posthumous publication: *Omnes epistolas D. Pavli apostoli Commentarius plenissimus* . . . (Leipzig: Jacob Apelius, 1595), I:175-229 on Rom. 8 and 9 (pp. 205-29 are devoted to a systematic summary of the doctrine), II:2-9 on Eph. 1. Other exegetes in the Wittenberg circle were also able to treat those passages without reference to Luther or his *De servo arbitrio:* Matthias Flacius, *Novvm Testamentvm Iesv Christi* . . . *Glossa compendiaria* . . . (Basel: Peter Perna and Theobald Dietrich, 1570), on Rom. 8 and 9, 703-19; on Eph. 1, 916-25; Tilemann Heshusius, *Explicatio epistolae Pavli ad Romanos* (Jena: Günther Hüttich, 1571), on Rom. 8:28–9:33, 261b-330b (including a systematic discussion of predestination, 271b-308 [= 310]b). See also Erasmus Sarcerius, *In epistolam ad Romanos, pia & erudita scholia* . . . (Frankfurt am Main: Christoph Egenolph, 1541); Johannes Wigand, *In epistolam S. Pavli ad Romanos annotationes* (Frankfurt am Main: Georg Corvinus, 1580); Christoph Körner, *In epistolam D. Pavli ad Romanos scriptus Commentarivs* (Heidelberg: Johannes Spies, 1583); and on Eph. 1, Sarcerius, *In epistolas D. Pavli, ad Galatas et Ephesios, piae atque eruditae Annotationes* . . . (Frankfurt am Main: Christian Egenolph, 1542); Hieronymus Weller, *In Epistolam diui Pauli ad Ephesios, Enarrationes piae, breues & eruditae* (Nuremberg: Johannes Berg and Ulrich Neuber, 1559); Johannes Wigand, *In S. Pavli ad Ephesios epistolam, annotationes* (Erfurt: Isaiah Mechler, 1581).

5. See chap. II, pp. 86-87, above. Cf. Robert Kolb, "The Ordering of the *Loci Communes Theologici:* The Structuring of the Melanchthonian Dogmatic Tradition," *Concordia Journal* 23 (1997): 329-31.

6. Judex bore major responsibility for this section; Heinz Scheible, *Die Entstehung der Magdeburger Zenturien* (Gütersloh: Mohn, 1966), 52.

7. Wigand and Judex, *Syntagma, seu Corpus doctrinae Christi, ex novo testamento tantum* . . . , 2nd ed. (Basel, 1563), 841-50; *SYNTAGMA; sev corpvs doctrinae veri & omnipotentis Dei, ex ueteri Testamento* . . . (Basel, 1564), 952-61.

8. Wigand and Judex, *Syntagma* . . . *ex novo testamento,* 841-46.

9. Wigand and Judex, *Syntagma* . . . *ex novo testamento,* 847-48.

10. Kirchner, *Thesavrvs: explicationvm omnivm articvlorvm ac capitvm, catholicae, orthodoxae, verae, ac piae doctrinae Christianae, quae hac aetate controuersa sunt, ex reuerendi, vereque Dei viri, ac summi Theologi D. Martini Lutheri* . . . *operibus* . . . (Frankfurt am Main: Thomas Rhebart and Sigismund Feierabend, 1566), 353-63. The eight citations come from the Genesis commentary (5), the preface to Romans (1), and comments on Isa. 34 (1) and Ps. 5 (1). In Johann Aurifaber's *Tischreden oder Colloquia doct. Mart. Luthers* . . . (Eisleben: Urban

Gaubisch, 1566), "predestination" or "election" was not listed among the eighty topics; "the free will" was.

11. Walther, *Erste [-Sechste] Theil der Heubtartickel/Christlicher Lere. In Fragstu[e]cken verfasset/vnd mit Gottes Wort/vnd fu[e]rnamen Spru[e]chen D. Lutheri/vnd D. Melanthonis erkleret vnd bekrefftiget . . .* (Magdeburg: Matthaeus Gieseke, 1573). Predestination is treated in *Dritte Theil der Heuptartickel;* see f4b-f5a, a paraphrase and summary of passages in WA 18:615.12-17; *LW* 33:37; and WA 18:622.16–623.5; *LW* 33:47.

12. Walther, *Dritte Theil der Heuptartickel,* g6b-g7b; WA 18:688.27–689.17; *LW* 33:145-46.

13. Walther, *Dritte Theil der Heuptartickel,* i1b-i2b; WA 18:618.19–619.21; *LW* 33:42-43.

14. Richard Muller, *Christ and the Decree: Christology and Predestination in Reformed Theology from Calvin to Perkins* (Durham: Labyrinth, 1986), 111.

15. See in addition to Muller, *Christ and the Decree,* esp. 110-25, Christopher J. Burchill, "Girolamo Zanchi: Portrait of a Reformed Theologian and His Work," *SCJ* 15 (1984): 185-207, esp. 194-99; John Patrick Donnelly, S.J., "Calvinist Thomism," *Viator* 7 (1976): 441-55; Donnelly, "Italian Influences on the Development of Calvinist Scholasticism," *SCJ* 7, no. 2 (1976): 81-101; Jürgen Moltmann, *Prädestination und Perseveranz, Geschichte und Bedeutung der reformierten Lehre "de perseverantia sanctorum"* (Neukirchen: Neukirchener Verlag, 1961), 72-109, esp. on the roots of the dispute, 75-91; and Otto Gründler, *Die Gotteslehre Girolamo Zanchi und ihre Bedeutung für seine Lehre von der Prädestination* (Neukirchen: Neukirchener Verlag, 1965).

16. WA 39.II:204-32.

17. On Marbach and the general situation in Strasbourg, see James M. Kittelson, *Toward an Established Church: Strasbourg from 1500 to the Dawn of the Seventeenth Century* (Mainz: Zabern, 2000), esp. 63-137; Kittelson, "Marbach vs. Zanchi: The Resolution of Controversy in Late Reformation Strasbourg," *SCJ* 8, no. 3 (1977): 31-44; and Lorna Jane Abray, *The People's Reformation: Magistrates, Clergy, and Commons in Strasbourg, 1500-1598* (Ithaca, N.Y.: Cornell University Press, 1985). On Sturm, including his relationship to Marbach, see Lewis W. Spitz and Barbara Sher Tinsley, *Johann Sturm on Education: The Reformation and Humanist Learning* (Saint Louis: Concordia, 1995). See also Walter Sohm, *Die Schule Johann Sturms und die Kirche Strassburgs in ihrem gegenseitigen Verhältnis 1530-1581* (Munich and Berlin: Oldenbourg, 1912), on the dispute between Marbach and Zanchi, 161-236.

18. Some details of the deteriorating relationship are portrayed from Zanchi's side in his correspondence with Calvin, recited by Joseph N. Tylenda, "Girolamo Zanchi and John Calvin: A Study in Discipleship as Seen through Their Correspondence," *Calvin Theological Journal* 10 (1975): 101-40. Moltmann, *Prädestination,* 75, asserts that Marbach was responsible for the appearance of "an unexpected and continuing disagreement between Calvinism and Lutheranism," ignoring the tensions between Melanchthon and Calvin over predestination twenty years earlier; see chap. II, n. 79, above. That he probably had not read the sources is suggested also by Moltmann's labeling Marbach's view that of "the semipelagian-appearing theology of the late Melanchthon" ("Bei [Zanchi's] lutherischen Gegner findet sich die semipelagianisch erscheinende Theologie des späten Melanchthon vermehrt im Züge gnesiolutherischer Sakramentstheologie"), p. 82.

19. Heshusius, *De praesentia corporis Christi in Coena Domini. Contra Sacramentarios* (Jena: Richtzenhan, 1560).

20. Cited by Moltmann, *Prädestination*, 72. See Willem van't Spijker, "Bucer als Zeuge Zanchis im Straßburger Prädestinationsstreit," in *Das Reformiertes Erbe, Festschrift für Gottfried W. Locher zu seinem 80. Geburtstag*, ed. Heiko A. Oberman et al. (= *Zwingliana* 19 [1991, 1992]), 2:327-42.

21. Throughout his "De Praedestinatione sanctorum . . . Confessio," presented to the Strasbourg senate, Zanchi cited extensively from Luther, particularly but not exclusively from *De servo arbitrio*, as well as from Bucer, from Brenz, and occasionally from Melanchthon's *Loci communes* of 1521; see Zanchi's *Opervm Theologicorvm Tomus Septimus* . . . ([Geneva]: Petrus Aubertus, 1613), 282-388; cf. also 251-56; cf. WA 18:615.31-33; *LW* 33:37-38; and WA 18:619.1-3; *LW* 33:42, cited by Moltmann, *Prädestination*, 83.

22. Tylenda, "Girolamo Zanchi," 123-24.

23. Muller, *Christ and the Decree*, 110-25.

24. Burchill aptly notes that his position was much like that finally expressed in FC XI; Burchill, "Girolamo Zanchi," 194.

25. Kittelson, *Toward an Established Church*, 101-3.

26. Moltmann, *Prädestination*, 83-89, and Kittelson, *Toward an Established Church*, 99-106.

27. Kittelson, *Toward an Established Church*, 64-66, and "The Significance of Humanist Educational Methods for Reformation Theology," *LuJ* 66 (1999): 229-36. Kittelson ("The Significance," 235) finds that Melanchthon's treatment of predestination was "foreign both to his student and to the 'Formula of Concord'" because "for Melanchthon, predestination was a pastoral elaboration on the bondage of the will, while for his student [Marbach] it concerned the hidden and revealed will of God." Indeed, by the time Marbach studied with Melanchthon, predestination was more a stumbling block to proper pastoral care than a pastoral elaboration on the bondage of the will for the Preceptor. For Marbach, as for Luther, it served indeed as a pastoral elaboration of the bondage of the will, but one that had to be used carefully.

28. See Zanchi's summary of their dispute, *Tomus Septimus*, 2:207-454.

29. Kittelson, *Toward an Established Church*, 106-7. Flinsbach was an associate of Marbach, Andreae a committed Lutheran, and Sultzer was viewed by many as having Lutheran leanings; see Hans Guggisberg, *Basel in the Sixteenth Century: Aspects of the City Republic before, during, and after the Reformation* (Saint Louis: Center for Reformation Research, 1982), 45-47.

30. Georg Biundo, *Die evangelischen Geistlichen der Pfalz seit der Reformation (Pfälzisches Pfarrerbuch)* (Neustadt an der Aisch: Degener, 1968), 119.

31. The date was important in view of the controversy over whether the original text of the confession's tenth article was valid or whether the revised version of 1540 (the *Confessio Augustana Variata*) could be used as a proper interpretation of its text. In 1561 the assembly of evangelical princes had struggled with this question and came to at best an ambiguous answer. At the request of Elector Johann Friedrich and apparently with the approval of his colleagues, Melanchthon had updated the confession in 1540: its adherents regarded the 1530 text as a working paper in the decade after he had composed it, and not a sacred and inalterable text. Later views of confessional documents had not yet been established. This retooled statement of what the Protestant estates confessed served as an agenda for colloquy with Roman Catholics, and in 1540 the Saxon elector, along with his colleagues and theological advis-

ers, wanted to sharpen the presentation in its Latin version. In elaborating the Wittenberg position on a number of articles, Melanchthon had changed the wording on the Lord's Supper to reflect the Wittenberg Concord of 1536; he held that the body of Christ is present *"cum pane,"* and substituted the word *exhibere*, which meant not only to show or present but also to deliver or give, for "are truly present and distributed" in the sentence "Concerning the Lord's Supper [the evangelical churches] teach that the body and blood of Christ are truly present and are distributed to those who eat the Lord's Supper" (*BSLK*, 64-65; *Book of Concord*, 44/45). This alteration had not become a theological issue until Elector Friedrich III of the Palatinate wanted to use it as a cover for his introduction of Calvinism in his lands. Then he pressed for a recognition of the "Altered Augsburg Confession" of 1540 as the official version, so that under the terms of the Religious Peace of Augsburg (1555) his Calvinist beliefs would be legal. Lutherans protested, but at Naumburg in 1561 both versions were recognized. The most complete treatment of the Naumburg diet remains Robert Calinich, *Der Naumburger Fürstentag, 1561* (Gotha: Perthes, 1870).

32. "Consensus inter theologos et professores in ecclesia et scholia Argentoratensi factus A.D. MDLXIII die 18. Martii," *CR* 47; *Calvini Opera*, 19:671-75.

33. *CR* 47:672-74.

34. Burchill, "Girolamo Zanchi," 195-99; Tylenda, "Girolamo Zanchi," 128-36.

35. On Palhöfer see Martin Bauer, *Evangelische Theologen in und um Erfurt im 16. bis 18. Jahrhundert* (Neustadt an der Aisch: Degener, 1992), 246. Dinckel, former student in Erfurt and at the time superintendent in Coburg (see Bauer, 129), published Palhöfer's two writings together under the title, *Zwey notwendige nu[e]zliche Lehr vnd Trostbu[e]chlein. Das Erste/Von der Ewigen Vorsehung des Menschen/in Christo Jesu zum ewigen Leben/Kurtzer Bericht auß Gottes Wort/welchem D. M. Lutherus/vnd alle reine Lehrer Zeugnus geben. Das Andere/Wider diese Proposition: Das Gott nicht alle Menschen wo[e]lle selig werden*, ed. Johannes Dinckel (Coburg: Valentin Kröner, 1593). Dinckel believed that Palhöfer's position was that of the Formula of Concord, which does teach particular election; see FC SD XI:23, 54; *BSLK*, 1070, 1079; *Book of Concord*, 644, 649.

36. E.g., in the second of his treatises, in *Zwey notwendige nu[e]zliche Lehr vnd Trostbu[e]chlein*, 94-97. Page numbers from the second treatise appear in parentheses in the following text.

37. Palhöfer, *Zwey notwendige nu[e]zliche Lehr vnd Trostbu[e]chlein*, 46-48, 92-93. Cf. WA 18:679.23-29; *LW* 33:130.

38. See pp. 265-66 below.

39. Karl Heussi, *Geschichte der theologischen Fakultät zu Jena* (Weimar: Böhlau, 1954), 70-74. Compare the judgment of the counselor in Pfalz-Neuburg, Wolfgang von Kötteritz, who reported to Johann Marbach on Jan. 1, 1568, "Deus mirabiliter vindicat nunc injurias & persecutiones D. Ilyrico illatas. Nam certum est, quod Dux Saxoniae, Wilhelmus, serio coepit reformare Ecclesias suas & Scholas, contaminatas fermento Victorini & Stosselii. Nam *Juristen boe[e]se Christen.* D. Dangel & D. Dürfeld, defensores corruptelarum, cum indignatione dimisit, Stosselium vero & Selneccerum ob officio deposuit & obligavit, ne pedem moverent." Johann Fecht, ed., *Historiae ecclesiasticae seculi A.N.C. XVI. Supplementum; plurimorum et celeberrimorum ex illo aevo theologorum epistolis, ad Joannem, Erasmum et Philippum, Marbachios . . .* (Durlach: Martin Muller, 1684), 219. On Selnecker see Werner Klän, "Der 'vierte Mann'. Auf den Spuren von Nikolaus Selnecker (1530-1592). Beitrag zu

Entstehung und Verbreitung der Konkordienformel," *Lutherische Theologie und Kirche* 17 (1993): 145-74.

40. Selnecker, *Doctrina de praedestinatione, Item de fato qvaedam vtilia et necessaria* (Frankfurt am Main: Peter Brubach, 1565).

41. Selnecker, *Paedagogia christiana, continens capita et locos doctrinae Christianae, forma & serie catechetica uerē & perspicuē explicata . . .* (1565; Frankfurt am Main: Peter Brubach, 1567), 911-34. The observation of Rune Söderlund, *Ex praevisa Fide. Zum Verständnis der Prädestinationslehre in der lutherischen Orthodoxie* (Hannover: Lutherisches Verlagshaus, 1983), that Selnecker taught a "rationalizing" doctrine of predestination that did not follow a strict law/gospel distinction is true for this work. It is not true for Selnecker's later treatment; see n. 42.

42. Selnecker, *Institvtionis Christianae religionis, pars secvnda, continens locos doctrinae Christianae . . .* (Jena: Jakob Tröster, 1579), 338. The entire text of the note reads: "Peccatum in spiritum sanctum est hominem peccando cum Deo ludere, & ira vndique sententia legis diuinae constrictum teneri, vt, quo euadat, nesciat, sed ipse sese reum aeternae damnationis pronunciet, quod mihi misero nunc accidit, vt aeternis damnationibus addictus detrudar ad non finienda tartara: externa sanctitate Deum fallere non possumus. O me infeliciβimum omnium, qui satius fuisset, me unquam natum. Verum est, certum esse numerum saluandorum. Hoc ex me: sed quid ad me? hoc ita necessario fieri debuit. Ego sum ex numero damnatorum, & nunquam Deo asscribi possum, damnatus ab initio. Vado igitur aeternum dedecus patriae, figmentum & vas formatum in ignominiam. Omnium peccatorum me aggressa est magnitudo, & horror Diaboli. Discedo ad claus infernales. Deo vos commendo, cuius misericordia mihi negata est. Occultior autem est huius rei causa, quam vt humana ratio perspicere poβit, &c. Perditiβimus P.I. subscripsit ipse." Cf. the report on the incident in Andreas Celichius, *Nu[e]tzlicher vnd notwendiger bericht/Von den Leuten/so sich selbst aus angstverzweiffelung/oder andern vrsachen/entleiben vnd hinrichten* (Magdeburg: Wolffgang Kirchner, 1578), E5a-b: "Also ists auch Anno 1562. mit einem Schulmeister ergangen/welcher aus Angstuerzweifelung sein Henckermeister geworden/vnd hat in einer hinterlassenen schrifft diese Lesterwort gesetzt/er were von Ewigkeit her zum Verdamniss predestiniert vnd verordnet/dru[e]mb mu[e]ste er auch nun seine Hellefart halten/vnd verloren sein." "P.I." is identified as Petrus Ilesuanus in the work by the Saxon electoral theologians, *Endlicher Bericht vnd Erklerung der Theologen beider Vniuersiteten/Leipzig vnd Wittemberg Auch der Superintendenten der Kirchen in des Churfu[e]rsten zu Sachsen Landen/belangend die Lere . . .* (Wittenberg: Hans Lufft, 1570), 188a. See also the comments on the association of a Calvinist doctrine of predestination with melancholy and suicide by later sixteenth- and seventeenth-century Lutheran theologians by Winfried Schleiner, *Melancholy, Genius, and Utopia in the Renaissance* (Wiesbaden: Harrassowitz, 1991), 74-75. On p. 74 Schleiner implies that the charge of "crypto-Calvinism" included the attribution of a doctrine of double predestination to the electoral Saxon theologians. In fact, all their contemporaries recognized that the Saxon "crypto-Calvinists" of the 1570s held synergistic views on the bondage or freedom of the will. See above, chap. VII, n. 10.

43. Celichius, *Nu[e]tzlicher vnd notwendiger bericht*, P6b-S5v.

44. Selnecker, *Institvtionis Christianae religionis, pars secvnda*, 338.

45. Selnecker, *Doctrina de praedestinatione*, 3.

46. Selnecker, *Doctrina de praedestinatione*, 3-5. Selnecker used the third edition of

Melanchthon's *Loci communes theologici* quite directly to fashion his seven *regulae*. Only the fifth *regula* is not expressly stated in its locus in *De praedestinatione*, but Selnecker conveyed Melanchthon's point of view also with that rule. In fact, most of the Bible passages he cited also come from his preceptor's discussion of the topic. He also repeated Melanchthon's fundamental concerns: to warn against speculation in regard to this doctrine, to avoid assigning God the responsibility for evil, to anchor any discussion of predestination firmly in the promise of God conveyed in the means of grace, and to bring comfort to despairing consciences. See *CR* 22:913-16.

47. Selnecker, *Doctrina de praedestinatione*, 5.

48. Selnecker, *Doctrina de praedestinatione*, 5-6.

49. Selnecker ignored Luther's translation of this verse, "Welcher wil/das allen Menschen geholffen werde/vnd zur erkentnis der warheit komen," and followed the Vulgate, "Vult enim Deus omnes homines saluos fieri." See chap. I, n. 136.

50. Selnecker, *Doctrina de praedestinatione*, 6-7.

51. *CR* 22:919; Melanchthon developed this interpretation in the several editions of his commentary on Romans, see, e.g., *StA* 5:257-58 (1532); *CR* 15:684 (1540); *CR* 15:981 (1556). See also Robert Kolb, "Melanchthon's Influence on the Exegesis of His Students: The Case of Romans 9," in *Philip Melanchthon (1497-1560) and the Commentary*, ed. M. Patrick Graham and Timothy J. Wengert (Sheffield: Sheffield Academic Press, 1997), 210.

52. Selnecker, *Doctrina de praedestinatione*, 7-8.

53. Selnecker, *Doctrina de praedestinatione*, 8.

54. Selnecker, *Doctrina de praedestinatione*, 8-9.

55. Selnecker, *Doctrina de praedestinatione*, 9.

56. Selnecker, *Doctrina de praedestinatione*, 9-10.

57. Melanchthon based the believer's comfort on membership in the assembly of the called, the church, gathered around the ministry of the gospel. Secondly, comfort is to be found in God's promise that he will never separate his choosing of his people from the call in the means of grace. Thirdly, believers take comfort in knowing that God is present in the visible assembly where his call is repeated through the means of grace. He then rephrased his expressions of comfort by pointing to the faith in Christ which the church produces and to the fact that the cause of God's choice of his people lies not in the law but in God's mercy in Christ; *CR* 22:917-18.

58. *CR* 22:919-20.

59. This definition was used in the Formula of Concord, SD XI:6-7; *BSLK*, 1065-66; *Book of Concord*, 642, and comes originally from Prosper of Aquitaine; see n. 75 below.

60. Selnecker, *Doctrina de praedestinatione*, 10-12.

61. Selnecker, *Doctrina de praedestinatione*, 12-13.

62. Selnecker, *Doctrina de praedestinatione*, 13-23.

63. See the citation from his fellow student and later Rostock colleague, Lucas Backmeister, in his funeral sermon for Chytraeus of 1600, as given by Rudolf Keller, "David Chytraeus (1530-1600). Melanchthons Geist im Luthertum," in *Melanchthon in seinen Schüler*, ed. Heinz Scheible (Wiesbaden: Harrassowitz, 1997), 362 n. 3.

64. Rudolf Keller, *Die Confessio Augustana im theologischen Wirken des Rostocker Professors David Chyträus (1530-1600)* (Göttingen: Vandenhoeck & Ruprecht, 1994), 132-57.

65. Rudolf Keller has accumulated evidence on this point, *Confessio Augustana*, 119-32.

See also Chytraeus's statement that God had led him to the knowledge of his Word through both Luther and Melanchthon, as cited in Thomas Kaufmann, *Universität und lutherische Konfessionalisierung. Die Rostocker Theologieprofessoren und ihr Beitrag zur theologischen Bildung und kirchlichen Gestaltung im Herzogtum Mecklenburg zwischen 1550 und 1675* (Gütersloh: Gütersloher Verlagshaus, 1997), 264.

66. Keller, *Confessio Augustana,* 134-41.

67. Green, "The Three Causes of Conversion in Philipp Melanchthon, Martin Chemnitz, David Chytraeus, and the 'Formula of Concord,'" *LuJ* 47 (1980): 89-114. Green does not discuss *necessitas.*

68. Chytraeus, *Piae & vtilliss. explicationes vocabvlorvm: Necessitatis. Determinationis Diuinae. Fati. Contingentiae. Virivm hvmanarvm. Liberi arbitrii* (Rostock: Jacobus Transylvanus, 1565).

69. Martin Helsing returned to Sweden with Melanchthon's recommendation after receiving a master of arts degree in Wittenberg in 1550. After serving as rector of the school in Uppsala and court preacher for King Erik XIV, he became superintendent in Gävle in 1562 and bishop of Linköping in 1569. Deposed in 1571 for his opposition to the catholicizing tendencies of King Johann III and the Counter-Reformation activities of Antonio Possevino, S.J., in Sweden, he supported the revolt of Karl IX and became pastor in Nyköping in 1580, dying in 1585 or 1587. See *Förteckning på Biskopar i Sverige och Finland* (Christianstad: Cedergréen, 1830), 8; *Upsala Ärkestifts Herdaminne* (Uppsala: Wahlström & Lästrom, 1842), 447-48; and Johann Israel Håhl, *Linköpings Stifts Herdaminne* (Norköping: Östlund & Berling, 1846), 20-21.

70. Michael Roberts, *The Early Vasas: A History of Sweden, 1523-1611* (Cambridge: University Press, 1968), 174-75. See also Sven Kjöllerström, *Striden kring kalvinismen i Sverige under Erik XIV* (Lund: Gleerup, 1935).

71. According to *Fortsetzung und Erga[e]nzungen zu Christian Gottlieb Jo[e]chers allgemeinen Gelehrten-Lexico,* ed. Johann Christoph Adelung, 2 (Leipzig: Gleditsch, 1787), 1897; it was entitled *Epistola ad Archiepiscopum Laurensium de Calvino et Beza religionisque Calvinianae progressu in Helvetia . . .* and was published in 1559.

72. It is inconclusive but interesting that in Calvin's *Institutes of the Christian Religion* 1.16.9, the terms Chytraeus analyzed in his tract, *necessitas, determinatio, eventus* (a synonym for *fatum*), and *providentia,* are discussed, and in a manner that is opposed to Chytraeus's view; *CR* 30; *Ioannis Calvini Opera,* ed. Wilhelm Baum et al., II (Brunswick: Schwetschke, 1864), 152-53; Calvin, *Institutes of the Christian Religion,* ed. John T. McNeill, trans. Ford Lewis Battles, Library of Christian Classics 20 (Philadelphia: Westminster, 1960), 208-10.

73. Chytraeus, *Piae & vtilliss,* A1b. The page references in the following text are to this work.

74. See chap. I, pp. 26-27, above.

75. Prosper of Aquitaine, *Pro Augusto Responsiones ad Capitula Gallorum; PL* 51:167-70, 174.

76. Chytraeus, *Piae & vtilliss,* B7a-C1a. In 1595, in comments on the dispute between Samuel Huber and Aegidius Hunnius, Chytraeus repeated his rejection of Luther's assertion of divine necessity in *De servo arbitrio;* see Gottfried Adam, *Der Streit um die Prädestination im ausgehenden 16. Jahrhundert, eine Untersuchung zu den Entwürfen vom Samuel Huber und Aegidius Hunnius* (Neukirchen: Neukirchener Verlag, 1970), 184-85.

77. See chap. II, pp. 86-87.

78. Although neither Chytraeus nor Selnecker practiced astrology as had Melanchthon and some of his students, they did not remove this from the list of definitions they found in the Preceptor's work.

79. Chytraeus, *Piae & vtilliss,* C3b-C8b. The page references in the following text are to this work.

80. *Von der Freiheit eines Christenmenschen;* WA 7:26-73; *LW* 31:333-77.

81. *Defense and Explanation of All Articles,* 1521; WA 7:444.30–451.7; *LW* 32:92-94.

Notes to Chapter VI

1. Cyriakus Spangenberg, *De praedestinatione. Von der Ewigen Vorsehung/vnd Go[e]tlichen/Gnadenwahl. Sieben Predigten* (Erfurt: Georg Bawman, 1567). A second edition with the same title was published in Eisleben by Andreas Petri in 1568.

2. Robert Kolb, *Martin Luther as Prophet, Teacher, and Hero: Images of the Reformer, 1520-1620* (Grand Rapids: Baker, 1999), esp. 46-55.

3. Cyriakus Spangenberg, *Der Briefwechsel des M. Cyriacus Spangenberg,* ed. Heinrich Rembe (Dresden: Naumann, 1887), 1:2-3; *CR* 7: 644-45, #4773, *MBW* #5879.

4. See Irene Dingel, *Concordia controversa, Die öffentlichen Diskussionen um das lutherische Konkordienwerk am Ende des 16. Jahrhunderts* (Gütersloh: Gütersloher Verlagshaus, 1996), esp. 468-92, and Robert Kolb, "The Flacian Rejection of the Concordia: Prophetic Style and Action in the German Late Reformation," *ARG* 73 (1982): 196-217.

5. Oliver K. Olson, "The Rise and Fall of the Antwerp Martinists," *LQ* 1 (1987): 105-11.

6. Spangenberg registered his views in his report on their meeting, *Colloqvivm So den 9. Septembris des 1577. Jars zu Sangerhausen/Zwischen D. Jacob Andreen vnd M. Cyriacum Spangenberg gehalten worden* (n.p., 1578). Spangenberg appraised Andreae's treatment of another adherent of Flacius, Tobias Rupp, as much the same, when he edited the report of their meeting, *Von dem Lindauwischen Colloquio/zwischen Doctor Jacob Andreen/vnd Herrn Tobia Ruppio/Anno 1575. Im Augusto gehalten* (n.p., 1577). The former work has been edited by Helmut Neumaier: Cyriakus Spangenberg, "Jakob Andreae im Streit mit Cyriakus Spangenberg — Quellen zur Disputation von Sangerhausen 1577," *Blätter für württembergische Kirchengeschichte* 95 (1995): 49-88. On the underground lay defense of Spangenberg's ideas in Mansfeld after his exile, see Robert J. Christman, "Heretics in Luther's Homeland: The Controversy over Original Sin in Late Sixteenth-Century Mansfeld" (Ph.D. dissertation, University of Arizona, 2004).

7. Wilhelm Hotz, "Cyriakus Spangenbergs Leben und Schicksale als Pfarrer in Schlitz von 1580-1590," *Beiträge zur Hessischen Kirchengeschichte. Ergänzungsband III zum Archiv für Hessische Geschichte und Altertumskunde,* n.s., 1908, 205-96.

8. See Robert Kolb, "Philipp's Foes but Followers Nonetheless: Late Humanism among the Gnesio-Lutherans," in *The Harvest of Humanism in Central Europe: Essays in Honor of Lewis W. Spitz,* ed. Manfred P. Fleischer (Saint Louis: Concordia, 1992), 168-74. On the *Adelspiegel,* see H. C. Erik Midelfort, "The German Nobility and Their Crisis of Legitimacy in the Late Sixteenth Century," in *Germania Illustrata: Essays on Early Modern Germany Presented to Gerald Strauss,* ed. Andrew C. Fix and Susan C. Karant-Nunn (Kirksville, Mo.: Sixteenth Century Journal, 1992), 217-42; Robert Kolb, "Cyriakus Spangenberg's Adelspiegel: A

Theologian's View of the Duties of the Nobleman," in *Social Groups and Religious Ideas in the Sixteenth Century*, ed. Miriam U. Chrisman and Otto Gründler (Kalamazoo, Mich.: Medieval Institute, 1977), 12-21; and Kolb, "'A Beautiful, Delightful Jewel': Cyriakus Spangenberg's Plan for the Sixteenth Century Noble's Library," *Journal of Library History* 24 (1979): 129-59.

9. Irene Dingel, "'Recht glauben, Christlich leben, und seliglich sterben,' die Leichenpredigt als evangelische Verkündigung im 16. Jahrhundert," in *Leichenpredigten als Quellen historischer Wissenschaft*, vol. 4, ed. Rudolf Lenz (Stuttgart: Frommann-Holzboog, 2004), 9-36.

10. Miriam Ussher Chrisman, *Lay Culture, Learned Culture, Books and Social Change in Strasbourg, 1480-1599* (New Haven: Yale University Press, 1982), 242. Cf. Robert Kolb, "Learning to Drink from the Fountains of Israel: Cyriakus Spangenberg Learns Hermeneutics from Luther," "On Eternal Predestination and God's Election by Grace: The Exegetical Basis of the Lutheran Teaching in Cyriakus Spangenberg's Commentary on Romans 8 and 9," and "Preaching and Hearing in Luther's Congregations: Village Pastors and Peasant Congregations," all in *Lutheran Synod Quarterly* 34 (1994): 2-31, 32-59, 60-91, respectively, with abridged versions of the first and third essays in *Luther's Heirs*, chap. 13.

11. Particularly important background can be found in his commentary on the first eight chapters of Romans: *Auslegung der Ersten Acht Capitel der Episteln S. Pavli an die Ro[e]mer* (Strasbourg: Samuel Emmel, 1566); chap. 8 addresses the topic of God's election of his own. The sermons on the last eight chapters appeared three years later, in 1569: *Auslegung der Letsten Acht Capitel der Episteln S. PAVLI an die Ro[e]mer* (Strasbourg, 1569), and contained the seven sermons on predestination originally published in 1567. They formed an appendix to an extensive exposition of Rom. 9, also a chapter that requires a discussion of predestination.

12. Cyriakus Spangenberg, *Die erste vnd andere Episteln des heyligen Apostels S. Pauli an die Thessalonicher . . .* (1557; Strasbourg: Samuel Emmel, 1564), 25a-b. Subsequent references are to this work.

13. Melanchthon's 1540 commentary on Romans; *CR* 15:668-74.

14. Cyriakus Spangenberg, *Auslegung der Ersten Acht Capitel*, 325a-328a. The page references in the following text are to this work.

15. Cyriakus Spangenberg, *Auslegung der Ersten Acht Capitel*, 348b-349b.

16. Cyriakus Spangenberg, *Auslegung der Ersten Acht Capitel*, 350b.

17. E.g., in his Romans commentary of 1556; *CR* 15:977.

18. Cyriakus Spangenberg, *Auslegung der Letsten Acht Capitel*, 140b; cf. 131a.

19. Cyriakus Spangenberg, *Auslegung der Ersten Acht Capitel*, 251a.

20. Cyriakus Spangenberg, *Auslegung der Letsten Acht Capitel*, 211b.

21. Cyriakus Spangenberg, *Auslegung der Letsten Acht Capitel*, 130b-131a.

22. Cyriakus Spangenberg, *Auslegung der Ersten Acht Capitel*, 351a.

23. Cyriakus Spangenberg, *Auslegung der Ersten Acht Capitel*, 348b-353a. Cf. Bernard's "Sermo 78" of his *Sermones in Cantica Canticorum*; *PL* 183:1159-62.

24. Cyriakus Spangenberg, *Auslegung der Ersten Acht Capitel*, 353b-357a.

25. Cyriakus Spangenberg, *Auslegung der Ersten Acht Capitel*, 358a-363a.

26. Cyriakus Spangenberg, *Apologia Bericht vnd Erklerung M. Cyria. Spangenberg: Der Sieben Predigten halben/von der Praedestination: Go[e]ttlichen Versehung/vnd Ewigen Gnadenwahl in Druck geben* (Eisleben: Andreas Petri, 1568). In a letter of Dec. 27, 1567, to Countess Dorothea of Mansfeld, Spangenberg wrote of the necessity of issuing such a defense; *Briefwechsel*, 1:48-49.

27. Cyriakus Spangenberg, *Apologia*, B4v-B5a.

28. Cyriakus Spangenberg, *De praedestinatione*, B7a-C5a.

29. Cyriakus Spangenberg, *De praedestinatione*, C2a-b; WA 18:719.9-12; *LW* 33:190.

30. Cyriakus Spangenberg, *De praedestinatione*, C3a-C5b.

31. Cyriakus Spangenberg, *Apologia*, C2a-C3b. References in the following text are to this work.

32. Cyriakus Spangenberg, *Briefwechsel*, 1:38.

33. Cyriakus Spangenberg, *De praedestinatione*, R2a-b; Augustine, N8a-b; Theodulus, N8a-O1a. Patristic argumentation occurred often in Spangenberg's preaching; see Robert Kolb, "Patristic Citation as Homiletical Tool in the Vernacular Sermon of the German Late Reformation," in *Die Patristik in der Bibelexegese des 16. Jahrhunderts*, ed. David C. Steinmetz (Wiesbaden: Harrassowitz, 1999), 151-79.

34. Cyriakus Spangenberg, *Ausslegung der Ersten Acht Capitel*, xb-xiiija. See Kolb, "Learning to Drink from the Fountains of Israel," in *Luther's Heirs*, 13:3-12.

35. Cyriakus Spangenberg, *De praedestinatione*, D1b; cf. N4b-N6b, N8a-O1a.

36. Cyriakus Spangenberg, *Apologia*, B8a-C2a.

37. Cyriakus Spangenberg, *De praedestinatione*, D1b-D2a; cf. N6b-N8a.

38. Cyriakus Spangenberg, *De praedestinatione*, D2a; cf. D5a-b, G4a-b. Melanchthon expressed concern over Calvin's use of philosophy to defend his doctrine of double predestination; see Timothy J. Wengert, "'We Will Feast Together in Heaven Forever': The Epistolary Friendship of John Calvin and Philip Melanchthon," in *Melanchthon in Europe: His Work and Influence beyond Wittenberg*, ed. Karin Maag (Grand Rapids: Baker, 1999), 26-33.

39. Cyriakus Spangenberg, *De praedestinatione*, D2a.

40. Cyriakus Spangenberg, *De praedestinatione*, O4b-P1a. Cf. G1b, N1b-N2b. WA Br 10:488-95, #3956. The Formula of Concord affirmed this position, SD XI:28; *BSLK*, 1071-72; and *Book of Concord*, 645.

41. Cyriakus Spangenberg, *De praedestinatione*, D2a-D3a.

42. Cyriakus Spangenberg, *De praedestinatione*, D3a-b.

43. Cyriakus Spangenberg, *De praedestinatione*, D7a. "Die Go[e]tliche versehung/ dauon wir jetzt dieses orts reden/Jst ein ewiger/gewieser/vnwandelbarer/krefftiger rhat vnd beschlus bey Gott/aus dem gantzen Menschlichen Geschlecht einen treflichen hauffen/ welche Er wil/nach seinem wolgefallen Gerecht/Selig/vnd herrlich zu machen."

44. Cyriakus Spangenberg, *De praedestinatione*, D7a-b. "So ist dieselbige ein gewiser beschlossener rhat bey GOTT/von zuku[e]nfftigen dingen/wie er entweder das gute schaffen/fortsetzen vnd erhalten/Oder dagegen das bo[e]se straffen/wehren/hindern/vnd zu nicht machen wolle/Wie er sich dessen in seinem Wort ausdrucklich verkleret/daraus man erkennen kan/seine vnuerdiente Gnade vnd gu[e]te gegen die/so da selig werden sollen/Vnd hinwider seine ernste vnd strenge Gerechtigkeit gegen die/so da sollen verdampt werden/vnd also allenthalben seine Almechtigkeit vnd vnermesliche gewalt in gnediger wolthat vnd gerechter straffe erscheine. Es ist der endliche vnd bestendige Beschlus bey Gott/dardurch er seine auserwelten von den andern bey jhm selbst absondert/zu deme/das den andern/von welchen er solches nicht beschlossen hat/nicht widerfehret. Denn Gott hat alhie die freye/ vngebundene/vngezwungene Wahle/das er erwehlet welche Er wil/vnd dieselbigen erwehleten seinem Son JHesu Christo schencket/sie zum ewigen leben zu bringen/welchem HErrn Christo niemand diese erwehleten vnd geschenckten aus seiner hand kan reissen/Dagegen

den andern/die nicht erwehlet sind/nach Go[e]tlicher Gerechtigkeit die ewige verdamnus vnd das Hellische fewer bereitet ist/wie CHristus selbst sagt/Matt. Am 25."

45. Cyriakus Spangenberg, *De praedestinatione*, F1a-F2b. References in the following text are to *De praedestinatione*.

46. WA 18:706.13-23; *LW* 33:171.

47. WA DB 7:22.26-39, 24.1-10 (1522), and 23.26-39, 25.1-10 (1546).

48. Cf. the same material treated in greater detail in the fourth sermon, H6b-K7a.

49. WA 18:615.13-14; *LW* 33:37.

50. See p. 193 above.

51. *Mammeluke* is a term derived from an Arabic word for slave and used in sixteenth-century German for apostates or defectors.

52. Cyriakus Spangenberg, *De praedestinatione*, M3b-M7b. Remigius, *Enarrationes in Psalmos;* PL 131:153B; cf. Augustine, *Contra Julianum* 6.3; PL 44:824.

53. Cyriakus Spangenberg, *De praedestinatione*, F8b-G1a.

54. Cyriakus Spangenberg, *De praedestinatione*, F3a-F6a. Spangenberg called upon Augustine, *De correptione et gratia* 13; PL 44:940-42, and Bede, *In Lucae Evangelium Expositio;* PL 92:383B, for support.

55. Cyriakus Spangenberg, *De praedestinatione*, C5b-D1b. Spangenberg cited Luther's sermon on 2 Pet. 2:10; WA 14:23.11–26.5, paraphrased, and his preface to Romans regarding Rom. 9; WA Bib 7:22.26-39, 24.1-10 (1522), and 23.26-39, 25.1-10 (1546), as well as Augustine, *De bono perseuerantiae* 14; PL 45:1013-16.

56. WA TR 6:39-41, #6961; WA Br 11:165-66.

57. Cyriakus Spangenberg, *Apologia*, B6b-B8b.

58. Cyriakus Spangenberg, *De praedestinatione*, E8a. "Die gnedige versehung ist der vnwandelbare fursatz Gottes/die jenigen so er in Christo Jhesu seinem Son erwelet hat vnd geliebet/zu beruffen/gerecht zu machen/zu heiligen/zu riegeren/vnd letztlich auch zur Herrligkeit zuerheben/vnd damit den reichtumb seiner grossen gu[e]te vnd Herrligkeit kundt zu machen. Widerumb ist die ernste verwerffung vnd reprobatio/auch der vnwandelbare fursatz GOttes/die andern/so er nicht erwehlet/in jrer art zu lassen/vnd vmb jhrer vngerechtigkeit willen endlich mit ewiger pein zu straffen/dadurch seinen gerechten zorn zu erzeigen/vnd seine macht kundt zu thun."

59. Cyriakus Spangenberg, *De praedestinatione*, L3b. "In der Erwelung verordnet Gott die mittel/schaffet/vbet/vnd treibet auch dieselbigen/dadurch die Auserwelten zur gerechtigkeit/vnd denn fo[e]rder zur Herrligkeit komen mo[e]gen. In der verwerffung aber hat er wol beschlossen/das er die Gotlosen mit ewiger verdamnus zuletzt straffen wo[e]lle/Er verordnet aber nicht die Su[e]nde/die sie thun musten/viel weniger schaffet/vbet vnd treibet er dieselbige durch sie."

60. Cyriakus Spangenberg, *Fu[e]nff Predigten vber den anfang des Euangelij S. Johannis. Im anfang war das Wort etc. . . . .* (Eisleben: Urban Gaubisch, 1559), G1b.

61. Cyriakus Spangenberg, *Die erste Epistel Paulj. An Timotheum. Außgelegt vnd gepredigt* (Strasbourg: Samuel Emmel, 1564), 36a-37a.

62. Cyriakus Spangenberg, *Die erste Epistel Paulj,* 40a.

63. Cyriakus Spangenberg, *Fu[e]nff Predigten,* G7b, G8b. Spangenberg follows Luther in his *Weihnachtspostille;* WA 10.I:220.18–225.4, and Melanchthon in his *Annotationes in Johannem; CR* 15:19.

64. Cyriakus Spangenberg, *De praedestinatione*, E4b-E7b.

65. Cyriakus Spangenberg, *Briefwechsel*, 1:27 (24-27).

66. In a letter of Apr. 20, 1567; *Briefwechsel*, 1:34.

67. See Timothy J. Wengert, "Georg Major (1502-1574): Defender of Wittenberg's Faith and Melanchthonian Exegete," in *Melanchthon in seinen Schülern*, ed. Heinz Scheible (Wiesbaden: Harrassowitz, 1997), 129-56, and Robert Kolb, "Georg Major as Controversialist: Polemics in the Late Reformation," *Church History* 45 (1976): 455-68.

68. See correspondence regarding the summons, in Cyriakus Spangenberg, *Briefwechsel*, 1:43-44, 46-47, 61.

69. Hans-Peter Hasse, *Zensur theologischer Bücher in Kursachsen im konfessionellen Zeitalter, Studien zur kursächsischen Literatur- und Religionspolitik in den Jahren 1569 bis 1575* (Leipzig: Evangelische Verlagsanstalt, 2000), 394; cf. 71-83.

70. Saxony, electoral theologians, *Endlicher Bericht vnd Erklerung der Theologen beider Vniuersiteten/Leipzig vnd Wittemberg Auch der Superintendenten der Kirchen in des Churfu[e]rsten zu Sachsen Landen/belangend die Lere/so gemelte Vniuersiteten vnd Kirchen von anfang der Augspurgischen Confession bis auff diese zeit/laut vnd vermu[e]ge derselben/zu allen Artickeln gleichfo[e]rmig/eintrechtig vnd bestendig gefu[e]ret haben/vber der sie auch durch hu[e]lff des allmechtigen Gottes gedencken fest zu halten* (Wittenberg: Hans Lufft, 1570), 185a-198a.

71. Saxony, electoral theologians, *Von der Person vnd Menschwerdung vnsers HERRN Jhesu Christi/Der waren Christlichen Kirchen Grundfest/Wider die newen Marcioniten/ Samosatener/Sabellianer/Arianer/Nestorianer/Eutychianer vnd Monotheleten/vnter dem Flacianischen hauffen. Durch die Theologen zu Wittemberg/aus der heiligen Schrifft/aus den Symbolis/aus den fu[e]rnemesten Concilijs vnd einhelligem Consenss aller bewerten Lerer. Widerholet vnd Gestellet/zu trewer lere vnd ernster verwarnung an alle frome vnd Gottselige Christen. Neben warhaffter vorantwortung/auff die gifftigen vnd boshaftigen verleumbdungen/ so von den Propositionibus vnd Catechismo zu Wittemberg ausgangen/von vielen dieser zeit ausgesprenget werden . . .* (Wittenberg: Hans Lufft, 1571). The focus of this work was Christology, and only brief mention of other "Flacian" heresies, including that of predestination, occurred at the beginning of the book (7b). Not Spangenberg specifically but "a part of the Flacians" was accused of teaching that predestination rested upon the secret, hidden, and inscrutable plan of God apart from the preaching of the gospel. In fact, neither Spangenberg nor any others held such a position.

72. Saxony, electoral theologians, *Endlicher Bericht*, 185a. Subsequent references to this work have been placed in the text.

73. Cf. the *Loci* of 1543; *StA* 2.2:592-603.

74. Saxony, electoral theologians, *Von der Erwehlung vnd ewigen Versehung Gottes. D. Mart. Luth. Philip. Melanchon* (Leipzig: Jakob Berwäld's heirs, n.d. [ca. 1570, 1571]).

75. E.g., in their *Bericht/der Prediger in der Graffschafft Mansfeld/Der irrungen halben/so zwischen jhnen/vnd etlichen Gelarten/in Vniuersiteten/vnd wie ferne sie mit denselbigen streitig* (Eisleben: Andreas Petri, 1568).

76. Mansfeld Ministerium, *Kurtze Antwort vnd Gegenbericht/Der Prediger/in der Graffschafft Mansfeldt. Vff Der Herrn Theologen/beider Vniuersiteten/Leiptzig/Vnd Wittemberg/Vnd Churfu[e]rstlichen Sechsischen Superintendenten/Endtlichen Bericht vnd Erklerung/ etc. Auch M. Cyriaci Spangenbergs su[e]nderliche Antwort/auff derselben Theologen/vber jhn*

gefelletes Endurtel (Eisleben: Andreas Petri, 1570); "Antwort: M. Cyriaci Spangenbergs/auff der Theologen zu Leiptzig vnd Wittenberg/vber jhn gefelletes Endurtel" is found on leaves E2a-K3a. References in the following text are to *Kurze Antwort.*

77. Mansfeld Ministerium, *Kurtze Antwort,* E2a-b.

78. Mansfeld Ministerium, *Kurtze Antwort,* E3a-F2b. He repeated this point in H1a-H2a.

79. Mansfeld Ministerium, *Kurtze Antwort,* F2b-F3a. Johann Spangenberg, in his *Margarita theologica, continens praecipuos locos doctrinae, per quaestiones, breuiter & ordine explicatos . . .* (1540; Frankfurt am Main: Christoph Egenolph, 1557), 92-93. He defined predestination: "Est certa Dei praeordinatio, qua eueniunt omnia cum interna, tum externa opera & cogitationes, in omnibus creaturis, iuxta decretum uoluntatis suae. Electio est, qua eligit nos Deus in ipso, antequam iacerentur fundamenta mundi, ut essemus irreprehensibiles coram illo per charitatem, ut adoptaret nos in filios per Iesum Christum in sese, iuxta beneplacitum uoluntatis usae, Ephes. 1 & Matth. 10. Nonne duo passeres &c." On universal or particular election, the father held to universal election, rejecting particular election as destructive of assurance (94-95), a position his son rejected.

80. Mansfeld Ministerium, *Kurtze Antwort,* F3b-G2b.

81. Rhegius, *Von volkomenhait vnd frucht des leidens Christi/Sampt erkla[e]rung der wort Pauli Colos. 1. Ich erfull/das abgeet den leyden Christi etc.* (n.p., n.d.), B2b-B4a.

82. Mansfeld Ministerium, *Kurtze Antwort,* G2b-G3b. He elaborated on this point in H1a-b.

83. Mansfeld Ministerium, *Kurtze Antwort,* G4a-H1a. WA Bib 7:22.26-39, 24.1-10 (1522); and 23.26-39, 25.1-10 (1546); Melanchthon, *Annotationes . . . in Epistolas Pauli Ad Rhomanos Et Corinthios* (Nuremberg: Johannes Stuchs, 1522), H1a-H3b.

84. Mansfeld Ministerium, *Kurtze Antwort,* H3b-H4b.

85. Mansfeld Ministerium, *Kurtze Antwort,* J3b-K2a.

86. Mansfeld Ministerium, *Kurtze Antwort,* H4b-J3b.

87. Chemnitz, *Martini Chemnitii . . . ad Matthiam Ritterum . . . Epistolae,* ed. Georg Christian Joannis (Frankfurt am Main: Hocker, 1712), 63, a letter of Dec. 13, 1567.

88. Robert Kolb, "The Braunschweig Resolution: The *Corpus Doctrinae Prutenicum* of Joachim Mörlin and Martin Chemnitz as an Interpretation of Wittenberg Theology," in *Confessionalization in Europe, 1555-1700: Essays in Honor and Memory of Bodo Nischan,* ed. John M. Headley and Hans J. Hillerbrand (Aldershot: Ashgate, 2004), 67-89.

89. Chemnitz, *De Controversiis quibusdam, quae superiori tempore circa quosdam Augustanae Confessionis articulos motae et agitatae sunt, Iudicium D. Martini Chemnitii,* ed. Polycarp Leyser (Wittenberg: Gronenberg, 1594), 20-30, translated in *Sources and Contexts,* 204-8. Cf. WA 43:457.32–463.17; *LW* 5:42-50. Chemnitz had also tried carefully to avoid that charge while affirming God's lordship over all in his commentary on Melanchthon's *Loci;* see Bengt Hägglund, "Wie hat Martin Chemnitz zu Luthers *De servo arbitrio* Stellung genommen?" in *Der zweite Martin der Lutherischen Kirche, Festschrift zum 400. Todestag von Martin Chemnitz,* ed. W. A. Jünke (Brunswick: Ev. Luth. Stadtkirchenverband und Propstei Braunschweig, 1986), 48-59, reprinted in Hägglund, *Chemnitz — Gerhard — Arndt — Rudbeckius. Aufsätze zum Studium der altlutherischen Theologie,* ed. Alexander Bitzel and Johann Anselm Steiger (Waltrop: Spenner, 2003), 65-76.

90. See chap. III, pp. 127-28, above.

91. As Chemnitz explains in the preface of *Eine Predigt vber das Euangelion Matth. 22. Von dem Ko[e]nig der seinem Sohn Hochzeit machet etc. Dahin der Hohe Artickel von der Versehung Gottes auffs aller einfeltigest erkleret wird* . . . (Heinrichstadt [Wolfenbüttel]: Conrad Horn, 1573), 2b. Julius was familiar with Spangenberg's earlier work. In 1565, two years before the publication of the Mansfeld preacher's *De praedestinatione,* Julius asked Chemnitz to bind together Spangenberg's works, "as many or as few as they may be," in lacquered brown or red pigskin; see his letter of Oct. 22, 1565, in Johann Georg Leuckfeld, *Historia Spangenbergensis, oder Historische Nachricht Von dem Leben, Lehre vnd Schriften Cyriace Spangenbergs* (Quedlinberg and Aschersleben: Gottlob Ernst Struntz, 1712), 26.

Only one other extant sermon of Chemnitz treats God's choosing of his elect children, the postil sermon for Septuagesima, on Matt. 20:1-16, the parable of the workers in the vineyard. The date on which it was originally preached is not known, and therefore it is impossible to use it in tracing the chronological development of Chemnitz's thinking on the doctrine of election. In this sermon God's choice of those he would bring to faith is not the only concern in his proclamation of the parable. Indeed, the preacher announced five points to be treated in the sermon: (1) how God deals with his church on earth; (2) how God wants the lofty article of faith on his eternal election, a subtle, dangerous article, to be taught for the admonition and comfort of his people, and for instruction on how they are to live in repentance and new life when God calls them; (3) how God calls his people in different ways and in different circumstances; (4) how God's people do not earn a wage but receive all from him only because of his grace and goodness; and (5) how to apply this text through the Holy Spirit's help for the good of the people of God. See Chemnitz, *Postilla Oder Außlegung der Euangelien/welche auff die Sontage/vnd fu[e]nemste Feste/durchs gantze Jahr in der gemeine Gottes erkleret werden* . . . , ed. Melchior Neukirch (Magdeburg: Johann Franck, 1594), 348-57. Luther had not explained the passage from Matt. 22 in his postil sermons for the twentieth Sunday after Trinity; WA 10.III:407-19; WA 22:333-45; and 52:505-18 (Hauspostil).

92. Chemnitz, *Postilla*, 2:484-97. Neukirch was son of a Braunschweig pastor; after studying at Rostock, he returned to Braunschweig as rector and then pastor of the Petrikirche. Two years before the appearance of the sermon on Matt. 22 in the *Postilla,* it had been published with eight other previously published Chemnitz sermons or short treatises in *D. Martini Chemnitii Richtige/vnd inn H. Schrifft wolgegru[e]ndte Erkla[e]rung/etlicher hochwichtiger vnd no[e]tiger Artickel vnser Christlichen Religion* . . . (Frankfurt am Main: Johann Spieß, 1592). Another printing of the sermon, together with excerpts from Chemnitz's *Handtbu[e]chlein* on the topic, appeared in 1594, in *Eine Predigt vber das Evangelion Matthaei am 22. Vom Ko[e]nige der seinem Son Hochzeit machte/ec. Darinn der hohe Artickel von der Versehung Gottes auffs aller einfeltigest erkleret wird. Gethan Von dem Hochgelarten Gottseligen Herrn Martin Chemnitio* . . . (Coburg: Valentin Kröner, 1594), perhaps in connection with the effort of the local superintendent Johannes Dinckel, which brought Palhöfer's work into print.

93. Chemnitz, *Handtbu[e]chlein Der Fu[e]rnemsten Heupstu[e]ck der Christlichen Lehre/Durch Frag vnd Antwort aus Gottes Worte einfeltig vnd gru[e]ndlich erkleret* . . . , 2nd ed. (Heinrichstadt, 1574), translated as *Ministry, Word, and Sacraments, an Enchiridion,* trans. Luther Poellot (Saint Louis: Concordia, 1981). Because this translation is a hybrid based on the 1593 German edition and the 1603 Latin edition, its text does not always correspond exactly to the 1574 edition.

94. Chemnitz, *Eine Predigt*, 2b-4b. This attempt to formulate public teaching in simple terms at the "catechetical" level was the approach used by Jakob Andreae at just this time to lay a basis for concord among the Lutheran churches; see Robert Kolb, "Jakob Andreae's Concern for the Laity," *Concordia Journal* 4 (1978): 58-67.

95. Chemnitz, *Eine Predigt*, A2a-b.

96. Philipp Julius Rehtmeyer, *Historiae ecclesiasticae inclytae urbis Brunsvigae Pars III. Oder: Der beru[e]hmten Stadt Braunschweig Kirchen-Historie Dritter Theil* . . . (Brunswick: Zilliger, 1710), supplement #38, 240, a letter to Duke Wolfgang of Braunschweig-Lüneburg, Aug. 28, 1576.

97. Chemnitz, *Handtbu[e]chlein*, 158-59; *Ministry*, 85.

98. Chemnitz, *Handtbu[e]chlein*, 159-60; *Ministry*, 86-87.

99. Chemnitz, *Eine Predigt*, A3a.

100. Rune Söderlund, *Ex praevisa Fide. Zum Verständnis der Prädestinationslehre in der lutherischen Orthodoxie* (Hannover: Lutherisches Verlagshaus, 1983), 40, states that among the authors of the Formula of Concord, Chemnitz most clearly operated with a "broken" doctrine of predestination, that is, he most clearly distinguished law and gospel.

101. Chemnitz, *Eine Predigt*, B1b-B3a.

102. Chemnitz, *Handtbu[e]chlein*, 162-70; *Ministry*, 86-89.

103. Chemnitz, *Eine Predigt*, A3b-B1a.

104. Chemnitz, *Eine Predigt*, B1a-b.

105. Chemnitz, *Handtbu[e]chlein*, 171-73; *Ministry*, 89-90. On Melanchthon rejecting a fixed number of elect children of God, see chap. II, n. 44 above.

106. Chemnitz, *Handtbu[e]chlein*, 173-81; *Ministry*, 90-92.

107. Chemnitz, *Handtbu[e]chlein*, 181-86; *Ministry*, 92-94.

108. WA 18:784.14-15; *LW* 33:290.

109. Chemnitz, *Handtbu[e]chlein*, 186-91; *Ministry*, 94-96.

110. Chemnitz, *Eine Predigt*, B3a-B4b. B4a: "Nicht das die Menschliche natur der Gottheit sey gleich worden/Sondern das sie durch die Perso[e]nliche vereinigung in die gemeinschafft der Ehren/Wirden vnd Gu[e]tter des Sohns Gottes gesetzt. . . ." Cf. Chemnitz, *De duabus naturis in Christo* (Jena: Donatus Richtzenhan, 1570; 2nd ed., Leipzig: Johannes Rhamba, 1578); in translation, *The Two Natures in Christ*, trans. J. A. O. Preus (Saint Louis: Concordia, 1971).

111. Chemnitz, *Eine Predigt*, C1a. The references in the following text are to *Eine Predigt*.

112. Chemnitz took this occasion to warn his hearers against "the new false Calvinist catechism, whether it comes from the Palatinate or from Wittenberg," D1b, a reference to the Heidelberg Catechism of 1562 and the Wittenberg Catechism of the crypto-Philippists of 1571.

113. Chemnitz also used 1 Thess. 5:23-24 and 1 Pet. 5:10 at this point.

114. Andreae published his report on their meeting, *Colloquium de Peccato originis Inter D. Iacobvm Andreae, et M. Matthiam Flacivm Illyricvm Argentorati 1571* . . . (Tübingen: Georg Gruppenbach, 1571). See Wilhelm Preger, *Matthias Flacius Illyricus und seine Zeit*, 2 vols. (Erlangen: Bläsing, 1859-61), 2:364-73.

115. Andreae, *Disputatio de viribus humanis, seu de Libero Arbitrio* . . . (Tübingen: Georg Gruppenbach, 1571).

116. Andreae, *Dispvtatio de electione et praedestinatione diuina* . . . (Tübingen: Georg Gruppenbach, 1574), 1-3, theses 1-14.

117. Andreae, *Dispvtatio de electione,* 3-5, theses 15-32.

118. *CR* 51; *Calvini Opera,* 23:52-72 (see the larger discussion of Gen. 3, 51-81). It is unclear to what Andreae refers since Calvin concedes that Satan could have tempted Adam and Eve only with the permission of God but places responsibility for the fall into sin on Satan and human creatures, not on God.

119. Andreae, *Dispvtatio de electione,* 5-23, theses 33-148. Andreae debated Calvin's successor, Theodore Beza, on predestination, among other topics, at the Colloquy of Montbéliard in 1586; see Andreae, *Acta Colloquij Montis Belligartensis: Quod habitum est, Anno Christi 1586* . . . (Tübingen: Georg Gruppenbach, 1587), and Jill Raitt, *The Colloquy of Montbéliard: Religion and Politics in the Sixteenth Century* (New York: Oxford University Press, 1993), 147-56, and Gottfried Adam, *Der Streit um die Prädestination im ausgehenden 16. Jahrhundert, eine Untersuchung zu den Entwürfen vom Samuel Huber und Aegidius Hunnius* (Neukirchen: Neukirchener Verlag, 1970), 29-49. In 1586 Andreae led another disputation on predestination, in which he also was critical of the Calvinist teaching: *Disputatio de praedestinatione* . . . (Tübingen: Georg Gruppenbach, 1586).

120. WA 18:723.28–727.2; *LW* 33:197-202.

121. *BSLK,* 448-49; *Book of Concord,* 318-19.

122. Andreae, *Dispvtatio de electione,* 23-26, theses 149-81.

123. H. Hachfeld, "Die schwäbische Confession (liber Tubingensis). Nach einer Wolfenbüttler Handschrift," *Zeitschrift für historische Theologie* 36 (1866): 288-92. See Friedrich Hübner, "Über den freien Willen. Artikel II: 'De libero arbitrio' aus seinen historischen Grundlagen heraus interpretiert," in *Widerspruch, Dialog und Einigung. Studien zur Konkordienformel der Lutherischen Reformation* (Stuttgart: Calwer Verlag, 1977), 147-49.

124. Hachfeld, "Die schwäbische Confession," 292-95.

125. Hachfeld, "Die schwäbische Confession," 295-96.

Notes to Chapter VII

1. See Oliver K. Olson, *Matthias Flacius and the Survival of Luther's Reform* (Wiesbaden: Harrassowitz, 2002), 309-17; Wilhelm Preger, *Matthias Flacius Illyricus und seine Zeit,* 2 vols. (Erlangen: Bläsing, 1861), 2:1-102.

2. Irene Dingel, "Melanchthons Einigungsbemühen zwischen den Fronten: Der Frankfurter Rezeß," in *Philipp Melanchthon, Ein Wegbereiter für die Ökumene,* ed. Jörg Haustein (Göttingen: Vandenhoeck & Ruprecht, 1997), 121-43.

3. See chap. III, pp. 111-13.

4. See chap. III, pp. 128-33.

5. Inge Mager, "Jakob Andreaes lateinische Unionsartikel von 1568," *ZKG* 98 (1987): 70-86; Hans Christian Brandy, "Jacob Andreaes Fünf Artikel von 1568/69," *ZKG* 98 (1987): 338-51; and Robert Kolb, *Andreae and the Formula of Concord: Six Sermons on the Way to Lutheran Unity* (Saint Louis: Concordia, 1977), 43-48.

6. Andreae, *Sechs Christliche Predigt Von den Spaltungen so sich zwischen den Theologen Augspurgischer Confession von Anno 1548. biss auff diss 1573. Jar nach vnnd nach erhaben. Wie*

sich ein einfa[e]ltiger Pfarrer vnd gemeiner Christlicher Leye so dardurch mo[e]cht verergert sein worden auß seinem Catechismo darein schicken soll (Tübingen: Gruppenbach, 1573); translated in Kolb, *Andreae*, 61-120. See Jobst Ebel, "Jacob Andreae (1528-1590) als Verfasser der Konkordienformel," *ZKG* 89 (1978): 78-119; Inge Mager, *Die Konkordienformel im Fürstentum Braunschweig-Wolfenbüttel. Entstehungsbeitrag — Rezeption — Geltung* (Göttingen: Vandenhoeck & Ruprecht, 1993), 33-125, 175-259; and Rosemarie Müller-Streisand, "Theologie und Kirchenpolitik bei Jacob Andreä bis zum Jahr 1568," *Blätter für württembergische Kirchengeschichte* 60/61 (1960/61): 224-395.

7. Andreae, *Sechs Christliche Predigt,* 34-39; Kolb, *Andreae,* 84-87.

8. Andreae, *Sechs Christliche Predigt,* 39-43; Kolb, *Andreae,* 87-89.

9. Andreae, *Sechs Christliche Predigt,* 43-46; Kolb, *Andreae,* 89-91.

10. Although these Wittenberg theologians held a view of the presence of Christ in the Lord's Supper similar to that of Calvin and his colleagues, and although they were in epistolary contact with Swiss reformers, their views represent their own working out of what they believed Melanchthon had taught.

11. Ernst Koch, "Auseinandersetzungen um die Autorität von Philipp Melanchthon und Martin Luther in Kursachsen im Vorfeld der Konkordienformel von 1577," *LuJ* 59 (1992): 128-59, and the more narrowly focused study of one example, Irene Dingel, "Die Torgauer Artikel (1574) als Vermittlungsversuch zwischen der Theologie Luthers und der Melanchthons," in *Praxis Pietatis. Beiträge zu Theologie und Frömmigkeit in der Frühen Neuzeit. Wolfgang Sommer zum 60. Geburtstag,* ed. Hans-Jörg Nieden and Marcel Nieden (Stuttgart: Kohlhammer, 1999), 119-34.

12. Irene Dingel, "The Preface of *The Book of Concord* as a Reflection of Sixteenth-Century Confessional Development," *LQ* 15 (2001): 171-95.

13. Irene Dingel, *Concordia controversa, Die öffentlichen Diskussionen um das lutherische Konkordienwerk am Ende des 16. Jahrhunderts* (Gütersloh: Gütersloher Verlagshaus, 1996).

14. A good survey of this scholarly opinion is found in Rune Söderlund, *Ex praevisa fide. Zum Verständnis der Prädestinationslehre in der lutherischen Orthodoxie* (Hannover: Lutherisches Verlagshaus, 1983), 13-47.

15. Frank, *Die Theologie der Concordienformel* 1 (Erlangen: Blaesing, 1858), 113-240.

16. Muehlenberg, "Synergia and Justification by Faith," in *Discord, Dialogue, and Concord: Studies in the Lutheran Reformation's Formula of Concord,* ed. Lewis W. Spitz and Wenzel Lohff (Philadelphia: Fortress, 1977), 16.

17. Muehlenberg, "Synergia," 18. Muehlenberg did not recognize the way in which Luther and Melanchthon as well as their students fashioned their understanding of the interaction between Creator and human creature within a paradox of two responsibilities, and so he concluded, for instance, that the Formula "teaches the responsibility of sinful man for rejecting God's grace, but it also implies [!] individual predestination" (19) (article XI rather explicitly teaches individual predestination). Muehlenberg finds the Formula in contradiction regarding the "forced nature" of conversion because he completely ignores Luther's understanding of conversion as a new creation through God's Word (21-23).

18. FC SD II, 55; *BSLK,* 893; *Book of Concord,* 554; Söderlund, *Ex praevisa fide,* 29-38.

19. Friedrich Hübner, "Über den freien Willen. Artikel II: 'De libero arbitrio' aus seinen historischen Grundlagen heraus interpretiert," in *Widerspruch, Dialog und Einigung. Studien zur Konkordienformel der Lutherischen Reformation* (Stuttgart: Calwer Verlag, 1977), 153.

20. Söderlund, *Ex praevisa fide,* 15-28.

21. Prussian Ministerium, "Erklerung der Preussischen Theologen," Sächsisches Hauptstaatsarchiv, Dresden: Geheimrat (Geheimes Archiv) Locat. 10308/4, 258r-290v. Chemnitz had kept the two Prussian leaders, Wigand and Heshusius, informed of developments in the process of concord; cf. his letter of Mar. 1, 1576, to them regarding the Swabian-Saxon Concord; Philipp Julius Rehtmeyer, *Historiae ecclesiasticae inclytae urbis Brunsvigae Pars III. Oder: Der beru[e]hmten Stadt Braunschweig Kirchen-Historie Dritter Theil . . .* (Brunswick: Zilliger, 1710), supplement #43, 250-52. Chemnitz's close relationship to the Prussians can be seen in a report he sent Heshusius on June 23, 1576, regarding the proceedings at Torgau; Rehtmeyer, supplement #47, 255-59.

22. Jobst Ebel, "Die Herkunft des Konzeptes der Konkordienformel, Die Funktionen der fünf Verfasser neben Andreae beim Zustandekommen der Formel," *ZKG* 91 (1980): 263-64. Chytraeus's later claim that Andreae's imposition of changes on the Torgau text had eliminated his contributions to the Formula completely is clearly an exaggeration in view of the fact that just less than half of article II and more than three-quarters of article VII, on the Lord's Supper in the Solid Declaration, come from his pen; see the citation of his letter to Aegidius Hunnius of 1591 in Inge Mager, "Der Beitrag des David Chytraeus zur Entstehung und Rezeption der Konkordienformel," *Berliner Theologische Zeitschrift* 18 (2001): 218. Her judgment that "on the basis of fear [presumably that of Chemnitz and Andreae] of an alleged loss of the exclusive responsibility of God for salvation," decisions regarding the treatment of the human will in conversion fell "one-sidedly in favor of Luther, to Melanchthon's disadvantage," is an oversimplified assessment of the texts, ignoring the Formula's affirmation of the activity of the human will. Compare pp. 208, 221. See also Hübner, "Über den freien Willen," 149-53, on the composition of the article on the will; he concludes that "stofflich bildet [Chytraeus'] Werk zweifellos die Substanz des Artikels" (152).

23. *BSLK,* 866-67. The parts of the text that originally stood in the Torgau book from Chytraeus are found in the apparatus of the *BSLK.*

24. *BSLK,* 871; *Book of Concord,* 543. Cf. Sächsisches Hauptstaatsarchiv, 261v-263r.

25. *BSLK,* 867-68.

26. *BSLK,* 868.

27. *BSLK,* 868-70.

28. Sächsisches Hauptstaatsarchiv, 262r-263r.

29. Sächsisches Hauptstaatsarchiv, 263v-264r. The topic of the law as pedagogue had long occupied the Wittenberg theologians; see Timothy J. Wengert, *Law and Gospel: Philip Melanchthon's Debate with John Agricola of Eisleben over Poenitentia* (Grand Rapids: Baker, 1997), 156-59.

30. Sächsisches Hauptstaatsarchiv, 264v.

31. FC SD II:7; *BSLK,* 873-74; *Book of Concord,* 544.

32. FC SD II:9-10; *BSLK,* 874-75; *Book of Concord,* 545.

33. FC SD II:14-16; *BSLK,* 876-77; *Book of Concord,* 545-47.

34. WA 18:783.3-4; *LW* 33:288.

35. FC SD II:17-24; *BSLK,* 878-82; *Book of Concord,* 547-49.

36. See chap. III, pp. 116-17.

37. FC SD II:24-26; *BSLK,* 882-83; *Book of Concord,* 549. Mager's claim that Chytraeus made an "anti-gnesiolutheran strike" by rejecting the definition of the fallen sinner as an

"unmovable, lifeless block" of wood is of course false. Flacius had used this language, but even he had taught that the fallen will performs acts of willing. Chytraeus's position matches that of the Gnesio-Lutherans, such as Gallus. Indeed, the Gnesio-Lutherans from Prussia did call for a strengthening of this section, which was done at the Bergen meeting in March, but without essentially altering Chytraeus's position, already close to that of Wigand, Heshusius, and their colleagues; cf. Sächsisches Hauptstaatsarchiv, 265r.

38. FC SD II:43; *BSLK*, 888-89; *Book of Concord*, 552; WA 26:502.16/35–503.6/24; *LW* 37:362-63.

39. FC SD II:44; *BSLK*, 889; *Book of Concord*, 552.

40. FC SD II:46-56; *BSLK*, 890-94; *Book of Concord*, 552-54.

41. FC SD II:55; *BSLK*, 893; *Book of Concord*, 554.

42. FC SD II:56; *BSLK*, 893-94; *Book of Concord*, 554.

43. FC SD II:57-60; *BSLK*, 894-96; *Book of Concord*, 555.

44. FC SD II:67-72; *BSLK*, 898-901; *Book of Concord*, 555-58.

45. FC SD II:44; *BSLK*, 889; *Book of Concord*, 552.

46. FC SD II:59; *BSLK*, 894-96; *Book of Concord*, 555.

47. FC SD II:82-85; *BSLK*, 905-7; *Book of Concord*, 560. The Prussian theologians agreed with this point, rejecting the *coactio Illyrici*; Sächsisches Hauptstaatsarchiv, 265v.

48. FC SD II:61-62; *BSLK*, 896; *Book of Concord*, 555-56. On Strigel see chap. III, p. 119.

49. FC SD II:63-67; *BSLK*, 897-99; *Book of Concord*, 556-57.

50. FC SD II:89; *BSLK*, 909-10; *Book of Concord*, 561.

51. Sächsisches Hauptstaatsarchiv, 266r-v.

52. FC SD II:78; *BSLK*, 904; *Book of Concord*, 559.

53. I am grateful to Timothy J. Wengert for this insight.

54. Sächsisches Hauptstaatsarchiv, 266v-267r.

55. FC SD II:86-87; *BSLK*, 907-9; *Book of Concord*, 560-61.

56. Sächsisches Hauptstaatsarchiv, 267r-v.

57. FC SD II:90; *BSLK*, 910-12; *Book of Concord*, 561-62.

58. Hübner, "Über den freien Willen," 159.

59. FC SD XI:1-3; *BSLK*, 1063-64; *Book of Concord*, 640-41.

60. FC SD XI:2; *BSLK*, 1064; *Book of Concord*, 641.

61. Rehtmeyer, *Historiae*, supplement, 240-41, a letter to Duke Wolfgang of Braunschweig-Lüneburg of Aug. 28, 1576.

62. FC SD XI:23 and 24-59; *BSLK*, 1070-81; *Book of Concord*, 644-50.

63. See chap. III.

64. FC SD XI:4-8; *BSLK*, 1064-66; *Book of Concord*, 641-42.

65. See chap. VI, p. 231.

66. FC SD XI:9-14; *BSLK*, 1066-69; *Book of Concord*, 642-43.

67. FC SD XI:45-50; *BSLK*, 1077-78; *Book of Concord*, 648-49.

68. FC SD XI:15-22; *BSLK*, 1069-70; *Book of Concord*, 643-44.

69. FC SD XI:73; *BSLK*, 1084; *Book of Concord*, 652.

70. FC SD XI:54-59; *BSLK*, 1079-81; *Book of Concord*, 649-50.

71. FC SD XI:76-77; *BSLK*, 1085; *Book of Concord*, 652-53.

72. FC SD XI:23-32; *BSLK*, 1070-73; *Book of Concord*, 644-46.

73. FC SD XI:78, 81-86; *BSLK*, 1085-88; *Book of Concord*, 653-54.

74. FC SD XI:33-41; *BSLK,* 1073-76; *Book of Concord,* 646-47.

75. FC SD XI:42; *BSLK,* 1076; *Book of Concord,* 647-48.

76. FC SD XI:52-64; *BSLK,* 1079-82; *Book of Concord,* 649-50. Note that this passage is used in the conclusion of *De servo arbitrio.*

77. FC SD XI:65-72; *BSLK,* 1082-84; *Book of Concord,* 650-52.

78. See chap. VI, pp. 240-41. Cf. FC SD XI:75, 89; *BSLK,* 1084-85, 1089; *Book of Concord,* 652, 655.

79. FC SD XI:79; *BSLK,* 1086; *Book of Concord,* 653.

80. FC SD XI:83-86; *BSLK,* 1087-88; *Book of Concord,* 653-54.

81. Söderlund, *Ex praevisa fide,* 25-27.

82. FC SD XI:91-92; *BSLK,* 1089-90; *Book of Concord,* 655.

83. In his essay "Vom Lehren der Prädestination zur Lehre von der Prädestination, FC XI im Lichte der Prädestinationsaussagen Luthers," in *Widerspruch, Dialog und Einigung. Studien zur Konkordienformel der Lutherischen Reformation,* 249-73, Klaus Schwarzwäller regrets this development from teaching or proclaiming predestination to a formal doctrine of predestination. That is, however, the nature of the task of the theologian over against the task of the preacher and pastor as the ecumenical necessities of meeting the thought of other sixteenth-century theological systems defined that task.

84. Gottfried Adam, *Der Streit um die Prädestination im ausgehenden 16. Jahrhundert, eine Untersuchung zu den Entwürfen vom Samuel Huber und Aegidius Hunnius* (Neukirchen: Neukirchener Verlag, 1970), 80-83.

85. Söderlund, *Ex praevisa fide,* esp. 49-132; cf. Adam, *Streit,* 128-65.

86. Söderlund reviews the positions held by Georg Calixt and his student Johannes Latermann and mentions the positions of Johannes Musaeus and others in the later seventeenth century. The former two he demonstrates to be synergistic; the latter he regards as more guarded and cautious in their description of the role of the human will in coming to faith, as they tried to retain the prevenient nature of the Holy Spirit's action in conversion while describing predestination as the result of the faith God foresees the Holy Spirit would create; *Ex praevisa fide,* 133-77. Cf. also the judgment of Adam, *Streit,* 197-207, and Otto Ritschl, *Dogmengeschichte des Protestantismus* IV (Leipzig: Hinrichs, 1927), 126-27, 154-55.

87. *BSLK,* 75; *Book of Concord,* 52/53.

88. Söderlund, *Ex praevisa fide,* 25-28.

Notes to the Conclusion

1. Brecht, *Martin Luther. Zweiter Band. Ordnung und Abgrenzung der Reformation, 1521-1532* (Stuttgart: Calwer Verlag, 1986), 231; ET, *Martin Luther, Shaping and Defining the Reformation, 1521-1532,* trans. James L. Schaaf (Minneapolis: Fortress, 1990), 235.

2. Robert Kolb, *Martin Luther as Prophet, Teacher, and Hero: Images of the Reformer, 1520-1620* (Grand Rapids: Baker, 1999).

3. Hans-Günter Leder, "Luthers Beziehungen zu seinen Wittenberger Freunden," in *Leben und Werk Martin Luthers von 1526 bis 1546, Festgabe zu seinem 500. Geburtstag,* ed. Helmar Junghans (Berlin: Evangelische Verlagsanstalt, 1983), 1:419.

4. Reinhard Flogaus, "Luther versus Melanchthon? Zur Frage der Einheit der Wittenberger Reformation in der Rechtfertigungslehre," *ARG* 91 (2000): 6-46.

5. Flogaus, "Luther versus Melanchthon?" 32-35.

6. Hartmut Oskar Günther, "Die Entwicklung der Willenslehre Melanchthons in der Auseinandersetzung mit Luther und Erasmus" (Th.D. diss., University of Erlangen, 1963), 9.

7. Flacius, *Bericht M. Fla. Illyrici/Von etlichen Artikeln der Christlichen Lehr/vnd von seinem Leben* . . . (n.p., 1559), C1a-b.

8. Nikolaus Gallus, *Erklerung der Religions streite/zu nottu[e]rfftigem vnterricht der Kirche/vnd ablenung falscher Calumnien. Wider die verfelscher der waren Augspurgischen Confession* (Regensburg: Heinrich Geissler, 1559), A2b-B1b. See chap. III, pp. 115-16, above.

9. *CR* 21:375.

10. WA 18:754.4-8; *LW* 33:243.

Bibliography

Manuscripts

Amsdorf, Nikolaus von. "Annotationes quibus indicatur paucis quae in locis communibus Philippi Melanchthonis displicent per N.A." 1541. Weimar, Goethe-Schiller Archiv der Nationale Forschungs- und Gedenkstätten der klassischen deutschen Literatur: Ehemalige Thüringische Landesbibliothek folio Band XL: 301-309.

———. "De contingentia. Disputatione prima pars." 1536. Dresden, Sächsische Landesbibliothek, Ms. Dres. A180, 752-770.

Prussian Ministerium. "Erklerung der Preussischen Theologen." 1576. Dresden, Sächsisches Hauptstaatsarchiv: Geheimrat (Geheimes Archiv) Locat. 10308/4, 258r-290v.

Primary Printed Documents

Altenstaig, Joannes, and Joannes Tytz. *Lexicon Theologicum.* Cologne, 1619. Hildesheim: Olms, 1974.

Amsdorf, Nikolaus von. *Das D. Pfeffinger seine missethat bo[e]slich vnd felschlicht leugnet/ vnd gewaltiglich vberzeugt wird/das er die Kirchen Christi zusto[e]rt vnd zuru[e]ttet/ vnd die Schrifft verfelschet vnd verkert hab.* Magdeburg, 1559.

———. *Offentliche Bekentnis der reinen Lehre des Euangelij/Vnd Confutatio der jtzigen Schwermer.* Jena: Thomas Rhebart, 1558.

———. *Wider die Synergia Victorini. Nemlich Das der Mensch in seiner Bekerung/kein Synergiam noch modum agendi, habe noch haben kan/das ist/allerding nichts mit wircke in seiner Bekerung/Sondern sey Gottes gnedige wirckung allein.* N.p., 1564.

Andreae, Jakob. *Acta Colloquij Montis Belligartensis: Quod habitum est, Anno Christi 1586. . . .* Tübingen: Georg Gruppenbach, 1587.

———. *Colloquium de Peccato originis Inter D. Iacobvm Andreae, et M. Matthiam Flacivm Illyricvm Argentorati 1571. . . .* Tübingen: Georg Gruppenbach, 1571.

————. *Disputatio de praedestinatione.* . . . Tübingen: Georg Gruppenbach, 1586.

————. *Disputatio de viribus humanis, seu de Libero Arbitrio.* . . . Tübingen: Georg Gruppenbach, 1571.

————. *Dispvtatio de electione et praedestinatione diuina.* . . . Tübingen: Georg Gruppenbach, 1574.

————. *Sechs Christlicher Predig Von den Spaltungen so sich zwischen den Theologen Augspurgischer Confession von Anno 1548. biss auff diss 1573. Jar nach vnnd nach erhaben.* . . . Tübingen: Gruppenbach, 1573.

Brenz, Johannes. *In D. Iohannis Evangelion . . . Exegesis.* Hagenau: Johannes Secer, 1527.

Bugenhagen, Johannes. *Ain kurtze/wolgegründte Außlegung uber die Zehen nachgeenden Episteln S. Pauli.* N.p., 1524.

Canisius, Peter. *Commentariorvm de Verbi Dei corrvptelis liber primis . . . contra nouos Ecclesiasticae historiae consarcinatores siue Centuriatores pertractatur.* Dillingen: Sebald Mayer, 1581.

Capito, Wolfgang. *In Hoseam prophetam V. F. Capitonis Commentarius.* . . . Strasbourg: Ioannes Hervagius, 1528.

Celichius, Andreas. *Nu[e]tzlicher vnd notwendiger bericht/Von den Leuten/so sich selbst aus angstverzweiffelung/oder andern vrsachen/entleiben vnd hinrichten.* Magdeburg: Wolffgang Kirchner, 1578.

Chemnitz, Martin. *De Controversiis quibusdam, quae superiori tempore circa quosdam Augustanae Confessionis articulos motae et agitatae sunt, Iudicium D. Martini Chemnitii.* Edited by Polycarp Leyser. Wittenberg, 1594.

————. *De duabus naturis in Christo.* Jena: Donatus Richtzenhan, 1570; 2nd ed., Leipzig: Johannes Rhamba, 1578. Translated as *The Two Natures in Christ,* trans. J. A. O. Preus (Saint Louis: Concordia, 1971).

————. *D. Martini Chemnitii Richtige/vnd inn H. Schrifft wolgegru[e]ndte Erkla[e]rung/ etlicher hochwichtiger vnd no[e]tiger Artickel vnser Christlichen Religion.* . . . Frankfurt am Main: Johann Spieß, 1592.

————. *Eine Predigt vber das Euangelion Matth. 22. Von dem Ko[e]nig der seinem Sohn Hochzeit machet etc. Dahin der Hohe Artickel von der Versehung Gottes auffs aller einfeltigest erkleret wird.* . . . Heinrichstadt [Wolfenbüttel]: Conrad Horn, 1573.

————. *Eine Predigt vber das Evangelion Matthaei am 22. Vom Ko[e]nige der seinem Son Hochzeit machte/ec. Darinn der hohe Artickel von der Versehung Gottes auffs aller einfeltigest erkleret wird. Gethan Von dem Hochgelarten Gottseligen Herrn Martin Chemnitio . . .* Coburg: Valentin Kroner, 1594.

————. *Handtbu[e]chlein Der Fu[e]rnemsten Heupstu[e]ck der Christlichen Lehre/Durch Frag vnd Antwort aus Gottes Worte einfeltig vnd gru[e]ndlich erkleret . . .* , 156. 2nd ed. Heinrichstadt, 1574. Translated as *Ministry, Word, and Sacraments, an Enchiridion,* trans. Luther Poellot (Saint Louis: Concordia, 1981).

————. *Postilla Oder Außlegung der Euangelien/welche auff die Sontage/vnd fu[e]nemste Feste/durchs gantze Jahr in der gemeine Gottes erkleret werden.* . . . Edited by Melchior Neukirch. Magdeburg: Johann Franck, 1594.

Chytraeus, David. *Explicatio Malachiae prophetae.* . . . Rostock: Jacob Transylvanus, 1568.

————. *In Exodvm Enarratio.* Wittenberg: Johannes Crato, 1561.

————. *Jn evangelion Ioannis, Scholia.* Frankfurt am Main: Johannes Spies, 1588.

————. *Piae & vtilliss. explicationes vocabvlorvm: Necessitatis. Determinationis Diuinae. Fati. Contingentiae. Virivm hvmanarvm. Liberi arbitrii.* Rostock: Jacobus Transylvanus, 1565.

Cochlaeus, Johannes. *Commentaria de actis et scriptis Martini Lvtheri Saxonis, Chronographice, Ex ordine ab Anno Domini M.D.XVII. usque ad Annum M.D.XLVI. Inclusiuē, fideliter conscripta.* Mainz: Franz Behem, 1549.

————. *De libero arbitrio hominis adversvs locos communes Philippi Melanchthonis, libri duo.* Tübingen: Morhart, 1525.

Corvinus, Anton. *Qvatenvs expediat aeditam recens Erasmi de sarcienda Ecclesiae concordia Rationem sequi, tantisper dum adparatur Synodus, Iuditium.* Wittenberg: Nicolaus Schirlentz, 1534.

Eck, Johann. *Chrysopassus praedestinationis.* Augsburg: Miller, 1514.

Erasmus, Desiderius. *De libero arbitrio DIATRIBH; siue Collectae. . . .* Augsburg: Simprecht Ruff and Sigmund Grimm, 1524.

————. *De sarcienda ecclesiae Concordia deque sedandis opinionum dissidiis.* Basel: Hieronymus Froben and Nicolaus Episcopius, 1533.

————. *Eyn Vergleychung oder Zusamenhaltung der spruche vom freyen wyllen/Erasmi von Roterodam/durch Nicolaum Herman von Altdorff yns teutsch gebracht/von ersten ließ/darnach vrteyls.* Leipzig: Jacob Thanner, 1525.

————. *Hyperaspistae liber secundus aduersus librum Martini Lutheri, cui titulem fecit, Seruum arbitrium.* Nuremberg: Johann Petreius, 1527.

————. *Hyperaspistes Diatribae Aduersus Seruum Arbitrium Martini Lutheri. . . .* Cologne: Peter Quentel, 1526.

Flacius, Matthias, Illyricus. *Bericht M. Fla. Illyrici/Von etlichen Artikeln der Christlichen Lehr/vnd von seinem Leben. . . .* N.p., 1559.

————. *Censura de V. Strigilii apostatae declaratione s. potius errorum occultatione.* Regensburg: Heinrich Geissler, 1562.

————. *Clavis Scriptvrae S. seu de Sermone Sacrarum literarum . . . Altera pars.* Basel: Herwagen, 1580.

————. *Disputatio de originali peccato et libero arbitrio, inter Matthiam Flacium Illyricum & Victorinum Strigelium.* N.p., 1562; n.p., 1563; Eisleben, 1563.

————. *Dispvtatio de originali peccato, et libero arbitrio, contra praesentes errores.* N.p., 1559.

————. *Novvm Testamentvm Iesv Christi . . . Glossa compendiaria. . . .* Basel: Peter Perna and Theobald Dietrich, 1570.

————. *Warhafftige vnd bestendiger meinung vnd zeugnis/Von der Erbsu[e]nde vnd dem freien willen Des Ehrwirdigen tewren Mans Gottes D. Martin Luthers Aus allen seinen schrifften trewliche vnd mit vleis zusamen gezogen. . . .* Jena: Thomas Rhebart, 1560.

Flacius, Matthias, and Nikolaus Gallus. *Apologia . . . Das die Adiaphoristen/vnd nit sie/ trennung in vnsern Kirchen der Augspurgischen Confession/vnd vneinigkeit an-gericht. . . .* Regensburg: Hans Kohl, n.d.

Gallus, Nikolaus. *Auff des Herrn D. Maiors verantwortung vnd Declaration der Leiptzigischen Proposition/wie gute werck zur seligkeit no[e]tig sind. . . .* Magdeburg: Michael Lotther, 1552.

————. *Auff die newe subtile verfelschung des Euangelij Christi/in Doctor Maiors Comment vber seine Antichristische Proposition.* . . . Magdeburg: Michael Lotther, 1553.

————. *Erklerung der Religions streite/zu nottu[e]rfftigem vnterricht der Kirche/vnd ablenung falscher Calumnien. Wider die verfelscher der waren Augspurgischen Confession.* Regensburg: Heinrich Geissler, 1559.

————. *Erklerung vnd Consens vieler Christlichen Kirchen/der Augspurgischen Confession/ auff die newe verfelschung der Lehre vom Freyen willen/wie die aus dem INTERIM von etlichen noch gefu[e]rt vnd verteidigt wird.* Regensburg: Heinrich Geissler, 1559.

————. *Qvaestio libero arbitrio, qvatenvs illa qvibvsdam nunc disceptatur in Ecclesijs Augustanae Confessionis. Cvm adsertione ex perpetva propheticae et apostolicae scripturae sententia, & ex sententia Lutheri instauratoris doctrinae, authoris & interprecis Augustanae Confessionis.* Regensburg: Heinrich Geissler, 1559.

————. *Religion streite vnd Einigkeit.* Regensburg: Heinrich Geissler, 1560.

————. *Tafel der verkerten/vnd gleich vmbgekerten etlicher Lere/bey der wahren Christlichen Augsp. Conf.* Regensburg: Heinrich Geissler, 1560.

————. *Wa[e]chterstimme/Nic. Galli. Wo vnd in was Stücken/vnter dem Namen Lutheri/der Augspurgischen Confession vnd H. Schrift/Wider Lutherum/wider die Augspur. Conf. vnd H. Schrift jtzo gelehret wird.* Regensburg: Heinrich Geissler, n.d.

Gribaldi, Matthaeus. *Epistola . . . de tremendo diuini iudicij exemplo super eum, qui nominum metu pulsus, Christum & cognitam ueritatem abnegat.* . . . Basel, 1549. Translation: *Ein Epistel oder sendtbrieff . . . von einem erschrockenlichen exempel Go[e]ttliches gerichts/über einen gelerten man/welcher vß forcht der menschen getrungen/Christum vnd die erkante warheit verleügnet hat.* N.p., 1549.

Herbst (Autumnus), Georg. *Vom Freien Willen vnd Bekerung des Menschen zu Gott. Warhafftige/bestendige/vnd in Gottes wort wolgegru[e]ndte Lehr vnd meinung/des tewren vnd Seligen Mannes D. Martini Lvtheri.* . . . Eisleben: Andreas Petri, 1565.

Heshusius, Tilemann. *De servo hominis arbitrio: et conversione eivs per Dei gratiam aduersus Synergiae adsertores.* Magdeburg: Wolfgang Kirchner, 1562.

————. *Explicatio epistolae Pavli ad Romanos.* Jena: Günther Hüttich, 1571.

Irenaeus, Christoph. *Symbolvm Apostolicvm. Das ist. Die Artickel vnsers Christlichen Glaubens/ausgelegt.* . . . Eisleben: Urban Gaubisch, 1562. With an attached section with its own title page, *Der dritte Artickel Vnsers Christlichen Glaubens/von der Heiligung/Ausgelegt. Mit Vermeldung vnd widerlegung allerley Irthumb vnd Ketzereyen/beide alt vnd new/so dawider entstanden.* Eisleben: Urban Gaubisch, 1562.

Jena University Theological Faculty. *Bekentnis Vom Freien Willen. So im Colloquio zu Altenburg/hat sollen vorbracht werden/von Fu[e]rstlichen Sechsischen Theologen.* Jena, 1570.

————. *Bekentnis Von Fu[e]nff Streittigen Religions Artickeln.* Jena, 1570.

————. *Bericht Vom Colloquio zu Altenburgk. Auff den endlichen Bericht/etc.* Jena, 1570.

————. *Der Chur vnd Fu[e]rstlichen Sa[e]shsischen Theologen schrifft vnd Gegenschrifft/ vom Aldenburgischen Colloquio/durch wen/aus was vrsachen/vnnd welcher gestalt dasselbige zerschlagen vnnd zergangen.* N.p., 1569.

————. *Colloqvivm zu Altenburgk in Meissen/Vom Artikel der Rechtfertigung vor Gott. Zwischen Den Churfu[e]rstlichen vnd Fu[e]rstlichen zu Sachsen etc. Theologen gehalten. Vom 20. Octobris Anno 1568. bis auff den 9. Martij/Anno 1569. Es ist auch von den zweien hinderstelligen Artikeln/Nemlich vom Freien Willen/vnd von den Mitteldingen/was da ferner im Colloquio/von Fu[e]rstlichen Sechsischen Theologen/ hette sollen vorbracht werden/hinzu gedruckt.* Jena, 1569.

———. *Wie das Aldenburgisch Colloquium zergangen.* N.p., 1569.

Jurieau, Pierre. *De pace inter Protestantes ineunde consultatio. Sive disquisitio Circa quaestiones de gratia quae remorantur unionem Protestantium utriusque confessionis Augustanae & Reformatae.* . . . Utrecht: Franciscus Halma, 1688.

Kirchner, Timotheus. *Deudscher Thesaurus. Des Hochgelerten weit berumbten vnd thewren Mans D. Mart. Luthers/Darinnen alle Heubtartickel/Christlicher/Catholischer vnd Apostolischer Lere vnd glaubens erklert vnd ausgelegt.* . . . Frankfurt am Main: Peter Schmidt and Hieronymus Feierabent, 1568.

———. *Thesavrvs: explicationvm omnivm articvlorvm ac capitvm, catholicae, orthodoxae, verae, ac piae doctrinae Christianae, quae hac aetate controuersa sunt, ex reuerendi, vereque Dei viri, ac summi Theologi D. Martini Lutheri . . . operibus.* . . . Frankfurt am Main: Thomas Rhebart and Sigismund Feierabend, 1566.

Körner, Christoph. *In epistolam D. Pavli ad Romanos scriptus Commentarivs.* Heidelberg: Johannes Spies, 1583.

Lasius, Christoph. *Fundament Warer vnd Christlicher Bekerung/Wider die Flacianische Klotzbus/aus vier Irrthumen widers Fundament ersetzt/Klerlich erwisen/vnd gru[e]ndlich widerlegt.* Frankfurt an der Oder: Johann Eichorn; Wittenberg: Peter Seitz, 1568.

———. *Praelibatio Flaciani dogmatis de prodigiosa conversione hominis, ad gustum totius controversiae proposita.* Wittenberg: Peter Seitz, 1568.

Luther, Martin. *Das der freie Wille nichts sey/Antwort D. Martini Luther an Erasmum Roterdamum. Verdeutscht durch D. Justum Jonam.* Wittenberg: Hans Lufft, 1526.

———. *Das der freie wille nichts sey/Antwort D. Martini Luther an Erasmum Roterdam. Verdeutscht durch Justum Jonam.* Edited by Nikolaus Gallus. Regensburg: Geißler, 1559.

———. *De servo arbitrio Martini Lvtheri, ad D. Erasmvm Roterodamvm.* . . . Neustadt: Matthaeus Harnisch, 1591.

———. *Der Sechste teil der Bu[e]cher des Ehrnwirdigen Herrn Doctoris Martini Lutheri.* . . . Wittenberg: Hans Lufft, 1553; Wittenberg: Lorenz Schwenck, 1570.

———. *Tomvs secvndvs omnivm opervm Reverendi Domini Martini Lvtheri.* . . . Wittenberg: Johannes Lufft, 1546; Wittenberg: Seitz, 1552; Wittenberg: Lorenz Schwenck, 1562.

———. *Tomvs tertivs omnivm opervm Reverendi Patris Viri Dei, D.M.L.* . . . Jena: Rödinger, 1557; Jena: Richtzenhan/Rhebart, 1567.

Magdeburg Ministerium. *Bekentnis Vnterricht vnd vermanung/der Pfarrhern vnd Prediger/ der Christlichen Kirchen zu Magdeburgk. Anno 1550. Den 13. Aprilis.* . . . Magdeburg: Michael Lotther, 1550.

———. *Confessio et Apologia pastorum & reliquorum ministrorum Ecclesiae Magdeburgensis. Anno 1550. Idibus Aprilis.* . . . Magdeburg: Michael Lotther, 1550.

Mansfeld Ministerium. *Bericht/der Prediger in der Graffschafft Mansfelt/Der irrungen halben/so zwischen jhnen/vnd etlichen Gelarten/in Vniuersiteten/vnd wie ferne sie mit denselbigen streitig.* Eisleben: Andreas Petri, 1568.

———. *Kurtze Antwort vnd Gegenbericht/Der Prediger/in der Graffschafft Mansfeldt. Vff*

Der Herrn Theologen/beider Vniuersiteten/Leiptzig/Vnd Wittemberg/Vnd Chur-fu[e]rstlichen Sechsischen Superintendenten/Endtlichen Bericht vnd Erklerung/etc. Auch M. Cyriaci Spangenbergs su[e]nderliche Antwort/auff derselben Theologen/vber jhn gefelletes Endurteil. Eisleben: Andreas Petri, 1570.

————. *Kurtzer Bericht/Wes sich die Prediger/Jn der Graff vnd Herrschafft Mansfelt . . . der fur zweien jaren in Deutscher vnd Lateinischer sprach/ausgegangenen Confession halben wider alle Secten/erklerungs weise/vnd sonst in aldern no[e]tigen stu[e]cken/ einhellig vergliechen haben.* Eisleben: Urban Gaubisch, 1563.

————. *Responsio Ministrorum verbi in Comitatu Mansfeldensi. Ad Apologiam D. Johannis Stosselii. . . .* Eisleben: Urban Gaubisch, 1566.

————. *Sententia ministrorvm verbi in comitatv Mansfeldiensi de formvla declarationis Victorini Strigelii in qvestione de libro hominis arbitrio.* N.p., 1562.

Mathesius, Johann. *Historien/Von des Ehrwirdigen in Gott Seligen thewren Manns Gottes/ Doctoris Martini Luthers/anfang/lehr/leben vnd sterben. . . .* Nuremberg: Heirs of Johann vom Berg and Ulrich Neuber, 1566.

Melanchthon, Philip. *Annotationes . . . in Epistolas Pauli Ad Rhomanos Et Corinthios.* Nuremberg: Johannes Stuchs, 1522.

————. *Responsiones scriptae a Philippo Melanthone ad impios articvlos bavaricae inqvisitionis.* Wittenberg: Georg Rhau, 1558.

Menzel, Hieronymus. *Vom Freyenn willen des Menschen. Eine Predigt vber den Spruch Christi/Matth. 23. . . .* Eisleben: Urban Gaubisch, 1564.

Mörlin, Joachim. *Wie die Bu[e]cher vnd Schrifften/des tewren vnd Seligen Manns Gottes D. Martini Lutheri nu[e]tzlich zu lesen. . . .* Eisleben: Andreas Petri, 1565.

Obenhin, Christoph. *Einfa[e]ltiger vnd wahrhaftiger bericht/von dem Freyen Willen vnd bekerung des Menschen/aus heiliger Go[e]ttlicher Schrift/vnnd bewerten alten Kirchenlerern genomen/in diesen letzten vnd betru[e]bten Zeiten . . . wider etliche Ferber vnd Verfelscher der reinen religion. Sampt zugethanen lateinischen Zeugnissen/ aus den ersten ausgegangenen Schrifften/des E. W. H. Philippi Melanchtonis/seliger Gedechtnis/trewlich gezogen/zu erklerung dieses Tractats. . . .* N.p., 1569.

Oecolampadius, Johannes. *De libero arbitrio Divorum Prosperi, Augustini et Ambrosii opuscula perquam erudita.* Basel: Wolff, 1524.

Palhöfer, Leonhardt. *Zwey notwendige nu[e]zliche Lehr vnd Trostbu[e]chlein. Das Erste/Von der Ewigen Vorsehung des Menschen/in Christo Jesu zum ewigen Leben/Kurtzer Bericht auß Gottes Wort/welchem D. M. Lutherus/vnd alle reine Lehrer Zeugnus geben. Das Andere/Wider diese Proposition: Das Gott nicht alle Menschen wo[e]lle selig werden.* Edited by Johannes Dinckel. Coburg: Valentin Kröner, 1593.

Pfeffinger, Johann. *Antwort: D. Johan Pfeffingers/Pastoris der Kirchen zu Leiptzig. Auff die Offentliche Bekentnis der reinen Lare des Euangelij/vnd Confutation der jtzigen Schwermerey/Niclasen von Ambsdorff.* Wittenberg, 1558.

————. *De Libertate Voluntatis humanae Quaestiones quinque.* Leipzig: Georg Hantsch, 1555.

————. *Demonstratio manifesti mendacii, qvo infamare conatvr Doctorem Iohannem Pfeff. Libellvs qvidam maledicus & Sycophanticus germanicē editus titulo Nicolai ab Amsdorff, Necessaria propter Veritatis assertionem & auersionem Scandali, & tuendam existimationem sincereae doctrinae.* Wittenberg, 1558.

————. *In hoc Libello continentvr vtiles dispvtationes de praecipuis capitibus doctrinae Christianae, quae propositae fuerunt in academia Lipsica.* Frankfurt am Main: Peter Brubach, 1558.

————. *Nochmals gru[e]ndlicher/klarer/warhafftiger Bericht vnd Bekentnis/der bittern lautern Warheit/reiner Lere/vnd strefflichen Handlungen/vnd vnuermeidliche notwendige Verantwortunge Johannis Pfeffingers Doctoris.* . . . Wittenberg: Lorentz Schwenck, 1559.

Porta, Conrad. *Oratio continens adhortationem, ad assidvam Lectionem scriptorum Reuerendi Patris & Praeceptoris nostri D. Martini Lvtheri, vltimi Eliae & Prophetae Germaniae.* Jena: Donatus Richtzenhan, 1571.

Pufendorf, Samuel von. *Heiliges Religions-Recht/Darinnen angezeiget wird/in welchen Lehr-Puncten die Protestanten einig sind oder nicht.* . . . Frankfurt an der Oder: Johann Völcker, 1696.

Rabus, Ludwig. *Historien. Der Heyligen Außerwo[e]lten Gottes Zeügen/Bekennern vnnd Martyrern . . . Der vierdte Theyl.* Strassburg: Samuel Emmel, 1556.

————. *Historien der Martyrer/Ander Theil.* . . . Strassburg: Johann Rihel, 1572.

Rhegius, Urbanus. *Formvlae qvaedam cavte et citra Scandalum loquendi de praecipuis Christianae doctrinae locis, pro iunioribus Verbi Ministris in Ducatu Luneburgensi.* Leipzig: Michael Blum, 1544. Translated as *Preaching the Reformation: The Homiletical Handbook of Urbanus Rhegius,* trans. and ed. Scott Hendrix (Milwaukee: Marquette University Press, 2003).

————. *Von volkomenhait vnd frucht des leidens Christi/Sampt erkla[e]rung der wort Pauli Colos. 1. Ich erfull/das abgeet den leyden Christi etc.* N.p., n.d.

Sarcerius, Erasmus. *In epistolam ad Romanos, pia & erudita scholia.* . . . Frankfurt am Main: Christoph Egenolph, 1541.

————. *In epistolas D. Pavli, ad Galatas et Ephesios, piae atque eruditae Annotationes.* . . . Frankfurt am Main: Christian Egenolph, 1542.

Saxony, ducal government. *Confutation. Gru[e]ndlicher vnd ausfu[e]hrlicher Beweis/aus Gottes Wort/der Veter schrifften . . . Das Victorini Strigelij Declaration . . . falsch verfu[e]risch vnd verwerfflich. Auf . . . verordnung . . . Herrn Johans Wilhelmen/ Hertzogen zu Sachssen . . . gestellet.* Jena: Thomas Rhebart, 1567.

————. *Des Durchleuchtigen . . . Herrn Johans Friderichen des Mittlern . . . in Gottes wort/ Prophetischer vnd Apostolischer schrifft/gegru[e]ndete Confutationes/Widerlegungen vnd verdammung etlicher . . . Corruptelen/Secten vnd Irrthumen.* . . . Jena: Thomas Rhebart, 1559.

————. *Illvstrissimi principis . . . Iohannis Friderici secvndi . . . Confutatio & condemnatio praecipuarum Corruptelarum, Sectarum, & errorum.* . . . Jena: Thomas Rhebart, 1559.

Saxony, ducal pastors. *Warhafftiger vnnd Gru[e]ndtlicher Summarien Bericht Etlicher Predicanten Wie vnd Worumb sie in LXII. Vnd LXIII. Jare in Thu[e]ringen seind jres Ampts entsetzt vnd zum theil verjagt worden.* . . . N.p., 1564.

Saxony, electoral theologians. *Endlicher Bericht vnd Erklerung der Theologen beider Vniuersiteten/Leipzig vnd Wittemberg Auch der Superintendenten der Kirchen in des Churfu[e]rsten zu Sachsen Landen/belangend die Lere/so gemelte Vniuersiteten vnd Kirchen von anfang der Augspurgischen Confession bis auff diese zeit/laut vnd vermu[e]ge derselben/zu allen Artickeln gleichfo[e]rmig/eintrechtig vnd bestendig gefu[e]ret haben/vber der sie auch durch hu[e]lff des allmechtigen Gottes gedencken fest zu halten.* Wittenberg: Hans Lufft, 1570.

———. *Gantze vnd Vnuerfelschete Acta vnd handlung des Colloquij/zwischen den Churfu[e]rstlichen vnd Fu[e]rstlichen zu Sachsen etc. Theologen/vom artickel der Gerechtigkeit des Menschen fur Gott/vnd von guten Wercken/zu Aldenburgk in Meissen gehalten. Vom 20. Octobris Anno 1568. bis auff den 9. Martij/Anno 1569.* Wittenberg: Hans Lufft, 1570.

———. *Von der Erwehlung vnd ewigen Versehung Gottes. D. Mart. Luth. Philip. Melanthon.* Leipzig: Jakob Berwäld's heirs, n.d. (ca. 1570, 1571).

———. *Von der Person vnd Menschwerdung vnsers HERRN Jhesu Christi/Der waren Christlichen Kirchen Grundfest/Wider die newen Marcioniten/Samosatener/Sabellianer/Arianer/Nestorianer/Eutychianer vnd Monotheleten/vnter dem Flacianischen hauffen. Durch die Theologen zu Wittemberg/aus der heiligen Schrifft/aus den Symbolis/aus den fu[e]rnemesten Concilijs vnd einhelligem Consenss aller bewerten Lerer. Widerholet vnd Gestellet/zu trewer lere vnd ernster verwarnung an alle frome vnd Gottselige Christen. Neben warhaffter vorantwortung/auff die gifftigen vnd boshaftigen verleumbdungen/so von den Propositionibus vnd Catechismo zu Wittemberg ausgangen/von vielen dieser zeit ausgesprenget werden. . . .* Wittenberg: Hans Lufft, 1571.

———. *Warhafftiger bericht vnd kurtze Warnung der Theologen/beider Vniuersitet Leiptzig vnd Wittemberg Von Den newlich zu Jhena im Druck ausgangenen Acten des Colloquij/so zu Aldenburg in Meissen gehalten.* N.p., 1570.

Schlüsselburg, Conrad. *Haereticorum Catalogus.* Frankfurt am Main: Saurius, 1597-99.

Schmidt, Sebastian. *Beati Patris Martini Lutheri Liber De servo arbitrio, contra Desid. Erasmum Roterdamum: Cum brevibus Annotationibus, Quibus B. Vir ab accusatione, quasi absolutum Calviniorum, vel durius aliquod Dei decretum in libro ipso statuerit. . . .* Strasbourg: Nagel, 1664.

Schoppe, Andreas. *Rettung Des Heiligen Catechismi wider den Schwarm der newen Manicheer vnd Substantijsten.* Jena: Donatus Richtzenhan, 1572.

Scultetus, Abraham. *Vitalia, das ist ein christlich und freundlich Reyß-Gespräch. . . .* Hanau: Aubrius and Clement, 1618.

Selnecker, Nikolaus. *Doctrina de praedestinatione, Item de fato qvaedam vtilia et necessaria.* Frankfurt am Main: Peter Brubach, 1565.

———. *Institvtionis Christianae religionis, pars secvnda, continens locos doctrinae Christianae. . . .* Jena: Jakob Tröster, 1579.

———. *Omnes epistolas D. Pavli apostoli Commentarius plenissimus. . . .* Leipzig: Jacob Apelius, 1595.

———. *Paedagogia christiana, continens capita et locos doctrinae Christianae, forma & serie catechetica uerē & perspicuē explicata. . . . 1565.* Frankfurt am Main: Peter Brubach, 1567.

Sleidan, Johann. *De statv religionis et reipvblicae, Carolo Qvinto, Caesare, Commentarij.* Strasbourg: Wendelin Rihel, 1555.

Spangenberg, Cyriakus. *Apologia Bericht vnd Erklerung M. Cyria. Spangenberg: Der Sieben Predigten halben/von der Praedestination: Go[e]ttlichen Versehung/vnd Ewigen Gnadenwahl in Druck geben.* Eisleben: Andreas Petri, 1568.

————. *Ausslegung der Ersten Acht Capitel der Episteln S. Pavli an die Ro[e]mer.* Strasbourg: Samuel Emmel, 1566.

————. *Ausslegung der Letsten Acht Capitel der Episteln S. PAVLI an die Ro[e]mer.* Strasbourg, 1569.

————. *Colloqvivm So den 9. Septembris des 1577. Jars zu Sangerhausen/Zwischen D. Jacob Andreen vnd M. Cyriacum Spangenberg gehalten worden.* N.p., 1578.

————. *De praedestinatione. Von der Ewigen Vorsehung/vnd Go[e]tlichen/Gnadenwahl. Sieben Predigten.* Erfurt: Georg Bawman, 1567; Eisleben: Andreas Petri, 1568.

————. *Die erste Epistel Paulj. An Timotheum. Außgelegt vnd gepredigt.* Strasbourg: Samuel Emmel, 1564.

————. *Die erste vnd andere Episteln des heyligen Apostels S. Pauli an die Thessalonicher. . . .* 1557. Strasbourg: Samuel Emmel, 1564.

————. *Fu[e]nff Predigten vber den anfang des Euangelij S. Johannis. Im anfang war das Wort etc. . . .* Eisleben: Urban Gaubisch, 1559.

————. *Theander Lutherus. Von des werthen Gottes Manne Doctor Martin Luthers Geistlicher Haushaltung vnd Ritterschafft. . . .* Ursel: Nicolaus Heinrich, 1589.

————. *Von dem Lindauwischen Colloquio/zwischen Doctor Jacob Andreen/vnd Herrn Tobia Ruppio/Anno 1575. Im Augusto gehalten.* N.p., 1577.

————. *Wider den vermeinten Freyen Willen des Menschen/vnd mitwirckung desselben/in bekerung sein selbst. Eine Predigt vber das Euangelium Marci VII.* Frankfurt am Main: Nicolaus Basse, 1562.

Spangenberg, Johann. *Margarita theologica, continens praecipuos locos doctrinae, per quaestiones, breuiter & ordine explicatos. . . .* 1540. Frankfurt am Main: Christoph Egenolph, 1557.

Staupitz, Johannes von. *De executione aeternae praedestinationis.* Nuremberg: Friedrich Peypus, 1517.

Stoltz, Johann. *Refutatio propositionum Pfeffingeri de Libero arbitrio. . . .* Edited by Johannes Aurifaber. N.p., 1558.

Tübingen, theological faculty. *Acta Colloquij Montis Belligartensis: Quod habitum est, Anno Christi 1586. . . .* Tübingen: Georg Gruppenbach, 1587.

Walther, Christoph. *Bericht Von den Wittembergischen Tomis der Bücher des Ehrnwirdigen Herrn Doctoris Martini Lutheri. Wider Matthes Flacium Illyricum.* Wittenberg: Hans Lufft, 1558.

Walther, Georg. *Erste [-Sechste] Theil der Heubtartickel/Christlicher Lere. In Fragstu[e]cken verfasset/vnd mit Gottes Wort/vnd fu[e]rnamen Spru[e]chen D. Lutheri/vnd D. Melanthonis erkleret vnd bekrefftiget. . . .* Magdeburg: Matthaeus Gieseke, 1573.

Weller, Hieronymus. *In Epistolam diui Pauli ad Ephesios, Enarrationes piae, breues & eruditae.* Nuremberg: Johannes Berg and Ulrich Neuber, 1559.

Wesenbeck, Matthias. *Papianus.* Wittenberg, 1567.

Wigand, Johannes. *De confessione in doctrina divina, & necessarijs factis.* Jena: Rödinger, 1569.

————. *De Libero arbitrio Hominis, INTEGRO. CORRVPTO in rebus externis. MORTVO in rebus spiritualibus. RENATO. Doctrina solidē ac Methodicē Verbo Dei tradita & explicata. . . .* Ursel: Heinrich, 1562.

————. *In epistolam S. Pavli ad Romanos annotationes.* Frankfurt am Main: Georg Corvinus, 1580.

————. *In evangelivm S. Johannis explicationes.* Königsberg: Johannes Daubmann, 1575.

————. *In S. Pavli ad Ephesios epistolam, annotationes.* Erfurt: Isaiah Mechler, 1581.

————. *In XII. Prophetas minores explicationes svccinctae.* . . . Frankfurt am Main: Johannes Wolf, 1569.

————. *Von der Erbs[e]nde/Lere aus Gottes wort/aus dem Du[e]ringischen Corpore Doctrinae/vnd aus D. Luthers Bu[e]chern.* . . . Jena: Donatus Richtzenhan, 1571.

Wigand, Johannes, and Matthaeus Judex. *Syntagma, seu Corpus doctrinae Christi, ex novo testamento tantum.* . . . 2nd ed. Basel, 1563.

————. *SYNTAGMA; sev corpvs doctrinae veri & omnipotentis Dei, ex ueteri Testamento.* . . . Basel, 1564.

Wimpina, Konrad. *De divina providentia.* Frankfurt an der Oder: Johannes Hanau, 1516.

Zanchi, Hieronymus. *Opervm Theologicorvm Tomus Septimus.* . . . [Geneva]: Petrus Aubertus, 1613.

Edited Sources

Amsdorf, Nikolaus von. "Nicolai Amsdorfii Conclusiones." In *Abhandlungen Alexander von Oettingen zum siebzigsten Geburtstag.* Munich: Beck, 1898.

Augsburger Interim von 1548, Das. Edited by Joachim Mehlhausen. 2nd ed. Neukirchen: Neukirchener Verlag, 1996.

Calvin, John. *Corpus Reformatorum 30. Ioannis Calvini Opera,* edited by Wilhelm Baum et al., II. Brunswick: Schwetschke, 1864.

————. *Institutes of the Christian Religion.* Edited by John T. McNeill. Translated by Ford Lewis Battles. Library of Christian Classics 20 and 21. Philadelphia: Westminster, 1960.

Chemnitz, Martin. *Martini Chemnitii . . . ad Matthiam Ritterum . . . Epistolae.* Edited by Georg Christian Joannis. Frankfurt am Main: Hocker, 1712.

D. Johann Ecks Vierhundertundvier Artikel zum Reichstag von Augsburg 1530. Edited by Wilhelm Gussmann. Kassel: Picardy, 1930.

Erasmus, Desiderius. *Collected Works of Erasmus 76, Controversies.* Edited by Charles Trinkaus. Toronto: University of Toronto Press, 1999.

————. *Desiderii Erasmi Roterodami Opera Omnia.* . . . Edited by J. Clericus. 10 vols. Leiden, 1703-6.

————. *Opvs epistolarvm Des. Erasmi Roterodami.* Edited by P. S. Allen. Vol. 3. Oxford: Clarendon, 1913.

Fecht, Johann, ed. *Historiae ecclesiasticae seculi A.N.C. XVI. Supplementum; plurimorum et celeberrimorum ex illo aevo theologorum epistolis, ad Joannem, Erasmum et Philippum Marbachios.* . . . Durlach: Martin Muller, 1684.

Hachfeld, H. "Die schwäbische Confession (liber Tubingensis). Nach einer Wolfenbüttler Handschrift." *Zeitschrift für historische Theologie* 36 (1866): 234-301.

Luther, Martin. *Dr. Martin Luthers Werke.* Weimar: Böhlau, 1883-.

―――. *Luther's Epistle Sermons, Advent and Christmas Season*. Translated by John Nicolaus Lenker, I. In *Luther's Complete Works* VII. Minneapolis: Luther Press, 1908.

―――. *Luther's Works*. Saint Louis and Philadelphia: Concordia and Fortress, 1958-86.

Melanchthon, Philip. *Corpus Reformatorum. Opera quae supersunt omnia*. Edited by C. G. Bretschneider and H. E. Bindweil. Halle and Brunswick: Schwetschke, 1834-60.

―――. *Melanchthons Werke in Auswahl [Studien-Ausgabe]*. Edited by Robert Stupperich. 6 vols. Gütersloh: Bertelsmann, 1955.

―――. *Supplementa Melanchthonia*. 6/1 (*Melanchthons Briefwechsel* 1). 1926. Frankfurt am Main: Minerva, 1968.

Rehtmeyer, Philipp Julius. *Historiae ecclesiasticae inclytae urbis Brunsvigae Pars III. Oder: Der beru[e]hmten Stadt Braunschweig Kirchen-Historie Dritter Theil. . . .* Brunswick: Zilliger, 1710.

Saxony, ducal government. "Superdeclaration." 1564. In Christian F. Paullini, *Historia Isenacensis*, 192-94. Frankfurt am Main: Bauer, 1698.

Spangenberg, Cyriakus. *Der Briefwechsel des M. Cyriacus Spangenberg*. Edited by Heinrich Rembe. Dresden: Naumann, 1887.

―――. "Jakob Andreae im Streit mit Cyriakus Spangenberg — Quellen zur Disputation von Sangerhausen 1577." Edited by Helmut Neumaier. *Blätter für württembergische Kirchengeschichte* 95 (1995): 49-88.

Spiegel, B. "Zwei ungedruckte Briefe Philipp Melanchthon's." *Zeitschrift für wissenschaftliche Theologie* 11 (1868): 457.

Secondary Literature

Abray, Lorna Jane. *The People's Reformation: Magistrates, Clergy, and Commons in Strasbourg, 1500-1598*. Ithaca, N.Y.: Cornell University Press, 1985.

Adam, Gottfried. *Der Streit um die Prädestination im ausgehenden 16. Jahrhundert, eine Untersuchung zu den Entwürfen vom Samuel Huber und Aegidius Hunnius*. Neukirchen: Neukirchener Verlag, 1970.

Adams, Marilyn McCord. "Ockham on Will, Nature and Morality." In *Cambridge Companion to Ockham*, edited by Paul Vincent Spade, 245-72. Cambridge: Cambridge University Press, 1999.

Adelung, Johann Christoph, ed. *Fortsetzung und Erga[e]nzungen zu Christian Gottlieb Jo[e]chers allgemeinen Gelehrten-Lexico*. 2. Leipzig: Gleditsch, 1787.

Althaus, Paul. *The Theology of Martin Luther*. Translated by Robert C. Schultz. Philadelphia: Fortress, 1966.

Arand, Charles P. *That I May Be His Own: An Overview of Luther's Catechisms*. Saint Louis: Concordia, 2000.

―――. "Two Kinds of Righteousness as a Framework for Law and Gospel in the Apology." *LQ* 15 (2001): 417-39.

Asendorf, Ulrich. *Eschatologie bei Luther*. Göttingen: Vandenhoeck & Ruprecht, 1967.

―――. *Luther und Hegel: Untersuchungen zur Grundlegung einer neuen systematischen Theologie*. Wiesbaden: Steiner, 1982.

Barton, Peter F. *Um Luthers Erbe. Studien und Texte zur Spätreformation, Tilemann Heshusius (1527-1559)*. Witten: Luther-Verlag, 1972.

Bauer, Martin. *Evangelische Theologen in und um Erfurt im 16. bis 18. Jarhundert*. Neustadt an der Aisch: Degener, 1992.

Beck, August. *Johann Friedrich der Mittlere, Herzog zu Sachsen*. Weimar: Böhlau, 1858.

Bentley, Jerry, *Humanists and Holy Writ: New Testament Scholarship in the Renaissance*. Princeton: Princeton University Press, 1983.

Biundo, Georg. *Die evangelischen Geistlichen der Pfalz seit der Reformation (Pfälzisches Pfarrerbuch)*. Neustadt an der Aisch: Degener, 1968.

Bornkamm, Heinrich. "Erasmus und Luther." *LuJ* 25 (1958): 3-22.

Boyle, Marjorie O'Rourke. *Rhetoric and Reform: Erasmus' Civil Dispute with Luther*. Cambridge: Harvard University Press, 1983.

Brandy, Hans Christian. "Jacob Andreaes Fünf Artikel von 1568/69." *ZKG* 98 (1987): 338-51.

Brecht, Martin. *Die frühe Theologie des Johannes Brenz*. Tübingen: Mohr (Siebeck), 1966.

———. *Martin Luther. Dritter Band. Die Erhaltung der Kirche 1532-1546*. Stuttgart: Calwer, 1987.

———. *Martin Luther. Zweiter Band. Ordnung und Abgrenzung der Reformation, 1521-1532*. Stuttgart: Calwer Verlag, 1986. Translated as *Martin Luther, Shaping and Defining the Reformation, 1521-1532*, trans. James L. Schaaf (Minneapolis: Fortress, 1990).

Brown, Christopher B. *Singing the Gospel: Lutheran Hymns and the Success of the Reformation in Joachimsthal*. Cambridge: Harvard University Press, 2005.

Bundschuh, Benno. *Das Wormser Religionsgespräch von 1557, unter besonderer Berücksichtigung der kaiserlichen Religionspolitik*. Münster: Aschendorff, 1988.

Burchill, Christopher J. "Girolamo Zanchi: Portrait of a Reformed Theologian and His Work." *SCJ* 15 (1984): 185-207.

Calinich, Robert. *Der Naumburger Fürstentag, 1561*. Gotha: Perthes, 1870.

Chrisman, Miriam Ussher. *Lay Culture, Learned Culture, Books and Social Change in Strasbourg, 1480-1599*. New Haven: Yale University Press, 1982.

Christman, Robert J. "Heretics in Luther's Homeland: The Controversy over Original Sin in Late Sixteenth-Century Mansfeld." Ph.D. dissertation, University of Arizona, 2004.

Dingel, Irene. *Concordia controversa, Die öffentlichen Diskussionen um das lutherische Konkordienwerk am Ende des 16. Jahrhunderts*. Gütersloh: Gütersloher Verlagshaus, 1996.

———. "Melanchthons Einigungsbemühen zwischen den Fronten: Der Frankfurter Rezeß." In *Philipp Melanchthon, Ein Wegbereiter für die Ökumene*, edited by Jörg Haustein, 121-43. Göttingen: Vandenhoeck & Ruprecht, 1997.

———. "Melanchthon und die Normierung des Bekenntnisses." In *Der Theologe Melanchthon*, edited by Günter Frank, 195-211. Stuttgart: Thorbecke, 2000.

———. "Melanchthon und Westeuropa." In *Philipp Melanchthon als Politiker zwischen Reich, Reichsständen und Konfessionsparteien*, edited by Günther Wartenberg and Matthias Zenter, 105-22. Themata Leucoreana. Wittenberg: Drei Kastanien Verlag, 1998.

———. "The Preface of *The Book of Concord* as a Reflection of Sixteenth-Century Confessional Development." *LQ* 15 (2001): 171-95.

―――. "'Der rechten Lehre zuwider,' Die Beurteilung des Interims in ausgewählten theologischen Reaktionen." In *Das Interim 1548/50, Herrschaftskrise und Glaubenskonflikt. Symposion des Verein für Reformationsgeschichte in der Leucorea, Wittenberg, 3.10–6.10.2001,* ed. Luise Schorn-Schütte. Gütersloh: Gütersloher Verlagshaus, forthcoming.

―――. "'Recht glauben, Christlich leben, und seliglich sterben,' die Leichenpredigt als evangelische Verkündigung im 16. Jahrhundert." In *Leichenpredigten als Quellen historischer Wissenschaft,* vol. 4, edited by Rudolf Lenz, 9-36. Stuttgart, 2004.

―――. "Die Torgauer Artikel (1574) als Vermittlungsversuch zwischen der Theologie Luthers und der Melanchthons." In *Praxis Pietatis. Beiträge zu Theologie und Frömmigkeit in der Frühen Neuzeit. Wolfgang Sommer zum 60. Geburtstag,* edited by Hans-Jörg Nieden and Marcel Nieden, 119-34. Stuttgart: Kohlhammer, 1999.

Doerne, Martin. "Gottes Ehre am gebundenen Willen. Evangelische Grundlagen und theologische Spitzensätze in *De servo arbitrio*." *LuJ* 20 (1938): 45-92.

Donnelly, John Patrick, S.J. "Calvinist Thomism." *Viator* 7 (1976): 441-55.

―――. "Italian Influences on the Development of Calvinist Scholasticism." *SCJ* 7, no. 2 (1976): 81-101.

Ebel, Jobst. "Die Herkunft des Konzeptes der Konkordienformel, Die Funktionen der fünf Verfasser neben Andreae beim Zustandekommen der Formel." *ZKG* 91 (1980): 245-73.

―――. "Jacob Andreae (1528-1590) als Verfasser der Konkordienformel." *ZKG* 89 (1978): 78-119.

Flogaus, Reinhard. "Luther versus Melanchthon? Zur Frage der Einheit der Wittenberger Reformation in der Rechtfertigungslehre." *ARG* 91 (2000): 6-46.

Forde, Gerhard O. *The Captivation of the Will.* Grand Rapids: Eerdmans, 2005.

―――. *On Being a Theologian of the Cross: Reflections on Luther's Heidelberg Disputation, 1518.* Grand Rapids: Eerdmans, 1997.

Förteckning på Biskopar i Sverige och Finland. Christianstad: Cedergréen, 1830.

Frank, Günter. *Die theologische Philosophie Philipp Melanchthons (1497-1560).* Leipzig: Benno, 1995.

Gensichen, Hans-Werner. *We Condemn: How Luther and Sixteenth Century Lutheranism Condemned False Doctrine.* Translated by Herbert J. A. Bouman. Saint Louis: Concordia, 1967.

Geyer, Hans-Georg. "Zur Rolle der Prädestinationslehre Augustins beim jungen Melanchthon." In *Studien zur Geschichte und Theologie der Reformation. Festschrift für Ernst Bizer,* edited by Luise Abramowski and J. F. Gerhard Goeters, 175-87. Neukirchen: Neukirchener Verlag, 1969.

Grane, Leif. "Erasmus und Luther vor dem Streit 1524/25." In *Widerspruch. Luthers Auseinandersetzung mit Erasmus von Rotterdam,* edited by Kari Kopperi, 9-25. Helsinki: Luther-Agricola-Gesellschaft, 1997.

―――. *Martinus Noster: Luther in the German Reform Movement, 1518-1521.* Mainz: Zabern, 1994.

Green, Lowell C. *How Melanchthon Helped Luther Discover the Gospel: The Doctrine of Justification in the Reformation.* Fallbrook, Calif.: Verdict, 1980.

————. "Luther's Understanding of the Freedom of God and the Salvation of Man: His Interpretation of 1 Timothy 2:4." *ARG* 87 (1996): 57-73.

————. "The Problem of the 'Universal Will of God unto Salvation' of 1 Timothy 2:4 in Sixteenth-Century Thought." *LQ* 9 (1995): 281-300.

————. "The Three Causes of Conversion in Philipp Melanchthon, Martin Chemnitz, David Chytraeus, and the Formula of Concord." *LuJ* 47 (1980): 89-114.

Greschat, Martin. *Luther neben Melanchthon. Studien zur Gestalt der Rechtfertigungslehre zwischen 1528 und 1537*. Witten: Luther-Verlag, 1965.

————. "Luthers Haltung im Bauernkrieg." *ARG* 57 (1965): 31-47.

Gründler, Otto. *Die Gotteslehre Girolamo Zanchi und ihre Bedeutung für seine Lehre von der Prädestination*. Neukirchen: Neukirchener Verlag, 1965.

Guggisberg, Hans. *Basel in the Sixteenth Century: Aspects of the City Republic before, during, and after the Reformation*. Saint Louis: Center for Reformation Research, 1982.

Günther, Hartmut Oskar. "Die Entwicklung der Willenslehre Melanchthons in der Auseinandersetzung mit Luther und Erasmus." Th.D. diss., University of Erlangen, 1963.

Hägglund, Bengt. *The Background of Luther's Doctrine of Justification in Late Medieval Theology*. Philadelphia: Fortress, 1971.

————. "Die Frage der Willensfreiheit in der Auseinandersetzung zwischen Erasmus und Luther." In *Renaissance — Reformation. Gegensätze und Gemeinsamkeiten*, edited by August Buck, 181-95. Wiesbaden: Harrassowitz, 1984.

————. *Theologie und Philosophie bei Luther und in der Occamistischen Tradition, Luthers Stellung zur Theorie von der doppelten Wahrheit*. Lund: Gleerup, 1955.

————. "Wie hat Martin Chemnitz zu Luthers *De servo arbitrio* Stellung genommen?" In *Der zweite Martin der Lutherischen Kirche, Festschrift zum 400. Todestag von Martin Chemnitz*, edited by W. A. Jünke, 48-59. Brunswick: Ev. Luth. Stadtkirchenverband und Propstei Braunschweig, 1986. Reprinted in Hägglund, *Chemnitz — Gerhard — Arndt — Rudbeckius. Aufsätze zum Studium der altlutherischen Theologie*, ed. Alexander Bitzel and Johann Anselm Steiger (Waltrop: Spenner, 2003), 65-76.

Håhl, Johann Israel. *Linköpings Stifts Herdaminne*. Norköping: Östlund & Berling, 1846.

Hase, Hans Christoph von. *Die Gestalt der Kirche Luthers. Der casus confessionis im Kampf des Matthias Flacius gegen das Interim von 1548*. Göttingen: Vandenhoeck & Ruprecht, 1940.

Hasse, Hans-Peter. *Zensur theologischer Bücher in Kursachsen im konfessionellen Zeitalter, Studien zur kursächsischen Literatur- und Religionspolitik in den Jahren 1569 bis 1575*. Leipzig: Evangelische Verlagsanstalt, 2000.

Headley, John M. *Luther's View of Church History*. New Haven: Yale University Press, 1963.

Hendrix, Scott. "Urbanus Rhegius, Frontline Reformer." *LQ* 18 (2004): 76-87.

Herms, Eilert. "Gewißheit in Martin Luthers 'De servo arbitrio.'" *LuJ* 67 (2000): 23-50.

Heussi, Karl. *Geschichte der theologischen Fakultät zu Jena*. Weimar: Böhlau, 1954.

Holeczek, Heinz. "Erasmus' Stellung zur Reformation: Studia humanitatis und Kirchenreform." In *Renaissance — Reform. Gegensätze und Gemeinsamkeiten*, edited by August Buck, 136-45. Wiesbaden: Harrassowitz, 1984.

Hotz, Wilhelm. "Cyriakus Spangenbergs Leben und Schicksale als Pfarrer in Schlitz von

1580-1590." *Beiträge zur Hessischen Kirchengeschichte. Ergänzungsband III zum Archiv für Hessische Geschichte und Altertumskunde,* n.s., 1908, 205-96.

Hübner, Friedrich. "Über den freien Willen. Artikel II: 'De libero arbitrio' aus seinen historischen Grundlagen heraus interpretiert." In *Widerspruch, Dialog und Einigung. Studien zur Konkordienformel der Lutherischen Reformation,* 137-70. Stuttgart: Calwer Verlag, 1977.

Iwand, Hans Joachim. *Um den rechten Glauben, Gesammelte Aufsätze.* Edited by Karl Gerhard Steck. Munich: Kaiser, 1959.

Junghans, Helmar. *Der junge Luther und die Humanisten.* Weimar: Böhlau, 1984.

————. *Ockham im Lichte der neuen Forschung.* Berlin: Lutherisches Verlagshaus, 1968.

Kaufmann, Thomas. *Universität und lutherische Konfessionalisierung. Die Rostocker Theologieprofessoren und ihr Beitrag zur theologischen Bildung und kirchlichen Gestaltung im Herzogtum Mecklenburg zwischen 1550 und 1675.* Gütersloh: Gütersloher Verlagshaus, 1997.

Kawerau, Gustav. Art. Strigel. *RE* 19:97-102.

Keller, Rudolf. *Die Confessio Augustana im theologischen Wirken des Rostocker Professors David Chyträus (1530-1600).* Göttingen: Vandenhoeck & Ruprecht, 1994.

————. "David Chytraeus (1530-1600). Melanchthons Geist im Luthertum." In *Melanchthon in seinen Schüler,* edited by Heinz Scheible, 361-71. Wiesbaden: Harrassowitz, 1997.

————. *Der Schlüssel zur Schrift, Die Lehre vom Wort Gottes bei Matthias Flacius Illyricus.* Hannover: Lutherisches Verlagshaus, 1984.

Kinsman, Robert S., ed. *The Darker Vision of the Renaissance: Beyond the Fields of Reason.* Berkeley: University of California Press, 1974.

Kittelson, James M. "Marbach vs. Zanchi: The Resolution of Controversy in Late Reformation Strasbourg." *SCJ* 8, no. 3 (1977): 31-44.

————. "The Significance of Humanist Educational Methods for Reformation Theology." *LuJ* 66 (1999): 229-36.

————. *Toward an Established Church: Strasbourg from 1500 to the Dawn of the Seventeenth Century.* Mainz: Zabern, 2000.

————. *Wolfgang Capito: From Humanist to Reformer.* Leiden: Brill, 1975.

Kjöllerström, Sven. *Striden kring kalvinismen i Sverige under Erik XIV.* Lund: Gleerup, 1935.

Klän, Werner. "Der 'vierte Mann'. Auf den Spuren von Nikolaus Selnecker (1530-1592). Beitrag zu Entstehung und Verbreitung der Konkordienformel." *Lutherische Theologie und Kirche* 17 (1993): 145-74.

Kleinhans, Robert G. "Luther and Erasmus, Another Perspective." *Church History* 39 (1970): 459-69.

Koch, Ernst. "Auseinandersetzungen um die Autorität von Philipp Melanchthon und Martin Luther in Kursachsen im Vorfeld der Konkordienformel von 1577." *LuJ* 59 (1992): 128-59.

Kohls, Ernst-Wilhelm. *Die Theologie des Erasmus.* 2 vols. Basel: Reinhardt, 1966.

Kolb, Robert. "The Advance of Dialectic in Lutheran Theology: The Role of Johannes Wigand (1523-1587)." In *Regnum, Religio et Ratio: Essays Presented to Robert M. Kingdon,* edited by Jerome Friedman, 93-102. Kirksville, Mo.: Sixteenth Century Journal, 1987. In *Luther's Heirs,* chap. 16.

―――. *Andreae and the Formula of Concord: Six Sermons on the Way to Lutheran Unity.* Saint Louis: Concordia, 1977.

―――. "'A Beautiful, Delightful Jewel': Cyriakus Spangenberg's Plan for the Sixteenth Century Noble's Library." *Journal of Library History* 24 (1979): 129-59.

―――. "The Braunschweig Resolution: The *Corpus Doctrinae Prutenicum* of Joachim Mörlin and Martin Chemnitz as an Interpretation of Wittenberg Theology." In *Confessionalization in Europe, 1555-1700: Essays in Honor and Memory of Bodo Nischan,* edited by John M. Headley and Hans J. Hillerbrand, 67-89. Aldershot: Ashgate, 2004.

―――. *Confessing the Faith: Reformers Define the Church, 1530-1580.* Saint Louis: Concordia, 1991.

―――. "Cyriakus Spangenberg's Adelspiegel: A Theologian's View of the Duties of the Nobleman." In *Social Groups and Religious Ideas in the Sixteenth Century,* edited by Miriam U. Chrisman and Otto Gründler, 12-21. Kalamazoo, Mich.: Medieval Institute, 1977.

―――. "Dynamics of Party Conflict in the Saxon Late Reformation: Gnesio-Lutherans vs. Philippists." *Journal of Modern History* 49 (1977): D1289-1305. In *Luther's Heirs,* chap. 1.

―――. "The Flacian Rejection of the Concordia: Prophetic Style and Action in the German Late Reformation." *ARG* 73 (1982): 196-217. In *Luther's Heirs,* chap. 6.

―――. "Georg Major as Controversialist: Polemics in the Late Reformation." *Church History* 45 (1976): 455-68. In *Luther's Heirs,* chap. 4.

―――. "The German Lutheran Reaction to the Third Period of the Council of Trent." *LuJ* 51 (1984): 63-95. In *Luther's Heirs,* chap. 5.

―――. "God Kills to Make Alive: Romans 6 and Luther's Understanding of Justification (1535)." *LQ* 12, no. 1 (1998): 33-56.

―――. "Jakob Andreae's Concern for the Laity." *Concordia Journal* 4 (1978): 58-67.

―――. "Learning to Drink from the Fountains of Israel: Cyriakus Spangenberg Learns Hermeneutics from Luther." *Lutheran Synod Quarterly* 34 (1994): 2-31. In *Luther's Heirs,* chap. 13.

―――. "Luther on the Two Kinds of Righteousness: Reflections on His Two-Dimensional Definition of Humanity at the Heart of His Theology." *LQ* 13 (1999): 449-66. Also in *Harvesting Martin Luther's Reflections on Theology, Ethics, and the Church,* ed. Timothy J. Wengert (Grand Rapids: Eerdmans, 2003), 38-55.

―――. *Luther's Heirs Define His Legacy: Studies on Lutheran Confessionalization.* Aldershot: Variorum, 1996.

―――. *Martin Luther as Prophet, Teacher, and Hero: Images of the Reformer, 1520-1620.* Grand Rapids: Baker, 1999.

―――. "Matthaeus Judex's Condemnation of Princely Censorship of Theologians' Publications." *Church History* 50 (1981): 401-14. In *Luther's Heirs,* chap. 14.

―――. "Melanchthon's Doctrinal Last Will and Testament: The *Responsiones ad articulos Bavaricae inquisitionis* as His Final Confession of Faith." *SCJ* 35 (2004): 97-114.

―――. "Melanchthon's Influence on the Exegesis of His Students: The Case of Romans 9." In *Philip Melanchthon (1497-1560) and the Commentary,* edited by M. Patrick Graham and Timothy J. Wengert, 198-217. Sheffield: Sheffield Academic Press, 1997.

———. "Nikolaus Gallus' Critique of Philip Melanchthon's Teaching on the Freedom of the Will." *ARG* 91 (2000): 87-110.

———. *Nikolaus von Amsdorf (1483-1565): Popular Polemics in the Preservation of Luther's Legacy.* Nieuwkoop: De Graaf, 1978.

———. "Nikolaus von Amsdorf on Vessels of Wrath and Vessels of Mercy: A Lutheran's Doctrine of Double Predestination." *Harvard Theological Review* 69 (1976): 325-43. In *Luther's Heirs,* chap. 2.

———. "On Eternal Predestination and God's Election by Grace: The Exegetical Basis of the Lutheran Teaching in Cyriakus Spangenberg's Commentary on Romans 8 and 9." *Lutheran Synod Quarterly* 34 (1994): 32-59. In *Luther's Heirs,* chap. 13.

———. "The Ordering of the *Loci Communes Theologici:* The Structuring of the Melanchthonian Dogmatic Tradition." *Concordia Journal* 23 (1997): 317-37.

———. "Patristic Citation as Homiletical Tool in the Vernacular Sermon of the German Late Reformation." In *Die Patristik in der Bibelexegese des 16. Jahrhunderts,* edited by David C. Steinmetz, 151-79. Wiesbaden: Harrassowitz, 1999.

———. "Philipp's Foes but Followers Nonetheless: Late Humanism among the Gnesio-Lutherans." In *The Harvest of Humanism in Central Europe: Essays in Honor of Lewis W. Spitz,* edited by Manfred P. Fleischer, 159-77. Saint Louis: Concordia, 1992. In *Luther's Heirs,* chap. 15.

———. "Preaching and Hearing in Luther's Congregations: Village Pastors and Peasant Congregations." *Lutheran Synod Quarterly* 34 (1994): 60-91. In *Luther's Heirs,* chap. 13.

———. "'Saint John Hus' and 'Jerome Savonarola, Confessor of God': The Lutheran 'Canonization' of Late Medieval Martyrs." *Concordia Journal* 17 (1991): 404-18.

———. *Teaching God's Children His Teaching: A Guide for the Study of Luther's Catechism.* Hutchinson, Minn.: Crown, 1992.

———. "'What Benefit Does the Soul Receive from a Handful of Water?' Luther's Preaching on Baptism, 1528-1539." *Concordia Journal* 25 (1999): 346-63.

Korf, August. *Geschichte der evangelischen Gemeinde in Oberursel a. Taunus.* Oberursel: Evang. Pfarramt, 1902.

Kress, Christine. *Gottes Allmacht angesichts von Leiden, Zur Interpretation der Gotteslehre in den systematisch-theologischen Entwürfen von Paul Althaus, Paul Tillich und Karl Barth.* Neukirchen-Vluyn: Neukirchener Verlag, 1999.

Kristeller, Paul O. *Renaissance Thought and Its Sources.* New York: Columbia University Press, 1979.

Krodel, Gottfried G. "Erasmus — Luther: One Theology, One Method, Two Results." *Concordia Theological Monthly* 41 (1970): 648-67.

Kropatscheck, Hans. "Das Problem theologischer Anthropologie auf dem Weimarer Gespräch von 1560 zwischen Matthias Flacius Illyricus und Viktorin Strigel." Licentiate diss., University of Göttingen, 1943.

Kruse, Martin. *Speners Kritik am landesherrlichen Kirchenregiment und ihre Vorgeschichte.* Witten: Luther-Verlag, 1971.

Kunze, Johannes. *Erasmus und Luther. Der Einfluss des Erasmus auf die Kommentierung des Galaterbriefes und der Psalmen durch Luther 1519-1521.* Münster: LIT, 2000.

Lane, Anthony N. S. "The Influence upon Calvin of His Debate with Pighius." In

Auctoritas Patrum II. Neue Beiträge zur Rezeption der Kirchenväter im 15. und 16. Jahrhundert, edited by Leif Grane, Alfred Schindler, and Markus Wriedt, 125-39. Mainz: Zabern, 1998.

Leder, Hans-Günter. "Luthers Beziehungen zu seinen Wittenberger Freunden." In *Leben und Werk Martin Luthers von 1526 bis 1546, Festgabe zu seinem 500. Geburtstag*, edited by Helmar Junghans, 1:419-40. Berlin: Evangelische Verlagsanstalt, 1983.

Leppin, Volker. *Antichrist und Jüngster Tag. Das Profil apokalyptischer Flugschriftenpublizistik im deutschen Luthertum 1548-1618*. Gütersloh: Gütersloher Verlagshaus, 1999.

———. *Geglaubte Wahrheit, Das Theologieverständnis Wilhelms von Ockham*. Göttingen: Vandenhoeck & Ruprecht, 1995.

Levi, Anthony. *Renaissance and Reformation: The Intellectual Genesis*. New Haven: Yale University Press, 2002.

Liebmann, Maximilian. *Urbanus Rhegius und die Anfänge der Reformation. Beiträge zu seinem Leben, seiner Lehre und seinem Wirken bis zum Augsburger Reichstag von 1530*. Münster: Aschendorff, 1980.

Lindhardt, Jan. "Valla and Luther on the Free Will." In *Widerspruch. Luthers Auseinandersetzung mit Erasmus von Rotterdam*, edited by Kari Kopperi, 46-53. Helsinki: Luther-Agricola-Gesellschaft, 1997.

Lohse, Bernhard. "Dogma und Bekenntnis in der Reformation: Von Luther bis zum Konkordienbuch." In *Handbuch der Dogmen- und Theologiegeschichte, Zweiter Band: Die Lehrentwicklung im Rahmen der Konfessionalität*, edited by Carl Andresen, 1-166. Göttingen: Vandenhoeck & Ruprecht, 1980.

———. *Martin Luther's Theology, Its Historical and Systematic Development*. Translated by Roy A. Harrisville. Minneapolis: Fortress, 1999.

———, ed. *Der Durchbruch der reformatorischen Erkenntnis bei Luther*. Darmstadt: Wissenschaftliche Buchgesellschaft, 1968.

———. *Der Durchbruch der reformatorischen Erkenntnis bei Luther, Neue Untersuchungen*. Stuttgart: Steiner, 1988.

Mager, Inge. "Der Beitrag des David Chytraeus zur Entstehung und Rezeption der Konkordienformel." *Berliner Theologische Zeitschrift* 18 (2001): 207-21.

———. "Jakob Andreaes lateinische Unionsartikel von 1568." *ZKG* 98 (1987): 70-86.

———. *Die Konkordienformel im Fürstentum Braunschweig-Wolfenbüttel. Entstehungsbeitrag — Rezeption — Geltung*. Göttingen: Vandenhoeck & Ruprecht, 1993.

Martikainen, Eeva. "Der Begriff 'Gott' in *De servo arbitrio*." In *Widerspruch. Luthers Auseinandersetzung mit Erasmus von Rotterdam*, edited by Kari Kopperi, 26-45. Helsinki: Luther-Agricola-Gesellschaft, 1997.

Masaki, Makito. "Luther's Two Kinds of Righteousness and His Wartburg Postil (1522): How Luther Exhorted People to Live Christian Lives." Ph.D. diss., Concordia Seminary, Saint Louis, forthcoming.

Matheson, Peter. *The Rhetoric of the Reformation*. Edinburgh: T. & T. Clark, 1998.

Matthias, Walter. "Über die Lehre von der Willensfreiheit in der altlutherischen Theologie." *ZKG* 74 (1963): 109-33.

Matz, Wolfgang. *Der befreite Mensch. Die Willenslehre in der Theologie Philipp Melanchthons*. Göttingen: Vandenhoeck & Ruprecht, 2001.

McSorley, Harry J. *Luther: Right or Wrong? An Ecumenical-Theological Study of Luther's Major Work, "The Bondage of the Will."* New York: Newman; Minneapolis: Augsburg, 1969.

Mennecke-Haustein, Ute. *Luthers Trostbriefe.* Gütersloh: Mohn, 1989.

Meusel, O. "Die Reussische oder Reussisch-Schönburgische Konfession." *Beiträge zur sächsischen Kirchengeschichte* 14 (1899): 149-87.

Midelfort, H. C. Erik. "The German Nobility and Their Crisis of Legitimacy in the Late Sixteenth Century." In *Germania Illustrata: Essays on Early Modern Germany Presented to Gerald Strauss,* edited by Andrew C. Fix and Susan C. Karant-Nunn, 217-42. Kirksville, Mo.: Sixteenth Century Journal, 1992.

Moltmann, Jürgen. *Prädestination und Perseveranz, Geschichte und Bedeutung der reformierten Lehre "de perseverantia sanctorum."* Neukirchen: Neukirchener Verlag, 1961.

Muehlenberg, Ekkehard. "Synergia and Justification by Faith." In *Discord, Dialogue, and Concord: Studies in the Lutheran Reformation's Formula of Concord,* edited by Lewis W. Spitz and Wenzel Lohff, 15-37. Philadelphia: Fortress, 1977.

Muller, Richard. *Christ and the Decree: Christology and Predestination in Reformed Theology from Calvin to Perkins.* Durham: Labyrinth, 1986.

Müller-Streisand, Rosemarie. "Theologie und Kirchenpolitik bei Jacob Andreä bis zum Jahr 1568." *Blätter für württembergische Kirchengeschichte* 60/61 (1960/61): 224-395.

Neuroth, Ferdinand. *Geschichte der Stadt Oberursel und der Hohemark.* Oberursel: Altkönig-Verlag, 1955.

Oberman, Heiko Augustinus. *The Harvest of Medieval Theology: Gabriel Biel and Late Medieval Nominalism.* Durham: Labyrinth, 1983.

———. *Luther, Man between God and the Devil.* Translated by Eileen Walliser-Schwarzbart. New Haven: Yale University Press, 1989.

Olson, Oliver K. *Matthias Flacius and the Survival of Luther's Reform.* Wiesbaden: Harrassowitz, 2002.

———. "The Rise and Fall of the Antwerp Martinists." *LQ* 1 (1987): 105-11.

O'Malley, John W. "Erasmus and Luther, Continuity and Discontinuity as Key to Their Conflict." *SCJ* 5, no. 2 (1974): 47-65.

Payne, John B. "The Significance of Lutheranizing Changes in Erasmus' Interpretation of Paul's Letters to the Romans and the Galatians in His Annotations (1527) and Paraphrases (1532)." In *Histoire de l'exégèse au XVIe siècle. Textes du Colloque International tenu à Genève en 1976,* 312-30. Geneva: Droz, 1978.

Périgot, Béatrice. "La *disputatio* comme méthode dans la confrontation sur le libre-arbitre d'Erasme et de Luther." *Université de Genève Institut d'Histoire de la Reformation Bulletin Annuel* 23 (2001-2): 31-52.

Pommerien, Albert. *Viktorin Strigels Lehre von dem Peccatum originis.* Hannover: Stephanusstift, 1917.

Preger, Wilhelm. *Matthias Flacius Illyricus und seine Zeit.* 2 vols. Erlangen: Bläsing, 1859-61.

Raitt, Jill. *The Colloquy of Montbéliard: Religion and Politics in the Sixteenth Century.* New York: Oxford University Press, 1993.

Raunio, Antti. "Das liberum arbitrium als göttliche Eigenschaft in Luthers De servo arbitrio." In *Widerspruch. Luthers Auseinandersetzung mit Erasmus von Rotterdam,* edited by Kari Kopperi, 63-91. Helsinki: Luther-Agricola-Gesellschaft, 1997.

Reinhuber, Thomas. *Kämpfender Glaube. Studien zu Luthers Bekenntnis am Ende von De servo arbitrio.* Berlin: De Gruyter, 2000.

Ritschl, Albrecht. *Die christliche Lehre von der Rechtfertigung und Versöhnung. Bd. 1.* Bonn: Marcus, 1870.

Ritschl, Otto. *Dogmengeschichte des Protestantismus IV.* Leipzig: Hinrichs, 1927.

Roberts, Michael. *The Early Vasas: A History of Sweden, 1523-1611.* Cambridge: University Press, 1968.

Rosin, Robert. *Reformers, the Preacher, and Skepticism: Luther, Brenz, Melanchthon, and Ecclesiastes.* Mainz: Zabern, 1997.

Rost, Gerhard. *Der Prädestinationsgedanke in der Theologie Martin Luthers.* Berlin: Evangelische Verlagsanstalt, 1966.

Schäfer, Rolf. "Zur Prädestinationslehre beim jungen Melanchthon." *ZKG* 63 (1966): 352-78.

Scheible, Heinz. *Die Entstehung der Magdeburger Zenturien.* Gütersloh: Mohn, 1966.

———. *Melanchthon, eine Biographie.* Munich: Beck, 1997.

———. "Melanchthon zwischen Luther und Erasmus." In *Renaissance — Reformation. Gegensätze und Gemeinsamkeiten,* edited by August Buck, 155-80. Wiesbaden: Harrassowitz, 1984.

Schleiner, Winfried. *Melancholy, Genius, and Utopia in the Renaissance.* Wiesbaden: Harrassowitz, 1991.

Schmidt, Kurt Dietrich. "Der Göttinger Bekehrungsstreit." *Zeitschrift der Gesellschaft für niedersächsische Kirchengeschichte* 34/35 (1929): 66-121.

Schneider, John R. *Philip Melanchthon's Rhetorical Construal of Biblical Authority: Oratio Sacra.* Lewiston, N.Y.: Mellen, 1990.

Schwarzwäller, Klaus. "The Bondage of the Free Human." In *By Faith Alone: Essays on Justification in Honor of Gerhard O. Forde,* edited by Joseph A. Burgess and Marc Kolden, 46-66. Grand Rapids: Eerdmans, 2004.

———. *sibboleth. Die Interpretation von Luthers Schrift de servo arbitrio seit Theodosius Harnack. Ein systematisch-kritischer Überblick.* Munich: Kaiser, 1969.

———. *Theologia crucis. Luthers Lehre von Prädestination nach De servo arbitrio, 1525.* Munich: Kaiser, 1970.

Söderlund, Rune. *Ex praevisa fide. Zum Verständnis der Prädestinationslehre in der lutherischen Orthodoxie.* Hannover: Lutherisches Verlagshaus, 1983.

Sohm, Walter. *Die Schule Johann Sturms und die Kirche Strassburgs in ihrem gegenseitigen Verhältnis 1530-1581.* Munich and Berlin: Oldenbourg, 1912.

Spijker, Willem van't. "Bucer als Zeuge Zanchis im Straßburger Prädestinationsstreit." In *Das Reformiertes Erbe, Festschrift für Gottfried W. Locher zu seinem 80. Geburtstag,* edited by Heiko A. Oberman et al., 2:327-42. = *Zwingliana* 19 (1991, 1992).

Spitz, Lewis W. "Man on This Isthmus." In *Luther for an Ecumenical Age,* edited by Carl S. Meyer, 23-66. Saint Louis: Concordia, 1967.

———. *The Religious Renaissance of the German Humanists.* Cambridge: Harvard University Press, 1963.

Spitz, Lewis W., and Barbara Sher Tinsley. *Johann Sturm on Education: The Reformation and Humanist Learning.* Saint Louis: Concordia, 1995.

Stählin, Friedrich. *Humanismus und Reformation im bürgerlichen Raum.* Leipzig: Heinsius, 1936.

Steinmetz, David C. *Luther and Staupitz: An Essay in the Intellectual Origin of the Protestant Reformation.* Durham, N.C.: Duke University Press, 1980.

————. *Luther in Context.* Bloomington: Indiana University Press, 1986.

Tracy, James D. "Two Erasmuses, Two Luthers: Erasmus' Strategy in Defense of *De libero arbitrio.*" *ARG* 78 (1987): 37-60.

Trinkaus, Charles. *The Scope of Renaissance Humanism.* Ann Arbor: University of Michigan Press, 1983.

Tylenda, Joseph N. "Girolamo Zanchi and John Calvin: A Study in Discipleship as Seen through Their Correspondence." *Calvin Theological Journal* 10 (1975): 101-40.

Upsala Ärkestifts Herdaminne. Uppsala: Wahlström & Lästrom, 1842.

Voit, Hartmut. *Nikolaus Gallus, Ein Beitrag zur Reformationsgeschichte der nachlutherischen Zeit.* Neustadt an der Aisch: Degener, 1977.

Wabel, Thomas. *Sprache als Grenze in Luthers theologischer Hermeneutik und Wittgensteins Sprachphilosophie.* Berlin: De Gruyter, 1998.

Wartenberg, Günther. "Philipp Melanchthon und die sächsisch-albertinische Interimspolitik." *LuJ* 55 (1988): 60-80.

Watson, Philip S. *Let God Be God! An Interpretation of the Theology of Martin Luther.* Philadelphia: Muhlenberg, 1947.

Wengert, Timothy J. *Human Freedom, Christian Righteousness: Philip Melanchthon's Exegetical Dispute with Erasmus of Rotterdam.* New York and Oxford: Oxford University Press, 1998.

————. *Law and Gospel: Philip Melanchthon's Debate with John Agricola of Eisleben over Poenitentia.* Grand Rapids: Baker, 1997.

————. "Melanchthon and Luther/Luther and Melanchthon." *LuJ* 66 (1999): 55-88.

————. "Philip Melanchthon's Contribution to Luther's Debate with Erasmus over the Bondage of the Will." In *By Faith Alone: Essays on Justification in Honor of Gerhard O. Forde,* edited by Joseph A. Burgess and Marc Kolden, 110-24. Grand Rapids: Eerdmans, 2004.

————. "'We Will Feast Together in Heaven Forever': The Epistolary Friendship of John Calvin and Philip Melanchthon." In *Melanchthon in Europe: His Work and Influence beyond Wittenberg,* edited by Karin Maag, 19-44. Texts and Studies in Reformation and Post-Reformation Thought. Grand Rapids: Baker, 1999.

Whitford, David Mark. *Tyranny and Resistance: The Magdeburg Confession and the Lutheran Tradition.* Saint Louis: Concordia, 2001.

Wriedt, Markus. *Gnade und Erwählung, eine Untersuchung zu Johann von Staupitz und Martin Luther.* Mainz: Zabern, 1991.

Zickendraht, Karl. *Der Streit zwischen Erasmus und Luther über die Willensfreiheit.* Leipzig: Hinrichs, 1909.

Zschoch, Helmut. *Reformatorische Existenz und konfessionelle Identität. Urbanus Rhegius als evangelischer Theologe in den Jahren 1520 bis 1530.* Tübingen: Mohr (Siebeck), 1995.

Index of Names

Agricola, Johann (1494-1566), 75, 78
Amsdorf, Nikolaus von (1483-1565), 7, 70, 95-96, 105, 107, 110-11
Andreae, Jakob (1528-1590), 121, 133, 176, 199, 236-42, 245-48, 254, 261-66, 277
August, elector of Saxony (1526-1586), 112, 128, 182, 220-21, 246-47
Augustine (354-430), 20, 68, 75-76, 123-24, 132, 163, 178, 192, 195, 208, 213, 216, 223, 226
Aurifaber, Johannes (1519-1575), 110-11, 220
Autumnus, Georg. *See* Herbst, Georg

Basil (= Pseudo-Basil), 91, 93-94, 256
Bede, the Venerable (673-735), 216
Bernard of Clairvaux (1090-1153), 76, 203-4
Bernardi, Bernhard (1487-1551), 11
Beza, Theodore (1519-1605), 265
Biel, Gabriel (c. 1420-1495), 23, 29, 131, 281
Binder, Christoph (1519-1596), 121
Boethius (c. 480-c.524), 193
Brenz, Johannes (1499-1570), 69-70, 208, 224, 226, 236, 238
Bucer, Martin (1491-1551), 96, 173-74, 178
Bugenhagen, Johannes, Jr. (1524-1592), 277

Bugenhagen, Johannes, Sr. (1485-1558), 4, 67-68, 101, 108
Bullinger, Heinrich (1504-1575), 224

Calvin, John (1590-1564), 88-90, 171, 173-74, 188, 208, 224
Camerarius, Joachim (1500-1574), 14
Capito, Wolfgang (1478-1541), 15, 68
Celichius, Andreas (d. 1599), 182-83
Charles V, emperor (1500-1558), 103-4
Chemnitz, Martin (1522-1586), 88, 127, 144, 146, 162, 164, 166, 172, 197, 226-36, 245-47, 254, 258, 260-66, 277, 287-88
Christoph, duke of Württemberg (1515-1568), 121, 128, 236, 244-45
Chrysostom, John (c. 345-407), 91, 93, 185, 223, 256
Chytraeus, David (1531-1600), 121, 161, 164, 179, 190-98, 207, 212, 220, 236, 242-43, 246-47, 249-56, 260, 266, 277, 288, 322(n.5)
Coccius, Ulrich, 176
Cochlaeus, Johannes (1479-1552), 7, 75, 78, 280
Cruciger, Caspar, Jr. (1525-1597), 277
Cruciger, Caspar, Sr. (1504-1548), 40

Dedekind, Friedrich (d. 1598), 127

Dinckel, Johannes (1545-1601), 180, 324(n.92)

Eber, Paul (1511-1569), 89-90, 128, 220, 294(n.4)
Eck, John (1486-1543), 81, 88, 280
Erasmus, Desiderius (1466/9-1536), 1, 7, 8, 12-16, 18-28, 42, 47, 49, 53, 58, 62, 67-69, 71-75, 78, 114, 123-24, 131, 134, 136, 139-42, 148, 150-52, 154-57, 159-60, 162-63, 168, 249, 270, 273, 279, 281-82

Fisher, John (1469-1535), 13
Flacius, Matthias, Illyricus (1520-1575), 105, 107-8, 110, 112-14, 118-20, 122, 134-36, 138, 140, 157, 159-61, 165, 198-99, 222, 237-38, 244-46, 251, 257, 277, 284-85, 288
Flinsbach, Cunmann (1527-1571), 176-78, 197, 212, 220, 242, 264, 277
Freyhub, Andreas (1526-1585), 128, 182
Fricius, Andreas Modrzewski (1503-1572), 224
Fulgentius (c. 467-533), 208

Gallus, Nikolaus (1516-1570), 105, 107-10, 112-17, 122, 138, 143, 147, 159, 162, 164, 166, 246, 253, 277, 284-85
Gerson, Jean (1363-1429), 231
Gribaldi, Matthias (d. 1564), 100

Hardenberg, Albert (c. 1510-1574), 108
Helsing, Martin Olai, 190-91
Henry VIII, King of England (1491-1547), 13
Herbst, Georg (1529-1598), 125, 136, 138, 140-41, 143-45, 148, 150, 153-60, 163-64, 167-68
Herrmann, Nikolaus (ca. 1480-1561), 68
Heshusius, Tilemann (1527-1588), 124, 140, 144, 146, 160, 175, 209, 246, 249, 256, 258, 267, 277
Huber, Samuel (c. 1547-1624), 181, 265-66
Hunnius, Aegidius (1550-1603), 181, 266
Hyperius, Andreas (151-564), 224

Ilesuanus, Petrus, 182-83, 189-90, 222

Irenaeus, Christoph (1522-1595), 124, 129, 138, 155-56, 159, 164, 277

Jerome (c. 342-420), 142
Johann Albrecht, duke of Mecklenburg (1525-1576), 220
Johann Friedrich I, elector of Saxony (1503-1554), 103-4
Johann Friedrich the Middler, duke of Saxony (1529-1595), 110-11, 118-20, 122, 125, 128, 182
Johann Wilhelm, duke of Saxony (1530-1573), 110-11, 122, 128-29, 182
John, elector of Saxony (1468-1532), 14
Jonas, Justus (1493-1555), 4, 67-68, 114
Judex, Matthaeus (1528-1564), 147, 172, 198, 242, 287
Julius, duke of Braunschweig-Wolfenbüttel (1529-1589), 227, 245
Jurieau, Pierre (1637-1713), 293(n.25)

Keyser, Philip (d. 1585), 127-28
Kirchner, Timotheus (1533-1587), 125-26, 129, 136, 138-40, 143, 147, 149-58, 162, 164, 168, 172, 242, 277
Körner, Christoph (1518-1594), 247
Köteritz, Wolfgang von, 176
Krell, Paul (1531-1579), 220

Lasius, Christoph (1504-1572), 122
Latomus, Jacob Masson (c. 1475-1544), 14, 17
Leibniz, Gottfried Wilhelm (1646-1716), 19
Likirchen, Barbara, 41
Luther, Martin (1483-1546), 1-75, 78, 103, 108, 110-12, 114-15, 120, 123-26, 131, 134-78, 192-93, 196, 198-99, 203, 206, 208, 220, 222-27, 234, 237, 241-43, 247, 249, 252, 258-59, 269-90; interpretation of Genesis 26:7, 17, 40, 65, 131, 146, 162, 178, 222, 227, 267

Major, Georg (1502-1574), 106, 108, 135, 220
Marbach, Johannes (1521-1581), 173-78, 197, 212, 220, 242, 262, 264, 277

Martyr, Peter, Vermigli. *See* Vermigli, Peter Martyr

Mathesius, Johannes (1504-1565), 7-8, 108

Meister, Joachim, 127-28

Melanchthon, Philipp (1497-1560), 4, 6, 7, 10, 17-19, 67-68, 70-118, 121, 125-26, 150, 156, 159-61, 165, 167-68, 171-76, 179, 188, 190, 192, 196-200, 202-3, 208, 210, 219, 222-27, 234, 242-43, 248-49, 251, 256, 258, 262, 269-73, 275, 277-86, 288-90

Menzel, Hieronymus (1517-1590), 124, 198, 221

Möller, Rudolf, 127

Mörlin, Joachim (1514-1571), 8, 111, 119, 159, 226

Mörlin, Maximilian (1516-1584), 111

Moller, Heinrich (1530-1589), 277

Moritz, elector of Saxony (1521-1553), 104-5

Musaeus, Simon (1521-1576), 118-20, 246

Musculus, Andreas (1514-1581), 247

Neukirch, Melchior (c. 1540-1597), 227

Obenhin, Christoph, 126-27, 138

Ockham, William of (c. 1300-c. 1349), 29

Oecolampadius, Johannes (1482-1531), 69

Origen (c. 185-c.254), 53, 142, 162

Palhöfer, Leonhardt (d. 1566), 179-81, 197-8, 207, 212, 220, 242, 265

Petri, Laurentius (1499-1573), 191

Peucer, Caspar (1525-1602), 220, 277

Pfeffinger, Johann (1493-1573), 110, 120, 122, 159, 165, 277, 285

Philip, Landgrave of Hesse (1504-1567), 103-4

Poach, Andreas (1515/6-1585), 179-81, 207, 220

Porta, Conrad (1541-1585), 8

Prosper of Aquitaine (c. 390-c. 463), 193, 208, 214, 238, 240, 259, 264

Pufendorf, Samuel von (1632-1694), 293(n.25)

Rabus, Ludwig (1524-1592), 8

Rhegius, Urbanus (1489-1541), 68-69, 208, 224

Rörer, Georg (1492-1557), 28, 135, 192

Salmuth, Heinrich (1522-1576), 128, 182

Sarcerius, Erasmus (1501-1559), 111, 198

Schlüsselburg, Conrad (1543-1619), 226-27

Schmidt, Sebastian (1617-1696), 293(n.25)

Scultetus, Abraham (1566-1625), 293(n.25)

Schwenckfeld, Caspar von (c. 1490-1561), 112

Selnecker, Nikolaus (1530-1592), 162, 164, 179, 182-90, 196-98, 212, 220, 236, 242-43, 245, 247, 266, 277

Silberschlag, Georg (1535-1572), 180, 220

Sleidan, Johann (1506-1556), 7

Spalatin, Georg (1484-1545), 13

Spangenberg, Cyriacus (1528-1604), 8, 124, 134. 138, 171-72, 197-226, 230, 240, 242, 259-60, 264, 266, 277, 284, 287

Spangenberg, Johann (1484-1550), 198-200, 224

Spiera, Francisco (1502-1548), 100, 222

Sporckhof, Bartholomaeus, 127

Staupitz, Johann von (c. 1470-1524), 38-39, 294(n.4)

Stössel, Johann (1524-1578), 119

Stoltz, Johann (1514-1556), 110

Strigel, Viktorin (1524-1569), 111-12, 118-22, 124, 140, 157, 160-61, 164-65, 182, 246, 255, 266, 277, 284-85

Sturm, Johannes (1507-1589), 174

Sultzer, Simon (1508-1585), 176, 242

Tetelbach, Johannes (1517-c. 1598), 125

Valla, Lorenzo (c. 1406-1457), 90, 193

Vermigli, Peter Martyr (1500-1562), 173-74, 224

Walther, Georg (ca. 1530-1580), 160, 172-73

Weller, Hieronymus (1499-1572), 41

Westphal, Joachim (1510/11-1574), 105

Widebram, Friedrich (1532-1585), 277

Wigand, Johannes (1523-1587), 118, 120, 122-24, 129, 131, 137-38, 140-44, 146-47,

149-50, 155-56, 159, 162, 164, 166, 168, 172, 198-99, 209, 242, 246, 249, 256, 258, 267, 277, 287

Wimpina, Konrad (1460-1531), 294(n.4)

Winter, Balthasar, 119

Wycliffe, John (c. 1329-1384), 1, 13, 162

Zanchi, Girolamo (1516-1590), 173-78, 262, 287

Zasius, Ulrich (1461-1535), 67

Index of Subjects

Altenburg Colloquy, 128-34, 221, 244, 284
Apology of the Augsburg Confession, 81, 253
Apostasy, falling from grace, 100, 222, 235, 240, 262
Assertion as confession of faith, 16, 45
Augsburg Confession, 81-82, 104-5, 115-16, 129, 253, 259; Variata of the Augsburg Confession, 81-82
Augsburg Interim (1548), 103-7

Bible. *See* Scripture

Calvinists' use of *De servo arbitrio*, 9, 293(n.25)
Catechisms, Luther's, 125, 182, 245, 253
Causae tres (of conversion), 83, 93, 121, 130-31, 256, 258
Christ: work of, 3, 37, 58, 205, 219, 229-30, 265, 267; two natures, 229-30, 233
Confutation, Book of (1559), 111-13, 118, 120, 190, 244
Contingency, 32-33, 73, 87-91, 99, 193-94
Conversion, 93-94, 110-12, 114-17, 127-33, 148-50, 177, 187

Doctrine, method of teaching, 1-5, 16-21, 42, 44-45, 65-66, 78, 133-34, 137, 250, 270-72, 277-90

Double predestination. *See* Reprobation

Election, 33, 38-43, 67-70, 76-87, 147, 170-243, 249, 259-70, 287; universal election/predestination, 180-81, 259, 265-66

Facultas applicandi se(se) ad gratiam, 94, 114-15, 131-32, 159-60, 256, 258, 288
Fate, 90, 188-89, 191-92
Freedom: Christian, 2, 195; divine, 32-33, 151; of the will, 11-31, 33-34, 48-60, 67-70, 73-86, 91-102, 106-69, 194-96, 235, 237-38, 245-46, 248-58, 266, 268-69, 278-82, 284-85

God: as cause of sin/evil, 62-65, 75, 80, 88-90, 97, 114-16, 166-69, 177, 179, 183-87, 189, 191, 194, 208, 214, 225, 227, 231, 239, 241, 254, 261-64, 268-69, 285, 287; as Creator, 2, 5-6, 11-12, 21-22, 29-34, 47-66, 76-77, 133-34, 139-46, 151-56, 191, 193, 213, 285, 288-89; God Hidden/God Revealed, 35-39, 144-46, 176, 208-9, 214, 239, 241, 267-68
Göttingen ministerium, 127-28, 227

Humanism, 72-73, 248
Humanity, 28-30, 47-61, 96-97, 139-61, 164-66, 194-96, 257-58, 267-68, 281-89

Intuitu fidei, 266

Jena theological faculty, 128-34, 140, 155, 158-60, 163-64

Law/gospel distinction, 3, 6, 23, 43, 45-47, 61-62, 70, 92, 112, 115-16, 134, 137, 149-51, 155, 175, 178, 208-9, 211, 216-17, 220-21, 233, 236, 238, 249, 253-54, 260, 262, 264, 269-70, 283-89
Leipzig "Interim," 104-7, 108

Magdeburg *Confession* (1550), 107-8
Mansfeld ministerium, 124, 225
Maulbronn Formula, 247, 249, 253-54, 259
Means of Grace (Word of God), 34, 40, 43-48, 100-101, 113, 116, 132, 134, 146-51, 172-73, 176, 181, 183-85, 200-206, 213-17, 219, 223, 225, 228-35, 238-40, 246, 253-55, 257-58, 260-65, 267-68, 273, 276, 284-86
Modus agendi, 90, 119, 121, 126, 238, 255-56, 258, 284, 288

Necessity, divine, 1, 26-28, 38, 52-55, 87-91, 95-96, 99, 107-9, 112, 115-17, 138, 161-64, 167, 184-85, 188-89, 191-96, 227, 239, 255, 258, 267, 274-75, 282-83, 285, 287-88

Ockhamism, 28-31
Order of salvation *(ordo salutis),* 204-5, 213-14, 229-30, 260-61

Parables, rules for interpretation, 228
Particular predestination, predestination of individuals, 77-78, 86-87, 100-101, 208, 217, 221-22, 225, 231-33, 242, 259, 264-65
Passivē purē, or *merē,* 115, 140, 153, 160, 255-56, 258, 288
Pastoral care/concern, 21-23, 39-42, 62-65, 92, 113, 170, 176-77, 187-88, 208, 210-11, 215-16, 219-21, 228-29, 232, 236, 241, 251, 253-54, 260, 262, 264-65, 270
Pharaoh's heart, hardening of, 53, 64, 87-88, 93, 135, 142, 162, 167, 185-86, 241, 263
Predestination. *See* Election

Predestination to Damnation. *See* Reprobation
Prussian critique of the Torgau Book, 249-52, 256, 259, 267

Reception, 6-10, 272-75, 281-90
Repentance, 3, 61-62, 99-100, 112, 115-16, 127-28, 154, 165-66, 178, 211, 216-17, 231, 234, 242, 252, 254, 260, 262-63, 269-70, 281, 284, 287
Repetition of the Augsburg Confession/ Saxon Confession (1551), 82-83
Reprobation, 28, 42-43, 69-70, 94-96, 99, 100-101, 130, 144-46, 171, 182-89, 207, 217-19, 221, 239-40, 261-62
Righteousness: civil, 60, 80, 91-92, 97-98, 116, 251-52, 285; divine, 34; two kinds of (passive and active), 3, 34, 49-52, 55, 59-60, 79-80, 92, 98-100, 153-56, 210, 250, 276, 289
Rostock theological faculty, 121

Sanctification (new obedience), 80, 82, 172-73, 213, 219, 251-52, 261
Satan, in conflict with God, 18, 41, 47, 56-57, 98, 143, 157-58, 160, 165, 284
Saxon, electoral, ministerium, 128-34, 162, 220-26, 231, 246-47
Scholasticism, 2, 14, 17, 24-26, 28-31, 38-39, 52-53, 281-82
Scripture, authority and interpretation of, 22-23, 44, 79, 136-37, 209-11, 273-74
Sin, 55-59, 77, 85, 92, 98-101, 119-20, 156-61, 216, 234, 237-39, 245, 252, 257-58, 268-69, 280, 283, 285
Smalcald Articles, 253
Suicide, 182-83
Swabian Concord or Binding Summary, 238, 240-41, 247, 249, 259
Swabian Saxon Concord, 247, 249-56, 258-59, 262
Synergistic controversy, 106-69, 248-58, 277

Theodicy, 19, 21-23, 43, 62-65, 143-46, 167-69, 206-7, 246, 268-69, 288

Theology of the cross, 2-3, 36, 59, 63-64, 148

Universal promise of salvation, 41, 83, 86, 113, 130, 144-46, 172, 180-81, 183-84, 221-22, 238-39, 241, 246, 253, 261, 265, 286, 302(n.136)

Visitation, Saxon (1528), 80

Weimar Disputation (1560), 118-20, 155, 159-60, 164

Wittenberg theological faculty, 147, 221-25, 259, 275-76

Worms, Colloquy of (1557), 97, 111, 159

Index of Scripture References

OLD TESTAMENT

Genesis

1:1-31	47
1:26	151
2:7	151
3:15	219
6:5	111
8:21	111, 252
15:5	212
17	166
18:16-19	214
26:9	37-38, 65, 146
27:43-45	28
39:1-18	98
50:20-21	213

See also Luther, Martin, interpretation of Genesis

26:7

Exodus

3:19-20	214
4:11	63
4:21	142, 185
7:3	142
9:7	12, 142
9:12	263
9:16	178
14:3-4	214
14:21-31	192
32:32-33	216
33:20	209
33:23	209
50:20-21	213

Numbers

23:19	213

Deuteronomy

7:6-9	212, 214
10:14-15	214
29:4	253
30:6	253

Joshua

3:7-13	192
11:20	214

1 Samuel

2:6	61
9–10	95
13	95

2 Samuel

12:1-14	240
15:29	213
24:1	186

1 Kings

12	95

2 Kings

20:1-6	193

1 Chronicles

21:1	186

Psalms

1:3	202
5:4	184
5:4-5	177
21:5	47
37:5	202
39:9	207
45:8-10	236
51:4	111
51:10, 12	253
65:4	214
69:28	216
73:22	252
73:22-23	57
79	186
95:7-8	130
106:4-5	214
119	252
119:124	185
139	177

Proverbs

16:4	77
16:9	77
20:24	77

Ecclesiastes

3:14	213

Isaiah

14:24	213
37	194
38:1-8	193
40:1-2	58
45:7	63
45:9	140
46:10	231
49:15	215
53:4-5	215
59:2	239
61	158
61:10	236
64:6	236

Jeremiah

1:1-29	35
5:3	252
10:23	77, 96, 163
17:9	252
18:6	140
18:8	193
24:7	112
31:28	185
31:33	112
32:40	112

Lamentations

3:38	186

Ezekiel

1:3	35
11:19	112, 253
18:23	145, 177
18:30	177
18:32	41, 177
33:11	215, 239, 241, 253
33:12-13	216
36:26	112, 252-53

Daniel

3:8-30	192
6	188
12:1	216

Hosea

1:1	35
6:5	252
13:9	184-85, 239, 263, 269

Amos

3:6	63, 186

Jonah

3:10	193

Micah

1:1	35

Nahum

2:13	184

Malachi

1:2-3	69, 141, 240
3:6	40, 213

APOCRYPHA

Sirach

15:14-17	49-50, 154-55, 194

Wisdom of Solomon

11:20	217

NEW TESTAMENT

Matthew

5:6	261
5:20	251
10:22	216
10:29	77, 95
10:30	185
11:25	177
11:25-30	177
11:27	253
11:28	177, 210, 215, 238-39, 261
13:11	252
13:13	252
13:15	253
17:5	37, 239
18:3	286
18:14	239
20:16	96
20:22	261
22:1-14	227-36
22:14	185, 215-16, 239, 261
22:37-40	49
23:37	42, 147, 262
24:13	216, 261
26:28	96

Mark

16:16	225

Luke

8:13	262
10:20	216
11:13	286
11:21	57
11:24-25	262
13:24	130
22:20	96
24:45	253
24:47	261

John

1:1-4	43
1:1-18	47
1:5	252
1:9	219
1:12	51, 153, 160
1:12-13	140
1:14	35, 43, 273
1:18	36, 43
1:29	143, 261
3:3	91, 286
3:3-5	62
3:5-8	196
3:6	111

3:8	148	1:18	178	9:19-24	146, 160	
3:15	86	2:14	251	9:20	187, 269	
3:16	177, 210, 215, 221,	3 and 4	143	9:20-24	140	
	225, 253, 261	3:11-12	252	9:22-23	263	
3:17	187	3:21-25	153	9:22-24	178	
5:27	210	3:22	86, 261	9:23	215	
6:29	253	3:28	51	9:24	219	
6:37-40	177	5:12	158	10:8	235	
6:39	215, 261	5:18	219	10:12	86, 219, 261	
6:40	261	6:3-11	3, 58, 62	10:17	181	
6:44	91, 143, 148, 253	6:13	100	10:19-21	219	
6:44-45	185	6:23	58	11:2	203	
6:44-46	201	7:14-23	252	11:7-8	219	
6:51	261	8 and 9	177, 207	11:11-14	219	
8:34	252	8:6	178	11:29	231, 235	
8:44	47	8:7	252	11:32	219, 261	
8:44-47	177	8:9	14, 91	11:33	36, 65, 95, 168, 177,	
10:27-28	235, 261	8:14	235		187, 233, 265, 268	
10:28	178	8:17	201	11:33-36	212, 288	
10:28-29	1	8:18	202	11:34	233, 263	
10:29	215	8:20-21	202	11:36	77	
13:18	231	8:23	202	11:40	231, 235	
14:6	37, 112, 143, 202	8:24-25	202	15:4	177, 229, 238, 264-	
14:9	37, 209	8:25	261		65	
14:16-17	91	8:26	82	15:8-13	219	
14:23	202	8:26-27	202			
15:5	82, 253	8:28	203	**1 Corinthians**		
16:8-9	143	8:28-30	202	1:8	235	
16:14	253	8:29	208, 215, 231	1:9	210, 235	
17:12	207	8:29-30	187, 204, 230	1:18–2:16	3, 44, 58	
		8:29-39	215	1:21	252	
Acts		8:30	224	2:6-7	215	
2:5	219	8:31-34	204	2:9-10	215	
2:23	203, 219	8:31-37	202	2:10	235	
3:20	219	8:31	35-38, 235	2:14	79, 91, 93, 112, 129,	
5:31	253	8:34	202		209, 252	
10:1-48	219	8:35-37	205	2:14-16	235	
10:34	86, 167, 221, 286	8:38-39	202	4:7	253	
10:41	219	9:10-13	69	5:2-4	236	
13:48	224, 239	9:11-12	231	6:9-10	178	
14:16	229	9:13	141	10:11	229	
15:1-29	219	9:14-28	268	12:6	152	
17:26	229	9:16	86, 130, 222, 239	12:3	185, 253	
26:18	252	9:17	178, 263	15:3-4	219	
		9:17-18	219	15:16	58	
Romans		9:18	142			
1:16	229	9:19-23	241			

2 Corinthians

3:3	229
3:4-6	235
3:5	253
5:17, 62	253, 286
6:16	219

Galatians

1:15	39, 170
3:10	46
3:14	82
3:27	236
5:1, 13	272
5:17	252
6:15	62, 253

Ephesians

1:3-4	230
1:3-11	39, 210, 219, 222
1:3-14	172, 177, 201, 204, 241
1:4	69, 177
1:4-5	260
1:4-6	207
1:11	77, 204
1:13	235
1:13-14	187
1:18	215
2:1	64
2:1, 5	252
2:2	252
2:3, 65	168
2:8	253
2:8-10	69
4:17-18	252
5:8	252
5:15	99

Philippians

1:6	235, 261
1:9-10	252
1:29	177, 253
2:13	69, 112, 121, 185, 253
4:3	216, 231

Colossians

1:9-11	252
2:3	36
2:11-15	62, 95
2:13	252

2 Thessalonians

2:13-14	210
2:13-17	200-201

1 Timothy

1:9	251
1:9-10	203
2:4, 41	86, 96, 185, 187, 218, 238-39, 241, 302(n.136)
2:5	218
4:10	218
6:16, 62	146

2 Timothy

1:9	222, 231
13:13, 11	252
1:9-10	203
2:13	200, 203
2:19	39, 207, 212, 239
2:20-21	212
2:21	141, 178
2:25	253

| | |
|---|---|
| 2:26, 57 | 252 |
| 3:16 | 229-30 |

Titus

3:3-8	62
3:5	251, 253

Hebrews

2:1-2	35
10:20	209
10:26	262

James

1:17	253

1 Peter

1:12-16	219
1:23	229

2 Peter

1:19	44
2:10	262
3:9	261

1 John

1:7	261
1:10	55
2:2	261
3:8	184

Revelation

3:20	130
20:12-15	216
21:27	216